The Flower Adornment Sutra

An Annotated Translation of the Avataṃsaka Sutra

With a Commentarial Synopsis Of the Flower Adornment Sutra

Volume Five
Chapter 39

Kalavinka Press
8603 39th Ave SW / Seattle, WA 98136 USA
(www.kalavinkapress.org)

Kalavinka Press is associated with the Kalavinka Dharma Association, a non-profit organized exclusively for religious educational purposes as allowed within the meaning of section 501(c)3 of the Internal RevenueCode. Kalavinka Dharma Association was founded in 1990 and gained formal approval in 2004 by the United States Internal Revenue Service as a 501(c)3 non-profit organization to which all donations are tax deductible.

To refrain from doing any manner of evil,
to respectfully perform all varieties of good,
and to purify one's own mind—
This is the teaching of all buddhas.

The Ekottara Āgama Sūtra (T02 n.125 p.551a 13–14)

A Note on the Proper Care of Dharma Materials

Traditional Buddhist cultures treat books on Dharma as sacred. Hence it is considered disrespectful to place them in a low position, to read them when lying down, or to place them where they might be damaged by food or drink.

Kalavinka Press books are printed on acid-free paper.
Cover and interior designed by Bhikshu Dharmamitra.
Printed in the United States of America

The Flower Adornment Sutra

The Great Expansive
Buddha's Flower Adornment Sutra

An Annotated English Translation of the Avataṃsaka Sutra
By Bhikshu Dharmamitra

With a Commentarial Synopsis Of the Flower Adornment Sutra

Volume Five

Kalavinka Press
Seattle, Washington
www.kalavinkapress.org

Edition: HY-SA-1025-1.0 / Kalavinka Buddhist Classics Book 15a
The Six-Volume Set ISBN (paperback): 978-1-935413-47-9
This Volume Five ISBN: 978-1-935413-52-3
Vol. 1 ISBN: 978-1-935413-48-6
Vol. 2 ISBN: 978-1-935413-49-3
Vol. 3 ISBN: 978-1-935413-50-9
Vol. 4 ISBN: 978-1-935413-51-6
Vol. 6 ISBN: 978-1-935413-53-0
The Six-Volume Set ISBN (Adobe PDF): 978-1-935413-54-7
Library of Congress Control Number: 2025947392

Publisher's Cataloging-in-Publication Data

Names: Dharmamitra, Bhikshu, 1948, translator. | Śikṣānanda, 652 CE, translator. | Prajñā, 734 CE, translator.

Title: The Flower Adornment Sutra. An Annotated Translation of the Avataṃsaka Sutra. With a Commentarial Synopsis of the Flower Adornment Sutra.

Other titles: *Mahāvaipulya Buddha Avataṃsaka Sūtra*. English

Description: HY-SA-1025-1.0-chinese/english. | Seattle, Washington : Kalavinka Press, 2025. | Series: Kalavinka Buddhist Classics, Book 15a | Includes bibliographical references. | English and Chinese. | Summary: "The Flower Adornment Sutra is Bhikshu Dharmamitra's extensively annotated original translation of the Mahāvaipulya Buddha Avataṃsaka Sūtra or "The Great Expansive Buddha's Flower Adornment Sutra" which he has rendered from Tripiṭaka Master Śikṣānanda's circa 699 ce Sanskrit-to-Chinese 80-fascicle translation as Da Fangguang Fo Huayan Jing (Taisho Vol. 10, no. 279). Appended here as the conclusion to Chapter 39 is Dharmamitra's English translation of Tripiṭaka Master Prajñā's translation into Chinese of "The Conduct and Vows of Samantabhadra" which is traditionally included as the conclusion of Chinese language editions of this sutra. Altogether, this sutra consists of 39 chapters that introduce an interpenetrating, infinitely expansive, and majestically grand multiverse of countless buddha worlds while explaining in great detail the cultivation of the bodhisattva path to buddhahood, most notably the ten highest levels of bodhisattva practice known as "the ten bodhisattva grounds." To date, this is the first and only complete English translation of the Avataṃsaka Sutra. This special bilingual edition (English / Chinese) includes the facing-page simplified and traditional Chinese scripts to facilitate close study by academic buddhologists, students in Buddhist universities, and Buddhists in Taiwan, Hong Kong, Mainland China, and the West."-- Provided by publisher.

Identifiers: LCCN 2025947392 | ISBN 9781935413479 (paperback) | ISBN 9781935413547 (adobe pdf)

Subjects: LCSH: Tripiṭaka. Sūtrapiṭaka. Avataṃsakasūtra. | Bodhisattva stages (Mahayana Buddhism)

LC record available at https://lccn.loc.gov/2025947392

Volume Five Table of Contents

Chapter 39 – Entering the Dharma Realm 3137

1 – Meghaśrī 3281

2 – Sāgaramegha 3291

3 – Supratiṣṭhita 3305

4 – Megha 3317

5 – Muktaka 3327

6 – Sāgaradhvaja 3345

7 – Āśā 3375

8 – Bhīṣmottaranirghoṣa 3397

9 – Jayoṣmāyatana 3407

10 – Maitrāyaṇī 3427

11 – Sudarśana 3439

12 – Indriyeśvara 3451

13 – Prabhūtā 3459

14 – Vidvān 3471

15 – Ratnacūḍa 3483

16 – Samantanetra 3491

17 – Anala 3497

18 – Mahāprabha 3507

19 – Acalā 3525

20 – Sarvagāmin 3545

21 – Utpalabhūti 3551

22 – Vaira 3559

23 – Jayottama 3569

24 – Siṁhavijṛmbhitā 3577

25 – Vasumitrā 3595

26 – Veṣṭhila 3605

27 – Avalokiteśvara 3611

28 – Ananyagāmin 3619

29 – Mahādeva 3623

30 – Sthāvarā 3631

31 – Vāsantī 3635

32 – Samantagambhīraśrīvimalaprabhā 3663

The Flower Adornment Sutra

Volume Five

The Great Expansive Buddha's Flower Adornment Sutra

The Mahāvaipulya Buddha Avataṃsaka Sūtra

(Taisho T10, no. 279)

Translated under Imperial Auspices by
Tripiṭaka Master Śikṣānanda from the State of Khotan

English Translation by Bhikshu Dharmamitra

正體字

319a02║ 大方廣佛華嚴經卷第六十
319a05║ 入法界品第三十九之一
319a06║ 爾時世尊。在室羅筏國逝多林給孤獨園大
319a07║ 莊嚴重閣。與菩薩摩訶薩。五百人俱。普賢菩
319a08║ 薩。文殊師利菩薩。而為上首。其名曰光焰幢
319a09║ 菩薩。須彌幢菩薩。寶幢菩薩。無礙幢菩薩。華
319a10║ 幢菩薩。離垢幢菩薩。日幢菩薩。妙幢菩薩。離
319a11║ 塵幢菩薩。普光幢菩薩。地威力菩薩。寶威力
319a12║ 菩薩。大威力菩薩。金剛智威力菩薩。離塵垢
319a13║ 威力菩薩。正法日威力菩薩。功德山威力菩
319a14║ 薩。智光影威力菩薩。普吉祥威力菩薩。地藏
319a15║ 菩薩。虛空藏菩薩。蓮華藏菩薩。寶藏菩薩。日
319a16║ 藏菩薩。淨德藏菩薩。法印藏菩薩。光明藏菩
319a17║ 薩。臍藏菩薩。蓮華德藏菩薩。善眼菩薩。淨眼
319a18║ 菩薩。離垢眼菩薩。無礙眼菩薩。普見眼菩薩。
319a19║ 善觀眼菩薩。青蓮華眼菩薩。金剛眼菩薩。寶
319a20║ 眼菩薩。虛空眼菩薩。喜眼菩薩。普眼菩薩。天
319a21║ 冠菩薩。普照法界智慧冠菩薩。道場冠菩薩。
319a22║ 普照十方冠菩薩。一切佛藏冠菩薩。超出一
319a23║ 切世間冠菩薩。

简体字

大方广佛华严经卷第六十

入法界品第三十九之一

尔时，世尊在室罗筏国逝多林给孤独园大庄严重阁，与菩萨摩诃萨五百人俱，普贤菩萨、文殊师利菩萨而为上首。其名曰：光焰幢菩萨、须弥幢菩萨、宝幢菩萨、无碍幢菩萨、华幢菩萨、离垢幢菩萨、日幢菩萨、妙幢菩萨、离尘幢菩萨、普光幢菩萨、地威力菩萨、宝威力菩萨、大威力菩萨、金刚智威力菩萨、离尘垢威力菩萨、正法日威力菩萨、功德山威力菩萨、智光影威力菩萨、普吉祥威力菩萨、地藏菩萨、虚空藏菩萨、莲华藏菩萨、宝藏菩萨、日藏菩萨、净德藏菩萨、法印藏菩萨、光明藏菩萨、脐藏菩萨、莲华德藏菩萨、善眼菩萨、净眼菩萨、离垢眼菩萨、无碍眼菩萨、普见眼菩萨、善观眼菩萨、青莲华眼菩萨、金刚眼菩萨、宝眼菩萨、虚空眼菩萨、喜眼菩萨、普眼菩萨、天冠菩萨、普照法界智慧冠菩萨、道场冠菩萨、普照十方冠菩萨、一切佛藏冠菩萨、超出一切世间冠菩萨、

Chapter 39
Entering the Dharma Realm

At that time, the Bhagavat was abiding in the state of Śrāvastī in the multistory Great Adornment Pavilion in the Jeta Grove within the Garden of the Benefactor of Orphans and the Solitary,[1] together with a congregation of five hundred bodhisattva-mahāsattvas headed by Samantabhadra Bodhisattva and Mañjuśrī Bodhisattva. Their names were:[2]

Flaming Radiance Banner Bodhisattva, Sumeru Banner Bodhisattva, Jewel Banner Bodhisattva, Unimpeded Banner Bodhisattva, Floral Banner Bodhisattva, Stainless Banner Bodhisattva, Solar Banner Bodhisattva, Sublimity Banner Bodhisattva, Transcendence of the Dusts Banner Bodhisattva, Universal Light Banner Bodhisattva, and Awesome Power of the Earth Bodhisattva.

Awesome Power of Jewels Bodhisattva, Great Awesome Power Bodhisattva, Awesome Power of Vajra Wisdom Bodhisattva, Awesome Power of Transcending the Defilement Bodhisattva, Awesome Power of the Right Dharma Sun Bodhisattva, Awesome Power of a Mountain of Meritorious Qualities Bodhisattva, Awesome Power of Wisdom Radiance Bodhisattva, and Awesome Power of Universal Auspiciousness Bodhisattva.

Earth Matrix Bodhisattva, Space Matrix Bodhisattva, Lotus flower Matrix Bodhisattva, Jewel Matrix Bodhisattva, Solar Matrix Bodhisattva, Pure Virtue Matrix Bodhisattva, Dharma Seal Matrix Bodhisattva, Light Matrix Bodhisattva, Navel Matrix Bodhisattva, and Lotus Flower Virtue Matrix Bodhisattva.

Fine Eye Bodhisattva, Pure Eye Bodhisattva, Stainless Eye Bodhisattva, Unimpeded Eye Bodhisattva, Universally Seeing Eye Bodhisattva, Skillfully Contemplating Eye Bodhisattva, Blue Lotus Eye Bodhisattva, Vajra Eye Bodhisattva, Jewel Eye Bodhisattva, Empty Space Eye Bodhisattva, Joyous Eye Bodhisattva, and Universal Eye Bodhisattva.

Celestial Crown Bodhisattva, Wisdom Crown Everywhere Illuminating the Dharma Realm Bodhisattva, Bodhimaṇḍa Crown Bodhisattva, Crown Everywhere Illuminating the Ten Directions Bodhisattva, Crown of All Buddhas' Matrix Bodhisattva, Crown Transcending All Worlds Bodhisattva, Universally Illuminating

正體字

普照冠菩薩。不可壞冠菩薩。
319a24║ 持一切如來師子座冠菩薩。普照法界虛空
319a25║ 冠菩薩。梵王髻菩薩。龍王髻菩薩。一切化
319a26║ 佛光明髻菩薩。[2]一切道場髻菩薩。一切願海
319a27║ 音寶王髻菩薩。一切佛光明摩尼髻菩薩。示
319a28║ 現一切虛空平等相摩尼王莊嚴髻菩薩。示
319a29║ 現一切如來神變摩尼王幢網垂覆髻菩薩。
319b01║ 出一切佛轉法輪音髻菩薩。說三世一切名
319b02║ 字音髻菩薩。大光菩薩。離垢光菩薩。寶光菩
319b03║ 薩。離塵光菩薩。焰光菩薩。法光菩薩。寂靜光
319b04║ 菩薩。日光菩薩。自在光菩薩。天光菩薩。福德
319b05║ 幢菩薩。智慧幢菩薩。法幢菩薩。神通幢菩薩。
319b06║ 光幢菩薩。華幢菩薩。摩尼幢菩薩。菩提幢菩
319b07║ 薩。梵幢菩薩。普光幢菩薩。梵音菩薩。海[3]音
319b08║ 菩薩。大地音菩薩。世主音菩薩。山相擊音菩
319b09║ 薩。遍一切法界音菩薩。震一切法海雷音菩
319b10║ 薩。降魔音菩薩。大慈方便雲雷音菩薩。息一
319b11║ 切世間苦安慰音菩薩。法上菩薩。勝上菩薩。
319b12║ 智上菩薩。福德須彌上菩薩。功德珊瑚上菩
319b13║ 薩。名稱上菩薩。普光上菩薩。大慈上菩薩。智
319b14║ 海上菩薩。佛種上菩薩。光勝菩薩。德勝菩薩。
319b15║ 上勝菩薩。

简体字

普照冠菩萨、不可坏冠菩萨、持一切如来师子座冠菩萨、普照法界虚空冠菩萨、梵王髻菩萨、龙王髻菩萨、一切化佛光明髻菩萨、道场髻菩萨、一切愿海音宝王髻菩萨、一切佛光明摩尼髻菩萨、示现一切虚空平等相摩尼王庄严髻菩萨、示现一切如来神变摩尼王幢网垂覆髻菩萨、出一切佛转法轮音髻菩萨、说三世一切名字音髻菩萨、大光菩萨、离垢光菩萨、宝光菩萨、离尘光菩萨、焰光菩萨、法光菩萨、寂静光菩萨、日光菩萨、自在光菩萨、天光菩萨、福德幢菩萨、智慧幢菩萨、法幢菩萨、神通幢菩萨、光幢菩萨、华幢菩萨、摩尼幢菩萨、菩提幢菩萨、梵幢菩萨、普光幢菩萨、梵音菩萨、海音菩萨、大地音菩萨、世主音菩萨、山相击音菩萨、遍一切法界音菩萨、震一切法海雷音菩萨、降魔音菩萨、大慈方便云雷音菩萨、息一切世间苦安慰音菩萨、法上菩萨、胜上菩萨、智上菩萨、福德须弥上菩萨、功德珊瑚上菩萨、名称上菩萨、普光上菩萨、大慈上菩萨、智海上菩萨、佛种上菩萨、光胜菩萨、德胜菩萨、上胜菩萨、

Crown Bodhisattva, Indestructible Crown Bodhisattva, Crown Holding all Tathāgatas' Lion Throne Bodhisattva, and Crown Universally Illuminating the Dharma Realm's Empty Space Bodhisattva.

Brahman King Topknot Bodhisattva, Dragon King Topknot Bodhisattva, Light of All Transformation Buddhas' Topknots Bodhisattva, All Bodhimaṇḍas' Topknot Bodhisattva, Sound of the Ocean of All Vows Sovereign Jewel Topknot Bodhisattva, All Buddhas' Light Maṇi Jewel Topknot Bodhisattva, Topknot Adorned with Sovereign Jewels Revealing the Identical Character of All Space Bodhisattva, Topknot Draped with Sovereign Maṇi Jewel Banners and Nets Revealing All Tathāgatas' Spiritual Transformations Bodhisattva, Topknot Emanating the Sound of All Buddhas' Turning of the Dharma Wheel Bodhisattva, and Topknot Speaking the Sound of All Names of the Three Periods of Time Bodhisattva.

Great Light Bodhisattva, Stainless Light Bodhisattva, Jewel Light Bodhisattva, Dust-Transcending Light Bodhisattva, Flaming Light Bodhisattva, Dharma Light Bodhisattva, Quiescent Light Bodhisattva, Solar Light Bodhisattva, Light of the Sovereign Masteries Bodhisattva, and Celestial Light Bodhisattva.

Merit Banner Bodhisattva, Wisdom Banner Bodhisattva, Dharma Banner Bodhisattva, Spiritual Superknowledges Banner Bodhisattva, Light Banner Bodhisattva, Floral Banner Bodhisattva, Jewel Banner Bodhisattva, Bodhi Banner Bodhisattva, Brahman Banner Bodhisattva, and Universal Light Banner Bodhisattva.

Brahman Sound Bodhisattva, Ocean Sound Bodhisattva, Great Earth Sound Bodhisattva, World Leaders' Sound Bodhisattva, Sound of Colliding Mountains Bodhisattva, Sound Pervading the Entire Dharma Realm Bodhisattva, Thunder Sound Shaking the Ocean of All Dharmas Bodhisattva, Māra-Vanquishing Sound Bodhisattva, Thunder Sound of the Cloud of Great Kindness and Skillful Means Bodhisattva, and Comforting Sound Extinguishing All Worlds' Sufferings Bodhisattva.

Risen from Dharma Bodhisattva, Risen from Victory Bodhisattva, Risen from Wisdom Bodhisattva, Risen from a Sumeru of Merit Bodhisattva, Risen from Merit Coral Bodhisattva, Risen from Fame Bodhisattva, Risen from Universal Light Bodhisattva, Risen from Great Kindness Bodhisattva, Risen from a Wisdom Sea Bodhisattva, and Risen from the Buddha's Lineage Bodhisattva.

Light Supremacy Bodhisattva, Virtue Supremacy Bodhisattva, Ascendant Supremacy Bodhisattva, Universal Radiance Supremacy

正體字

普明勝菩薩。法勝菩薩。月勝菩薩。
319b16║ 虛空勝菩薩。寶勝菩薩。幢勝菩薩。智勝菩薩。
319b17║ 娑羅自在王菩薩。法自在王菩薩。象自在王
319b18║ 菩薩。梵自在王菩薩。山自在王菩薩。眾自
319b19║ 在王菩薩。速疾自在王菩薩。寂靜自在王菩
319b20║ 薩。不動自在王菩薩。勢力自在王菩薩。最勝
319b21║ 自在王菩薩。寂靜音菩薩。無礙音菩薩。地震
319b22║ 音菩薩。海震音菩薩。雲音菩薩。法光音菩薩。
319b23║ 虛空音菩薩。說一切眾生善根音菩薩。示一
319b24║ 切大願音菩薩。道場音菩薩。須彌光覺菩薩。
319b25║ 虛空覺菩薩。離染覺菩薩。無礙覺菩薩。善覺
319b26║ 菩薩。普照三世覺菩薩。廣大覺菩薩。普明覺
319b27║ 菩薩。法界光明覺菩薩。如是等菩薩摩訶薩
319b28║ 五百人俱。此諸菩薩。皆悉成就普賢行願。境
319b29║ 界無礙。普遍一切諸佛剎故。現身無量。親近
319c01║ 一切諸如來故。淨眼無障。見一切佛神變事
319c02║ 故。至處無限。一切如來成正覺所。恒普詣故。
319c03║ 光明無際。以智慧光。普照一切實法海故。說
319c04║ 法無盡。清淨辯才。無邊際劫。無窮盡故。等虛
319c05║ 空界。智慧所行。悉清淨故。

简体字

普明胜菩萨、法胜菩萨、月胜菩萨、虚空胜菩萨、宝胜菩萨、幢胜菩萨、智胜菩萨、娑罗自在王菩萨、法自在王菩萨、象自在王菩萨、梵自在王菩萨、山自在王菩萨、众自在王菩萨、速疾自在王菩萨、寂静自在王菩萨、不动自在王菩萨、势力自在王菩萨、最胜自在王菩萨、寂静音菩萨、无碍音菩萨、地震音菩萨、海震音菩萨、云音菩萨、法光音菩萨、虚空音菩萨、说一切众生善根音菩萨、示一切大愿音菩萨、道场音菩萨、须弥光觉菩萨、虚空觉菩萨、离染觉菩萨、无碍觉菩萨、善觉菩萨、普照三世觉菩萨、广大觉菩萨、普明觉菩萨、法界光明觉菩萨，如是等菩萨摩诃萨五百人俱。此诸菩萨皆悉成就普贤行愿，境界无碍，普遍一切诸佛刹故；现身无量，亲近一切诸如来故；净眼无障，见一切佛神变事故；至处无限，一切如来成正觉所恒普诣故；光明无际，以智慧光普照一切实法海故；说法无尽，清净辩才无边际劫无穷尽故；等虚空界，智慧所行悉清净故；

Bodhisattva, Dharma Supremacy Bodhisattva, Moon Supremacy Bodhisattva, Empty Space Supremacy Bodhisattva, Jewel Supremacy Bodhisattva, Banner Supremacy Bodhisattva, and Wisdom Supremacy Bodhisattva.

Śāla Sovereign King Bodhisattva, Dharma Sovereign King Bodhisattva, Elephant Sovereign King Bodhisattva, Brahman Sovereign King Bodhisattva, Mountain Sovereign King Bodhisattva, Manifold Sovereign King Bodhisattva, Swift Sovereign King Bodhisattva, Quiescent Sovereign King Bodhisattva, Motionless Sovereign King Bodhisattva, Strength Sovereign King Bodhisattva, and Supreme Sovereign King Bodhisattva.

Quiescent Sound Bodhisattva, Unimpeded Sound Bodhisattva, Earthquake Sound Bodhisattva, Oceanic Quaking Sound Bodhisattva, Cloud Sound Bodhisattva, Dharma Light Sound Bodhisattva, Empty Space Sound Bodhisattva, Sound Proclaiming All Beings' Roots of Goodness Bodhisattva, Sound Manifesting All Great Vows Bodhisattva, and Bodhimaṇḍa Sound Bodhisattva.

Sumeru Light Awakening Bodhisattva, Empty Space Awakening Bodhisattva, Transcending Defilement Awakening Bodhisattva, Unimpeded Awakening Bodhisattva, Thorough Awakening Bodhisattva, Universal Illumination of the Three Times Awakening Bodhisattva, Vast Awakening Bodhisattva, Universal Clarity Awakening Bodhisattva, and Dharma Realm Light Awakening Bodhisattva.

In all, there were five hundred bodhisattva-mahāsattvas such as these. All of these bodhisattvas had entirely perfected the conduct and vows of Samantabhadra:

Their spheres of cognition were unimpeded, for they pervaded the *kṣetras* of all buddhas;

They manifested countless bodies, for they drew near to all *tathāgatas*;

The vision of their purified eyes was unobstructed, for they observed all buddhas' spiritual transformations;

They were unlimited in the places to which they went, for they were forever traveling to pay their respects where all *tathāgatas* achieved the right enlightenment;

Their radiance was boundless, for their wisdom light everywhere illuminated the ocean of all true dharmas;

They were inexhaustible in speaking Dharma, for they could hold forth endlessly, doing so with pure eloquence throughout boundless kalpas;

They were commensurate with the realm of empty space, for their wisdom's actions were all completely purified;

正體字

無所依止。隨眾生
319c06║ 心。現色身故。除滅癡翳。了眾生界。無眾生
319c07║ 故。等虛空智。以大光網。照法界故。及與五百
319c08║ 聲聞眾俱。悉覺真諦。皆證實際。深入法性。永
319c09║ 出有海。依佛功德。離結使縛。住無礙處。其心
319c10║ 寂靜。猶如虛空。於諸佛所。永斷疑惑。於佛智
319c11║ 海。深信趣入。及與無量諸世主俱。悉曾供養
319c12║ 無量諸佛。常能利益一切眾生。為不請友。恒
319c13║ 勤守護。誓願不捨。入於世間殊勝智門。從佛
319c14║ 教生。護佛正法。起於大願。不斷佛種。生如來
319c15║ 家。求一切智
319c16║ 時諸菩薩大德聲聞。世間諸王。并其眷屬。咸
319c17║ 作是念。如來境界。如來智行。如來加持。如來
319c18║ 力。如來無畏。如來三昧。如來所住。如來自
319c19║ 在。如來身。如來智。一切世間。諸天及人。無
319c20║ 能通達。無能趣入。無能信解。無能了知。無能
319c21║ 忍受。無能觀察。無能揀擇。無能開示。無能宣
319c22║ 明。無有能令眾生解了。

简体字

无所依止，随众生心现色身故；除灭痴翳，了众生界无众生故；等虚空智，以大光网照法界故。及与五百声闻众俱，悉觉真谛，皆证实际，深入法性，永出有海；依佛功德，离结、使、缚，住无碍处；其心寂静犹如虚空，于诸佛所永断疑惑，于佛智海深信趣入。及与无量诸世主俱，悉曾供养无量诸佛，常能利益一切众生，为不请友，恒勤守护，誓愿不舍；入于世间殊胜智门，从佛教生，护佛正法，起于大愿，不断佛种，生如来家，求一切智。

　　时，诸菩萨大德、声闻、世间诸王并其眷属，咸作是念：“如来境界、如来智行、如来加持、如来力、如来无畏、如来三昧、如来所住、如来自在、如来身、如来智，一切世间诸天及人无能通达、无能趣入、无能信解、无能了知、无能忍受、无能观察、无能拣择、无能开示、无能宣明、无有能令众生解了，

They had no particular place in which they dwelt, for they adapted to the minds of beings in manifesting their form bodies;

They had extinguished the cataracts of the delusions, for they completely understood that the realms of beings contained no beings at all; and

They possessed wisdom commensurate with empty space, for they illuminated the Dharma realm with an immense net of light.

He was also together with a congregation of five hundred *śrāvaka* disciples, all of whom had awakened to the truths and all of whom had achieved realization of ultimate reality, had deeply penetrated the nature of dharmas, had forever escaped the ocean of existence, had, in reliance upon the qualities of the Buddha, left behind the bonds of the fetters, had come to dwell in the unimpeded stations, had made their minds so quiescent as to be like empty space, had forever cut off any doubts in the buddhas, and had developed deep faith in and proceeded into the ocean of the Buddha's knowledge.

He was also together with countless world leaders, all of whom had made offerings to countless buddhas. They were always able to benefit all beings, serving them as unsolicited friends. They were constantly diligent in protecting them, having made vows to never forsake them. They had entered the gateways of the world's especially excellent wisdom and had been born from the Buddha's teaching. They protected the Buddha's right Dharma and generated great vows to prevent the severance of the lineage of the buddhas. They had been born into the clan of the Tathāgata and sought to acquire all-knowledge.

At that time, the bodhisattvas, the venerable *śrāvaka* disciples, the world leaders, and those in their retinues all had this thought:

As for the Tathāgata's sphere of action, the range in which the Tathāgata's knowledge functions, the Tathāgata's empowerments, the Tathāgata's powers, the Tathāgata's fearlessnesses, the Tathāgata's samādhis, the Tathāgata's dwelling places, the Tathāgata's sovereign masteries, the Tathāgata's bodies, and the Tathāgata's knowledge, these are all such that, of all the world's devas or humans, none would be able to reach a penetrating comprehension of them, none would be able to enter them, none would be able to have resolute faith in them, none would be able to completely know them, none would be able to accept them, none would be able to contemplate them, none would be able to selectively distinguish among them, none would be able to explain them, none would be able to elucidate them; and none would be able to cause beings to completely understand them.

正體字

唯除諸佛加被之力。
319c23‖ 佛神通力。佛威德力。佛本願力。及其宿世善
319c24‖ 根之力。諸善知識。攝受之力。深淨信力。大明
319c25‖ 解力。趣向菩提。清淨心力。求一切智。廣大願
319c26‖ 力。唯願世尊。隨順我等及諸眾生。種種欲。種
319c27‖ 種解。種種智。種種語。種種自在。種種住地。
319c28‖ 種種根清淨。種種意方便。種種心境界。種種
319c29‖ 依止如來功德。種種聽受諸所說法。顯示如
320a01‖ 來往昔趣求一切智心。往昔所起菩薩大願
320a02‖ 往昔所淨諸波羅蜜。往昔所入菩薩諸地。往
320a03‖ 昔圓滿諸菩薩行。往昔成就方便。往昔修行
320a04‖ 諸道。往昔所得出離法。往昔所作神通事。往
320a05‖ 昔所有。本事因緣。及成等正覺。轉妙法輪。淨
320a06‖ 佛國土。調伏眾生。開一切智法城。示一切眾
320a07‖ 生道。入一切眾生所住。受一切眾生所施。為
320a08‖ 一切眾生。說布施功德。為一切眾生。現諸佛
320a09‖ 影像。如是等法。願皆為說

简体字

唯除诸佛加被之力、佛神通力、佛威德力、佛本愿力，及其宿世善根之力、诸善知识摄受之力、深净信力、大明解力、趣向菩提清净心力、求一切智广大愿力。唯愿世尊随顺我等及诸众生种种欲、种种解、种种智、种种语、种种自在、种种住地、种种根清净、种种意方便、种种心境界、种种依止如来功德、种种听受诸所说法，显示如来往昔趣求一切智心、往昔所起菩萨大愿、往昔所净诸波罗蜜、往昔所入菩萨诸地、往昔圆满诸菩萨行、往昔成就方便、往昔修行诸道、往昔所得出离法、往昔所作神通事、往昔所有本事因缘，及成等正觉、转妙法轮、净佛国土、调伏众生、开一切智法城、示一切众生道、入一切众生所住、受一切众生所施、为一切众生说布施功德、为一切众生现诸佛影像；如是等法，愿皆为说！”

They would remain unable to do so unless they were assisted by the power of all buddhas' assistance, by the power of the Buddha's spiritual superknowledges, by the power of the Buddha's awesome virtue, by the power of the Buddha's original vows, by the power of past-life roots of goodness, by the power of having been drawn forth and sustained by good spiritual guides, by the power of deep and pure faith, by the power of immensely clear understanding, by the power of pure resolve to progress toward bodhi, and by the power of a vast vow to seek all-knowledge.

We only wish that the Bhagavat would adapt to us and to all beings in accordance with our many different desires, many different understandings, many different kinds of knowledge, many different languages, many different masteries, many different dwelling grounds, many different degrees of purification of the faculties, many different motivations and methods, many different spheres of mind, many different ways of relying on the meritorious qualities of the Tathāgata, and many different ways of hearing and accepting all the Dharma that has been proclaimed. Then, having done so, may the Bhagavat reveal:

His past resolve to set out in the quest for all-knowledge;
His past generation of the bodhisattva's great vows;
His past purification of the *pāramitās;*
His past entry onto the bodhisattva grounds;
His past fulfillment of the bodhisattva practices;
His past perfection of expedient means;
His past cultivation of all paths;
His past acquisition of the dharmas of emancipation;
His past feats of the spiritual superknowledges; and
The causes and conditions of his previous lifetimes as well as:

His realization of the universal and right enlightenment;
His turning of the wheel of the sublime Dharma;
His purification of his buddha land;
His training of beings;
His opening of the Dharma city of all-knowledge;
His revealing of all beings' paths;
His entry into the places in which all beings dwell;
His acceptance of the gifts of all beings;
His instruction to all beings about the merit of giving; and
His displaying for all beings the appearance of all buddhas.

We wish that, for our sakes, he will speak about all dharmas such as these.

正體字

320a10 ‖ 爾時世尊。知諸菩薩心之所念。大悲為身。大
320a11 ‖ 悲為門。大悲為首。以大悲法。而為方便。充遍
320a12 ‖ 虛空。入師子[1]頻申三昧。入此三昧已。一切
320a13 ‖ 世間。普皆嚴淨。于時此大莊嚴樓閣。忽然廣
320a14 ‖ 博。無有邊際。金剛為地。寶王覆上。無量寶
320a15 ‖ 華。及諸摩尼。普散其中。處處盈滿。瑠璃為
320a16 ‖ 柱。眾寶合成。大光摩尼之所莊嚴。閻浮檀金
320a17 ‖ 如意寶王。周置其上。以為嚴飾。危樓[2]迴帶。
320a18 ‖ 閣道傍出。棟宇相承窓闥交映。階墀軒檻。
320a19 ‖ 種種備足。一切皆以妙寶莊嚴。其寶悉作人
320a20 ‖ 天形像。堅固妙好。世中第一。摩尼寶網。彌覆
320a21 ‖ 其上。於諸門側。悉建幢幡。咸放光明。普周法
320a22 ‖ 界道場之外。階隥欄楯。其數無量不可稱說。
320a23 ‖ 靡不咸以摩尼所成。爾時復以佛神力故。其
320a24 ‖ 逝多林。忽然廣博。與不可說佛剎微塵數諸
320a25 ‖ 佛國土。其量正等。一切妙寶。間錯莊嚴。不可
320a26 ‖ 說寶。遍布其地。阿僧祇寶。以為垣牆。寶多羅
320a27 ‖ 樹。莊嚴道側。其間復有無量香河。香水盈滿。
320a28 ‖ 湍激洄澓。一切寶華。隨流右轉。自然演出佛
320a29 ‖ 法音聲。

简体字

尔时，世尊知诸菩萨心之所念，大悲为身，大悲为门，大悲为首，以大悲法而为方便，充遍虚空，入师子频申三昧；入此三昧已，一切世间普皆严净。于时，此大庄严楼阁忽然广博无有边际。金刚为地，宝王覆上，无量宝华及诸摩尼普散其中处处盈满。琉璃为柱，众宝合成，大光摩尼之所庄严，阎浮檀金如意宝王周置其上以为严饰。危楼迴带，阁道傍出，栋宇相承，窗闼交映，阶、墀、轩、槛种种备足，一切皆以妙宝庄严；其宝悉作人、天形像，坚固妙好，世中第一，摩尼宝网弥覆其上。于诸门侧悉建幢幡，咸放光明普周法界道场之外。阶蹬、栏楯，其数无量不可称说，靡不咸以摩尼所成。

尔时，复以佛神力故，其逝多林忽然广博，与不可说佛刹微尘数诸佛国土其量正等。一切妙宝间错庄严，不可说宝遍布其地，阿僧祇宝以为垣墙，宝多罗树庄严道侧。其间复有无量香河，香水盈满，湍激洄澓；一切宝华随流右转，自然演出佛法音声；

Then, aware of the thoughts that had arisen in the minds of all the bodhisattvas and taking the great compassion as his body, the great compassion as his gateway, the great compassion as foremost, and taking the dharma of great compassion as his method, the Bhagavat then filled all of empty space and entered the lion sprint samādhi. Having entered this samādhi, the entire world became everywhere purified.[3]

At this time, the Greatly Adorned Pavilion suddenly became boundlessly vast. The ground beneath it became composed of vajra covered by kings of jewels. Countless jewel flowers and all kinds of *maṇi* jewels were spread about everywhere within it so that every place overflowed with them. *Vaiḍūrya* formed its pillars and it was composed of combinations of the many kinds of jewels. It was adorned with greatly radiant *maṇi* jewels with *jambūnada* gold and sovereign wishing jewels arranged around its top as adornments. It was surrounded by tall towers off in the distance and roads ran off from its sides so that the buildings connected with each other and the windows and doorways each shone light on the other. The steps and railings were fully adorned in many ways with all kinds of marvelous jewels. All of those jewels displayed images of humans and devas. They were solid, marvelously fine, and foremost in the entire world.

A net of *maṇi* jewels stretched all across it from above and banners and pennants stood alongside all the doors. They all emanated brilliant light that everywhere pervaded the Dharma realm. Outside of this site of enlightenment, there were so innumerably many cascades of steps and railings as to be indescribable. None of them were not made entirely of *maṇi* jewels.

Then, again because of the Buddha's spiritual powers, that Jeta Grove suddenly became so expansively vast as to equal in its dimensions buddha lands as numerous as the atoms in inconceivably many buddha *kṣetras*. It was inlaid with adornments created from all the marvelous jewels. Indescribably many jewels were spread all about across its grounds. *Asaṃkhyeyas* of jewels composed its walls. Jeweled palm trees served as adornments along its pathways where, in addition, between them, there were countless fragrant streams brimming with scented waters the currents of which stirred whirling eddies in which jeweled blossoms twirled to the right, following the direction of the flow, spontaneously proclaiming the sounds of the Buddha's Dharma.

正體字

不思議寶。芬陀利華。菡萏芬敷。彌布
320b01‖ 水上。眾寶華樹。列植其岸。種種臺榭。不可思
320b02‖ 議。皆於岸上。次第行列。摩尼寶網之所彌覆。
320b03‖ 阿僧祇寶。放大光明。阿僧祇寶。莊嚴其地。燒
320b04‖ 眾妙香。香氣[3]氛氳。復建無量種種寶幢。所
320b05‖ 謂寶香幢。寶[表>衣]幢。寶幡幢。寶繒幢。寶華幢。
320b06‖ 寶瓔珞幢。寶鬘幢。寶鈴幢。摩尼寶蓋幢。大摩
320b07‖ 尼寶幢。光明遍照摩尼寶幢。出一切如來名
320b08‖ 號音聲摩尼王幢。師子摩尼王幢。說一切如
320b09‖ 來本事海摩尼王幢。現一切法界影像摩尼
320b10‖ 王幢。周遍十方。行列莊嚴。時逝多林上虛空
320b11‖ 之中。有不思議天宮殿雲。無數香樹雲。不可
320b12‖ 說須彌山雲。不可說妓樂雲。出美妙音歌讚
320b13‖ 如來不可說寶蓮華雲。不可說寶座雲。敷以
320b14‖ 天衣菩薩坐上歎佛功德不可說諸天王形像
320b15‖ 摩尼寶雲。不可說白真珠雲。不可說赤珠樓
320b16‖ 閣莊嚴具雲。不可說雨金剛堅固珠雲。皆住
320b17‖ 虛空。周匝遍滿。以為嚴飾。何以故。

简体字

不思议宝芬陀利华，菡萏芬敷，弥布水上；众宝华树列植其岸；种种台榭不可思议，皆于岸上次第行列，摩尼宝网之所弥覆。阿僧祇宝放大光明，阿僧祇宝庄严其地。烧众妙香，香气氛氲。复建无量种种宝幢，所谓：宝香幢、宝衣幢、宝幡幢、宝缯幢、宝华幢、宝璎珞幢、宝鬘幢、宝铃幢、摩尼宝盖幢、大摩尼宝幢、光明遍照摩尼宝幢、出一切如来名号音声摩尼王幢、师子摩尼王幢、说一切如来本事海摩尼王幢、现一切法界影像摩尼王幢，周遍十方，行列庄严。

时，逝多林上虚空之中，有不思议天宫殿云、无数香树云、不可说须弥山云、不可说妓乐云、出美妙音歌赞如来不可说宝莲华云、不可说宝座云、敷以天衣菩萨坐上叹佛功德不可说诸天王形像摩尼宝云、不可说白真珠云、不可说赤珠楼阁庄严具云、不可说雨金刚坚固珠云，皆住虚空，周匝遍满，以为严饰。何以故？

Inconceivably many buds of *puṇḍarīka* lotus flowers made of inconceivably fine jewels blossomed fragrantly all across the surface of these waters. Trees with blossoms made of the many kinds of jewels were planted all along the banks. All kinds of different terraces and open halls, inconceivably marvelous in appearance, were arrayed in sequential rows along the shore, all of them draped with *maṇi* jewel nets from which *asaṃkhyeyas* of jewels emanated brilliant light. *Asaṃkhyeyas* of jewels graced those grounds on which many varieties of sublime incense burned, sending forth mists of fragrant vapors.

Countless jeweled banners of every different sort also stood there, namely jeweled incense banners, jeweled robe banners, jeweled pennant banners, jeweled silk banners, jeweled blossom banners, jeweled necklace banners, jeweled garland banners, jeweled bell banners, *maṇi* jewel canopy banners, and great *maṇi* jewel banners.

In addition, there was a *maṇi* jewel banner that shone with pervasively illuminating radiance, a sovereign *maṇi* jewel banner that recited the sounds of all *tathāgatas'* names, a leonine sovereign *maṇi* jewel banner, a sovereign *maṇi* jewel banner that narrated stories of the ocean of all *tathāgatas'* previous lives, and a sovereign *maṇi* jewel banner that displayed images of the entire Dharma realm. These were present in stately rows everywhere throughout the ten directions.

Then, in the sky above the Jeta Grove, there were:

Inconceivably[4] many celestial palace clouds;
Countless incense tree clouds;
Ineffably many Mount Sumeru clouds;
Ineffably many music clouds emanating sublime sounds singing the praises of the Tathāgata;
Ineffably many clouds of lotus flowers made of jewels;
Ineffably many clouds of jeweled thrones draped with celestial robes on which bodhisattvas sat, praising the Buddha's meritorious qualities;
Ineffably many *maṇi* jewel clouds displaying the images of heavenly kings;
Ineffably many clouds of real white pearls;
Ineffably many clouds of ruby towers adorned with ornaments; and
Ineffably many clouds that sprinkled down solid-vajra pearls.

These phenomena all remained there in the sky, everywhere encircling the area, serving as adornments. And why did this occur? It did so:

正體字

如來善
320b18‖ 根。不思議故。如來白法不思議故。如來威力
320b19‖ 不思議故。如來能以一身。自在變化。遍一切
320b20‖ 世界。不思議故。如來能以神力。令一切佛及
320b21‖ 佛國莊嚴。皆入其身。不思議故。如來能於一
320b22‖ 微塵內。普現一切法界影像。不思議故。如來
320b23‖ 能於一毛孔中。示現過去一切諸佛。不思議
320b24‖ 故。如來隨放一一光明。悉能遍照一切世界。
320b25‖ 不思議故。如來能於一毛孔中。出一切佛刹
320b26‖ 微塵數變化雲。充滿一切諸佛國土。不思議
320b27‖ 故。如來能於一毛孔中。普現一切十方世界。
320b28‖ 成住壞劫。不思議故。如於此逝多林給孤獨
320b29‖ 園。見佛國土。清淨莊嚴。十方一切。盡法界虛
320c01‖ 空界。一切世界。亦如是見。所謂見如來身。住
320c02‖ 逝多林。菩薩眾會。皆悉遍滿。見普雨一切莊
320c03‖ 嚴雲。見普雨一切寶光明照曜雲。見普雨一
320c04‖ 切摩尼寶雲。見普雨一切莊嚴蓋彌覆佛刹
320c05‖ 雲。見普雨一切天身雲。見普雨一切華樹雲。
320c06‖ 見普雨一切衣樹雲。見普雨一切寶鬘瓔珞
320c07‖ 相續不絕周遍一切大地雲。見普雨一切莊
320c08‖ 嚴具雲。見普雨一切如眾生形種種香雲。

简体字

如来善根不思议故，如来白法不思议故，如来威力不思议故，如来能以一身自在变化遍一切世界不思议故，如来能以神力令一切佛及佛国庄严皆入其身不思议故，如来能于一微尘内普现一切法界影像不思议故，如来能于一毛孔中示现过去一切诸佛不思议故，如来随放一一光明悉能遍照一切世界不思议故，如来能于一毛孔中出一切佛刹微尘数变化云充满一切诸佛国土不思议故，如来能于一毛孔中普现一切十方世界成、住、坏劫不思议故。如于此逝多林给孤独园见佛国土清净庄严，十方一切尽法界、虚空界、一切世界亦如是见。所谓：见如来身住逝多林，菩萨众会皆悉遍满；见普雨一切庄严云，见普雨一切宝光明照曜云，见普雨一切摩尼宝云，见普雨一切庄严盖弥覆佛刹云，见普雨一切天身云，见普雨一切华树云，见普雨一切衣树云，见普雨一切宝鬘、璎珞相续不绝周遍一切大地云，见普雨一切庄严具云，见普雨一切如众生形种种香云，

Due to the inconceivability of the Tathāgata's roots of goodness;
Due to the inconceivability of the Tathāgata's pure dharmas;
Due to the inconceivability of the Tathāgata's awesome powers;
Due to the inconceivability of the Tathāgata's ability to miraculously transform one body so that it pervades all worlds;
Due to the inconceivability of the Tathāgata's ability to use his spiritual powers to cause all buddhas and their buddha lands' adornments to enter into his own body;
Due to the inconceivability of the Tathāgata's ability to everywhere manifest reflected images of the entire Dharma realm within one atom;
Due to the inconceivability of the Tathāgata's ability to reveal all buddhas of the past within one pore;
Due to the inconceivability of the Tathāgata's emanation of rays of light, each one of which is able to everywhere illuminate all worlds;
Due to the inconceivability of the Tathāgata's ability to emanate from one pore clouds of transformations as numerous as the atoms in all buddha *kṣetras* that completely fill all buddha lands; and
Due to the inconceivability of the Tathāgata's ability to reveal within but one pore the kalpas of formation, abiding, and destruction of all worlds of the ten directions.

And just as one observed the pure adornments of the Buddha's land here within this Jeta Grove's Garden of the Benefactor of Orphans and the Solitary, so too could one also observe this in all worlds of the ten directions throughout the entire Dharma realm and the realm of empty space, as follows:

One saw the body of the Tathāgata dwelling in the Jeta Grove together with a congregation full of bodhisattvas;
One saw clouds everywhere raining all kinds of adornments;
One saw clouds everywhere raining all kinds of jewels that shone with dazzling radiance;
One saw clouds everywhere raining all kinds of *maṇi* jewels;
One saw clouds everywhere raining all kinds of adorned canopies that completely covered the buddha *kṣetra*;
One saw clouds everywhere raining all kinds of heavenly bodies;
One saw clouds everywhere raining all kinds of flowering trees;
One saw clouds everywhere raining all kinds of robe-bearing trees;[5]
One saw clouds continuously and uninterruptedly raining all kinds of jeweled garlands and necklaces all over the great earth;
One saw clouds everywhere raining all kinds of articles of adornment;
One saw clouds everywhere raining incense vapors in the shapes of all kinds of beings;

正體字

見
320c09 普雨一切微妙寶華網相續不斷雲。見普雨
320c10 一切諸天女持寶幢幡於虛空中周旋來去
320c11 雲。見普雨一切眾寶蓮華於華葉間自然而
320c12 出種種樂音雲。見普雨一切師子座寶網瓔
320c13 珞而為莊嚴雲
320c14 爾時東方。過不可說佛剎微塵數世界海外。
320c15 有世界。名金燈雲幢。佛號毘盧遮那勝德王。
320c16 彼佛眾中。有菩薩。名毘盧遮那願光明。與不
320c17 可說佛剎微塵數菩薩俱。來向佛所。悉以神
320c18 力。興種種雲。所謂天華雲。天香雲。天末香
320c19 雲。天鬘雲。天寶雲。天莊嚴具雲。天寶蓋雲。
320c20 天微妙衣雲。天寶幢幡雲。天一切妙寶。諸莊
320c21 嚴雲。充滿虛空。至佛所已。頂禮佛足。即於東
320c22 方。化作寶莊嚴樓閣。及普照十方寶蓮華藏
320c23 師子之座。如意寶網。羅覆其身。與其眷屬。結
320c24 [4]跏趺坐。南方過不可說佛剎微塵數世界海
320c25 外。有世界。名金剛藏。佛號普光明無勝藏王。
320c26 彼佛眾中。有菩薩。名不可壞精進王。與不可
320c27 說佛剎微塵數菩薩俱。

简体字

见普雨一切微妙宝华网相续不断云，见普雨一切诸天女持宝幢幡于虚空中周旋来去云，见普雨一切众宝莲华于华叶间自然而出种种乐音云，见普雨一切师子座宝网璎珞而为庄严云。

尔时，东方过不可说佛刹微尘数世界海外有世界，名金灯云幢，佛号毗卢遮那胜德王。彼佛众中有菩萨，名毗卢遮那愿光明，与不可说佛刹微尘数菩萨俱，来向佛所，悉以神力兴种种云，所谓：天华云、天香云、天末香云、天鬘云、天宝云、天庄严具云、天宝盖云、天微妙衣云、天宝幢幡云、天一切妙宝诸庄严云，充满虚空。至佛所已，顶礼佛足，即于东方化作宝庄严楼阁及普照十方宝莲华藏师子之座，如意宝网罗覆其身，与其眷属结跏趺坐。

南方过不可说佛刹微尘数世界海外有世界，名金刚藏，佛号普光明无胜藏王。彼佛众中有菩萨，名不可坏精进王，与不可说佛刹微尘数菩萨俱，

One saw clouds everywhere continuously raining all kinds of nets of subtle and marvelous flowers made of jewels;

One saw clouds everywhere raining all kinds of celestial maidens who held jeweled banners and pennants as they circled about hither and thither up in the sky;

One saw clouds everywhere raining all kinds of lotus flowers made of the many kinds of jewels that spontaneously emanated the sounds of many different types of music from between their flower petals; and

One saw clouds everywhere raining all kinds of lion thrones adorned with jeweled nets and necklaces.

Then, off in the easterly direction, beyond an ocean of worlds as numerous as the atoms in an ineffably great number of buddha *kṣetras,* there was a world known as Golden Lamp Cloud Banner with a buddha named Vairocana's Supreme Virtue King. Within that buddha's congregation, there was a bodhisattva named Light of Vairocana's Vows who, accompanied by bodhisattvas as numerous as the atoms in an ineffably great number of buddha *kṣetras,* came to where the Buddha dwelt, whereupon they all used their spiritual powers to cause all kinds of different clouds to come forth and fill the entire sky, namely clouds of heavenly flowers, clouds of heavenly incense, clouds of heavenly powdered incense, clouds of heavenly garlands, clouds of heavenly jewels, clouds of heavenly adornments, clouds of heavenly jeweled canopies, clouds of fine heavenly robes, clouds of jeweled heavenly banners, and clouds adorned with all kinds of marvelous heavenly jewels.

After those bodhisattvas had all arrived in the presence of the Buddha, they bowed down in reverence at the Buddha's feet and then transformationally created off in the easterly direction a jewel-adorned tower with a jeweled lotus dais lion throne that everywhere illuminated the ten directions. Over it hung a net canopy made of wish-fulfilling jewels that spread forth and covered them all. Then, together with his entire retinue, that bodhisattva sat down there in the lotus posture.

Then, off in the southerly direction, beyond an ocean of worlds as numerous as the atoms in an ineffably great number of buddha *kṣetras,* there was a world known as Vajra Treasury with a buddha named Invincible Treasury King of Universal Light. Within that buddha's congregation, there was a bodhisattva named King of Indestructible Vigor who, together with bodhisattvas as numerous as the atoms in an ineffably great number of buddha *kṣetras,* came to

正體字

來向佛所。持一切寶
320c28║ 香網。持一切寶瓔珞。持一切寶華帶。持一切
320c29║ 寶鬘帶。持一切金剛瓔珞。持一切摩尼寶網。
321a01║ 持一切寶衣帶。持一切寶瓔珞帶。持一切最
321a02║ 勝光明摩尼帶。持一切師子。摩尼寶瓔珞。悉
321a03║ 以神力。充遍一切諸世界海。到佛所已。頂禮
321a04║ 佛足。即於南方。化作遍照世間摩尼寶莊嚴
321a05║ 樓閣。及普照十方寶蓮華藏師子之座。以一
321a06║ 切寶華網。羅覆其身。與其眷屬。結[1]跏趺坐。
321a07║ 西方過不可說佛剎微塵數世界海外。有世
321a08║ 界。名摩尼寶燈須彌山幢。佛號法界智燈。彼
321a09║ 佛眾中。有菩薩。名普勝無上威德王。與世界
321a10║ 海微塵數菩薩俱。來向佛所。悉以神力。興不
321a11║ 可說佛剎微塵數種種塗香燒香須彌山雲。不
321a12║ 可說佛剎微塵數種種色香水須彌山雲。不
321a13║ 可說佛剎微塵數一切大地微塵等光明摩尼
321a14║ 寶王須彌山雲。不可說佛剎微塵數種種光
321a15║ 焰輪莊嚴幢須彌山雲。

简体字

来向佛所，持一切宝香网，持一切宝瓔珞，持一切宝华带，持一切宝鬘带，持一切金刚瓔珞，持一切摩尼宝网，持一切宝衣带，持一切宝瓔珞带，持一切最胜光明摩尼带，持一切师子摩尼宝瓔珞，悉以神力充遍一切诸世界海。到佛所已，顶礼佛足，即于南方化作遍照世间摩尼宝庄严楼阁及普照十方宝莲华藏师子之座，以一切宝华网罗覆其身，与其眷属结跏趺坐。

西方过不可说佛刹微尘数世界海外有世界，名摩尼宝灯须弥山幢，佛号法界智灯。彼佛众中有菩萨，名普胜无上威德王，与世界海微尘数菩萨俱，来向佛所，悉以神力兴不可说佛刹微尘数种种涂香烧香须弥山云、不可说佛刹微尘数种种色香水须弥山云、不可说佛刹微尘数一切大地微尘等光明摩尼宝王须弥山云、不可说佛刹微尘数种种光焰轮庄严幢须弥山云、

where the Buddha dwelt, carrying nets consisting of all kinds of precious incense, carrying necklaces made of all kinds of jewels, carrying floral sashes made of all kinds of jewels, carrying garlands made of all kinds of jewels, carrying all kinds of vajra necklaces, carrying all kinds of nets made of *maṇi* jewels, carrying sashes made of all kinds of jeweled robes, carrying sashes made of all kinds of jeweled necklaces, carrying sashes made of all kinds of supremely radiant *maṇi* jewels, and carrying necklaces made of all kinds of leonine *maṇi* jewels. Using their spiritual powers, they caused all these adornments to fill up that entire ocean of worlds.

After those bodhisattvas had all arrived in the presence of the Buddha, they bowed down in reverence at the Buddha's feet and then transformationally created off in the southerly direction a tower adorned with *maṇi* jewels that everywhere illuminated the world together with a jeweled lotus dais lion throne that everywhere illuminated the ten directions. Over it hung a net canopy made of all kinds of jeweled flowers that spread forth and covered them all. Then, together with his entire retinue, that bodhisattva sat down there in the lotus posture.

Then, off in the westerly direction, beyond an ocean of worlds as numerous as the atoms in an ineffably great number of buddha *kṣetras,* there was a world known as Sumeru Mountain Banner of *Maṇi* Jewel Lamps with a buddha named Dharma Realm Wisdom Lamp. Within that buddha's congregation, there was a bodhisattva named King of Universally Supreme and Unsurpassable Awesome Virtue who, together with bodhisattvas as numerous as the atoms in an ocean of worlds, then came to where the Buddha dwelt and, all using their spiritual powers, conjured phenomena that filled the entire Dharma realm, namely:

Sumeru Mountain clouds as numerous as the atoms in an ineffably great number of buddha *kṣetras* consisting of all different kinds of perfumes and burning incense;

Sumeru Mountain clouds as numerous as the atoms in an ineffably great number of buddha *kṣetras* consisting of all different kinds of varicolored perfumes;

Sumeru Mountain clouds as numerous as the atoms in an ineffably great number of buddha *kṣetras* consisting of radiant sovereign *maṇi* jewels as numerous as all the atoms in the entire great earth;

Sumeru Mountain clouds as numerous as the atoms in an ineffably great number of buddha *kṣetras* consisting of all kinds of different banners adorned with flaming-light wheels;

正體字

不可說佛剎微塵數
321a16║ 種種色金剛藏摩尼王莊嚴須彌山雲。不可
321a17║ 說佛剎微塵數普照一切世界閻浮檀摩尼寶
321a18║ 幢須彌山雲。不可說佛剎微塵數現一切法
321a19║ 界摩尼寶須彌山雲。不可說佛剎微塵數現一
321a20║ 切諸佛相好摩尼寶王須彌山雲。不可說佛
321a21║ 剎微塵數現一切如來本事因緣說諸菩薩所
321a22║ 行之行摩尼寶王須彌山雲。不可說佛剎微
321a23║ 塵數現一切佛坐菩提場摩尼寶王須彌山
321a24║ 雲。充滿法界至佛所已。頂禮佛足。即於西方。
321a25║ 化作一切香王樓閣。真珠寶網。彌覆其上。及
321a26║ 化作帝釋影幢寶蓮華藏師子之座。以妙色
321a27║ 摩尼網。羅覆其身。心王寶冠。以嚴其首。與其
321a28║ 眷屬。結[＊]跏趺坐。北方過不可說佛剎微塵數
321a29║ 世界海外。有世界。名寶衣光明幢。佛號照虛
321b01║ 空法界大光明。彼佛眾中。有菩薩。名無礙勝
321b02║ 藏王。與世界海微塵數菩薩俱。來向佛所。

简体字

不可说佛刹微尘数种种色金刚藏摩尼王庄严须弥山云、不可说佛刹微尘数普照一切世界阎浮檀摩尼宝幢须弥山云、不可说佛刹微尘数现一切法界摩尼宝须弥山云、不可说佛刹微尘数现一切诸佛相好摩尼宝王须弥山云、不可说佛刹微尘数现一切如来本事因缘说诸菩萨所行之行摩尼宝王须弥山云、不可说佛刹微尘数现一切佛坐菩提场摩尼宝王须弥山云，充满法界。至佛所已，顶礼佛足，即于西方化作一切香王楼阁，真珠宝网弥覆其上，及化作帝释影幢宝莲华藏师子之座，以妙色摩尼网罗覆其身，心王宝冠以严其首，与其眷属结跏趺坐。

北方过不可说佛刹微尘数世界海外有世界，名宝衣光明幢，佛号照虚空法界大光明。彼佛众中有菩萨，名无碍胜藏王，与世界海微尘数菩萨俱，来向佛所，

Sumeru Mountain clouds as numerous as the atoms in an ineffably great number of buddha *kṣetras* consisting of all different kinds of colored vajra treasuries adorned with sovereign *maṇi* jewels;

Sumeru Mountain clouds as numerous as the atoms in an ineffably great number of buddha *kṣetras* consisting of banners made of *jambūnada* gold and *maṇi* jewels that everywhere illuminated all worlds;

Sumeru Mountain clouds as numerous as the atoms in an ineffably great number of buddha *kṣetras* consisting of *maṇi* jewels that manifested the appearance of the entire Dharma realm;

Sumeru Mountain clouds as numerous as the atoms in an ineffably great number of buddha *kṣetras* consisting of sovereign *maṇi* jewels that manifested the appearance of the major marks and secondary characteristics of all buddhas;

Sumeru Mountain clouds as numerous as the atoms in an ineffably great number of buddha *kṣetras* consisting of sovereign *maṇi* jewels that manifested the appearance of the causes and conditions of the events of all *tathāgatas'* previous lives while also proclaiming the practices in which all bodhisattvas engage; and

Sumeru Mountain clouds as numerous as the atoms in an ineffably great number of buddha *kṣetras* consisting of sovereign *maṇi* jewels that manifested the appearance of all buddhas sitting in the site of enlightenment.

After those bodhisattvas had all arrived in the presence of the Buddha, they bowed down in reverence at the Buddha's feet and then transformationally created off in the westerly direction a tower made of the king of all types of incense that had a jeweled net of real pearls draped over it. They also transformationally created a jeweled lotus dais lion throne adorned with banners reflecting images of Indra. Over it hung a net canopy that spread forth and covered them all which was composed of marvelously colored *maṇi* jewels. Crowns of sovereign wish-fulfilling gems adorned their heads. Then, together with his entire retinue, that bodhisattva sat down there in the lotus posture.

Then, off in the northerly direction, beyond an ocean of worlds as numerous as the atoms in an ineffably great number of buddha *kṣetras*, there was a world known as Jeweled Robe Radiance Banner with a buddha named Great Radiance Illuminating the Spacious Dharma Realm. Within that buddha's congregation there was a bodhisattva named Unimpeded Supremacy Treasury King who, together with bodhisattvas as numerous as the atoms in an ocean of worlds, came to where the Buddha dwelt, whereupon, using their spiritual

正體字

悉
321b03║ 以神力。興一切寶衣雲。所謂黃色寶光明衣
321b04║ 雲。種種香所熏衣雲。日幢摩尼王衣雲。金色
321b05║ 熾然摩尼衣雲。一切寶光焰衣雲。一切星辰
321b06║ 像上妙摩尼衣雲。白玉光摩尼衣雲。光明遍
321b07║ 照殊勝赫奕摩尼衣雲。光明遍照威勢熾盛
321b08║ 摩尼衣雲。莊嚴海摩尼衣雲。充遍虛空。至佛
321b09║ 所已。頂禮佛足。即於北方。化作摩尼寶海莊
321b10║ 嚴樓閣。及毘瑠璃寶蓮華藏師子之座。以師
321b11║ 子威德摩尼王網。羅覆其身。清淨寶王。為髻
321b12║ 明珠。與其眷屬。結跏趺坐。東北方過不可說
321b13║ 佛剎微塵數世界海外。有世界。名一切歡喜
321b14║ 清淨光明網。佛號無礙眼。彼佛眾中。有菩薩。
321b15║ 名化現法界願月王。與世界海微塵數菩薩
321b16║ 俱。來向佛所。悉以神力。興寶樓閣雲。香樓閣
321b17║ 雲。燒香樓閣雲。華樓閣雲。栴檀樓閣雲。金剛
321b18║ 樓閣雲。摩尼樓閣雲。金樓閣雲。衣樓閣雲。
321b19║ 蓮華樓閣雲。彌覆十方一切世界。

简体字

悉以神力兴一切宝衣云，所谓：黄色宝光明衣云、种种香所熏衣云、日幢摩尼王衣云、金色炽然摩尼衣云、一切宝光焰衣云、一切星辰像上妙摩尼衣云、白玉光摩尼衣云、光明遍照殊胜赫奕摩尼衣云、光明遍照威势炽盛摩尼衣云、庄严海摩尼衣云，充遍虚空。至佛所已，顶礼佛足，即于北方化作摩尼宝海庄严楼阁及毗琉璃宝莲华藏师子之座，以师子威德摩尼王网罗覆其身，清净宝王为髻明珠，与其眷属结跏趺坐。

东北方过不可说佛刹微尘数世界海外有世界，名一切欢喜清净光明网，佛号无碍眼。彼佛众中有菩萨，名化现法界愿月王，与世界海微尘数菩萨俱，来向佛所，悉以神力兴宝楼阁云、香楼阁云、烧香楼阁云、华楼阁云、栴檀楼阁云、金刚楼阁云、摩尼楼阁云、金楼阁云、衣楼阁云、莲华楼阁云，弥覆十方一切世界。

powers, they all conjured an adorning array of all kinds of jeweled robe clouds that completely filled all of empty space, namely:

- Clouds of yellow-colored jewel light robes;
- Clouds of robes imbued with the fragrance of all different kinds of incense;
- Clouds of robes adorned with solar banner sovereign *maṇi* jewels;
- Clouds of robes adorned with gold-colored flaming *maṇi* jewels;
- Clouds of robes adorned with the flaming light of every sort of jewel;
- Clouds of robes adorned with supremely marvelous *maṇi* jewels arrayed in the images of all the stars and constellations;
- Clouds of robes adorned with *maṇi* jewels emanating the radiance of white jade;
- Clouds of robes adorned with *maṇi* jewels emanating universally illuminating radiance of especially excellent refulgence;
- Clouds of robes adorned with *maṇi* jewels emanating a universally illuminating radiance possessed of awesomely powerful flaming brilliance; and
- Clouds of *maṇi* jewel robes forming an ocean of adornments.

After those bodhisattvas had all arrived in the presence of the Buddha, they bowed down in reverence at the Buddha's feet and then transformationally created off in the northerly direction a tower adorned with an ocean of *maṇi* jewels along with a lotus dais lion throne composed of *vaiḍūrya* gems. Over it hung a net canopy that spread forth and covered them all which was composed of leonine awesomeness sovereign *maṇi* jewels. Pristine sovereign jewels formed the bright pearls in their topknots. Then, together with his entire retinue, that bodhisattva sat down there in the lotus posture.

Then, off in the northeasterly direction, beyond an ocean of worlds as numerous as the atoms in an ineffably great number of buddha *kṣetras*, there was a world known as Net of Pure Light Inspiring Universal Joyousness with a buddha named Unimpeded Eye. Within that buddha's congregation, there was a bodhisattva named Moon King Manifesting Dharma Realm Vows who, together with bodhisattvas as numerous as the atoms in an ocean of worlds, came to where the Buddha dwelt, whereupon, using their spiritual powers, they all conjured an adorning array of tower clouds that spread completely over all worlds of the ten directions, namely jeweled tower clouds, incense tower clouds, burning incense tower clouds, floral tower clouds, sandalwood tower clouds, vajra tower clouds, *maṇi* jewel tower clouds, gold tower clouds, robe tower clouds, and lotus flower tower clouds.

正體字

至佛所已。
321b20‖ 頂禮佛足。即於東北方。化作一切法界門大
321b21‖ 摩尼樓閣。及無等香王蓮華藏師子之座。摩
321b22‖ 尼華網。羅覆其身。著妙寶藏摩尼王冠。與其
321b23‖ 眷屬。結跏趺坐。東南方。過不可說佛刹微塵
321b24‖ 數世界海外。有世界。名香雲莊嚴幢。佛號龍
321b25‖ 自在王。彼佛眾中。有菩薩。名法慧光焰王。與
321b26‖ 世界海微塵數菩薩俱。來向佛所。悉以神力。
321b27‖ 興金色圓滿光明雲。無量寶色圓滿光明雲。
321b28‖ 如來毫相圓滿光明雲。種種寶色圓滿光明
321b29‖ 雲。蓮華藏圓滿光明雲。眾寶樹枝圓滿光明
321c01‖ 雲。如來頂髻圓滿光明雲。閻浮檀金色圓滿
321c02‖ 光明雲。日色圓滿光明雲。星月色圓滿光明
321c03‖ 雲。悉遍虛空。到佛所已。頂禮佛足。即於東南
321c04‖ 方。化作毘盧遮那最上寶光明樓閣金剛摩
321c05‖ 尼蓮華藏師子之座。眾寶光焰摩尼王網。羅
321c06‖ 覆其身。與其眷屬。結跏趺坐。

简体字

至佛所已，顶礼佛足，即于东北方化作一切法界门大摩尼楼阁及无等香王莲华藏师子之座，摩尼华网罗覆其身，著妙宝藏摩尼王冠，与其眷属结跏趺坐。

东南方过不可说佛刹微尘数世界海外有世界，名香云庄严幢，佛号龙自在王。彼佛众中有菩萨，名法慧光焰王，与世界海微尘数菩萨俱，来向佛所，悉以神力兴金色圆满光明云、无量宝色圆满光明云、如来毫相圆满光明云、种种宝色圆满光明云、莲华藏圆满光明云、众宝树枝圆满光明云、如来顶髻圆满光明云、阎浮檀金色圆满光明云、日色圆满光明云、星月色圆满光明云，悉遍虚空。到佛所已，顶礼佛足，即于东南方化作毗卢遮那最上宝光明楼阁、金刚摩尼莲华藏师子之座，众宝光焰摩尼王网罗覆其身，与其眷属结跏趺坐。

After those bodhisattvas had all arrived in the presence of the Buddha, they bowed down in reverence at the Buddha's feet and then transformationally created off in the northeasterly direction a tower graced with immense *maṇi* jewels and gateways to the entire Dharma realm along with a lotus dais lion throne made of the peerless king of all types of incense. Over it hung a net canopy that spread forth and covered them all which was composed of *maṇi* jewel flowers. They wore crowns of sovereign *maṇi* jewels from the treasury of marvelous jewels. Then, together with his entire retinue, that bodhisattva sat down there in the lotus posture.

Then, off in the southeasterly direction, beyond an ocean of worlds as numerous as the atoms in an ineffably great number of buddha *kṣetras*, there was a world known as Banner Adorned with Incense Clouds with a buddha named Dragon's Sovereign Mastery King. Within that buddha's congregation, there was a bodhisattva named King of the Dharma's Flaming Wisdom Light who, together with bodhisattvas as numerous as the atoms in an ocean of worlds, came to where the Buddha dwelt, whereupon, using their spiritual powers, they all conjured an adorning array of clouds that completely pervaded all of empty space, namely:

Clouds of light spheres the color of gold;[6]
Clouds of light spheres the color of countless jewels;
Clouds of light spheres the color of the Tathāgata's mid-brow hair mark;
Clouds of light spheres the color of various jewels;
Clouds of light spheres the color of a lotus flower seed pod;
Clouds of light spheres the color of many-jeweled trees;
Clouds of light spheres the color of the Tathāgata's crowning *uṣṇīṣa;*
Clouds of light spheres the color of *jambūnada* gold;
Clouds of light spheres the color of the sun; and
Clouds of light spheres the color of the stars and moon.

After those bodhisattvas had all arrived in the presence of the Buddha, they bowed down in reverence at the Buddha's feet and then transformationally created off in the southeasterly direction a tower of light made of the most supreme *vairocana* jewels and a vajra *maṇi* jewel lotus flower dais lion throne. Over it hung a net canopy that spread forth and covered them all which was composed of sovereign *maṇi* jewels emanating the fiery radiance of the many kinds of jewels. Then, together with his entire retinue, that bodhisattva sat down there in the lotus posture.

Then, off in the southwesterly direction, beyond an ocean of worlds as numerous as the atoms in an ineffably great number of buddha

正體字

西南方。過不可
321c07║ 說佛剎微塵數世界海外有世界。名日光摩
321c08║ 尼藏。佛號普照諸法智月王。彼佛眾中。有菩
321c09║ 薩。名摧破一切魔軍智幢王。與世界海微塵
321c10║ 數菩薩俱。來向佛所。於一切毛孔中。出等虛
321c11║ 空界華焰雲。香焰雲。寶焰雲。金剛焰雲。燒香
321c12║ 焰雲。電光焰雲。毘盧遮那摩尼寶焰雲。一切
321c13║ 金光焰雲。勝藏摩尼王光焰雲。等三世如來
321c14║ 海光焰雲。一一皆從毛孔中出。遍虛空界。到
321c15║ 佛所已。頂禮佛足。即於西南方。化作普現十
321c16║ 方法界光明網大摩尼寶樓閣及香燈焰寶蓮
321c17║ 華藏師子之座。以離垢藏摩尼網。羅覆其身。
321c18║ 著出一切眾生發趣音摩尼王嚴飾冠。與其
321c19║ 眷屬。結跏趺坐。西北方。過不可說佛剎微塵
321c20║ 數世界海外。有世界。名毘盧遮那願摩尼王
321c21║ 藏。佛號普光明最勝須彌王。

简体字

西南方过不可说佛刹微尘数世界海外有世界，名日光摩尼藏，佛号普照诸法智月王。彼佛众中有菩萨，名摧破一切魔军智幢王，与世界海微尘数菩萨俱，来向佛所，于一切毛孔中出等虚空界华焰云、香焰云、宝焰云、金刚焰云、烧香焰云、电光焰云、毗卢遮那摩尼宝焰云、一切金光焰云、胜藏摩尼王光焰云、等三世如来海光焰云，一一皆从毛孔中出，遍虚空界。到佛所已，顶礼佛足，即于西南方化作普现十方法界光明网大摩尼宝楼阁及香灯焰宝莲华藏师子之座，以离垢藏摩尼网罗覆其身，著出一切众生发趣音摩尼王严饰冠，与其眷属结跏趺坐。

西北方过不可说佛刹微尘数世界海外，有世界，名毗卢遮那愿摩尼王藏，佛号普光明最胜须弥王。

kṣetras, there was a world known as Sunlight Maṇi Jewel Matrix with a buddha named Wisdom Moon King Who Everywhere Illuminates All Dharmas. Within that buddha's congregation, there was a bodhisattva named Wisdom Banner King Who Vanquishes All Demon Armies who, together with bodhisattvas as numerous as the atoms in an ocean of worlds, came to where the Buddha dwelt, whereupon he emanated from all his pores phenomena that were commensurate in their vastness with the entire realm of empty space, namely sending forth:

Floral flaming-radiance clouds;
Incense flaming-radiance clouds;
Jewel flaming-radiance clouds;
Vajra flaming-radiance clouds;
Burning incense flaming-radiance clouds;
Lightning flash flaming-radiance clouds;
Vairocana *maṇi* jewel flaming-radiance clouds;
All kinds of golden light flaming-radiance clouds;
Flaming-radiance clouds of light from supreme treasuries of sovereign *maṇi* jewels; and
Flaming-radiance clouds matching the light of the ocean of all *tathāgatas* of the three periods of time.

Every one of these phenomena issued from his pores and everywhere filled the realms of space.

After those bodhisattvas had all arrived in the presence of the Buddha, they bowed down in reverence at the Buddha's feet and then transformationally created off in the southwesterly direction an immense tower made of *maṇi* jewels that everywhere revealed a web of brilliant light throughout the Dharma realm's ten directions. They also created a fragrant flaming-radiance lamp jeweled lotus flower dais lion throne. Over it hung a net canopy that spread forth and covered them all which was composed of immaculate matrix *maṇi* jewels. They wore crowns adorned with sovereign *maṇi* jewels that emanated the sounds of all beings setting forth on the path. Then, together with his entire retinue, that bodhisattva sat down there in the lotus posture.

Then, off in the northwesterly direction, beyond an ocean of worlds as numerous as the atoms in an ineffably great number of buddha *kṣetras*, there was a world known as Sovereign Maṇi Jewel Treasury of Vairocana's Vows with a buddha named Universally Radiant Supreme Sumeru King. Within that buddha's congregation, there was

正體字

彼佛眾中。有
321c22‖ 菩薩。名願智光明幢。與世界海微塵數菩薩
321c23‖ 俱。來向佛所。於念念中。一切相好。一切毛
321c24‖ 孔。一切身分。皆出三世一切如來形像雲。一
321c25‖ 切菩薩形像雲。一切如來眾會形像雲。一切
321c26‖ 如來變化身形像雲。一切如來本生身形像
321c27‖ 雲。一切聲聞辟支佛形像雲。一切如來菩提
321c28‖ 場形像雲。一切如來神變形像雲。一切世間
321c29‖ 主形像雲。一切清淨國土形像雲。充滿虛空。
322a01‖ 至佛所已。頂[理>禮]佛足。即於西北方。化作普照
322a02‖ 十方摩尼寶莊嚴樓閣及普照世間寶蓮華藏
322a03‖ 師子之座。以無能勝光明真珠網。羅覆其身。
322a04‖ 著普光明摩尼寶冠。與其眷屬。結跏趺坐。下
322a05‖ 方。過不可說佛剎微塵數世界海外。有世界。
322a06‖ 名一切如來圓滿光普照。佛號虛空無礙相
322a07‖ 智幢王。彼佛眾中。有菩薩。名破一切障勇猛
322a08‖ 智王。與世界海微塵數菩薩俱。來向佛所。於
322a09‖ 一切毛孔中。出說一切眾生語言海音聲雲。
322a10‖ 出說一切三世菩薩修行方便海音聲雲。

简体字

彼佛众中有菩萨，名愿智光明幢，与世界海微尘数菩萨俱，来向佛所，于念念中，一切相好、一切毛孔、一切身分，皆出三世一切如来形像云、一切菩萨形像云、一切如来众会形像云、一切如来变化身形像云、一切如来本生身形像云、一切声闻辟支佛形像云、一切如来菩提场形像云、一切如来神变形像云、一切世间主形像云、一切清净国土形像云，充满虚空。至佛所已，顶礼佛足，即于西北方化作普照十方摩尼宝庄严楼阁及普照世间宝莲华藏师子之座，以无能胜光明真珠网罗覆其身，著普光明摩尼宝冠，与其眷属结跏趺坐。

下方过不可说佛刹微尘数世界海外有世界，名一切如来圆满光普照，佛号虚空无碍相智幢王。彼佛众中有菩萨，名破一切障勇猛智王，与世界海微尘数菩萨俱，来向佛所，于一切毛孔中，出说一切众生语言海音声云，出说一切三世菩萨修行方便海音声云，

a bodhisattva named Banner of the Light of Vows and Wisdom[7] who, together with bodhisattvas as numerous as the atoms in an ocean of worlds, came to where the Buddha dwelt, whereupon, in each succeeding moment, he emanated clouds of images from all of his major marks, secondary signs, pores, and other parts of his body, emanating image clouds that completely filled all of empty space, namely:

Clouds of images of all *tathāgatas* of the three periods of time;
Clouds of images of all bodhisattvas;
Clouds of images of all *tathāgatas'* congregations;
Clouds of images of all *tathāgatas'* transformation bodies;
Clouds of images of all *tathāgatas'* previous-life bodies;
Clouds of images of all *śrāvaka* disciples and *pratyekabuddhas;*
Clouds of images of all *tathāgatas'* sites of enlightenment;
Clouds of images of all *tathāgatas'* spiritual transformations;
Clouds of images of all world leaders; and
Clouds of images of all pure lands.

After those bodhisattvas had all arrived in the presence of the Buddha, they bowed down in reverence at the Buddha's feet and then transformationally created off in the northwesterly direction a tower adorned with *maṇi* jewels that everywhere illuminated the ten directions and a jeweled lotus dais lion throne that everywhere illuminated the world. Over it hung a net canopy that spread forth and covered them all which was composed of true pearls emanating insuperable radiance. They wore *maṇi* jewel crowns emanating pervasively radiant light. Then, together with his entire retinue, that bodhisattva sat down there in the lotus posture.

Then, off in the direction of the nadir, beyond an ocean of worlds as numerous as the atoms in an ineffably great number of buddha *kṣetras,* there was a world known as Universal Illumination of the Halos of All Tathāgatas with a buddha named King Having a Banner of Marks and Wisdom as Unimpeded as Space. Within that buddha's congregation, there was a bodhisattva named King of Valiant Wisdom Demolishing All Obstacles who, together with bodhisattvas as numerous as the atoms in an ocean of worlds, came to where the Buddha dwelt, whereupon, he emanated sound clouds from all of his pores:

Emanating sound clouds speaking of the ocean of all beings' languages;
Emanating sound clouds speaking of the ocean of methods of cultivation used by all bodhisattvas of the three periods of time;

正體字

出
322a11‖ 說一切菩薩所起願方便海音聲雲。出說一
322a12‖ 切菩薩成滿清淨波羅蜜方便海音聲雲。出
322a13‖ 說一切菩薩圓滿行遍一切剎音聲雲。出說
322a14‖ 一切菩薩成就自在用音聲雲。出說一切如
322a15‖ 來[住>往]詣道場破魔軍眾成等正覺自在用音聲
322a16‖ 雲。出說一切如來轉法輪契經門名號海音
322a17‖ 聲雲。出說一切隨應教化調伏眾生法方便
322a18‖ 海音聲雲。出說一切隨時隨善根隨願力普
322a19‖ 令眾生證得智慧方便海音聲雲。到佛所已。
322a20‖ 頂禮佛足。即於下方。化作現一切如來宮殿
322a21‖ 形像眾寶莊嚴樓閣及一切寶蓮華藏師子之
322a22‖ 座。著普現道場影摩尼寶冠。與其眷屬。結跏
322a23‖ 趺坐。上方。過不可說佛剎微塵數世界海外。
322a24‖ 有世界。名說佛種性無有盡。佛號普智輪光
322a25‖ 明音。彼佛眾中。有菩薩。名法界差別願。與世
322a26‖ 界海。微塵數菩薩俱。發彼道場來。向此娑婆
322a27‖ 世界釋迦牟尼佛所。於一切相好。一切毛孔。
322a28‖ 一切身分。一切[1]肢節。一切莊嚴具。一切衣
322a29‖ 服中。現毘盧遮那等。過去一切諸佛。未來一
322b01‖ 切諸佛。

简体字

出说一切菩萨所起愿方便海音声云，出说一切菩萨成满清净波罗蜜方便海音声云，出说一切菩萨圆满行遍一切刹音声云，出说一切菩萨成就自在用音声云，出说一切如来往诣道场破魔军众成等正觉自在用音声云，出说一切如来转法轮契经门名号海音声云，出说一切随应教化调伏众生法方便海音声云，出说一切随时、随善根、随愿力普令众生证得智慧方便海音声云。到佛所已，顶礼佛足，即于下方化作现一切如来宫殿形像众宝庄严楼阁及一切宝莲华藏师子之座，著普现道场影摩尼宝冠，与其眷属结跏趺坐。

上方过不可说佛刹微尘数世界海外有世界，名说佛种性无有尽，佛号普智轮光明音。彼佛众中有菩萨，名法界差别愿，与世界海微尘数菩萨俱，发彼道场来向此娑婆世界释迦牟尼佛所，于一切相好、一切毛孔、一切身分、一切肢节、一切庄严具、一切衣服中，现毗卢遮那等过去一切诸佛、未来一切诸佛、

Emanating sound clouds speaking of the ocean of methods of bringing forth vows used by all bodhisattvas;
Emanating sound clouds speaking of the ocean of all bodhisattvas' methods for achieving complete purification of the *pāramitās*;
Emanating sound clouds speaking of all bodhisattvas' complete fulfillment of the practices throughout all *kṣetras*;
Emanating sound clouds speaking of all bodhisattvas' perfection of the use of feats of spiritual powers;[8]
Emanating sound clouds speaking of all *tathāgatas'* reaching the site of enlightenment, vanquishing Māra's armies, gaining the universal and right enlightenment, and using feats of spiritual power;
Emanating sound clouds speaking of the ocean of names of sutra gateways taught by all *tathāgatas* in turning the Dharma wheel;
Emanating sound clouds speaking of the ocean of all skillful means used in implementing dharmas adapted to what is appropriate in instructing and training beings; and
Emanating sound clouds speaking of the ocean of all skillful means adapted to the time, adapted to roots of goodness, and adapted to vows in everywhere causing beings to gain wisdom.

After those bodhisattvas had all arrived in the presence of the Buddha, they bowed down in reverence at the Buddha's feet and then transformationally created off in the direction of the nadir a tower adorned with many kinds of jewels that displayed the appearance of all *tathāgatas'* temple halls as they also created a lotus dais lion throne made from all types of jewels. They wore crowns of *maṇi* jewels displaying reflected images of all sites of enlightenment. Together with his entire retinue, he then sat there in the lotus posture.

Then, off in the direction of the zenith, beyond an ocean of worlds as numerous as the atoms in an ineffably great number of buddha *kṣetras*, there was a world known as Proclamation of the Endlessness of the Buddha Lineages with a buddha named Voice of the Sphere of Light of Universal Knowledge. Within that buddha's congregation, there was a bodhisattva named Different Vows of the Dharma Realm[9] who, together with bodhisattvas as numerous as the atoms in an ocean of worlds, came forth from the site of their own Dharma assembly to the place in this Sahā World where Śākyamuni Buddha dwelt. Then, from his major marks and secondary characteristics, from all of his pores, from all parts of his body, from all of his joints, from all of his adornments, and from all parts of his robes, he displayed images of all buddhas of the past, including Vairocana and the others, displayed images of all buddhas of the future, including those

正體字

已得授記。未授記者。現在十方一切
322b02‖ 國土。一切諸佛。并其眾會。亦現過去行檀那
322b03‖ 波羅蜜。及其一切受布施者。諸本事海。亦現
322b04‖ 過去行尸羅波羅蜜。諸本事海。亦現過去行
322b05‖ 羼提波羅蜜。割截[*]肢體。心無動亂。諸本事
322b06‖ 海。亦現過去行精進波羅蜜。勇猛不退。諸
322b07‖ 本事海。亦現過去求一切如來。禪波羅蜜海。
322b08‖ 而得成就。諸本事海。亦現過去求一切佛所
322b09‖ 轉法輪。所成就法。發勇猛心。一切皆捨。諸本
322b10‖ 事海。亦現過去樂見一切佛。樂行一切菩薩
322b11‖ 道。樂化一切眾生界。諸本事海。亦現過去
322b12‖ 所發一切菩薩大願。清淨莊嚴。諸本事海。亦
322b13‖ 現過去菩薩所成。力波羅蜜。勇猛清淨。諸本
322b14‖ 事海。亦現過去一切菩薩。所修圓滿。智波羅
322b15‖ 蜜。諸本事海。如是一切本事海。悉皆遍滿廣
322b16‖ 大法界。至佛所已。頂禮佛足。即於上方。化作
322b17‖ 一切金剛藏莊嚴樓閣及帝青金剛王蓮華藏
322b18‖ 師子之座。

简体字

已得授记、未授记者，现在十方一切国土、一切诸佛并其众会，亦现过去行檀那波罗蜜及其一切受布施者诸本事海，亦现过去行尸罗波罗蜜诸本事海，亦现过去行羼提波罗蜜割截肢体心无动乱诸本事海，亦现过去行精进波罗蜜勇猛不退诸本事海，亦现过去求一切如来禅波罗蜜海而得成就诸本事海，亦现过去求一切佛所转法轮所成就法发勇猛心一切皆舍诸本事海，亦现过去乐见一切佛、乐行一切菩萨道、乐化一切众生界诸本事海，亦现过去所发一切菩萨大愿清净庄严诸本事海，亦现过去菩萨所成力波罗蜜勇猛清净诸本事海，亦现过去一切菩萨所修圆满智波罗蜜诸本事海；如是一切本事海，悉皆遍满广大法界。至佛所已，顶礼佛足，即于上方化作一切金刚藏庄严楼阁及帝青金刚王莲华藏师子之座，

who have already acquired their predictions and those who have not yet received their predictions, and displayed images of all buddhas of the present throughout the ten directions along with all their lands and their congregations. Furthermore:[10]

He also displayed images from the ocean of their previous lives' practice of *dāna pāramitā*,[11] while also showing all beneficiaries of their giving;

He also displayed images from the ocean of their previous lives' practice of *śīla pāramitā*;[12]

He also displayed images from the ocean of their previous lives' practice of *kṣānti pāramitā*[13] during which they endured the severance of limbs and yet their minds remained undisturbed;

He also displayed images from the ocean of their previous lives' valiant and unretreating practice of vigor *pāramitā*;

He also displayed images from the ocean of their previous lives' quest to practice the ocean of all *tathāgatas' dhyāna pāramitā*[14] and their subsequent attainment of success in this;

He also displayed images from the ocean of their previous lives' production of valiant resolve and sacrifice of everything in seeking the Dharma established by all buddhas' turning of the Dharma wheel;

He also displayed images from the ocean of their previous lives' delight in seeing all buddhas, delight in practicing the path of all bodhisattvas, and delight in teaching all realms of beings;

He also displayed images from the ocean of their previous lives' great vows of all bodhisattvas that they brought forth and then used as means of purification and adornment;

He also displayed images from the ocean of their previous lives' valiant and pure practice of the powers *pāramitā* as perfected by the bodhisattvas of the past; and

He also displayed images from the ocean of their previous lives' practice of the knowledge *pāramitā* as completely fulfilled by all bodhisattvas of the past.

Such images of those oceans of their previous lives' practices completely filled the vast Dharma realm.

After those bodhisattvas had all arrived in the presence of the Buddha, they bowed down in reverence at the Buddha's feet and then transformationally created off in the direction of the zenith a tower adorned with a treasury of all varieties of vajra as well as a lotus dais lion throne made of *indranīla* sapphires and sovereign vajra gems. Over it hung a net canopy that spread forth and covered them all that was composed of sovereign *maṇi* jewels that shone with the

正體字

以一切寶光明摩尼王網。羅覆其
322b19 | 身。以演說三世如來名摩尼寶王。為髻明珠。
322b20 | 與其眷屬。結跏趺坐。如是十方一切菩薩。并
322b21 | 其眷屬。皆從普賢菩薩行願中生。以淨智眼。
322b22 | 見三世佛。普聞一切諸佛如來。所轉法輪。修
322b23 | 多羅海。已得至於一切菩薩自在彼岸。於念
322b24 | 念中。現大神變。親近一切諸佛如來。一身
322b25 | 充滿一切世界一切如來眾會道場。於一塵
322b26 | 中。普現一切世間境界。教化成[2]熟一切眾
322b27 | 生。未曾失時。一毛孔中。出一切如來說法音
322b28 | 聲。知一切眾生悉皆如幻。知一切佛悉皆如
322b29 | 影。知一切諸趣受生悉皆如夢。知一切業報
322c01 | 如鏡中像。知一切諸有生起如熱時焰。知一
322c02 | 切世界皆如變化。成就如來十力無畏。勇猛
322c03 | 自在。能師子吼。深入無盡。辯才大海。得一切
322c04 | 眾生言辭海諸法智。於虛空法界。所行無礙。
322c05 | 知一切法。無有障礙。一切菩薩。神通境界。悉
322c06 | 已清淨。勇猛精進。摧伏魔軍。恒以智慧。了達
322c07 | 三世。知一切法猶如虛空。無有違諍。

简体字

以一切宝光明摩尼王网罗覆其身，以演说三世如来名摩尼宝王为髻明珠，与其眷属结跏趺坐。

如是十方一切菩萨并其眷属，皆从普贤菩萨行愿中生，以净智眼见三世佛，普闻一切诸佛如来所转法轮、修多罗海，已得至于一切菩萨自在彼岸；于念念中现大神变，亲近一切诸佛如来，一身充满一切世界一切如来众会道场，于一尘中普现一切世间境界，教化成就一切众生未曾失时，一毛孔中出一切如来说法音声；知一切众生悉皆如幻，知一切佛悉皆如影，知一切诸趣受生悉皆如梦，知一切业报如镜中像，知一切诸有生起如热时焰，知一切世界皆如变化；成就如来十力、无畏，勇猛自在，能师子吼，深入无尽辩才大海，得一切众生言辞海诸法智；于虚空法界所行无碍，知一切法无有障碍；一切菩萨神通境界悉已清净，勇猛精进，摧伏魔军；恒以智慧了达三世，知一切法犹如虚空，无有违诤，

light of all jewels. Sovereign *maṇi* jewels proclaiming the names of all *tathāgatas* of the three periods of time formed the bright pearls in their topknots. Then, together with his entire retinue, that bodhisattva sat down there in the lotus posture.

All such bodhisattvas of the ten directions and their retinues were born from the conduct and vows of Samantabhadra Bodhisattva. They used their purified wisdom eyes to see all buddhas of the three periods of time and everywhere hear the ocean of sutras proclaimed by all the buddhas, the *tathāgatas,* as they turned the wheel of Dharma.

They had already arrived at the far shore of perfection in all bodhisattvas' sovereign masteries. In each successive mind-moment, they manifested great spiritual transformations and drew near to all the buddhas, the *tathāgatas.* With but one body, they completely filled up all worlds and were thus present in the congregations at the Dharma assemblies of all *tathāgatas.*

They were everywhere able to manifest a sphere of cognition in which all worlds appeared within one atom. In their teaching and maturation of all beings, they never missed the correct timing and, from within but one of their pores, there came forth the sounds of all *tathāgatas* teaching the Dharma. Furthermore:

They knew all beings were like conjured illusions, knew all buddhas were like reflections, knew all instances of taking on births in any of the rebirth destinies were like dreams, knew all karmic consequences were like images reflected in a mirror, knew all instances of production were like mirages seen in the hot season, and knew all worlds were like mere transformations.

They had perfected the Tathāgata's ten powers, fearlessnesses, heroic bravery, and sovereign masteries, had become able to roar the lion's roar, had deeply entered the great ocean of inexhaustible eloquence, had acquired the knowledge of all dharmas of the ocean of all beings' languages, and had reached the point that whatever they practiced throughout the realm of empty space and the Dharma realm had become entirely unimpeded;

They knew all dharmas unimpededly. They had already purified the spheres of cognition of all bodhisattvas' spiritual superknowledges, had become heroically brave in their practice of vigor, had vanquished the armies of Māra, and constantly used their wisdom to achieve a completely penetrating comprehension of the three periods of time;

They knew all dharmas as like empty space, were entirely free of any indulgence in disputation, and were free of any grasping or

正體字

亦無取
322c08‖ 著。雖勤精進。而知一切智終無所來。雖觀境
322c09‖ 界。而知一切有悉不可得。以方便智。入一
322c10‖ 切法界。以平等智。入一切國土。以自在力。令
322c11‖ 一切世界。展轉相入於一切世界。處處受生。
322c12‖ 見一切世界種種形相。於微細境。現廣大剎。
322c13‖ 於廣大境。現微細剎。於一佛所一念之頃。得
322c14‖ 一切佛。威神所加。普見十方。無所迷惑。於剎
322c15‖ 那頃。悉能往詣。如是等一切菩薩。滿逝多林。
322c16‖ 皆是如來威神之力。于時上首諸大聲聞。舍
322c17‖ 利弗。大目揵連。摩訶迦葉。離婆多。須菩提。
322c18‖ 阿[少/兔]樓馱。難陀。劫賓那。迦旃延。富樓那等。
322c19‖ 諸大聲聞。在逝多林。皆悉不見如來神力。如
322c20‖ 來嚴好。如來境界。如來遊戲。如來神變。如來
322c21‖ 尊勝。如來妙行。如來威德。如來住持。如來淨
322c22‖ 剎。亦復不見不可思議菩薩境界。菩薩大會。
322c23‖ 菩薩普入。菩薩普至。菩薩普詣。菩薩神變。菩
322c24‖ 薩遊戲。

简体字

亦无取著；虽勤精进而知一切智终无所来，虽观境界而知一切有悉不可得；以方便智入一切法界，以平等智入一切国土，以自在力令一切世界展转相入于一切世界；处处受生，见一切世界种种形相；于微细境现广大刹，于广大境现微细刹；于一佛所一念之顷，得一切佛威神所加，普见十方无所迷惑，于刹那顷悉能往诣。如是等一切菩萨满逝多林，皆是如来威神之力。

于时，上首诸大声闻——舍利弗、大目揵连、摩诃迦葉、离婆多、须菩提、阿[少/兔]楼驮、难陀、劫宾那、迦旃延、富楼那等诸大声闻，在逝多林皆悉不见如来神力、如来严好、如来境界、如来游戏、如来神变、如来尊胜、如来妙行、如来威德、如来住持、如来净刹，亦复不见不可思议菩萨境界、菩萨大会、菩萨普入、菩萨普至、菩萨普诣、菩萨神变、菩萨游戏、

attachment. Although they were diligently vigorous, they knew that all-knowledge finally had no place from which it comes forth and, although they contemplated the spheres of cognition, they knew that anything that exists is ultimately inapprehensible.[15]

They used their knowledge of skillful means to enter the entire Dharma realm, used the wisdom that knows uniform equality to enter all lands, used their powers of transformation to cause all worlds to mutually interpenetrate with all other worlds, and took on births in all places.

They saw the many different forms and characteristics of all worlds. Within extremely tiny realms, they manifested vast *kṣetras*. Within vast realms, they manifested extremely tiny *kṣetras*. In one mind-moment's instant in the dwelling place of one buddha, they acquired the assistance of all buddhas' awesome spiritual powers so that they everywhere saw the ten directions without any confusion. In but one *kṣaṇa*'s instant, they were able to go forth to visit all of them.

That all of these bodhisattvas filled up the Jeta Grove in this way was entirely due to the awesome spiritual powers of the Tathāgata.

At that time, although the most senior *śrāvaka* disciples including Śāriputra, Mahāmaudgalyāyana, Mahākāśyapa, Revata, Subhuti, Aniruddha, Nanda, Kapphiṇa, Kātyāyana, Pūrṇa, and others were present there in the Jeta Grove, none of them saw:

The Tathāgata's spiritual powers;
The Tathāgata's adornments;
The Tathāgata's sphere of action;
The Tathāgata's easeful mastery;
The Tathāgata's spiritual transformations;
The Tathāgata's venerable supremacy;
The Tathāgata's marvelous practices;
The Tathāgata's awesome virtue;
The Tathāgata's sovereign power; or
The Tathāgata's purification of the *kṣetra*.

Nor did they see:

The bodhisattvas' inconceivable realms;
The bodhisattvas' great congregations;
The bodhisattvas' universal interpenetration;
The bodhisattvas' universal reach;
The bodhisattvas' universal paying of respects;
The bodhisattvas' spiritual transformations;
The bodhisattvas' easeful mastery;

正體字

菩薩眷屬。菩薩方所。菩薩莊嚴師子
322c25║ 座。菩薩宮殿。菩薩住處。菩薩所入三昧自在。
322c26║ 菩薩觀察。菩薩[*]頻申。菩薩勇猛。菩薩供養。
322c27║ 菩薩受記。菩薩成熟。菩薩勇健。菩薩法身清
322c28║ 淨。菩薩智身圓滿。菩薩願身示現。菩薩色身
322c29║ 成就。菩薩諸相具足清淨。菩薩常光眾色莊
323a01║ 嚴。菩薩放大光網。菩薩起變化雲。菩薩身遍
323a02║ 十方。菩薩諸行圓滿。如是等事。一切聲聞。諸
323a03║ 大弟子。皆悉不見。何以故。以善根不同故。本
323a04║ 不修習見佛自在善根故。本不讚說十方世
323a05║ 界一切佛剎清淨功德故。本不稱歎諸佛世尊
323a06║ 種種神變故。本不於生死流轉之中。發阿
323a07║ 耨多羅三藐三菩提心故。本不令他住菩提
323a08║ 心故。本不能令如來種性不斷絕故。

简体字

菩萨眷属、菩萨方所、菩萨庄严师子座、菩萨宫殿、菩萨住处、菩萨所入三昧自在、菩萨观察、菩萨频申、菩萨勇猛、菩萨供养、菩萨受记、菩萨成熟、菩萨勇健、菩萨法身清净、菩萨智身圆满、菩萨愿身示现、菩萨色身成就、菩萨诸相具足清净、菩萨常光众色庄严、菩萨放大光网、菩萨起变化云、菩萨身遍十方、菩萨诸行圆满。如是等事，一切声闻诸大弟子皆悉不见。何以故？以善根不同故，本不修习见佛自在善根故，本不赞说十方世界一切佛刹清净功德故，本不称叹诸佛世尊种种神变故，本不于生死流转之中发阿耨多罗三藐三菩提心故，本不令他住菩提心故，本不能令如来种性不断绝故，

The bodhisattvas' retinues;
The bodhisattvas' regions;
The bodhisattvas' adorned lion thrones;
The bodhisattvas' palaces;
The bodhisattvas' dwelling places;
The bodhisattvas' sovereign mastery in the samādhis they enter;
The bodhisattvas' contemplations;
The bodhisattvas' emergence;
The bodhisattvas' heroic bravery;
The bodhisattvas' offerings;
The bodhisattvas' receiving of predictions;
The bodhisattvas' ripening;
The bodhisattvas' heroic stalwart strength;
The bodhisattvas' purification of the Dharma body;
The bodhisattvas' perfect fulfillment of the wisdom body;
The bodhisattvas' manifestations of the vow body;
The bodhisattvas' perfection of the physical body;
The bodhisattvas' purity of complete fulfillment of their major marks;
The bodhisattvas' adornment with the many hues of their eternally shining radiance;
The bodhisattvas' emanation of nets of great radiance;
The bodhisattvas' generation of clouds of transformations;
The bodhisattvas' pervasive physical presence throughout the ten directions; or
The bodhisattvas' perfect fulfillment of the practices.

All of the phenomena such as these were not seen at all by any of the great disciples in the *śrāvaka*-disciple sangha. And why is this? It is for these reasons:

Because their roots of goodness were not of the same sort;
Because they did not previously cultivate the roots of goodness of the sovereign masteries that enable one to see the buddhas;
Because they did not previously praise the pure qualities of all buddha *kṣetras* among the worlds of the ten directions;
Because they did not previously praise the many different spiritual transformations of the buddhas, the *bhagavats*;
Because, while in the midst of transmigration in *saṃsāra*, they did not previously resolve to gain *anuttara-samyak-saṃbodhi*;
Because they did not previously influence others to abide in the resolve to realize bodhi;
Because they were previously incapable of preventing the lineage of the Tathāgata from being cut off;

正體字

本不攝
323a09║ 受諸眾生故。本不勸他修習菩薩波羅蜜故。
323a10║ 本在生死流轉之時。不勸眾生求於最勝大
323a11║ 智眼故。本不修習生一切智諸善根故。本不
323a12║ 成就如來出世諸善根故。本不得嚴淨佛剎
323a13║ 神通智故。本不得諸菩薩眼所知境故。本不
323a14║ 求超出世間不共菩提諸善根故。本不發一
323a15║ 切菩薩諸大願故。本不從如來加被之所生
323a16║ 故。本不知諸法如幻菩薩如夢故。本不得諸
323a17║ 大菩薩廣大歡喜故。如是皆是普賢菩薩。智
323a18║ 眼境界。不與一切二乘所共。以是因緣。諸大
323a19║ 聲聞。不能見不能知。不能聞不能入。不能
323a20║ 得不能念。不能觀察。不能籌量。不能思惟。不
323a21║ 能分別。是故。雖在逝多林中。不見如來諸大
323a22║ 神變。

简体字

本不摄受诸众生故，本不劝他修习菩萨波罗蜜故，本在生死流转之时不劝众生求于最胜大智眼故，本不修习生一切智诸善根故，本不成就如来出世诸善根故，本不得严净佛刹神通智故，本不得诸菩萨眼所知境故，本不求超出世间不共菩提诸善根故，本不发一切菩萨诸大愿故，本不从如来加被之所生故，本不知诸法如幻、菩萨如梦故，本不得诸大菩萨广大欢喜故。如是皆是普贤菩萨智眼境界，不与一切二乘所共。以是因缘，诸大声闻不能见、不能知、不能闻、不能入、不能得、不能念、不能观察、不能筹量、不能思惟、不能分别；是故，虽在逝多林中，不见如来诸大神变。

Because they did not previously attract all beings;
Because they did not previously encourage others to cultivate the bodhisattva's *pāramitās;*
Because previously, when abiding in the midst of *saṃsāra's* births and deaths, they did not exhort beings to seek the Supremely Victorious One's eye of great wisdom;
Because they did not previously cultivate the roots of goodness that produce all-knowledge;
Because they did not previously perfect the Tathāgata's world-transcending roots of goodness;
Because they did not previously acquire knowledge of the spiritual superknowledges used in purifying buddha *kṣetras;*
Because they did not previously acquire the sphere of cognition known to the eyes of all bodhisattvas;
Because they did not previously seek the world-transcending roots of goodness conducive to exclusive realizations of bodhi;
Because they did not previously bring forth the great vows of all bodhisattvas;
Because they were not previously born through the aid of the Tathāgata's assistance;
Because they did not previously realize all dharmas are like an illusion and bodhisattvas are like a dream; and
Because they did not previously acquire the great bodhisattvas' vast joyous delight.

All of these phenomena are spheres of cognition perceived by Samantabhadra Bodhisattva's wisdom eye that are not held in common with any adherents of the two vehicles. It is for these reasons that the great *śrāvaka* disciples:

Were not able to see them;
Were not able to know them;
Were not able to hear them;
Were not able to enter into them;
Were not able to acquire them;
Were not able to bear them in mind;
Were not able to contemplate them;
Were not able to assess them;
Were not able to meditate on them; and
Were not able to distinguish them.

Consequently, although they were abiding in the Jeta Grove, they did not witness any of the Tathāgata's great spiritual transformations. Furthermore, the great *śrāvaka* disciples:

正體字

復次諸大聲聞。無如是善根故。無如是
323a23║ 智眼故。無如是三昧故。無如是解脫故。無如
323a24║ 是神通故。無如是威德故。無如是勢力故。無
323a25║ 如是自在故。無如是住處故。無如是境界故。
323a26║ 是故於此。不能知不能見。不能入不能證。不
323a27║ 能住不能解。不能觀察。不能忍受。不能趣向。
323a28║ 不能遊履。又亦不能廣為他人開闡解說。稱
323a29║ 揚示現。引導勸進。令其趣向。令其修習。令其
323b01║ 安住。令其證入。何以故。諸大弟子。依聲聞
323b02║ 乘。而出離故。成就聲聞道。滿足聲聞行。安住
323b03║ 聲聞果。於無有諦。得決定智。

简体字

复次，诸大声闻无如是善根故，无如是智眼故，无如是三昧故，无如是解脱故，无如是神通故，无如是威德故，无如是势力故，无如是自在故，无如是住处故，无如是境界故，是故于此不能知、不能见、不能入、不能证、不能住、不能解、不能观察、不能忍受、不能趣向、不能游履；又亦不能广为他人，开阐解说，称扬示现，引导劝进，令其趣向，令其修习，令其安住，令其证入。何以故？诸大弟子依声闻乘而出离故，成就声闻道，满足声闻行，安住声闻果，于无有谛得决定智，

Did not have roots of goodness such as these;
Did not have wisdom eyes such as these;[16]
Did not have samādhis such as these;[17]
Did not have liberations such as these;
Did not have spiritual superknowledges such as these;
Did not have qualities of awesome virtue such as these;
Did not have powers such as these;
Did not have sovereign masteries such as these;
Did not have stations in which they dwelt such as these; and
Did not have spheres of cognition such as these.

Therefore, as regards phenomena such as these:

They were not able to know them;
They were not able to see them;
They were not able to enter into them;
They were not able to realize them;
They were not able to abide in them;
They were not able to understand them;
They were not able to contemplate them;
They were not able to endure them;
They were not able to progress toward them; and
They were not able to roam about within them.

They were also unable to extensively:

Expound on them for others;
Explain them for others;
Praise them for others;
Reveal them for others;
Lead others into them;
Encourage others to advance into them;
Induce others to progress toward them;
Induce others to cultivate them;
Induce others to abide securely within them; or
Induce others to realize and enter them.

And why was this? It was because all of those great disciples:

Had relied upon the *śrāvaka*-disciple vehicle to gain emancipation;
Had achieved success in the *śrāvaka*-disciple path;
Had fulfilled the *śrāvaka*-disciple practices;
Had come to abide securely in the fruits of the path acquired by the *śrāvaka* disciples;
Had acquired definitive knowledge of the truth of absence of inherent existence;

正體字

常住實際。究竟
323b04║ 寂靜。遠離大悲。捨於眾生。住於自事。於彼智
323b05║ 慧。不能積集。不能修行。不能安住。不能願
323b06║ 求。不能成就。不能清淨。不能趣入。不能通
323b07║ 達。不能知見。不能證得。是故。雖在逝多林中
323b08║ 對於如來。不見如是廣大神變。佛子。如恒河
323b09║ 岸。有百千億無量餓鬼。裸形飢渴。舉體焦然。
323b10║ 烏鷲豺狼。競來搏撮。為渴所逼。欲求水飲。雖
323b11║ 住河邊。而不見河。設有見者。見其枯竭。何以
323b12║ 故。深厚業障之所覆故。彼大聲聞。亦復如是。
323b13║ 雖復住在逝多林中。不見如來廣大神力。捨
323b14║ 一切智。無明[1]瞖瞙。覆其眼故。不曾種植薩
323b15║ 婆若地諸善根故。譬如有人。於大會中。昏睡
323b16║ 安寢。忽然夢見須彌山頂帝釋所住善見大
323b17║ 城。宮殿園林。種種嚴好。

简体字

常住实际究竟寂静，远离大悲，舍于众生，住于自事；于彼智慧，不能积集，不能修行，不能安住，不能愿求，不能成就，不能清净，不能趣入，不能通达，不能知见，不能证得。是故，虽在逝多林中对于如来，不见如是广大神变。

佛子，如恒河岸有百千亿无量饿鬼，裸形饥渴，举体焦然，乌鹫豺狼竞来搏撮，为渴所逼，欲求水饮，虽住河边而不见河；设有见者，见其枯竭。何以故？深厚业障之所覆故。彼大声闻亦复如是，虽复住在逝多林中，不见如来广大神力，舍一切智，无明瞖瞙覆其眼故，不曾种植萨婆若地诸善根故。譬如有人，于大会中昏睡安寝，忽然梦见须弥山顶帝释所住善见大城，宫殿、园林种种严好，

Had come to always abide in the apex of reality;[18]
Had achieved the ultimate realization of quiescence;
Had abandoned the great compassion;
Had become indifferent to beings; and
Had come to abide in their own endeavors.[19]

It was also because, with regard to [the Buddha's] wisdom:[20]

They were unable to accumulate it;
They were unable to cultivate it;
They were unable to securely abide in it;
They were unable to vow to seek it;
They were unable to successfully develop it;
They were unable to purify it;
They were unable to progress into it;
They were unable to completely comprehend it;
They were unable to know or see it; and
They were unable to realize and attain it.

Consequently, although they did reside within the Jeta Grove, facing the Tathāgata, they still did not see such vast spiritual transformations as these that he manifested there.

Sons of the Buddha, this is comparable to the circumstance found along the banks of the Ganges River where there are countless hundreds of thousands of *koṭīs* of hungry ghosts who are naked, famished, thirsty, their entire bodies burning, over whom the crows, vultures, and wolves struggle with each other to come and pounce on them and seize them.

They are driven by thirst and wish to find water to drink, yet, even though they live there on the banks of the river, they still do not see the river. If they were to see it at all, they would only see it as completely dried up. Why? This is because they are covered by deep and thick karmic obstacles.

So too it is with those great *śrāvaka* disciples, for, although they reside within the Jeta Grove, they still do not see the Tathāgata's vast spiritual powers. This is because their eyes are covered by cataracts of ignorance that lead to forsaking all-knowledge. This is due to their never having planted roots of goodness in the ground of omniscience.

It is as if there is someone in the midst of a great congregation who, having fallen into a peaceful sleep, suddenly sees in his dreams the great city of Śakra, lord of the devas, that is known as Sudarśana or "Good to Behold," along with his palace, gardens, groves, many different kinds of refined adornments, hundreds of thousands of

正體字

天子天女。百千萬
323b18║ 億。普散天華。遍滿其地。種種衣樹。出妙衣
323b19║ 服。種種華樹。開敷妙華。諸音樂樹。奏天音
323b20║ 樂。天諸[2]采女。歌詠美音。無量諸天。於中戲
323b21║ 樂。其人自見著天衣服。普於其處。住止周旋。
323b22║ 其大會中。一切諸人。雖同一處。不知不見。何
323b23║ 以故。夢中所見。非彼大眾所能見故。一切菩
323b24║ 薩。世間諸王。亦復如是。以久積集善根力故。
323b25║ 發一切智廣大願故。學習一切佛功德故。修
323b26║ 行菩薩莊嚴道故。圓滿一切智智法故。滿足
323b27║ 普賢諸行願故。趣入一切菩薩智地故。遊戲
323b28║ 一切菩薩所住諸三昧故。已能觀察一切菩
323b29║ 薩智慧境界無障礙故。是故悉見如來世尊
323c01║ 不可思議自在神變。一切聲聞。諸大弟子。皆
323c02║ 不能見。皆不能知。以無菩薩清淨眼故。譬如
323c03║ 雪山具眾藥草。良醫詣彼。悉能分別。其諸捕
323c04║ 獵放牧之人。恒住彼山。不[具>見]其藥。此亦如是。
323c05║ 以諸菩薩入智境界。

简体字

天子、天女百千万亿，普散天华遍满其地，种种衣树出妙衣服，种种华树开敷妙华，诸音乐树奏天音乐，天诸婇女歌咏美音，无量诸天于中戏乐；其人自见著天衣服，普于其处住止周旋。其大会中一切诸人虽同一处，不知不见。何以故？梦中所见，非彼大众所能见故。一切菩萨、世间诸王亦复如是，以久积集善根力故，发一切智广大愿故，学习一切佛功德故，修行菩萨庄严道故，圆满一切智智法故，满足普贤诸行愿故，趣入一切菩萨智地故，游戏一切菩萨所住诸三昧故，已能观察一切菩萨智慧境界无障碍故，是故悉见如来世尊不可思议自在神变。一切声闻诸大弟子，皆不能见，皆不能知，以无菩萨清净眼故。譬如雪山具众药草，良医诣彼悉能分别；其诸捕猎、放牧之人恒住彼山，不见其药。此亦如是，以诸菩萨入智境界，

myriads of *koṭīs* of devas' sons and devas' daughters everywhere scattering heavenly flower petals completely covering those grounds, seeing too the many different kinds of robe trees that produce marvelous robes, the many different kinds of flowering trees that bloom with marvelous blossoms, the music trees that emanate the sounds of celestial music, the heavenly consorts singing with lovely voices, and the countless devas who delight in the pleasures there. Even as that person sees himself dressed in celestial robes, living there and wandering around everywhere there, everyone in that immense congregation, although residing in the same place, neither knows of nor sees any of this.

And how could this be so? It would be because everything seen in that dream remained invisible to everyone in that great congregation. So too it is in the case of all these bodhisattvas and world rulers[21] [who were able to see these phenomena]:

Because they had long accumulated the power of roots of goodness;
Because they had made the vast vow to attain all-knowledge;
Because they had trained in all buddhas' meritorious qualities;
Because they had cultivated the adorned path of the bodhisattvas;
Because they had perfectly fulfilled the dharmas of the wisdom of all-knowledge;
Because they had completely fulfilled the conduct and vows of Samantabhadra;
Because they had progressed into the wisdom grounds of all bodhisattvas;
Because they roamed and delighted in the samādhis in which all bodhisattvas dwell; and
Because they had already become able to unimpededly contemplate the realms of all bodhisattvas' wisdom.

Therefore they were all able to witness the inconceivable freely implemented spiritual transformations manifested by the Tathāgata, the Bhagavat, whereas all the great disciples in the community of *śrāvaka* disciples remained unable to see them and unable to know them. This was because they did not possess the purified eyes of the bodhisattvas.

It is as if, in the Himalaya Mountains where there are many kinds of medicinal herbs, there was an especially good physician who, on encountering them, was able to distinguish them all, whereas all the hunters and herders that constantly dwell in those mountains did not even see those herbs. This circumstance is just like that, for all those bodhisattvas had entered wisdom's spheres of cognition and become

正體字

具自在力。能見如來廣
323c06║ 大神變。諸大弟子。唯求自利。不欲利他。唯求
323c07║ 自安。不欲安他。雖在林中。不知不見。譬如地
323c08║ 中有諸寶藏。種種珍異。悉皆充滿。有一丈夫。
323c09║ 聰慧明達。善能分別一切伏藏。其人復有大
323c10║ 福德力。能隨所欲。自在而取。奉養父母。賑恤
323c11║ 親屬。老病窮乏。靡不均贍。其無智慧。無福德
323c12║ 人雖亦至於寶藏之處。不知不見。不得其益。
323c13║ 此亦如是。諸大菩薩。有淨智眼。能入如來不
323c14║ 可思議甚深境界。能見佛神力。能入諸法門。
323c15║ 能遊三昧海。能供養諸佛。能以正法開悟眾
323c16║ 生。能以四攝攝受眾生。諸大聲聞。不能得見
323c17║ 如來神力。亦不能見諸菩薩眾。譬如盲人至
323c18║ 大寶洲。若行若住。若坐若臥。不能得見。一切
323c19║ 眾寶。以不見故。不能採取。不得受用。此亦如
323c20║ 是。諸大弟子。雖在林中親近世尊。不見如來
323c21║ 自在神力。亦不得見菩薩大會。何以故。

简体字

具自在力，能见如来广大神变；诸大弟子唯求自利，不欲利他，唯求自安，不欲安他，虽在林中，不知不见。譬如地中有诸宝藏，种种珍异悉皆充满，有一丈夫聪慧明达，善能分别一切伏藏，其人复有大福德力，能随所欲自在而取，奉养父母，赈恤亲属，老、病、穷乏靡不均赡；其无智慧、无福德人，虽亦至于宝藏之处，不知不见，不得其益。此亦如是，诸大菩萨有净智眼，能入如来不可思议甚深境界，能见佛神力，能入诸法门，能游三昧海，能供养诸佛，能以正法开悟众生，能以四摄摄受众生；诸大声闻不能得见如来神力，亦不能见诸菩萨众。譬如盲人至大宝洲，若行、若住、若坐、若卧，不能得见一切众宝；以不见故，不能采取，不得受用。此亦如是，诸大弟子虽在林中亲近世尊，不见如来自在神力，亦不得见菩萨大会。何以故？

equipped with the powers of their sovereign masteries. Hence they were able to see the vast spiritual transformations manifested by the Tathāgata.

All the great disciples sought only to serve their own self-benefit and did not wish to benefit others. They sought only to gain peace for themselves and did not wish to bestow peace on others. Thus, even though they dwelt within this grove, they still did not know or see this.

By way of analogy, suppose that the earth contained deposits of the many different precious and rare jewels and there was some man possessed of clearly penetrating intelligence who was well able to distinguish everything contained in those hidden treasuries. Because this man also possessed the power of immense merit, he was able to take whatever he pleased to care for his parents, provide compassionate relief to his relatives and retinue, and ensure that, among those who are old, sick, or destitute, there were none who were not equally provided with material support. Suppose, too, that there was someone who had no wisdom and no merit. Although he, too, might go to that place where there are repositories of jewels, he would not be able to recognize them, would not even notice them, and would not acquire any benefit for himself.

This circumstance is just the same, for the great bodhisattvas, possessed as they were of the purified wisdom eye, were able to enter the Tathāgata's inconceivable and extremely profound spheres of cognition, were able to observe the Buddha's spiritual powers, were able to enter the Dharma's gateways, were able to roam about in the ocean of samādhis, were able to make offerings to all buddhas, were able to use right Dharma to awaken beings, and were able to use the four means of attraction to attract beings, whereas the great *śrāvaka* disciples were unable to see the Tathāgata's spiritual powers and were unable to see the congregation of bodhisattvas.

It is as if there were a blind man who had arrived at a great isle of precious jewels where, whether walking, standing, sitting, or lying down, he was unable to see any of those many jewels, and, because he could not see them, he was unable to pick them up and unable to put them to use. So too it was in this circumstance, for, even though the great disciples dwelt in this grove close to the Bhagavat, they still did not see the Tathāgata's freely implemented spiritual powers and could not see the great congregation of bodhisattvas. Why not? This was because they did not possess the bodhisattvas' unimpeded

正體字

無
323c22║ 有菩薩無礙淨眼。不能次第悟入法界。見於
323c23║ 如來自在力故。譬如有人。得清淨眼。名離垢
323c24║ 光明。一切暗色。不能為障。爾時彼人。於夜暗
323c25║ 中。處在無量百千萬億人眾之內。或行或住。
323c26║ 或坐或臥。彼諸人眾。形相威儀。此明眼人。莫
323c27║ 不具見。其明眼者。威儀進退。彼諸人眾。悉不
323c28║ 能覩。佛亦如是。成就智眼。清淨無礙。悉能明
323c29║ 見一切世間。其所示現。神通變化。大菩薩眾。
324a01║ 所共圍遶。諸大弟子。悉不能見。譬如比丘在
324a02║ 大眾中。入遍處定。所謂地遍處定。水遍處定。
324a03║ 火遍處定。風遍處定。[清>青]遍處定。黃遍處定。赤
324a04║ 遍處定。白遍處定。天遍處定。種種眾生身遍
324a05║ 處定。一切語言音聲遍處定。一切所緣遍處
324a06║ 定。入此定者。見其所緣。其餘大眾。悉不能
324a07║ 見。唯除有住此三昧者。如來所現。不可思議。
324a08║ 諸佛境界。亦復如是。菩薩具見。聲聞莫覩。

简体字

无有菩萨无碍净眼，不能次第悟入法界见于如来自在力故。譬如有人得清净眼，名离垢光明，一切暗色不能为障。尔时，彼人于夜暗中，处在无量百千万亿人众之内，或行、或住、或坐、或卧，彼诸人众形相威仪，此明眼人莫不具见；其明眼者威仪进退，彼诸人众悉不能睹。佛亦如是，成就智眼，清净无碍，悉能明见一切世间；其所示现神通变化，大菩萨众所共围绕，诸大弟子悉不能见。譬如比丘在大众中入遍处定，所谓：地遍处定、水遍处定、火遍处定、风遍处定、青遍处定、黄遍处定、赤遍处定、白遍处定、天遍处定、种种众生身遍处定、一切语言音声遍处定、一切所缘遍处定；入此定者见其所缘，其余大众悉不能见，唯除有住此三昧者。如来所现不可思议诸佛境界亦复如是，菩萨具见，声闻莫睹。

and purified eyes, could not awaken to and sequentially enter the Dharma realm, and could not see the freely implemented powers of the Tathāgata.

It is as if there were someone who had acquired the purified eye known as "stainless radiance" so that his vision was unimpeded by any darkness or physical forms. In that case, even in the dark of night, when dwelling in a population of countless hundreds of thousands of myriads of *koṭīs* of people, whether walking, standing, sitting, or lying down, there would be no forms, features, or manners of deportment that this clear-eyed person could not see in their entirety, whereas no one in that population of people would be able to observe the deportment or the goings and comings of that clear-eyed man.

So too it was with the Buddha who had completely developed the wisdom eye's unimpeded purification so that he was able to clearly see everything in the entire world, whereas none of the great disciples were able to see either any of his spiritual transformations or any of the congregation of great bodhisattvas surrounding him.

It is also as if there were a bhikshu in the midst of the great assembly who had entered the universal-pervasion meditative absorptions, namely:

The universal pervasion of earth absorption;
The universal pervasion of water absorption;
The universal pervasion of fire absorption;
The universal pervasion of wind absorption;
The universal pervasion of blue absorption;
The universal pervasion of yellow absorption;
The universal pervasion of red absorption;
The universal pervasion of white absorption;
The universal pervasion of heavens absorption;
The universal pervasion of the bodies of the various beings absorption;
The universal pervasion of the sound of all languages absorption; and
The universal pervasion of all objective conditions absorption;

Those who had entered these meditative absorptions would see whatever objective condition they focused on, whereas, with the sole exception of others who had entered this same samādhi, no one else in that great assembly would be able to see any of these things. So too it was with the buddhas' inconceivable realm of cognition as revealed by the Tathāgata. The bodhisattvas saw it entirely, whereas none of the *śrāvaka* disciples could see it at all.

正體字

譬
324a09 | 如有人。以翳形藥。自塗其眼。在於眾會。去來
324a10 | 坐立。無能見者。而能悉覩眾會中事。應知如
324a11 | 來。亦復如是。超過於世。普見世間。非諸聲聞
324a12 | 所能得見。唯除趣向一切智境。諸大菩薩。如
324a13 | 人生已。則有二天。恒相隨逐。一曰同生。二曰
324a14 | 同名。天常見人。人不見天。應知如來。亦復如
324a15 | 是。在諸菩薩大集會中。現大神通。諸大聲聞。
324a16 | 悉不能見。譬如比丘得心自在。入滅盡定。六
324a17 | 根作業。皆悉不行。一切語言。不知不覺。定力
324a18 | 持故。不般涅槃。一切聲聞。亦復如是。雖復住
324a19 | 在逝多林中。具足六根。而不知不見。不解不
324a20 | 入。如來自在。菩薩眾會。諸所作事。何以故。
324a21 | 如來境界。甚深廣大。難見難知。難測難量。超
324a22 | 諸世間。不可思議。無能壞者。非是一切二乘
324a23 | 境界。是故如來。自在神力。菩薩眾會。及逝多
324a24 | 林。普遍一切清淨世界。如是等事。諸大聲聞。
324a25 | 悉不知見。非其器故。

简体字

譬如有人以翳形药自涂其眼，在于众会去、来、坐、立无能见者，而能悉睹众会中事。应知如来亦复如是，超过于世，普见世间，非诸声闻所能得见，唯除趣向一切智境诸大菩萨。如人生已，则有二天，恒相随逐，一曰：同生，二曰：同名；天常见人，人不见天。应知如来亦复如是，在诸菩萨大集会中现大神通，诸大声闻悉不能见。譬如比丘得心自在，入灭尽定，六根作业皆悉不行，一切语言不知不觉；定力持故，不般涅槃。一切声闻亦复如是，虽复住在逝多林中，具足六根，而不知不见不解不入如来自在、菩萨众会诸所作事。何以故？如来境界甚深广大，难见难知，难测难量，超诸世间，不可思议，无能坏者，非是一切二乘境界；是故，如来自在神力、菩萨众会及逝多林普遍一切清净世界，如是等事，诸大声闻悉不知见，非其器故。

It is also as if there were someone who had an invisibility elixir that, when he applied it to his eyes, while in the midst of some assembly, he could go and come or sit down and stand up without anyone there being able to witness this, whereas he himself would still be able to see everything happening in that congregation. One should realize that the Tathāgata is just like this, for he has transcended the world and yet he is able to see everywhere within the world. With the exception of the great bodhisattvas who have set out toward the realm of all-knowledge, [no one else could see these phenomena], for this is not something that the *śrāvaka* disciples would be able to see.

Again, this is like when, once a man[22] is born, two devas constantly follow him, one of whom is called "Identically Born" and the other of whom is called "Identically Named." Those devas are always able to see that man, whereas that man does not see those devas. One should realize that the Tathāgata's circumstance is just like this, for, as he manifests great spiritual superknowledges in the midst of an immense congregation of bodhisattvas, the great *śrāvaka* disciples are all still unable to see this.

It is as if there were a bhikshu who had acquired the sovereign mastery of mind by which he entered the complete cessation absorption in which none of the actions of the six sense faculties continue to function and he no longer apprehends or is even aware of anything that is spoken. Because he is sustained in this by the power of meditative concentration, he does not enter *parinirvāṇa*. So too it was with the *śrāvaka* disciples. Although they continued to reside within the Jeta Grove and were completely endowed with the six sense faculties, they still did not know, did not see, did not understand, and did not enter the Tathāgata's sovereign masteries or any of the endeavors carried out by those in the congregation of bodhisattvas.

And why was this the case? This is because the Tathāgata's sphere of cognition is extremely deep and vast, difficult to perceive, difficult to know, difficult to fathom, and difficult to assess. It transcends all worlds and is inconceivable and indestructible. It is not a sphere of cognition accessible to any of the adherents of the two vehicles. Therefore the Tathāgata's freely implemented use of the spiritual powers, the assembly of bodhisattvas, the Jeta Grove's pervasive presence in all pure worlds, and all other phenomena such as these were such that none of the great *śrāvaka* disciples could know or see them because they were not suitable vessels for [being able to see] them.

正體字

爾時毘盧遮那願光明
324a26 | 菩薩。承佛神力。觀察十方。而說頌言
324a27 | 汝等應觀察　佛道不思議
324a28 | 於此逝多林　示現神通力
324a29 | 善逝威神力　所現無央數
324b01 | 一切諸世間　迷惑不能了
324b02 | 法王深妙法　無量難思議
324b03 | 所現諸神通　舉世莫能測
324b04 | 以了法無相　是故名為佛
324b05 | 而具相莊嚴　稱揚不可盡
324b06 | 今於此林內　示現大神力
324b07 | 甚深無有邊　言辭莫能辯
324b08 | 汝觀大威德　無量菩薩眾
324b09 | 十方諸國土　而來見世尊
324b10 | 所願皆具足　所行無障礙
324b11 | 一切諸世間　無能測量者
324b12 | 一切諸緣覺　及彼大聲聞
324b13 | 皆悉不能知　菩薩行境界
324b14 | 菩薩大智慧　諸地悉究竟
324b15 | 高建勇猛幢　難摧難可動

简体字

尔时，毗卢遮那愿光明菩萨，承佛神力，观察十方而说颂言：

“汝等应观察，佛道不思议，
于此逝多林，示现神通力。
善逝威神力，所现无央数；
一切诸世间，迷惑不能了。
法王深妙法，无量难思议，
所现诸神通，举世莫能测。
以了法无相，是故名为佛，
而具相庄严，称扬不可尽。
今于此林内，示现大神力，
甚深无有边，言辞莫能辩。
汝观大威德，无量菩萨众，
十方诸国土，而来见世尊。
所愿皆具足，所行无障碍；
一切诸世间，无能测量者。
一切诸缘觉，及彼大声闻，
皆悉不能知，菩萨行境界。
菩萨大智慧，诸地悉究竟，
高建勇猛幢，难摧难可动。

At that time, Light of Vairocana's Vows Bodhisattva, aided by the Buddha's spiritual powers, surveyed the ten directions and then spoke these verses:

You should all contemplate
the inconceivability of the Buddha's enlightenment[23]
as, within this Jeta Grove,
he manifests the power of his spiritual superknowledges.

The awe-inspiring spiritual powers of the Well Gone One
that he has displayed here are endlessly many.
Everyone in the entire world is deluded,
hence they are all unable to understand them.

The Dharma King's profound and marvelous dharmas
are measureless and inconceivable.
No one in the entire world
can fathom the spiritual superknowledges that he manifests.

Because he completely understands dharmas as signless,
he is therefore known as "the Buddha,"
yet he is endowed with the adornment of the signs
that one could never completely finish praising.

Now, within this grove,
he has displayed great spiritual powers
that are so extremely profound and boundless,
that words could never describe them.

You should contemplate the great awe-inspiring virtue
of this measurelessly vast assembly of bodhisattvas
that has come here from the lands of the ten directions
in order to see the Bhagavat.

They have completely fulfilled the vows they have made
and they are unimpeded in their spheres of action.
Of all who reside in the world,
there are none who can completely fathom them.

All the *pratyekabuddhas*
as well as those great *śrāvaka* disciples—
they are all unable to know
the range of the bodhisattvas' practice.

The great wisdom of the bodhisattvas
has reached its ultimate culmination on the grounds.
They have raised high their banner of heroic bravery
that is invincible and unshakable.

正體字

324b16 諸大名稱士　無量三昧力
324b17 所現諸神變　法界悉充滿
324b18 爾時不可壞精進王菩薩。承佛神力。觀察十
324b19 方。而說頌言
324b20 汝觀諸佛子　智慧功德藏
324b21 究竟菩提行　安隱諸世間
324b22 其心本明達　善入諸三昧
324b23 智慧無邊際　境界不可量
324b24 今此逝多林　種種皆嚴飾
324b25 菩薩眾雲集　親近如來住
324b26 汝觀無所著　無量大眾海
324b27 十方來詣此　坐寶蓮華座
324b28 無來亦無住　無依無戲論
324b29 離垢心無礙　究竟於法界
324c01 建立智慧幢　堅固不動搖
324c02 知無變化法　而現變化事
324c03 十方無量剎　一切諸佛所
324c04 同時悉往詣　而亦不分身
324c05 汝觀釋師子　自在神通力
324c06 能令菩薩眾　一切俱來集

简体字

诸大名称士，无量三昧力，
所现诸神变，法界悉充满。”
尔时，不可坏精进王菩萨，承佛神力，观察十方而说颂言：
“汝观诸佛子，智慧功德藏，
究竟菩提行，安隐诸世间。
其心本明达，善入诸三昧，
智慧无边际，境界不可量。
今此逝多林，种种皆严饰，
菩萨众云集，亲近如来住。
汝观无所著，无量大众海，
十方来诣此，坐宝莲华座。
无来亦无住，无依无戏论，
离垢心无碍，究竟于法界。
建立智慧幢，坚固不动摇，
知无变化法，而现变化事。
十方无量刹，一切诸佛所，
同时悉往诣，而亦不分身。
汝观释师子，自在神通力，
能令菩萨众，一切俱来集。

The spiritual transformations manifested
by the measureless samādhi power
of all these great and famous eminences
fill up the entire Dharma realm.

At that time, King of Indestructible Vigor Bodhisattva, aided by the Buddha's spiritual powers, surveyed the ten directions and then spoke these verses:

You should all contemplate these sons of the buddhas,
these treasuries of wisdom and meritorious qualities,
who have completed the bodhi practices
and who bring peace and security to the entire world.

Their minds originally possess clear and penetrating understanding
and they have skillfully entered all the samādhis.
Their wisdom is boundless
and its range of application is measureless.

Now, this Jeta Grove
is entirely adorned in many different ways.
This congregation of bodhisattvas has gathered like clouds
to dwell near to the Tathāgata.

Contemplate the ocean of this measurelessly vast assembly
which is entirely free of attachments.
They have come from the ten directions to pay their respects here
and have taken their seats on their jeweled lotus flower thrones.

They have neither any coming, nor any abiding,
nor anything on which they rely, nor any conceptual proliferation.
They are undefiled and possessed of unimpeded minds
that reach to the very ends of the Dharma realm.

They have raised up the banner of wisdom,
and are solid and unshakable.
They have realized the nonexistence of transformational dharmas
and yet manifest transformationally created phenomena.

They simultaneously go forth to pay their respects
wherever all buddhas are dwelling
in countless *kṣetras* throughout the ten directions,
and yet still do not divide their bodies as they do so.

You should contemplate this lion of the Śākya clan,
his sovereign mastery of the powers of spiritual superknowledges,
and his ability to cause the congregations of bodhisattvas
to all come forth and gather here.

正體字

324c07 | 一切諸佛法　法界悉平等
324c08 | 言說故不同　此眾咸通達
324c09 | 諸佛常安住　法界平等際
324c10 | 演說差別法　言辭無有盡
324c11 | 爾時普勝無上威德王菩薩。承佛神力。觀察
324c12 | 十方。而說頌言
324c13 | 汝觀無上士　廣大智圓滿
324c14 | 善達時非時　為眾演說法
324c15 | 摧伏眾外道　一切諸異論
324c16 | 普隨眾生心　為現神通力
324c17 | 正覺非有量　亦復非無量
324c18 | 若量若無量　牟尼悉超越
324c19 | 如日在虛空　照臨一切處
324c20 | 佛智亦如是　了達三世法
324c21 | 譬如十五夜　月輪無減缺
324c22 | 如來亦復然　白法悉圓滿
324c23 | 譬如空中日　運行無暫已
324c24 | 如來亦如是　神變恒相續
324c25 | 譬如十方剎　於空無所礙
324c26 | 世燈現變化　於世亦復然

简体字

一切诸佛法，法界悉平等，
言说故不同，此众咸通达。
诸佛常安住，法界平等际，
演说差别法，言辞无有尽。”

尔时，普胜无上威德王菩萨，承佛神力，观察十方而说颂言：

“汝观无上士，广大智圆满，
善达时非时，为众演说法；
摧伏众外道，一切诸异论，
普随众生心，为现神通力。
正觉非有量，亦复非无量；
若量若无量，牟尼悉超越。
如日在虚空，照临一切处；
佛智亦如是，了达三世法。
譬如十五夜，月轮无减缺；
如来亦复然，白法悉圆满。
譬如空中日，运行无暂已；
如来亦如是，神变恒相续。
譬如十方刹，于空无所碍，
世灯现变化，于世亦复然。

The Dharma of all buddhas is uniformly equal
throughout the Dharma realm.
It is due to the ways it is spoken that it differs.
Those in this assembly all thoroughly comprehend this.

All buddhas always dwell serenely
at the apex of the Dharma realm's uniformity
and expound on the different dharmas
with inexhaustibly many expressions.

At that time, King of Universally Supreme and Unsurpassable Awesome Virtue Bodhisattva, aided by the Buddha's spiritual powers, surveyed the ten directions and then spoke these verses:

You should contemplate the Unsurpassed Eminence[24]
and the fullness of his vast sphere of wisdom.[25]
He skillfully comprehends what is and is not the right time,
and expounds on the Dharma for beings.

He utterly demolishes all the heterodox theories
of the many adherents of non-Buddhist paths
and, everywhere adapting to beings' minds,
he manifests the powers of his spiritual superknowledges.

The Rightly Enlightened One is neither measurable
nor is he measureless.
Whether it be measurability or immeasurability,
the Muni has entirely transcended it all.

Just as it is with the sun in the sky
whose illumination reaches all places,
so too it is with the Buddha's wisdom
that completely penetrates all dharmas of the three times.

Just as on the fifteenth night of the month
when the orb of the moon is undiminished,[26]
so too it is with the Tathāgata
whose white dharmas[27] of pristine purity are all perfectly complete.

Just as the sun in the middle of the sky
moves along without pausing for even a moment,
so too it is with the Tathāgata
whose spiritual transformations continue constantly.

Just as the *kṣetras* of the ten directions
exist without being obstructed by space,
so too it is with the Lamp of the World's
manifesting of transformations in the world.

正體字

324c27 譬如世間地　群生之所依
324c28 照世燈法輪　為依亦如是
324c29 譬如猛疾風　所行無障礙
325a01 佛法亦如是　速遍於世間
325a02 譬如大水輪　世界所依住
325a03 智慧輪亦爾　三世佛所依
325a04 爾時無礙勝藏王菩薩。承佛神力。觀察十方。
325a05 而說頌言
325a06 譬如大寶山　饒益諸含識
325a07 佛山亦如是　普益於世間
325a08 譬如大海水　澄淨無垢濁
325a09 見佛亦如是　能除諸渴愛
325a10 譬如須彌山　出於大海中
325a11 世間燈亦爾　從於法海出
325a12 如海具眾寶　求者皆滿足
325a13 無師智亦然　見者悉開悟
325a14 如來甚深智　無量無有數
325a15 是故神通力　示現難思議
325a16 譬如工幻師　示現種種事
325a17 佛智亦如是　現諸自在力
325a18 譬如如意寶　能滿一切欲

简体字

譬如世间地，群生之所依；
照世灯法轮，为依亦如是。
譬如猛疾风，所行无障碍；
佛法亦如是，速遍于世间。
譬如大水轮，世界所依住；
智慧轮亦尔，三世佛所依。”

尔时，无碍胜藏王菩萨，承佛神力，观察十方而说颂言：

“譬如大宝山，饶益诸含识；
佛山亦如是，普益于世间。
譬如大海水，澄净无垢浊；
见佛亦如是，能除诸渴爱。
譬如须弥山，出于大海中；
世间灯亦尔，从于法海出。
如海具众宝，求者皆满足；
无师智亦然，见者悉开悟。
如来甚深智，无量无有数；
是故神通力，示现难思议。
譬如工幻师，示现种种事；
佛智亦如是，现诸自在力。
譬如如意宝，能满一切欲；

Just as the world's ground
is what the many kinds of beings depend on for support,
so, too, the Lamp of the World's Dharma wheel
is what they depend on in this very same way.

Just as a fiercely swift wind
is unimpeded in its motion,
so too it is with the Buddha's Dharma
in its swift pervasion of the entire world.

Just as a great sphere of water[28]
is what the world depends on to abide,
so too it is with the sphere of wisdom
on which all buddhas of the three times rely.

At that time, Unimpeded Supremacy Treasury King Bodhisattva, aided by the Buddha's spiritual powers, surveyed the ten directions and then spoke these verses:

Just as the great mountain of jewels
liberally benefits all sentient beings,
so too it is with the mountain of the Buddha
who everywhere benefits those in the world.

Just as the waters of the great sea
are clear, clean, and free of filth or turbidity,
so, too, when one sees the Buddha,
one is then able to dispel all thirst-driven cravings.

Just as Mount Sumeru
rises up from the midst of the great ocean,
so, too, the Lamp of the World
rises up from the ocean of the Dharma.

Just as the ocean is so replete with the many kinds of jewels
that all who seek them become completely satisfied,
so, too, it is with the wisdom he gained independent of a teacher.
All who perceive it become awakened.

The Tathāgata's extremely deep wisdom
is measureless and incalculable.
Hence the power of his superknowledges
makes manifest what is inconceivable.

Just as a master conjurer
manifests all different kinds of phenomena,
so, too, the wisdom of the Buddha
reveals the power of his miraculous transformations.[29]

Just as a wish-fulfilling jewel
is able to fulfill all desires,

正體字

325a19 最勝亦復然　滿諸清淨願
325a20 譬如明淨寶　普照一切物
325a21 佛智亦如是　普照群生心
325a22 譬如八面寶　等鑒於諸方
325a23 無礙燈亦然　普照於法界
325a24 譬如水清珠　能清諸濁水
325a25 見佛亦如是　諸根悉清淨
325a26 爾時化現法界願月王菩薩。承佛神力。觀察
325a27 十方。而說頌言
325a28 譬如帝青寶　能青一切色
325a29 見佛者亦然　悉發菩提行
325b01 一一微塵內　佛現神通力
325b02 令無量無邊　菩薩皆清淨
325b03 甚深微妙力　無邊不可知
325b04 菩薩之境界　世間莫能測
325b05 如來所現身　清淨相莊嚴
325b06 普入於法界　成就諸菩薩
325b07 難思佛國土　於中成正覺
325b08 一切諸菩薩　世主皆充滿
325b09 釋迦無上尊　於法悉自在
325b10 示現神通力　無邊不可量

简体字

最胜亦复然，满诸清净愿。
譬如明净宝，普照一切物；
佛智亦如是，普照群生心。
譬如八面宝，等鉴于诸方；
无碍灯亦然，普照于法界。
譬如水清珠，能清诸浊水；
见佛亦如是，诸根悉清净。”

尔时，化现法界愿月王菩萨，承佛神力，观察十方而说颂言：

“譬如帝青宝，能青一切色；
见佛者亦然，悉发菩提行。
一一微尘内，佛现神通力，
令无量无边，菩萨皆清净。
甚深微妙力，无边不可知；
菩萨之境界，世间莫能测。
如来所现身，清净相庄严，
普入于法界，成就诸菩萨。
难思佛国土，于中成正觉；
一切诸菩萨，世主皆充满。
释迦无上尊，于法悉自在，
示现神通力，无边不可量。

so, too, the Jina, the Supremely Victorious One,[30]
fulfills all pure aspirations.

Just as a luminous pristine jewel
everywhere illuminates all things,
so, too, the Buddha's wisdom
everywhere illuminates the minds of the many beings.

Just as an eight-faceted jewel
reflects light in all directions,
so, too, the Unobstructed Lamp
everywhere illuminates the Dharma realm.

Just as a water-clarifying pearl
is able to clarify all turbid waters,
so, too, when one sees the Buddha,
all one's faculties become completely purified.

At that time, the bodhisattva known as Moon King Manifesting Dharma Realm Vows, aided by the Buddha's spiritual powers, surveyed the ten directions and then spoke these verses:

Just as the *indranīla* sapphire gem
is able to make all colors turn blue,
so, too, those who see the Buddha
all then bring forth the bodhi practices.

Within each and every atom,
the Buddha manifests his spiritual powers,
causing measurelessly and boundlessly many
bodhisattvas to all achieve purity.

These extremely deep and sublime powers
are so boundless as to be unknowable.
No one in the world is able to fathom
the bodhisattvas' sphere of cognition.

The bodies manifested by the Tathāgata
are adorned with their marks of purity.
They everywhere enter the Dharma realm
and lead the bodhisattvas to perfection.

Within inconceivably many buddha lands,
they achieve the right enlightenment.
They are all completely full
of all the bodhisattvas and world leaders.

The unexcelled honored one of the Śākya clan
who has achieved sovereign mastery in all dharmas
manifests spiritual powers
that are boundless and immeasurable.

正體字

325b11║ 菩薩種種行　無量無有盡
325b12║ 如來自在力　為之悉示現
325b13║ 佛子善修學　甚深諸法界
325b14║ 成就無礙智　明了一切法
325b15║ 善逝威神力　為眾轉法輪
325b16║ 神變普充滿　令世皆清淨
325b17║ 如來智圓滿　境界亦清淨
325b18║ 譬如大龍王　普濟諸群生
325b19║ 爾時法慧光焰王菩薩。承佛神力。觀察十方。
325b20║ 而說頌言
325b21║ 三世諸如來　聲聞大弟子
325b22║ 悉不能知佛　舉足下足事
325b23║ 去來現在世　一切諸緣覺
325b24║ 亦不知如來　舉足下足事
325b25║ 況復諸凡夫　結使所纏縛
325b26║ 無明覆心識　而能知導師
325b27║ 正覺無礙智　超過語言道
325b28║ 其量不可測　孰有能知見
325b29║ 譬如明月光　無能測邊際
325c01║ 佛神通亦爾　莫見其終盡

简体字

菩萨种种行，无量无有尽；
如来自在力，为之悉示现。
佛子善修学，甚深诸法界，
成就无碍智，明了一切法。
善逝威神力，为众转法轮，
神变普充满，令世皆清净。
如来智圆满，境界亦清净；
譬如大龙王，普济诸群生。”

尔时，法慧光焰王菩萨，承佛神力，观察十方而说颂言：

“三世诸如来，声闻大弟子，
悉不能知佛，举足下足事。
去来现在世，一切诸缘觉，
亦不知如来，举足下足事。
况复诸凡夫，结使所缠缚，
无明覆心识，而能知导师！
正觉无碍智，超过语言道，
其量不可测，孰有能知见！
譬如明月光，无能测边际；
佛神通亦尔，莫见其终尽。

The many different practices of the bodhisattva
are immeasurable and inexhaustible.
The Tathāgata's miraculous powers[31]
are all revealed for their sakes.

These sons of the Buddha thoroughly cultivate and train
in the realm of extremely deep dharmas,
and become perfectly accomplished in the unimpeded knowledge
by which they clearly understand all dharmas.

It is with the Well Gone One's awesome spiritual powers
that he turns the wheel of the Dharma for the sake of the many.
His spiritual transformations are everywhere fully present,
causing the entire world to become purified.

The Tathāgata's wisdom is perfectly fulfilled
and its domain is pure as well.
Like a great dragon king,[32]
he everywhere rescues the many kinds of beings.

At that time, King of the Dharma's Flaming Wisdom Light Bodhisattva, aided by the Buddha's spiritual powers, surveyed the ten directions and then spoke these verses:

None of the great *śrāvaka* disciples
of any of the *tathāgatas* of the three periods of time
could ever know of a buddha
what transpires even as he merely lifts or sets down his foot.

Nor could any of the *pratyekabuddhas*
of the past, the future, or present
ever know of a *tathāgata*
what transpires even as he merely lifts or sets down his foot.

How much the less might a common person,
entangled by the bonds of the fetters
and having a mind and consciousness blanketed by ignorance,
then ever be able to know the Master Guide?

The unimpeded wisdom of the Rightly Enlightened One
utterly surpasses the path of verbal description
and his capacities are unfathomable.
Who then could possibly know or perceive this?

Just as no one could fathom the farthest boundaries
of the radiance of the brightly shining moon,
so too it is with the Buddha's spiritual powers,
for there is no one who could see where they end.

正體字

325c02║ 一一諸方便　念念所變化
325c03║ 盡於無量劫　思惟不能了
325c04║ 思惟一切智　不可思議法
325c05║ 一一方便門　邊際不可得
325c06║ 若有於此法　而興廣大願
325c07║ 彼於此境界　知見不為難
325c08║ 勇猛勤修習　難思大法海
325c09║ 其心無障礙　入此方便門
325c10║ 心意已調伏　志願亦寬廣
325c11║ 當獲大菩提　最勝之境界
325c12║ 爾時破一切魔軍智幢王菩薩。承佛神力。觀
325c13║ 察十方。而說頌言
325c14║ 智身非是身　無礙難思議
325c15║ 設有思議者　一切無能及
325c16║ 從不思議業　起此清淨身
325c17║ 殊特妙莊嚴　不著於三界
325c18║ 光明照一切　法界悉清淨
325c19║ 開佛菩提門　出生眾智慧
325c20║ 譬如世間日　普放慧光明
325c21║ 遠離諸塵垢　滅除一切障

简体字

一一诸方便，念念所变化，
尽于无量劫，思惟不能了。
思惟一切智，不可思议法，
一一方便门，边际不可得。
若有于此法，而兴广大愿；
彼于此境界，知见不为难。
勇猛勤修习，难思大法海；
其心无障碍，入此方便门。
心意已调伏，志愿亦宽广，
当获大菩提，最胜之境界。”

尔时，破一切魔军智幢王菩萨，承佛神力，观察十方而说颂言：

“智身非是身，无碍难思议；
设有思议者，一切无能及。
从不思议业，起此清净身，
殊特妙庄严，不著于三界。
光明照一切，法界悉清净，
开佛菩提门，出生众智慧。
譬如世间日，普放慧光明，
远离诸尘垢，灭除一切障，

Every one of the skillful means and transformations
he produces in each successive mind-moment
are such that one could never completely comprehend them
even by exhausting limitless kalpas in attempting to do so.

If one were to ponder his all-knowledge,
his inconceivable dharmas,
and each one of his gateways of skillful means,
one could never discover their boundaries.

However, if one were to make a vast vow
intent on gaining this Dharma,
one would not find it difficult
to know and see this realm of cognition.

If one were to arouse heroic bravery and then diligently cultivate
this inconceivably vast ocean of Dharma,
then one's resolve would remain unimpeded
as one entered these gateways of skillful means.

Once one's mind has become disciplined
and one's resolute vows have also become broadly inclusive and vast,
then one will become bound to acquire the great bodhi,
the domain of the Jina, the Supremely Victorious One.

At that time, Wisdom Banner King Who Vanquishes All Demon Armies Bodhisattva, aided by the Buddha's spiritual powers, surveyed the ten directions and then spoke these verses:

The wisdom body is not this body.
It is unimpeded and inconceivable.
If there was anyone who attempted to conceive of it,
none of them could even come close to doing so.

It is through inconceivable karmic works
that one produces this pure body.
It is extraordinary in its marvelous adornments
and it is not attached to any of the three realms of existence.

Its radiance illuminates everything
and thus the Dharma realm becomes entirely purified.
It opens the gates of the Buddha's bodhi
and produces the many varieties of wisdom.

Just like the sun that shines in the world,
it everywhere sends forth the light of wisdom,
leaves all of the dusts' defilements far behind,
and utterly extinguishes all obstacles.

正體字

325c22 ‖ 普淨三有處　永絕生死流
325c23 ‖ 成就菩薩道　出生無上覺
325c24 ‖ 示現無邊色　此色無依處
325c25 ‖ 所現雖無量　一切不思議
325c26 ‖ 菩提一念頃　能覺一切法
325c27 ‖ 云何欲測量　如來智邊際
325c28 ‖ 一念悉明達　一切三世法
325c29 ‖ 故說佛智慧　無盡無能壞
326a01 ‖ 智者應如是　專思佛菩提
326a02 ‖ 此思難思議　思之不可得
326a03 ‖ 菩提不可說　超過語言路
326a04 ‖ 諸佛從此生　是法難思議
326a05 ‖ 爾時願智光明幢王菩薩。承佛神力。觀察十
326a06 ‖ 方。而說頌言
326a07 ‖ 若能善觀察　菩提無盡海
326a08 ‖ 則得離癡念　決定受持法
326a09 ‖ 若得決定心　則能修妙行
326a10 ‖ 禪寂自思慮　永斷諸疑惑
326a11 ‖ 其心不疲倦　亦復無懈怠
326a12 ‖ 展轉增進修　究竟諸佛法
326a13 ‖ 信智已成就　念念令增長

简体字

普净三有处，永绝生死流，
成就菩萨道，出生无上觉。
示现无边色，此色无依处；
所现虽无量，一切不思议。
菩提一念顷，能觉一切法；
云何欲测量，如来智边际？
一念悉明达，一切三世法；
故说佛智慧，无尽无能坏。
智者应如是，专思佛菩提；
此思难思议，思之不可得。
菩提不可说，超过语言路；
诸佛从此生，是法难思议。”

尔时，愿智光明幢王菩萨，承佛神力，观察十方而说颂言：

“若能善观察，菩提无尽海，
则得离痴念，决定受持法。
若得决定心，则能修妙行，
禅寂自思虑，永断诸疑惑。
其心不疲倦，亦复无懈怠，
展转增进修，究竟诸佛法。
信智已成就，念念令增长，

It everywhere purifies the abodes in the three realms of existence,
forever cuts off the stream of births and deaths,
brings about complete success in the bodhisattva path,
and produces the unexcelled awakening.

He manifests boundlessly many forms,
yet there is nothing in these forms that he relies on.
Although his manifestations are countless,
all of them are inconceivable.

When, in but one instant of bodhi,
he is able to awaken to all dharmas,
how could one ever hope to fathom
the bounds of the Tathāgata's wisdom?

In but one mind-moment, he clearly comprehends
all dharmas of the three periods of time.
Hence it is said that the Buddha's wisdom
is endless and unassailable.

It is in this way that the wise
should focus their contemplations on the Buddha's bodhi.
This contemplation is inconceivable, for,
in contemplating it, one finds it cannot be grasped.

Bodhi is indescribable,
for it entirely surpasses the path of speech.
All buddhas come forth from this,
This Dharma is inconceivable.

At that time, King of the Banner of the Light of Vows and Wisdom Bodhisattva, aided by the Buddha's spiritual powers, surveyed the ten directions and then spoke these verses:

If they[33] are able to skillfully contemplate
the endless ocean of bodhi,
they will be able to abandon deluded thought
and decisively resolve to uphold the Dharma.

If they acquire such decisively resolute mind,
they will be able to cultivate the marvelous practices,
pursue inward reflection in the stillness of *dhyāna*,
and forever cut off all doubts.

Their resolve will remain invulnerable to weariness
and they will remain free of indolence as well.
They will continuously increase in the progress of their cultivation
toward the ultimate realization of the Dharma of all buddhas.

Their faith and wisdom have already been completely developed.
Still, in each successive mind-moment, they are caused to increase.

正體字

326a14 | 常樂常觀察　無得無依法
326a15 | 無量億千劫　所修功德行
326a16 | 一切悉迴向　諸佛所求道
326a17 | 雖在於生死　而心無染著
326a18 | 安住諸佛法　常樂如來行
326a19 | 世間之所有　蘊界等諸法
326a20 | 一切皆捨離　專求佛功德
326a21 | 凡夫嬰妄惑　於世常流轉
326a22 | 菩薩心無礙　救之令解脫
326a23 | 菩薩行難稱　舉世莫能思
326a24 | 遍除一切苦　普與群生樂
326a25 | 已獲菩提智　復愍諸群生
326a26 | 光明照世間　度脫一切眾
326a27 | 爾時破一切障勇猛智王菩薩。承佛神力。觀
326a28 | 察十方。而說頌言
326a29 | 無量億千劫　佛名難可聞
326b01 | 況復得親近　永斷諸疑惑
326b02 | 如來世間燈　通達一切法
326b03 | 普生三世福　令眾悉清淨
326b04 | 如來妙色身　一切所欽歎
326b05 | 億劫常瞻仰　其心無厭足

简体字

常乐常观察，无得无依法。
无量亿千劫，所修功德行；
一切悉回向，诸佛所求道。
虽在于生死，而心无染著，
安住诸佛法，常乐如来行。
世间之所有，蕴界等诸法；
一切皆舍离，专求佛功德。
凡夫婴妄惑，于世常流转；
菩萨心无碍，救之令解脱。
菩萨行难称，举世莫能思，
遍除一切苦，普与群生乐。
已获菩提智，复愍诸群生，
光明照世间，度脱一切众。”

尔时，破一切障勇猛智王菩萨，承佛神力，观察十方而说颂言：

“无量亿千劫，佛名难可闻；
况复得亲近，永断诸疑惑！
如来世间灯，通达一切法，
普生三世福，令众悉清净。
如来妙色身，一切所钦叹，
亿劫常瞻仰，其心无厌足。

They always delight in and always contemplate the Dharma
that has nothing that can be grasped and nothing on which it depends.

They entirely dedicate
all meritorious practices they have cultivated
throughout countless *koṭīs* of thousands of kalpas
to the path that all buddhas have sought.

Although they abide within *saṃsāra,*
their minds still remain free of any defiling attachments.
They abide securely in the Dharma of all buddhas
and always delight in the Tathāgata's practices.

Everything within the world—
the aggregates, the sense realms, and other such dharmas—
They entirely abandon them all
for they seek only to acquire the qualities of the Buddha.

Common people, entangled in falseness and delusion,
always flow along in the world's cyclic existence.
The bodhisattvas' minds are unimpeded
in striving to rescue them and bring about their liberation.

The bodhisattvas' practices are difficult to completely praise
for no one in the entire world could even conceive of them.
They everywhere dispel all sufferings
and universally bestow happiness on all the many kinds of beings.

They have already acquired the wisdom of bodhi
and also take pity on all the many kinds of beings.
Their light illuminates the world
as they proceed to liberate all beings.

At that time, King of Valiant Wisdom Demolishing All Obstacles Bodhisattva, aided by the Buddha's spiritual powers, surveyed the ten directions and then spoke these verses:

Even in countless thousands of *koṭīs* of kalpas,
it would be difficult to even hear the word "buddha,"
how much the more so to also draw near to him
and then forever cut off all one's doubts.

The Tathāgata, the Lamp of the World,
has a penetrating comprehension of all dharmas.
He everywhere generates merit[34] throughout the three times
and thereby enables all beings to become purified.

The Tathāgata's marvelous form body
is admired and praised by everyone.
If one always gazed up at it for a *koṭī* of kalpas,
one's mind would still never be fully satisfied.

正體字

326b06 | 若有諸佛子　觀佛妙色身
326b07 | 必捨諸有著　迴向菩提道
326b08 | 如來妙色身　恒演廣大音
326b09 | 辯才無障礙　開佛菩提門
326b10 | 曉悟諸眾生　無量不思議
326b11 | 令入智慧門　授以菩提記
326b12 | 如來出世間　為世大福田
326b13 | 普導諸含識　令其集福行
326b14 | 若有供養佛　永除惡道畏
326b15 | 消滅一切苦　成就智慧身
326b16 | 若見兩足尊　能發廣大心
326b17 | 是人恒值佛　增長智慧力
326b18 | 若見人中勝　決意向菩提
326b19 | 是人能自知　必當成正覺
326b20 | 爾時法界差別願智神通王菩薩。承佛神力。
326b21 | 觀察十方。而說頌言
326b22 | 釋迦無上尊　具一切功德
326b23 | 見者心清淨　迴向大智慧
326b24 | 如來大慈悲　出現於世間
326b25 | 普為諸群生　轉無上法輪

简体字

若有诸佛子，观佛妙色身，
必舍诸有著，回向菩提道。
如来妙色身，恒演广大音，
辩才无障碍，开佛菩提门；
晓悟诸众生，无量不思议，
令入智慧门，授以菩提记。
如来出世间，为世大福田，
普导诸含识，令其集福行。
若有供养佛，永除恶道畏，
消灭一切苦，成就智慧身。
若见两足尊，能发广大心；
是人恒值佛，增长智慧力。
若见人中胜，决意向菩提；
是人能自知，必当成正觉。”

尔时，法界差别愿智神通王菩萨，承佛神力，观察十方而说颂言：

“释迦无上尊，具一切功德；
见者心清净，回向大智慧。
如来大慈悲，出现于世间，
普为诸群生，转无上法轮。

Wherever there are sons of the Buddha
who contemplate the Buddha's marvelous form body,
they will certainly forsake all attachments to existence
and dedicate their efforts to the path that leads to bodhi.

The Tathāgata's marvelous form body
constantly expounds teachings with a far-reaching voice
that speaks with unimpeded eloquence
and opens the gates leading to the Buddha's bodhi.

He enlightens beings,
countlessly and inconceivably many,
causes them to enter the gateway of wisdom,
and gives them predictions of future bodhi.

The Tathāgata comes forth into the world
and serves as a great field of merit for the world.
He everywhere guides all sentient beings
and causes them to accumulate meritorious practices.

If anyone makes offerings to the Buddha,
they will forever eliminate any peril of the wretched destinies,
will do away with all their sufferings,
and will perfect the wisdom body.

If on seeing the one most revered of all two-legged beings,
one is able to bring forth the great resolve,
such a person shall always encounter the Buddha
and grow in the power of his wisdom.

If on seeing the one supreme among men,
one decisively resolves to progress toward bodhi,
such a person shall be able to realize of himself
that he is definitely bound to realize right enlightenment.

At that time, the Bodhisattva known as King of the Different Vows, Wisdom, and Spiritual Superknowledges of the Dharma Realm, aided by the Buddha's spiritual powers, surveyed the ten directions and then spoke these verses:

The supremely honored one among the Śakyans
is replete in all the meritorious qualities.
The minds of those who see him become purified
whereupon they dedicate themselves to gaining great wisdom.

The Tathāgatas,[35] possessed of the great kindness and compassion,
come forth and appear within the world
to turn the unexcelled wheel of Dharma
for the universal benefit of all the many kinds of beings.

正體字

326b26 如來無數劫　勤苦為眾生
326b27 云何諸世間　能報大師恩
326b28 寧於無量劫　受諸惡道苦
326b29 終不捨如來　而求於出離
326c01 寧代諸眾生　備受一切苦
326c02 終不捨於佛　而求得安樂
326c03 寧在諸惡趣　恒得聞佛名
326c04 不願生善道　暫時不聞佛
326c05 寧生諸地獄　一一無數劫
326c06 終不遠離佛　而求出惡趣
326c07 何故願久住　一切諸惡道
326c08 以得見如來　增長智慧故
326c09 若得見於佛　除滅一切苦
326c10 能入諸如來　大智之境界
326c11 若得見於佛　捨離一切障
326c12 長養無盡福　成就菩提道
326c13 如來能永斷　一切眾生疑
326c14 隨其心所樂　普皆令滿足
326c18 大方廣佛華嚴經卷第六十一
326c21 入法界品第三十九之二
326c22 爾時普賢菩薩摩訶薩。普觀一切菩薩眾會。
326c23 以等法界方便。等虛空界方便。

简体字

如来无数劫，勤苦为众生；
云何诸世间，能报大师恩？
宁于无量劫，受诸恶道苦；
终不舍如来，而求于出离。
宁代诸众生，备受一切苦；
终不舍于佛，而求得安乐。
宁在诸恶趣，恒得闻佛名；
不愿生善道，暂时不闻佛。
宁生诸地狱，一一无数劫；
终不远离佛，而求出恶趣。
何故愿久住，一切诸恶道？
以得见如来，增长智慧故。
若得见于佛，除灭一切苦；
能入诸如来，大智之境界。
若得见于佛，舍离一切障；
长养无尽福，成就菩提道。
如来能永断，一切众生疑，
随其心所乐，普皆令满足。”

大方广佛华严经卷第六十一

入法界品第三十九之二

尔时，普贤菩萨摩诃萨普观一切菩萨众会，以等法界方便、等虚空界方便、

For countless kalpas, the Tathāgata
has diligently toiled for the sake of beings.
How could all those in the world
ever be able to repay the Great Teacher's kindness?

One should rather endure all manner of sufferings
for countless kalpas within the wretched destinies
than ever abandon the Tathāgata
and thus thereby seek to gain emancipation.

One should rather substitute for all beings
in completely undergoing all their sufferings
than ever abandon the Buddha
and thereby seek to gain peace and happiness.

One should rather reside in the wretched destinies
and yet still always be able to hear the Buddha's name
than wish to be reborn in the good destinies
and have even a short time where one never hears the Buddha's name.

One should rather be born into the hells
enduring each one of them for countless kalpas
than ever become distantly separated from the Buddha
and thereby seek to escape the wretched destinies.

Why might one prefer to abide for a long time
in all the wretched destinies?
It would be in order to be able to see the Tathāgata
and bring about the growth of one's wisdom.

If one were to succeed in seeing the Buddha,
one could thereby do away with all sufferings
and be able to enter the domain
of all *tathāgatas'* great wisdom.

Were one to succeed in seeing the Buddha,
one could abandon all one's obstacles,
bring about the growth of endless merit,
and perfect the path to bodhi.

The Tathāgata is able to forever sever
all the doubts entertained by beings.
By according with their aspirations,
he everywhere enables them all to gain complete satisfaction.

At that time, Samantabhadra Bodhisattva-mahāsattva completely surveyed this entire congregation of bodhisattvas and, adopting methods[36] commensurate with[37] the Dharma realm, methods commensurate with the realm of empty space, methods commensurate

正體字

等眾生界方
326c24║ 便。等三世。等一切劫。等一切眾生業。等一切
326c25║ 眾生欲。等一切眾生解。等一切眾生根。等一
326c26║ 切眾生成熟時。等一切法光影方便。為諸菩
326c27║ 薩以十種法句。開發顯示照明演說此師子
326c28║ [3]頻[4]申三昧。何等為十。所謂演說能示現等法
326c29║ 界。一切佛剎微塵中。諸佛出興次第。諸剎成
327a01║ 壞。次第法句。演說能示現等虛空界。一切佛
327a02║ 剎中。盡未來劫。讚歎如來功德音聲法句。演
327a03║ 說能示現等虛空界。一切佛剎中。如來出世。
327a04║ 無量無邊。成正覺門法句。演說能示現等虛
327a05║ 空界。一切佛剎中。佛坐道場。菩薩眾會法句。
327a06║ 演說於一切毛孔。念念出現等三世一切佛
327a07║ 變化身。充滿法界法句。演說能令一身充滿
327a08║ 十方一切剎海。平等顯現法句。演說能令一
327a09║ 切諸境界中。普現三世諸佛神變法句。演說
327a10║ 能令一切佛剎微塵中。普現三世一切佛剎
327a11║ 微塵數佛。種種神變。經無量劫法句。

简体字

等众生界方便，等三世、等一切劫、等一切众生业、等一切众生欲、等一切众生解、等一切众生根、等一切众生成熟时、等一切法光影方便，为诸菩萨，以十种法句开发、显示、照明、演说此师子频申三昧。何等为十？所谓：演说能示现等法界一切佛刹微尘中，诸佛出兴次第、诸刹成坏次第法句；演说能示现等虚空界一切佛刹中，尽未来劫赞叹如来功德音声法句；演说能示现等虚空界一切佛刹中，如来出世无量无边成正觉门法句；演说能示现等虚空界一切佛刹中，佛坐道场菩萨众会法句；演说于一切毛孔，念念出现等三世一切佛变化身充满法界法句；演说能令一身充满十方一切刹海，平等显现法句；演说能令一切诸境界中，普现三世诸佛神变法句；演说能令一切佛刹微尘中，普现三世一切佛刹微尘数佛种种神变经无量劫法句；

with the realms of beings, and methods commensurate with the three periods of time, commensurate with all kalpas, commensurate with all beings' karma, commensurate with all beings' aspirations, commensurate with all beings' convictions, commensurate with all beings' faculties, commensurate with all beings' time of maturation, and commensurate with the reflections of the light of all dharmas, he then used these methods to present for the bodhisattvas ten kinds of Dharma instructions with which to open, reveal, illuminate, and expound on this lion sprint samādhi. What then were those ten? They were as follows:

Dharma instructions in which he expounded on its capacity to reveal on a scale commensurate[38] with the Dharma realm the sequence of all buddhas' emergence and the sequence of all *kṣetras'* creation and destruction as these phenomena occur within all buddha *kṣetras'* atoms.

Dharma instructions in which he expounded on its capacity to reveal on a scale commensurate with the realm of empty space, within all Buddha *kṣetras,* the sounds of praises of the Tathāgata's qualities which continue on to the end of all future kalpas;

Dharma instructions in which he expounded on its capacity to reveal on a scale commensurate with the realm of empty space the *tathāgatas'* emergence in the world within all buddha *kṣetras* and their teaching of measurelessly and boundlessly many gateways to right enlightenment;

Dharma instructions in which he expounded on its capacity to reveal on a scale commensurate with the realm of empty space the presence in all buddha *kṣetras* of buddhas sitting in their sites of enlightenment, surrounded by congregations of bodhisattvas;

Dharma instructions in which he expounded on the emanation of transformation bodies that stream forth from their pores in every mind-moment, filling the Dharma realm in numbers equal to that of all buddhas of the three periods of time;

Dharma instructions in which he expounded on its capacity to cause one body to fill up the ocean of all *kṣetras* of the ten directions, manifesting equally everywhere.

Dharma instructions in which he expounded on its capacity to cause the appearance of the spiritual transformations of all buddhas of the three periods of time to manifest everywhere in all spheres of cognition.

Dharma instructions in which he expounded on its capacity to cause the appearance within all buddha *kṣetras'* atoms of the various spiritual transformations performed for countless kalpas by all buddhas

正體字

演說能
327a12║ 令一切毛孔。出生三世一切諸佛。大願海音。
327a13║ 盡未來劫。開發化導一切菩薩法句。演說能
327a14║ 令佛師子座。量同法界。菩薩眾會。道場莊嚴。
327a15║ 等無差別。盡未來劫。轉於種種微妙法輪法
327a16║ 句。佛子。此十為首。有不可說佛剎微塵數法
327a17║ 句。皆是如來。智慧境界。爾時普賢菩薩。欲重
327a18║ 宣此義。承佛神力。觀察如來。觀察眾會。觀察
327a19║ 諸佛難思境界。觀察諸佛無邊三昧。觀察不
327a20║ 可思議諸世界海。觀察不可思議如幻法智。
327a21║ 觀察不可思議三世諸佛悉皆平等。觀察一
327a22║ 切無量無邊諸言辭法。而說頌言
327a23║ 一一毛孔中　微塵數剎海
327a24║ 悉有如來坐　皆具菩薩眾
327a25║ 一一毛孔中　無量諸剎海
327a26║ 佛處菩提座　如是遍法界
327a27║ 一一毛孔中　一切剎塵佛
327a28║ 菩薩眾圍遶　為說普賢行

简体字

演说能令一切毛孔出生三世一切诸佛大愿海音，尽未来劫开发化导一切菩萨法句；演说能令佛师子座量同法界，菩萨众会道场庄严等无差别，尽未来劫转于种种微妙法轮法句。

“佛子，此十为首，有不可说佛刹微尘数法句，皆是如来智慧境界。”

尔时，普贤菩萨欲重宣此义，承佛神力，观察如来，观察众会，观察诸佛难思境界，观察诸佛无边三昧，观察不可思议诸世界海，观察不可思议如幻法智，观察不可思议三世诸佛悉皆平等，观察一切无量无边诸言辞法，而说颂言：

“一一毛孔中，微尘数刹海，
悉有如来坐，皆具菩萨众。
一一毛孔中，无量诸刹海，
佛处菩提座，如是遍法界。
一一毛孔中，一切刹尘佛，
菩萨众围绕，为说普贤行。

of the three periods of time who are as numerous as the atoms in all buddha *kṣetras*.

Dharma instructions in which he expounded on its capacity to cause all of their pores to send forth until the very end of all future kalpas the sound of the ocean of great vows made by all buddhas of the three periods of time which serves for all bodhisattvas as a means of initiation and transformative guidance; and

Dharma instructions in which he expounded on its capacity to cause the Buddha's lion throne to become equal in size to the Dharma realm, to cause the bodhisattva congregation and the adornments of the site of enlightenment to become equally large and no different, and to also cause the turning of the Dharma wheel and the exposition of the many different kinds of sublime teachings to continue on to the very end of all future kalpas.

"Sons of the Buddha, these ten are chief among them. Still, there are additional Dharma instructions such as these that are as numerous as the atoms in an ineffable number of buddha *kṣetras*. However,[39] all of these lie solely within the sphere of the Tathāgata's wisdom."

At that time, wishing to proclaim this meaning once again, aided by the Buddha's spiritual powers, Samantabhadra Bodhisattva contemplated the Tathāgata, contemplated the congregation, contemplated all buddhas' inconceivable sphere of action, contemplated the countless samādhis of the buddhas, contemplated the inconceivable ocean of worlds, contemplated the inconceivable knowledge that knows dharmas to be like magical illusions, contemplated the inconceivable identity of all buddhas of the three periods of time, and contemplated their measureless and boundless means of expression through language, whereupon he spoke these verses:

Within each and every pore,
there are oceans of *kṣetras* as numerous as atoms.
In all of them there are *tathāgatas* seated there,
all of whom are accompanied by assemblies of bodhisattvas.

Within each and every pore,
there is an ocean of countless *kṣetras*
in which buddhas abide on the throne of bodhi
and appear in this way throughout the Dharma realm.

Within each and every pore,
there are buddhas as numerous as the atoms in all *kṣetras*
who are surrounded by assemblies of bodhisattvas
for whom they speak on Samantabhadra's practices.

正體字

327a29║ 佛坐一國土　充滿十方界
327b01║ 無量菩薩雲　咸來集其所
327b02║ 億剎微塵數　菩薩功德海
327b03║ 俱從會中起　遍滿十方界
327b04║ 悉住普賢行　皆遊法界海
327b05║ 普現一切剎　等入諸佛會
327b06║ 安坐一切剎　聽聞一切法
327b07║ 一一國土中　億劫修諸行
327b08║ 菩薩所修行　普明法海行
327b09║ 入於大願海　住佛境界地
327b10║ 了達普賢行　出生諸佛法
327b11║ [1]具佛功德海　廣現神通事
327b12║ 身雲等塵數　充遍一切剎
327b13║ 普雨甘露法　令眾住佛道
327b14║ 爾時世尊。欲令諸菩薩。安住如來師子頻申
327b15║ 廣大三昧故。從眉間白毫相。放大光明。其光
327b16║ 名普照三世法界門。以不可說佛剎微塵數
327b17║ 光明。而為眷屬。普照十方一切世界海諸佛
327b18║ 國土。時逝多林菩薩大眾。悉見一切盡法界
327b19║ 虛空界一切佛剎。一一微塵中。各有一切佛
327b20║ 剎微塵數諸佛國土。

简体字

佛坐一国土，充满十方界，
无量菩萨云，咸来集其所。
亿刹微尘数，菩萨功德海，
俱从会中起，遍满十方界。
悉住普贤行，皆游法界海，
普现一切刹，等入诸佛会。
安坐一切刹，听闻一切法；
一一国土中，亿劫修诸行。
菩萨所修行，普明法海行，
入于大愿海，住佛境界地。
了达普贤行，出生诸佛法，
具佛功德海，广现神通事。
身云等尘数，充遍一切刹，
普雨甘露法，令众住佛道。”

尔时，世尊欲令诸菩萨安住如来师子频申广大三昧故，从眉间白毫相放大光明，其光名普照三世法界门，以不可说佛刹微尘数光明而为眷属，普照十方一切世界海诸佛国土。时，逝多林菩萨大众，悉见一切尽法界、虚空界一切佛刹一一微尘中，各有一切佛刹微尘数诸佛国土，

Even as the Buddha sits within one land,
he completely fills the realms of the ten directions
and clouds of countless bodhisattvas
all come forth and gather wherever he dwells.

These bodhisattvas, the oceans of meritorious qualities,
as numerous as the atoms in a *koṭī* of *kṣetras*
all come forth from within these assemblies
and everywhere fill the realms of the ten directions.

They all abide in Samantabhadra's practices
and all roam the ocean of the Dharma realm,
everywhere appearing in all *kṣetras,*
where they equally enter the assemblies of all buddhas.

They sit peacefully within all the *kṣetras,*
listening to teachings on all dharmas,
and in each and every one of those lands,
they cultivate the practices throughout a *koṭī* of kalpas.

The practices that the bodhisattvas cultivate
are universally radiant practices from the ocean of Dharma.
They enter the ocean of great vows
and dwell on the grounds of the Buddha's sphere of action.

They completely comprehend the practices of Samantabhadra,
bring forth the dharmas of all buddhas,
become fully possessed of the Buddha's ocean of qualities,
and extensively manifest feats of the spiritual superknowledges.

Their clouds of bodies as numerous as atoms
fill up and pervade all the *kṣetras,*
everywhere rain down the Dharma as the elixir of immortality,
and enable beings to abide in the path of the Buddha.

At that time, because the Bhagavat wished to enable the bodhisattvas to abide securely in the Tathāgata's vast lion sprint samādhi, he then emanated an immense beam of light from the white hair mark between his brows. That light known as "universal illumination of the Dharma realm's gateways of the three periods of time" had a retinue of light rays as numerous as the atoms in an ineffable number of buddha *kṣetras*. It everywhere illuminated all buddha lands in the oceans of worlds throughout the ten directions.

At that time, that great assembly of bodhisattvas within the Jeta Grove all saw that, in every atom in all buddha *kṣetras* throughout the Dharma realm and the realm of empty space, there were buddha lands as numerous as the atoms in all buddha *kṣetras*, buddha lands

正體字

種種名。種種色。種種清
327b21║ 淨。種種住處。種種形相。如是一切諸國土中。
327b22║ 皆有大菩薩。坐於道場師子座上。成等正覺。
327b23║ 菩薩大眾。前後圍遶。諸世間主。而為供養。或
327b24║ 見於不可說佛剎量。大眾會中。出妙音聲。充
327b25║ 滿法界。轉正法輪。或見在天宮殿。龍宮殿夜
327b26║ 叉宮殿。乾闥婆阿脩羅迦樓羅緊那羅摩睺
327b27║ 羅伽人非人等諸宮殿中。或在人間村邑聚
327b28║ 落。王都大處。現種種姓。種種名。種種身。種
327b29║ 種相。種種光明。住種種威儀。入種種三昧。現
327c01║ 種種神變。或時自以種種言音。或令種種諸
327c02║ 菩薩等。在於種種大眾會中。種種言辭。說種
327c03║ 種法。如此會中。菩薩大眾。見於如是諸佛如
327c04║ 來甚深三昧大神通力。如是盡法界虛空界。
327c05║ 東西南北。四維上下。一切方海中。依於眾生
327c06║ 心想而住。始從前際至今現在。一切國土身。
327c07║ 一切眾生身。一切虛空道。其中一一毛端量
327c08║ 處。

简体字

种种名、种种色、种种清净、种种住处、种种形相。如是一切诸国土中，皆有大菩萨坐于道场师子座上成等正觉，菩萨大众前后围绕，诸世间主而为供养；或见于不可说佛刹量大众会中，出妙音声充满法界，转正法轮；或见在天宫殿、龙宫殿、夜叉宫殿，乾闼婆、阿修罗、迦楼罗、紧那罗、摩睺罗伽、人非人等诸宫殿中，或在人间村邑聚落、王都大处，现种种姓、种种名、种种身、种种相、种种光明，住种种威仪，入种种三昧，现种种神变，或时自以种种言音，或令种种诸菩萨等在于种种大众会中种种言辞说种种法。

如此会中，菩萨大众见于如是诸佛如来甚深三昧大神通力；如是尽法界、虚空界，东、西、南、北、四维、上、下一切方海中，依于众生心想而住，始从前际至今现在，一切国土身、一切众生身、一切虚空道，其中一一毛端量处，

that had many different names, many different physical forms, many different manifestations of purity, many different abodes, and many different shapes and characteristics.

In each one of all those lands such as these, there was a great bodhisattva within a site of enlightenment, seated on a lion throne, realizing the universal and right enlightenment, who was entirely surrounded by an immense congregation of bodhisattvas as the world's rulers then presented offerings to him.

In some cases, they saw him in the midst of an immense congregation spanning the breadth of an ineffable number of buddha *kṣetras*, emanating a marvelous voice that pervaded the Dharma realm as he turned the wheel of right Dharma.

In some cases, they saw him in a deva palace, a dragon palace, a *yakṣa* palace, or a palace of the *gandharvas, asuras, garuḍas, kiṃnaras, mahoragas*, humans, nonhumans, or others.

In some cases, they saw him among humans, within a town or village, or within a grand dwelling place in the royal capital at which times he would appear as a member of many different clans, as bearing many different names, as possessing many different kinds of bodies, as displaying many different kinds of appearances, as emanating many different kinds of light, as adopting many different kinds of personal deportment, as entering many different kinds of samādhis, or as manifesting many different kinds of spiritual transformations.

And in some cases, [they saw him] using various different voices himself or else saw him causing various different bodhisattvas in various different great assemblies to use various different modes of expression to teach various different dharmas.

And just as, in this very assembly, an immense congregation of bodhisattvas observed the great supernatural powers used by all these buddhas, these *tathāgatas*, in their extremely deep samādhis, so too did this also occur in this same way throughout the oceans of all regions to the very ends of the Dharma realm and the realm of empty space, off in the directions of the east, west, south, north, the four midpoints, the zenith, and the nadir where they dwelt in a manner reliant upon the minds and mental conceptions of those beings there, doing so from the very beginnings of the past on through to the present, wherein, in every place so large as the point of a hair within the physical body of a land, within the physical body of any being, or within all the paths throughout all of empty space—in every one of these places, there existed in a sequentially orderly fashion *kṣetras*

正體字

一一各有微塵數剎。種種業起。次第而住。
327c09║ 悉有道場菩薩眾會。皆亦如是。見佛神力。不
327c10║ 壞三世。不壞世間。於一切眾生心中。現其影
327c11║ 像。隨一切眾生心樂。出妙言音。普入一切眾
327c12║ 會中。普現一切眾生前。色相有別。智慧無
327c13║ 異。隨其所應。開示佛法。教化調伏一切眾生。
327c14║ 未曾休息。其有見此佛神力者。皆是毘盧遮
327c15║ 那如來。於往昔時。善根攝受。或昔曾以四攝
327c16║ 所攝。或是見聞憶念親近之所成熟。或是往
327c17║ 昔教其令發阿耨多羅三藐三菩提心。或是
327c18║ 往昔於諸佛所。同種善根。或是過去以一切
327c19║ 智。善巧方便。教化成熟。是故皆得入於如來
327c20║ 不可思議甚深三昧。盡法界虛空界大神通
327c21║ 力。或入法身。或入色身。或入往昔所成就行。
327c22║ 或入圓滿諸波羅蜜。或入莊嚴清淨行輪。或
327c23║ 入菩薩諸地。或入成正覺力。

简体字

一一各有微尘数刹种种业起次第而住，悉有道场菩萨众会，皆亦如是见佛神力，不坏三世，不坏世间，于一切众生心中现其影像，随一切众生心乐出妙言音，普入一切众会中，普现一切众生前，色相有别，智慧无异，随其所应开示佛法，教化调伏一切众生未曾休息。其有见此佛神力者，皆是毗卢遮那如来于往昔时善根摄受，或昔曾以四摄所摄，或是见闻忆念亲近之所成熟，或是往昔教其令发阿耨多罗三藐三菩提心，或是往昔于诸佛所同种善根，或是过去以一切智善巧方便教化成熟，是故皆得入于如来不可思议甚深三昧；尽法界、虚空界大神通力，或入法身，或入色身，或入往昔所成就行，或入圆满诸波罗蜜，或入庄严清净行轮，或入菩萨诸地，或入成正觉力，

as numerous as atoms that all arose from many different kinds of karma. All of them had sites of enlightenment and congregations of bodhisattvas, all of whom saw in this very same way that the buddhas' spiritual powers did not interfere with the three periods of time and did not interfere with those worlds even as they manifested their appearance to the minds of all those beings in a manner adapted to all of those beings' aspirations, sending forth to them sublime voices that everywhere entered into the midst of all of those congregations in which they everywhere appeared directly before all beings in different kinds of physical forms, yet with wisdom that did not vary as they never desisted either from presenting appropriately adapted explanations of the Buddha's Dharma for their sakes or from continuing to teach and train all beings.

As for those who observed these spiritual powers of the Buddha, they were:

Those who had been attracted and sustained by Vairocana Tathāgata through the power of past-life roots of goodness;

Those who had been drawn forth in the past through the use of the four means of attraction;

Those who had become ripened by seeing, hearing, recalling, or drawing near to him;

Those whom he had taught in the past, thereby enabling them to arouse the resolve to realize *anuttara-samyak-saṃbodhi*;

Those who, in the past, had planted the same kinds of roots of goodness under other buddhas; or

Those who had been taught and ripened in the past through skillful means for attaining all-knowledge.

It was for reasons such as these that they had each entered the Tathāgata's inconceivable and extremely deep samādhis and his powers of the great spiritual superknowledges that manifested throughout the Dharma realm and the realm of empty space:

Some entered by way of the Dharma body;

Some entered by way of the form body;

Some entered by way of practices perfected in the past;

Some entered by way of perfect fulfillment of the *pāramitās*;

Some entered by way of pure adornments related to his sphere of action;

Some entered by way of the bodhisattva grounds;

Some entered by way of the powers arising through realization of right enlightenment;

正體字

或入佛所住三
327c24‖ 昧無差別大神變。或入如來力無畏智。或入
327c25‖ 佛無礙辯才海。彼諸菩薩。以種種解。種種道。
327c26‖ 種種門。種種入。種種理趣。種種隨順。種種智
327c27‖ 慧。種種助道。種種方便。種種三昧。入如是
327c28‖ 等十不可說佛刹微塵數佛神變海方便門。
327c29‖ 云何種種三昧。所謂普莊嚴法界三昧。普照
328a01‖ 一切三世無礙境界三昧。法界無差別智光
328a02‖ 明三昧。入如來境界不動轉三昧。普照無邊
328a03‖ 虛空三昧。入如來力三昧。佛無畏勇猛奮迅
328a04‖ 莊嚴三昧。一切法界旋轉藏三昧。如月普現
328a05‖ 一切法界以無礙音大開演三昧。普清淨法
328a06‖ 光明三昧。無礙繒法王幢三昧。一一境界中
328a07‖ 悉見一切諸佛海三昧。於一切世間悉現身
328a08‖ 三昧。入如來無差別身境界三昧。隨一切世
328a09‖ 間轉大悲藏三昧。知一切法無有[1]迹三昧。

简体字

或入佛所住三昧无差别大神变，或入如来力、无畏智，或入佛无碍辩才海。

彼诸菩萨以种种解、种种道、种种门、种种入、种种理趣、种种随顺、种种智慧、种种助道、种种方便、种种三昧，入如是等十不可说佛刹微尘数佛神变海方便门。云何种种三昧？所谓：普庄严法界三昧、普照一切三世无碍境界三昧、法界无差别智光明三昧、入如来境界不动转三昧、普照无边虚空三昧、入如来力三昧、佛无畏勇猛奋迅庄严三昧、一切法界旋转藏三昧、如月普现一切法界以无碍音大开演三昧、普清净法光明三昧、无碍缯法王幢三昧、一一境界中悉见一切诸佛海三昧、于一切世间悉现身三昧、入如来无差别身境界三昧、随一切世间转大悲藏三昧、知一切法无有迹三昧、

Some entered by way of undifferentiated great spiritual transformations arising from the samādhis in which the Buddha abides;
Some entered by way of the Tathāgata's knowledge of the powers and fearlessnesses; and
Some entered by way of the Buddha's ocean of unimpeded eloquence.

All of those bodhisattvas relied upon many different convictions, many different paths, many different gateways, many different means of entry, many different means of penetration through reasoning, many different modes of compliance, many different kinds of wisdom, many different provisions for enlightenment, many different kinds of skillful means, and many different kinds of samādhis to enter such gateways of skillful means emerging from the Buddha's ocean of spiritual superknowledges, gateways that are as numerous as the atoms in ten ineffables[40] of Buddha *kṣetras*.

What then is meant by "many different kinds of samādhis"? They are as follows:

The samādhi of the universal adornment of the Dharma realm;
The samādhi of the unimpeded sphere of action that everywhere illuminates all three periods of time;
The samādhi of the Dharma realm's undifferentiated light of wisdom;
The samādhi of entry into the Tathāgata's realm of unshakability and irreversibility;
The samādhi of the universal illumination of boundless space;
The samādhi of entry into the Tathāgata's powers;
The samādhi of adornment by the Buddha's fearless and valiant swiftness;
The samādhi of the treasury of the swirling rotation of the entire Dharma realm;
The samādhi of the moon-like omnipresent appearance throughout the Dharma realm by using an unimpeded sound to commence the great proclamation of Dharma;
The samādhi of the universally pure light of Dharma;
The samādhi of the silken banner of the unimpeded Dharma king;
The samādhi of the complete vision of the ocean of all buddhas in all objects;
The samādhi of the manifestation of bodies in all worlds;
The samādhi of entry into the realm of the Tathāgata's undifferentiated body;
The samādhi of the treasury of great compassion that adapts to the transformations in all worlds;
The samādhi of the realization of the traceless nature of all dharmas;

正體字

知
328a10║ 一切法究竟寂滅三昧。雖無所得而能變化
328a11║ 普現世間三昧。普入一切刹三昧。莊嚴一切
328a12║ 佛刹成正覺三昧。觀一切世間主色相差別
328a13║ 三昧。觀一切眾生境界無障礙三昧。能出生
328a14║ 一切如來母三昧。能修行入一切佛海功德
328a15║ 道三昧。一一境界中出現神變盡未來際三
328a16║ 昧。入一切如來本事海三昧。盡未來際護持
328a17║ 一切如來種性三昧。以決定解力令現在十
328a18║ 方一切佛刹海皆清淨三昧。一念中普照一
328a19║ 切佛所住三昧。入一切境界無礙際三昧。令
328a20║ 一切世界為一佛刹三昧。出一切佛變化身
328a21║ 三昧。以金剛王智知一切諸根海三昧。知一
328a22║ 切如來同一身三昧。知一切法界所安立悉
328a23║ 住心念際三昧。於一切法界廣大國土中示
328a24║ 現涅槃三昧。令住最上處三昧。於一切佛刹
328a25║ 現種種眾生差別身三昧。普入一切佛智慧
328a26║ 三昧。知一切法性相三昧。

简体字

知一切法究竟寂灭三昧、虽无所得而能变化普现世间三昧、普入一切刹三昧、庄严一切佛刹成正觉三昧、观一切世间主色相差别三昧、观一切众生境界无障碍三昧、能出生一切如来母三昧、能修行入一切佛海功德道三昧、一一境界中出现神变尽未来际三昧、入一切如来本事海三昧、尽未来际护持一切如来种性三昧、以决定解力令现在十方一切佛刹海皆清净三昧、一念中普照一切佛所住三昧、入一切境界无碍际三昧、令一切世界为一佛刹三昧、出一切佛变化身三昧、以金刚王智知一切诸根海三昧、知一切如来同一身三昧、知一切法界所安立悉住心念际三昧、于一切法界广大国土中示现涅槃三昧、令住最上处三昧、于一切佛刹现种种众生差别身三昧、普入一切佛智慧三昧、知一切法性相三昧、

The samādhi of the realization that all dharmas are ultimately quiescent;

The samādhi in which, even though one cannot apprehend the inherent existence of anything at all, one is still able to manifest transformations that appear throughout the world;

The samādhi of the universal entry into all *kṣetras;*

The samādhi of the adornment of all buddha *kṣetras* through the realization of right enlightenment;

The samādhi of the contemplation of the different physical features of all world leaders;

The samādhi of the unimpeded contemplation of all beings' spheres of experience;

The samādhi able to produce the mother of all *tathāgatas;*

The samādhi enabling cultivation and entry into the path of all buddhas' oceans of qualities;

The samādhi of the manifestation of spiritual transformations in every realm to the end of future time;

The samādhi of entry into the ocean of all *tathāgatas'* past lives' practices;

The samādhi of the protection and preservation of the lineage of all *tathāgatas'* to the end of future time;

The samādhi of the complete purification of the ocean of all buddha *kṣetras* of the present throughout the ten directions by the power of definite understanding;

The samādhi of the instantaneous illumination of all buddhas' abodes;

The samādhi of the unimpeded entry into all objective realms;

The samādhi causing all worlds to become one buddha *kṣetra;*

The samādhi producing all buddhas' transformation bodies;

The samādhi of the knowledge of the ocean of all faculties through sovereign vajra wisdom;

The samādhi of the knowledge of all *tathāgatas* as possessing the same single body;

The samādhi in which everything arrayed throughout the entire Dharma realm abides in one mind-moment;

The samādhi in which everything contained in the vast lands throughout the entire Dharma realm appears as a manifestation of nirvāṇa;

The samādhi that enables one to dwell in the most superior abodes;

The samādhi displaying the appearances of the different types of bodies of the various kinds of beings that live in all buddha *kṣetras.*

The samādhi in which one everywhere enters the wisdom of all buddhas;

The samādhi of the knowledge of the nature and characteristics of all dharmas.

正體字

一念普知三世法
328a27║ 三昧。念念中普現法界身三昧。以師子勇猛
328a28║ 智知一切如來出興次第三昧。於一切法界
328a29║ 境界慧眼圓滿三昧。勇猛趣向十力三昧。放
328b01║ 一切功德圓滿光明普照世間三昧。不動藏
328b02║ 三昧。說一法普入一切法三昧。於一法以一
328b03║ 切言音差別訓釋三昧。演說一切佛無二法三
328b04║ 昧。知三世無礙際三昧。知一切劫無差別三
328b05║ 昧。入十力微細方便三昧。於一切劫成就一
328b06║ 切菩薩行不斷絕三昧。十方普現身三昧。於
328b07║ 法界自在成正覺三昧。生一切安隱受三昧。
328b08║ 出一切莊嚴具莊嚴虛空界三昧。念念中出
328b09║ 等眾生數變化身雲三昧。如來淨空月光明
328b10║ 三昧。常見一切如來住虛空三昧。開示一切
328b11║ 佛莊嚴三昧。照明一切法義燈三昧。照十力
328b12║ 境界三昧。三世一切佛幢[2]想三昧。一切佛一
328b13║ 密藏三昧。念念中所作皆究竟三昧。

简体字

一念普知三世法三昧、念念中普现法界身三昧、以师子勇猛智知一切如来出兴次第三昧、于一切法界境界慧眼圆满三昧、勇猛趣向十力三昧、放一切功德圆满光明普照世间三昧、不动藏三昧、说一法普入一切法三昧、于一法以一切言音差别训释三昧、演说一切佛无二法三昧、知三世无碍际三昧、知一切劫无差别三昧、入十力微细方便三昧、于一切劫成就一切菩萨行不断绝三昧、十方普现身三昧、于法界自在成正觉三昧、生一切安隐受三昧、出一切庄严具庄严虚空界三昧、念念中出等众生数变化身云三昧、如来净空月光明三昧、常见一切如来住虚空三昧、开示一切佛庄严三昧、照明一切法义灯三昧、照十力境界三昧、三世一切佛幢相三昧、一切佛一密藏三昧、念念中所作皆究竟三昧、

The samādhi of the instantaneous knowledge of the dharmas of the three periods of time;
The samādhi in which, in every instant, the Dharma realm body appears everywhere;
The samādhi in which, with the lion's courageous wisdom, one knows the sequence of all *tathāgatas'* coming forth into the world;
The samādhi of the perfect fulfillment of the wisdom eye in all objective realms throughout the Dharma realm;
The samādhi of the courageous progression into the ten powers;
The samādhi of the emanation of all qualities' perfectly full radiance to everywhere illuminate the world;
The samādhi of the treasury of immovability;
The samādhi in which teaching one dharma causes the universal penetration of all dharmas;
The samādhi of the explanation of one dharma through the discussion of all kinds of linguistic distinctions;
The samādhi of expounding on all buddhas' non-dual Dharma;
The samādhi of the knowledge of the unimpeded boundaries of the three periods of time;
The samādhi of the knowledge of all kalpas as no different;
The samādhi of entry into the ten powers' subtle methods;[41]
The samādhi of the uninterrupted perfection of all bodhisattva practices in all kalpas;
The samādhi of the manifestation of bodies throughout the ten directions;
The samādhi of sovereign mastery in realizing the right enlightenment throughout the Dharma realm;
The samādhi of the production of all peaceful and secure feelings;
The samādhi of the adornment of the realm of empty space through the production of all adornments;
The samādhi of the emanation in every instant of a cloud of transformation bodies as numerous as all beings;
The samādhi of the Tathāgata's moonlight in empty space;
The samādhi of the constant vision of all *tathāgatas* dwelling in space;
The samādhi of the revelation of all buddhas' adornments;
The samādhi of the lamp illuminating all dharmas' meanings;
The samādhi of the illumination of the sphere of the ten powers;
The samādhi of the appearance of the banners of all buddhas of the three periods of time;[42]
The samādhi of the single esoteric matrix of all buddhas;
The samādhi of the moment-to-moment accomplishment of all endeavors;

正體字

無盡福
328b14║ 德藏三昧。見無邊佛境界三昧。堅住一切法
328b15║ 三昧。現一切如來變化悉令知見三昧。念念
328b16║ 中佛日常出現三昧。一[3]日中悉知三世所有
328b17║ 法三昧。普音演說一切法性寂滅三昧。見一
328b18║ 切佛自在力三昧。法界開敷蓮華三昧。觀諸
328b19║ 法如虛空無住處三昧。十方海普入一方三
328b20║ 昧。入一切法界無源底三昧。一切法海三昧。
328b21║ 以寂靜身放一切光明三昧。一念中現一切
328b22║ 神通大願三昧。一切時一切處成正覺三昧。
328b23║ 以一莊嚴入一切法界三昧。普現一切諸佛
328b24║ 身三昧。知一切眾生廣大殊勝神通智三昧。
328b25║ 一念中其身遍法界三昧。現一乘淨法界三
328b26║ 昧。入普門法界示現大莊嚴三昧。住持一切
328b27║ 佛法輪三昧。以一切法門莊嚴一法門三昧。
328b28║ 以因陀羅網願行攝一切眾生界三昧。

简体字

无尽福德藏三昧、见无边佛境界三昧、坚住一切法三昧、现一切如来变化悉令知见三昧、念念中佛日常出现三昧、一日中悉知三世所有法三昧、普音演说一切法性寂灭三昧、见一切佛自在力三昧、法界开敷莲华三昧、观诸法如虚空无住处三昧、十方海普入一方三昧、入一切法界无源底三昧、一切法海三昧、以寂静身放一切光明三昧、一念中现一切神通大愿三昧、一切时一切处成正觉三昧、以一庄严入一切法界三昧、普现一切诸佛身三昧、知一切众生广大殊胜神通智三昧、一念中其身遍法界三昧、现一乘净法界三昧、入普门法界示现大庄严三昧、住持一切佛法轮三昧、以一切法门庄严一法门三昧、以因陀罗网愿行摄一切众生界三昧、

The samādhi of the inexhaustible treasury of merit;
The samādhi of the vision of the Buddha's boundless domain;
The samādhi of the solid abiding in all dharmas;
The samādhi of the revelation of all *tathāgatas'* transformations causing all to know and see;
The samādhi of the constant appearance of the buddha sun in every moment;
The samādhi of the complete knowledge of all dharmas of the three periods of time in but one day;
The samādhi of the omnipresent voice proclaiming the nature of all dharmas to be quiescence;
The samādhi of the vision of the power of all buddhas' sovereign mastery;
The samādhi of the Dharma realm's blooming lotus flower;
The samādhi of the contemplation of all dharmas as like empty space in their having no place to abide;
The samādhi of the ocean of the ten directions' entry into one region;
The samādhi of entry into the entire Dharma realm's beginningless basis;
The samādhi of the ocean of all dharmas;
The samādhi in which one uses a quiescent body to emanate every kind of radiance;
The samādhi of the instantaneous manifestation of all spiritual superknowledges and great vows;
The samādhi of the realization of right enlightenment at all times and in all places;
The samādhi of entry into the entire Dharma realm through one adornment;
The samādhi of the omnipresent appearance of the body of all buddhas;
The samādhi of the vast and especially excellent superknowledges that know all beings;
The samādhi in which one's body instantaneously pervades the entire Dharma realm;
The samādhi of the revelation of the One Vehicle's pure Dharma realm;
The samādhi of entry into the universal gateway's Dharma realm by which one manifests the great adornments;
The samādhi of the sustenance of the Dharma wheel of all buddhas;
The samādhi in which one uses all Dharma gateways to adorn one Dharma gateway;
The samādhi in which one uses an Indra's net of conduct and vows to gather in all realms of beings;

正體字

分別
328b29‖ 一切世界門三昧。乘蓮華自在遊步三昧。知
328c01‖ 一切眾生種種差別神通智三昧。令其身恒
328c02‖ 現一切眾生前三昧。知一切眾生差別音聲
328c03‖ 言辭海三昧。知一切眾生差別智神通三昧。
328c04‖ 大悲平等藏三昧。一切佛入如來際三昧。觀
328c05‖ 察一切如來解脫處師子[＊]頻申三昧。菩薩以
328c06‖ 如是等不可說佛剎微塵數三昧。入毘盧遮
328c07‖ 那如來念念充滿一切法界三昧神變海。其
328c08‖ 諸菩薩。皆悉具足大智神通。明利自在。住
328c09‖ 於諸地。以廣大智。普觀一切。從諸智慧種性
328c10‖ 而生。一切智智。常現在前。得離癡翳清淨智
328c11‖ 眼。為諸眾生。作調御師。住佛平等。於一切
328c12‖ 法。無有分別。了達境界。知諸世間。性皆寂
328c13‖ 滅。無有依處。普詣一切諸佛國土而無所著。
328c14‖ 悉能觀察一切諸法。而無所住。遍入一切妙
328c15‖ 法宮殿。而無所來。

简体字

分别一切世界门三昧、乘莲华自在游步三昧、知一切众生种种差别神通智三昧、令其身恒现一切众生前三昧、知一切众生差别音声言辞海三昧、知一切众生差别智神通三昧、大悲平等藏三昧、一切佛入如来际三昧、观察一切如来解脱处师子频申三昧。菩萨以如是等不可说佛刹微尘数三昧，入毗卢遮那如来念念充满一切法界三昧神变海。

其诸菩萨皆悉具足大智神通，明利自在，住于诸地，以广大智普观一切；从诸智慧种性而生，一切智智常现在前，得离痴翳清净智眼，为诸众生作调御师；住佛平等，于一切法无有分别；了达境界，知诸世间性皆寂灭无有依处；普诣一切诸佛国土而无所著，悉能观察一切诸法而无所住，遍入一切妙法宫殿而无所来；

The samādhi in which one distinguishes all the world's gateways;
The samādhi in which one sits on a lotus flower and roams about using feats of spiritual power;[43]
The samādhi of spiritual superknowledges by which one knows all beings' many kinds of differences;
The samādhi in which one causes one's body to constantly appear before all beings;
The samādhi by which one knows all beings' ocean of different voices and languages;
The samādhi of spiritual superknowledges that know all beings' different kinds of knowledge;
The samādhi of the treasury of the great compassion's equal regard for all;
The samādhi of all buddhas' entry into the Tathāgata's apex of realization; and
The lion sprint samādhi by which one contemplates all *tathāgatas'* stations of liberation.

It is through the use of just such samādhis as numerous as the atoms in an ineffable number of buddha *kṣetras* that those bodhisattvas entered the ocean of spiritual transformations of Vairocana Tathāgata's samādhi in which, in each successive mind-moment, one completely fills the entire Dharma realm.

All of those bodhisattvas had become completely endowed with acuity and sovereign mastery in great wisdom and the spiritual superknowledges. They dwelt on the grounds and used vast wisdom to everywhere contemplate everything. They were born from the lineage of wisdom. The wisdom of all-knowledge always manifested directly before them. They had acquired the purified wisdom eye that had left behind all the obscurations of delusion.

They served all beings as teachers who train them. They dwelt in the Buddha's uniform equality and remained free of any discriminations regarding any dharmas. They possessed a completely penetrating comprehension of the objective realms and knew the entire world to be by nature quiescent.

They had no place upon which they depended. They went forth everywhere to pay their respects in all buddha lands, and yet, in doing so, they remained free of any attachment. They were entirely able to contemplate all dharmas and yet, in doing so, they had no place in which dwelt.

They everywhere entered the palace of all wondrous dharmas and yet they had no place from which they came. They taught and trained

正體字

教化調伏一切世間。普為
328c16‖ 眾生。現安隱處。智慧解脫。為其所行。恒以智
328c17‖ 身。住離貪際。超諸有海。示真實際。智光圓
328c18‖ 滿。普見諸法。住於三昧。堅固不動。於諸眾
328c19‖ 生。恒起大悲。知諸法門悉皆如幻。一切眾
328c20‖ 生悉皆如夢。一切如來悉皆如影。一切言音
328c21‖ 悉皆如響。一切諸法悉皆如化。善能積集殊
328c22‖ 勝行願。智慧圓滿。清淨善巧。心極寂靜。善入
328c23‖ 一切總持境界。具三昧力。勇猛無怯。獲明智
328c24‖ 眼。住法界際。到一切法無所得處。修習無涯
328c25‖ 智慧大海。到智波羅蜜究竟彼岸。為般若波
328c26‖ 羅蜜之所攝持。以神通波羅蜜。普入世間。依
328c27‖ 三昧波羅蜜。得心自在。以不顛倒智。知一
328c28‖ 切義。以巧分別智。開示法藏。以現了智。訓釋
328c29‖ 文[4]辭。以大願力。說法無盡。以無所畏大師
329a01‖ 子吼。常樂觀察無依處法。以淨法眼。普觀一
329a02‖ 切。以淨智月。照世成壞。以智慧光。照真實
329a03‖ 諦。

简体字

教化调伏一切世间，普为众生现安隐处；智慧解脱，为其所行；恒以智身住离贪际，超诸有海，示真实际；智光圆满，普见诸法；住于三昧，坚固不动；于诸众生恒起大悲，知诸法门悉皆如幻，一切众生悉皆如梦，一切如来悉皆如影，一切言音悉皆如响，一切诸法悉皆如化；善能积集殊胜行愿，智慧圆满，清净善巧，心极寂静；善入一切总持境界，具三昧力，勇猛无怯；获明智眼，住法界际，到一切法无所得处；修习无涯智慧大海，到智波罗蜜究竟彼岸，为般若波罗蜜之所摄持；以神通波罗蜜普入世间，依三昧波罗蜜得心自在；以不颠倒智知一切义，以巧分别智开示法藏，以现了智训释文辞，以大愿力说法无尽，以无所畏大师子吼；常乐观察无依处法，以净法眼普观一切，以净智月照世成坏，以智慧光照真实谛；

everyone in all worlds. They everywhere revealed for beings the station of peace and security. Wisdom and liberation constituted the bases of their practices.

They constantly relied on the wisdom body and dwelt at the very peak of the transcendence of desire. They stepped beyond the ocean of all stations of existence and unveiled the very apex of reality.[44] The light of their wisdom was perfectly full. They everywhere perceived all dharmas and dwelt in solid and unshakable samādhi.

They constantly aroused the great compassion for all beings even as they realized all gateways into the Dharma were like illusions, realized all beings were like dreams, realized all *tathāgatas* were like reflections, realized all speech was like echoes, and realized all dharmas were like transformationally created phenomena.

They were well able to accumulate especially superior practices and vows. Through skillfulness in purification, they had achieved the perfect fulfillment of wisdom. Their minds had reached the utmost degree of quiescence. They skillfully entered the domain of the complete-retention *dhāraṇīs*. By being well equipped with the power of samādhi, they were heroically brave and free of timidity.

Having acquired the bright wisdom eye, they dwelt at the furthest reaches of the Dharma realm and had reached the station where no inherent existence can be apprehended in any dharma. They had cultivated the great ocean of boundless wisdom, reached the far shore of the perfection of the knowledge *pāramitā*, and were sustained by the *prajñā pāramitā*.

With the superknowledges *pāramitā*, they everywhere entered the world;

Relying on the samādhi *pāramita*, they acquired the sovereign masteries of the mind;

With knowledge free of inverted views, they knew all meanings;

With their skillfully distinguishing knowledge, they provided instruction in the treasury of Dharma;

With their completely manifesting knowledge, they provided explanations of phrases in the texts;

With the power of great vows, they are endlessly devoted to teaching the Dharma;

With their fearlessnesses, they roared the great roar of the lion and always delighted in contemplating the dharma of baselessness;[45]

With the pure Dharma eye, they everywhere contemplated all things;

With the moon of pure wisdom, they illuminated the creation and destruction of worlds; and

With the light of wisdom, they illuminated the real truths.

正體字

福德智慧如金剛山。一切譬[1]諭所不能
329a04║ 及。善觀諸法。慧根增長。勇猛精進。摧伏眾
329a05║ 魔。無量智慧。威光熾盛。其身超出一切世間。
329a06║ 得一切法無礙智慧。善能悟解盡無盡際。住
329a07║ 於普際。入真實際。無相觀智。常現在前。善巧
329a08║ 成就諸菩薩行。以無二智。知諸境界。普見一
329a09║ 切世間諸趣。遍往一切諸佛國土。智燈圓滿。
329a10║ 於一切法。無諸暗障。放淨法光。照十方界。為
329a11║ 諸世間真實福田。若見若聞。所願皆滿。福德
329a12║ 高大。超諸世間。勇猛無畏。摧諸外道。演微妙
329a13║ 音。遍一切剎。普見諸佛。心無厭足。於佛法
329a14║ 身。已得自在。隨所應化。而為現身。一身充
329a15║ 滿一切佛剎。已得自在清淨神通。乘大智舟。
329a16║ 所往無礙。智慧圓滿。周遍法界。譬如日出普
329a17║ 照世間。隨眾生心。現其色像。知諸眾生根
329a18║ 性欲樂。入一切法無諍境界。知諸法性無生
329a19║ 無起。能令小大。自在相入。

简体字

福德智慧如金刚山，一切譬喻所不能及；善观诸法，慧根增长；勇猛精进，摧伏众魔；无量智慧，威光炽盛；其身超出一切世间，得一切法无碍智慧，善能悟解尽、无尽际；住于普际，入真实际，无相观智常现在前；善巧成就诸菩萨行，以无二智知诸境界，普见一切世间诸趣，遍往一切诸佛国土；智灯圆满，于一切法无诸暗障，放净法光照十方界；为诸世间真实福田，若见若闻所愿皆满，福德高大超诸世间，勇猛无畏摧诸外道；演微妙音遍一切刹，普见诸佛心无厌足；于佛法身已得自在，随所应化而为现身，一身充满一切佛刹；已得自在清净神通，乘大智舟，所往无碍，智慧圆满周遍法界；譬如日出普照世间，随众生心现其色像；知诸众生根性欲乐，入一切法无诤境界；知诸法性无生无起，能令小大自在相入；

Their merit and wisdom were like a vajra mountain and were indescribable even by resort to any analogy. Through their thorough contemplation of all dharmas, their wisdom and faculties increased. With their courage and vigor, they utterly vanquished the many kinds of *māras*. Their measureless wisdom's awesome radiance burned with flaming brilliance. Their bodies were superior to those of everyone in the world.

They had acquired unimpeded wisdom in fathoming all dharmas by which they were well able to awaken to the bounds of the finite and the infinite, dwell at the apex of universality, and enter the apex of reality.[46] The contemplative wisdom of signlessness always manifested directly before them. They had skillfully perfected the bodhisattva practices. They used non-dual wisdom to know all objective spheres, everywhere saw all of the worlds' destinies, and went forth everywhere to all buddha lands. Their lamps of wisdom shone in perfect fullness so that no darkness interfered with their perception of all dharmas. They emanated the light of pure Dharma which illuminated the realms of the ten directions.

They served the entire world as genuine fields for the planting of merit. If anyone so much as saw or heard them, then whatever they wished for would always be fulfilled. Their merit was so lofty and immense that it surpassed that of everyone in the world. They courageously and fearlessly vanquished all proponents of non-Buddhist paths. They expounded with sublime voices that reached everywhere in all *kṣetras*. Their minds never grew weary of going everywhere to see all buddhas. They had already achieved sovereign mastery in the Buddha's Dharma body. Adapting to those who should be taught, they manifested bodies for their sakes by causing [the manifestations of] one body to fill all buddha *kṣetras*.

They had already achieved sovereign mastery in the use of the pure spiritual superknowledges and had already boarded the ship of wisdom that is unimpeded in sailing wherever it chooses. Their wisdom had become so perfectly full that it reached everywhere throughout the entire Dharma realm. They were like the sun which, when it rises, it illuminates the entire world. Adapting to beings' minds, they manifested their physical appearance. Knowing all beings' faculties, natures, and aspirations, they entered the realm of noncontentiousness with respect to all dharmas. They realized that the nature of all dharmas was one of nonproduction and non-arising. They were able to cause the small and the large to freely interpenetrate.

正體字

決了佛地甚深之
329a20║ 趣。以無盡句。說甚深義。於一句中。演說一切
329a21║ 修多羅海。獲大智慧陀羅尼身。凡所受持。永
329a22║ 無忘失。一念能憶無量劫事。一念悉知三世
329a23║ 一切諸眾生智。恒以一切陀羅尼門。演說無
329a24║ 邊諸佛法海。常轉不退清淨法輪。令諸眾生
329a25║ 皆生智慧。得佛境界。智慧光明。入於善見
329a26║ 甚深三昧。入一切法無障礙際。於一切法。勝
329a27║ 智自在。一切境界。清淨莊嚴。普入十方一切
329a28║ 法界。隨其方所。靡不咸至。一一塵中。現成正
329a29║ 覺。於無色性。現一切色。以一切方。普入一
329b01║ 方。其諸菩薩。具如是等無邊福智功德之藏。
329b02║ 常為諸佛之所稱歎。種種言辭。說其功德。不
329b03║ 能令盡。靡不咸在逝多林中。深入如來功德
329b04║ 大海。悉見於佛光明所照。爾時諸菩薩。得
329b05║ 不思議正法光明。心大歡喜。各於其身及以
329b06║ 樓閣。諸莊嚴具。并其所坐。師子之座。遍逝多
329b07║ 林一切物中。化現種種大莊嚴雲。充滿一切
329b08║ 十方法界。所謂於念念中。放大光明雲。充滿
329b09║ 十方。悉能開悟一切眾生。

简体字

决了佛地甚深之趣，以无尽句说甚深义，于一句中演说一切修多罗海；获大智慧陀罗尼身，凡所受持永无忘失；一念能忆无量劫事，一念悉知三世一切诸众生智；恒以一切陀罗尼门，演说无边诸佛法海，常转不退清净法轮，令诸众生皆生智慧；得佛境界智慧光明，入于善见甚深三昧；入一切法无障碍际，于一切法胜智自在，一切境界清净庄严；普入十方一切法界，随其方所靡不咸至；一一尘中现成正觉，于无色性现一切色，以一切方普入一方。其诸菩萨具如是等无边福智功德之藏，常为诸佛之所称叹，种种言辞说其功德不能令尽，靡不咸在逝多林中，深入如来功德大海，悉见于佛光明所照。

尔时，诸菩萨得不思议正法光明，心大欢喜，各于其身及以楼阁、诸庄严具，并其所坐师子之座，遍逝多林一切物中，化现种种大庄严云，充满一切十方法界，所谓：于念念中放大光明云，充满十方，悉能开悟一切众生；

They decisively and completely understood the extremely profound import of the ground of buddhahood, used endless statements in explaining extremely profound meanings and, with but one statement, expounded on the ocean of all sutras. They acquired the body equipped with the great wisdom *dhāraṇī* with which, whatever they took in and retained, they never forgot. In but one mind-moment, they could recall the events occurring in countless kalpas and, in but a single mind-moment, knew all the knowledge possessed by all beings of the three periods of time. They constantly used all *dhāraṇī* gateways to expound on the boundless ocean of the Buddha's dharmas. They always turned the irreversible wheel of pure Dharma, thereby enabling all beings to develop wisdom.

They had acquired the wisdom light of the Buddha's sphere of cognition and entered into the extremely deep "superior vision" samādhi. They had entered the apex of nonattachment to any dharmas and possessed sovereign mastery in the supreme knowledge of all dharmas. All their spheres of experience were as if adorned with purity. They everywhere entered the ten directions of the entire Dharma realm and, no matter what region it might be, there were none they had not reached. Even in every dust mote, they manifested the realization of right enlightenment. Whatever was colorless by nature, they could cause to appear in every hue and they could cause all regions to completely enter but one region.

All of those bodhisattvas possessed a treasury of boundlessly many qualities of merit and wisdom such as these. They were always praised by all buddhas and were such that, even if one used many different kinds of phrasing to describe their meritorious qualities, one would never be able to finish doing so. None of them were not present there in the Jeta Grove where they deeply entered the great ocean of the Tathāgata's qualities and were all illuminated by the radiance of the Buddha.

At that time, as they attained the light of the inconceivable right Dharma, those bodhisattvas' minds became suffused with immense joyous delight whereupon they each transformationally manifested many different kinds of great adornment clouds. Those clouds streamed forth from their bodies, their towers, their adornments, the lion thrones on which they sat, and everything in the Jeta Grove and filled up the ten directions of the entire Dharma realm as, in each successive mind-moment:

They emanated immense clouds of light that filled the ten directions, all of which were able to awaken all beings;

正體字

出一切摩尼寶鈴
329b10║ 雲。充滿十方。出微妙音稱揚讚歎三世諸佛
329b11║ 一切功德。出一切音樂雲。充滿十方。音中演
329b12║ 說一切眾生諸業果報。出一切菩薩種種願
329b13║ 行色相雲。充滿十方。說諸菩薩所有大願。出
329b14║ 一切如來自在變化雲。充滿十方。演出一切
329b15║ 諸佛如來語言音聲。出一切菩薩相好莊嚴
329b16║ 身雲。充滿十方。說諸如來。於一切國土。出興
329b17║ 次第。出三世如來道場雲。充滿十方。現一
329b18║ 切如來成等正覺。功德莊嚴。出一切龍王雲。
329b19║ 充滿十方。雨一切諸香。出一切世主身雲。充
329b20║ 滿十方。演說普賢菩薩之行。出一切寶莊嚴
329b21║ 清淨佛剎雲。充滿十方。現一切如來轉正法
329b22║ 輪。是諸菩薩。以得不思議法光明故。法應如
329b23║ 是。出興此等不可說佛剎微塵數大神變莊
329b24║ 嚴雲。爾時文殊師利菩薩。承佛神力。欲重
329b25║ 宣此逝多林中。諸神變事。觀察十方。而說頌
329b26║ 言
329b27║ 汝應觀此逝多林　以佛威神廣無際

简体字

出一切摩尼宝铃云，充满十方，出微妙音，称扬赞叹三世诸佛一切功德；出一切音乐云，充满十方，音中演说一切众生诸业果报；出一切菩萨种种愿行色相云，充满十方，说诸菩萨所有大愿；出一切如来自在变化云，充满十方，演出一切诸佛如来语言音声；出一切菩萨相好庄严身云，充满十方，说诸如来于一切国土出兴次第；出三世如来道场云，充满十方，现一切如来成等正觉功德庄严；出一切龙王云，充满十方，雨一切诸香；出一切世主身云，充满十方，演说普贤菩萨之行；出一切宝庄严清净佛刹云，充满十方，现一切如来转正法轮。是诸菩萨以得不思议法光明故，法应如是，出兴此等不可说佛刹微尘数大神变庄严云。

尔时，文殊师利菩萨，承佛神力，欲重宣此逝多林中诸神变事，观察十方而说颂言：

“汝应观此逝多林，以佛威神广无际，

They emanated clouds of all kinds of bells adorned with *maṇi* jewels that, as they filled the ten directions, emitted sublime sounds spreading the praises of the qualities of all buddhas of the three periods of time;

They emanated clouds of all kinds of music that, as they filled the ten directions, expounded in their musical sounds on the consequences of all beings' karma;

They emanated clouds of all bodhisattvas' many different kinds of vows, practices, and physical features that, as they filled the ten directions, expounded on the bodhisattvas' great vows;

They emanated clouds of all *tathāgatas'* freely implemented spiritual transformations that, as they filled the ten directions, broadcast the sounds of the speech of all the buddhas, the *tathāgatas;*

They emanated clouds of all bodhisattvas' bodies adorned with the major marks and secondary signs that, as they filled the ten directions, spoke of the sequential order of all *tathāgatas'* appearing in all lands;

They emanated clouds of the sites of enlightenment of the *tathāgatas* of the three periods of time that, as they filled the ten directions, revealed the adornment with meritorious qualities of all *tathāgatas* when they reached the universal and right enlightenment;

They emanated clouds of dragon kings that, as they filled the ten directions, rained down all kinds of fragrances;

They emanated clouds of the bodies of world leaders that, as they filled the ten directions, proclaimed the practices of Samantabhadra Bodhisattva; and

They emanated clouds of pure buddha *kṣetras* adorned with all kinds of jewels that, as they filled the ten directions, revealed all *tathāgatas* turning the wheel of right Dharma.

It was because they had attained the light of the inconceivable Dharma and because it is the way of the Dharma that matters occur in this way—it was for these reasons that these bodhisattvas emanated such clouds of adornment as numerous as the atoms in an ineffable number of buddha *kṣetras,* all of which emanations were transformationally produced by their great spiritual powers.

At that time, Mañjuśrī Bodhisattva, aided by the Buddha's spiritual powers and wishing to summarize the feats of spiritual transformation that had just occurred in this Jeta Grove, surveyed the ten directions and spoke these verses:

You should all contemplate this Jeta Grove that,
due to Buddha's awesome spiritual powers, is limitlessly vast.

正體字

329b28 | 一切莊嚴皆示現　十方法界悉充滿
329b29 | 十方一切諸國土　無邊品類大莊嚴
329c01 | 於其座等境界中　色像分明皆顯現
329c02 | 從諸佛子毛孔出　種種莊嚴寶焰雲
329c03 | 及發如來微妙音　遍滿十方一切剎
329c04 | 寶樹華中現妙身　其身色相等梵王
329c05 | 從禪定起而遊步　進止威儀恒寂靜
329c06 | 如來一一毛孔內　常現難思變化身
329c07 | 皆如普賢大菩薩　種種諸相為嚴好
329c08 | 逝多林上虛空[2]中　所有莊嚴發妙音
329c09 | 普說三世諸菩薩　成就一切功德海
329c10 | 逝多林中諸寶樹　亦出無量妙音聲
329c11 | 演說一切諸群生　種種業海各差別
329c12 | 林中所有眾境界　悉現三世諸如來
329c13 | 一一皆起大神通　十方剎海微塵數
329c14 | 十方所有諸國土　一切剎海微塵數
329c15 | 悉入如來毛孔中　次第莊嚴皆現覩
329c16 | 所有莊嚴皆現佛　數等眾生遍世間
329c17 | 一一咸放大光明　種種隨宜化群品
329c18 | 香焰眾華及寶藏　一切莊嚴殊妙雲

简体字

一切庄严皆示现，十方法界悉充满。
十方一切诸国土，无边品类大庄严，
于其座等境界中，色像分明皆显现。
从诸佛子毛孔出，种种庄严宝焰云，
及发如来微妙音，遍满十方一切刹。
宝树华中现妙身，其身色相等梵王，
从禅定起而游步，进止威仪恒寂静。
如来一一毛孔内，常现难思变化身，
皆如普贤大菩萨，种种诸相为严好。
逝多林上虚空中，所有庄严发妙音，
普说三世诸菩萨，成就一切功德海。
逝多林中诸宝树，亦出无量妙音声，
演说一切诸群生，种种业海各差别。
林中所有众境界，悉现三世诸如来，
一一皆起大神通，十方刹海微尘数。
十方所有诸国土，一切刹海微尘数，
悉入如来毛孔中，次第庄严皆现睹。
所有庄严皆现佛，数等众生遍世间，
一一咸放大光明，种种随宜化群品。
香焰众华及宝藏，一切庄严殊妙云，

Every sort of adornment has been manifested here
and it has filled all ten directions of the Dharma realm.

All the lands throughout the ten directions
have become arrayed with countless kinds of great adornment.
Within the scenes appearing in his throne and the other objects,
the physical appearances of those phenomena are all clearly shown.

There flow forth from the pores of all these sons of the Buddha
jeweled flaming-light clouds with their many different adornments
as well as resounding emanations[47] of the Tathāgata's wondrous voice,
all of which everywhere pervade all *kṣetras* of the ten directions.

Within the jeweled trees' blossoms these marvelous bodies appear.
Their bodies' forms and features the same as a Brahma Heaven king's.
When they rise from *dhyāna* absorption and proceed to roam about,
their awesome deportment in going and stopping is forever serene.

Within every one of the pores of the Tathāgata,
there always appear inconceivably many transformation bodies,
all of which resemble that of Samantabhadra, the great bodhisattva,
in the ways they are adorned with the many different signs.

Up in the sky above the Jeta Grove,
all those adornments send forth wondrous voices
that everywhere speak of the bodhisattvas of the three periods of time
and their perfection of the ocean of all meritorious qualities.

All the jeweled trees within the Jeta Grove
also emanate the sounds of countless wondrous voices
expounding on each of the differences in the ocean of various deeds
as they are carried out by all the many types of beings.

In all the phenomena there within the Grove,
there appear every feat of great spiritual powers
as numerous as the atoms in the oceans of *kṣetras* in the ten directions
that ever were produced by all *tathāgatas* of the three periods of time.

All the lands throughout the ten directions,
as numerous as the atoms in the ocean of all *kṣetras*,
all enter into the pores of the Tathāgata
in which the sequences in their adornment are all shown and seen.

All of those adornments show the buddhas
as numerous as the beings throughout the world.
Every one of them emanates rays of bright light as, in various ways,
they adapt to what is fitting in teaching the many kinds of beings.

Of all those clouds of especially marvelous adornments, including
fragrances, flaming light, many kinds of flowers, and jewel treasuries,

正體字

329c19 | 靡不廣大等虛空　遍滿十方諸國土
329c20 | 十方三世一切佛　所有莊嚴妙道場
329c21 | 於此園林境界中　一一色像皆明現
329c22 | 一切普賢諸佛子　百千劫海莊嚴剎
329c23 | 其數無量等眾生　莫不於此林中見
329c24 | 爾時彼諸菩薩。以佛三昧光明照故。即時得
329c25 | 入如是三昧。一一皆得不可說佛剎微塵數
329c26 | 大悲門。利益安樂一切眾生。於其身上一一
329c27 | 毛孔。皆出不可說佛剎微塵數光明。一一光
329c28 | 明。皆化現不可說佛剎微塵數菩薩。其身形
329c29 | 相。如世諸主。普現一切眾生之前。周匝遍
330a01 | 滿十方法界。種種方便。教化調伏。或現不可
330a02 | 說佛剎微塵數諸天宮殿無常門。或現不可
330a03 | 說佛剎微塵數一切眾生受生門。或現不可
330a04 | 說佛剎微塵數一切菩薩修行門。或現不可
330a05 | 說佛剎微塵數夢境門。或現不可說佛剎微
330a06 | 塵數菩薩大願門。或現不可說佛剎微塵數
330a07 | 震動世界門。

简体字

靡不广大等虚空，遍满十方诸国土。
十方三世一切佛，所有庄严妙道场，
于此园林境界中，一一色像皆明现。
一切普贤诸佛子，百千劫海庄严刹，
其数无量等众生，莫不于此林中见。”

尔时，彼诸菩萨，以佛三昧光明照故，即时得入如是三昧，一一皆得不可说佛刹微尘数大悲门，利益安乐一切众生；于其身上一一毛孔，皆出不可说佛刹微尘数光明；一一光明，皆化现不可说佛刹微尘数菩萨。其身形相如世诸主，普现一切众生之前，周匝遍满十方法界，种种方便教化调伏，或现不可说佛刹微尘数诸天宫殿无常门，或现不可说佛刹微尘数一切众生受生门，或现不可说佛刹微尘数一切菩萨修行门，或现不可说佛刹微尘数梦境门，或现不可说佛刹微尘数菩萨大愿门，或现不可说佛刹微尘数震动世界门，

there are none not so vast as to equal the expanse of empty space
as they everywhere pervade all the lands of the ten directions.

All of the adorned and marvelous sites of enlightenment
of all buddhas of the ten directions and three periods of time—
the images of every one of their forms are all clearly shown
in the scene arrayed here within this garden and grove.

All these sons of the Buddha of Samantabhadra
have adorned *kṣetras* for an ocean of hundreds of thousands of kalpas.
Their numbers are so measureless as to equal the number of all beings.
There are none of them not seen here within this grove.

At that time, because they were illuminated by the light of the Buddha's samādhi, all those bodhisattvas then gained entry into samādhis like those described earlier, whereupon every one of them acquired entryways into the great compassion as numerous as the atoms in an ineffable number of buddha *kṣetras* with which they bestowed benefit and happiness on all beings.

From every one of the pores on their bodies, there streamed forth rays of light as numerous as the atoms in an ineffable number of buddha *kṣetras* and every light ray transformationally manifested bodhisattvas as numerous as the atoms in an ineffable number of buddha *kṣetras*. With forms and features resembling those of world leaders, those transformation bodies appeared directly before all beings everywhere throughout the ten directions of the Dharma realm where they adopted many different kinds of skillful means in teaching and training those beings:

Some showed gateways as numerous as the atoms in ineffably many buddha *kṣetras* portraying the impermanence of all the heavenly palaces;

Some showed gateways as numerous as the atoms in ineffably many buddha *kṣetras* portraying the manner in which all beings take on rebirths;

Some showed gateways as numerous as the atoms in ineffably many buddha *kṣetras* portraying all bodhisattvas' cultivation of the practices;

Some showed gateways as numerous as the atoms in ineffably many buddha *kṣetras* portraying spheres of experience as like dreams;[48]

Some showed gateways as numerous as the atoms in ineffably many buddha *kṣetras* portraying bodhisattvas' great vows;

Some showed gateways as numerous as the atoms in ineffably many buddha *kṣetras* portraying the shaking and movement of worlds;

正體字

或現不可說佛剎微塵數分別
330a08║ 世界門。或現不可說佛剎微塵數現生世界
330a09║ 門。或現不可說佛剎微塵數檀波羅蜜門。或
330a10║ 現不可說佛剎微塵數一切如來修諸功德種
330a11║ 種苦行尸波羅蜜門。或現不可說佛剎微塵數
330a12║ 割截[1]肢體羼提波羅蜜門。或現不可說佛剎
330a13║ 微塵數勤修毘梨耶波羅蜜門。或現不可說
330a14║ 佛剎微塵數一切菩薩修諸三昧禪定解脫
330a15║ 門。或現不可說佛剎微塵數佛道圓滿智光
330a16║ 明門。或現不可說佛剎微塵數勤求佛法為
330a17║ 一文一句故捨無數身命門。或現不可說佛
330a18║ 剎微塵數親近一切佛諮問一切法心無疲厭
330a19║ 門。或現不可說佛剎微塵數隨諸眾生時節
330a20║ 欲樂往詣其所方便成熟令住一切智海光明
330a21║ 門。或現不可說佛剎微塵數降伏眾魔制諸
330a22║ 外道顯現菩薩福智力門。或現不可說佛剎
330a23║ 微塵數知一切工巧明智門。

简体字

或现不可说佛刹微尘数分别世界门，或现不可说佛刹微尘数现生世界门，或现不可说佛刹微尘数檀波罗蜜门，或现不可说佛刹微尘数一切如来修诸功德种种苦行尸波罗蜜门，或现不可说佛刹微尘数割截肢体羼提波罗蜜门，或现不可说佛刹微尘数勤修毗梨耶波罗蜜门，或现不可说佛刹微尘数一切菩萨修诸三昧禅定解脱门，或现不可说佛刹微尘数佛道圆满智光明门，或现不可说佛刹微尘数勤求佛法为一文一句故舍无数身命门，或现不可说佛刹微尘数亲近一切佛咨问一切法心无疲厌门，或现不可说佛刹微尘数随诸众生时节欲乐往诣其所方便成熟令住一切智海光明门，或现不可说佛刹微尘数降伏众魔制诸外道显现菩萨福智力门，或现不可说佛刹微尘数知一切工巧明智门，

Some showed gateways as numerous as the atoms in ineffably many buddha *kṣetras* portraying the distinctions between worlds;

Some showed gateways as numerous as the atoms in ineffably many buddha *kṣetras* portraying the appearance of taking birth in the world;[49]

Some showed gateways as numerous as the atoms in ineffably many buddha *kṣetras* portraying the practice of *dāna pāramitā*;[50]

Some showed gateways as numerous as the atoms in ineffably many buddha *kṣetras* portraying all *tathāgatas'* cultivation of meritorious qualities and many different austere practices as they practice *śīla pāramitā*;

Some showed gateways as numerous as the atoms in ineffably many buddha *kṣetras* portraying even the severance of limbs while practicing *kṣānti pāramitā*;

Some showed gateways as numerous as the atoms in ineffably many buddha *kṣetras* portraying the diligent cultivation of *vīrya pāramitā*;

Some showed gateways as numerous as the atoms in ineffably many buddha *kṣetras* portraying all bodhisattvas' cultivation of the samādhis, the *dhyāna* absorptions, and the liberations;

Some showed gateways as numerous as the atoms in ineffably many buddha *kṣetras* portraying the perfect fulfillment of the light of wisdom arising from the path to buddhahood;

Some showed gateways as numerous as the atoms in ineffably many buddha *kṣetras* portraying instances of so diligently seeking the Buddha's Dharma that, for the sake of single passages or one sentence, they sacrificed countless physical lives;

Some showed gateways as numerous as the atoms in ineffably many buddha *kṣetras* portraying instances of drawing near to all buddhas and, with tireless mind, posing questions to them about all dharmas;

Some showed gateways as numerous as the atoms in ineffably many buddha *kṣetras* portraying adaptation to beings' timing and aspirations, going to where they abide, and using skillful means to enable their ripening, thereby causing them to abide in the light of the ocean of all-knowledge;

Some showed gateways as numerous as the atoms in ineffably many buddha *kṣetras* portraying the quelling of many kinds of *māras*, the restraint of non-Buddhist traditions, and the manifestations of the bodhisattva's merit and wisdom;

Some showed gateways of knowledge as numerous as the atoms in ineffably many buddha *kṣetras* portraying the knowledge of all skills and arts;

正體字

或現不可說佛
330a24‖ 剎微塵數知一切眾生差別明智門。或現不可
330a25‖ 說佛剎微塵數知一切法差別明智門。或現
330a26‖ 不可說佛剎微塵數知一切眾生心樂差別明
330a27‖ 智門。或現不可說佛剎微塵數知一切眾生
330a28‖ 根行煩惱習氣明智門。或現不可說佛剎微
330a29‖ 塵數知一切眾生種種業明智門。或現不可
330b01‖ 說佛剎微塵數開悟一切眾生門。以如是等
330b02‖ 不可說佛剎微塵數方便門。往詣一切眾生
330b03‖ 住處。而成熟之。所謂或往天宮。或往龍宮。
330b04‖ 或往夜叉乾闥婆阿脩羅迦樓羅緊那羅摩睺
330b05‖ 羅伽宮。或往梵王宮。或往人王宮。或往閻羅
330b06‖ 王宮。或往畜生餓鬼地獄之所住處。以平等
330b07‖ 大悲。平等大願。平等智慧。平等方便。攝諸眾
330b08‖ 生。或有見已而調伏者。或有聞已而調伏者。
330b09‖ 或有憶念而調伏者。或聞音聲而調伏者。或
330b10‖ 聞名號而調伏者。或見圓光而調伏者。

简体字

或现不可说佛刹微尘数知一切众生差别明智门，或现不可说佛刹微尘数知一切法差别明智门，或现不可说佛刹微尘数知一切众生心乐差别明智门，或现不可说佛刹微尘数知一切众生根行、烦恼、习气明智门，或现不可说佛刹微尘数知一切众生种种业明智门，或现不可说佛刹微尘数开悟一切众生门。以如是等不可说佛刹微尘数方便门，往诣一切众生住处而成熟之，所谓：或往天宫，或往龙宫，或往夜叉、乾闼婆、阿修罗、迦楼罗、紧那罗、摩睺罗伽宫，或往梵王宫，或往人王宫，或往阎罗王宫，或往畜生、饿鬼、地狱之所住处，以平等大悲、平等大愿、平等智慧、平等方便摄诸众生。或有见已而调伏者，或有闻已而调伏者，或有忆念而调伏者，或闻音声而调伏者，或闻名号而调伏者，或见圆光而调伏者，

Some showed gateways of knowledge as numerous as the atoms in ineffably many buddha *kṣetras* portraying the knowledge of the distinctions existing among all beings;

Some showed gateways of knowledge as numerous as the atoms in ineffably many buddha *kṣetras* portraying the knowledge of all the distinctions existing among all dharmas;

Some showed gateways of knowledge as numerous as the atoms in ineffably many buddha *kṣetras* portraying the knowledge of the distinctions existing in all beings' aspirations;

Some showed gateways of knowledge as numerous as the atoms in ineffably many buddha *kṣetras* portraying the knowledge of all beings' faculties, practices, afflictions, and habitual karmic propensities;

Some showed gateways of knowledge as numerous as the atoms in ineffably many buddha *kṣetras* portraying the knowledge of all beings' many different kinds of karmic actions; and

Some showed gateways as numerous as the atoms in ineffably many buddha *kṣetras* portraying the awakening of all beings.

Using gateways of skillful means such as these that are as numerous as the atoms in ineffably many buddha *kṣetras*, they go wherever beings dwell and ripen them, doing so in these ways:

Perhaps they go to the palaces of devas;

Or they go to the palaces of dragons;

Or they go to the palaces of *yakṣas, gandharvas, asuras, garuḍas, kiṃnaras,* or *mahoragas;*

Or they go to the palaces of Brahma Heaven kings;

Or they go to the palaces of human kings;

Or they go to the palace of King Yama;

Or they go to the abodes of animals, hungry ghosts, or hell-dwellers.

Then, using impartially bestowed great compassion, impartially bestowed great vows, impartially bestowed wisdom, and impartially bestowed skillful means, they attract those beings, among whom:

There are some who, having seen them, become susceptible to training;

There are some who, having heard about them, become susceptible to training;

There are some who, having brought them to mind, become susceptible to training;

There are some who, having heard the sounds of their voices, become susceptible to training;

There are some who, having heard their names, become susceptible to training;

There are some who, having seen the light of their auras, become susceptible to training;

正體字

或見
330b11║ 光網而調伏者。隨諸眾生心之所樂。皆詣其
330b12║ 所。令其獲益。佛子。此逝多林。一切菩薩。為
330b13║ 欲成熟諸眾生故。或時現處種種嚴飾諸宮
330b14║ 殿中。或時示現住自樓閣寶師子座。道場眾
330b15║ 會所共圍遶。周遍十方皆令得見。然亦不離
330b16║ 此逝多林如來之所。佛子。此諸菩薩。或時示
330b17║ 現無量化身雲。或現其身。獨一無侶。所謂或
330b18║ 現沙門身。或現婆羅門身。或現苦行身。或
330b19║ 現充盛身。或現醫王身。或現商主身。或現淨
330b20║ 命身。或現[2]妓樂身。或現奉事諸天身。或現
330b21║ 工巧[3]技術身。往詣一切村營城邑。王都聚
330b22║ 落。諸眾生所。隨其所應。以種種形相。種種威
330b23║ 儀。種種音聲。種種言論。種種住處。於一切世
330b24║ 間。猶如帝網。行菩薩行。或說一切世間工巧
330b25║ 事業。或說一切智慧照世明燈。或說一切眾
330b26║ 生業力所莊嚴。

简体字

或见光网而调伏者；随诸众生心之所乐，皆诣其所令其获益。

佛子，此逝多林一切菩萨，为欲成熟诸众生故，或时现处种种严饰诸宫殿中，或时示现住自楼阁宝师子座，道场众会所共围绕，周遍十方皆令得见，然亦不离此逝多林如来之所。佛子，此诸菩萨，或时示现无量化身云，或现其身独一无侣。所谓：或现沙门身，或现婆罗门身，或现苦行身，或现充盛身，或现医王身，或现商主身，或现净命身，或现妓乐身，或现奉事诸天身，或现工巧技术身。往诣一切村营城邑、王都聚落、诸众生所，随其所应，以种种形相、种种威仪、种种音声、种种言论、种种住处，于一切世间犹如帝网行菩萨行。或说一切世间工巧事业，或说一切智慧照世明灯，或说一切众生业力所庄严，

Or there are some who, having observed their nets of light, become susceptible to training.

So it is that, adapting to beings' inclinations, they go wherever they may dwell and enable them to benefit.

Sons of the Buddha, because they wish to ripen all beings, all the bodhisattvas in this Jeta Grove sometimes appear as dwelling in palaces with many different kinds of adornments or sometimes they manifest as dwelling in their own tower, sitting on a jeweled lion throne, surrounded by a congregation at a site of enlightenment where everyone throughout the ten directions is enabled to see this. And, even as this occurs in this way, they still never leave the presence of the Tathāgata here in this Jeta Grove.

Sons of the Buddha, these bodhisattvas sometimes manifest clouds of countless transformation bodies and sometimes manifest their bodies as dwelling alone without any companions at all, in particular as follows:

They may manifest in the body of a *śramaṇa*;
Or they may manifest in the body of a brahman;
Or they may manifest in the body of an ascetic;
Or they may manifest in a body that is robust and strong;
Or they may manifest in the body of a master physician;[51]
Or they may manifest in the body of a leader of merchants;
Or they may manifest in the body of one who practices a pure livelihood;
Or they may manifest in the body of a female musician or performer;
Or they may manifest in the body of someone devoted to serving the devas;
Or they may manifest in the body of a skilled craftsman or artisan.

They travel to every village, town, city, royal capital, or hamlet, where, adapting to whatever is appropriate for the residents, they adopt various forms and appearances, various styles of deportment, various voices, various ways of speaking, and live in various dwelling places where they carry out the bodhisattva practices in all worlds [interconnected] like the net of Indra.

In so doing, they sometimes expound on all the world's skilled crafts and livelihoods, sometimes expound on all the world-illuminating lamps of wisdom, sometimes expound on the adornments created by the power of all beings' karmic actions, sometimes expound on the establishment of the stages of all the vehicles [for

正體字

或說十方國土建立諸乘位。
330b27‖ 或說智燈所照一切法境界。教化成就一切
330b28‖ 眾生。而亦不離此逝多林如來之所
330b29‖ 爾時文殊師利童子。從善住樓閣出。與無量
330c01‖ 同行菩薩。及常隨侍衛諸金剛神。普為眾生。
330c02‖ 供養諸佛諸身眾神。久發堅誓願常隨從諸
330c03‖ 足行神。樂聞妙法主地神。常修大悲主水神。
330c04‖ 智光照[4]耀主火神。摩尼為冠主風神。明練十
330c05‖ 方一切儀式主方神。專勤除滅無明黑暗主
330c06‖ 夜神。一心匪懈闡明佛日主晝神。莊嚴法界
330c07‖ 一切虛空主空神。普度眾生超諸有海主海
330c08‖ 神。常勤積集趣一切智助道善根高大如山主
330c09‖ 山神。常勤守護一切眾生菩提心城主城神。
330c10‖ 常勤守護一切智智無上法城諸大龍王。常
330c11‖ 勤守護一切眾生諸夜叉王。常令眾生增長
330c12‖ 歡喜乾闥婆王。常勤除滅諸餓鬼趣鳩槃[＊]荼
330c13‖ 王。恒願拔濟一切眾生出諸有海迦樓羅王。
330c14‖ 願得成就諸如來身高出世間阿脩羅王。

简体字

或说十方国土建立诸乘位，或说智灯所照一切法境界，教化成就一切众生，而亦不离此逝多林如来之所。

尔时，文殊师利童子从善住楼阁出，与无量同行菩萨，及常随侍卫诸金刚神、普为众生供养诸佛诸身众神、久发坚誓愿常随从诸足行神、乐闻妙法主地神、常修大悲主水神、智光照耀主火神、摩尼为冠主风神、明练十方一切仪式主方神、专勤除灭无明黑暗主夜神、一心匪懈阐明佛日主昼神、庄严法界一切虚空主空神、普度众生超诸有海主海神、常勤积集趣一切智助道善根高大如山主山神、常勤守护一切众生菩提心城主城神、常勤守护一切智智无上法城诸大龙王、常勤守护一切众生诸夜叉王、常令众生增长欢喜乾闼婆王、常勤除灭诸饿鬼趣鸠槃荼王、恒愿拔济一切众生出诸有海迦楼罗王、愿得成就诸如来身高出世间阿修罗王、

gaining liberation] throughout the lands of the ten directions, and sometimes expound on the sphere of all dharmas illuminated by the lamp of wisdom, thereby teaching and ripening all beings. And yet, even as they do, they still never leave the Tathāgata's presence in this Jeta Grove.

At that time, Mañjuśrī the Youth came out from his Tower of Skillful Abiding together with countless bodhisattvas who cultivated the same practices as well as:

Vajra spirits who always followed along, serving and protecting him;

Many-bodied spirits who everywhere make offerings to buddhas on behalf of beings;

Foot-travel spirits[52] that long ago made the solid vow to always follow him;

Earth spirits who delight in listening to the sublime Dharma;

Water spirits who always cultivate the great compassion;

Fire spirits whose wisdom light emanates intensely bright illumination;

Wind spirits with *maṇi* jewel crowns;

Regional spirits who are knowledgeable and experienced in all ceremonial protocols pertaining to the ten directions;

Night spirits who diligently extinguish the darkness of ignorance;

Day spirits who are single-minded and tireless in expounding on the Buddha as the sun;

Sky spirits who adorn the entire sky throughout the Dharma realm;

Ocean spirits who everywhere liberate beings by helping them across the ocean of existence;

Mountain spirits who always diligently accumulate a stock of roots of goodness as high as a mountain which serves them as provisions for the path to all-knowledge;

City spirits who always diligently guard all beings' city of the resolve to attain bodhi;

Great dragon kings who always diligently guard the unexcelled city of the wisdom of all-knowledge;

Yakṣa kings who always diligently guard all beings;

Gandharva kings who always increase beings' happiness;

Kumbhāṇḍa kings who are always diligent in doing away with the rebirth destiny of the hungry ghosts;

Garuḍa kings who constantly vow to rescue all beings by pulling them out of the ocean of the stations of existence;

Asura kings who have vowed to develop the *tathāgatas'* body that is taller than that of anyone else in the world;

正體字

見
330c15‖ 佛歡喜曲躬恭敬摩睺羅伽王。常厭生死恒
330c16‖ 樂見佛諸大天王。尊重於佛讚歎供養諸大
330c17‖ 梵王。文殊師利。與如是等功德莊嚴諸菩薩
330c18‖ 眾。出自住處。來詣佛所。右遶世尊。經無量
330c19‖ 匝。以諸供具種種供養。供養畢已。辭退南行。
330c20‖ 往於人間
330c21‖ 爾時尊者舍利弗。承佛神力。見文殊師利菩
330c22‖ 薩。與諸菩薩眾會莊嚴。出逝多林。往於南方。
330c23‖ 遊行人間。作如是念。我今當與文殊師利。俱
330c24‖ 往南方。時尊者舍利弗。與六千比丘。前後圍
330c25‖ 遶。出自住處。來詣佛所。頂禮佛足。具白世尊。
330c26‖ 世尊聽許。右遶三匝。辭退而去。往文殊師利
330c27‖ 所。此六千比丘。是舍利弗自所同住。出家未
330c28‖ 久。所謂海覺比丘。善生比丘。福光比丘。大童
330c29‖ 子比丘。電生比丘。淨行比丘。天德比丘君慧
331a01‖ 比丘。梵勝比丘。寂慧比丘。如是等其數六千。
331a02‖ 悉曾供養無量諸佛。深植善根。解力廣大。信
331a03‖ 眼明徹。其心寬博。觀佛境界。了法本性。饒益
331a04‖ 眾生。常樂勤求諸佛功德。皆是文殊師利說
331a05‖ 法教化之所成就。

简体字

见佛欢喜曲躬恭敬摩睺罗伽王、常厌生死恒乐见佛诸大天王、尊重于佛赞叹供养诸大梵王。文殊师利与如是等功德庄严诸菩萨众，出自住处，来诣佛所，右绕世尊，经无量匝，以诸供具种种供养；供养毕已，辞退南行，往于人间。

尔时，尊者舍利弗承佛神力，见文殊师利菩萨，与诸菩萨众会庄严，出逝多林，往于南方，游行人间；作如是念：“我今当与文殊师利俱往南方。”时，尊者舍利弗与六千比丘，前后围绕，出自住处，来诣佛所，顶礼佛足，具白世尊；世尊听许，右绕三匝，辞退而去，往文殊师利所。此六千比丘是舍利弗自所同住，出家未久，所谓：海觉比丘、善生比丘、福光比丘、大童子比丘、电生比丘、净行比丘、天德比丘、君慧比丘、梵胜比丘、寂慧比丘。如是等其数六千，悉曾供养无量诸佛，深植善根，解力广大，信眼明彻，其心宽博，观佛境界，了法本性，饶益众生，常乐勤求诸佛功德，皆是文殊师利说法教化之所成就。

Mahoraga kings who, whenever they see the Buddha, are filled with delight, and bow in reverence;
Great deva kings who always abhor involvement in *saṃsāra* and constantly delight in seeing the Buddha;
Kings of the Mahābrahmā Heaven who revere, praise, and make offerings to the Buddha.

Together with a congregation of bodhisattvas such as these who were adorned with such meritorious qualities, Mañjuśrī emerged from his dwelling place and came forth to pay his respects to the Buddha, whereupon he circumambulated the Bhagavat countless times with his right side toward him and then made many different kinds of offerings to him of various gifts. After making these offerings, they withdrew and then headed south where they sojourned among the people.

At that time, aided by the Buddha's spiritual powers, the Venerable Śāriputra saw Mañjuśrī Bodhisattva with the congregation of bodhisattvas adorning his presence as they left the Jeta Grove and headed south to travel among the people. He then thought, "I should now go off toward the south with Mañjuśrī."

Then, surrounded by six thousand bhikshus, the Venerable Śāriputra emerged from his dwelling place and came to pay his respects to the Buddha, whereupon he bowed down in reverence at the Buddha's feet and reported this to the Bhagavat. Then, after receiving the Bhagavat's assent, Śāriputra circumambulated him three times and then withdrew, proceeding then toward where Mañjuśrī had gone.

These six thousand bhikshus were those who had been dwelling together with Śāriputra and who had not left the home life for long. In particular, they were: Oceanic Awakening Bhikshu, Well Born Bhikshu, Merit Light Bhikshu, Great Youth Bhikshu, Born of Lightning Bhikshu, Pure Conduct Bhikshu, Celestial Virtue Bhikshu, Sovereign Wisdom Bhikshu, Supreme Brahman Bhikshu, Serene Wisdom Bhikshu, and others such as these, six thousand in all. They had all made offerings to countless buddhas, had deeply planted roots of goodness, possessed vast powers of comprehension, had brilliantly penetrating eyes of faith, were possessed of expansive minds, contemplated the realms of the Buddha, completely understood the fundamental nature of dharmas, liberally benefited beings, and always delighted in diligently seeking to acquire the Buddha's meritorious qualities. They had all been brought to complete development by the teachings contained in Mañjuśrī's discourses on the Dharma.

正體字

爾時尊者舍利弗。在行道
331a06║ 中。觀諸比丘。告海覺言。海覺。汝可觀察文殊
331a07║ 師利菩薩清淨之身相好莊嚴。一切天人莫
331a08║ 能思議。汝可觀察文殊師利圓光映徹。令無
331a09║ 量眾生。發歡喜心。汝可觀察文殊師利光網
331a10║ 莊嚴。除滅眾生無量苦惱。汝可觀察文殊師
331a11║ 利眾會具足。皆是菩薩往昔善根之所攝受。
331a12║ 汝可觀察文殊師利所行之路。左右八步。平
331a13║ 坦莊嚴。汝可觀察文殊師利所住之處。周迴
331a14║ 十方。常有道場。隨逐而轉。汝可觀察文殊師
331a15║ 利所行之路。具足無量福德莊嚴。左右兩邊。
331a16║ 有大伏藏。種種珍寶。自然而出。汝可觀察文
331a17║ 殊師利曾供養佛。善根所流。一切樹間。出
331a18║ 莊嚴藏。汝可觀察文殊師利。諸世間主雨供
331a19║ 具雲。頂禮恭敬。以為供養。汝可觀察文殊師
331a20║ 利。十方一切諸佛如來。將說法時。悉放眉間
331a21║ 白毫相光。來照其身。從頂上入。爾時尊者舍
331a22║ 利弗。為諸比丘。稱揚讚歎。開示演說文殊師
331a23║ 利童子。有如是等。無量功德具足莊嚴。彼諸
331a24║ 比丘。聞是說已。心意清淨。信解堅固。喜不自
331a25║ 持。舉身踊躍。形體柔軟。諸根悅豫。憂苦悉
331a26║ 除。垢障咸盡。

简体字

尔时，尊者舍利弗在行道中观诸比丘，告海觉言："海觉，汝可观察文殊师利菩萨清净之身相好庄严，一切天人莫能思议。汝可观察文殊师利圆光映彻，令无量众生发欢喜心。汝可观察文殊师利光网庄严，除灭众生无量苦恼。汝可观察文殊师利众会具足，皆是菩萨往昔善根之所摄受。汝可观察文殊师利所行之路，左右八步，平坦庄严。汝可观察文殊师利所住之处，周回十方常有道场随逐而转。汝可观察文殊师利所行之路，具足无量福德庄严，左右两边有大伏藏，种种珍宝自然而出。汝可观察文殊师利曾供养佛，善根所流，一切树间出庄严藏。汝可观察文殊师利，诸世间主雨供具云，顶礼恭敬以为供养。汝可观察文殊师利，十方一切诸佛如来将说法时，悉放眉间白毫相光来照其身，从顶上入。"

尔时，尊者舍利弗为诸比丘称扬赞叹、开示演说文殊师利童子有如是等无量功德具足庄严。彼诸比丘闻是说已，心意清净，信解坚固，喜不自持，举身踊跃，形体柔软，诸根悦豫，忧苦悉除，垢障咸尽，

At that time, as the Venerable Śāriputra traveled along the road, he contemplated all those bhikshus and then spoke to Oceanic Awakening Bhikshu, saying:

Oceanic Awakening, you should observe Mañjuśrī Bodhisattva's adornment with the major marks and secondary signs of physical purity that no god or man could ever conceive of;

You should observe the penetrating brilliance of Mañjuśrī's aura that causes countless beings to feel joyous delight;

You should observe Mañjuśrī's adornment with a net of light rays which extinguish beings' measureless suffering and anguish;

You should observe the abundance of Mañjuśrī's congregation of followers, all of whom were attracted and sustained by that bodhisattva's past roots of goodness;

You should observe the road on which Mañjuśrī travels that is level and adorned to a distance of eight paces to the left and right;

You should observe Mañjuśrī's abode, for, even as he goes all around throughout the ten directions, his site of enlightenment always follows along and turns with him;

You should observe the road on which Mañjuśrī travels that is abundantly replete in adornments with measureless merit and which, on both the left and right sides, has great treasuries of many different kinds of precious jewels which just spontaneously emerge there;

You should observe the treasuries of adornments emerging between every tree, all of which flow forth from the roots of goodness produced by Mañjuśrī's past offerings to the buddhas;

You should observe the world leaders' raining down of clouds of gifts and their bowing down in reverence, doing so in order to make offerings to Mañjuśrī; and

You should observe that, when all buddhas, the Tathāgatas, are about to teach the Dharma, they all emanate light from the white hair mark between their brows which comes, illuminates Mañjuśrī's body, and then enters the crown of his head.

Then, for the sake of those bhikshus, the Venerable Śāriputra proclaimed, praised, explained, and expounded on Mañjuśrī the Youth's complete adornment with countless meritorious qualities such as these.

After those bhikshus heard him speak in this way, their minds were purified, their resolute faith was strengthened, they felt joy they could not contain, their entire bodies felt uplifted with delight, their bodies acquired a state of pliancy, their faculties were suffused with blissful contentment, they became rid of all their worries, and their defilement obstacles were all extinguished.

正體字

常見諸佛。深求正法。具菩薩
331a27‖ 根。得菩薩力。大悲大願。皆自出生。入於諸度
331a28‖ 甚深境界。十方佛海。常現在前。於一切智。深
331a29‖ 生信樂。即白尊者舍利弗言。唯願大師。將引
331b01‖ 我等。往詣於彼勝人之所。時舍利弗。即與俱
331b02‖ 行。至其所已。白言仁者。此諸比丘。願得奉
331b03‖ 覲。爾時文殊師利童子。無量自在菩薩圍遶。
331b04‖ 并其大眾。如象王迴。觀諸比丘。時諸比丘。頂
331b05‖ 禮其足。合掌恭敬。作如是言。我今奉見。恭敬
331b06‖ 禮拜。及餘所有一切善根。唯願仁者文殊師
331b07‖ 利。和尚舍利弗。世尊釋迦牟尼。皆悉證知。如
331b08‖ 仁所有。如是色身。如是音聲。如是相好。如是
331b09‖ 自在。願我一切悉當具得。爾時文殊師利菩
331b10‖ 薩。告諸比丘言。比丘。若善男子善女人。成就
331b11‖ 十種趣大乘法。則能速入如來之地。況菩薩
331b12‖ 地。何者為十。所謂積集一切善根心無疲厭。
331b13‖ 見一切佛承事供養心無疲厭。求一切佛法
331b14‖ 心無疲厭。行一切波羅[1]蜜心無疲厭。成就一
331b15‖ 切菩薩三昧心無疲厭。

简体字

常见诸佛，深求正法，具菩萨根，得菩萨力，大悲大愿皆自出生，入于诸度甚深境界，十方佛海常现在前，于一切智深生信乐；即白尊者舍利弗言：“唯愿大师将引我等，往诣于彼胜人之所。”时，舍利弗即与俱行，至其所已，白言：“仁者，此诸比丘，愿得奉觐。”

尔时，文殊师利童子，无量自在菩萨围绕并其大众，如象王回观诸比丘。时，诸比丘顶礼其足，合掌恭敬，作如是言：“我今奉见，恭敬礼拜，及余所有一切善根。唯愿仁者文殊师利、和尚舍利弗、世尊释迦牟尼，皆悉证知！如仁所有如是色身、如是音声、如是相好、如是自在，愿我一切悉当具得。”

尔时，文殊师利菩萨告诸比丘言：“比丘，若善男子、善女人，成就十种趣大乘法，则能速入如来之地，况菩萨地！何者为十？所谓：积集一切善根，心无疲厌。见一切佛承事供养，心无疲厌。求一切佛法，心无疲厌。行一切波罗蜜，心无疲厌。成就一切菩萨三昧，心无疲厌。

They were then always able to see buddhas, they deeply sought right Dharma, they became equipped with the faculties of bodhisattvas, they acquired the bodhisattva's powers, and they spontaneously developed the great compassion and made the great vows. They then entered into the extremely profound realm of the perfections whereupon the ocean of the buddhas of the ten directions thenceforth always appeared directly before them.

They experienced the deep arising of aspiring faith in all-knowledge and then straightaway addressed the Venerable Śāriputra, saying, "We wish only that the Great Master would lead us to that *ārya*'s dwelling place so that we might pay our respects to him."

Śāriputra then traveled on together with them. Once they had arrived there, he addressed Mañjuśrī, saying, "O Worthy One. These bhikshus wish to pay their respects to you."

Then Mañjuśrī the Youth who was surrounded by countless bodhisattvas possessed of spiritual powers,[53] turned toward them together with his immense congregation, doing so in the same way that an elephant king turns, whereupon he cast his gaze upon those bhikshus.

Those bhikshus then bowed down in reverence at his feet, respectfully pressed their palms together, and spoke these words:

> May the Worthy One, Mañjuśrī, our preceptor, Śāriputra, and the Bhagavat, Śākyamuni, all bear witness to this request: We only pray that, by the power of the roots of goodness of our paying respects, bowing in reverence, and all of our other actions, we may be able to completely acquire just as the Worthy One has them, a physical form like this, a voice like this, major marks and secondary signs like these, and spiritual powers like these.

Mañjuśrī Bodhisattva then told those bhikshus:

> O Bhikshus, if there be any son of good family or daughter of good family who perfects ten dharmas by which one progresses into the Great Vehicle, they will be able to swiftly enter onto the ground of the Tathāgata, how much the more so might they reach the bodhisattva grounds. What then are those ten? They are as follows:
>
> With tireless resolve, accumulate all roots of goodness;
>
> With tireless resolve, see all buddhas, serve them, and make offerings to them;
>
> With tireless resolve, seek to acquire all dharmas of the Buddha;
>
> With tireless resolve, practice all the *pāramitās*;
>
> With tireless resolve, perfect all the bodhisattva samādhis;

正體字

次第入一切三世心
331b16‖ 無疲厭。普嚴淨十方佛剎心無疲厭。教化調
331b17‖ 伏一切眾生心無疲厭。於一切剎一切劫中
331b18‖ 成就菩薩行心無疲厭。為成[2]熟一眾生故修
331b19‖ 行一切佛剎微塵數波羅蜜成就如來[3]一力
331b20‖ 如是次第為成熟一切眾生界成就如來一切
331b21‖ 力心無疲厭。比丘若善男子善女人。成就深
331b22‖ 信。發此十種無疲厭心。則能長養一切善根。
331b23‖ 捨離一切諸生死趣。超過一切世間種[4]姓。
331b24‖ 不墮聲聞辟支佛地。生一切如來家。具一切
331b25‖ 菩薩願。學習一切如來功德。修行一切菩薩
331b26‖ 諸行。得如來力。摧伏眾魔及諸外道。亦能除
331b27‖ 滅一切煩惱。入菩薩地。近如來地。時諸比
331b28‖ 丘。聞此法已。則得三昧。名無礙眼見一切佛
331b29‖ 境界。得此三昧故。悉見十方無量無邊一切
331c01‖ 世界諸佛如來。及其所有道場眾會。亦悉見
331c02‖ 彼十方世界一切諸趣所有眾生。亦悉見彼
331c03‖ 一切世界種種差別。亦悉見彼一切世界所
331c04‖ 有微塵。亦悉見彼諸世界中一切眾生所住
331c05‖ 宮殿。以種種寶而為莊嚴。及亦聞彼諸佛如
331c06‖ 來種種言音演說諸法文辭訓釋。悉皆解了。
331c07‖ 亦能觀察彼世界中一切眾生諸根心欲。

简体字

次第入一切三世，心无疲厌。普严净十方佛刹，心无疲厌。教化调伏一切众生，心无疲厌。于一切刹一切劫中成就菩萨行，心无疲厌。为成就一众生故，修行一切佛刹微尘数波罗蜜，成就如来一力；如是次第，为成熟一切众生界，成就如来一切力，心无疲厌。

“比丘，若善男子、善女人，成就深信，发此十种无疲厌心，则能长养一切善根，舍离一切诸生死趣，超过一切世间种性，不堕声闻、辟支佛地，生一切如来家，具一切菩萨愿，学习一切如来功德，修行一切菩萨诸行，得如来力，摧伏众魔及诸外道，亦能除灭一切烦恼，入菩萨地，近如来地。”

时，诸比丘闻此法已，则得三昧，名无碍眼见一切佛境界。得此三昧故，悉见十方无量无边一切世界诸佛如来，及其所有道场众会；亦悉见彼十方世界一切诸趣所有众生；亦悉见彼一切世界种种差别；亦悉见彼一切世界所有微尘；亦悉见彼诸世界中，一切众生所住宫殿，以种种宝而为庄严；及亦闻彼诸佛如来种种言音演说诸法文辞训释，悉皆解了；亦能观察彼世界中一切众生诸根心欲；

With tireless resolve, enter all three periods of time in succession;

With tireless resolve, everywhere accomplish the purification of buddha *kṣetras* throughout the ten directions;

With tireless resolve, teach and train all beings;

With tireless resolve, perfect the bodhisattva practices in all *kṣetras* and in all kalpas; and

With tireless resolve, for the sake of ripening one being, cultivate *pāramitās* as numerous as the atoms in all buddha *kṣetras*, perfect one of the Tathāgata's powers, and then, for the sake of ripening all realms of beings, sequentially perfect all of the other powers of the Tathāgata.

O Bhikshus. If a son of good family or daughter of good family were to perfect deep faith and bring forth these ten kinds of tireless resolve, then they would be able to increase all types of roots of goodness, would leave behind all the rebirth destinies within *saṃsāra*, would step entirely beyond all worldly lineages, would never fall onto the grounds of *śrāvaka* disciples or *pratyekabuddhas*, would attain birth into the family of all *tathāgatas*, would become equipped with all the bodhisattva vows, would train in all the Tathāgata's meritorious qualities, would cultivate all the bodhisattva practices, would acquire the Tathāgata's powers, would vanquish the many kinds of *māras* and the adherents of non-Buddhist paths, and would also extinguish all afflictions, enter the bodhisattva grounds, and draw near to the ground of the Tathāgata.

At that time, having just listened to this Dharma, those bhikshus then acquired a samādhi known as "the unimpeded eye that sees all buddhas' sphere of action." Because they acquired this samādhi:

They saw all buddhas, *tathāgatas*, with all their congregations in all of the measureless and boundlessly many worlds of the ten directions;

They also saw all beings in all the rebirth destinies throughout those worlds of the ten directions;

They also saw all the various differences in all those worlds;

They also saw all the atoms in all those worlds;

They also saw all the palaces adorned with many different kinds of jewels in which all the beings in those worlds dwelt;

They also heard all those buddhas, *tathāgatas'*, use of many different languages and voices and completely understood their exposition of dharmas through the use of particular phrases, expressions, and close explanations;

They were also able to observe the faculties and mental dispositions of all those beings in all those worlds;

正體字

亦
331c08║ 能憶念彼世界中一切眾生前後十生。亦能
331c09║ 憶念彼世界中過去未來各十劫事。亦能憶
331c10║ 念彼諸如來十本生事。十成正覺。十轉法輪。
331c11║ 十種神通。十種說法。十種教誡。十種辯才。又
331c12║ 即成就十千菩提心。十千三昧。十千波羅蜜。
331c13║ 悉皆清淨。得大智慧圓滿光明。得菩薩十神
331c14║ 通。柔軟微妙。住菩薩心。堅固不動。爾時文殊
331c15║ 師利菩薩。勸諸比丘。住普賢行。住普賢行已
331c16║ 入大願海。入大願海已成就大願海。以成就
331c17║ 大願海故心清淨。心清淨故身清淨。身清淨
331c18║ 故身輕利。身清淨輕利故得大神通無有退
331c19║ 轉。得此神通故不離文殊師利足下。普於十
331c20║ 方一切佛所。悉現其身。具足成就一切佛法
331c24║ 大方廣佛華嚴經卷第六十二
331c27║ 入法界品第三十九之三
331c28║ 爾時文殊師利菩薩。勸諸比丘。發阿耨多羅
331c29║ 三藐三菩提心已。漸次南行。經歷人間。至福
332a01║ 城東。住莊嚴幢娑羅林中。往昔諸佛曾所止
332a02║ 住。教化眾生。大塔廟處。亦是世尊。於往昔
332a03║ 時。修菩薩行。

简体字

亦能忆念彼世界中一切众生前后十生；亦能忆念彼世界中过去、未来各十劫事；亦能忆念彼诸如来十本生事、十成正觉、十转法轮、十种神通、十种说法、十种教诫、十种辩才；又即成就十千菩提心、十千三昧、十千波罗蜜，悉皆清净；得大智慧圆满光明，得菩萨十神通，柔软微妙，住菩萨心，坚固不动。

尔时，文殊师利菩萨劝诸比丘住普贤行；住普贤行已，入大愿海；入大愿海已，成就大愿海。以成就大愿海故，心清净；心清净故，身清净；身清净故，身轻利；身清净、轻利故，得大神通无有退转；得此神通故，不离文殊师利足下，普于十方一切佛所悉现其身，具足成就一切佛法。

大方广佛华严经卷第六十二

入法界品第三十九之三

尔时，文殊师利菩萨劝诸比丘发阿耨多罗三藐三菩提心已，渐次南行，经历人间，至福城东，住庄严幢娑罗林中往昔诸佛曾所止住教化众生大塔庙处，亦是世尊于往昔时修菩萨行

They were also able to bring to mind ten past and future lifetimes of all beings in those worlds;
They were also able to bring to mind the events that transpired in each of those worlds throughout ten past and future kalpas; and
They were also able to bring to mind with regard to all those *tathāgatas* the events occurring in ten of their previous lives, including ten instances of their attaining right enlightenment, ten instances of their turning the Dharma wheel, ten kinds of use of their spiritual superknowledges, ten ways in which they expounded on the Dharma, ten kinds of teachings and remonstrances, and ten ways in which they spoke with eloquence.

Moreover, they immediately perfected a myriad ways of invoking their bodhi resolve, a myriad samādhis, and a myriad *pāramitās,* all of which they purified. They also acquired the perfectly fulfilled light of great wisdom and acquired ten kinds of bodhisattva superknowledges whereby, with gentleness and sublimity, they dwelt in a solid and unshakable bodhi resolve.

Mañjuśrī Bodhisattva then exhorted all those bhikshus, instructing them to abide in Samantabhadra's practices. Then, having dwelt in Samantabhadra's practices, they would be able to enter the ocean of great vows. Having entered the ocean of great vows, they would then be able to perfect the ocean of great vows. Due to perfecting the ocean of great vows, they would then be able to gain purity of mind. Due to gaining purity of mind, they would then be able to acquire physical purity. Due to acquiring physical purity, they would then be able to acquire buoyant physical agility. Due to acquiring physical purity and buoyant physical agility, they would be able to irreversibly acquire great spiritual superknowledges. Due to acquiring these spiritual superknowledges, they would then be able, even without ever leaving the presence of Mañjuśrī, to manifest their bodies in the dwelling places of all buddhas everywhere throughout the ten directions, whereupon they would then be able to completely perfect all dharmas of the Buddha.

At that time, after exhorting those bhikshus to resolve to attain *anuttara-samyak-saṃbodhi,* Mañjuśrī Bodhisattva gradually traveled south, passing through inhabited areas until, having reached a place to the east of Dhanyākara, or Merit City, he then dwelt at the site of a great stupa temple in the Adornment Banner *Śāla* Tree Grove, a place in which buddhas of the past had dwelt as they taught beings. This was also a place where, in the past, the Bhagavat had cultivated bodhisattva practices, a place where he had been able to relinquish in

正體字

能捨無量難捨之處。是故此林。
332a04 名稱普聞無量佛剎。此處常為天龍夜叉乾
332a05 闥婆阿脩羅迦樓羅緊那羅摩睺羅伽人與非
332a06 人之所供養。時文殊師利。與其眷屬。到此處
332a07 已。即於其處。說普照法界修多羅。百萬億那
332a08 由他修多羅。以為眷屬。說此經時。於大海中。
332a09 有無量百千億諸龍。而來其所。聞此法已。深
332a10 厭龍趣。正求佛道。咸捨龍身。生天人中。一萬
332a11 諸龍。於阿耨多羅三藐三菩提。得不退轉。復
332a12 有無量無數眾生。於三乘中。各得調伏。時福
332a13 城人。聞文殊師利童子。在莊嚴幢娑羅林中
332a14 大塔廟處。無量大眾。從其城出。來詣其所。時
332a15 有優婆塞。名曰大智。與五百優婆塞眷屬俱。
332a16 所謂須達多優婆塞。婆須達多優婆塞。福德
332a17 光優婆塞。有名稱優婆塞。施名稱優婆塞。月
332a18 德優婆塞。善慧優婆塞。大慧優婆塞。賢護優
332a19 婆塞。賢勝優婆塞。如是等五百優婆塞俱。來
332a20 詣文殊師利童子所。頂禮其足。右遶三匝。退
332a21 坐一面。復有五百優婆夷。所謂大慧優婆夷。
332a22 善光優婆夷。妙身優婆夷。可樂身優婆夷。賢
332a23 優婆夷。賢德優婆夷。賢光優婆夷。幢光優婆
332a24 夷。德光優婆夷。善目優婆夷。如是等五百優
332a25 婆夷。來詣文殊師利童子所。頂禮其足。右
332a26 遶三匝。退坐一面。

简体字

能舍无量难舍之处。是故，此林名称普闻无量佛刹，此处常为天、龙、夜叉、乾闼婆、阿修罗、迦楼罗、紧那罗、摩睺罗伽、人与非人之所供养。

时，文殊师利与其眷属到此处已，即于其处说普照法界修多罗，百万亿那由他修多罗以为眷属。说此经时，于大海中有无量百千亿诸龙而来其所；闻此法已，深厌龙趣，正求佛道，咸舍龙身，生天人中。一万诸龙，于阿耨多罗三藐三菩提得不退转；复有无量无数众生，于三乘中各得调伏。

时，福城人闻文殊师利童子在庄严幢娑罗林中大塔庙处，无量大众从其城出，来诣其所。时，有优婆塞，名曰：大智，与五百优婆塞眷属俱，所谓：须达多优婆塞、婆须达多优婆塞、福德光优婆塞、有名称优婆塞、施名称优婆塞、月德优婆塞、善慧优婆塞、大慧优婆塞、贤护优婆塞、贤胜优婆塞，如是等五百优婆塞俱，来诣文殊师利童子所，顶礼其足，右绕三匝，退坐一面。复有五百优婆夷，所谓：大慧优婆夷、善光优婆夷、妙身优婆夷、可乐身优婆夷、贤优婆夷、贤德优婆夷、贤光优婆夷、幢光优婆夷、德光优婆夷、善目优婆夷，如是等五百优婆夷，来诣文殊师利童子所，顶礼其足，右绕三匝，退坐一面。

countless ways what is difficult to relinquish. It is for this reason that the fame of this grove was known everywhere in countless buddha *kṣetras*. This place is one in which offerings are always being made by devas, dragons, *yakṣas, gandharvas, asuras, garuḍas, kiṃnaras, mahoragas,* humans and nonhumans.

At that time, after Mañjuśrī and his retinue had arrived there, he then taught in this very place The Sutra on the Universal Illumination of the Dharma Realm, a sutra that had a retinue of a hundred myriads of *koṭīs* of *nayutas* of sutras. When he taught this sutra, countless hundreds of thousands of *koṭīs* of dragons living in the great ocean all came to where he was. Having heard this Dharma, they felt a deep revulsion toward the dragon rebirth destiny and sought to correctly pursue the path to buddhahood, whereupon they became able to relinquish their dragon bodies and take rebirth among devas and humans.

A myriad dragons then achieved irreversibility in their quest to gain *anuttara-samyak-saṃbodhi*. In addition, there were measurelessly and countlessly many beings who were able to receive training in the Three Vehicles.

Then, having heard that Mañjuśri the Youth was at the great stupa temple in the Adornment Banner Sāla Tree Grove, the inhabitants of Dhanyākara came forth from that city as a great congregation of countless people wishing to pay their respects where he was staying.

At that time, there was an *upāsaka* named Great Wisdom together with a retinue of five hundred other *upāsakas,* namely: Sudatta Upāsaka, Vasumitra Upāsaka, Merit Light Upāsaka, Possessed of Fame Upāsaka, Benevolence Fame Upāsaka, Moon Virtue Upāsaka, Fine Intelligence Upāsaka, Great Intelligence Upāsaka, Worthy Protector Upāsaka, Worthy Supremacy Upāsaka, and other such *upāsakas,* five hundred in all, who came to pay their respects to Mañjuśrī the Youth. They bowed down in reverence at his feet, circumambulated him three times to his right, withdrew, and then sat off to one side.

There were also five hundred *upāsikās,* namely: Great Intelligence Upāsikā, Light of Goodness Upāsikā, Marvelous Body Upāsikā, Delightful Body Upāsikā, Worthy Upāsikā, Worthy Virtue Upāsikā, Worthy Light Upāsikā, Banner Light Upāsikā, Virtue Light Upāsikā, Fine Eyes Upāsikā, and other such *upāsikās,* five hundred in all, who came to pay their respects to Mañjuśrī the Youth. They bowed down in reverence at his feet, circumambulated him three times to his right, withdrew, and then sat off to one side.

正體字

復有五百童子。所謂善財
332a27 童子。善行童子。善戒童子。善威儀童子。善勇
332a28 猛童子。善思童子。善慧童子。善覺童子。善眼
332a29 童子。善臂童子。善光童子。如是等五百童子。
332b01 來詣文殊師利童子所。頂禮其足。右遶三匝。
332b02 退坐一面。復有五百童女。所謂善賢童女。大
332b03 智居士女童女。賢稱童女。美顏童女。堅慧童
332b04 女。賢德童女。有德童女。梵授童女。德光童
332b05 女。善光童女。如是等五百童女。來詣文殊師
332b06 利童子所。頂禮其足。右遶三匝。退坐一面
332b07 爾時文殊師利童子。知福城人。悉已來集。隨
332b08 其心樂。現自在身威光赫奕。蔽諸大眾。以自
332b09 在大慈。令彼清涼。以自在大悲。起說法心。以
332b10 自在智慧。知其心樂。以廣大辯才。將為說法。
332b11 復於是時。觀察善財。以何因緣。而有其名。知
332b12 此童子初入胎時。於其宅內。自然而出七寶
332b13 樓閣。其樓閣下。有七伏藏。於其藏上。地自開
332b14 裂。生七寶[1]芽。所謂金銀瑠璃。[2]玻瓈真珠硨
332b15 磲碼碯。善財童子。處胎十月。然後誕生。形體
332b16 [3]肢分。端正具足。其七大藏。縱廣高下。各滿
332b17 七肘。從地[4]涌出。光明照[5]耀。

简体字

复有五百童子，所谓：善财童子、善行童子、善戒童子、善威仪童子、善勇猛童子、善思童子、善慧童子、善觉童子、善眼童子、善臂童子、善光童子，如是等五百童子，来诣文殊师利童子所，顶礼其足，右绕三匝，退坐一面。复有五百童女，所谓：善贤童女、大智居士女童女、贤称童女、美颜童女、坚慧童女、贤德童女、有德童女、梵授童女、德光童女、善光童女，如是等五百童女，来诣文殊师利童子所，顶礼其足，右绕三匝，退坐一面。

尔时，文殊师利童子知福城人悉已来集，随其心乐现自在身，威光赫奕蔽诸大众；以自在大慈令彼清凉，以自在大悲起说法心，以自在智慧知其心乐，以广大辩才将为说法。复于是时，观察善财以何因缘而有其名？知此童子初入胎时，于其宅内自然而出七宝楼阁，其楼阁下有七伏藏，于其藏上，地自开裂，生七宝牙，所谓：金、银、琉璃、玻璃、真珠、砗磲、玛瑙。善财童子处胎十月然后诞生，形体肢分端正具足；其七大藏，纵广高下各满七肘，从地涌出，光明照耀。

There were also five hundred youths, namely: the youth Sudhana or "Good Wealth," the youth Good Practice, the youth Good Moral Virtue, the youth Good Deportment, the youth Good Courage, the youth Good Contemplation, the youth Good Intelligence, the youth Good Awakening, the youth Good Eyes, the youth Good Arms, and the youth Good Light and other such youths, five hundred in all, who came to pay their respects to Mañjuśrī the Youth. They bowed down in reverence at his feet, circumambulated him three times to his right, withdrew, and then sat off to one side.

There were also five hundred maidens, namely: the maiden Fine Worthy who was the daughter of the householder Great Wisdom, the maiden Worthy Name, the maiden Beautiful Countenance, the maiden Solid Intelligence, the maiden Worthy Virtue, the maiden Possessed of Virtue, the maiden Brahman Legacy, the maiden Virtue Light, the maiden Good Light, and other such maidens, five hundred in all who came to pay their respects to Mañjuśrī the Youth. They bowed down in reverence at his feet, circumambulated him three times to his right, withdrew, and then sat off to one side.

At that time, Mañjuśrī the Youth, on seeing that the people of Dhanyākara had all arrived and gathered there, adapted to their dispositions by manifesting a body possessed of the sovereign masteries that emanated such awesomely splendorous light that it obscured the appearance of that great assembly. With masterful great kindness, he caused them to experience clarity and coolness. With masterful great compassion, he aroused the intention to teach the Dharma. With masterful wisdom, he knew the nature of their dispositions. And with vast eloquence, he began to teach the Dharma for them.

At this time, he also contemplated the causes and conditions by which Sudhana, "Good Wealth," came to have his name. He then perceived that: When this youth first entered the womb, a tower made of the seven precious things spontaneously emerged in his household; beneath this tower, there had been seven buried treasuries; the earth covering those treasuries spontaneously split open and sent forth sprouts of the seven precious things, namely gold, silver, *lapis lazuli*, crystal, true pearls, mother-of-pearl, and carnelian; after the youth Sudhana had dwelt in the womb for ten months, he was born with a physical form and limbs that were handsome and fully formed; his seven great treasuries, each fully seven cubits in length, width, and depth, rose up from the earth and shone with dazzling radiance; and, within that household, there spontaneously appeared five hundred

正體字

復於宅中。自然
332b18‖ 而有五百寶器。種種諸物。自然盈滿。所謂金
332b19‖ 剛器中盛一切香。於香器中盛種種衣。美玉
332b20‖ 器中盛滿種種上味飲食。摩尼器中盛滿種
332b21‖ 種殊異珍寶。金器盛銀。銀器盛金。金銀器中
332b22‖ 盛滿瑠璃及摩尼寶。[*]玻瓈器中盛滿硨磲。硨
332b23‖ 磲器中盛滿[*]玻瓈。碼碯器中盛滿真珠。真珠
332b24‖ 器中盛滿碼碯。火摩尼器中盛滿水摩尼。水
332b25‖ 摩尼器中盛滿火摩尼。如是等五百寶器。自
332b26‖ 然出現。又雨眾寶及諸財物。一切庫藏。悉令
332b27‖ 充滿。以此事故。父母親屬。及善相師。共呼此
332b28‖ 兒。名曰善財。又知此童子。已曾供養過去諸
332b29‖ 佛。深種善根。信解廣大常樂親近諸善知識。
332c01‖ 身語意業。皆無過失。淨菩薩道。求一切智。成
332c02‖ 佛法器。其心清淨。猶如虛空。迴向菩提。無所
332c03‖ 障礙。爾時文殊師利菩薩。如是觀察善財童
332c04‖ 子已。安慰開[6]諭。而為演說一切佛法。所謂
332c05‖ 說一切佛積集法。說一切佛相續法。

简体字

复于宅中自然而有五百宝器，种种诸物自然盈满，所谓：金刚器中盛一切香，于香器中盛种种衣，美玉器中盛满种种上味饮食，摩尼器中盛满种种殊异珍宝，金器盛银，银器盛金，金银器中盛满琉璃及摩尼宝，玻璃器中盛满砗磲，砗磲器中盛满玻璃，玛瑙器中盛满真珠，真珠器中盛满玛瑙，火摩尼器中盛满水摩尼，水摩尼器中盛满火摩尼，如是等五百宝器，自然出现。又雨众宝及诸财物，一切库藏悉令充满。以此事故，父母亲属及善相师共呼此儿，名曰善财。又知此童子，已曾供养过去诸佛，深种善根，信解广大，常乐亲近诸善知识，身、语、意业皆无过失，净菩萨道，求一切智，成佛法器，其心清净犹如虚空，回向菩提无所障碍。

尔时，文殊师利菩萨如是观察善财童子已，安慰开喻，而为演说一切佛法，所谓：说一切佛积集法，说一切佛相续法，

jeweled vessels which in turn were spontaneously filled to the brim with many different kinds of things. In particular, there were:

Vajra vessels filled with all kinds of incense;
Incense wood vessels filled with all different kinds of robes;
Beautiful jade vessels filled with all different kinds of supremely flavored food and drinks;
Maṇi jewel vessels filled with many different kinds of extraordinary precious jewels;
Gold vessels filled with silver;
Silver vessels filled with gold;
Gold and silver vessels filled with *lapis lazuli* and *maṇi* jewels;
Crystal vessels filled with mother-of-pearl;
Mother-of-pearl vessels filled with crystal;
Carnelian vessels filled with true pearls;
True pearl vessels filled with carnelian;
Fiery *maṇi* jewel vessels filled with water-clarifying *maṇi* jewels; and
Water-clarifying *maṇi* jewel vessels filled with fiery *maṇi* jewels.

In this way, there were five hundred jeweled vessels that spontaneously appeared while, at the same time, a rain of the many kinds of jewels sprinkled down along with all kinds of other valuables that caused all the storerooms in the house to become completely filled. Due to the occurrence of these phenomena, his parents, relatives, and fortune tellers henceforth called this child "Sudhana" or "Good Wealth." Mañjuśrī also knew of this youth:

That he already made offerings to past buddhas;
That he had deeply planted roots of goodness;
That he possessed vast resolute faith;
That he always delighted in drawing near to good spiritual guides;
That he was free of fault in all his physical, verbal, and mental actions;
That he had purified the bodhisattva path;
That he sought to acquire all-knowledge;
That he was a vessel with the capacity to attain buddhahood;
That his intentions were as pure as empty space; and
That his dedications directed toward attaining bodhi were free of any obstacles.

At that time, after Mañjuśrī Bodhisattva had contemplated Sudhana the Youth in this way, he provided him with kind and gentle instruction and expounded for his benefit on all dharmas of the buddhas, in particular:

He explained the dharma of all buddhas' accumulation;[54]
He explained the dharma of all buddhas' continuity;[55]

正體字

說一切
332c06 佛次第法。說一切佛眾會清淨法。說一切佛
332c07 法輪化導法。說一切佛色身相好法。說一切
332c08 佛法身成就法。說一切佛言辭辯才法。說一
332c09 切佛光明照[*]耀法。說一切佛平等無二法。爾
332c10 時文殊師利童子。為善財童子及諸大眾。說
332c11 此法已。慇懃勸[*]諭。增長勢力。令其歡喜。發
332c12 阿耨多羅三藐三菩提心。又令憶念過去善
332c13 根。作是事已。即於其處。復為眾生。隨宜說
332c14 法。然後而去。爾時善財童子。從文殊師利所。
332c15 聞佛如是種種功德。一心勤求阿耨多羅三
332c16 藐三菩提。隨文殊師利。而說頌曰
332c17 三有為城廓　憍慢為垣牆
332c18 諸趣為門戶　愛水為池塹
332c19 愚癡闇所覆　貪恚火熾然
332c20 魔王作君主　童蒙依止住
332c21 貪愛為徽纆　諂誑為轡勒
332c22 疑惑蔽其眼　趣入諸邪道
332c23 慳嫉憍盈故　入於三惡處
332c24 或墮諸趣中　生老病死苦

简体字

说一切佛次第法，说一切佛众会清净法，说一切佛法轮化导法，说一切佛色身相好法，说一切佛法身成就法，说一切佛言辞辩才法，说一切佛光明照耀法，说一切佛平等无二法。尔时，文殊师利童子为善财童子及诸大众说此法已，殷勤劝喻，增长势力，令其欢喜，发阿耨多罗三藐三菩提心，又令忆念过去善根；作是事已，即于其处，复为众生随宜说法，然后而去。

尔时，善财童子从文殊师利所闻佛如是种种功德，一心勤求阿耨多罗三藐三菩提，随文殊师利而说颂曰：

“三有为城郭，憍慢为垣墙，
诸趣为门户，爱水为池堑。
愚痴暗所覆，贪恚火炽然，
魔王作君主，童蒙依止住。
贪爱为徽[给-合+墨]，谄诳为辔勒，
疑惑蔽其眼，趣入诸邪道。
悭嫉憍盈故，入于三恶处，
或堕诸趣中，生老病死苦。

He explained the dharma of all buddhas' sequential appearance;
He explained the dharma of the purity of all buddhas' congregations;
He explained the dharma of all buddhas' turning of the Dharma wheel to provide teaching and guidance;
He explained the dharma of all buddhas' possession of the major marks and secondary signs;
He explained the dharma of the perfection of all buddhas' Dharma body;
He explained the dharma of all buddhas' eloquence in verbal expression;
He explained the dharma of all buddhas' brilliantly shining light; and
He explained the dharma of all buddhas' non-dual identity.

At that time, after Mañjuśrī the Youth had explained these dharmas for Sudhana the Youth and that immense congregation, he earnestly encouraged and instructed them so that they felt empowered and delighted and then resolved to attain *anuttara-samyak-saṃbodhi*. He also caused them to recall their past lives' roots of goodness. Then, having accomplished these matters, he continued to teach Dharma for those beings according to what was fitting, after which he departed.

At that time, after Sudhana the Youth had heard from Mañjuśrī about all of these many different meritorious qualities of the Buddha, he single-mindedly and diligently sought to attain *anuttara-samyak-saṃbodhi*. Then, as he followed along after Mañjuśrī, he spoke these verses:

The three realms of existence form the city's outer walls,
pride makes up its inner walls,
the rebirth destinies serve as the city's gates,
and the waters of desire fill the city's moat.

Blanketed by the darkness of delusion,
burned by the blazing flames of greed and hatred,
and taking the king of *māras* as their ruler,
the young and foolish all dwell within it.

With craving acting as the rope that binds,
flattery and deviousness serving as the bit and bridle,
and doubts covering their eyes,
they enter the paths of wrong action.

Due to the flourishing of miserliness, jealousy, and arrogance,
they enter the three wretched destinies
or fall into the other rebirth destinies
to endure the sufferings of birth, aging, sickness, and death.

正體字

332c25 | 妙智清淨日　大悲圓滿輪
332c26 | 能竭煩惱海　願賜少觀察
332c27 | 妙智清淨月　大慈無垢輪
332c28 | 一切悉施安　願垂照察我
332c29 | 一切法界王　法寶為先導
333a01 | 遊空無所礙　願垂教勅我
333a02 | 福智大商主　勇猛求菩提
333a03 | 普利諸群生　願垂守護我
333a04 | 身被忍辱甲　手提智慧劍
333a05 | 自在降魔軍　願垂拔濟我
333a06 | 住法須彌頂　定女常恭侍
333a07 | 滅惑阿脩羅　帝釋願觀我
333a08 | 三有凡愚宅　惑業地趣因
333a09 | 仁者悉調伏　如燈示我道
333a10 | 捨離諸惡趣　清淨諸善道
333a11 | 超諸世間者　示我解脫門
333a12 | 世間顛倒執　常樂我淨想
333a13 | 智眼悉能離　開我解脫門
333a14 | 善知邪正道　分別心無怯
333a15 | 一切決了人　示我菩提路

简体字

妙智清净日，大悲圆满轮，
能竭烦恼海，愿赐少观察！
妙智清净月，大慈无垢轮，
一切悉施安，愿垂照察我！
一切法界王，法宝为先导，
游空无所碍，愿垂教敕我！
福智大商主，勇猛求菩提，
普利诸群生，愿垂守护我！
身被忍辱甲，手提智慧剑，
自在降魔军，愿垂拔济我！
住法须弥顶，定女常恭侍，
灭惑阿修罗，帝释愿观我！
三有凡愚宅，惑业地趣因；
仁者悉调伏，如灯示我道！
舍离诸恶趣，清净诸善道；
超诸世间者，示我解脱门！
世间颠倒执，常乐我净想；
智眼悉能离，开我解脱门！
善知邪正道，分别心无怯；
一切决了人，示我菩提路！

May the pure sun of your sublime wisdom
and the perfectly full orb of your great compassion
be able to dry up the ocean of our afflictions.
I pray that you will devote some of your attention to this.

May the pure moon of your sublime wisdom
and the immaculate orb of your loving-kindness
be able to bestow peace on everyone.
I pray that you will let their illumination fall on me.

O King who rules over the entire Dharma realm
for whom the Dharma jewel serves as the guide
as you roam unimpeded through the sky of Dharma—
I pray you will assent to instruct me.

O great caravan leader equipped with merit and wisdom
who courageously leads the quest to attain bodhi
and everywhere bestows benefit on the many kinds of beings—
Please offer me your protection.

O you whose body has donned the armor of patience
and whose hand has raised up the sword of wisdom,
by masterfully subduing the armies of Māra,
I pray that you will assent to rescue me.

O you who dwell on the summit of the Sumeru of Dharma
and are always respectfully served by the maidens of samādhi,
may you eradicate now the *asuras* of the afflictions.
I pray, O Indra, that you will extend your regard to me.[56]

In the foolish common person's abode of the three realms of existence,
actions influenced by the afflictions are the cause of earthly destinies.
O Worthy One who bestows the training on everyone,
please, like a lamp, reveal the path to me.

O you who have left behind all the wretched destinies,
have purified all the courses of good karmic action,
and have stepped entirely beyond all worldly existences,
please show me the gateway to gain liberation.

Worldlings are held in the grasp of the inverted views,
the perceptions of permanence, pleasure, self, and purity.
O you who, with the wisdom eye, was able to abandon them all,
please open the gateway by which I may gain liberation.

O you who know well the wrong and right paths,
who distinguish between them with a fearless mind,
and who decisively understands all things,
please show me the road to the attainment of bodhi.

正體字	333a16 | 住佛正見地　長佛功德樹 333a17 | 雨佛妙法華　示我菩提道 333a18 | 去來現在佛　處處悉周遍 333a19 | 如日出世間　為我說其道 333a20 | 善知一切業　深達諸乘行 333a21 | 智慧決定人　示我摩訶衍 333a22 | 願輪大悲轂　信軸堅忍[1]鎋 333a23 | 功德寶莊校　令我載此乘 333a24 | 總持廣大箱　慈愍莊嚴蓋 333a25 | 辯才鈴[2]震響　使我載此乘 333a26 | 梵行為茵蓐　三昧為采女 333a27 | 法鼓[*]震妙音　願與我此乘 333a28 | 四攝無盡藏　功德莊嚴寶 333a29 | 慚愧為羈鞅　願與我此乘 333b01 | 常轉布施輪　恒塗淨戒香 333b02 | 忍辱牢莊嚴　令我載此乘 333b03 | 禪定三昧[3]箱　智慧方便軛 333b04 | 調伏不退轉　令我載此乘 333b05 | 大願清淨輪　總持堅固力 333b06 | 智慧所成就　令我載此乘
简体字	住佛正见地，长佛功德树， 雨佛妙法华，示我菩提道！ 去来现在佛，处处悉周遍， 如日出世间，为我说其道！ 善知一切业，深达诸乘行； 智慧决定人，示我摩诃衍！ 愿轮大悲毂，信轴坚忍辖， 功德宝庄校，令我载此乘！ 总持广大箱，慈愍庄严盖， 辩才铃震响，使我载此乘！ 梵行为茵褥，三昧为采女， 法鼓震妙音，愿与我此乘！ 四摄无尽藏，功德庄严宝， 惭愧为羁鞅，愿与我此乘！ 常转布施轮，恒涂净戒香， 忍辱牢庄严，令我载此乘！ 禅定三昧箱，智慧方便轭， 调伏不退转，令我载此乘！ 大愿清净轮，总持坚固力， 智慧所成就，令我载此乘！

O you who stand on the ground of the Buddha's right views,
who causes the tree of the Buddha's qualities to grow,
and who rains down the blossoms of the Buddha's sublime Dharma,
please show me the path to the attainment of bodhi.

The buddhas of the past, the future, and the present
who, in place after place, appear everywhere
are like the sun which rises and shines on the world.
Please explain for me the path that they have taught.

O you who know well the nature of all karmic actions,
who deeply comprehend all vehicles' practices,
and who are a man possessed of decisive wisdom,
please show me the path of the Mahāyāna's Great Vehicle.

Great compassion forms the hubs for its wheels of vows,
faith serves as its axles, solid patience acts as its linchpins,
and it is adorned with the jewels of the meritorious qualities.
Please enable me to enter this vehicle.

The complete-retention *dhāraṇīs* act as its great cargo trunk,
kindly sympathy forms its well-adorned canopy,
and the bells of eloquence resound as they shake.
Please enable me to enter this vehicle.

The *brahmacarya* is what serves as its cushions,
samādhi is what serves as its maiden attendants,
and its Dharma drum reverberates with a marvelous sound.
Please bestow this vehicle on me.

The four means of attraction are its inexhaustible treasury,
the meritorious qualities are its adorning jewels,
and a sense of shame and dread of blame are its bridle and harness.
Please bestow this vehicle on me.

It always turns the wheel of giving,
it is constantly scented with the incense of pure moral precepts,
and it is adorned with solid patience.
Please enable me to enter this vehicle.

It has a storage chest of *dhyāna* samādhi,
a yoke made of wisdom and skillful means,
and it never turns back from its training of beings.
Please enable me to enter this vehicle.

The purity of great vows serves as its wheels,
the complete-retention *dhāraṇīs* provide its enduring power,
and it is brought to completion by its possession of wisdom.
Please enable me to enter this vehicle.

正體字

333b07║ 普行為周校　悲心作徐轉
333b08║ 所向皆無怯　令我載此乘
333b09║ 堅固如金剛　善巧如幻化
333b10║ 一切無障礙　令我載此乘
333b11║ 廣大極清淨　普與眾生樂
333b12║ 虛空法界等　令我載此乘
333b13║ 淨諸業惑輪　斷諸流轉苦
333b14║ 摧魔及外道　令我載此乘
333b15║ 智慧滿十方　莊嚴遍法界
333b16║ 普洽眾生[4]類　令我載此乘
333b17║ 清淨如虛空　愛見悉除滅
333b18║ 利益一切眾　令我載此乘
333b19║ 願力速疾行　定心安隱住
333b20║ 普運諸含識　令我載此乘
333b21║ 如地不傾動　如水普饒益
333b22║ 如是運眾生　令我載此乘
333b23║ 四攝圓滿輪　總持清淨光
333b24║ 如是智慧日　願示我令見
333b25║ 已入法王[5]城　已著智王冠
333b26║ 已繫妙法繒　願[6]能慈顧我

简体字

普行为周校，悲心作徐转，
所向皆无怯，令我载此乘！
坚固如金刚，善巧如幻化，
一切无障碍，令我载此乘！
广大极清净，普与众生乐，
虚空法界等，令我载此乘！
净诸业惑轮，断诸流转苦，
摧魔及外道，令我载此乘！
智慧满十方，庄严遍法界，
普洽众生愿，令我载此乘！
清净如虚空，爱见悉除灭，
利益一切众，令我载此乘！
愿力速疾行，定心安隐住，
普运诸含识，令我载此乘！
如地不倾动，如水普饶益，
如是运众生，令我载此乘！
四摄圆满轮，总持清净光；
如是智慧日，愿示我令见！
已入法王位，已著智王冠，
已系妙法缯，愿能慈顾我！”

The practices of Samantabhadra form its pervasive adornments,[57]
the mind of compassion guides its slow rolling on,
and, wherever it goes, it is fearless.
Please enable me to enter this vehicle.

It is as solid as vajra,[58]
its skillful means are like magical conjurations,
and it is unimpeded in all things.
Please enable me to enter this vehicle.

It is vast in scope and utterly pure,
it everywhere bestows happiness on beings,
and it is equal in its range to empty space and the Dharma realm.
Please enable me to enter this vehicle.

Its wheels which purify all karma and afflictions
cut off all the sufferings of cyclic existence,
and it vanquishes *māras* and the adherents of non-Buddhist paths.
Please enable me to enter this vehicle.

Its wisdom fills up the ten directions,
its adornments pervade the Dharma realm,
and it everywhere fulfills beings' aspirations.[59]
Please enable me to enter this vehicle.

It is as pure as empty space,
it entirely extinguishes cravings and views,
and it benefits all beings.
Please enable me to enter this vehicle.

By the power of vows, it travels swiftly,
with the mind of meditative absorption, it abides securely,
and it everywhere transports all sentient beings.
Please enable me to enter this vehicle.

Like the earth itself, it does not tremble at all,
and, like water, it benefits everyone.
It is in these ways that it transports beings.
Please enable me to enter this vehicle.

The four means of attraction are its round and full orb and
the complete-retention *dhāraṇīs* create its pure radiance.
Please show me and enable me to see
a sun of wisdom like this.

O you who have already entered the city of the Dharma King,
have already donned the crown of the Wisdom King,
and have already put on the fine robes of the sublime Dharma,
I pray that you will be able to look on me with kindness.

正體字

333b27 爾時文殊師利菩薩。如象王迴。觀善財童子。
333b28 作如是言。善哉善哉。善男子。汝已發阿耨多
333b29 羅三藐三菩提心。復欲親近諸善知識。問菩
333c01 薩行。修菩薩道。善男子。親近供養諸善知識。
333c02 是具一切智。最初因緣。是故於此。勿生疲厭。
333c03 善財白言。唯願聖者。廣為我說。菩薩應云何
333c04 學菩薩行。應云何修菩薩行。應云何趣菩薩
333c05 行。應云何行菩薩行。應云何淨菩薩行。應云
333c06 何入菩薩行。應云何成就菩薩行。應云何隨
333c07 順菩薩行。應云何憶念菩薩行。應云何增廣
333c08 菩薩行。應云何令普賢行速得圓滿。爾時文
333c09 殊師利菩薩。為善財童子。而說頌言
333c10 善[7]哉功德藏　能來至我所
333c11 發起大悲心　勤求無上覺
333c12 已發廣大願　除滅眾生苦
333c13 普為諸世間　修行菩薩行
333c14 若有諸菩薩　不厭生死苦
333c15 則具普賢道　一切無能壞
333c16 福光福威力　福處福淨海

简体字

尔时，文殊师利菩萨如象王回，观善财童子，作如是言："善哉！善哉！善男子，汝已发阿耨多罗三藐三菩提心，复欲亲近诸善知识，问菩萨行，修菩萨道。善男子，亲近供养诸善知识，是具一切智最初因缘，是故于此勿生疲厌。"

善财白言："唯愿圣者广为我说，菩萨应云何学菩萨行？应云何修菩萨行？应云何趣菩萨行？应云何行菩萨行？应云何净菩萨行？应云何入菩萨行？应云何成就菩萨行？应云何随顺菩萨行？应云何忆念菩萨行？应云何增广菩萨行？应云何令普贤行速得圆满？"

尔时，文殊师利菩萨为善财童子而说颂言：

"善哉功德藏，能来至我所，
发起大悲心，勤求无上觉。
已发广大愿，除灭众生苦，
普为诸世间，修行菩萨行。
若有诸菩萨，不厌生死苦，
则具普贤道，一切无能坏。
福光福威力，福处福净海；

At that time, Mañjuśrī Bodhisattva turned around just as an elephant king turns, cast his gaze on Sudhana the Youth, and spoke thus: "Good indeed! Good indeed! Son of Good Family, you have already resolved to attain *anuttara-samyak-saṃbodhi* and also wish to draw near to the good spiritual guide to inquire about the bodhisattva practices and cultivate the bodhisattva path.

"Son of Good Family, drawing near to and making offerings to the good spiritual guide is the very first of the causes and conditions essential to achieving all-knowledge. Therefore, you must not grow weary of this."

Sudhana addressed him, saying:

I wish only that the Ārya will extensively explain for me:

How one should train in the bodhisattva practices;
How one should cultivate the bodhisattva practices;
How one should progress into the bodhisattva practices;
How one should carry out the bodhisattva practices;
How one should purify the bodhisattva practices;
How one should reach a penetrating comprehension of the bodhisattva practices;
How one should perfect the bodhisattva practices;
How one should comply with the bodhisattva practices;
How one should bear in mind the bodhisattva practices;
How one should broaden the bodhisattva practices; and
How one should bring about the swift fulfillment of Samantabhadra's practices?

Then, for the sake of Sudhana the Youth, Mañjuśrī Bodhisattva spoke these verses:

It is good indeed, O Treasury of Meritorious Qualities,
that you have been able to come to me.
You have aroused the mind of great compassion
and diligently seek the unexcelled enlightenment.

You have already made the vast vow
to extinguish the sufferings of beings
and cultivate the bodhisattva practices
for the sake of everyone in the world.

If there be any bodhisattva
who is not wearied by the sufferings of *saṃsāra*,
then he may fully accomplish Samantabhadra's path
and remain unconquered by anything.

O you light of merit, you awesome force of merit,
you abode of merit, you ocean of pure merit—

正體字

333c17 | 汝為諸眾生　願修普賢行
333c18 | 汝見無邊際　十方一切佛
333c19 | 皆悉聽聞法　受持不忘失
333c20 | 汝於十方界　普見無量佛
333c21 | 成就諸願海　具足菩薩行
333c22 | 若入方便海　安住佛菩提
333c23 | 能隨導師學　當成一切智
333c24 | 汝遍一切剎　微塵等諸劫
333c25 | 修行普賢行　成就菩提道
333c26 | 汝於無量剎　無邊諸劫海
333c27 | 修行普賢行　成滿諸大願
333c28 | 此無量眾生　聞汝願歡喜
333c29 | 皆發菩提意　願學普賢乘
334a01 | 爾時文殊師利菩薩。說此頌已。告善財童子
334a02 | 言。善哉善哉。善男子。汝已發阿耨多羅三藐
334a03 | 三菩提心。求菩薩行。善男子。若有眾生。能發
334a04 | 阿耨多羅三藐三菩提心。是事為難。能發心
334a05 | 已。求菩薩行。倍更為難。善男子。若欲成就一
334a06 | 切智智。應決定求真善知識。善男子。求善
334a07 | 知識勿生疲懈。見善知識勿生厭足。於善知
334a08 | 識所有教誨皆應隨順。於善知識善巧方便
334a09 | 勿見過失。

简体字

汝为诸众生，愿修普贤行。
汝见无边际，十方一切佛，
皆悉听闻法，受持不忘失。
汝于十方界，普见无量佛，
成就诸愿海，具足菩萨行。
若入方便海，安住佛菩提，
能随导师学，当成一切智。
汝遍一切刹，微尘等诸劫，
修行普贤行，成就菩提道。
汝于无量刹，无边诸劫海，
修行普贤行，成满诸大愿。
此无量众生，闻汝愿欢喜，
皆发菩提意，愿学普贤乘。”

尔时，文殊师利菩萨说此颂已，告善财童子言：“善哉！善哉！善男子，汝已发阿耨多罗三藐三菩提心，求菩萨行。善男子，若有众生能发阿耨多罗三藐三菩提心，是事为难；能发心已，求菩萨行，倍更为难。

“善男子，若欲成就一切智智，应决定求真善知识。善男子，求善知识勿生疲懈，见善知识勿生厌足，于善知识所有教诲皆应随顺，于善知识善巧方便勿见过失。

You have vowed to cultivate Samantabhadra's practices
for the sake of all living beings.

You will see all the boundlessly many buddhas
abiding throughout the ten directions,
will hear the Dharma proclaimed by all of them,
and will retain it all without ever forgetting it.

Throughout the ten directions,
you will everywhere see countless buddhas.
You will perfect the ocean of vows
and will completely accomplish the bodhisattva practices.

If you enter the ocean of skillful means,
if you dwell securely in the Buddha's bodhi,
and if you remain able to follow the training of the Master Guide,
you are bound to attain all-knowledge.

Throughout all the *kṣetras*
and for kalpas as numerous as their atoms,
you have cultivated Samantabhadra's practices
and have perfected the path to bodhi.

In countless *kṣetras,*
across a boundless ocean of kalpas,
you have cultivated Samantabhadra's practices
and completely fulfill all the great vows.

All of these countless beings,
on hearing of your vow, are delighted.
They all arouse the resolve to attain bodhi
and vow to train in the vehicle of Samantabhadra.

At that time, after Mañjuśrī Bodhisattva had spoken these verses, he told Sudhana the Youth, "It is good indeed, good indeed, Son of Good Family, that you have resolved to attain *anuttara-samyak-saṃbodhi* and seek the bodhisattva practices. Son of Good Family, it is a rarity for there to be any being at all who can resolve to attain *anuttara-samyak-saṃbodhi.* But to be able after having aroused the resolve to then seek the bodhisattva practices—that is doubly rare.

Son of Good Family, if one wishes to perfect the wisdom of all-knowledge, he should resolutely seek a true good spiritual guide. Son of Good Family, when searching for a good spiritual guide, one must not be overcome by weariness, and when one sees one's good spiritual guide, one must not develop a sense of self-satisfaction. One should comply with all instruction provided by the good spiritual guide. One must not find fault with any of the skillful means adopted by one's good spiritual guide.

正體字

善男子。於此南方。有一國土。名為
334a10║ 勝樂。其國有山。名曰妙峯。於彼山中。有一比
334a11║ 丘。名曰德雲。汝可往問。菩薩云何學菩薩行。
334a12║ 菩薩云何修菩薩行。乃至菩薩云何於普賢
334a13║ 行。[疲>疾]得圓滿。德雲比丘。當為汝說。爾時善財
334a14║ 童子。聞是語已。歡喜踊躍。頭頂禮足。遶無數
334a15║ 匝。慇懃瞻仰。悲泣流淚。辭退南行。向勝樂
334a16║ 國。登妙峯山。於其山上。東西南北。四維上
334a17║ 下。觀察求覓。渴仰欲見德雲比丘。經[1]于七
334a18║ 日。見彼比丘在別山上徐步經行。見已往詣。
334a19║ 頂禮其足。右遶三匝。於前而住。作如是言。聖
334a20║ 者我已先發阿耨多羅三藐三菩提心。而未知
334a21║ 菩薩云何學菩薩行。云何修菩薩行。乃至應
334a22║ 云何於普賢行疾得圓滿。我聞聖者。善能誘
334a23║ 誨。唯願垂慈。為我宣說。云何菩薩。而得成就
334a24║ 阿耨多羅三藐三菩提。時德雲比丘。告善財
334a25║ 言。善哉善哉。善男子。汝已能發阿耨多羅三
334a26║ 藐三菩提心。復能請問諸菩薩行。如是之事。
334a27║ 難中之難。所謂

简体字

"善男子，于此南方有一国土，名为胜乐；其国有山，名曰妙峰；于彼山中，有一比丘，名曰德云。汝可往问：菩萨云何学菩萨行？菩萨云何修菩萨行？乃至菩萨云何于普贤行疾得圆满？德云比丘当为汝说。"

尔时，善财童子闻是语已，欢喜踊跃，头顶礼足，绕无数匝，殷勤瞻仰，悲泣流泪。

辞退南行，向胜乐国，登妙峰山，于其山上东、西、南、北、四维、上、下观察求觅，渴仰欲见德云比丘。经于七日，见彼比丘在别山上徐步经行。见已往诣，顶礼其足，右绕三匝，于前而住，作如是言："圣者，我已先发阿耨多罗三藐三菩提心，而未知菩萨云何学菩萨行？云何修菩萨行？乃至应云何于普贤行疾得圆满？我闻圣者善能诱诲，唯愿垂慈，为我宣说：云何菩萨而得成就阿耨多罗三藐三菩提？"

时，德云比丘告善财言："善哉！善哉！善男子，汝已能发阿耨多罗三藐三菩提心，复能请问诸菩萨行。如是之事，难中之难，所谓：

Son of Good Family, south of here, there is a country known as Rāmāvarānta or 'Supreme Bliss.' There is a mountain in that land known as Sugrīvo, or 'Marvelous Peak.' On that mountain, there is a bhikshu named Meghaśrī, or 'Virtue Cloud.' You may go there and ask him how a bodhisattva trains in the bodhisattva practices, how a bodhisattva cultivates the bodhisattva practices, and so forth, including asking him how a bodhisattva may swiftly fulfill Samantabhadra's practices. Meghaśrī Bhikshu should be able to explain these matters for you."

At that time, after hearing these words, Sudhana the Youth was filled with joyous delight and exultation. He bowed down his head in reverence at Mañjuśrī's feet, circumambulated him countless times, and gazed up at him in attentive admiration as tears of sadness flowed down his countenance. He then respectfully withdrew and traveled south.

1 – Meghaśrī

[At that time, Sudhana the Youth traveled south] toward Rāmāvarānta where he climbed up Sugrīvo Mountain and looked all over that mountain, searching to the east, west, south, north, the four midpoints, above, and below, all the while feeling admiration for Meghaśrī Bhikshu and yearning to meet him. Then, after doing this for seven days, he saw that bhikshu on another mountain where he was engaged in slow walking meditation.

After seeing him, he then went there to pay his respects, bowed down in reverence at his feet, circumambulated him three times, stood before him, and said, "Oh, Ārya, I have already resolved to attain *anuttara-samyak-saṃbodhi*. However, I do not yet know how a bodhisattva should train in the bodhisattva practices, how he should cultivate the bodhisattva practices, and so forth, including how he should go about swiftly fulfilling Samantabhadra's practices. I have heard that the Ārya is well able to guide and instruct me on these matters. Please bestow your kindness on me and teach me how a bodhisattva may attain *anuttara-samyak-saṃbodhi*."

At that time, Meghaśrī Bhikshu spoke to Sudhana, saying:

It is, good indeed, good indeed, Son of Good Family, that you have been able to resolve to attain *anuttara-samyak-saṃbodhi* while also being able to inquire about the bodhisattva practices. A circumstance such as this is a rarity among rarities. This refers to:

正體字

求菩薩行。求菩薩境界。求菩
334a28 薩出離道。求菩薩清淨道。求菩薩清淨廣大
334a29 心。求菩薩成就神通。求菩薩示現解脫門。求
334b01 菩薩示現世間所作業。求菩薩隨順眾生心。
334b02 求菩薩生死涅槃門。求菩薩觀察有為無為
334b03 心無所著。善男子。我得自在決定解力。信眼
334b04 清淨。智光照曜。普觀境界。離一切障。善巧觀
334b05 察。普眼明徹。具清淨行。往詣十方一切國土。
334b06 恭敬供養一切諸佛。常念一切諸佛如來。總
334b07 持一切諸佛正法。常見一切十方諸佛。所謂
334b08 見於東方一佛二佛十佛百佛。千佛百千佛。
334b09 億佛百億佛。千億佛百千億佛。那由他億佛。
334b10 百那由他億佛。千那由他億佛。百千那由他
334b11 億佛。乃至見無數無量無邊無等。不可數不
334b12 可稱。不可思不可量。不可說。不可說不可
334b13 說佛。乃至見閻浮提微塵數佛。四天下微塵
334b14 數佛。千世界微塵數佛。二千世界微塵數佛。
334b15 三千世界微塵數佛。佛刹微塵數佛。

简体字

求菩萨行，求菩萨境界，求菩萨出离道，求菩萨清净道，求菩萨清净广大心，求菩萨成就神通，求菩萨示现解脱门，求菩萨示现世间所作业，求菩萨随顺众生心，求菩萨生死涅槃门，求菩萨观察有为、无为心无所著。

“善男子，我得自在决定解力，信眼清净，智光照耀，普观境界，离一切障，善巧观察，普眼明彻，具清净行，往诣十方一切国土，恭敬供养一切诸佛，常念一切诸佛如来，总持一切诸佛正法，常见一切十方诸佛，所谓：见于东方一佛、二佛、十佛、百佛、千佛、百千佛、亿佛、百亿佛、千亿佛、百千亿佛、那由他亿佛、百那由他亿佛、千那由他亿佛、百千那由他亿佛，乃至见无数、无量、无边、无等、不可数、不可称、不可思、不可量、不可说、不可说不可说佛，乃至见阎浮提微尘数佛、四天下微尘数佛、千世界微尘数佛、二千世界微尘数佛、三千世界微尘数佛、佛刹微尘数佛，

Seeking the bodhisattva practices;[60]
Seeking the bodhisattva's sphere of cognition;
Seeking the bodhisattva's path of transcendence;
Seeking the bodhisattva's path of purification;
Seeking the bodhisattva's purification of the vast resolve;
Seeking the bodhisattva's perfection of the spiritual superknowledges;
Seeking the bodhisattva's manifestation of the gates to liberation;
Seeking the bodhisattva's manifestation of the accomplishment of karmic works within the world;
Seeking the bodhisattva's adaptation to beings' mental dispositions;
Seeking the bodhisattva's gateways to nirvāṇa and *saṃsāra*;[61] and
Seeking the bodhisattva's contemplation of both the conditioned and the unconditioned with a mind that remains free of attachment.

Son of Good Family, having acquired mastery over the power of resolute conviction, the purified eye of faith, and the brilliantly shining light of wisdom, I everywhere contemplate all spheres of cognition, leave behind all obstacles, skillfully contemplate with the brightly penetrating and universally seeing eye, and embody the pure practices. I travel to pay my respects in all lands throughout the ten directions where I reverently make offerings to all buddhas. Remaining ever mindful of all the buddhas, the *tathāgatas*, and comprehensively upholding all buddhas' right Dharma, I always see all buddhas throughout the ten directions. That is to say, off to the east, I see one buddha, two buddhas, ten buddhas, a hundred buddhas, a thousand buddhas, a hundred thousand buddhas, a *koṭī* of buddhas, a hundred *koṭīs* of buddhas, a thousand *koṭīs* of buddhas, a hundred thousand *koṭīs* of buddhas, a *nayuta* of *koṭīs* of buddhas, a hundred *nayutas* of *koṭīs* of buddhas, a thousand *nayutas* of *koṭīs* of buddhas, a hundred thousand *nayutas* of *koṭīs* of buddhas, and so forth until we come to my seeing numberlessly many, measurelessly many, boundlessly many, incomparably many, innumerably many, indescribably many, inconceivably many, immeasurably many, ineffably many, and ineffably-ineffably many buddhas, and so forth until we come to my seeing buddhas as numerous as all the atoms on the continent of Jambudvīpa, buddhas as numerous as the atoms on all four continents, buddhas as numerous as the atoms in a thousand worlds, buddhas as numerous as the atoms in two thousand worlds, buddhas as numerous as the atoms in three thousand worlds, buddhas as numerous as the atoms in a buddha *kṣetra*, and

正體字

乃至不
334b16 可說不可說佛剎微塵數佛。如東方。南西北
334b17 方。四維上下。亦復如是。一一方中。所有諸
334b18 佛。種種色相。種種形貌。種種神通。種種遊
334b19 戲。種種眾會莊嚴道場。種種光明無邊照
334b20 [*]耀。種種國土。種種壽命隨諸眾生。種種心
334b21 樂示現種種成正覺門。於大眾中。而師子吼。
334b22 善男子我唯得此憶念一切諸佛境界智慧光
334b23 明普見法門。豈能了知諸大菩薩無邊智慧
334b24 清淨行門。所謂智光普照念佛門。常見一切
334b25 諸佛國土種種宮殿。悉嚴淨故。令一切眾生
334b26 念佛門。隨諸眾生心之所樂。皆令見佛。得
334b27 清淨故。令安住力念佛門。令入如來十力中
334b28 故。令安住法念佛門。見無量佛。聽聞法故。照
334b29 [*]耀諸方念佛門。悉見一切諸世界中。等無
334c01 差別諸佛海故。入不可見處念佛門。悉見一
334c02 切微細境中。諸佛自在。神通事故。住於諸劫
334c03 念佛門。

简体字

乃至不可说不可说佛刹微尘数佛；如东方，南、西、北方，四维、上、下，亦复如是。一一方中所有诸佛，种种色相、种种形貌、种种神通、种种游戏、种种众会庄严道场、种种光明无边照耀、种种国土、种种寿命，随诸众生种种心乐，示现种种成正觉门，于大众中而师子吼。

“善男子，我唯得此忆念一切诸佛境界智慧光明普见法门，岂能了知诸大菩萨无边智慧清净行门？所谓：智光普照念佛门，常见一切诸佛国土种种宫殿悉严净故；令一切众生念佛门，随诸众生心之所乐，皆令见佛得清净故；令安住力念佛门，令入如来十力中故；令安住法念佛门，见无量佛，听闻法故；照耀诸方念佛门，悉见一切诸世界中等无差别诸佛海故；入不可见处念佛门，悉见一切微细境中诸佛自在神通事故；住于诸劫念佛门，

so forth until we come to my seeing buddhas as numerous as the atoms in an ineffable-ineffable number of buddha *kṣetras*.[62]

And just as it is in the east, so too it is in the south, west, and north, in the four midpoints, and in the zenith and the nadir where, in every one of those regions, I see all of those buddhas' many different forms and characteristic signs, many different appearances, many different spiritual superknowledges, many different ways in which they freely wander at will, many different variously adorned congregations, many different forms of boundlessly illuminating brilliant radiance, many different lands, many different life spans, and many different manifestations of gateways to achieving right enlightenment adapted to beings' many different kinds of mental dispositions as, in all those circumstances, they roar the lion's roar in the midst of their immense congregations.

Son of Good Family, I have acquired only this Dharma gateway of the universal vision with which I bear in mind all buddha's spheres of cognition and light of wisdom. How then could I completely know the boundless wisdom and gateways of pure practice that are possessed by all the great bodhisattvas, namely:

[Those who have attained] the mindfulness-of-the-Buddha gateway of "universal illumination with the light of wisdom" by which they always see the many different kinds of palaces in the buddha lands of all buddhas, all of which are purified;

[Those who have attained] the mindfulness-of-the-Buddha gateway of "enabling all beings" by which they adapt to all beings' mental dispositions and enable them all to see the Buddha and attain purity;

[Those who have attained] the mindfulness-of-the-Buddha gateway of "enabling secure establishment in the powers" by which they are caused to enter the ten powers of the Tathāgata;

[Those who have attained] the mindfulness-of-the-Buddha gateway of "enabling secure establishment in the Dharma" by which they see countless buddhas and hear the Dharma;

[Those who have attained] the mindfulness-of-the-Buddha gateway of "the brilliant illumination of all regions" by which they see in all worlds the ocean of all buddhas who are all the same and no different;

[Those who have attained] the mindfulness-of-the-Buddha gateway of "entry into the invisible regions" by which they see all buddhas' masterful feats of the spiritual powers in even the tiniest spheres of objective experience;

[Those who have attained] the mindfulness-of-the-Buddha gateway of "abiding in all kalpas" by which they always see in all

正體字

一切劫中。常見如來諸所施為。無暫
334c04‖ 捨故。住一切時念佛門。於一切時。常見如來。
334c05‖ 親近同住。不捨離故。住一切剎念佛門。一切
334c06‖ 國土。咸見佛身。超過一切無與等故。住一切
334c07‖ 世念佛門。隨於自心之所欲樂。普見三世諸
334c08‖ 如來故。住一切境念佛門。普於一切諸境界
334c09‖ 中。見諸如來次第現故。住寂滅念佛門。於一
334c10‖ 念中。見一切剎。一切諸佛。示涅槃故。住遠離
334c11‖ 念佛門。於一[2]日中。見一切佛。從其所住。而
334c12‖ 出去故。住廣大念佛門。心常觀察一一佛身。
334c13‖ 充遍一切諸法界故。住微細念佛門。於一毛
334c14‖ 端。有不可說如來出現。悉至其所。而承事故。
334c15‖ 住莊嚴念佛門。於一念中。見一切剎。皆有諸
334c16‖ 佛成等正覺。現神變故。住能事念佛門。見一
334c17‖ 切佛出現世間。放智慧光。轉法輪故。

简体字

一切劫中常见如来诸所施为无暂舍故；住一切时念佛门，于一切时常见如来，亲近同住不舍离故；住一切刹念佛门，一切国土咸见佛身超过一切无与等故；住一切世念佛门，随于自心之所欲乐普见三世诸如来故；住一切境念佛门，普于一切诸境界中见诸如来次第现故；住寂灭念佛门，于一念中见一切刹一切诸佛示涅槃故；住远离念佛门，于一念中见一切佛从其所住而出去故；住广大念佛门，心常观察一一佛身充遍一切诸法界故；住微细念佛门，于一毛端有不可说如来出现，悉至其所而承事故；住庄严念佛门，于一念中见一切刹皆有诸佛成等正觉现神变故；住能事念佛门，见一切佛出现世间放智慧光转法轮故；

kalpas all of the endeavors of the Tathāgata and never even briefly lose sight of them;

[Those who have attained] the mindfulness-of-the-Buddha gateway of "dwelling at all times" by which they always see the *tathāgatas* at all times, draw near to them, and never separate from them;

[Those who have attained] the mindfulness-of-the-Buddha gateway of "abiding in every *kṣetra*" by which, in all lands, they see the buddhas' peerless bodies which surpass all others;

[Those who have attained] the mindfulness-of-the-Buddha gateway of "abiding in all periods of time" by which, in accordance with their own mental dispositions, they everywhere see all *tathāgathas* of the three periods of time;

[Those who have attained] the mindfulness-of-the-Buddha gateway of "abiding in all objective spheres" by which they see in all spheres of experience all *tathāgatas'* sequential appearance in the world;

[Those who have attained] the mindfulness-of-the-Buddha gateway of "abiding in quiescence" by which, in one mind-moment, they see in all *kṣetras* all buddhas' manifesting entry into nirvāṇa;

[Those who have attained] the mindfulness-of-the-Buddha gateway of "abiding in detachment" by which, in one day, they see all buddhas leaving their abodes;

[Those who have attained] the mindfulness-of-the-Buddha gateway of "abiding in vastness" by which their minds always contemplate the bodies of every buddha filling up and pervading the entire Dharma realm;

[Those who have attained] the mindfulness-of-the-Buddha gateway of "abiding in the extremely minute" by which they see that, even on the tip of one hair, there are an ineffable number of *tathāgatas* appearing in the world, whereupon they go to wherever they are dwelling to serve them;

[Those who have attained] the mindfulness-of-the-Buddha gateway of "abiding in adornments" by which, in one mind-moment, they see that all *kṣetras* have buddhas attaining the universal and right enlightenment and manifesting spiritual transformations;

[Those who have attained] the mindfulness-of-the-Buddha gateway of "abiding of the capacity to serve" by which they see all buddhas appearing in the world, emanating the light of wisdom, and turning the wheel of the Dharma.

正體字

住自在
334c18║ 心念佛門。知隨自心所有欲樂。一切諸佛。現
334c19║ 其像故。住自業念佛門。知隨眾生所積集業。
334c20║ 現其影像。令覺悟故。住神變念佛門。見佛所
334c21║ 坐廣大蓮華。周遍法界。而開敷故。住虛空念
334c22║ 佛門。觀察如來所有身雲。莊嚴法界虛空界
334c23║ 故。而我云何能知能說彼功德行。善男子。南
334c24║ 方有國。名曰海門。彼有比丘。名為海雲。汝往
334c25║ 彼問。菩薩云何學菩薩行。修菩薩道。海雲
334c26║ 比丘。能分別說發起廣大善根因緣。善男子。
334c27║ 海雲比丘。當令汝入廣大助道位。當令汝生
334c28║ 廣大善根力。當為汝說發菩提心因。當令汝
334c29║ 生廣大乘光明。當令汝修廣大波羅蜜。當令
335a01║ 汝入廣大諸行海。當令汝滿廣大誓願輪。當
335a02║ 令汝淨廣大莊嚴門。當令汝生廣大慈悲力。
335a03║ 時善財童子。禮德雲比丘足。右遶觀察。辭退
335a04║ 而去

简体字

住自在心念佛门，知随自心所有欲乐，一切诸佛现其像故；住自业念佛门，知随众生所积集业，现其影像令觉悟故；住神变念佛门，见佛所坐广大莲华周遍法界而开敷故；住虚空念佛门，观察如来所有身云庄严法界、虚空界故。而我云何能知能说彼功德行？

“善男子，南方有国，名曰海门；彼有比丘，名为海云。汝往彼问：‘菩萨云何学菩萨行、修菩萨道？’海云比丘能分别说发起广大善根因缘。善男子，海云比丘当令汝入广大助道位，当令汝生广大善根力，当为汝说发菩提心因，当令汝生广大乘光明，当令汝修广大波罗蜜，当令汝入广大诸行海，当令汝满广大誓愿轮，当令汝净广大庄严门，当令汝生广大慈悲力。”

时，善财童子礼德云比丘足，右绕观察，辞退而去。

[Those who have attained] the mindfulness-of-the-Buddha gateway of "abiding in the mind of sovereign mastery" by which they realize that all buddhas may manifest their appearances in ways adapted to one's own mental dispositions;

[Those who have attained] the mindfulness-of-the-Buddha gateway of "abiding in individual karma" by which they realize that, in order to enable them to awaken, they may manifest mirroring appearances corresponding to beings' accumulated karma;

[Those who have attained] the mindfulness-of-the-Buddha gateway of "abiding in spiritual transformations" by which they see the vast lotus flower on which the Buddha sits pervading the Dharma realm and then fully blooming; and

[Those who have attained] the mindfulness-of-the-Buddha gateway of "abiding in empty space" by which they contemplate the cloud of all the Tathāgata's bodies that adorn the Dharma realm and the realm of empty space?

How could I know of or be able to speak about their meritorious qualities and practices?

Son of Good Family, in a country to the south of here known as Sāgaramukha or "Ocean Gateway," there is a bhikshu known as Sāgaramegha or "Ocean Cloud." You should go to him and ask him, "How should the bodhisattva train in the bodhisattva practices and how should he cultivate the bodhisattva path?" Sāgaramegha Bhikshu will be able to distinguish and explain the causes and conditions for developing vast roots of goodness. Son of Good Family, Sāgaramegha Bhikshu:

Will enable you to enter the vast ground of the provisions for enlightenment;

Will enable you to develop the power of vast roots of goodness;

Will explain for you the causes for resolving to attain bodhi;

Will enable you to produce the light of the vast vehicle;

Will enable you to cultivate the vast *pāramitās*;

Will enable you to enter vast ocean of practices;

Will enable you to fulfill the vast sphere of vows;

Will enable you to purify the gateway to vast adornments; and

Will enable you to develop the power of vast kindness and compassion.

At that time, Sudhana the Youth bowed down in reverence at the feet of Meghaśrī Bhikshu and circumambulated him to his right as he gazed up at him. He then respectfully withdrew and departed.

正體字

335a05║ 爾時善財童子。一心思惟善知識教。正念觀
335a06║ 察智慧光明門。正念觀察菩薩解脫門。正念
335a07║ 觀察菩薩三昧門。正念觀察菩薩大海門。正
335a08║ 念觀察諸佛現前門。正念觀察諸佛方所門。
335a09║ 正念觀察諸佛軌則門。正念觀察諸佛等虛
335a10║ 空界門。正念觀察諸佛出現次第門。正念觀
335a11║ 察諸佛所入方便門。漸次南行。至海門國。向
335a12║ 海雲比丘所。頂禮其足。右遶畢[1]已。於前合
335a13║ 掌。作如是言。聖者。我已先發阿耨多羅三藐
335a14║ 三菩提心。欲入一切無上智海。而未知菩薩
335a15║ 云何能捨世俗家生如來家。云何能度生死
335a16║ 海入佛智海。云何能離凡夫地入如來地。云
335a17║ 何能斷生死流入菩薩行流。

简体字

尔时，善财童子一心思惟善知识教，正念观察智慧光明门，正念观察菩萨解脱门，正念观察菩萨三昧门，正念观察菩萨大海门，正念观察诸佛现前门，正念观察诸佛方所门，正念观察诸佛轨则门，正念观察诸佛等虚空界门，正念观察诸佛出现次第门，正念观察诸佛所入方便门。

渐次南行，至海门国，向海云比丘所顶礼其足，右绕毕，于前合掌，作如是言："圣者，我已先发阿耨多罗三藐三菩提心，欲入一切无上智海，而未知菩萨云何能舍世俗家，生如来家？云何能度生死海，入佛智海？云何能离凡夫地，入如来地？云何能断生死流，入菩萨行流？

2 – Sāgaramegha

At that time, Sudhana the Youth single-mindedly reflected on the teachings of the good spiritual guide:

He contemplated with right mindfulness the gateways of the light of wisdom;

He contemplated with right mindfulness the gateways of the bodhisattva liberations;

He contemplated with right mindfulness the gateways of the bodhisattva samādhis;

He contemplated with right mindfulness the gateways of the bodhisattvas [which were like] a great ocean;[63]

He contemplated with right mindfulness the gateways of all buddhas' direct manifestations;

He contemplated with right mindfulness the gateways of all buddhas' locations in the [ten] directions;[64]

He contemplated with right mindfulness the gateways of all buddhas' guiding regulations and principles;

He contemplated with right mindfulness the gateways of all buddhas' co-extensiveness with the realm of empty space;

He contemplated with right mindfulness the gateways of all buddhas' successive appearance [in the world]; and

He contemplated with right mindfulness the gateways of skillful means that all buddhas enter.

He then traveled gradually toward the south until he reached the country of Sāgaramukha where he went to the abode of Sāgaramegha Bhikshu and bowed down in reverence at his feet. After circumambulating him, with palms pressed together, he addressed him with words such as these: "O Ārya, I have already resolved to attain *anuttara-samyak-saṃbodhi*. I wish to enter the ocean of unexcelled knowledge. However, I do not yet know with regard to the bodhisattva:

How can one leave behind one's worldly lineage and acquire birth into the lineage of the Tathāgata?

How can one cross beyond the ocean of *saṃsāra* and enter the ocean of the Buddha's knowledge?

How can one leave the ground of the common person and enter the ground of the Tathāgata?

How can one cut off the stream of *saṃsāra* and enter the stream of the bodhisattva practices?

正體字

云何能破生死
335a18‖ 輪成菩薩願輪。云何能滅魔境界顯佛境界。
335a19‖ 云何能竭愛欲海長大悲海。云何能閉眾難
335a20‖ 惡趣門開諸[2]天涅槃門。云何能出三界城入
335a21‖ 一切智城。云何能棄捨一切玩好之物悉以
335a22‖ 饒益一切眾生。時海雲比丘。告善財言。善男
335a23‖ 子。汝已發阿耨多羅三藐三菩提心耶。善財
335a24‖ 言唯。我已先發阿耨多羅三藐三菩提心。海
335a25‖ 雲言。善男子。若諸眾生。不種善根。則不能發
335a26‖ 阿耨多羅三藐三菩提心。要得普門善根光
335a27‖ 明。具真實道三昧智光。出生種種廣大福海。
335a28‖ 長白淨法無有懈息。事善知識不生疲厭。不
335a29‖ 顧身命無所藏積。等心如地無有高下。性常
335b01‖ 慈愍一切眾生。於諸有趣。專念不捨。恒樂
335b02‖ 觀察如來境界。如是乃能發菩提心。發菩提
335b03‖ 心者。所謂發大悲心。普救一切眾生故。

简体字

云何能破生死轮，成菩萨愿轮？云何能灭魔境界，显佛境界？云何能竭爱欲海，长大悲海？云何能闭众难恶趣门，开诸大涅槃门？云何能出三界城，入一切智城？云何能弃舍一切玩好之物，悉以饶益一切众生？”

时，海云比丘告善财言：“善男子，汝已发阿耨多罗三藐三菩提心耶？”

善财言：“唯！我已先发阿耨多罗三藐三菩提心。”

海云言：“善男子，若诸众生不种善根，则不能发阿耨多罗三藐三菩提心。要得普门善根光明，具真实道三昧智光，出生种种广大福海，长白净法无有懈息，事善知识不生疲厌，不顾身命无所藏积，等心如地无有高下，性常慈愍一切众生，于诸有趣专念不舍，恒乐观察如来境界，如是乃能发菩提心。

“发菩提心者，所谓：发大悲心，普救一切众生故；

How can one demolish the wheel of *saṃsāra* and perfect the wheel of the bodhisattva vows?
How can one demolish the realms of Māra and manifest the realms of the Buddha?
How can one dry up the ocean of desire and increase the ocean of the great compassion?
How can one close the gates of the manifold difficulties and the wretched rebirth destinies and open the gates to the heavens and nirvāṇa?
How can one escape from the city of the three realms of existence and enter the city of all-knowledge?
And how can one relinquish all objects of enjoyment and use them to greatly benefit all beings?

Then Sāgaramegha Bhikshu spoke to Sudhana, saying, "Son of Good Family, have you already resolved to attain *anuttara-samyak-saṃbodhi*?"

Sudhana replied, "Yes, I have already resolved to attain *anuttara-samyak-saṃbodhi*."

Sāgaramegha then said:

Son of Good Family, if beings have failed to plant roots of goodness, then they will be unable to resolve to attain *anuttara-samyak-saṃbodhi*. Hence it is essential:

To acquire the universal gateway of the light of roots of goodness;
To acquire the light of the true path's samādhi and wisdom;
To produce a vast ocean of many different kinds of merit;
To incessantly increase the white dharmas of pristine purity;
To tirelessly serve the good spiritual guide;
To not be concerned for one's own body or life and not hoard anything;
To have nothing that one stores up on one's own behalf;
To maintain a mind that is as equanimous as the earth and that regards no one as either above or below one;
To be inclined by nature to always regard all beings with kindness and sympathy;
To remain attentively mindful of and never forsake those in any of the rebirth destinies in any of the realms of existence; and
To constantly delight in contemplating the realm of the Tathāgata.

If one proceeds in this manner, only then can one bring forth the resolve to attain bodhi. By "bringing forth the resolve to attain bodhi," I refer to the following:

Bringing forth the mind of great compassion with which one rescues all beings everywhere;

正體字

發大
335b04‖ 慈心。等祐一切世間故。發安樂心。令一切
335b05‖ 眾生滅諸苦故。發饒益心。令一切眾生離惡
335b06‖ 法故。發哀愍心。有怖畏者。咸守護故。發無礙
335b07‖ 心。捨離一切。諸障礙故。發廣大心。一切法
335b08‖ 界。咸遍滿故。發無邊心。等虛空界。無不往
335b09‖ 故。發寬博心。悉見一切諸如來故。發清淨心。
335b10‖ 於三世法。智無違故。發智慧心。普入一切智
335b11‖ 慧海故。善男子。我住此海門國。十有二年。常
335b12‖ 以大海。為其境界。所謂思惟大海廣大無量。
335b13‖ 思惟大海甚深難測。思惟大海漸次深廣。思
335b14‖ 惟大海無量眾寶奇妙莊嚴。思惟大海積無
335b15‖ 量水。思惟大海水色不同不可思議。思惟大
335b16‖ 海無量眾生之所住處。思惟大海容受種種大
335b17‖ 身眾生。思惟大海能受大雲所雨之雨。思惟
335b18‖ 大海無增無減。

简体字

发大慈心，等祐一切世间故；发安乐心，令一切众生灭诸苦故；发饶益心，令一切众生离恶法故；发哀愍心，有怖畏者咸守护故；发无碍心，舍离一切诸障碍故；发广大心，一切法界咸遍满故；发无边心，等虚空界无不往故；发宽博心，悉见一切诸如来故；发清净心，于三世法智无违故；发智慧心，普入一切智慧海故。

“善男子，我住此海门国十有二年，常以大海为其境界，所谓：思惟大海广大无量，思惟大海甚深难测，思惟大海渐次深广，思惟大海无量众宝奇妙庄严，思惟大海积无量水，思惟大海水色不同不可思议，思惟大海无量众生之所住处，思惟大海容受种种大身众生，思惟大海能受大云所雨之雨，思惟大海无增无减。

Bringing forth the mind of great kindness with which one equally protects everyone in all worlds;

Bringing forth the blissful mind with which one causes all beings to extinguish all their sufferings;

Bringing forth the beneficent mind with which one causes all beings to abandon evil dharmas;

Bringing forth the sympathetic mind with which, wherever there are those beset with fear, one protects them all;

Bringing forth the unimpeded mind with which one abandons all obstacles;

Bringing forth the vast mind with which one completely pervades the entire Dharma realm;

Bringing forth the boundless mind commensurate with the realm of empty space with which there is no place one does not go;

Bringing forth the expansive mind with which one sees all *tathāgatas*;

Bringing forth the pure mind with which one's knowledge does not oppose any dharmas of the three periods of time; and

Bringing forth the mind of wisdom with which one everywhere enters the ocean of all-knowledge.

Son of Good Family, I have dwelt in this country of Sāgaramukha for twelve years during which I have always taken the great ocean as my object of contemplation. In particular, I refer to the following:

I have contemplated the great ocean as measurelessly vast;

I have contemplated the great ocean as extremely deep and difficult to fathom;

I have contemplated the great ocean as becoming gradually more deep and vast;

I have contemplated the great ocean as adorned with countless extraordinary and marvelous jewels;

I have contemplated the great ocean as having accumulated a measureless amount of water;

I have contemplated the great ocean's waters as having inconceivably many different colorations;

I have contemplated the great ocean as the dwelling place for countless creatures;

I have contemplated the great ocean as containing many different kinds of large-bodied creatures;

I have contemplated the great ocean as able to take in the rains sent down by immense clouds; and

I have contemplated the great ocean as neither increasing nor decreasing.

正體字

善男子。我思惟時。復作是念。
335b19║ 世間之中。頗有廣博過此海不。頗有無量過
335b20║ 此海不。頗有甚深過此海不。頗有殊特過此
335b21║ 海不。善男子。我作是念時。此海之下。有大蓮
335b22║ 華。忽然出現。以無能勝因陀羅尼羅寶為莖。
335b23║ [3]吠瑠璃寶為[4]藏。閻浮檀金為葉。沈水為臺。
335b24║ 碼碯為鬚。芬敷布[5]濩。彌覆大海。百萬阿脩
335b25║ 羅王執持其莖。百萬摩尼寶莊嚴網彌覆其
335b26║ 上。百萬龍王雨以香水。百萬迦樓羅王[6]銜諸
335b27║ 瓔珞及寶繒帶周匝垂下。百萬羅剎王慈心
335b28║ 觀察。百萬夜叉王恭敬禮拜。百萬乾闥婆王
335b29║ 種種音樂讚歎供養。百萬天王雨諸天華。天
335c01║ 鬘天香。天燒香。天塗香。天末香。天妙衣服。
335c02║ 天幢幡蓋。百萬梵王頭頂禮敬。百萬淨居
335c03║ 天合掌作禮。百萬轉輪王各以七寶莊嚴供
335c04║ 養。百萬海神俱時出現恭敬頂禮。百萬味光
335c05║ 摩尼寶光明普照。

简体字

“善男子，我思惟时，复作是念：‘世间之中，颇有广博过此海不？颇有无量过此海不？颇有甚深过此海不？颇有殊特过此海不？’

“善男子，我作是念时，此海之下，有大莲华忽然出现，以无能胜因陀罗尼罗宝为茎，吠琉璃宝为藏，阎浮檀金为叶，沉水为台，玛瑙为须，芬敷布濩，弥覆大海。百万阿修罗王执持其茎，百万摩尼宝庄严网弥覆其上，百万龙王雨以香水，百万迦楼罗王衔诸璎珞及宝缯带周匝垂下，百万罗刹王慈心观察，百万夜叉王恭敬礼拜，百万乾闼婆王种种音乐赞叹供养，百万天王雨诸天华，天鬘、天香、天烧香、天涂香、天末香、天妙衣服、天幢幡盖，百万梵王头顶礼敬，百万净居天合掌作礼，百万转轮王各以七宝庄严供养，百万海神俱时出现恭敬顶礼，百万味光摩尼宝光明普照，

Son of Good Family, as I was engaged in these contemplations, I also had these thoughts regarding what exists in the world:

Could there be anything that surpasses this ocean in its vastness, or not?

Could there be anything that surpasses this ocean in its measurelessness, or not?

Could there be anything that surpasses this ocean in its depth, or not?

And could there be anything that surpasses this ocean in its extraordinariness, or not?

Son of Good Family, as I was pondering these thoughts, an immense lotus flower suddenly emerged from the depths of this ocean. It had a stem made of unexcelled *indranīla* sapphires,[65] a seed pod made of *vaiḍūrya* gems, petals made of *jambūnada* gold, a dais made of *kālaguru* incense, and stamens made of emeralds. Releasing its fragrance, it blossomed fully, spreading out over the great ocean.

A hundred myriad *asura* kings supported its stem.

A hundred myriad *maṇi* jewels formed an adorning net canopy that spread out over it from above.

A hundred myriad dragon kings rained down fragrant waters.

A hundred myriad *garuḍa* kings held in their beaks pearl strands and jeweled silken sashes that draped down and encircled it.

A hundred myriad *rākṣasa* kings looked on with minds imbued with loving-kindness.

A hundred myriad *yakṣa* kings bowed down in reverence.

A hundred myriad *gandharva* kings played many different kinds of musical praises as offerings.

A hundred myriad heavenly kings rained down heavenly flowers, heavenly garlands, heavenly incense, heavenly burning incense, heavenly perfume, heavenly powdered incense, and marvelous heavenly robes as well as heavenly banners, pennants, and canopies.

A hundred myriad Brahma Heaven kings bowed down in reverence.

A hundred myriad devas from the Pure Abodes pressed their palms together in reverence.

A hundred myriad wheel-turning kings each made offerings of seven-jeweled adornments.

A hundred myriad ocean spirits simultaneously appeared and bowed down in reverence.

A hundred myriad delectable-light *maṇi* jewels shone forth with universal illumination.

正體字

百萬淨福摩尼寶以為莊
335c06║ 嚴。百萬普光摩尼寶為清淨藏。百萬殊勝摩
335c07║ 尼寶其光赫奕。百萬妙藏摩尼寶光照無邊。
335c08║ 百萬閻浮幢摩尼寶次第行列。百萬金剛師
335c09║ 子摩尼寶不可破壞清淨莊嚴。百萬日藏摩
335c10║ 尼寶廣大清淨。百萬可樂摩尼寶具種種色。
335c11║ 百萬如意摩尼寶莊嚴無盡。光明照[＊]耀此大
335c12║ 蓮華。如來出世。善根所起。一切菩薩。皆生信
335c13║ 樂。十方世界。無不現前。從如幻法生。如夢法
335c14║ 生。清淨業生。無諍法門之所莊嚴。入無為
335c15║ 印。住無礙門。充滿十方一切國土。隨順諸佛
335c16║ 甚深境界。於無數百千劫。歎其功德。不可得
335c17║ 盡。我時見彼蓮華之上。有一如來。結[7]跏趺
335c18║ 坐。其身從此上至有頂寶蓮華座不可思議
335c19║ 道場眾會不可思議。諸相成就不可思議。隨
335c20║ 好圓滿不可思議。神通變化不可思議。色相
335c21║ 清淨不可思議。無見頂相不可思議。廣長舌
335c22║ 相不可思議。

简体字

百万净福摩尼宝以为庄严，百万普光摩尼宝为清净藏，百万殊胜摩尼宝其光赫奕，百万妙藏摩尼宝光照无边，百万阎浮幢摩尼宝次第行列，百万金刚师子摩尼宝不可破坏清净庄严，百万日藏摩尼宝广大清净，百万可乐摩尼宝具种种色，百万如意摩尼宝庄严无尽光明照耀。此大莲华，如来出世善根所起，一切菩萨皆生信乐，十方世界无不现前，从如幻法生、如梦法生、清净业生，无诤法门之所庄严，入无为印，住无碍门，充满十方一切国土，随顺诸佛甚深境界，于无数百千劫叹其功德不可得尽。

“我时见彼莲华之上，有一如来结跏趺坐，其身从此上至有顶。宝莲华座不可思议，道场众会不可思议，诸相成就不可思议，随好圆满不可思议，神通变化不可思议，色相清净不可思议，无见顶相不可思议，广长舌相不可思议，

A hundred myriad pure-merit *maṇi* jewels served as adornments.

A hundred myriad universal-radiance *maṇi* jewels formed a pure treasury.

A hundred myriad especially superior *maṇi* jewels shone with resplendent radiance.

A hundred myriad marvelous-core *maṇi* jewels shone with boundless illumination.

A hundred myriad *jambu*-banner *maṇi* jewels were arrayed in sequential rows.

A hundred myriad vajra lion *maṇi* jewels served as indestructible and immaculate adornments.

A hundred myriad solar-core *maṇi* jewels provided a vast display of purity.

A hundred myriad delightful *maṇi* jewels contained many different colorations.

And a hundred myriad wish-fulfilling *maṇi* jewels formed an endless array of adornments that shone with dazzling radiance.

This immense lotus flower arising through the power of the Tathāgata's roots of world-transcending goodness inspired faith and delight in all the bodhisattvas. It was born from the illusory nature of dharmas, was born from the dream-like nature of dharmas, and was born from pure karma. It was adorned by the dharma gateway of noncontentiousness, penetrated the seal of the unconditioned, and dwelt within the gateway of the unimpeded.

It completely filled all lands of the ten directions and accorded with the extremely deep realm of all buddhas. Even if one praised its qualities for countless hundreds of thousands of kalpas, one could still never come to the end of them.

At that time, I saw that atop that lotus flower there was:

A *tathāgata* seated in the lotus posture whose body extended from here up to the peak of existence;

His inconceivable jeweled lotus flower throne;

His inconceivable congregation at the site of enlightenment;

His inconceivable and completely perfected major marks;

His inconceivable perfectly fulfilled secondary signs;

His inconceivable transformations produced by the spiritual superknowledges;

His inconceivable pure form and appearance;

His inconceivable summit mark the peak of which none could ever see;

His inconceivable mark of the vast and long tongue;

正體字

善巧言說不可思議。圓滿音聲
335c23‖ 不可思議。無邊際力不可思議。清淨無畏不
335c24‖ 可思議。廣大辯才不可思議。又念彼佛往修
335c25‖ 諸行不可思議。自在成道不可思議。妙音演
335c26‖ 法不可思議。普門示現種種莊嚴不可思議。
335c27‖ 隨其左右見各差別不可思議。一切利益皆
335c28‖ 令圓滿不可思議。時此如來。即伸右手。而
335c29‖ 摩我頂。為我演說普眼法門。開示一切如來
336a01‖ 境界。顯發一切菩薩諸行。闡明一切諸佛妙
336a02‖ 法。一切法輪。悉入其中。能淨一切諸佛國土。
336a03‖ 能摧一切異道邪論。能滅一切諸魔軍眾。能
336a04‖ 令眾生。皆生歡喜。能照一切眾生心行。能了
336a05‖ 一切眾生諸根。隨眾生心。悉令開悟。我從於
336a06‖ 彼如來之所聞此法門。受持讀誦。憶念觀察。
336a07‖ 假使有人。以大海量墨。須彌聚筆。書寫於此
336a08‖ 普眼法門。一品中一門。一門中一法。一法
336a09‖ 中一義。一義中一句。不得少分。何況能盡。善
336a10‖ 男子。我於彼佛所。千二百歲。受持如是普眼
336a11‖ 法門。於日日中。

简体字

善巧言说不可思议，圆满音声不可思议，无边际力不可思议，清净无畏不可思议，广大辩才不可思议。又念彼佛往修诸行不可思议，自在成道不可思议，妙音演法不可思议，普门示现种种庄严不可思议，随其左右见各差别不可思议，一切利益皆令圆满不可思议。

“时，此如来即伸右手而摩我顶，为我演说普眼法门，开示一切如来境界，显发一切菩萨诸行，阐明一切诸佛妙法，一切法轮悉入其中，能净一切诸佛国土，能摧一切异道邪论，能灭一切诸魔军众，能令众生皆生欢喜，能照一切众生心行，能了一切众生诸根，随众生心悉令开悟。

“我从于彼如来之所闻此法门，受持读诵，忆念观察。假使有人，以大海量墨，须弥聚笔，书写于此普眼法门，一品中一门，一门中一法，一法中一义，一义中一句，不得少分，何况能尽？

“善男子，我于彼佛所千二百岁，受持如是普眼法门，于日日中，

His inconceivable skillful discourse;
His inconceivable perfectly fulfilled voice;
His inconceivable boundless powers;
His inconceivable pure fearlessnesses; and
His inconceivable great eloquence.

I also then brought to mind that buddha's inconceivable past cultivation of the practices and saw his inconceivable use of spiritual transformations in attaining enlightenment,[66] his inconceivable sublime voice in expounding the Dharma, his inconceivable manifestation of adornments of the universal gateway, his various inconceivable phenomena to his left and right, and his inconceivable fulfillment of benefit for everyone.

At that very time, this *tathāgata* straightaway extended his right hand and stroked the crown of my head, whereupon he expounded for my sake on the Dharma gateway of the universal eye by which:

One opens and reveals the realms of all *tathāgatas;*
One reveals the generation of all bodhisattvas' practices;
One clearly explains all buddhas' sublime Dharma in which the sphere of all dharmas is entirely subsumed;
One is able to purify all buddha lands;
One is able to vanquish the adherents of all heterodox paths and their erroneous doctrines;
One is able to destroy all armies of *māras;*
One is able to cause all beings to be filled with joyous delight;
One is able to illuminate the actions of all beings' minds;
One is able to completely understand all beings' faculties; and
One is able to adapt to beings' minds and thereby enable them all to awaken.

It is from that *tathāgata* that I heard this Dharma gateway, absorbed and retained it, studied and recited it, bore it in mind, and meditated on it.

Even if there were to be some person who used enough ink to fill a great ocean and used a heap of brushes the size of Mount Sumeru in an attempt to record the contents of this gateway of the universal eye, even so, he could not thereby manage to record even a minor fraction of what is contained within but one statement on but one meaning of but one dharma contained in one gateway topic within but one of its chapters. How much the less might he be able to record all that it contains.

Son of Good Family, I spent twelve hundred years under that buddha absorbing and retaining contents of this universal eye Dharma gateway such as these. In every one of those days:

正體字

以聞持陀羅尼光明。領受無
336a12║ 數品。以寂靜門陀羅尼光明。趣入無數品。以
336a13║ 無邊旋陀羅尼光明。普入無數品。以隨地觀
336a14║ 察陀羅尼光明。分別無數品。以威力陀羅尼
336a15║ 光明。普攝無數品。以蓮華莊嚴陀羅尼光明。
336a16║ 引發無數品。以清淨言音陀羅尼光明。開演
336a17║ 無數品。以虛空藏陀羅尼光明。顯示無數品。
336a18║ 以光聚陀羅尼光明。增廣無數品。以海藏陀
336a19║ 羅尼光明。[1]辨析無數品。若有眾生。從十方
336a20║ 來。若天若天王。若龍若龍王。若夜叉若夜叉
336a21║ 王。若乾闥婆若乾闥婆王。若阿脩羅若阿脩
336a22║ 羅王。若迦樓羅若迦樓羅王。若緊那羅若緊
336a23║ 那羅王。若摩睺羅伽若摩睺羅伽王。若人若
336a24║ 人王。若梵若梵王。如是一切。來至我所。我悉
336a25║ 為其。開示解釋。稱揚讚歎。咸令愛樂。趣入安
336a26║ 住此諸佛菩薩行光明普眼法門。善男子。我
336a27║ 唯知此普眼法門。如諸菩薩摩訶薩。深入一
336a28║ 切菩薩行海。隨其願力。而修行故。入大願海。
336a29║ 於無量劫住世間故。入一切眾生海。隨其心
336b01║ 樂廣利益故。入一切眾生心海。出生十力無
336b02║ 礙智光故。

简体字

以闻持陀罗尼光明，领受无数品；以寂静门陀罗尼光明，趣入无数品；以无边旋陀罗尼光明，普入无数品；以随地观察陀罗尼光明，分别无数品；以威力陀罗尼光明，普摄无数品；以莲华庄严陀罗尼光明，引发无数品；以清净言音陀罗尼光明，开演无数品；以虚空藏陀罗尼光明，显示无数品；以光聚陀罗尼光明，增广无数品；以海藏陀罗尼光明，辩析无数品。若有众生从十方来，若天、若天王，若龙、若龙王，若夜叉、若夜叉王，若乾闼婆、若乾闼婆王，若阿修罗、若阿修罗王，若迦楼罗、若迦楼罗王，若紧那罗、若紧那罗王，若摩睺罗伽、若摩睺罗伽王，若人、若人王，若梵、若梵王，如是一切来至我所，我悉为其开示解释、称扬赞叹，咸令爱乐、趣入、安住此诸佛菩萨行光明普眼法门。

“善男子，我唯知此普眼法门。如诸菩萨摩诃萨深入一切菩萨行海，随其愿力而修行故；入大愿海，于无量劫住世间故；入一切众生海，随其心乐广利益故；入一切众生心海，出生十力无碍智光故；

By the light of the "retaining what has been heard" *dhāraṇī*, I received countless chapters;
By the light of the "quiescence gateway" *dhāraṇī*, I entered countless chapters;
By the light of the "boundless turnings" *dhāraṇī*, I comprehensively penetrated countless chapters;
By the light of the "grounds-adapted contemplation" *dhāraṇī*, I analyzed countless chapters;
By the light of the "awesome powers" *dhāraṇī*, I comprehensively absorbed countless chapters;
By the light of the "lotus flower adornment" *dhāraṇī*, I drew forth and implemented the meaning of countless chapters;
By the light of the "pure speech" *dhāraṇī*, I expounded on countless chapters;
By the light of the "empty space treasury" *dhāraṇī*, I revealed countless chapters;
By the light of the "mass of light" *dhāraṇī*, I deduced the broader implications of countless chapters; and
By the light of the "oceanic treasury" *dhāraṇī*, I analytically distinguished the contents of countless chapters.

Whenever any being comes to me from the ten directions, whether he be a deva or deva king, a dragon or dragon king, a *yakṣa* or *yakṣa* king, a *gandharva* or *gandharva* king, an *asura* or *asura* king, a *garuḍa* or *garuḍa* king, a *kiṃnara* or a *kiṃnara* king, a *mahoraga* or a *mahoraga* king, a human or a human king, a brahma heaven deva or a brahma heaven king—in all such circumstances as these in which someone comes to me, I introduce and explain all of these matters for them, extolling and praising these matters in ways that cause them to cherish and delight in them, progress into them, and then become securely established in this universal eye Dharma gateway into the light of the practices of buddhas and bodhisattvas.

Son of Good Family, I know only this universal eye Dharma gateway. As for the bodhisattva-mahāsattvas:

Who have deeply entered the ocean of all bodhisattva practices and cultivate in accordance with the power of their vows;
Who have entered the ocean of great vows to dwell in the world for countless kalpas;
Who have entered the ocean of all beings to benefit them extensively by adapting to their mental dispositions in doing so;
Who have entered the ocean of all beings' minds to bring forth the ten powers and the light of unimpeded wisdom;

正體字

入一切眾生根海。應[2]時教化悉令
336b03║ 調伏故。入一切剎海。成滿本願嚴淨佛剎故。
336b04║ 入一切佛海。願常供養諸如來故。入一切法
336b05║ 海。能以智慧咸悟入故。入一切功德海。一
336b06║ 一修行令具足故。入一切眾生言辭海。於一
336b07║ 切剎轉正法輪故。而我云何。能知能說彼功
336b08║ 德行。善男子。從此南行。六十由旬。楞伽道
336b09║ 邊。有一聚落。名為海岸。彼有比丘。名曰善
336b10║ 住。汝詣彼問。菩薩云何淨菩薩行。時善財童
336b11║ 子。禮海雲足。右遶瞻仰。辭退而去
336b12║ 爾時善財童子。專念善知識教。專念普眼法
336b13║ 門。專念佛神力。專持法句雲。專入法海門。專
336b14║ 思法差別。深入法[3]漩澓。普入法虛空。淨[4]治
336b15║ 法[5]翳障。觀察法寶處。

简体字

入一切众生根海，应时教化悉令调伏故；入一切刹海，成满本愿严净佛刹故；入一切佛海，愿常供养诸如来故；入一切法海，能以智慧咸悟入故；入一切功德海，一一修行令具足故；入一切众生言辞海，于一切刹转正法轮故。而我云何能知能说彼功德行？

“善男子，从此南行六十由旬，楞伽道边有一聚落，名为海岸；彼有比丘，名曰善住。汝诣彼问：菩萨云何净菩萨行？”

时，善财童子礼海云足，右绕瞻仰，辞退而去。

尔时，善财童子专念善知识教，专念普眼法门，专念佛神力，专持法句云，专入法海门，专思法差别，深入法漩澓，普入法虚空，净持法翳障，观察法宝处。

Who have entered the ocean of all beings' faculties to enable the training of them all by teaching them in accordance with the appropriate timing;

Who have entered the ocean of all *kṣetras* to fulfill their original vows to purify the buddha *kṣetras;*

Who have entered the ocean of all buddhas due to their vow to always make offerings to all *tathāgatas;*

Who have entered the ocean of all dharmas to be able to use wisdom to awaken to and penetrate them all;

Who have entered the ocean of all meritorious qualities to cultivate every one of them and thus enable their complete fulfillment; and

Who have entered the ocean of all beings' languages to turn the wheel of right Dharma in all *kṣetras*—

How could I know of or be able to speak about their meritorious qualities and practices?

Son of Good Family, traveling to the south from here for a distance of sixty *yojanas,* off to the side of Laṅka Road, there is a village known as Sāgaratīra or "Ocean Shore" where there is a bhikshu known as Supratiṣṭhita or "Well Established." You should go pay your respects to him and inquire of him about how one is to purify the bodhisattva practices.

Then Sudhana the Youth bowed down in reverence at the feet of Sāgaramegha, circumambulated him to his right as he gazed up at him in admiration, respectfully withdrew, and then departed.

3 – Supratiṣṭhita

At that time, Sudhana the Youth:

Single-mindedly recalled the teachings of that good spiritual guide;
Single-mindedly recalled that universal eye Dharma gateway;
Single-mindedly recalled the Buddha's spiritual powers;
Single-mindedly retained the cloud of Dharma statements;
Single-mindedly entered the gateways into the ocean of Dharma;
Single-mindedly contemplated the distinctions among the dharmas;
Deeply entered the vortex of the Dharma;
Everywhere entered the sky of Dharma;
Purified and cured the cataract-like obstacles to seeing the Dharma; and
Closely contemplated the location of the jewels of the Dharma.

正體字

漸次南行。至楞伽[6]道
336b16║ 海岸聚落。觀察十方。求覓善住。見此比丘於
336b17║ 虛空中來往經行。無數諸天。恭敬圍遶。散諸
336b18║ 天華。作天妓樂。幡幢繒綺。悉各無數。遍滿虛
336b19║ 空。以為供養。諸大龍王。於虛空中。興不思
336b20║ 議。沈水香雲。震雷激電。以為供養。緊那羅
336b21║ 王。奏眾樂音。如法讚美。以為供養。摩睺羅伽
336b22║ 王。以不思議極微細衣。於虛空中。周迴布設。
336b23║ 心生歡喜。以為供養。阿脩羅王。興不思議摩
336b24║ 尼寶雲。無量光明。種種莊嚴。遍滿虛空。以為
336b25║ 供養。迦樓羅王。作童子形無量采女之所圍
336b26║ 遶。究竟成就無殺害心。於虛空中。合掌供養。
336b27║ 不思議數諸羅剎王。無量羅剎之所圍遶。其
336b28║ 形長大甚可怖畏。見善住比丘。慈心自在。曲
336b29║ 躬合掌。瞻仰供養。不思議數諸夜叉王。各各
336c01║ 悉有自眾圍遶。四面周匝。恭敬守護。不思議
336c02║ 數諸梵天王。於虛空中。曲躬合掌。以人間法。
336c03║ 稱揚讚歎。不思議數諸淨居天。於虛空中。與
336c04║ 宮殿俱。恭敬合掌。發弘誓願。

简体字

渐次南行，至楞伽道边海岸聚落，观察十方，求觅善住。见此比丘于虚空中来往经行，无数诸天恭敬围绕，散诸天华，作天妓乐，幡幢缯绮悉各无数，遍满虚空以为供养；诸大龙王，于虚空中兴不思议沉水香云，震雷激电以为供养；紧那罗王奏众乐音，如法赞美以为供养；摩睺罗伽王以不思议极微细衣，于虚空中周回布设，心生欢喜，以为供养；阿修罗王兴不思议摩尼宝云，无量光明种种庄严，遍满虚空以为供养；迦楼罗王作童子形，无量采女之所围绕，究竟成就无杀害心，于虚空中合掌供养；不思议数诸罗刹王，无量罗刹之所围绕，其形长大，甚可怖畏，见善住比丘慈心自在，曲躬合掌瞻仰供养；不思议数诸夜叉王，各各悉有自众围绕，四面周匝恭敬守护；不思议数诸梵天王，于虚空中曲躬合掌，以人间法称扬赞叹；不思议数诸净居天，于虚空中与宫殿俱，恭敬合掌发弘誓愿。

He then gradually traveled southward until he arrived at the village on Laṅka Road known as Sāgaratīra or "Ocean Shore" where he searched the ten directions, wishing to see Supratiṣṭhita, whereupon he saw this bhikshu engaged in walking meditation as he walked back and forth up in the sky where countless devas reverently circumambulated him, scattered celestial flowers, and played heavenly music. Countless pennants, banners, and silk streamers everywhere filled the sky where they had been presented to him there as offerings.

Up in the open sky, the great dragon kings created as an offering an inconceivable display of *agaru* incense clouds, quaking thunder, and lightning.

As an offering, the *kiṃnara* kings played many kinds of music with which they praised him in accordance with the Dharma.

With minds full of joyous delight, as an offering, the *mahoraga* kings spread across the sky a circular array of inconceivably beautiful robes of the finest sorts.

As an offering, the *asura* kings released an inconceivable array of *maṇi* jewel clouds, countless rays of light, and many different kinds of adornments, all of which completely filled the sky.

Up in the sky, the *garuḍa* kings manifested in the form of pure youths who were surrounded by countless maiden attendants, youths who, having ultimately perfected the mind free of any intention to kill or injure, pressed their palms together as an offering.

There were inconceivably many *rākṣasa* kings surrounded by countless *rākṣasas* whose physical forms had grown immense and extremely fearsome in their appearance. On observing Supratiṣṭhita Bhikshu's freely invoked thoughts of loving-kindness, they bent their bodies deferentially low and pressed their palms together as they gazed up in admiration, doing so as an offering.

All around the four sides of this scene, respectfully serving as protectors, there were inconceivably many *yakṣa* kings, each of whom was surrounded by his own retinue.

Inconceivably many Brahma Heaven kings up in the sky stood with bodies bowing deferentially low and palms pressed together as they deferred to the customs of humans in praising him.

Inconceivably many devas of the Pure Abode Heavens floated up in the sky, together with their palaces, reverently pressing their palms together as they made vast vows.

正體字

時善財童子。見
336c05║ 是事已。心生歡喜。合掌敬禮。作如是言。聖
336c06║ 者。我已先發阿耨多羅三藐三菩提心。而未
336c07║ 知菩薩云何修行佛法。云何積集佛法。云
336c08║ 何備具佛法。云何熏習佛法。云何增長佛法。
336c09║ 云何總攝佛法。云何究竟佛法。云何淨治佛
336c10║ 法。云何深淨佛法。云何通達佛法。我聞聖
336c11║ 者。善能誘誨。唯願慈哀。為我宣說。菩薩云何
336c12║ 不捨見佛。常於其所。精勤修習。菩薩云何不
336c13║ 捨菩薩。與諸菩薩。同一善根。菩薩云何不捨
336c14║ 佛法。悉以智慧。而得明證。菩薩云何不捨大
336c15║ 願。能普利益一切眾生。菩薩云何不捨眾
336c16║ 行。住一切劫。心無疲厭。菩薩云何不捨佛剎。
336c17║ 普能嚴淨一切世界。

简体字

时，善财童子见是事已，心生欢喜，合掌敬礼，作如是言："圣者，我已先发阿耨多罗三藐三菩提心，而未知菩萨云何修行佛法？云何积集佛法？云何备具佛法？云何熏习佛法？云何增长佛法？云何总摄佛法？云何究竟佛法？云何净治佛法？云何深净佛法？云何通达佛法？我闻圣者善能诱诲，唯愿慈哀，为我宣说：菩萨云何不舍见佛，常于其所精勤修习？菩萨云何不舍菩萨，与诸菩萨同一善根？菩萨云何不舍佛法，悉以智慧而得明证？菩萨云何不舍大愿，能普利益一切众生？菩萨云何不舍众行，住一切劫心无疲厌？菩萨云何不舍佛刹，普能严净一切世界？

At that time, having observed these phenomena, the mind of Sudhana the Youth became filled with joyous delight, whereupon he pressed his palms together, bowed down in reverence, and spoke as follows:

O Ārya, I am one who has already resolved to attain *anuttara-samyak-saṃbodhi*. However, I do not yet know with regard to the bodhisattva:

How does he cultivate the dharmas of the Buddha?

How does he accumulate the dharmas of the Buddha?

How does he become completely equipped with the dharmas of the Buddha?

How does he become habitually imbued with the dharmas of the Buddha?

How does he bring about the growth of the dharmas of the Buddha?

How does he assemble the dharmas of the Buddha?

How does he achieve the ultimate realization of the dharmas of the Buddha?

How does he purify the dharmas of the Buddha?

How does he deeply purify the dharmas of the Buddha?

And how does he reach a penetrating comprehension of the dharmas of the Buddha?

I have heard that the Ārya is well able to lead and provide instruction. I wish only that you would feel kindness and pity for me and expound on these matters for my sake:

How can the bodhisattva never lose the ability to see the Buddha and always be able to diligently cultivate in his presence?

How can the bodhisattva never be separated from the bodhisattvas and develop the same roots of goodness as the bodhisattvas possess?

How can the bodhisattva never become separated from the dharmas of the Buddha and use wisdom to understand and realize them all?

How can the bodhisattva never abandon the great vows and be able to benefit all beings everywhere?

How can the bodhisattva never abandon the many practices and tirelessly abide in them throughout all kalpas?

How can the bodhisattva never leave the buddha *kṣetras* and become everywhere able to accomplish the purification of all worlds?

正體字

菩薩云何不捨佛力。悉
336c18║ 能知見如來自在。菩薩云何不捨有為。亦
336c19║ 復不住。普於一切諸有趣中。猶如變化。示
336c20║ 受生死。修菩薩行。菩薩云何不捨聞法。悉能
336c21║ 領受諸佛正教。菩薩云何不捨智光。普入
336c22║ 三世智所行處。時善住比丘。告善財言。善哉
336c23║ 善哉。善男子。汝已能發阿耨多羅三藐三菩
336c24║ 提心。今復發心。求問佛法一切智法自然者
336c25║ 法。善男子。我已成就菩薩無礙解脫門。若來
336c26║ 若去。若行若止。隨順思惟。修習觀察。即時獲
336c27║ 得智慧光明。名究竟無礙。得此智慧光明故。
336c28║ 知一切眾生心行。無所障礙。知一切眾生沒
336c29║ 生。無所障礙。知一切眾生宿命。無所障礙。
337a01║ 知一切眾生未來劫事。無所障礙。知一切眾
337a02║ 生現在世事。無所障礙。知一切眾生言語音
337a03║ 聲種種差別。無所障礙。決一切眾生所有疑
337a04║ 問。無所障礙。知一切眾生諸根。無所障礙。隨
337a05║ 一切眾生應受化時。悉能往赴。無所障礙。知
337a06║ 一切剎那羅[1]婆。牟呼栗多日夜時分。無所障
337a07║ 礙。

简体字

菩萨云何不舍佛力，悉能知见如来自在？菩萨云何不舍有为亦复不住，普于一切诸有趣中犹如变化，示受生死，修菩萨行？菩萨云何不舍闻法，悉能领受诸佛正教？菩萨云何不舍智光，普入三世智所行处？”

时，善住比丘告善财言：“善哉！善哉！善男子，汝已能发阿耨多罗三藐三菩提心，今复发心求问佛法、一切智法、自然者法。

“善男子，我已成就菩萨无碍解脱门，若来若去，若行若止，随顺思惟，修习观察，即时获得智慧光明，名究竟无碍。得此智慧光明故，知一切众生心行无所障碍，知一切众生殁生无所障碍，知一切众生宿命无所障碍，知一切众生未来劫事无所障碍，知一切众生现在世事无所障碍，知一切众生言语音声种种差别无所障碍，决一切众生所有疑问无所障碍，知一切众生诸根无所障碍，随一切众生应受化时悉能往赴无所障碍，知一切刹那、罗婆、牟呼栗多、日夜时分无所障碍，

How can the bodhisattva never be separated from the Buddha's powers and be able to know and see all of the Tathāgata's masterful feats of spiritual power?

How can the bodhisattva never abandon the realm of the conditioned and still never abide in it so that, everywhere in all the rebirth destinies of existence, as if producing spiritual transformations, he may manifest the appearance of undergoing births and deaths as he cultivates the bodhisattva practices?

How can the bodhisattva never lose the ability to hear the Dharma and be able to receive all the right teachings of all buddhas?

And how can the bodhisattva never be separated from the light of wisdom and everywhere enter the stations of wisdom practice throughout all three periods of time?

At that time, Supratiṣṭhita Bhikshu spoke to Sudhana, saying:

It is good indeed, good indeed, Son of Good Family, that you have already been able to bring forth the resolve to attain *anuttara-samyak-saṃbodhi* and now have also resolved to ask about the dharmas of the Buddha, the dharmas of all-knowledge, and the dharmas of a self-accomplished one.[67]

Son of Good Family, I have already perfected the gateway of a bodhisattva's unimpeded liberations. Whether coming or going or walking or standing, as I engage in meditative reflection and cultivate investigative contemplation, I immediately acquire the light of wisdom that is known as "ultimately unimpeded." Because I have acquired this wisdom light:

I am unimpeded in knowing all beings' mental actions;

I am unimpeded in knowing all beings' deaths and births;

I am unimpeded in knowing all beings' past lives;

I am unimpeded in knowing all beings' circumstances in future kalpas;

I am unimpeded in knowing all beings' present-life circumstances;

I am unimpeded in knowing the many different distinctions in all beings' languages and speech;

I am unimpeded in resolving all beings' doubting questions;

I am unimpeded in knowing all beings' faculties;

I am unimpeded in being able to go to all beings when they should be amenable to accepting the teachings;

I am unimpeded in knowing all the divisions of time on down even to all of the *kṣaṇas*, *lavas*, and *muhūrtas* of the day and night;[68]

正體字

知三世海流轉次第。無所障礙。能以其
337a08║ 身遍往十方一切佛剎。無所障礙。何以故。得
337a09║ 無住無作神通力故。善男子。我以得此神通
337a10║ 力故。於虛空中。或行或住。或坐或臥。或隱或
337a11║ 顯。或現一身。或現多身。穿度牆壁。猶如虛
337a12║ 空。於虛空中。結[2]跏趺坐。往來自在。猶如飛
337a13║ 鳥。入地如水。履水如地。遍身上下。普出煙
337a14║ 焰。如大火聚。或時震動一切大地。或時以手
337a15║ 摩觸日月。或現其身。高至梵宮。或現燒香雲。
337a16║ 或現寶焰雲。或現變化雲。或現光網雲。皆悉
337a17║ 廣大。彌覆十方。或一念中。過於東方一世界
337a18║ 二世界。百世界千世界。百千世界。乃至無量
337a19║ 世界。乃至不可說不可說世界。或過閻浮提
337a20║ 微塵數世界。或過不可說不可說佛剎微塵
337a21║ 數世界。於彼一切諸佛國土佛世尊前。聽聞
337a22║ 說法。一一佛所。現無量佛剎微塵數差別身。
337a23║ 一一身。雨無量佛剎微塵數供養雲。所謂一
337a24║ 切華雲。一切香雲。一切鬘雲。一切末香雲。一
337a25║ 切塗香雲。一切蓋雲。

简体字

知三世海流转次第无所障碍，能以其身遍往十方一切佛刹无所障碍。何以故？得无住无作神通力故。

“善男子，我以得此神通力故，于虚空中或行、或住、或坐、或卧、或隐、或显，或现一身，或现多身，穿度墙壁犹如虚空；于虚空中结跏趺坐，往来自在犹如飞鸟；入地如水，履水如地，遍身上下普出烟焰如大火聚。或时震动一切大地，或时以手摩触日月，或现其身高至梵宫。或现烧香云，或现宝焰云，或现变化云，或现光网云，皆悉广大弥覆十方。或一念中过于东方一世界、二世界、百世界、千世界、百千世界，乃至无量世界，乃至不可说不可说世界；或过阎浮提微尘数世界，或过不可说不可说佛刹微尘数世界。于彼一切诸佛国土佛世尊前听闻说法，一一佛所现无量佛刹微尘数差别身，一一身雨无量佛刹微尘数供养云，所谓：一切华云、一切香云、一切鬘云、一切末香云、一切涂香云、一切盖云、

I am unimpeded in knowing the sequences involved in the flowing on of the ocean of the three periods of time; and

I am unimpeded in being able to use my body to go to the buddha *kṣetras* everywhere throughout the ten directions.

And why is this so? This is due to having acquired spiritual powers associated with non-abiding and karmic inaction.[69]

Son of Good Family, because I have acquired these spiritual powers, I may walk, stand, sit, or lie down in space, may become invisible or visible, may manifest one body or many bodies, may pass through walls as if they were empty space, may sit in space in the lotus posture, may freely come and go like a bird in flight, may enter the earth as if it were water, may walk on water as if it were the earth, or may send forth smoke and flames from my entire body either upward or downward as if from an immense bonfire. So, too:

Sometimes I may cause the entire great earth to quake;

Sometimes I may use my hand to rub the sun or moon;

Or I may manifest a body so tall that it reaches all the way up to the palaces of the Brahma Heaven;

Or I may manifest clouds of burning incense;

Or I may manifest clouds of flaming jewel light;

Or I may manifest clouds of transformations;

Or I may manifest clouds of light-ray nets, all so vast as to spread across the ten directions;

Or, in but a single mind-moment, I may pass beyond one world to the east, two worlds, a hundred worlds, a thousand worlds, a hundred thousand worlds, and so forth until we come to the passing of countless worlds on up to the passing of an ineffable-ineffable number of worlds;

Or I may pass beyond worlds as numerous as the atoms in Jambudvīpa;

Or I may pass beyond worlds as numerous as the atoms in an ineffable-ineffable number of buddha *kṣetras* in which, in the presence of each of those buddhas, the *bhagavats,* I listen to them teach the Dharma, whereupon I manifest in each of those buddhas' lands different bodies as numerous as the atoms in countless buddha *kṣetras*. Then each of these bodies sends down a rain of offering gift clouds as numerous as the atoms in countless buddha *kṣetras,* including: clouds of all kinds of flower blossoms; clouds of all kinds of incense; clouds of all kinds of garlands; clouds of all kinds of powdered incense; clouds of all kinds of perfume; clouds of all kinds of canopies; clouds of all

正體字

一切衣雲。一切幢雲。一
337a26‖ 切幡雲。一切帳雲。以一切身雲。而為供養。一
337a27‖ 一如來。所有宣說。我皆受持。一一國土。所有
337a28‖ 莊嚴。我皆憶念。如東方。南西北方。四維上
337a29‖ 下。亦復如是。如是一切諸世界中。所有眾生。
337b01‖ 若見我形。皆決定得阿耨多羅三藐三菩提。
337b02‖ 彼諸世界。一切眾生。我皆明見。隨其大小勝
337b03‖ 劣苦樂。示同其形。教化成就。若有眾生。親近
337b04‖ 我者。悉令安住如是法門。善男子。我唯知此
337b05‖ 普速疾供養諸佛成就眾生無礙解脫門。如
337b06‖ 諸菩薩。持大悲戒。波羅蜜戒。大乘戒。菩薩道
337b07‖ 相應戒。無障礙戒。不退墮戒。不捨菩提心戒。
337b08‖ 常以佛法為所緣戒。於一切智常作意戒。如
337b09‖ 虛空戒。一切世間無所依戒。無失戒。無損
337b10‖ 戒。無缺戒。無雜戒。無濁戒。無悔戒。清淨戒。

简体字

一切衣云、一切幢云、一切幡云、一切帐云，以一切身云而为供养。一一如来所有宣说，我皆受持；一一国土所有庄严，我皆忆念。如东方，南、西、北方，四维、上、下，亦复如是。如是一切诸世界中所有众生，若见我形，皆决定得阿耨多罗三藐三菩提。彼诸世界一切众生，我皆明见，随其大小、胜劣、苦乐，示同其形，教化成就。若有众生亲近我者，悉令安住如是法门。

“善男子，我唯知此普速疾供养诸佛成就众生无碍解脱门。如诸菩萨持大悲戒、波罗蜜戒、大乘戒、菩萨道相应戒、无障碍戒、不退堕戒、不舍菩提心戒、常以佛法为所缘戒、于一切智常作意戒、如虚空戒、一切世间无所依戒、无失戒、无损戒、无缺戒、无杂戒、无浊戒、无悔戒、清净戒、

kinds of robes; clouds of all kinds of banners; clouds of all kinds of pennants; and clouds of all kinds of curtains.

I use clouds of all kinds of bodies to present these offerings. I take in and retain all that every one of these *tathāgatas* proclaims. I recall all the adornments of every one of those lands.

And just as described above with reference to the east, so too is this so with regard to the south, the west, the north, the four midpoints, the zenith, and the nadir. In all such worlds as these, any one of those beings who so much as sees my physical form shall definitely attain *anuttara-samyak-saṃbodhi.*

I clearly see all the beings in all those worlds and, as befits their large or small size, their superiority or inferiority, their suffering or their happiness, I manifest a form that matches theirs and then teach them and enable them to succeed in this. Wherever there are any beings at all who draw near to me, I enable them all to become securely established in a Dharma gateway such as this.

Son of Good Family, I know only this unimpeded gateway of liberation of swiftly making offerings to all buddhas everywhere and bringing about the development of beings. As for the bodhisattvas who observe:

The moral precepts of the great compassion;
The moral precepts of the *pāramitās;*
The moral precepts of the Great Vehicle;
The moral precepts of the bodhisattva path;
The unimpeded moral precepts;
The moral precepts of never retreating and falling away;
The moral precepts of never abandoning the resolve to attain bodhi;
The moral precepts of always taking the dharmas of a buddha as one's objective focus;
The moral precepts of always maintaining the intention to attain all-knowledge;
The moral precepts that are like the sky;
The moral precepts independent of anything in any world;
The faultless moral precepts;
The undamaged moral precepts;
The moral precepts free of deficiencies;
The unadulterated moral precepts;
The moral precepts free of turbidity;
The moral precepts free of regrets;
The pure moral precepts;

正體字

337b11║ 離塵戒。離垢戒。如是功德。而我云何能知能
337b12║ 說。善男子。從此南方有國。名達里鼻荼。城名
337b13║ 自在。其中有人。名曰彌伽。汝詣彼問。菩薩云
337b14║ 何學菩薩行。修菩薩道。時善財童子。頂禮其
337b15║ 足。右遶瞻仰。辭退而行
337b19║ 大方廣佛華嚴經卷第六十三
337b22║ 　　入法界品第三十九之四
337b23║ 爾時善財童子。一心正念法光明法門。深信
337b24║ 趣入。專念於佛。不斷三寶。歎離欲性。念善知
337b25║ 識。普照三世。憶諸大願。普救眾生。不著有
337b26║ 為。究竟思惟諸法自性。悉能嚴淨一切世界。
337b27║ 於一切佛眾會道場。心無所著。漸次南行。至
337b28║ 自在城。求覓彌伽。乃見其人。於市肆中。坐於
337b29║ 說法師子之座。十千人眾。所共圍遶。說輪字
337c01║ 莊嚴法門。時善財童子。頂禮其足。遶無量匝。
337c02║ 於前合掌。而作是言。聖者。我已先發阿耨多
337c03║ 羅三藐三菩提心。而我未知菩薩云何學菩
337c04║ 薩行。云何修菩薩道。云何流轉於諸有趣常
337c05║ 不忘失菩提之心。

简体字

离尘戒、离垢戒；如是功德，而我云何能知能说？

“善男子，从此南方有国，名达里鼻荼，城名自在；其中有人，名曰弥伽。汝诣彼问：菩萨云何学菩萨行、修菩萨道？”

时，善财童子顶礼其足，右绕瞻仰，辞退而行。

大方广佛华严经卷第六十三

入法界品第三十九之四

尔时，善财童子一心正念法光明法门，深信趣入，专念于佛，不断三宝，叹离欲性，念善知识普照三世，忆诸大愿普救众生，不著有为，究竟思惟诸法自性，悉能严净一切世界，于一切佛众会道场心无所著。

渐次南行，至自在城，求觅弥伽。乃见其人于市肆中，坐于说法师子之座，十千人众所共围绕，说轮字庄严法门。时，善财童子顶礼其足，绕无量匝，于前合掌，而作是言：“圣者，我已先发阿耨多罗三藐三菩提心，而我未知菩萨云何学菩萨行？云何修菩萨道？云何流转于诸有趣常不忘失菩提之心？

The unsullied moral precepts; and
The immaculate moral precepts—

How could I know of or be able to speak about meritorious qualities such as these?

Son of Good Family, south of here, there is a country known as Draviḍa. There, in a city named Vaṣitā[70] or "Sovereign Mastery" there is a man known as Megha. You should go pay your respects to him and ask him how one should train in the bodhisattva practices and how one should cultivate the bodhisattva path.

Sudhana the Youth then bowed down in reverence at his feet and circumambulated him to his right as he gazed up at him in admiration, after which he respectfully withdrew and departed.

4 – Megha

At that time, Sudhana the Youth single-mindedly recalled the Dharma light Dharma gateway, whereupon he progressed into it with deep faith, focused his attention on the Buddha and the uninterrupted lineage of the Three Jewels, and praised the lineage of dispassion.[71] He also bore in mind the good spiritual guides and their comprehensive illumination of the three periods of time, recalled the great vows to everywhere rescue all beings, nonattachment to the conditioned, ultimate reflective meditations on the inherent nature of all dharmas, the ability to purify all worlds, and the mind free of attachment even to the congregations of all buddhas.

He then gradually traveled south to the city of Vaśitā where he searched for Megha until he saw him in the marketplace, seated on a lion seat for teaching Dharma where he was surrounded by a crowd of ten thousand people, expounding on a Dharma gateway known as "the adornments of the syllabary wheel."[72]

Sudhana the Youth then bowed down in reverence at his feet, circumambulated him countless times, stood before him with palms pressed together, and spoke these words:

O Ārya, I am one who has previously resolved to attain *anuttara-samyak-saṃbodhi*. However, I do not yet know with regard to the bodhisattva:

How does he train in the bodhisattva practices?
How does he cultivate the bodhisattva path?
How does he never lose the resolve to attain bodhi even as he flows along in the rebirth destinies of all realms of existence?

正體字

云何得平等意堅固不動。
337c06 云何獲清淨心無能沮壞。云何生大悲力恒
337c07 不勞疲。云何入陀羅尼普得清淨。云何發生
337c08 智慧廣大光明。於一切法離諸暗障。云何具
337c09 無礙解辯才之力。決了一切甚深義藏。云何
337c10 得正念力。憶持一切差別法輪。云何得淨趣
337c11 力。於一切趣普演諸法。云何得智慧力。於
337c12 一切法悉能決定分別其義。爾時彌伽。告善
337c13 財言。善男子。汝已發阿耨多羅三藐三菩提
337c14 心耶。善財言唯。我已先發阿耨多羅三藐三
337c15 菩提心。彌伽遽即下師子座。於善財所。五體
337c16 投地。散金銀華無價寶珠。及以上妙碎末栴
337c17 檀無量種衣。以覆其上。復散無量種種香華。
337c18 種種供具。以為供養。然後起立。而稱歎言。善
337c19 哉善哉。善男子。乃能發阿耨多羅三藐三菩
337c20 提心。善男子。若有能發阿耨多羅三藐三菩
337c21 提心。則為不斷一切佛種。則為嚴淨一切佛
337c22 剎。則為成熟一切眾生。

简体字

云何得平等意坚固不动？云何获清净心无能沮坏？云何生大悲力恒不劳疲？云何入陀罗尼普得清净？云何发生智慧广大光明，于一切法离诸暗障？云何具无碍解辩才之力，决了一切甚深义藏？云何得正念力，忆持一切差别法轮？云何得净趣力，于一切趣普演诸法？云何得智慧力，于一切法悉能决定分别其义？”

尔时，弥伽告善财言：“善男子，汝已发阿耨多罗三藐三菩提心耶？”

善财言：“唯！我已先发阿耨多罗三藐三菩提心。”

弥伽遽即下师子座，于善财所五体投地，散金银华无价宝珠，及以上妙碎末栴檀、无量种衣以覆其上，复散无量种种香华、种种供具以为供养，然后起立而称叹言：“善哉！善哉！善男子，乃能发阿耨多罗三藐三菩提心。善男子，若有能发阿耨多罗三藐三菩提心，则为不断一切佛种，则为严净一切佛刹，则为成熟一切众生，

How does he maintain an impartial mind that is steadfast and unshakable?

How does he acquire a pure mind invulnerable to interference by anyone?

How does he produce the never-wearying power of great compassion?

How does he enter the *dhāraṇīs* and achieve thorough purification?

How does he produce the vast light of wisdom that dispels all darkness with regard to all dharmas?

How does he acquire the power of the unimpeded knowledge with respect to eloquence that demonstrates a decisive and complete understanding of the treasury of all extremely profound meanings?

How does he acquire the power of right mindfulness by which he recalls and retains the entire sphere of all the different dharmas?

How does he acquire the power to purify the rebirth destinies and everywhere expound on all dharmas in all the rebirth destinies?

And how does he acquire the power of wisdom that is able to decisively distinguish the meanings of all dharmas?

At that time, Megha spoke to Sudhana the Youth, asking, "Son of Good Family, are you one who has already resolved to attain *anuttara-samyak-saṃbodhi*?"

Sudhana replied, "Yes, I have already resolved to attain *anuttara-samyak-saṃbodhi*."

Megha then descended from the lion seat, went to Sudhana, and made a full reverential prostration, after which he scattered gold and silver flowers and priceless jewels and pearls, as well as supremely fine powdered sandalwood incense. He draped him with many different robes, scattered many different kinds of fragrant flowers, and presented him with many different gifts as offerings. After this, he stood before him and uttered praises, saying:

Son of Good Family, it is good indeed, good indeed that you have been able to bring forth the resolve to attain *anuttara-samyak-saṃbodhi*. Son of Good Family, if there is anyone who is able to bring forth the resolve to attain *anuttara-samyak-saṃbodhi*:

He becomes one who will never sever the lineage of all buddhas;

He becomes one who will purify all buddha *kṣetras*;

He becomes one who will ripen all beings;

正體字

則為了達一切法性。
337c23‖ 則為悟解一切業種。則為圓滿一切諸行。則
337c24‖ 為不斷一切大願。則如實解離貪種性。則能
337c25‖ 明見三世差別。則令信解永得堅固。則為一
337c26‖ 切如來所持。則為一切諸佛憶念。則與一切
337c27‖ 菩薩平等。則為一切賢聖讚喜。則為一切梵
337c28‖ 王禮覲。則為一切天主供養。則為一切夜叉
337c29‖ 守護。則為一切羅刹侍衛。則為一切龍王迎
338a01‖ 接。則為一切緊那羅王歌詠讚歎。則為一切
338a02‖ 諸世間主稱揚慶悅。則令一切諸眾生界悉
338a03‖ 得安隱。所謂令捨惡趣故。令出難處故。斷
338a04‖ 一切貧窮根本故。生一切天人快樂故。遇善
338a05‖ 知識親近故。聞廣大法受持故。生菩提心故。

简体字

则为了达一切法性，则为悟解一切业种，则为圆满一切诸行，则为不断一切大愿，则如实解离贪种性，则能明见三世差别，则令信解永得坚固，则为一切如来所持，则为一切诸佛忆念，则与一切菩萨平等，则为一切贤圣赞喜，则为一切梵王礼觐，则为一切天主供养，则为一切夜叉守护，则为一切罗刹侍卫，则为一切龙王迎接，则为一切紧那罗王歌咏赞叹，则为一切诸世间主称扬庆悦，则令一切诸众生界悉得安隐。所谓：令舍恶趣故，令出难处故，断一切贫穷根本故，生一切天人快乐故，遇善知识亲近故，闻广大法受持故，生菩提心故，

He becomes one who will completely comprehend the nature of all dharmas;
He becomes one who will awaken to and understand the seeds of all karmic actions;
He becomes one who will achieve the perfect fulfillment of all practices;
He becomes one who will never cut off [the lineage of] any of the great vows;
He becomes one who will understand in accordance with reality the lineage of dispassion;
He becomes one who will be able to clearly see the differences in the three periods of time;
He becomes one who will cause resolute faith to be forever solid;
He becomes one who will be supported by all *tathāgatas*;
He becomes one who will be borne in mind by all buddhas;
He becomes one who will be the same as all the bodhisattvas;
He becomes one who will elicit the praise and delight of all worthies and *āryas*;
He becomes one who will be revered by all Brahma Heaven kings;
He becomes one to whom all rulers of the devas will make offerings;
He becomes one who will be protected by all *yakṣas*;
He becomes one who will be served and guarded by all *rākṣasas*;
He becomes one who will be respectfully welcomed by all dragon kings;
He becomes one who will be praised in song by all *kiṃnara* kings;
He becomes one who will be praised and celebrated by all world leaders; and
He becomes one who enables all realms of beings to gain peace and security, doing so:
Because he causes them to abandon the wretched rebirth destinies;
Because he causes them to escape stations of rebirth beset by the difficulties;[73]
Because he severs the roots of all forms of poverty;
Because he produces happiness for all devas and humans;
Because, on meeting good spiritual guides, he draws near to them;
Because, when he hears [teachings of] the vast Dharma, he absorbs and retains them;
Because he resolves to attain bodhi;

正體字

338a06‖ 淨菩提心故。照菩薩道故。入菩薩智故。住菩
338a07‖ 薩地故。善男子。應知菩薩。所作甚難。難出難
338a08‖ 值。見菩薩者。倍更難有。菩薩為一切眾生恃
338a09‖ 怙。生長成就故。為一切眾生拯濟。拔諸苦難
338a10‖ 故。為一切眾生依處。守護世間故。為一切眾
338a11‖ 生救護。令免怖畏故。菩薩如風輪。持諸世
338a12‖ 間。不令墮落惡趣故。如大地。增長眾生善
338a13‖ 根故。如大海。福德充滿無盡故。如淨日。智慧
338a14‖ 光明普照故。如須彌。善根高出故。如明月。智
338a15‖ 光出現故。如猛將。摧伏魔軍故。如君主。佛法
338a16‖ 城中得自在故。如猛火。燒盡眾生我愛心故。
338a17‖ 如大雲。降霔無量妙法雨故。如時雨。增長一
338a18‖ 切信根芽故。如船師。示導法海津濟處故。

简体字

净菩提心故，照菩萨道故，入菩萨智故，住菩萨地故。

“善男子，应知菩萨所作甚难，难出难值，见菩萨者倍更难有。菩萨为一切众生恃怙，生长成就故；为一切众生拯济，拔诸苦难故；为一切众生依处，守护世间故；为一切众生救护，令免怖畏故。菩萨如风轮，持诸世间不令堕落恶趣故；如大地，增长众生善根故；如大海，福德充满无尽故；如净日，智慧光明普照故；如须弥，善根高出故；如明月，智光出现故；如猛将，摧伏魔军故；如君主，佛法城中得自在故；如猛火，烧尽众生我爱心故；如大云，降霔无量妙法雨故；如时雨，增长一切信根芽故；如船师，示导法海津济处故；

Because he purifies his resolve to attain bodhi;
Because he illuminates the bodhisattva path;
Because he enters the wisdom of the bodhisattvas; and
Because he dwells on the bodhisattva grounds.

Son of Good Family, you should realize that the endeavors of a bodhisattva are extremely difficult. It is difficult for them to come forth and it is difficult to encounter them. To actually see a bodhisattva is doubly rare. The bodhisattva:

Serves as a mother and father for all beings because he aids their growth and success;

Serves as a rescuer for all beings because he extricates them from every kind of suffering and difficulty;

He serves as a support for all beings because he protects the inhabitants of the world;

He serves as a rescuer and protector for all beings because he causes them to avoid terrifying circumstances;

He is like the wheel of wind which sustains the existence of all worlds because he prevents beings from falling into the wretched destinies;

He is like the great earth because he promotes the growth of beings' roots of goodness;

He is like the great ocean because he possesses a completely full and inexhaustible reservoir of merit;

He is like the shining sun because the light of his wisdom shines everywhere;

He is like Mount Sumeru because his roots of goodness reach soaring heights;

He is like a bright moon because the light of his wisdom comes forth and manifests;

He is like a courageous general because he crushes the armies of Māra;

He is like a ruler because he acts with sovereign mastery in the city of the Buddha's Dharma;

He is like a fierce blaze because he completely incinerates beings' self-cherishing thoughts;

He is like a great cloud because he sends down the measureless rain of the sublime Dharma;

He is like the seasonal rains because he produces growth in the sprouts of all roots of faith;

He is like a ship captain because he guides others to the places where they may cross the ocean of Dharma;

正體字

如
338a19‖ 橋梁。令其得度生死海故。彌伽如是。讚歎善
338a20‖ 財。令諸菩薩。皆歡喜已。從其面門。出種種
338a21‖ 光。普照三千大千世界。其中眾生。遇斯光
338a22‖ 已。諸龍神等。乃至梵天。悉皆來至彌伽之
338a23‖ 所。彌伽大士。即以方便。為開示演說分別解
338a24‖ 釋輪字品莊嚴法門。彼諸眾生。聞此法已。皆
338a25‖ 於阿耨多羅三藐三菩提。得不退轉。彌伽於
338a26‖ 是。還昇本座。告善財言。善男子。我已獲得妙
338a27‖ 音陀羅尼。能分別知三千大千世界中。諸天
338a28‖ 語言。諸龍夜叉乾闥婆阿脩羅迦樓羅緊那
338a29‖ 羅摩睺羅伽人與非人。及諸梵天。所有語言。
338b01‖ 如此三千大千世界十方無數。乃至不可說
338b02‖ 不可說世界。悉亦如是。善男子。我唯知此菩
338b03‖ 薩妙音陀羅尼光明法門。如諸菩薩摩訶薩。
338b04‖ 能普入一切眾生種種想海。種種施設海。種
338b05‖ 種名號海。種種語言海。能普入說一切深密
338b06‖ 法句海。說一切究竟法句海。說[1]一所緣中
338b07‖ 有一切三世所緣法句海。說上法句海。說上
338b08‖ 上法句海。說差別法句海。說一切差別法句

简体字

如桥梁，令其得度生死海故。”

弥伽如是赞叹善财，令诸菩萨皆欢喜已，从其面门出种种光，普照三千大千世界。其中众生遇斯光已，诸龙神等乃至梵天悉皆来至弥伽之所。弥伽大士即以方便，为开示、演说、分别、解释轮字品庄严法门。彼诸众生闻此法已，皆于阿耨多罗三藐三菩提得不退转。

弥伽于是还升本座，告善财言：“善男子，我已获得妙音陀罗尼，能分别知三千大千世界中诸天语言，诸龙、夜叉、乾闼婆、阿修罗、迦楼罗、紧那罗、摩睺罗伽、人与非人及诸梵天所有语言。如此三千大千世界，十方无数乃至不可说不可说世界，悉亦如是。

“善男子，我唯知此菩萨妙音陀罗尼光明法门。如诸菩萨摩诃萨，能普入一切众生种种想海、种种施设海、种种名号海、种种语言海，能普入说一切深密法句海、说一切究竟法句海、说一切所缘中有一切三世所缘法句海、说上法句海、说上上法句海、说差别法句海、说一切差别法句海，

He is like a bridge because he enables others to cross over the ocean of *saṃsāra.*

It was in ways such as these that Megha praised Sudhana. Having produced joyous delight in all the bodhisattvas, he then sent forth from his mouth many different kinds of light that everywhere illuminated the worlds of the great trichiliocosm. After the beings in them encountered this light, all the dragons, spirits, and other such beings on up to the Brahma Heaven devas came to where Megha was, whereupon Megha, that great eminence, immediately used skillful means to teach, expound, and explain in detail for them the Syllabary Wheel Chapter's adorning Dharma gateway. After those beings heard these dharmas, they all became irreversible in their progress toward *anuttara-samyak-saṃbodhi.*

At this point, Megha again ascended to his original seat and spoke to Sudhana, saying:

Son of Good Family, I have already acquired the "sublime sounds" *dhāraṇī* with which I can distinguish and know throughout the worlds of the great trichiliocosm all the deva languages as well as all the languages used by the dragons, *yakṣas, gandharvas, asuras, garuḍas, kiṃnaras, mahoragas,* humans, nonhumans, and Brahma Heaven devas. And just as this is true of the worlds within this great trichiliocosm, so too is this also true of the countless worlds throughout the ten directions which amount to as many as an ineffable-ineffable number of worlds.[74]

Son of Good Family, I know only this Dharma gateway of the light of the bodhisattva's sublime sounds *dhāraṇī.* But, as for the bodhisattva-mahāsattvas:

Who are able to everywhere enter the ocean of all beings' many different kinds of perception, the ocean of their many different kinds of [linguistic] conventions, the ocean of their many different kinds of designations, and the ocean of their many different kinds of languages;

Who are able to everywhere enter the explanations of the ocean of the deeply secret Dharma instructions, the explanations of the ocean of all ultimate Dharma instructions, the explanations of the ocean of Dharma instructions on the presence within but one objective condition of all objective conditions throughout all three periods of time, the explanations of the ocean of superior Dharma instructions, the explanations of the ocean of supremely superior Dharma instructions, the explanations of the ocean of different Dharma instructions, and the explanations of the ocean of all different Dharma instructions; and

正體字

338b09‖ 海。能普入一切世間呪術海。一切音聲莊嚴
338b10‖ 輪一切差別字輪際。如是功德。我今云何能
338b11‖ 知能說。善男子。從此南行。有一聚落。名曰住
338b12‖ 林。彼有長者。名曰解脫。汝詣彼問。菩薩云何
338b13‖ 修菩薩行。菩薩云何成菩薩行。菩薩云何集
338b14‖ 菩薩行。菩薩云何思菩薩行。爾時善財童子。
338b15‖ 以善知識故。於一切智法。深生尊重。深植淨
338b16‖ 信。深自增益。禮彌伽足。涕泗悲泣。遶無量
338b17‖ 匝。戀慕瞻仰。辭退而行
338b18‖ 爾時善財童子。思惟諸菩薩無礙解陀羅尼
338b19‖ 光明莊嚴門。深入諸菩薩語言海門。憶念諸
338b20‖ 菩薩知一切眾生微細方便門。觀察諸菩薩
338b21‖ 清淨心門。成就諸菩薩善根光明門。淨治諸
338b22‖ 菩薩教化眾生門。明利諸菩薩攝眾生智門。
338b23‖ 堅固諸菩薩廣大志樂門。[2]住持諸菩薩殊勝
338b24‖ 志樂門。淨治諸菩薩種種信解門。思惟諸菩
338b25‖ 薩無量善心門。

简体字

能普入一切世间咒术海、一切音声庄严轮、一切差别字轮际；如是功德，我今云何能知能说？

“善男子，从此南行，有一聚落，名曰住林；彼有长者，名曰解脱。汝诣彼问：菩萨云何修菩萨行？菩萨云何成菩萨行？菩萨云何集菩萨行？菩萨云何思菩萨行？”

尔时，善财童子以善知识故，于一切智法，深生尊重，深植净信，深自增益；礼弥伽足，涕泗悲泣，绕无量匝，恋慕瞻仰，辞退而行。

尔时，善财童子思惟诸菩萨无碍解陀罗尼光明庄严门，深入诸菩萨语言海门，忆念诸菩萨知一切众生微细方便门，观察诸菩萨清净心门，成就诸菩萨善根光明门，净治诸菩萨教化众生门，明利诸菩萨摄众生智门，坚固诸菩萨广大志乐门，任持诸菩萨殊胜志乐门，净治诸菩萨种种信解门，思惟诸菩萨无量善心门；

Who are able to everywhere enter the ocean of all the world's mantra techniques, all of its realms of adornment with sounds, and all of its different syllabary wheels—

How could I be able to know of or be able to speak about such meritorious qualities as these?

Son of Good Family, traveling south from here, there is a village known as Vanavāsī or "Forest Abode" in which there is an elder known as Muktaka or "Liberated One." You should go there, pay your respects to him, and ask him:

How should a bodhisattva cultivate the bodhisattva practices?
How should a bodhisattva perfect the bodhisattva practices?
How should a bodhisattva accumulate the bodhisattva practices?
And how should a bodhisattva reflect upon the bodhisattva practices?

Because of the good spiritual guide, Sudhana the Youth developed deep reverential esteem for the dharma of all-knowledge, deeply established roots of pure faith in it, and deeply increased the benefit he derived from it. He then bowed down at Megha's feet and, with a flood of tears of sadness streaming down his face, he circumambulated him countless times as he gazed up at him in fond admiration. He then respectfully withdrew and departed.

5 – Muktaka

At that time, Sudhana the Youth:

Reflected on the radiance-adorned gateway of all bodhisattvas' *dhāraṇī* of unimpeded understanding;
Deeply entered the gateway of all bodhisattvas' ocean of languages;
Brought to mind all bodhisattvas' gateway of knowing the subtle skillful means for all beings;
Contemplated all bodhisattvas' gateway of the pure mind;
Perfected all bodhisattvas' gateway of the light of roots of goodness;
Purified all bodhisattvas' gateway of teaching beings;
Clearly understood all bodhisattvas' wisdom gateway by which they attract beings;
Strengthened all bodhisattvas' gateway of vast aspiration;
Held firmly to all bodhisattvas' gateway of supreme aspiration;
Purified all bodhisattvas' gateway of the many different forms of resolute faith; and
Reflected upon all bodhisattvas' gateway of the measureless mind of goodness.

正體字

誓願堅固。心無疲厭。以諸
338b26║ 甲[胄>冑]。而自莊嚴。精進深心。不可退轉。具不壞
338b27║ 信。其心堅固。猶如金剛及那羅延。無能壞者。
338b28║ 守持一切善知識教。於諸境界。得不壞智。普
338b29║ 門清淨。所行無礙。智光圓滿。普照一切。具足
338c01║ 諸地。總持光明。了知法界種種差別。無依無
338c02║ 住。平等無二。自性清淨。而普莊嚴。於諸所
338c03║ 行。皆得究竟。智慧清淨。離諸執著。知十方差
338c04║ 別法。智無障礙。往十方差別處。身不疲懈。於
338c05║ 十方差別業。皆得明了。於十方差別佛。無不
338c06║ 現見。於十方差別時。悉得深入。清淨妙法。充
338c07║ 滿其心。普智三昧。明照其心。心恒普入平等
338c08║ 境界。如來智慧之所照觸。一切智流。相續
338c09║ 不斷。若身若心。不離佛法。一切諸佛。神力所
338c10║ 加。一切如來。光明所照。成就大願。願身周遍
338c11║ 一切剎網。一切法界普入其身。漸次遊行。十
338c12║ 有二年。至住林城。周遍推求解脫長者。既
338c13║ 得見已。五體投地。起立合掌。白言

简体字

誓愿坚固，心无疲厌；以诸甲胄而自庄严，精进深心不可退转，具不坏信；其心坚固，犹如金刚及那罗延，无能坏者；守持一切善知识教，于诸境界得不坏智；普门清净，所行无碍；智光圆满，普照一切；具足诸地总持光明，了知法界种种差别，无依无住，平等无二；自性清净而普庄严，于诸所行皆得究竟，智慧清净离诸执著；知十方差别法，智无障碍；往十方差别处，身不疲懈；于十方差别业，皆得明了；于十方差别佛，无不现见；于十方差别时，悉得深入；清净妙法充满其心，普智三昧明照其心，心恒普入平等境界；如来智慧之所照触，一切智流相续不断，若身若心不离佛法；一切诸佛神力所加，一切如来光明所照；成就大愿，愿身周遍一切刹网，一切法界普入其身。

渐次游行，十有二年，至住林城，周遍推求解脱长者。既得见已，五体投地，起立合掌，白言：

His vows became steadfast, his mind became free of weariness, he donned every form of armor, and his vigor's determination became irreversible. He became possessed of indestructible faith and his resolve became as solid as vajra and as invincible as a *nārāyaṇa* stalwart.[75]

He preserved and retained the teaching of all his good spiritual guides and, in all spheres of experience, he acquired indestructible wisdom and the purified universal gateway. He was unimpeded in whatever he practiced. His wisdom light became so perfectly full that it everywhere illuminated everything. He achieved the complete fulfillment of the *dhāraṇī* light of all the grounds.

He completely understood the Dharma realm's various distinctions have nothing on which they depend and have no basis for their abiding, that they are possessed of a uniform non-duality, and that their inherent nature is pure even as they everywhere manifest their adornment. In whatever he practiced, he achieved a state of ultimate realization characterized by pure wisdom and freedom from all attachments.

With unimpeded knowledge, he knew the different dharmas throughout the ten directions and traveled to the different places throughout the ten directions without any physical weariness. He acquired a complete understanding of all karmic actions throughout the ten directions. There were none of the different buddhas throughout the ten directions that he did not directly see and he deeply entered all of the different times throughout the ten directions. The pure and sublime Dharma completely filled his mind, the universal wisdom samādhi brightly illuminated his mind, and his mind constantly and everywhere entered the sphere of uniform equality.

He was illuminated and touched by the Tathāgata's wisdom and the current flowing toward all-knowledge continued without interruption. Whether in body or mind, he never departed from the Buddha's Dharma. He was aided by the spiritual powers of all buddhas and was illuminated by the light of all *tathāgatas*. He perfected the great vows, his vow-generated bodies everywhere pervaded the web of all *kṣetras*, and the entire Dharma realm entered his own body.

Sudhana gradually traveled for twelve years until he reached the city of Vanavāsī where he searched all around for Muktaka the Elder. Once he encountered him, he made full reverential prostrations, stood up, pressed his palms together, and addressed him, saying:

正體字

聖者。我今
338c14║ 得與善知識會。是我獲得廣大善利。何以故。
338c15║ 善知識者。難可得見。難可得聞。難可出現。難
338c16║ 得奉事。難得親近。難得承接。難可逢值。難得
338c17║ 共居。難令喜悅。難得隨逐。我今會遇為得善
338c18║ 利。聖者。我已先發阿耨多羅三藐三菩提心。
338c19║ 為欲事一切佛故。為欲值一切佛故。為欲見
338c20║ 一切佛故。為欲觀一切佛故。為欲知一切佛
338c21║ 故。為欲證一切佛平等故。為欲發一切佛大
338c22║ 願故。為欲滿一切佛大願故。為欲具一切佛
338c23║ 智光故。為欲成一切佛眾行故。為欲得一切
338c24║ 佛神通故。為欲具一切佛諸力故。為欲獲一
338c25║ 切佛無畏故。為欲聞一切佛法故。為欲受一
338c26║ 切佛法故。為欲持一切佛法故。為欲解一切
338c27║ 佛法故。為欲護一切佛法故。為欲與一切諸
338c28║ 菩薩眾同一體故。為欲與一切菩薩善根等
338c29║ 無異故。為欲圓滿一切菩薩波羅蜜故。為欲
339a01║ 成就一切菩薩所修行故。為欲出[世>生]一切菩
339a02║ 薩清淨願故。

简体字

“圣者，我今得与善知识会，是我获得广大善利。何以故？善知识者，难可得见，难可得闻，难可出现，难得奉事，难得亲近，难得承接，难可逢值，难得共居，难令喜悦，难得随逐。我今会遇，为得善利。

“圣者，我已先发阿耨多罗三藐三菩提心，为欲事一切佛故，为欲值一切佛故，为欲见一切佛故，为欲观一切佛故，为欲知一切佛故，为欲证一切佛平等故，为欲发一切佛大愿故，为欲满一切佛大愿故，为欲具一切佛智光故，为欲成一切佛众行故，为欲得一切佛神通故，为欲具一切佛诸力故，为欲获一切佛无畏故，为欲闻一切佛法故，为欲受一切佛法故，为欲持一切佛法故，为欲解一切佛法故，为欲护一切佛法故，为欲与一切诸菩萨众同一体故，为欲与一切菩萨善根等无异故，为欲圆满一切菩萨波罗蜜故，为欲成就一切菩萨所修行故，为欲出生一切菩萨清净愿故，

O Ārya, because I am now able to meet a good spiritual guide, I have obtained a vast and excellent benefit. How is this so? As for good spiritual guides:

They are only rarely met;
They are only rarely heard;
They only rarely appear;
One is only rarely able to serve them;
One is only rarely able to draw near to them;
One is only rarely able to receive what they pass on;
One only rarely encounters them;
One is only rarely able to dwell together with them;
One is only rarely able to please them; and
One is only rarely able to follow them.

That I have now been able to meet him is an excellent benefit for me.

O Ārya, I have already resolved to attain *anuttara-samyak-saṃbodhi*:

Because I wish to serve all buddhas;
Because I wish to meet all buddhas;
Because I wish to see all buddhas;
Because I wish to contemplate all buddhas;
Because I wish to know all buddhas;
Because I wish to realize all buddhas' uniform equality;
Because I wish to make the great vows of all buddhas;
Because I wish to fulfill all buddhas' great vows;
Because I wish to become equipped with all buddhas' wisdom light;
Because I wish to perfect all buddhas' many practices;
Because I wish to acquire all buddhas' spiritual superknowledges;
Because I wish to become equipped with all buddhas' powers;
Because I wish to acquire all buddhas' fearlessnesses;
Because I wish to hear all buddhas' Dharma;
Because I wish to receive all buddhas' Dharma;
Because I wish to uphold all buddhas' Dharma;
Because I wish to understand all buddhas' Dharma;
Because I wish to protect all buddhas' Dharma;
Because I wish to become of the same substance as the community of all bodhisattvas;[76]
Because I wish to possess roots of goodness that are the same as and no different from those of all bodhisattvas;
Because I wish to fulfill the *pāramitās* of all bodhisattvas;
Because I wish to perfect whatever all bodhisattvas cultivate;
Because I wish to make the pure vows of all bodhisattvas;

正體字

為欲得一切諸佛菩薩威神藏
339a03 故。為欲得一切菩薩法藏無盡智慧大光明
339a04 故。為欲得一切菩薩三昧廣大藏故。為欲成
339a05 就一切菩薩無量無數神通藏故。為欲以大
339a06 悲藏教化調伏一切眾生。皆令究竟到邊際
339a07 故。為欲顯現神變藏故。為於一切自在藏中
339a08 悉以自心得自在故。為欲入於清淨藏中以
339a09 一切相而莊嚴故。聖者我今。以如是心。如是
339a10 意。如是樂。如是欲。如是希求。如是思惟。如
339a11 是尊重。如是方便。如是究竟。如是謙下。至聖
339a12 者所。我聞聖者。善能誘誨諸菩薩眾。能以方
339a13 便。闡明所得。示其道路。與其津梁。授其法
339a14 門。令除迷倒障。拔猶豫箭。截疑惑網。照心稠
339a15 林。[1]澣心垢濁。令心潔白。使心清[2]涼。正心諂
339a16 曲。絕心生死。止心不善。解心執著。於執著
339a17 處。令心解脫。於染愛處。使心動轉。令其速入
339a18 一切智境。使其疾到無上法城。

简体字

为欲得一切诸佛菩萨威神藏故，为欲得一切菩萨法藏无尽智慧大光明故，为欲得一切菩萨三昧广大藏故，为欲成就一切菩萨无量无数神通藏故，为欲以大悲藏教化调伏一切众生皆令究竟到边际故，为欲显现神变藏故，为于一切自在藏中悉以自心得自在故，为欲入于清净藏中以一切相而庄严故。

“圣者，我今以如是心、如是意、如是乐、如是欲、如是希求、如是思惟、如是尊重、如是方便、如是究竟、如是谦下，至圣者所。我闻圣者善能诱诲诸菩萨众，能以方便阐明所得，示其道路，与其津梁，授其法门；令除迷倒障，拔犹豫箭，截疑惑网，照心稠林，浣心垢浊，令心洁白，使心清净，正心谄曲，绝心生死，止心不善，解心执著；于执著处令心解脱，于染爱处使心动转，令其速入一切智境，使其疾到无上法城；

Because I wish to acquire the awesome spiritual qualities of all buddhas and bodhisattvas;
Because I wish to acquire the inexhaustible light of great wisdom of the Dharma treasury of all bodhisattvas;
Because I wish to acquire the vast treasury of all bodhisattvas' samādhis;
Because I wish to perfect all bodhisattvas' measureless and incalculable treasury of spiritual superknowledges;
Because I wish to use the treasury of great compassion to teach and train all beings so that they are all enabled to achieve the ultimate goal;
Because I wish to manifest the treasury of spiritual transformations;
Because I wish with my own mind to achieve sovereign mastery of the treasury of all sovereign masteries; and
Because I wish to enter the treasury of purity and use all the marks as adornments.

O Ārya, I have now come to the Ārya with such resolve, such intentions, such inclinations, such wishes, such hopes, such considerations, such veneration, such skillful means, such ultimate aims, and such humility. I have heard that the Ārya is well able to guide and instruct the entire community of bodhisattvas and that he is able to use skillful methods:

To explain what they can acquire;
To show their path;
To provide their bridge for crossing over;
To transmit their Dharma gateways;
To do away with the obstacles of confusion and inverted views;
To extract the arrows of perplexity;
To rend the net of doubts;
To illuminate the dense thicket of the mind;
To wash away the mind's defilements and turbidity;
To enable the mind to gain pristine purity;
To cause the mind to become clear and cool;
To rectify any flattery or deviousness in the mind;
To cut off the mind's involvement in *saṃsāra;*
To halt the mind's involvement in what is bad;
To loosen the mind's attachments;
To liberate the mind from its points of attachment;
To turn the mind away from its objects of defiled craving;
To enable one to quickly enter the realm of all-knowledge;
To enable one to quickly reach the city of the unexcelled Dharma;

正體字

令住大悲。令
339a19 住大慈。令入菩薩行。令修三昧門。令入證位。
339a20 令觀法性。令增長力。令修習行。普於一切。其
339a21 心平等。唯願聖者。為我宣說。菩薩云何學
339a22 菩薩行。修菩薩道。隨所修習。疾得清淨。疾得
339a23 明了。時解脫長者。以過去善根力佛威神力。
339a24 文殊師利童子憶念力故。即入菩薩三昧門。
339a25 名普攝一切佛剎無邊旋陀羅尼。入此三昧
339a26 已。得清淨身。於其身中。顯現十方各十佛剎
339a27 微塵數佛。及佛國土。眾會道場。種種光明。諸
339a28 莊嚴事。亦現彼佛往昔所行。神通變化。一切
339a29 大願。助道之法。諸出離行。清淨莊嚴。亦見諸
339b01 佛成等正覺。轉妙法輪。教化眾生。如是一切。
339b02 於其身中。悉皆顯現。無所障礙。種種形相。種
339b03 種次第。如本而住。不相雜亂。所謂種種國土。
339b04 種種眾會。種種道場。種種嚴飾。

简体字

令住大悲，令住大慈，令入菩萨行，令修三昧门，令入证位，令观法性，令增长力，令修习行，普于一切，其心平等。唯愿圣者为我宣说：菩萨云何学菩萨行、修菩萨道？随所修习，疾得清净，疾得明了！”

时，解脱长者以过去善根力、佛威神力、文殊师利童子忆念力故，即入菩萨三昧门，名普摄一切佛刹无边旋陀罗尼。入此三昧已，得清净身。于其身中，显现十方各十佛刹微尘数佛，及佛国土、众会、道场、种种光明、诸庄严事，亦现彼佛往昔所行神通变化、一切大愿、助道之法、诸出离行、清净庄严，亦见诸佛成等正觉、转妙法轮、教化众生。如是一切，于其身中悉皆显现，无所障碍；种种形相、种种次第，如本而住，不相杂乱，所谓：种种国土、种种众会、种种道场、种种严饰。

To enable one to abide in the great compassion;
To enable one to abide in the great kindness;
To enable one to enter the bodhisattva practices;
To enable one to cultivate the gateways to samādhi;
To enable one to enter the stations of realization;
To enable one to contemplate the nature of dharmas;
To enable one to increase in strength; and
To enable one to cultivate the practices by which one maintains a mind of equal regard for everyone.

I hope, O Ārya, that you will explain for me how a bodhisattva should train in the bodhisattva practices, how he should cultivate the bodhisattva path, how he may accord with what is to be cultivated and then swiftly acquire purity, and how he may swiftly acquire complete clarity of understanding.

At that time, by the power of his past roots of goodness, by the power of the Buddha's awesome spiritual power, and by the power of being borne in mind by Mañjuśrī the Youth, Muktaka the Elder immediately entered a bodhisattva samādhi gateway known as "the boundless revolving *dhāraṇī* of the universal integration of all buddha *kṣetras*." Once he had entered this samādhi, he acquired a purified body in which, within that very body, he revealed in each of the ten directions buddhas as numerous as the atoms in ten buddha *kṣetras* along with their buddha lands, their congregations, all their different kinds of light, and all their adornments.

He also revealed the past practices of those buddhas, the spiritual transformations wrought by their spiritual superknowledges, all their great vows, their path-assisting dharmas, their practices leading to emancipation, and their pure adornments. He also revealed therein those buddhas' realization of the universal and right enlightenment, their turning of the wheel of the sublime Dharma, and their teaching of beings.

All such phenomena as these were entirely and unimpededly revealed within his body, including all their different physical forms and characteristics and all their different sequences of appearance in the world. All of these were shown there in accordance with the manner in which they originally occurred and without any of these appearances being mixed together with any others. These included their many different lands, their many different congregations, their many different sites of enlightenment, and their many different kinds of adornments.

正體字

其中諸佛。現
339b05 ‖ 種種神力。立種種乘道。示種種願門。或於一
339b06 ‖ 世界處兜率宮。而作佛事。或於一世界沒兜
339b07 ‖ 率宮。而作佛事。如是或有住胎。或復誕生。或
339b08 ‖ 處宮中。或復出家。或詣道場。或破魔軍。或諸
339b09 ‖ 天龍。恭敬圍遶。或諸世主。勸請說法。或轉法
339b10 ‖ 輪。或般涅槃。或分舍利。或起塔廟。彼諸如
339b11 ‖ 來。於種種眾會。種種世間。種種趣生。種種家
339b12 ‖ 族。種種欲樂。種種業行。種種語言。種種根
339b13 ‖ 性。種種煩惱。隨眠習氣。諸眾生中。或處微細
339b14 ‖ 道場。或處廣大道場。或處一由旬量道場。或
339b15 ‖ 處十由旬量道場。或處不可說不可說佛剎
339b16 ‖ 微塵數由旬量道場。以種種神通。種種言辭。
339b17 ‖ 種種音聲。種種法門。種種總持門。種種辯
339b18 ‖ 才門。以種種聖諦海。種種無畏。大師子吼。說
339b19 ‖ 諸眾生種種善根。種種憶念。授種種菩薩記。
339b20 ‖ 說種種諸佛法。彼諸如來。所有言說。善財童
339b21 ‖ 子。悉能聽受。

简体字

其中诸佛现种种神力、立种种乘道、示种种愿门，或于一世界处兜率宫而作佛事，或于一世界殁兜率宫而作佛事；如是，或有住胎，或复诞生，或处宫中，或复出家，或诣道场，或破魔军，或诸天、龙恭敬围绕，或诸世主劝请说法，或转法轮，或般涅槃，或分舍利，或起塔庙。彼诸如来于种种众会、种种世间、种种趣生、种种家族、种种欲乐、种种业行、种种语言、种种根性、种种烦恼随眠习气诸众生中，或处微细道场，或处广大道场，或处一由旬量道场，或处十由旬量道场，或处不可说不可说佛刹微尘数由旬量道场，以种种神通、种种言辞、种种音声、种种法门、种种总持门、种种辩才门，以种种圣谛海、种种无畏大师子吼，说诸众生种种善根、种种忆念，授种种菩萨记，说种种诸佛法。彼诸如来所有言说，善财童子悉能听受，

The buddhas who appeared therein manifested many different kinds of spiritual powers, established many different vehicles and paths, and showed many different approaches to establishing vows.

In some instances, they appeared as dwelling in a world's Tuṣita Heaven palace, accomplishing buddha works there. In other instances, they appeared as descending from a world's Tuṣita Heaven palace and then accomplishing buddha works. In this way, they were sometimes shown as dwelling in the womb, or as taking birth, or as dwelling in the palace, or as leaving the home life, or as going to the site of enlightenment, or as demolishing the armies of Māra, or as surrounded by devas and dragons, or as being requested to teach the Dharma by world leaders, or as turning the wheel of the Dharma, or as entering *parinirvāṇa,* or as having their *śarīra* relics divided up, or as having commemorative stupas and temples erected for them.

All of those *tathāgatas* were shown among beings, in the midst of all different kinds of congregations, in all different kinds of worlds, in all different kinds of rebirth destinies, and among those in all different kinds of clans, among those with all different kinds of dispositions, among those performing all different kinds of karmic actions, among those speaking all different kinds of languages, among those having all different kinds of faculties and natures, and among those beset by all different kinds of afflictions, latent tendencies, and habitual karmic propensities.

They were shown therein as abiding in extremely small congregations, in vast congregations, or as abiding in congregations an entire *yojana* wide, or as abiding in congregations ten *yojanas* wide, or as abiding in congregations as many *yojanas* wide as the number of atoms in an ineffable-ineffable number of buddha *kṣetras* in which, using all different kinds of spiritual superknowledges, all different kinds of phrasings, all different kinds of voices, all different kinds of Dharma gateways, all different kinds of complete-retention *dhāraṇī* gateways, all different kinds of eloquence gateways, oceans of all different kinds of truths of the *āryas,* and all different kinds of fearlessnesses, as they roared the lion's roar and spoke about beings' many different kinds of roots of goodness and many different kinds of mindfulness, as they transmitted the many different kinds of bodhisattva predictions, and as they explained the many different kinds of dharmas of the Buddha.

Sudhana the Youth was able to hear and take in all that was spoken by all those *tathāgatas.* He was also able to see all of those buddhas'

正體字

亦見諸佛及諸菩薩。不可思議。
339b22 | 三昧神變。爾時解脱長者。從三昧起。告善財
339b23 | 童子言。善男子。我已入出如來無礙莊嚴解
339b24 | 脱門。善男子。我入出此解脱門時。即見東
339b25 | 方閻浮檀金光明世界。龍自在王如來應正
339b26 | 等覺。道場眾會之所圍遶。毘盧遮那藏菩薩。
339b27 | 而為上首。又見南方速疾力世界。普香如來
339b28 | 應正等覺。道場眾會之所圍遶。心王菩薩。而
339b29 | 為上首。又見西方香光世界。須彌燈王如來
339c01 | 應正等覺。道場眾會之所圍遶。無礙心菩薩。
339c02 | 而為上首。又見北方袈裟幢世界。不可壞金
339c03 | 剛如來應正等覺。道場眾會之所圍遶。金剛
339c04 | 步勇猛菩薩。而為上首。又見東北方一切上
339c05 | 妙寶世界。無所得境界眼如來應正等覺。道
339c06 | 場眾會之所圍遶。無所得善變化菩薩。而為
339c07 | 上首。又見東南方。香焰光音世界。香燈如
339c08 | 來應正等覺。道場眾會之所圍遶。金剛焰慧
339c09 | 菩薩。而為上首。又見西南方智慧日普光明
339c10 | 世界。法界輪幢如來應正等覺。道場眾會之
339c11 | 所圍遶。現一切變化幢菩薩。而為上首。又
339c12 | 見西北方普清淨世界。一切佛寶高勝幢如
339c13 | 來應正等覺。道場眾會之所圍遶。法幢王菩
339c14 | 薩。而為上首。

简体字

亦见诸佛及诸菩萨不可思议三昧神变。

尔时，解脱长者从三昧起，告善财童子言："善男子，我已入出如来无碍庄严解脱门。

"善男子，我入出此解脱门时，即见东方阎浮檀金光明世界，龙自在王如来、应、正等觉，道场众会之所围绕，毗卢遮那藏菩萨而为上首；又见南方速疾力世界，普香如来、应、正等觉，道场众会之所围绕，心王菩萨而为上首；又见西方香光世界，须弥灯王如来、应、正等觉，道场众会之所围绕，无碍心菩萨而为上首；又见北方袈裟幢世界，不可坏金刚如来、应、正等觉，道场众会之所围绕，金刚步勇猛菩萨而为上首；又见东北方一切上妙宝世界，无所得境界眼如来、应、正等觉，道场众会之所围绕，无所得善变化菩萨而为上首；又见东南方香焰光音世界，香灯如来、应、正等觉，道场众会之所围绕，金刚焰慧菩萨而为上首；又见西南方智慧日普光明世界，法界轮幢如来、应、正等觉，道场众会之所围绕，现一切变化幢菩萨而为上首；又见西北方普清净世界，一切佛宝高胜幢如来、应、正等觉，道场众会之所围绕，法幢王菩萨而为上首；

and bodhisattvas' inconceivable samādhis and spiritual transformations.

At that time, Muktaka the Elder emerged from samādhi and spoke to Sudhana the Youth, saying:

Son of Good Family, I have already entered and emerged from the liberation gateway of the Tathāgata's unimpeded adornments. Son of Good Family, when I enter and emerge from this liberation gateway, I immediately see off to the east, in the Jambūnada Golden Light World, Sovereign Dragon King Tathāgata, the Arhat, the One of Right and Universal Enlightenment, surrounded by a congregation headed by Vairocana Treasury Bodhisattva.

I also see off to the south, in the Swift Powers World, Universal Fragrance Tathāgata, the Arhat, the One of Right and Universal Enlightenment, surrounded by a congregation headed by Mind King Bodhisattva.

I also see off to the west, in the Fragrant Light World, Sumeru Lamp King Tathāgata, the Arhat, the One of Right and Universal Enlightenment, surrounded by a congregation headed by Unimpeded Mind Bodhisattva.

I also see off to the north, in the Kaṣāya Banner World, Indestructible Vajra Tathāgata, the Arhat, the One of Right and Universal Enlightenment, surrounded by a congregation headed by Heroic Vajra Steps Bodhisattva.

I also see off to the northeast, in the All Supremely Marvelous Jewels World, Eye Beholding the Realm of the Inapprehensible Tathāgata, the Arhat, the One of Right and Universal Enlightenment, surrounded by a congregation headed by Skillful Transformations of the Inapprehensible Bodhisattva.

I also see off to the southeast, in the Fragrant Flame and Sound World, Fragrant Lamp Tathāgata, the Arhat, the One of Right and Universal Enlightenment, surrounded by a congregation headed by Vajra Flaming Wisdom Bodhisattva.

I also see off to the southwest, in the Universally Radiant Wisdom Sun World, Dharma Realm Wheel Banner Tathāgata, the Arhat, the One of Right and Universal Enlightenment, surrounded by a congregation headed by Banner Displaying All Transformations Bodhisattva.

I also see off to the northwest, in the Universally Pure World, All Buddha Jewels' Lofty and Supreme Banner Tathāgata, the Arhat, the One of Right and Universal Enlightenment, surrounded by a congregation headed by Dharma Banner King Bodhisattva.

正體字

又見上方佛次第出現無盡世
339c15║ 界。無邊智慧光圓滿幢如來應正等覺。道場
339c16║ 眾會之所圍遶。法界門幢王菩薩。而為上首。
339c17║ 又見下方佛光明世界。無礙智幢如來應正
339c18║ 等覺。道場眾會之所圍遶。一切世間剎幢王
339c19║ 菩薩。而為上首。善男子。我見如是等十方各
339c20║ 十佛剎微塵數如來。彼諸如來。不來至此。我
339c21║ 不往彼。我若欲見安樂世界阿彌陀如來。隨
339c22║ 意即見。我若欲見栴檀世界金剛光明如來。
339c23║ 妙香世界寶光明如來。蓮華世界寶蓮華光
339c24║ 明如來。妙金世界寂靜光如來。妙喜世界不
339c25║ 動如來。善住世界師子如來。鏡光明世界月
339c26║ 覺如來。寶師子莊嚴世界毘盧遮那如來。如
339c27║ 是一切。悉皆即見。然彼如來。不來至此。我身
339c28║ 亦不往詣於彼。知一切佛及與我心。悉皆
339c29║ 如夢。知一切佛猶如影像。自心如水。知一
340a01║ 切佛所有色相。及以自心。悉皆如幻。知一切
340a02║ 佛及以己心。悉皆如響。我如是知。如是憶念。
340a03║ 所見諸佛。皆由自心。善男子。當知菩薩修諸
340a04║ 佛法。淨諸佛剎。積集妙行。調伏眾生。發大誓
340a05║ 願。入一切智自在遊戲不可思議解脫之門。
340a06║ 得佛菩提。現大神通。遍往一切十方法界。以
340a07║ 微細智。普入諸劫如是一切。悉由自心。

简体字

又见上方佛次第出现无尽世界，无边智慧光圆满幢如来、应、正等觉，道场众会之所围绕，法界门幢王菩萨而为上首；又见下方佛光明世界，无碍智幢如来、应、正等觉，道场众会之所围绕，一切世间刹幢王菩萨而为上首。

“善男子，我见如是等十方各十佛刹微尘数如来。彼诸如来不来至此，我不往彼。我若欲见安乐世界阿弥陀如来，随意即见；我若欲见栴檀世界金刚光明如来、妙香世界宝光明如来、莲华世界宝莲华光明如来、妙金世界寂静光如来、妙喜世界不动如来、善住世界师子如来、镜光明世界月觉如来、宝师子庄严世界毗卢遮那如来，如是一切，悉皆即见。然彼如来不来至此，我身亦不往诣于彼。知一切佛及与我心，悉皆如梦；知一切佛犹如影像，自心如水；知一切佛所有色相及以自心，悉皆如幻；知一切佛及以己心，悉皆如响。我如是知，如是忆念：所见诸佛，皆由自心。

“善男子，当知菩萨修诸佛法，净诸佛刹，积集妙行，调伏众生，发大誓愿，入一切智自在游戏不可思议解脱之门，得佛菩提，现大神通，遍往一切十方法界，以微细智普入诸劫；如是一切，悉由自心。

I also see off in the direction of the zenith, in the Buddhas' Endless Sequential Appearances World, Banner of Boundless Perfectly Fulfilled Wisdom Light Tathāgata, the Arhat, the One of Right and Universal Enlightenment, surrounded by a congregation headed by Dharma Realm Gateway Banner King Bodhisattva.

I also see off in the direction of the nadir, in the Buddha Light World, Unimpeded Wisdom Banner Tathāgata, the Arhat, the One of Right and Universal Enlightenment, surrounded by a congregation headed by Banner King of All Worlds' Kṣetras Bodhisattva.

Son of Good Family, in each of the ten directions, I see *tathāgatas* such as these as numerous as the atoms in ten buddha *kṣetras*. Those *tathāgatas* do not come here to this place nor do I go to where they are located. If I wish to see Amitābha Tathāgata from the World of Bliss, then, in response to such a wish, I immediately see him. So too, if I wish to see the Sandalwood World's Vajra Radiance Tathāgata, the Sublime Fragrance World's Jewel Radiance Tathāgata, the Lotus Flower World's Jeweled Lotus Radiance Tathāgata, the Marvelous Gold World's Quiescent Light Tathāgata, the Sublime Joy World's Unshakable Tathāgata, the Fine Abiding World's Lion Tathāgata, the Mirror Light World's Lunar Enlightenment Tathāgata, or the Jeweled Lion Adornment World's Vairocana Tathāgata, then, in every case, I immediately see all the *tathāgatas* such as these.

In so doing, those *tathāgatas* do not come here, nor does my body go there to pay respects to them. I realize that all buddhas as well as my mind are all like a dream. I realize that all buddhas are like reflected images and that my mind is like the water [in which they are reflected]. I realize that all buddhas' forms and features as well as my own mind are all like conjured illusions. I realize that all buddhas on the one hand and my mind on the other—these are all like mere echoes. In this way, I realize that recollections such as these as well as the buddhas that are seen—they all arise from one's own mind.

Son of Good Family, you should realize that the bodhisattva's cultivation of the Buddha's dharmas, his purification of the buddha *kṣetras*, his accumulation of the marvelous practices, his training of beings, his generation of the great vows, his entry into the inconceivable liberation gateway of wandering and sporting with sovereign mastery in all-knowledge, his acquisition of the Buddha's bodhi, his manifestation of the great spiritual superknowledges, his going everywhere throughout the ten directions of the Dharma realm, and his use of subtle wisdom in everywhere entering all kalpas—all phenomena such as these arise from one's own mind.

正體字

是故。
340a08 善男子。應以善法。扶助自心。應以法水。潤澤
340a09 自心。應於境界。淨治自心。應以精進。堅固自
340a10 心。應以忍辱。坦蕩自心。應以智證。潔白自
340a11 心。應以智慧。明利自心。應以佛自在。開發自
340a12 心。應以佛平等。廣大自心。應以佛十力。照察
340a13 自心。善男子。我唯於此如來無礙莊嚴解脫
340a14 門。而得入出。如諸菩薩摩訶薩。得無礙智。住
340a15 無礙行。得常見一切佛三昧。得不住涅槃際
340a16 三昧。了達三昧。普門境界。於三世法。悉皆平
340a17 等。能善分身。遍一切剎。住於諸佛平等境界。
340a18 十方境界。皆悉現前。智慧觀察。無不明了。於
340a19 其身中。悉現一切世界成壞。而於己身及諸
340a20 世界。不生二想。如是妙行。而我云何。能知能
340a21 說。善男子。從此南行。至閻浮提畔。有一國
340a22 土。名摩利伽羅。

简体字

“是故，善男子，应以善法扶助自心，应以法水润泽自心，应于境界净治自心，应以精进坚固自心，应以忍辱坦荡自心，应以智证洁白自心，应以智慧明利自心，应以佛自在开发自心，应以佛平等广大自心，应以佛十力照察自心。

“善男子，我唯于此如来无碍庄严解脱门而得入出。如诸菩萨摩诃萨得无碍智住无碍行，得常见一切佛三昧，得不住涅槃际三昧，了达三昧普门境界，于三世法悉皆平等，能善分身遍一切刹，住于诸佛平等境界，十方境界皆悉现前，智慧观察无不明了，于其身中悉现一切世界成坏，而于己身及诸世界不生二想；如是妙行，而我云何能知能说？

“善男子，从此南行，至阎浮提畔，有一国土，名摩利伽罗；

Therefore, Son of Good Family:

One should use good dharmas to support one's mind;

One should use the waters of Dharma to moisten one's mind;

One should purify one's mind in the spheres of experience;

One should use vigor to fortify one's mind;

One should use patience to broaden one's mind;

One should use realizations of wisdom to enable one's mind to become immaculately pure;

One should use wisdom to clarify and sharpen one's mind;

One should use the Buddha's sovereign masteries to open and develop one's mind;

One should use the Buddha's equal regard for everyone to make one's mind vast in its scope; and

One should use the Buddha's ten powers to illuminate and investigate one's mind.

Son of Good Family, I have only achieved entry into and emergence from this liberation gateway of the Tathāgata's unimpeded adornments. As for the bodhisattva-mahāsattvas:

Who have acquired unimpeded wisdom;

Who abide in unimpeded practices;

Who have attained the samādhi in which one always sees all buddhas;

Who have attained the samādhi in which one does not reside beyond nirvāṇa's threshold and completely understands this samādhi's realm of the universal gateway;

Who abide in the uniform equality of all dharmas of the three periods of time;

Who are able to skillfully divide their bodies and go everywhere in all *kṣetras*;

Who abide in all buddhas' realm of uniform equality;

Who make all the realms of the ten directions manifest directly before them;

Who have nothing they do not completely understand through their wise contemplation; and

Who manifest within their own bodies the creation and destruction of all worlds and yet never generate any dualistic perceptions with respect to their own bodies and all worlds—

As for such marvelous practices as these, how could I know of or be able to speak about them?

Son of Good Family, traveling south from here to the very boundary of Jambudvīpa, there is a country known as Milaspharaṇa in

正體字

[1]彼有比丘。名曰海幢。汝詣
340a23║ 彼問。菩薩云何學菩薩行。修菩薩道。時善
340a24║ 財童子。頂禮解脫長者足。右遶觀察。稱揚讚
340a25║ 歎。思惟戀仰。悲泣流淚。一心憶念。依善知
340a26║ 識。事善知識。敬善知識。由善知識。見一切
340a27║ 智。於善知識。不生違逆。於善知識。心無諂
340a28║ 誑。於善知識。心常隨順。於善知識。起慈母
340a29║ 想。捨離一切無益法故。於善知識。起慈父想。
340b01║ 出生一切諸善法故。辭退而去
340b02║ 爾時善財童子。一心正念彼長者教。觀察彼
340b03║ 長者教。憶念彼不思議菩薩解脫門。思惟彼
340b04║ 不思議菩薩智光明。深入彼不思議法界門。
340b05║ 趣向彼不思議菩薩普入門。明見彼不思議
340b06║ 如來神變。解了彼不思議普入佛剎。分別彼
340b07║ 不思議佛力莊嚴。思惟彼不思議菩薩三昧
340b08║ 解脫境界分位。

简体字

彼有比丘，名曰海幢。汝诣彼问：菩萨云何学菩萨行、修菩萨道？”

时，善财童子顶礼解脱长者足，右绕观察，称扬赞叹，思惟恋仰，悲泣流泪，一心忆念：依善知识，事善知识，敬善知识，由善知识见一切智；于善知识不生违逆，于善知识心无谄诳，于善知识心常随顺；于善知识起慈母想，舍离一切无益法故；于善知识起慈父想，出生一切诸善法故。辞退而去。

尔时，善财童子一心正念彼长者教，观察彼长者教，忆念彼不思议菩萨解脱门，思惟彼不思议菩萨智光明，深入彼不思议法界门，趣向彼不思议菩萨普入门，明见彼不思议如来神变，解了彼不思议普入佛刹，分别彼不思议佛力庄严，思惟彼不思议菩萨三昧解脱境界分位，

which there is a bhikshu known as Sāgaradhvaja or "Ocean Banner." You should go there, pay your respects to him, and ask him how a bodhisattva should train in the bodhisattva practices and how he should cultivate the bodhisattva path.

Sudhana the Youth then bowed down in reverence at the feet of Muktaka the Elder, circumambulated him to his right as he gazed up at him, proclaimed his praises, and thought of him with fond longing as tears of sadness flowed down his face. He then single-mindedly brought to mind:

Reliance on the good spiritual guides;
Service to the good spiritual guides;
Reverence for the good spiritual guides;
That it is because of the good spiritual guides that one may attain the cognition of all-knowledge;
Refraining from opposition to the good spiritual guides;
Refraining from any flattery or deception in one's thoughts about the good spiritual guides;
Always mentally complying with the good spiritual guides;
Conceiving of the good spiritual guides as like a kindly mother due to whom one abandons all nonbeneficial dharmas; and
Conceiving of the good spiritual guides as like a kindly father due to whom one produces all good dharmas.

He then respectfully withdrew and departed.

6 – Sāgaradhvaja

At that time, Sudhana the Youth single-mindedly focused his right mindfulness on the teachings of that elder and contemplated the teachings of that elder:

He recollected his inconceivable gateways to bodhisattva liberation;
He reflected upon his inconceivable bodhisattva wisdom light;
He deeply entered his inconceivable gateways to the Dharma realm;
He progressed into his inconceivable gateways to the bodhisattva's universal penetration;
He clearly saw his inconceivable spiritual transformations of the *tathāgatas*;
He completely understood his inconceivable pervasive entry into the buddha *kṣetras*;
He distinguished among his inconceivable adornments with the Buddha's powers;
He reflected upon his inconceivable bodhisattva samādhis and liberations as well as his spheres of experience and stages [of the path];

正體字

了達彼不思議差別世界究
340b09 竟無礙。修行彼不思議菩薩堅固深心。發起
340b10 彼不思議菩薩大願淨業。漸次南行。至閻浮
340b11 提畔。摩利聚落。周遍求覓海幢比丘。乃見
340b12 其在經行地側。結[2]跏趺坐。入于三昧。離出
340b13 入息。無別思覺。身安不動。從其足下。出無數
340b14 百千億長者居士。婆羅門眾。皆以種種諸莊
340b15 嚴具。莊嚴其身。悉著寶冠。頂繫明珠。普往十
340b16 方一切世界。雨一切寶。一切瓔珞。一切衣服。
340b17 一切飲食。如法上味。一切華一切鬘。一切香
340b18 一切塗香。一切欲樂。資生之具。於一切處。救
340b19 攝一切貧窮眾生。安慰一切苦惱眾生。皆令
340b20 歡喜。心意清淨。成就無上菩提之道。從其兩
340b21 膝。出無數百千億剎帝利。婆羅門眾。皆悉
340b22 聰慧。種種色相。種種形貌。種種衣服。上妙莊
340b23 嚴。普遍十方一切世界。愛語同事。攝諸眾
340b24 生。所謂貧者令足。病者令愈。危者令安。怖者
340b25 令止。有憂苦者。咸使快樂。復以方便。而勸導
340b26 之。皆令捨惡。安住善法。

简体字

了达彼不思议差别世界究竟无碍，修行彼不思议菩萨坚固深心，发起彼不思议菩萨大愿净业。

渐次南行，至阎浮提畔摩利聚落，周遍求觅海幢比丘。乃见其在经行地侧结跏趺坐，入于三昧，离出入息，无别思觉，身安不动。

从其足下，出无数百千亿长者、居士、婆罗门众，皆以种种诸庄严具庄严其身，悉著宝冠，顶系明珠，普往十方一切世界，雨一切宝、一切璎珞、一切衣服、一切饮食如法上味、一切华、一切鬘、一切香、一切涂香、一切欲乐资生之具，于一切处救摄一切贫穷众生，安慰一切苦恼众生，皆令欢喜心意清净，成就无上菩提之道。

从其两膝，出无数百千亿刹帝利、婆罗门众，皆悉聪慧，种种色相、种种形貌、种种衣服上妙庄严，普遍十方一切世界，爱语、同事摄诸众生，所谓：贫者令足，病者令愈，危者令安，怖者令止，有忧苦者咸使快乐；复以方便而劝导之，皆令舍恶，安住善法。

He gained a complete comprehension of his inconceivable and ultimately unimpeded presence in different worlds;
He cultivated his possession of the bodhisattva's inconceivably strong determination; and
He made his inconceivable great bodhisattva vows and pure karmic works.

He then gradually traveled southward to the borderlands of Jambudvīpa, to the village of Mali where he searched all around for Sāgaradhvaja Bhikshu. He then saw him alongside his meditation walkway where, sitting in the lotus posture, he had entered samādhi. He had left behind outward and inward breathing, he had become free of discriminating thought and awareness, and his body remained calm and motionless.

From the bottom of his feet, he was sending forth countless groups of hundreds of thousands of *koṭīs* of elders, lay disciples, and brahmans, all of whose bodies were graced with all different kinds of adornments and all of whom wore jeweled crowns on their heads and had gleaming jewels set in their topknots. They all went forth everywhere throughout all the worlds of the ten directions in which they sent down a rain of all kinds of jewels, all kinds of necklaces, all kinds of robes, all kinds of food and beverages that accorded with the Dharma and were supreme in their flavors, all kinds of flower blossoms, all kinds of garlands, all types of incense, all sorts of perfumes, and all kinds of other desirable and delightful life-enhancing gifts. They everywhere rescued and gathered in all the poor and destitute beings and comforted all the beings who were tormented by sufferings. They then caused them all to be delighted, to acquire purified minds, and to attain complete success in the path to unexcelled bodhi.

From both of his knees, he sent forth countless groups of hundreds of thousands of *koṭīs* of *kṣatriya*s and brahmans, all of whom were possessed of sharp intelligence and all of whom, in their many different physical appearances, their many different physical forms, and their many different types of robes, were possessed of the most marvelous adornments. They went forth everywhere throughout all worlds of the ten directions in which, using pleasing words and joint endeavors, they attracted the many beings, in particular bringing sufficiency to the poor, bringing cures to the sick, bringing security to the endangered, halting threats to those in fear, and bringing happiness to those beset by suffering and despair. They also used skillful means by which they exhorted and guided them and caused them to abandon evil and securely establish themselves in good dharmas.

正體字

從其腰間。出等眾生
340b27 數無量仙人。或服草衣。或樹皮衣。皆執澡瓶。
340b28 威儀寂靜。周旋往返十方世界。於虛空中。以
340b29 佛妙音。稱讚如來。演說諸法。或說清淨梵行
340c01 之道。令其修習。調伏諸根。或說諸法皆無自
340c02 性。使其觀察。發生智慧。或說世間言論軌則。
340c03 或復開示一切智智出要方便。令隨次第各
340c04 修其業。從其兩脇。出不思議龍。不思議龍女。
340c05 示現不思議諸龍神變。所謂雨不思議香雲。
340c06 不思議華雲。不思議鬘雲。不思議寶蓋雲。不
340c07 思議寶幡雲。不思議妙寶莊嚴具雲。不思議
340c08 大摩尼寶雲。不思議寶瓔珞雲。不思議寶座
340c09 雲。不思議寶宮殿雲。不思議寶蓮華雲。不
340c10 思議寶冠雲。不思議天身雲。不思議采女雲。
340c11 悉遍虛空。而為莊嚴。充滿一切十方世界。諸
340c12 佛道場。而為供養。令諸眾生。皆生歡喜。從胸
340c13 前卍字中。出無數百千億阿脩羅王。

简体字

从其腰间，出等众生数无量仙人，或服草衣或树皮衣，皆执澡瓶，威仪寂静，周旋往返十方世界，于虚空中，以佛妙音，称赞如来，演说诸法；或说清净梵行之道，令其修习，调伏诸根；或说诸法皆无自性，使其观察，发生智慧；或说世间言论轨则，或复开示一切智智出要方便，令随次第各修其业。

从其两胁，出不思议龙、不思议龙女，示现不思议诸龙神变，所谓：雨不思议香云、不思议华云、不思议鬘云、不思议宝盖云、不思议宝幡云、不思议妙宝庄严具云、不思议大摩尼宝云、不思议宝璎珞云、不思议宝座云、不思议宝宫殿云、不思议宝莲华云、不思议宝冠云、不思议天身云、不思议采女云，悉遍虚空而为庄严，充满一切十方世界，诸佛道场而为供养，令诸众生皆生欢喜。

从胸前卍字中，出无数百千亿阿修罗王，

From his waist, he sent forth countless rishis just as numerous as beings themselves, some of whom wore robes made of grasses or robes made of tree bark and all of whom carried ablution pitchers. Serene in their deportment, they traveled around everywhere, going and coming throughout the worlds of the ten directions in which, from up in the sky, they used the sublime voice of a buddha to praise the Tathāgata and expound on all dharmas. In some cases, they expounded on the path of *brahmacarya*,[77] thereby causing beings to practice it and train their sense faculties. In some cases, they spoke of all dharmas' absence of any inherently existent nature, thereby causing beings to meditate on it and thus develop wisdom. In some cases they expounded on the principles contained in the world's treatises. Or then again, they offered instruction in attaining the wisdom of all-knowledge and the skillful means for gaining emancipation, thereby causing beings to follow the appropriate sequences for cultivating their own karma.

From both sides of his body, he sent forth an inconceivable number of dragons and an inconceivable number of dragon maidens who manifested all of the dragons' inconceivable spiritual transformations by sending down rains from:

Inconceivably many clouds of incense;
Inconceivably many clouds of flowers;
Inconceivably many clouds of garlands;
Inconceivably many clouds of jeweled canopies;
Inconceivably many clouds of jeweled banners;
Inconceivably many clouds of marvelous jeweled adornments;
Inconceivably many clouds of immense *maṇi* jewels;
Inconceivably many clouds of jewel necklaces;
Inconceivably many clouds of jeweled seats;
Inconceivably many clouds of jeweled palaces;
Inconceivably many clouds of jeweled lotus flowers;
Inconceivably many clouds of jeweled crowns;
Inconceivably many clouds of devas; and
Inconceivably many clouds of celestial nymphs.

These were present everywhere in the sky where they served as adornments. They filled all worlds throughout the ten directions where they were presented as offerings in the congregations of all buddhas and caused all the beings there to feel joyous delight.

From the *svastika* mark on the front of his chest, he sent forth countless hundreds of thousands of *koṭīs* of *asura* kings, all of whom

正體字

皆悉示
340c14║ 現不可思議自在幻力。令百世界。皆大震動。
340c15║ 一切海水。自然涌沸。一切山王。互相衝擊。諸
340c16║ 天宮殿。無不動搖。諸魔光明。無不隱蔽。諸魔
340c17║ 兵眾。無不摧伏。普令眾生捨憍慢心。除怒
340c18║ 害心。破煩惱山。息眾惡法。長無鬪諍。永共和
340c19║ 善。復以幻力。開悟眾生。令滅罪惡。令怖生
340c20║ 死。令出諸趣。令離染著。令住無上菩提之心。
340c21║ 令修一切諸菩薩行。令住一切諸波羅蜜。令
340c22║ 入一切諸菩薩地。令觀一切微妙法門。令知
340c23║ 一切諸佛方便。如是所作。周遍法界。從其
340c24║ 背上。為應以二乘而得度者。出無數百千億
340c25║ 聲聞獨覺。為著我者。說無有我。為執常者。說
340c26║ 一切行皆悉無常。為貪行者。說不淨觀。為瞋
340c27║ 行者。說慈心觀。為癡行者。說緣起觀。

简体字

皆悉示现不可思议自在幻力，令百世界皆大震动，一切海水自然涌沸，一切山王互相冲击，诸天宫殿无不动摇，诸魔光明无不隐蔽，诸魔兵众无不摧伏；普令众生，舍憍慢心，除怒害心，破烦恼山，息众恶法，长无斗诤，永共和善；复以幻力，开悟众生，令灭罪恶，令怖生死，令出诸趣，令离染著，令住无上菩提之心，令修一切诸菩萨行，令住一切诸波罗蜜，令入一切诸菩萨地，令观一切微妙法门，令知一切诸佛方便。如是所作，周遍法界。

从其背上，为应以二乘而得度者，出无数百千亿声闻、独觉；为著我者，说无有我；为执常者，说一切行皆悉无常；为贪行者，说不净观；为瞋行者，说慈心观；为痴行者，说缘起观；

manifested their sovereign mastery of the powers of conjuration with which they caused hundreds of worlds to all be seized by a great quaking movement, they caused the waters of all the oceans to spontaneously leap up as if boiling, and they caused the peaks of all the kings of mountains to knock against each other. Of all the heavens' palaces, there were none not shaken, of all the *māras'* light, there was none not obscured, and of all the armies of *māras*, there were none not vanquished.

This everywhere caused beings to relinquish their thoughts of arrogance, to rid themselves of angry or malicious thoughts, to smash their mountains of afflictions, to cease their dealing in the many kinds of evil dharmas, to increase their devotion to noncontentiousness, and to become forever joined in harmony and goodness.

In addition, they used the power of their conjurations to awaken beings, doing so:

By enabling them to extinguish the evil of karmic offenses;

By enabling them to fear existence in *saṃsāra*;

By enabling them to escape from all rebirth destinies;

By enabling them to abandon defiling attachments;

By enabling them to abide in the resolve to attain unexcelled bodhi;

By enabling them to cultivate all the bodhisattva practices;

By enabling them to abide in all the *pāramitās*;

By enabling them to enter into all the bodhisattva grounds;

By enabling them to contemplate all the gateways to the sublime Dharma; and

By enabling them to know all the skillful means of all buddhas.

Their endeavors such as these occurred everywhere throughout the Dharma realm.

Then, for those who should gain liberation through the teachings of the two vehicles, he sent forth from his upper back countless hundreds of thousands of *koṭīs* of *śrāvaka* disciples and *pratyekabuddhas* [who taught those beings in these ways]:

For those attached to the existence of a self, they taught the nonexistence of a self;

For those attached to the conception of permanence, they taught the impermanence of all conditioned things;

For those inclined to lust, they taught the meditation on impurity;[78]

For those inclined toward hatred, they taught meditation on the mind of loving-kindness;

For those inclined to delusion, they taught meditation on causal origination;

正體字

為等分
340c28║ 行者。說[3]與智慧相應境界法。為樂著境界
340c29║ 者。說無所有法。為樂著寂靜處者。說發大誓
341a01║ 願普饒益一切眾生法。如是所作。周遍法界。
341a02║ 從其兩肩。出無數百千億諸夜叉羅剎王。種
341a03║ 種形貌。種種色相。或長或短。皆可怖畏。無量
341a04║ 眷屬。而自圍遶。守護一切行善眾生。并諸賢
341a05║ 聖。菩薩眾會。若向正住。及正住者。或時現作
341a06║ 執金剛神。守護諸佛及佛住處。或遍守護一
341a07║ 切世間。有怖畏者。令得安隱。有疾病者。令得
341a08║ 除差。有苦惱者。令得免[1]離。有過惡者。令其
341a09║ 厭悔。有災橫者。令其息滅。如是利益一切眾
341a10║ 生。皆悉令其捨生死輪轉正法輪。從其腹出
341a11║ 無數百千億緊那羅王。各有無數緊那羅女。
341a12║ 前後圍遶。又出無數百千億乾闥婆王。各有
341a13║ 無數乾闥婆女。前後圍遶。各奏無數百千天
341a14║ 樂。歌詠讚歎諸法實性。歌詠讚歎一切諸佛。
341a15║ 歌詠讚歎發菩提心。

简体字

为等分行者，说与智慧相应境界法；为乐著境界者，说无所有法；为乐著寂静处者，说发大誓愿普饶益一切众生法。如是所作，周遍法界。

从其两肩，出无数百千亿诸夜叉、罗刹王，种种形貌、种种色相，或长或短，皆可怖畏，无量眷属而自围绕，守护一切行善众生，并诸贤圣、菩萨众会，若向正住及正住者；或时现作执金刚神，守护诸佛及佛住处，或遍守护一切世间。有怖畏者，令得安隐；有疾病者，令得除差；有苦恼者，令得免离；有过恶者，令其厌悔；有灾横者，令其息灭。如是利益一切众生，皆悉令其舍生死轮转正法轮。

从其腹，出无数百千亿紧那罗王，各有无数紧那罗女前后围绕；又出无数百千亿乾闼婆王，各有无数乾闼婆女前后围绕。各奏无数百千天乐，歌咏赞叹诸法实性，歌咏赞叹一切诸佛，歌咏赞叹发菩提心，

For those equally inclined to all of the afflictions, they taught the dharma of maintaining states of mind consistent with wisdom;

For those who delighted in attachment to their spheres of experience, they taught the dharma of the nonexistence of anything whatsoever;[79] and

For those who delighted in attachment to stations [of cultivation] characterized by quiescence, they taught the dharma of vowing to everywhere benefit all beings.

Their endeavors such as these occurred everywhere throughout the Dharma realm.

From both of his shoulders, he sent forth countless hundreds of thousands of *koṭīs* of *yakṣa* and *rākṣasa* kings who manifested in all different kinds of forms with all different kinds of appearances, some tall, some short, all of them fearsome. Surrounded by measurelessly large retinues, they served as guardians for all beings devoted to doing good deeds as well as for all of the worthies and *āryas* and the congregations of bodhisattvas whether they were still on the verge of reaching the stages of right abiding or had already reached the stages of right abiding.[80]

Some of them manifested as vajra-wielding spirits who guarded buddhas and the abodes of buddhas or manifested as those who everywhere guarded those in all worlds. Where there were those living in fear, they caused them to attain peace and security. Where there were those afflicted by sickness, they caused them to be cured. Where there were those tormented by sufferings, they caused them to avoid them. Where there were those who had committed evil deeds, they caused them to renounce them and repent of them. Where there were those beset by disastrous misfortunes, they caused those circumstances to disappear.

In ways such as these, they benefited all beings and enabled them all to abandon the wheel of *saṃsāra* and turn the wheel of right Dharma.

From his belly, he sent forth countless hundreds of thousands of *koṭīs* of *kiṃnara* kings, each of whom was surrounded by retinues of countless *kiṃnara* maidens. He also sent forth countless hundreds of thousands of *koṭīs* of *gandharva* kings, each of whom was surrounded by retinues of countless *gandharva* maidens. They each:

Played countless hundreds of thousands of types of celestial music;

Sang the praises of the true nature of all dharmas;

Sang the praises of all buddhas;

Sang the praises of resolving to attain bodhi;

正體字

歌詠讚歎修菩薩行。歌
341a16‖ 詠讚歎一切諸佛成正覺門。歌詠讚歎一切
341a17‖ 諸佛轉法輪門。歌詠讚歎一切諸佛現神變
341a18‖ 門。開示演說一切諸佛般涅槃門。開示演說
341a19‖ 守護一切諸佛教門。開示演說令一切眾生
341a20‖ 皆歡喜門。開示演說嚴淨一切諸佛剎門。開
341a21‖ 示演說顯示一切微妙法門。開示演說捨離
341a22‖ 一切諸障礙門。開示演說發生一切諸善根
341a23‖ 門。如是周遍十方法界。從其面門。出無數
341a24‖ 百千億轉輪聖[主>王]。七寶具足。四兵圍遶。放大
341a25‖ 捨光。雨無量寶。諸貧乏者。悉使充足。令其永
341a26‖ 斷不與取行。端正采女無數百千。悉以捨施
341a27‖ 心無所著。令其永斷邪婬之行。令生慈心。不
341a28‖ 斷生命。令其究竟常真實語。不作虛誑無益
341a29‖ 談說。令攝他語。不行離間。令柔軟語。無有麁
341b01‖ 惡。令常演說甚深決定明了之義。不作無義
341b02‖ 綺飾言辭。

简体字

歌咏赞叹修菩萨行，歌咏赞叹一切诸佛成正觉门，歌咏赞叹一切诸佛转法轮门，歌咏赞叹一切诸佛现神变门，开示演说一切诸佛般涅槃门，开示演说守护一切诸佛教门，开示演说令一切众生皆欢喜门，开示演说严净一切诸佛刹门，开示演说显示一切微妙法门，开示演说舍离一切诸障碍门，开示演说发生一切诸善根门。如是周遍十方法界。

从其面门，出无数百千亿转轮圣王，七宝具足，四兵围绕，放大舍光，雨无量宝；诸贫乏者悉使充足，令其永断不与取行；端正采女无数百千，悉以舍施心无所著，令其永断邪淫之行；令生慈心，不断生命；令其究竟常真实语，不作虚诳无益谈说；令摄他语，不行离间；令柔软语，无有粗恶；令常演说甚深决定明了之义，不作无义绮饰言辞；

Sang the praises of cultivating the bodhisattva practices;
Sang the praises of all buddhas' gateways to realizing right enlightenment;
Sang the praises of all buddhas' gateways to turning the Dharma wheel;
Sang the praises of all buddhas' gateways to the manifestation of spiritual transformations;
Revealed and expounded on all buddhas' gateways to *parinirvāṇa;*
Revealed and expounded on the gateways to preserving and protecting all buddhas' teachings;
Revealed and expounded on the gateways to delighting all beings;
Revealed and expounded on the gateways to the purification of all buddha *kṣetras;*
Revealed and expounded on the gateways to revealing all of the sublime dharmas;
Revealed and expounded on the gateways to abandoning all obstacles; and
Revealed and expounded on the gateways to producing all roots of goodness.

Their [actions] such as these occurred everywhere throughout the ten directions of the Dharma realm.

From his mouth,[81] he sent forth hundreds of thousands of *koṭīs* of wheel-turning sage kings fully endowed with their seven treasures and surrounded by their fourfold armies:

They emanated the light of great relinquishing and rained down countless jewels so that all who were poor and destitute became sufficiently endowed with wealth and were caused to forever cut off the practice of taking what has not been given;
They relinquished countless hundreds of thousands of beautiful female attendants, doing so with no thoughts of attachment, thereby causing beings to cut off the practice of sexual misconduct;
They caused beings to bring forth thoughts of loving-kindness and refrain from cutting short the lives of others;
They caused beings to ultimately always engage in truthful speech and refrain from false, devious, and nonbeneficial discourse;
They caused beings to adopt speech intended to attract others and refrain from speech conducive to estrangement;
They caused beings to practice gentle speech and refrain from harsh and evil speech;
They caused beings to always speak with profound, definite, and clear meaning while refraining from the use of meaningless and frivolous discourse;

正體字

為說少欲。令除貪愛。心無瑕垢。為
341b03║ 說大悲。令除忿怒意得清淨。為說實義。令其
341b04║ 觀察一切諸法。深入因緣。善明諦理。拔邪見
341b05║ 刺。破疑惑山。一切障礙。悉皆除滅。如是所
341b06║ 作。充滿法界。從其兩目。出無數百千億日輪。
341b07║ 普照一切諸大地獄及諸惡趣。皆令離苦。又
341b08║ 照一切世界中間。令除黑暗。又照一切十方
341b09║ 眾生。皆令捨離愚癡[2]翳障。於垢濁國土放清
341b10║ 淨光。白銀國土。放黃金色光。黃金國土。放白
341b11║ 銀色光。瑠璃國土。放[3]玻瓈色光。[*]玻瓈國土。
341b12║ 放瑠璃色光。硨磲國土。放碼碯色光。碼碯
341b13║ 國土。放硨磲色光。帝青國土。放日藏摩尼王
341b14║ 色光。日藏摩尼王國土。放帝青色光。赤真珠
341b15║ 國土。放月光網藏摩尼王色光。月光網藏摩
341b16║ 尼王國土。放赤真珠色光。一寶所成國土。放
341b17║ 種種寶色光。種種寶所成國土。放一寶色光。
341b18║ 照諸眾生心之稠林。[4]辨諸眾生無量事業。嚴
341b19║ 飾一切世間境界。令諸眾生。心得清涼。生
341b20║ 大歡喜。如是所作。充滿法界。從其眉間白毫
341b21║ 相中。出無數百千億帝釋。皆於境界。而得自
341b22║ 在。摩尼寶珠。繫其頂上。光照一切諸天宮殿。
341b23║ 震動一切須彌山王。

简体字

为说少欲，令除贪爱，心无瑕垢；为说大悲，令除忿怒，意得清净；为说实义，令其观察一切诸法，深入因缘，善明谛理，拔邪见刺，破疑惑山，一切障碍悉皆除灭。如是所作，充满法界。

从其两目，出无数百千亿日轮，普照一切诸大地狱及诸恶趣，皆令离苦；又照一切世界中间，令除黑暗；又照一切十方众生，皆令舍离愚痴翳障；于垢浊国土放清净光，白银国土放黄金色光，黄金国土放白银色光，琉璃国土放玻璃色光，玻璃国土放琉璃色光，砗磲国土放玛瑙色光，玛瑙国土放砗磲色光，帝青国土放日藏摩尼王色光，日藏摩尼王国土放帝青色光，赤真珠国土放月光网藏摩尼王色光，月光网藏摩尼王国土放赤真珠色光，一宝所成国土放种种宝色光，种种宝所成国土放一宝色光，照诸众生心之稠林，办诸众生无量事业，严饰一切世间境界，令诸众生心得清凉生大欢喜。如是所作，充满法界。

从其眉间白毫相中，出无数百千亿帝释，皆于境界而得自在，摩尼宝珠系其顶上，光照一切诸天宫殿，震动一切须弥山王，

They spoke on having but little desire, thereby causing beings to do away with lust and have minds free of defilements;

They spoke on the great compassion, thereby causing beings to do away with anger and purify their minds; and

They spoke on the ultimate truth, thereby causing beings to contemplate all dharmas, deeply penetrate causes and conditions, thoroughly understand the principles of the truths, extract the thorns of wrong views, smash the mountain of doubts, and do away with all obstacles.

Their endeavors such as these filled the entire Dharma realm.

From his eyes, he sent forth countless hundreds of thousands of *koṭīs* of suns that completely illuminated all the great hells and all the wretched destinies and enabled those within them to leave behind their sufferings. They also illuminated all the regions in those worlds and dispelled the darkness there. They also illuminated all beings throughout the ten directions and enabled them to leave behind the cataracts of their delusions.

They emanated pure light into defiled and turbid worlds, emanated yellow-gold light into silver worlds, emanated silver-colored light into yellow-gold worlds, emanated crystal-colored light into *vaiḍūrya* worlds, emanated *vaiḍūrya*-colored light into crystal worlds, emanated carnelian-colored light into *musāragalva* worlds, emanated *musāragalva*-colored light into carnelian worlds, emanated the colored light from solar-core sovereign *maṇi* jewels into *indranīla* sapphire worlds, emanated the colored light from *indranīla* sapphires into solar-core sovereign *maṇi* jewel worlds, emanated the colored light from moonlight net core sovereign *maṇi* jewels into red true pearl worlds, emanated the colored light from red true pearls into moonlight net core sovereign *maṇi* jewel worlds, emanated light the color of all different kinds of jewels into worlds consisting of but one type of jewel, emanated light the color of but one jewel into worlds consisting of many different kinds of jewels, illuminated the dense thickets of all beings minds, enabled the accomplishment[82] of beings' countless works, adorned the realms in all worlds, and enabled the minds of all beings to become clear and cool and filled with immense delight. Their endeavors such as these filled the entire Dharma realm.

From the white hair mark between his brows, he emanated countless hundreds of thousands of *koṭīs* of Śakras, lords of the devas, all of whom exercised sovereignty in all realms. The light from the *maṇi* jewels set in their topknots illuminated all the heavenly palaces, caused all the Sumerus, the kings of all mountains, to quake,

正體字

覺悟一切諸天大眾。歎
341b24‖ 福德力。說智慧力。生其樂力。持其志力。淨其
341b25‖ 念力。堅其所發菩提心力。讚樂見佛。令除世
341b26‖ 欲。讚樂聞法。令厭世境。讚樂觀智。令絕世
341b27‖ 染。止脩羅戰。斷煩惱[5]諍。滅怖死心。發降魔
341b28‖ 願。興立正法須彌山王。成[＊]辨眾生一切事
341b29‖ 業。如是所作。周遍法界。從其額上。出無數百
341c01‖ 千億梵天。色相端嚴。世間無比。威儀寂靜。言
341c02‖ 音美妙。勸佛說法。歎佛功德。令諸菩薩。悉皆
341c03‖ 歡喜。能[＊]辨眾生無量事業。普遍一切十方
341c04‖ 世界。從其頭上。出無量佛剎微塵數諸菩薩
341c05‖ 眾。悉以相好。莊嚴其身。放無邊光。說種種
341c06‖ 行。所謂讚歎布施。令捨慳貪。得眾妙寶。莊嚴
341c07‖ 世界。稱揚讚歎持戒功德。令諸眾生。永斷
341c08‖ 諸惡。住於菩薩大慈悲戒。說一切有悉皆如
341c09‖ 夢。說諸欲樂無有滋味。令諸眾生。離煩惱縛。
341c10‖ 說忍辱力。令於諸法。心得自在。

简体字

觉悟一切诸天大众；叹福德力，说智慧力，生其乐力，持其志力，净其念力，坚其所发菩提心力，赞乐见佛；令除世欲，赞乐闻法；令厌世境，赞乐观智；令绝世染，止修罗战，断烦恼诤，灭怖死心，发降魔愿，兴立正法须弥山王，成办众生一切事业。如是所作，周遍法界。

从其额上，出无数百千亿梵天，色相端严，世间无比，威仪寂静，言音美妙，劝佛说法，叹佛功德，令诸菩萨悉皆欢喜，能办众生无量事业，普遍一切十方世界。

从其头上，出无量佛刹微尘数诸菩萨众，悉以相好庄严其身，放无边光，说种种行。所谓：赞叹布施，令舍悭贪，得众妙宝庄严世界；称扬赞叹持戒功德，令诸众生永断诸恶，住于菩萨大慈悲戒；说一切有悉皆如梦，说诸欲乐无有滋味，令诸众生离烦恼缚；说忍辱力，令于诸法心得自在；

caused all the great congregations of devas to awaken, praised the power of merit, spoke about the power of wisdom, stimulated the power of their delight, sustained the power of their resolve, purified their power of mindfulness, strengthened the power of their resolve to attain bodhi, praised delight in seeing the Buddha, thus causing the elimination of worldly desires, praised delight in hearing the Dharma, thus causing weariness with worldly spheres of experience, and praised delight in contemplative wisdom, thus causing the severance of worldly defilements. This brought an end to warring with the *asuras*, brought about the severance of affliction-ridden disputation, extinguished thoughts fearful of death, inspired vows to quell the *māras*, proliferated the establishment of right Dharma as solid as Sumeru, the king of mountains, and facilitated the accomplishment[83] of all works undertaken by beings. Their endeavors such as these occurred everywhere throughout the Dharma realm.

From his forehead, he emanated countless hundreds of thousands of *koṭīs* of Brahma Heaven devas whose forms and appearances were handsome and without peer anywhere in the world. Their awesome deportment was serene and their voices were beautiful and sublime. They encouraged the buddhas to speak the Dharma, praised the meritorious qualities of the buddhas, caused all the bodhisattvas to feel delighted, and were able to bring about the accomplishment[84] of beings' countless works everywhere throughout the worlds of the ten directions.

From the top of his head, he emanated congregations of bodhisattvas as numerous as the atoms in countless buddha *kṣetras*, all of whom had the major marks and the secondary characteristics adorning their bodies. They all emanated boundless light and taught the many different kinds of practices, that is to say:

They praised giving, thereby causing beings to relinquish miserliness and encounter worlds adorned with the many kinds of marvelous jewels;

They proclaimed the praises of the meritorious qualities of upholding the moral precepts, thereby causing beings to forever cut off the many kinds of evil and abide in the bodhisattva's precepts of great kindness and compassion;

They taught that all stations of existence are like a dream;

They taught that all sensual pleasures are flavorless, thereby causing beings to escape the bonds of the afflictions;

They taught the power of patience, thereby causing beings' minds to acquire sovereign mastery in all dharmas;

正體字

讚金色身。令
341c11‖ 諸眾生。離瞋恚垢。起對治行。絕畜生道。歎精
341c12‖ 進行。令其遠離世間放逸。皆悉勤修無量妙
341c13‖ 法。又為讚歎禪波羅蜜。令其一切心得自在。
341c14‖ 又為演說般若波羅蜜。開示正見。令諸眾生。
341c15‖ 樂自在智。拔諸見毒。又為演說隨順世間種
341c16‖ 種所作。令諸眾生。雖離生死。而於諸趣。自在
341c17‖ 受生。又為示現神通變化。說壽命自在。令諸
341c18‖ 眾生。發大誓願。又為演說成就總持力。出生
341c19‖ 大願力。淨治三昧力。自在受生力。又為演
341c20‖ 說種種諸智。所謂普知眾生諸根智。普知一
341c21‖ 切心行智。普知如來十力智。普知諸佛自在
341c22‖ 智。如是所作。周遍法界。從其頂上。出無數百
341c23‖ 千億如來身。其身無等。諸相隨好。清淨莊嚴。
341c24‖ 威光赫奕。如真金山。無量光明。普照十方。出
341c25‖ 妙音聲。充滿法界。示現無量大神通力。為一
341c26‖ 切世間。普雨法雨。所謂

简体字

赞金色身，令诸众生离瞋恚垢，起对治行，绝畜生道；叹精进行，令其远离世间放逸，皆悉勤修无量妙法；又为赞叹禅波罗蜜，令其一切心得自在；又为演说般若波罗蜜，开示正见，令诸众生乐自在智拔诸见毒；又为演说随顺世间种种所作，令诸众生虽离生死，而于诸趣自在受生；又为示现神通变化，说寿命自在，令诸众生发大誓愿；又为演说成就总持力、出生大愿力、净治三昧力、自在受生力；又为演说种种诸智，所谓：普知众生诸根智、普知一切心行智、普知如来十力智、普知诸佛自在智。如是所作，周遍法界。

从其顶上，出无数百千亿如来身，其身无等，诸相随好，清净庄严，威光赫奕如真金山，无量光明普照十方，出妙音声充满法界，示现无量大神通力，为一切世间普雨法雨。所谓：

They praised the [Buddha's] golden-colored body, thereby causing beings to abandon the defilement of hatred, take up the counteractive practices, and cut off rebirths in the path of the animals;

They praised the practice of vigor, thereby causing them to leave worldly neglectfulness far behind and diligently cultivate the countless sublime dharmas;

They also praised *dhyāna pāramitā* for their sakes, thereby causing them to acquire sovereign mastery over all their thoughts;

They also expounded on *prajñāpāramitā* and explained right views for their sakes, thereby causing beings to delight in the masterful exercise of wisdom and in the elimination of the poison of wrong views;

They also expounded for their sakes on adapting to all the different endeavors occurring in the world, thereby enabling beings to freely take on births in all the rebirth destinies even though they have already escaped *saṃsāra;*

They also manifested spiritual transformations for their sakes and taught sovereign mastery over the length of one's life span, thereby causing beings to make the great vows;

They also expounded for their sakes on the successful development of the power of the complete-retention *dhāraṇīs,* on the power of bringing forth great vows, on the power of purifying samādhis, and on the power of sovereign mastery in taking on rebirths; and

They also expounded for their sakes on the many different kinds of knowledge, namely:

The knowledge that everywhere knows beings' faculties;

The knowledge that everywhere knows all their mental activity;

The knowledge that everywhere knows the Tathāgata's ten powers; and

The knowledge that everywhere knows all buddhas' sovereign masteries.

Their endeavors such as these occurred everywhere throughout the Dharma realm.

From the very summit of his head, he sent forth countless hundreds of thousands of *koṭīs* of *tathāgata* bodies. Their bodies were peerless and purely adorned with all the major marks and secondary signs. Their awesome radiance was gloriously bright, making them appear like mountains of real gold. Their countless light rays everywhere illuminated the ten directions and emanated marvelous sounds that, filling the entire Dharma realm, revealed the measureless powers of the great spiritual superknowledges.

They rained down the Dharma rains for the sake of everyone in the world, doing so in these ways:

正體字

為坐菩提道場諸菩
341c27 薩雨普知平等法雨。為灌頂位諸菩薩雨入
341c28 普門法雨。為法王子位諸菩薩雨普莊嚴法
341c29 雨。為童子位諸菩薩雨堅固山法雨。為不退
342a01 位諸菩薩雨海藏法雨。為成就正心位諸菩
342a02 薩雨普境界法雨。為方便具足位諸菩薩雨
342a03 自性門法雨。為生貴位諸菩薩雨隨順世間
342a04 法雨。為修行位諸菩薩雨普悲愍法雨。為新
342a05 學諸菩薩雨積集藏法雨。為初發心諸菩薩
342a06 雨攝眾生法雨。為信解諸菩薩雨無盡境界
342a07 普現前法雨。為色界諸眾生雨普門法雨。為
342a08 諸梵天雨普藏法雨。為諸自在天雨生力法
342a09 雨。為諸魔眾雨心幢法雨。為諸化樂天雨淨
342a10 念法雨。為諸兜率天雨生意法雨。

简体字

为坐菩提道场诸菩萨，雨普知平等法雨；为灌顶位诸菩萨，雨入普门法雨；为法王子位诸菩萨，雨普庄严法雨；为童子位诸菩萨，雨坚固山法雨；为不退位诸菩萨，雨海藏法雨；为成就正心位诸菩萨，雨普境界法雨；为方便具足位诸菩萨，雨自性门法雨；为生贵位诸菩萨，雨随顺世间法雨；为修行位诸菩萨，雨普悲愍法雨；为新学诸菩萨，雨积集藏法雨；为初发心诸菩萨，雨摄众生法雨；为信解诸菩萨，雨无尽境界普现前法雨；为色界诸众生，雨普门法雨；为诸梵天，雨普藏法雨；为诸自在天，雨生力法雨；为诸魔众，雨心幢法雨；为诸化乐天，雨净念法雨；为诸兜率天，雨生意法雨；

For the sake of bodhisattvas sitting in the sites of enlightenment, they rained down the Dharma rain of the universal realization of equality;

For the sake of bodhisattvas at the stage of the crown-anointing consecration, they rained down the Dharma rain of entry into the universal gateway;

For the sake of bodhisattvas at the stage of the Dharma prince, they rained down the Dharma rain of universal adornment;

For the sake of bodhisattvas at the stage of the pure youth, they rained down the Dharma rain of mountain-like solidity;

For the sake of bodhisattvas at the stage of irreversibility, they rained down the Dharma rain of the oceanic treasury;

For the sake of bodhisattvas at the stage of realization of right resolve, they rained down the Dharma rain of universal spheres of experience;

For the sake of bodhisattvas at the stage of complete repletion in skillful means, they rained down the Dharma rain of the inherent nature gateway;

For the sake of bodhisattvas at the stage of nobility, they rained down the Dharma rain of adaptation to the world;

For the sake of bodhisattvas at the stage of cultivation, they rained down the Dharma rain of universal compassionate sympathy;

For the sake of bodhisattvas at the stage of beginning training, they rained down the Dharma rain of treasury accumulation;

For the sake of bodhisattvas at the stage of initial generation of the resolve, they rained down the Dharma rain of the attraction of beings;

For the sake of bodhisattvas at the stage of resolute faith, they rained down the Dharma rain of the universal manifestation of endless spheres of experience;

For the sake of form realm beings, they rained down the Dharma rain of the universal gateway;

For the sake of Brahma Heaven devas, they rained down the Dharma rain of the universal treasury;

For the sake of the Paranirmita Vaśavartin Heaven devas, they rained down the Dharma rain of the generation of powers;

For the sake of the hordes of *māras*, they rained down the Dharma rain of the banner of the mind;

For the sake of Transformational Bliss Heaven devas, they rained down the Dharma rain of pure mindfulness;

For the sake of the Tuṣita Heaven devas, they rained down the Dharma rain of the generation of resolve;

正體字

為諸夜摩
342a11║ 天雨歡喜法雨。為諸忉利天雨疾莊嚴虛空
342a12║ 界法雨。為諸夜叉王雨歡喜法雨。為諸乾闥
342a13║ 婆王雨金剛輪法雨。為諸阿脩羅王雨大境
342a14║ 界法雨。為諸迦樓羅王雨無邊光明法雨。為
342a15║ 諸緊那羅王雨一切世間殊勝智法雨。為諸
342a16║ 人王雨無樂著法雨。為諸龍王雨歡喜幢法
342a17║ 雨。為諸摩睺羅伽王雨大休息法雨。為諸地
342a18║ 獄眾生雨正念莊嚴法雨。為諸畜生雨智慧
342a19║ 藏法雨。為閻羅王界眾生雨無畏法雨。為諸
342a20║ 厄難處眾生雨普安慰法雨。悉令得入賢聖
342a21║ 眾會。如是所作。充滿法界。海幢比丘。又於其
342a22║ 身一切毛孔。一一皆出阿僧祇佛剎微塵數
342a23║ 光明網。一一光明網。具阿僧祇色相。阿僧祇
342a24║ 莊嚴。阿僧祇境界。阿僧祇事業。充滿十方一
342a25║ 切法界。爾時善財童子。一心觀察海幢比丘。
342a26║ 深生渴仰。憶念彼三昧解脫。思惟彼不思議
342a27║ 菩薩三昧。

简体字

为诸夜摩天，雨欢喜法雨；为诸忉利天，雨疾庄严虚空界法雨；为诸夜叉王，雨欢喜法雨；为诸乾闼婆王，雨金刚轮法雨；为诸阿修罗王，雨大境界法雨；为诸迦楼罗王，雨无边光明法雨；为诸紧那罗王，雨一切世间殊胜智法雨；为诸人王，雨无乐著法雨；为诸龙王，雨欢喜幢法雨；为诸摩睺罗伽王，雨大休息法雨；为诸地狱众生，雨正念庄严法雨；为诸畜生，雨智慧藏法雨；为阎罗王界众生，雨无畏法雨；为诸厄难处众生，雨普安慰法雨。悉令得入贤圣众会。如是所作，充满法界。

海幢比丘又于其身一切毛孔，一一皆出阿僧祇佛刹微尘数光明网，一一光明网具阿僧祇色相、阿僧祇庄严、阿僧祇境界、阿僧祇事业，充满十方一切法界。

尔时，善财童子一心观察海幢比丘，深生渴仰，忆念彼三昧解脱，思惟彼不思议菩萨三昧，

For the sake of the Yāma Heaven devas, they rained down the Dharma rain of joyous delight;
For the sake of the Trāyastriṃśa Heaven devas, they rained down the Dharma rain of the swift adornment of the realm of empty space;
For the sake of the *yakṣa* kings, they rained down the Dharma rain of joyous delight;
For the sake of the *gandharva* kings, they rained down the Dharma rain of the vajra wheel;
For the sake of the *asura* kings, they rained down the Dharma rain of great spheres of experience;
For the sake of the *garuḍa* kings, they rained down the Dharma rain of boundless light;
For the sake of the *kiṃnara* kings, they rained down the Dharma rain of wisdom supreme throughout all worlds;
For the sake of the human kings, they rained down the Dharma rain of the absence of pleasure-based attachments;
For the sake of the dragon kings, they rained down the Dharma rain of banners of joyous delight;
For the sake of the *mahoraga* kings, they rained down the Dharma rain of the great cessation;
For the sake of the beings in the hells, they rained down the Dharma rain of adornment with right mindfulness;
For the sake of the animals, they rained down the Dharma rain of the treasury of wisdom;
For the sake of beings in the realms of King Yāma, they rained down the Dharma rain of fearlessness; and
For the sake of beings dwelling in the stations beset by the difficulties,[85] they rained down the Dharma rain of universal comfort.

They thereby enabled them all to enter the congregations of the worthies and *āryas*. Their endeavors such as these filled the entire Dharma realm.

From every one of the pores of his body, Sāgaradhvaja Bhikshu emitted nets of light rays as numerous as the atoms in an *asaṃkhyeya* of buddha *kṣetras* and every one of those nets of light rays included *asaṃkhyeyas* of forms and appearances, *asaṃkhyeyas* of adornments, *asaṃkhyeyas* of spheres of experience, and *asaṃkhyeyas* of karmic deeds that completely filled the ten directions of the entire Dharma realm.

At that time, Sudhana the Youth single-mindedly contemplated Sāgaradhvaja Bhikshu and felt deep admiration for him, whereupon:
He brought to mind his samādhis and liberations;
He contemplated his inconceivable bodhisattva samādhis;

正體字

思惟彼不思議利益眾生方便海。
342a28║ 思惟彼不思議無作用普莊嚴門。思惟彼莊
342a29║ 嚴法界清淨智。思惟彼受佛加持智。思惟彼
342b01║ 出生菩薩自在力。思惟彼堅固菩薩大願力。
342b02║ 思惟彼增廣菩薩諸行力。如是住立。思惟觀
342b03║ 察。經一日一夜。乃至經於七日七夜。半月一
342b04║ 月。乃至六月。復經六日。過此已後。海幢比
342b05║ 丘。從三昧出。善財童子。讚言聖者。希有奇
342b06║ 特。如此三昧最為甚深。如此三昧最為廣大。
342b07║ 如此三昧境界無量。如此三昧神力難思。如
342b08║ 此三昧光明無等。如此三昧莊嚴無數。如此
342b09║ 三昧威力難制。如此三昧境界平等。如此三
342b10║ 昧普照十方。如此三昧利益無限。以能除滅
342b11║ 一切眾生無量苦故。所謂能令一切眾生。離
342b12║ 貧苦故。出地獄故。免畜生故。閉諸難門故。開
342b13║ 人天道故。

简体字

思惟彼不思议利益众生方便海，思惟彼不思议无作用普庄严门，思惟彼庄严法界清净智，思惟彼受佛加持智，思惟彼出生菩萨自在力，思惟彼坚固菩萨大愿力，思惟彼增广菩萨诸行力。如是住立，思惟观察，经一日一夜，乃至经于七日七夜、半月、一月，乃至六月，复经六日。

过此已后，海幢比丘从三昧出。善财童子赞言：“圣者，希有奇特！如此三昧最为甚深，如此三昧最为广大，如此三昧境界无量，如此三昧神力难思，如此三昧光明无等，如此三昧庄严无数，如此三昧威力难制，如此三昧境界平等，如此三昧普照十方，如此三昧利益无限，以能除灭一切众生无量苦故。所谓：能令一切众生离贫苦故，出地狱故，免畜生故，闭诸难门故，开人、天道故，

He contemplated his ocean of inconceivable skillful means devoted to benefiting beings;
He contemplated his inconceivable gateways of effortless universal adornment;
He contemplated his pure knowledge regarding the adornments of the Dharma realm;
He contemplated his knowledge regarding receiving the Buddha's empowerments;
He contemplated his generation of the bodhisattva's powers of sovereign mastery;
He contemplated his strengthening of the power of the bodhisattva's great vows; and
He contemplated his broadening of the power of the bodhisattva's practices.

In this way, he stood there, meditatively contemplating him for one day and one night, and then on through seven days and seven nights, a half month, a month, and then for six months in all. He then continued doing so for an additional six days, after which Sāgaradhvaja Bhikshu arose from samādhi. Sudhana the Youth then praised him, saying:

O Ārya, this is so rare and extraordinary:
A samādhi such as this is the most extremely profound;
A samādhi such as this is the most vast;
A samādhi such as this has a measureless sphere of experience;
A samādhi such as this has inconceivable spiritual powers;
A samādhi such as this has incomparable radiance;
A samādhi such as this has countless adornments;
A samādhi such as this has indomitable awesome power;
A samādhi such as this has impartial spheres of experience;
A samādhi such as this everywhere illuminates the ten directions; and
A samādhi such as this bestows unlimited benefit because it is able to extinguish the measureless suffering of all beings, which is to say:
Because it is able to cause all beings to leave behind the suffering of poverty;
Because it allows them to escape from the hells;
Because it allows them to avoid rebirth in the animal realm;
Because it closes the gates to the difficulties;[86]
Because it opens the paths to rebirth among humans and devas;

正體字

令人天眾生喜樂故。令其愛樂禪
342b14‖ 境界故。能令增長有為樂故。能為顯示出有
342b15‖ 樂故。能為引發菩提心故。能使增長福智行
342b16‖ 故。能令增長大悲心故。能令生起大願力故。
342b17‖ 能令明了菩薩道故。能使莊嚴究竟智故。能
342b18‖ 令趣入大乘境故。能令照了普賢行故。能令
342b19‖ 證得諸菩薩地智光明故。能令成就一切菩
342b20‖ 薩諸願行故。能令安住一切智智境界中故。
342b21‖ 聖者。此三昧者。名為何等。海幢比丘言。善男
342b22‖ 子。此三昧。名普眼捨得。又名般若波羅蜜境
342b23‖ 界清淨光明。又名普莊嚴清淨門。善男子。我
342b24‖ 以修習般若波羅蜜故。得此普莊嚴清淨三
342b25‖ 昧等百萬阿僧祇三昧。善財童子言。聖者。此
342b26‖ 三昧境界。究竟唯如是耶。海幢言。

简体字

令人、天众生喜乐故，令其爱乐禅境界故，能令增长有为乐故，能为显示出有乐故，能为引发菩提心故，能使增长福智行故，能令增长大悲心故，能令生起大愿力故，能令明了菩萨道故，能使庄严究竟智故，能令趣入大乘境故，能令照了普贤行故，能令证得诸菩萨地智光明故，能令成就一切菩萨诸愿行故，能令安住一切智智境界中故。圣者，此三昧者，名为何等？”

海幢比丘言：“善男子，此三昧名普眼舍得，又名般若波罗蜜境界清净光明，又名普庄严清净门。善男子，我以修习般若波罗蜜故，得此普庄严清净三昧等百万阿僧祇三昧。”

善财童子言：“圣者，此三昧境界究竟唯如是耶？”

海幢言：

Because it causes joy and bliss for the beings in the human and deva realms;
Because it causes them to cherish and delight in the spheres of experience encountered in the *dhyānas*;
Because it is able to increase their happiness in conditioned existence;
Because it is able to reveal the bliss of escaping the stations of existence;
Because it is able to lead beings to resolve to attain bodhi;
Because it is able to cause them to increase the practices that produce merit and wisdom;
Because it is able to cause them to increase the mind of great compassion;
Because it is able to cause them to produce the power of great vows;
Because it is able to cause them to completely understand the bodhisattva path;
Because it is able to cause them to acquire the adornment of ultimate wisdom;
Because it is able to cause them to enter the realm of the Great Vehicle;
Because it is able to completely illuminate the practices of Samantabhadra;
Because it is able to cause them to attain the wisdom light of the bodhisattva grounds;
Because it is able to cause them to perfect all of the bodhisattva vows and practices; and
Because it is able to cause them to become securely established in the realm of the wisdom of all-knowledge.

O Ārya, please tell me: What is the name of this samādhi?

Sāgaradhvaja Bhikshu replied:

Son of Good Family, this samādhi is known as "the universal eye acquired through equanimity." It is also known as "the pure light of the realm of *prajñāpāramitā*" and as "the gateway of universal adornment and purification."

Son of Good Family, it is due to my cultivation of *prajñāpāramitā* that I have acquired this universal adornment and purification samādhi as well as a hundred myriads of *asaṃkhyeyas* of other such samādhis.

Sudhana the Youth then said, "O Ārya, are the spheres of experience of this samādhi ultimately only like these?"

Sāgaradhvaja replied:

正體字

善男子。入
342b27 此三昧時。了知一切世界。無所障礙。往詣
342b28 一切世界。無所障礙。超過一切世界。無所障
342b29 礙。莊嚴一切世界。無所障礙。修治一切世界。
342c01 無所障礙。嚴淨一切世界。無所障[1]礙。見一
342c02 切佛。無所障礙。觀一切佛廣大威德。無所障
342c03 礙。知一切佛自在神力。無所障礙。證一切佛
342c04 諸廣大力。無所障礙。入一切佛諸功德海。無
342c05 所障礙。受一切佛無量妙法。無所障礙。入一
342c06 切佛法中修習妙行。無所障礙。證一切佛轉
342c07 法輪平等智。無所障礙。入一切諸佛眾會道
342c08 場海。無所障礙。觀十方佛法。無所障礙。大
342c09 悲攝受十方眾生。無所障礙。常起大慈充滿
342c10 十方。無所障礙。見十方佛心無厭足。無所障
342c11 礙。入一切眾生海。無所障礙。知一切眾生根
342c12 海。無所障礙。知一切眾生諸根差別智。無所
342c13 障礙。善男子。我唯知此一般若波羅蜜三昧
342c14 光明。如諸菩薩。入智慧海。淨法界境。

简体字

“善男子，入此三昧时，了知一切世界，无所障碍；往诣一切世界，无所障碍；超过一切世界，无所障碍；庄严一切世界，无所障碍；修治一切世界，无所障碍；严净一切世界，无所障碍；见一切佛，无所障碍；观一切佛广大威德，无所障碍；知一切佛自在神力，无所障碍；证一切佛诸广大力，无所障碍；入一切佛诸功德海，无所障碍；受一切佛无量妙法，无所障碍；入一切佛法中修习妙行，无所障碍；证一切佛转法轮平等智，无所障碍；入一切诸佛众会道场海，无所障碍；观十方佛法，无所障碍；大悲摄受十方众生，无所障碍；常起大慈充满十方，无所障碍；见十方佛心无厌足，无所障碍；入一切众生海，无所障碍；知一切众生根海，无所障碍；知一切众生诸根差别智，无所障碍。

“善男子，我唯知此一般若波罗蜜三昧光明。如诸菩萨入智慧海，净法界境，

Son of Good Family, when one enters this samādhi:

One is unimpeded in completely knowing all worlds;
One is unimpeded in going to visit all worlds;
One is unimpeded in going beyond all worlds;
One is unimpeded in the adornment of all worlds;
One is unimpeded in the improvement of all worlds;
One is unimpeded in the purification of all worlds;
One is unimpeded in seeing all buddhas;
One is unimpeded in contemplating all buddhas' vast awesome virtue;
One is unimpeded in knowing all buddhas' sovereign mastery of the spiritual powers;
One is unimpeded in realizing all buddhas' vast powers;
One is unimpeded in entering the ocean of all buddhas' meritorious qualities;
One is unimpeded in receiving the countless sublime dharmas of all buddhas;
One is unimpeded in entering the cultivation of the marvelous practices in the Dharma of all buddhas;
One is unimpeded in realizing all buddhas' equal knowledge in turning the wheel of Dharma;
One is unimpeded in entering the ocean of all buddhas' congregations;
One is unimpeded in contemplating the Dharma of the buddhas of the ten directions;
One is unimpeded in using the great compassion to gather in the beings of the ten directions;
One is unimpeded in always filling the ten directions with the great kindness;
One is unimpeded in remaining mentally insatiable in seeing the buddhas of the ten directions;
One is unimpeded in entering the ocean of all beings;
One is unimpeded in knowing the ocean of all beings' faculties; and
One is unimpeded in knowing the different capacities for knowledge of all beings' faculties.

Son of Good Family, I know only this one "light of *prajñāpāramitā*" samādhi. As for the bodhisattvas:

Who have entered the ocean of wisdom;
Who have purified the sphere of the Dharma realm;

正體字

達一切
342c15 ║ 趣。遍無量剎。總持自在。三昧清淨。神通廣
342c16 ║ 大。辯才無盡。善說諸地。為眾生依。而我何能
342c17 ║ 知其妙行。[2]辨其功德。了其所行。明其境界。
342c18 ║ 究其願力。入其要門。達其所證。說其道分。住
342c19 ║ 其三昧。見其心境。得其所有。平等智慧。善男
342c20 ║ 子。從此南行。有一住處。名曰海潮。彼有園
342c21 ║ 林。名普莊嚴。於其園中。有優婆夷。名曰休
342c22 ║ 捨。汝往彼問。菩薩云何學菩薩行。修菩薩道。
342c23 ║ 時善財童子。於海幢比丘所。得堅固身。獲妙
342c24 ║ 法財。入深境界。智慧明徹。三昧照[＊]耀。住清
342c25 ║ 淨解。見甚深法。其心安住諸清淨門。智慧
342c26 ║ 光明。充滿十方。心生歡喜。踊躍無量。五體投
342c27 ║ 地。頂禮其足。遶無量匝。恭敬瞻仰。思惟觀
342c28 ║ 察。諮嗟戀慕。持其名號。想其容止。念其音
342c29 ║ 聲。思其三昧及彼大願所行境界。受其智慧
343a01 ║ 清淨光明。辭退而行

简体字

达一切趣，遍无量刹，总持自在，三昧清净，神通广大，辩才无尽，善说诸地，为众生依；而我何能知其妙行，辩其功德，了其所行，明其境界，究其愿力，入其要门，达其所证，说其道分，住其三昧，见其心境，得其所有平等智慧？

“善男子，从此南行，有一住处，名曰海潮；彼有园林，名普庄严；于其园中，有优婆夷，名曰休舍。汝往彼问：菩萨云何学菩萨行、修菩萨道？”

时，善财童子于海幢比丘所，得坚固身，获妙法财，入深境界，智慧明彻，三昧照耀，住清净解，见甚深法，其心安住诸清净门，智慧光明充满十方，心生欢喜，踊跃无量；五体投地，顶礼其足，绕无量匝，恭敬瞻仰，思惟观察，咨嗟恋慕，持其名号，想其容止，念其音声，思其三昧及彼大愿所行境界，受其智慧清净光明；辞退而行。

Who have a penetrating knowledge of the destinies [to which all dharmas lead];[87]
Who pervade countless *kṣetras;*
Who have achieved sovereign mastery of the complete-retention *dhāraṇīs;*
Who have purified the samādhis;
Whose spiritual superknowledges are vast;
Whose eloquence is inexhaustible;
Who skillfully explain the grounds; and
Who are refuges for beings—

How could I know their marvelous practices, explain[88] their meritorious qualities, comprehend what they practice, understand their spheres of experience, fathom their vow power, enter their essential gateways, acquire a penetrating comprehension of their realizations, speak about their aspects of the path, abide in their samādhis, see their minds' spheres of cognition, or acquire their wisdom of uniform equality?

Son of Good Family, traveling south from here, there is an abode known as Samudravetāḍī or "Ocean Tides," in which there is a park known as Samantavyūha or "Universal Adornment." There is an *upāsikā* in that park known as Āśā. You should go find her and ask, "How should one train in the bodhisattva practices?" and "How should one cultivate the bodhisattva path?"

Then, in the presence of Sāgaradhvaja Bhikshu, Sudhana the Youth, had acquired the solid body, had gained the wealth of sublime Dharma, had entered the deep spheres of experience, had developed brightly penetrating wisdom, had entered brilliantly luminous samādhis, had come to dwell in pure understanding,[89] and had perceived the extremely profound Dharma. His mind then dwelt securely in the pure gateways and the light of his wisdom filled the ten directions. His mind was filled with delight and he was overcome with measureless joy.

He then prostrated himself in reverence at the feet of Sāgaradhvaja Bhikshu and circumambulated him countless times as he gazed up at him respectfully, pondered and contemplating him, sighed with admiration, bore his name in mind, envisioned his countenance and demeanor, recollected the sound of his voice, and thought about his samādhi, his great vows, and the domain of his practice. Then, having received the pure light of his wisdom, he respectfully took his leave and traveled on.

正體字

343a05║大方廣佛華嚴經卷第六十四
343a08║　　入法界品第三十九之五
343a09║ 爾時善財童子。蒙善知識力。依善知識教。念
343a10║ 善知識語。於善知識。深心愛樂。作是念言。因
343a11║ 善知識。令我見佛。因善知識。令我聞法。善知
343a12║ 識者。是我師傅。示導於我諸佛法故。善知識
343a13║ 者。是我眼目。令我見佛如虛空故。善知識者。
343a14║ 是我津濟。令我得入諸佛如來蓮華池故。漸
343a15║ 漸南行。至海潮處。見普莊嚴園。眾寶垣牆。周
343a16║ 匝圍遶。一切寶樹。行列莊嚴。一切寶華樹。雨
343a17║ 眾妙華。布散其地。一切寶香樹。香氣氛氳。普
343a18║ 熏十方。一切寶鬘樹。雨大寶鬘。處處垂下。一
343a19║ 切摩尼寶王樹。雨大摩尼寶。遍布充滿。一切
343a20║ 寶衣樹。雨種種色衣。隨其所應。周匝敷布。一
343a21║ 切音樂樹。風動成音。其音美妙。過於天樂。一
343a22║ 切莊嚴具樹。各雨珍玩奇妙之物。處處分布。
343a23║ 以為嚴飾。其地清淨。無有高下。於中具有百
343a24║ 萬殿堂。大摩尼寶之所合成。百萬樓閣。

简体字

大方广佛华严经卷第六十四

入法界品第三十九之五

尔时，善财童子蒙善知识力，依善知识教，念善知识语，于善知识深心爱乐，作是念言："因善知识，令我见佛；因善知识，令我闻法。善知识者是我师傅，示导于我诸佛法故；善知识者是我眼目，令我见佛如虚空故；善知识者是我津济，令我得入诸佛如来莲华池故。"

渐渐南行，至海潮处，见普庄严园，众宝垣墙周匝围绕，一切宝树行列庄严；一切宝华树，雨众妙华，布散其地；一切宝香树，香气氛氲，普熏十方；一切宝鬘树，雨大宝鬘，处处垂下；一切摩尼宝王树，雨大摩尼宝，遍布充满；一切宝衣树，雨种种色衣，随其所应，周匝敷布；一切音乐树，风动成音，其音美妙，过于天乐；一切庄严具树，各雨珍玩奇妙之物，处处分布，以为严饰。

其地清净无有高下，于中具有百万殿堂，大摩尼宝之所合成；百万楼阁，

7 – Āśā

At that time, having received the powers bestowed by the good spiritual guide, Sudhana the Youth relied on the good spiritual guide's instruction, recalled the good spiritual guide's words, and felt deep affection for the good spiritual guide. He then had this thought: "It is because of the good spiritual guide that I have been enabled to see the Buddha and it is because of the good spiritual guide that I have been enabled to hear the Dharma. The good spiritual guide is my master teacher, for it is he who has shown and guided me in the Buddha's Dharma. The good spiritual guide is my very eyes, for it is he who has enabled me to see the Buddha as comparable to empty space. And the good spiritual guide is my bridge, for it is he who has enabled me to enter the lotus flower pond of the buddhas, the *tathāgatas*."

He then gradually traveled southward until he reached the place known as Ocean Tides where he saw Universal Adornment Park surrounded by a perimeter wall made of the many kinds of jewels. In it there were:

All kinds of jeweled trees arranged in beautifying rows;

All kinds of jeweled blossoming trees raining down many kinds of marvelous blossoms that scattered across its grounds;

All kinds of jeweled incense trees the fragrant vaporous mists from which everywhere scented the air throughout the ten directions;

All kinds of jeweled garland trees that rained down large garlands of jewels that hung down in place after place;

All kinds of sovereign *maṇi* jewel trees that rained down immense *maṇi* jewels that were spread about everywhere, completely covering those grounds;

All kinds of jeweled robe trees that rained down the many different colors of robes that, appearing in response to what was needed, were spread around everywhere;

All kinds of musical trees that, when blown and moved by the breeze, produced sounds that were more beautiful than heavenly music; and

All kinds of adornment-bearing trees, each of which rained down precious, unique, and marvelous objects of amusement that were spread about in place after place as adornments.

Its grounds were immaculate and free of either high or low places. Within it, there were hundreds of myriads of temple halls composed of immense *maṇi* jewels, hundreds of myriads of towers covered with

正體字

閻浮
343a25 ‖ 檀金。以覆其上。百萬宮殿。毘盧遮那摩尼寶。
343a26 ‖ 間錯莊嚴。一萬浴池。眾寶合成。七寶欄楯。周
343a27 ‖ 匝圍遶。七寶階道。四面分布。八功德水。湛然
343a28 ‖ 盈滿。其水香氣。如天栴檀。金沙布底。水清寶
343a29 ‖ 珠。周遍間錯。鳧鴈孔雀。俱枳羅鳥。遊戲其
343b01 ‖ 中。出和雅音。寶多羅樹。周匝行列。覆以寶
343b02 ‖ 網。垂諸金鈴。微風徐搖。恒出美音。施大寶
343b03 ‖ 帳。寶樹圍遶。建立無數摩尼寶幢。光明普照
343b04 ‖ 百千由旬。其中復有百萬陂池。黑栴檀泥。凝
343b05 ‖ 積其底。一切妙寶。以為蓮華。敷布水上。大摩
343b06 ‖ 尼華光色。照[1]耀園中。復有廣大宮殿。名莊
343b07 ‖ 嚴幢。海藏妙寶。以為其地。毘瑠璃寶。以為其
343b08 ‖ 柱。閻浮檀金。以覆其上。光藏摩尼。以為莊
343b09 ‖ 嚴。無數寶王。光焰熾然。重樓挾閣。種種莊
343b10 ‖ 飾。阿盧那香王。覺悟香王。皆出妙香。普熏一
343b11 ‖ 切。其宮殿中。復有無量寶蓮華座。周迴布列。
343b12 ‖ 所謂照耀十方摩尼寶蓮華座。

简体字

阎浮檀金以覆其上；百万宫殿，毗卢遮那摩尼宝间错庄严；一万浴池，众宝合成；七宝栏楯，周匝围绕；七宝阶道，四面分布；八功德水，湛然盈满，其水香气如天栴檀，金沙布底，水清宝珠周遍间错；凫雁、孔雀、俱枳罗鸟游戏其中，出和雅音；宝多罗树周匝行列，覆以宝网，垂诸金铃，微风徐摇，恒出美音；施大宝帐，宝树围绕，建立无数摩尼宝幢，光明普照百千由旬。其中复有百万陂池，黑栴檀泥凝积其底，一切妙宝以为莲华敷布水上，大摩尼华光色照耀园中。

复有广大宫殿，名庄严幢，海藏妙宝以为其地，毗琉璃宝以为其柱，阎浮檀金以覆其上，光藏摩尼以为庄严，无数宝王光焰炽然，重楼挟阁种种庄饰；阿卢那香王、觉悟香王，皆出妙香普熏一切。其宫殿中，复有无量宝莲华座周回布列，所谓：照耀十方摩尼宝莲华座、

jambūnada gold, hundreds of myriads of palaces adorned with inlaid *vairocana maṇi* jewels, and a myriad bathing ponds composed of the many different kinds of jewels. These had railings made of the seven types of precious jewels which encircled their perimeters and also had steps on all four sides which were made of the seven types of precious jewels.

These ponds were filled with clear waters possessed of the eight qualities that were fragrant with scents like those of celestial sandalwood incense. Gold sand was spread across their bottoms and their sides were inlaid all around with water-clarifying pearls. As geese, ducks, peacocks, and *kokila* birds sported about in them, their calls sent forth harmonious and lovely sounds.

Bejeweled *tāla* trees formed an encircling line of trees all around them. They were covered by suspended nets of jewels from which there hung all kinds of gold bells. As subtle breezes wafted through and gently shook them, they constantly sent forth beautiful sounds.

Immense curtains of jewels were set up there and jeweled trees encircled the area. Countless *maṇi* jewel banners had been raised there, the light from which sent its illumination everywhere to a distance of a hundred thousand *yojanas*.

In addition, there were a hundred myriad ponds the bottoms of which were coated with a clay consisting of *kālānusāri* sandalwood incense. All kinds of marvelous jewels formed blossoming lotus flowers that spread across the surface of their waters. The colored light from immense *maṇi* jewel flowers cast their brilliant radiance all about within that park.

There was also a vast palace known as Beautiful Banners which had marvelous jewels from the treasury of the ocean that formed its grounds and *vaiḍūrya* gems that composed its pillars. Its roof was made of *jambūnada* gold adorned with radiant-core *maṇi* jewels. Countless sovereign jewels emanated intensely brilliant flaming light.

The lateral chambers of the multistoried tower were decorated with many different kinds of adornments. Sovereign *anuracita* incense and sovereign awakening incense exuded marvelous fragrances that everywhere scented the air. Within that palace, there were also countless jeweled lotus flower thrones which were arrayed all around. In particular, there were:

Maṇi jewel lotus flower thrones casting their brilliant illumination in the ten directions;

正體字

毘盧遮那摩
343b13║ 尼寶蓮華座。照[＊]耀世間摩尼寶蓮華座。妙
343b14║ 藏摩尼寶蓮華座。師子藏摩尼寶蓮華座。離
343b15║ 垢藏摩尼寶蓮華座。普門摩尼寶蓮華座。光
343b16║ 嚴摩尼寶蓮華座。安住大海藏清淨摩尼王
343b17║ 寶蓮華座。金剛師子摩尼寶蓮華座。園中復
343b18║ 有百萬種帳。所謂衣帳鬘帳。香帳華帳。枝帳
343b19║ 摩尼帳。真金帳。莊嚴具帳。音樂帳。象王神變
343b20║ 帳。馬王神變帳。帝釋所著摩尼寶帳。如是等
343b21║ 其數百萬。有百萬大寶網。彌覆其上。所謂寶
343b22║ 鈴網。寶蓋網。寶身網。海藏真珠網。紺瑠璃摩
343b23║ 尼寶網。師子摩尼網。月光摩尼網。種種形像
343b24║ 眾香網。寶冠網。寶瓔珞網。如是等其數百萬。
343b25║ 有百萬大光明之所照[＊]耀。所謂焰光摩尼寶
343b26║ 光明。日藏摩尼寶光明。月幢摩尼寶光明。香
343b27║ 焰摩尼寶光明。勝藏摩尼寶光明。蓮華藏摩
343b28║ 尼寶光明。焰幢摩尼寶光明。大燈摩尼寶光
343b29║ 明。普照十方摩尼寶光明。香光摩尼寶光明。
343c01║ 如是等其數百萬。常雨百萬莊嚴具。百萬黑
343c02║ 栴檀香出妙音聲。

简体字

毗卢遮那摩尼宝莲华座、照耀世间摩尼宝莲华座、妙藏摩尼宝莲华座、师子藏摩尼宝莲华座、离垢藏摩尼宝莲华座、普门摩尼宝莲华座、光严摩尼宝莲华座、安住大海藏清净摩尼王宝莲华座、金刚师子摩尼宝莲华座。

园中复有百万种帐，所谓：衣帐、鬘帐、香帐、华帐、枝帐、摩尼帐、真金帐、庄严具帐、音乐帐、象王神变帐、马王神变帐、帝释所著摩尼宝帐，如是等其数百万。有百万大宝网弥覆其上，所谓：宝铃网、宝盖网、宝身网、海藏真珠网、绀琉璃摩尼宝网、师子摩尼网、月光摩尼网、种种形像众香网、宝冠网、宝璎珞网，如是等其数百万。有百万大光明之所照耀，所谓：焰光摩尼宝光明、日藏摩尼宝光明、月幢摩尼宝光明、香焰摩尼宝光明、胜藏摩尼宝光明、莲华藏摩尼宝光明、焰幢摩尼宝光明、大灯摩尼宝光明、普照十方摩尼宝光明、香光摩尼宝光明，如是等其数百万。常雨百万庄严具，百万黑栴檀香出妙音声，

Vairocana maṇi jewel lotus flower thrones;
World-illumining *maṇi* jewel lotus flower thrones;
Marvelous treasury *maṇi* jewel lotus flower thrones;
Lion treasury *maṇi* jewel lotus flower thrones;
Stainless treasury *maṇi* jewel lotus flower thrones;
Universal Gateway *maṇi* jewel lotus flower thrones;
Light-adorned *maṇi* jewel lotus flower thrones;
Lotus flower thrones made with pristine sovereign *maṇi* jewels from the great ocean's treasury; and
Vajra lion *maṇi* jewel lotus flower thrones.

Within that park, there were also a hundred myriad different kinds of canopies. In particular, there were robe canopies, garland canopies, incense canopies, flower canopies, branch canopies, *maṇi* jewel canopies, real gold canopies, adornment canopies, music canopies, elephant king canopies produced by spiritual transformations, horse king canopies produced by spiritual transformations, and canopies made of the *maṇi* jewels worn by Śakra, lord of the devas. There were a hundred myriad canopies such as these.

There were also a hundred myriad immense jeweled nets that stretched across and covered the area from above. In particular, there were jeweled bell nets, jeweled canopy nets, jeweled body nets, ocean treasury true pearl nets, nets of purple *vaiḍūrya* and *maṇi* jewels, lion *maṇi* jewel nets, moonlight *maṇi* jewel nets, nets of many different types of incense of all different forms and appearances, jeweled crown nets, and jewel necklace nets. There were a hundred myriad types of nets such as these.

[The park] was illuminated by the brilliant illumination of a hundred myriad kinds of great lights. In particular, there was light from flaming-light *maṇi* jewels, light from solar-core *maṇi* jewels, light from moon banner *maṇi* jewels, light from scented flaming-light *maṇi* jewels, light from supreme treasury *maṇi* jewels, light from lotus flower treasury *maṇi* jewels, light from flaming-light banner *maṇi* jewels, light from immense lamp *maṇi* jewels, light from *maṇi* jewels everywhere illuminating the ten directions, and light from scented radiance *maṇi* jewels. There were a hundred myriad types of brilliant illumination such as these.

And there was the constant raining down of:

Hundreds of myriads of adornments;
Hundreds of myriads of clouds of *kālānusāri* sandalwood incense emanating marvelous sounds;

正體字

百萬出過諸天曼陀羅華
343c03‖ 而以散之。百萬出過諸天瓔珞。以為莊嚴。百
343c04‖ 萬出過諸天妙寶鬘帶。處處垂下。百萬出過
343c05‖ 諸天眾色妙衣。百萬雜色摩尼寶。妙光普照。
343c06‖ 百萬天子。欣樂瞻仰。頭面作禮。百萬采女。於
343c07‖ 虛空中。投身而下。百萬菩薩。恭敬親近。常樂
343c08‖ 聞法。時休捨優婆夷。坐真金座。戴海藏真珠
343c09‖ 網。冠挂出過諸天真金寶釧。垂紺青髮。大摩
343c10‖ 尼網。莊嚴其首。師子口摩尼寶。以為耳璫。如
343c11‖ 意摩尼寶王。以為瓔珞。一切寶網。垂覆其身。
343c12‖ 百千億那由他眾生。曲躬恭敬。東方有無量
343c13‖ 眾生。來詣其所。所謂梵天梵眾天。大梵天梵
343c14‖ 輔天。自在天。乃至一切人及非人。南西北方。
343c15‖ 四維上下。皆亦如是。其有見此優婆夷者。一
343c16‖ 切病苦。悉得除滅。離煩惱垢。拔諸見刺。摧障
343c17‖ 礙山。入於無礙清淨境界。增明一切所有善
343c18‖ 根。長養諸根。入一切智慧門。入一切總持門。
343c19‖ 一切三昧門。一切大願門。一切妙行門。

简体字

百万出过诸天曼陀罗华而以散之，百万出过诸天璎珞以为庄严，百万出过诸天妙宝鬘带处处垂下，百万出过诸天众色妙衣，百万杂色摩尼宝妙光普照，百万天子欣乐瞻仰头面作礼，百万采女于虚空中投身而下，百万菩萨恭敬亲近常乐闻法。

时，休舍优婆夷坐真金座，戴海藏真珠网冠，挂出过诸天真金宝钏，垂绀青发，大摩尼网庄严其首，师子口摩尼宝以为耳珰，如意摩尼宝王以为璎珞，一切宝网垂覆其身，百千亿那由他众生曲躬恭敬。东方有无量众生来诣其所，所谓：梵天、梵众天、大梵天、梵辅天、自在天，乃至一切人及非人；南、西、北方，四维、上、下，皆亦如是。其有见此优婆夷者，一切病苦悉得除灭，离烦恼垢，拔诸见刺，摧障碍山，入于无碍清净境界，增明一切所有善根，长养诸根；入一切智慧门，入一切总持门；一切三昧门、一切大愿门、一切妙行门、

Hundreds of myriads of *mandārava* blossoms surpassing even those in the heavens that scattered down everywhere;

Hundreds of myriads of necklaces surpassing even those in the heavens that served there as adornments;

Hundreds of myriads of jeweled garland sashes surpassing even those in the heavens that were draped everywhere;

Hundreds of myriads of marvelous multicolored robes surpassing even those in the heavens;

Hundreds of myriads of varicolored *maṇi* jewels, the marvelous radiance from which sent their illumination everywhere;

Hundreds of myriads of deva sons who gazed up in delight and admiration and then made full reverential prostrations;

Hundreds of myriads of palace maidens who flew down from the sky; and

Hundreds of myriads of bodhisattvas who respectfully drew near and always delighted in hearing the Dharma.

At that time, Āśā, the Upāsikā, was sitting on a throne made of gold. She was wearing a filigree tiara of real pearls from the ocean treasury and her arms were adorned with jeweled gold bracelets that surpassed even those of the gods. She had flowing indigo hair, a net made of immense *maṇi* jewels that adorned her head, earrings made of lion mouth *maṇi* jewels, and a necklace made of wish-fulfilling sovereign *maṇi* jewels. A lace mesh made of every kind of jewel draped down and covered her body. A hundred thousand *koṭīs* of *nayutas* of beings bent their bodies low as a sign of respect as, off to the east, there were countless beings coming to pay respects to her, including devas from the Brahma Heaven, the Brahma Retinue Heaven, the Great Brahma Heaven, the Brahma Assistants Heaven, the Paranirmita Vaśavartin Heaven, and so forth. These also included all kinds of humans and nonhumans. This was also occurring in the south, the west, the north, the four midpoints, the zenith, and the nadir.

Of those who came to see this *upāsikā,* all of those suffering with illnesses found that they disappeared entirely. They left behind the defilement of the afflictions. The thorns of their wrong views were pulled out, the mountains of their various obstacles were crushed, and they entered unimpededly pure spheres of experience. They increased in the radiance of all their roots of goodness, increased in the development of their faculties, entered the gateway of all-knowledge, and entered the gateways of every kind of complete-retention *dhāraṇī.* The gateways of all of the samādhis, the gateways of all the great vows, the gateways of all the marvelous practices, and all the

正體字

一
343c20 切功德門。皆得現前。其心廣大。具足神通。身
343c21 無障礙。至一切處。爾時善財童子。入普莊嚴
343c22 園。周遍觀察。見休捨優婆夷。坐於妙座。往詣
343c23 其所。頂禮其足。遶無數匝。白言。聖者。我已
343c24 先發阿耨多羅三藐三菩提心。而未知菩薩
343c25 云何學菩薩行。云何修菩薩道。我聞聖者。善
343c26 能誘誨。願為我說。休捨告言。善男子。我唯得
343c27 菩薩一解脫門。若有見聞憶念於我。與我同
343c28 住。供給我者。悉不唐捐。善男子。若有眾生。
343c29 不種善根。不為善友之所攝受。不為諸佛之
344a01 所護念。是人終不得見於我。善男子。其有眾
344a02 生。得見我者。皆於阿耨多羅三藐三菩提。獲
344a03 不退轉。善男子。東方諸佛。常來至此。處於寶
344a04 座。為我說法。南西北方。四維上下。一切諸
344a05 佛。悉來至此。處於寶座。為我說法。善男子。
344a06 我常不離見佛聞法。與諸菩薩。而共同住。善
344a07 男子。我此大眾。有八萬四千億那由他。皆在
344a08 此園。與我同行。悉於阿耨多羅三藐三菩提。
344a09 得不退轉。其餘眾生。住此園者。亦皆普入不
344a10 退轉位。

简体字

一切功德门，皆得现前；其心广大，具足神通，身无障碍，至一切处。

尔时，善财童子入普庄严园，周遍观察，见休舍优婆夷坐于妙座，往诣其所，顶礼其足，绕无数匝，白言：“圣者，我已先发阿耨多罗三藐三菩提心，而未知菩萨云何学菩萨行？云何修菩萨道？我闻圣者善能诱诲，愿为我说！”

休舍告言：“善男子，我唯得菩萨一解脱门，若有见闻忆念于我，与我同住，供给我者，悉不唐捐。善男子，若有众生不种善根，不为善友之所摄受，不为诸佛之所护念，是人终不得见于我。善男子，其有众生得见我者，皆于阿耨多罗三藐三菩提获不退转。

“善男子，东方诸佛常来至此，处于宝座为我说法；南、西、北方，四维、上、下，一切诸佛悉来至此，处于宝座为我说法。善男子，我常不离见佛闻法，与诸菩萨而共同住。

“善男子，我此大众，有八万四千亿那由他，皆在此园与我同行，悉于阿耨多罗三藐三菩提得不退转；其余众生住此园者，亦皆普入不退转位。”

gateways to the meritorious qualities all manifested directly before them. Their minds became vast, they became fully possessed of the spiritual superknowledges, and their bodies became unimpeded in their ability to go everywhere.

At that time, Sudhana the Youth entered Universal Adornment Gardens, whereupon he searched all around and saw Āśā, the Upāsikā, seated on her marvelous throne. He then approached her to pay his respects, bowed down in reverence at her feet, circumambulated her countless times, and addressed her, saying, "O Ārya, I am one who has already resolved to attain *anuttara-samyak-saṃbodhi.* Still, I do not yet know how the bodhisattva should train in the bodhisattva practices and how one should cultivate the bodhisattva path. I have heard that the Ārya is well able to offer guidance and instruction on these matters. Please explain this for me."

Āśā then spoke to him, saying:

Son of Good Family, I have only acquired this single bodhisattva liberation gateway. Still, if there is anyone who sees me, hears me, brings me to mind, dwells together with me, or provides contributions to me, then they will not have done so in vain.

Son of Good Family, if there is any being who has not planted roots of goodness, who has not been drawn forth and accepted by the good spiritual friend, and who has not received the protection of the buddhas, then such a person would never even be able to see me.

Son of Good Family, where there are beings who do succeed in seeing me, then they all become irreversible in their progress toward *anuttara-samyak-saṃbodhi.*

Son of Good Family, buddhas from the east always come here, sit on a jeweled throne, and speak Dharma for me. So too do all buddhas come here from the south, the west, the north, the four midpoints, the zenith, and the nadir, whereupon they too sit on a jeweled throne and speak Dharma for me.

Son of Good Family, I never leave this circumstance in which I see the buddhas, hear them teach the Dharma, and dwell together with the bodhisattvas.

Son of Good Family, this immense congregation of mine consists of eighty-four thousand *koṭīs* of *nayutas* of beings, all of whom dwell together and practice with me in this park, and all of whom have become irreversible in their progress toward *anuttara-samyak-saṃbodhi.* All of the other beings dwelling in this park have also entered the station of irreversibility.

正體字

善財白言。聖者。發阿耨多羅三藐三
344a11║ 菩提心。為久近耶。答言。善男子。我憶過去。
344a12║ 於然燈佛所。修行梵行。恭敬供養。聞法受持。
344a13║ 次前於離垢佛所。出家學道。受持正法。次前
344a14║ 於妙幢佛所。次前於勝須彌佛所。次前於蓮
344a15║ 華德藏佛所。次前於毘盧遮那佛所。次前於
344a16║ 普眼佛所。次前於梵壽佛所。次前於金剛[1]齎
344a17║ 佛所。次前於婆樓那天佛所。善男子。我憶過
344a18║ 去。於無量劫無量生中。如是次第三十六恒
344a19║ 河沙佛所。皆悉承事。恭敬供養。聞法受持。淨
344a20║ 修梵行。於此已往。佛智所知。非我能測。善男
344a21║ 子。菩薩初發心無有量。充滿一切法界故。菩
344a22║ 薩大悲門無有量。普入一切世間故。菩薩大
344a23║ 願門無有量。究竟十方法界故。菩薩大慈門
344a24║ 無有量。普覆一切眾生故。菩薩所修行無有
344a25║ 量。於一切剎一切劫中修習故。菩薩三昧力
344a26║ 無有量。令菩薩道不退故。菩薩總持力無有
344a27║ 量。能持一切世間故。

简体字

善财白言："圣者发阿耨多罗三藐三菩提心为久近耶？"

答言："善男子，我忆过去，于燃灯佛所，修行梵行，恭敬供养，闻法受持；次前，于离垢佛所，出家学道，受持正法；次前，于妙幢佛所；次前，于胜须弥佛所；次前，于莲华德藏佛所；次前，于毗卢遮那佛所；次前，于普眼佛所；次前，于梵寿佛所；次前，于金刚脐佛所；次前，于婆楼那天佛所。善男子，我忆过去，于无量劫无量生中，如是次第三十六恒河沙佛所，皆悉承事，恭敬供养，闻法受持，净修梵行。于此已往，佛智所知，非我能测。

"善男子，菩萨初发心无有量，充满一切法界故；菩萨大悲门无有量，普入一切世间故；菩萨大愿门无有量，究竟十方法界故；菩萨大慈门无有量，普覆一切众生故；菩萨所修行无有量，于一切刹一切劫中修习故；菩萨三昧力无有量，令菩萨道不退故；菩萨总持力无有量，能持一切世间故；

Sudhana then asked, "O Ārya, was your own resolve to attain *anuttara-samyak-saṃbodhi* made long ago or more recently?"

She replied:

Son of Good Family, I recall that, in the past, under Burning Lamp Buddha, I cultivated the practice of *brahmacarya*, revered him, made offerings to him, listened to him teach the Dharma, absorbed it, and retained it. Before that, under Stainless Buddha, I left the householder's life, trained in the path, and then learned and retained right Dharma. Before that, I did so under Marvelous Banner Buddha. Before that, I did so under Supreme Sumeru Buddha. Before that, I did so under Lotus Virtue Treasury Buddha. Before that, I did so under Vairocana Buddha. Before that, I did so under Universal Eye Buddha. Before that, I did so under Brahman Lifespan Buddha. Before that, I did so under Vajra Navel Buddha. And before that, I did so under Varuṇa Deva Buddha.

Son of Good Family, I recall that, in this same way, throughout the past, during the course of countless lives in countless kalpas, under buddhas as numerous as the sands in thirty-six Ganges Rivers, I sequentially served, revered, and made offerings to them all, listened to them teach the Dharma, absorbed it, retained it, and purely cultivated the practice of *brahmacarya*. As for the time previous to that, since that is the exclusive domain of a buddha's knowledge, it is not a matter that I am able to assess.

Son of Good Family:

The bodhisattva's initial generation of the resolve is measureless, this because it completely fills the entire Dharma realm;

The bodhisattva's gateway of great compassion is measureless, because it everywhere enters all worlds;

The bodhisattva's gateway of great vows is measureless, because it reaches to the very ends of the ten directions of the Dharma realm;

The bodhisattva's gateway of great kindness is measureless, because it extends to all beings everywhere;

The practices cultivated by the bodhisattva are measureless, because they are cultivated in all *kṣetras* and in all kalpas;

The bodhisattva's samādhi power is measureless, because it makes him irreversible in the bodhisattva path;

The bodhisattva's power in the complete-retention *dhāraṇīs* is measureless, because it enables him to retain the contents of all worlds;

正體字

菩薩智光力無有量。普
344a28‖ 能證入三世故。菩薩神通力無有量。普現一
344a29‖ 切剎網故。菩薩辯才力無有量。一音一切悉
344b01‖ 解故。菩薩清淨身無有量。悉遍一切佛剎故。
344b02‖ 善財童子言。聖者。久如當得阿耨多羅三藐
344b03‖ 三菩提。答言。善男子。菩薩不為教化調伏一
344b04‖ 眾生故發菩提心。不為教化調伏百眾生故
344b05‖ 發菩提心。乃至不為教化調伏不可說不可
344b06‖ 說轉眾生故發菩提心。不為教化一世界眾生
344b07‖ 故發菩提心。乃至不為教化不可說不可說
344b08‖ 轉世界眾生故發菩提心。不為教化閻浮提
344b09‖ 微塵數世界眾生故發菩提心。不為教化三千
344b10‖ 大千世界微塵數世界眾生故發菩提心。乃
344b11‖ 至不為教化不可說不可說轉三千大千世界
344b12‖ 微塵數世界眾生故發菩提心。不為供養一
344b13‖ 如來故發菩提心。乃至不為供養不可說不
344b14‖ 可說轉如來故發菩提心。不為供養一世界
344b15‖ 中次第興世諸如來故發菩提心。

简体字

菩萨智光力无有量，普能证入三世故；菩萨神通力无有量，普现一切刹网故；菩萨辩才力无有量，一音一切悉解故；菩萨清净身无有量，悉遍一切佛刹故。”

善财童子言：“圣者久如当得阿耨多罗三藐三菩提？”

答言：“善男子，菩萨不为教化调伏一众生故发菩提心，不为教化调伏百众生故发菩提心，乃至不为教化调伏不可说不可说转众生故发菩提心；不为教化一世界众生故发菩提心，乃至不为教化不可说不可说转世界众生故发菩提心；不为教化阎浮提微尘数世界众生故发菩提心，不为教化三千大千世界微尘数世界众生故发菩提心，乃至不为教化不可说不可说转三千大千世界微尘数世界众生故发菩提心；不为供养一如来故发菩提心，乃至不为供养不可说不可说转如来故发菩提心；不为供养一世界中次第兴世诸如来故发菩提心，

The bodhisattva's power of the light of wisdom is measureless, because it enables him to enter all three periods of time;

The bodhisattva's power of the spiritual superknowledges is measureless, because it brings about his appearance everywhere throughout the network of all *kṣetras;*

The bodhisattva's power of eloquence is measureless, because, through his use of but one voice, everyone is able to gain complete understanding;

The bodhisattva's pure body is measureless, because it entirely pervades all buddha *kṣetras.*

Sudhana the Youth then asked, "O Ārya, how much longer will it be before you attain *anuttara-samyak-saṃbodhi*?"

She replied:

Son of Good Family:

It is not for the sake of teaching and training only one being that the bodhisattva[90] resolves to attain bodhi;

It is not for the sake of teaching and training only a hundred beings that the bodhisattva resolves to attain bodhi, and so forth on up to its not being for the sake of teaching and training only an ineffable-ineffable number times an ineffable-ineffable number of beings that the bodhisattva resolves to attain bodhi;[91]

It is not for the sake of teaching only the beings of one world that the bodhisattva resolves to attain bodhi, and so forth on up to its not being for the sake of teaching only the beings in an ineffable-ineffable number times an ineffable-ineffable number of worlds that the bodhisattva resolves to attain bodhi;

It is not for the sake of teaching only the beings in worlds as numerous as the atoms in the continent of Jambudvīpa that the bodhisattva resolves to attain bodhi;

It is not for the sake of teaching only the beings in worlds as numerous as the atoms in one great trichiliocosm that the bodhisattva resolves to attain bodhi, and so forth on up to its not being for the sake of teaching only the beings in worlds as numerous as the atoms in an ineffable-ineffable number times an ineffable-ineffable number of great trichiliocosms that the bodhisattva resolves to attain bodhi;

It is not for the sake of making offerings to only one *tathāgata* that the bodhisattva resolves to attain bodhi, and so forth on up to its not being for the sake of making offerings to only an ineffable-ineffable number times an ineffable-ineffable number of *tathāgatas* that the bodhisattva resolves to attain bodhi;

It is not for the sake of making offerings to only all the *tathāgatas* who have sequentially come forth into the world in one world that the bodhisattva resolves to attain bodhi, and so forth on up to its not be-

正體字

乃至不為
344b16║ 供養不可說不可說轉世界中次第興世諸如
344b17║ 來故發菩提心。不為供養一三千大千世界
344b18║ 微塵數世界中次第興世諸如來故發菩提
344b19║ 心。乃至不為供養不可說不可說轉佛剎微
344b20║ 塵數世界中次第興世諸如來故發菩提心。
344b21║ 不為嚴淨一世界故發菩提心。乃至不為嚴
344b22║ 淨不可說不可說轉世界故發菩提心。不為
344b23║ 嚴淨一三千大千世界微塵數世界故發菩提
344b24║ 心。乃至不為嚴淨不可說不可說轉三千大
344b25║ 千世界微塵數世界故發菩提心。不為住持
344b26║ 一如來遺法故發菩提心。乃至不為住持不
344b27║ 可說不可說轉如來遺法故發菩提心。不為
344b28║ 住持一世界如來遺法故發菩提心。乃至不
344b29║ 為住持不可說不可說轉世界如來遺法故發
344c01║ 菩提心。不為住持一閻浮提微塵數世界如
344c02║ 來遺法故發菩提心。乃至不為住持不可說
344c03║ 不可說轉佛剎微塵數世界如來遺法故發菩
344c04║ 提心。

简体字

乃至不为供养不可说不可说转世界中次第兴世诸如来故发菩提心；不为供养一三千大千世界微尘数世界中次第兴世诸如来故发菩提心，乃至不为供养不可说不可说转佛刹微尘数世界中次第兴世诸如来故发菩提心；不为严净一世界故发菩提心，乃至不为严净不可说不可说转世界故发菩提心；不为严净一三千大千世界微尘数世界故发菩提心，乃至不为严净不可说不可说转三千大千世界微尘数世界故发菩提心；不为住持一如来遗法故发菩提心，乃至不为住持不可说不可说转如来遗法故发菩提心；不为住持一世界如来遗法故发菩提心，乃至不为住持不可说不可说转世界如来遗法故发菩提心；不为住持一阎浮提微尘数世界如来遗法故发菩提心，乃至不为住持不可说不可说转佛刹微尘数世界如来遗法故发菩提心。

ing for the sake of making offerings only to the *tathāgatas* who have sequentially come forth into an ineffable-ineffable number times an ineffable-ineffable number of worlds that the bodhisattva resolves to attain bodhi;

It is not for the sake of making offerings only to the number of *tathāgatas* that have sequentially come forth into the world in worlds as numerous as the atoms in one great trichiliocosm that the bodhisattva resolves to attain bodhi, and so forth on up to its not being for the sake of making offerings only to *tathāgatas* that have sequentially come forth into the world in worlds as numerous as the atoms in an ineffable-ineffable number times an ineffable-ineffable number of buddha *kṣetras* that the bodhisattva resolves to attain bodhi;

It is not for the sake of purifying only one world that the bodhisattva resolves to attain bodhi, and so forth on up to its not being for the sake of purifying only an ineffable-ineffable number times an ineffable-ineffable number of worlds that the bodhisattva resolves to attain bodhi;

It is not for the sake of purifying only worlds as numerous as the atoms in all the worlds in a great trichiliocosm that the bodhisattva resolves to attain bodhi, and so forth on up to its not being for the sake of purifying only worlds as numerous as the atoms in all the worlds in an ineffable-ineffable number times an ineffable-ineffable number of great trichiliocosms that the bodhisattva resolves to attain bodhi;

It is not for the sake of sustaining and preserving the legacy Dharma of only one *tathāgata* that the bodhisattva resolves to attain bodhi, and so forth on up to its not being for the sake of sustaining and preserving the legacy Dharma of only an ineffable-ineffable number times an ineffable-ineffable number of *tathāgatas* that the bodhisattva resolves to attain bodhi;

It is not for the sake of sustaining and preserving the legacy Dharma of only all the *tathāgatas* appearing in one world that the bodhisattva resolves to attain bodhi, and so forth on up to its not being for the sake of sustaining and preserving the legacy Dharma of only all the *tathāgatas* appearing in an ineffable-ineffable number times an ineffable-ineffable number of worlds that the bodhisattva resolves to attain bodhi; and

It is not for the sake of sustaining and preserving the legacy Dharma of only the *tathāgatas* appearing in worlds as numerous as all the atoms on the continent of Jambudvīpa that the bodhisattva resolves to attain bodhi, and so forth on up to its not being for the sake of sustaining and preserving the legacy Dharma of only all the *tathāgatas* appearing in worlds as numerous as all the atoms in an ineffable-ineffable number times an ineffable-ineffable number of Buddha *kṣetras* that the bodhisattva resolves to attain bodhi.

正體字

如是略說。不為滿一佛誓願故。不為
344c05║ 往一佛國土故。不為入一佛眾會故。不為持
344c06║ 一佛法眼故。不為轉一佛法輪故。不為知一
344c07║ 世界中諸劫次第故。不為知一眾生心海故。
344c08║ 不為知一眾生根海故。不為知一眾生業海
344c09║ 故。不為知一眾生行海故。不為知一眾生煩
344c10║ 惱海故。不為知一眾生煩惱習海故。乃至不
344c11║ 為知不可說不可說轉佛剎微塵數眾生煩惱
344c12║ 習海故發菩提心。欲教化調伏一切眾生。悉
344c13║ 無餘故。發菩提心。欲承事供養一切諸佛。悉
344c14║ 無餘故。發菩提心。欲嚴淨一切諸佛國土。悉
344c15║ 無餘故。發菩提心。欲護持一切諸佛正教。悉
344c16║ 無餘故。發菩提心。欲成滿一切如來誓願。悉
344c17║ 無餘故。發菩提心。

简体字

如是略说，不为满一佛誓愿故，不为往一佛国土故，不为入一佛众会故，不为持一佛法眼故，不为转一佛法轮故，不为知一世界中诸劫次第故，不为知一众生心海故，不为知一众生根海故，不为知一众生业海故，不为知一众生行海故，不为知一众生烦恼海故，不为知一众生烦恼习海故，乃至不为知不可说不可说转佛刹微尘数众生烦恼习海故，发菩提心。

“欲教化调伏一切众生悉无余故发菩提心，欲承事供养一切诸佛悉无余故发菩提心，欲严净一切诸佛国土悉无余故发菩提心，欲护持一切诸佛正教悉无余故发菩提心，欲成满一切如来誓愿悉无余故发菩提心，

In this same way, and to state it simply:

It is not for the purpose of fulfilling only the vows of one buddha;
It is not for the purpose of going to only one buddha *kṣetra;*
It is not for the purpose of entering the congregation of only one buddha;
It is not for the purpose of sustaining the Dharma eye of only one buddha;
It is not for the purpose of turning the Dharma wheel of only one buddha;
It is not for the purpose of knowing the sequence of kalpas in only one world;
It is not for the purpose of knowing the ocean of thoughts of only one being;
It is not for the purpose of knowing the ocean of faculties of only one being;
It is not for the purpose of knowing the ocean of karmic deeds of only one being;
It is not for the purpose of knowing the ocean of conduct practiced by only one being;
It is not for the purpose of knowing the ocean of afflictions of only one being; and
It is not for the purpose of knowing the ocean of affliction-based habitual karmic propensities of only one being and so forth until we come to its not being for the purpose of knowing the ocean of affliction-based habitual karmic propensities of only beings as numerous as the atoms in an ineffable-ineffable number times an ineffable-ineffable number of buddha *kṣetras* that the bodhisattva resolves to attain bodhi.

Rather:

It is out of a wish to teach and train all beings without exception that the bodhisattva resolves to attain bodhi.
It is out of a wish to serve and make offerings to all buddhas without exception that the bodhisattva resolves to attain bodhi;
It is out of a wish to purify all buddha lands without exception that the bodhisattva resolves to attain bodhi;
It is out of a wish to protect and preserve the right teachings of all buddhas without exception that the bodhisattva resolves to attain bodhi;
It is out of a wish to completely fulfill the vows of all *tathāgatas* without exception that the bodhisattva resolves to attain bodhi;

正體字

欲往一切諸佛國土。悉無
344c18║ 餘故。發菩提心。欲入一切諸佛眾會。悉無
344c19║ 餘故。發菩提心。欲知一切世界中。諸劫次第。
344c20║ 悉無餘故。發菩提心。欲知一切眾生心海。悉
344c21║ 無餘故。發菩提心。欲知一切眾生根海。悉無
344c22║ 餘故。發菩提心。欲知一切眾生業海。悉無餘
344c23║ 故。發菩提心。欲知一切眾生行海。悉無餘故。
344c24║ 發菩提心。欲滅一切眾生。諸煩惱海。悉無餘
344c25║ 故。發菩提心。欲拔一切眾生。煩惱習海。悉無
344c26║ 餘故。發菩提心。善男子。取要言之。菩薩以如
344c27║ 是等百萬阿僧祇方便行故。發菩提心。善男
344c28║ 子。菩薩行。普入一切法。皆證得故。普入一切
344c29║ 剎。悉嚴淨故。是故善男子。嚴淨一切世界盡。
345a01║ 我願乃盡。拔一切眾生。煩惱習氣盡。我願乃
345a02║ 滿。善財童子言。聖者。此解脫名為何等。答
345a03║ 言。善男子。此解脫。名離憂安隱幢。善男子。
345a04║ 我唯知此一解脫門。如諸菩薩摩訶薩。

简体字

欲往一切诸佛国土悉无余故发菩提心，欲入一切诸佛众会悉无余故发菩提心，欲知一切世界中诸劫次第悉无余故发菩提心，欲知一切众生心海悉无余故发菩提心，欲知一切众生根海悉无余故发菩提心，欲知一切众生业海悉无余故发菩提心，欲知一切众生行海悉无余故发菩提心，欲灭一切众生诸烦恼海悉无余故发菩提心，欲拔一切众生烦恼习海悉无余故发菩提心。善男子，取要言之，菩萨以如是等百万阿僧祇方便行故发菩提心。

“善男子，菩萨行普入一切法皆证得故，普入一切刹悉严净故。是故，善男子，严净一切世界尽，我愿乃尽；拔一切众生烦恼习气尽，我愿乃满。”

善财童子言：“圣者，此解脱名为何等？”

答言：“善男子，此解脱名离忧安隐幢。善男子，我唯知此一解脱门。如诸菩萨摩诃萨，

It is out of a wish to go to all buddha lands without exception that the bodhisattva resolves to attain bodhi;

It is out of a wish to enter the congregations of all buddhas without exception that the bodhisattva resolves to attain bodhi;

It is out of a wish to know the sequences of kalpas of all worlds without exception that the bodhisattva resolves to attain bodhi;

It is out of a wish to know the ocean of thoughts of all beings without exception that the bodhisattva resolves to attain bodhi;

It is out of a wish to know the ocean of faculties of all beings without exception that the bodhisattva resolves to attain bodhi;

It is out of a wish to know the ocean of karma of all beings without exception that the bodhisattva resolves to attain bodhi;

It is out of a wish to know the ocean of conduct practiced by all beings without exception that the bodhisattva resolves to attain bodhi;

It is out of a wish to extinguish the ocean of afflictions of all beings without exception that the bodhisattva resolves to attain bodhi; and

It is out of a wish to rescue all beings without exception from their ocean of affliction-based habitual karmic propensities that the bodhisattva resolves to attain bodhi.

Son of Good Family, to state what is essential, it is for the purpose of adopting the practice of hundreds of myriads of *asaṃkhyeyas* of skillful means such as these that the bodhisattva resolves to attain bodhi.

Son of Good Family, the bodhisattva's practice everywhere penetrates all dharmas, this because he perfects them all, and everywhere enters all *kṣetras*, this because he purifies them all.

Therefore, Son of Good Family, it is only when the purification of all worlds has come to an end that my vows will come to an end, and it is only when the rescue of all beings from their affliction-based habitual karmic propensities has come to an end that my vows will be entirely fulfilled.

Sudhana the Youth then inquired, "O Ārya, what then is the name of this liberation?"

She replied:

Son of Good Family, this liberation is known as "the banner of sorrowless security."[92]

Son of Good Family, I know only this single gateway to liberation. As for the bodhisattva-mahāsattvas whose minds:

正體字

其心
345a05‖ 如海。悉能容受一切佛法。如須彌山。志意堅
345a06‖ 固。不可動搖。如善見藥。能除眾生煩惱重病。
345a07‖ 如明淨日。能破眾生無明闇障。猶如大地能
345a08‖ 作一切眾生依處。猶如好風能作一切眾生
345a09‖ 義利。猶如明燈能為眾生。生智慧光。猶如大
345a10‖ 雲能為眾生。雨寂滅法。猶如淨月能為眾生。
345a11‖ 放福德光。猶如帝釋悉能守護一切眾生。而
345a12‖ 我云何能知能說彼功德行。善男子。於此南
345a13‖ 方海潮之處。有一國土。名那羅素。中有仙人。
345a14‖ 名毘目瞿沙。汝詣彼問。菩薩云何學菩薩行。
345a15‖ 修菩薩道。時善財童子。頂禮其足。遶無數匝。
345a16‖ 慇懃瞻仰。悲泣流淚。作是思惟。得菩提難。近
345a17‖ 善知識難。遇善知識難。得菩薩諸根難。淨菩
345a18‖ 薩諸根難。值同行善知識難。如理觀察難。依
345a19‖ 教修行難。

简体字

其心如海，悉能容受一切佛法；如须弥山，志意坚固，不可动摇；如善见药，能除众生烦恼重病；如明净日，能破众生无明暗障；犹如大地，能作一切众生依处；犹如好风，能作一切众生义利；犹如明灯，能为众生生智慧光；犹如大云，能为众生雨寂灭法；犹如净月，能为众生放福德光；犹如帝释，悉能守护一切众生。而我云何能知能说彼功德行？

“善男子，于此南方海潮之处，有一国土，名那罗素；中有仙人，名毗目瞿沙。汝诣彼问：菩萨云何学菩萨行、修菩萨道？”

时，善财童子顶礼其足，绕无数匝，殷勤瞻仰，悲泣流泪，作是思惟：“得菩提难，近善知识难，遇善知识难，得菩萨诸根难，净菩萨诸根难，值同行善知识难，如理观察难，依教修行难，

Are like an ocean because they are able to contain the Dharma of all buddhas;
Are like Mount Sumeru because their resolve is unshakably solid;
Are like the "excellent when seen" medicine because they are able to cure the grave illnesses of beings which arise from afflictions;
Are like the brightly shining sun because they are able to dispel the darkness of beings' ignorance;
Are like the great earth because they are able to serve as the place that supports all beings;
Are like the good winds because they are able to benefit all beings;
Are like a bright lamp because they are able to produce the light of wisdom;
Are like a great cloud because they are able to send down the rain of the dharma of quiescence for all beings;
Are like the brightly shining moon because they are able to emanate the light of merit for all beings; and
Are like Śakra, lord of the devas because they are able to protect all beings—

How could I know of or be able to speak about their meritorious qualities and practices?

Son of Good Family, south of here, still in this Ocean Tides region, there is a country known as Nālayus in which there is a rishi known as Bhīsmottaranirghoṣa. You should go there to pay your respects and ask him, "How should the bodhisattva train in the bodhisattva practices and how should he cultivate the bodhisattva path?"

Sudhana the Youth then bowed down in reverence at her feet, circumambulated her countless times, and gazed up at her in attentive admiration as tears of sadness flowed down his face. He then reflected as follows:

To realize bodhi is difficult;
To draw near to a good spiritual guide is difficult;
To meet a good spiritual guide is difficult;
To acquire the faculties of a bodhisattva is difficult;
To purify the faculties of a bodhisattva is difficult;
To encounter a same-practice good spiritual friend[93] is difficult;
To carry out meditative contemplations in accordance with principle is difficult;
To carry out one's cultivation in accordance with the teachings is difficult;

正體字

值遇出生善心方便難。值遇增長
345a20 一切智法光明難。作是念已。辭退而行
345a21 爾時善財童子。隨順思惟菩薩正教。隨順思
345a22 惟菩薩淨行。生增長菩薩福力心。生明見一
345a23 切諸佛心。生出生一切諸佛心。生增長一切
345a24 大願心。生普見十方諸法心。生明照諸法實
345a25 性心。生普散一切障礙心。生觀察法界無闇
345a26 心。生清淨意寶莊嚴心。生摧伏一切眾魔心。
345a27 漸漸遊行。至那羅素國。周遍推求毘目瞿沙。
345a28 見一大林。阿僧祇樹。以為莊嚴。所謂種種葉
345a29 樹扶疎布濩。種種華樹開敷鮮榮。種種果樹
345b01 相續成熟。種種寶樹雨摩尼果。大栴檀樹處
345b02 處行列。諸沈水樹常出好香。悅意香樹妙香
345b03 莊嚴。波[1]吒羅樹四面圍遶。尼拘律樹其身聳
345b04 擢。閻浮檀樹常雨甘果。優鉢羅華波頭摩華
345b05 以嚴池沼。

简体字

值遇出生善心方便难，值遇增长一切智法光明难。”作是念已，辞退而行。

尔时，善财童子随顺思惟菩萨正教，随顺思惟菩萨净行，生增长菩萨福力心，生明见一切诸佛心，生出生一切诸佛心，生增长一切大愿心，生普见十方诸法心，生明照诸法实性心，生普散一切障碍心，生观察法界无暗心，生清净意宝庄严心，生摧伏一切众魔心。

渐渐游行，至那罗素国，周遍推求毗目瞿沙。见一大林，阿僧祇树以为庄严，所谓：种种叶树扶疏布濩，种种华树开敷鲜荣，种种果树相续成熟，种种宝树雨摩尼果，大栴檀树处处行列，诸沉水树常出好香，悦意香树妙香庄严，波吒罗树四面围绕，尼拘律树其身耸擢，阎浮檀树常雨甘果，优钵罗华、波头摩华以严池沼。

To encounter the skillful means by which one develops a wholesome mind is difficult; and
To encounter circumstances conducive to increasing the light of the dharmas of all-knowledge is difficult.

Having reflected in this manner, he respectfully took his leave and traveled on.

8 – Bhīṣmottaranirghoṣa

At that time, Sudhana the Youth reflected accordingly on the bodhisattva's right teaching and reflected accordingly on the bodhisattva's purification of his practice. He then:

Resolved to increase the power of his bodhisattva merit;
Resolved to clearly see all buddhas;
Resolved to bring forth [the enlightenment of] all buddhas;
Resolved to increase [his practice of] the great vows;
Resolved to everywhere perceive all dharmas of the ten directions;
Resolved to illuminate the true nature of all dharmas;
Resolved to demolish all obstacles;
Resolved to contemplate the Dharma realm without obscurations;
Resolved to become adorned with the jewel of pure intention; and
Resolved to vanquish all the many kinds of *māras*.

He then gradually traveled along until he reached the country of Nālayus where he searched around everywhere for Bhīsmottaranirghoṣa. He then saw a great forest adorned by the presence of an *asaṃkhyeya* of trees. In particular, there were:

Many different kinds of leafy trees with luxuriant foliage that spread out widely;
Many different kinds of flowering trees with blossoms that were fresh and gloriously beautiful;
Many different kinds of fruit trees with fruits that were continuously ripe;
Many different kinds of jeweled trees that rained down fruits made of *maṇi* jewels;
Immense sandalwood incense trees that were everywhere growing in rows;
All kinds of *agaru* incense trees that always emanated fine fragrances;
Mind-pleasing incense trees graced by their marvelous fragrance;
Pāṭalī trees that surrounded the area on all four sides;
Nyagrodha trees whose trunks were tall and straight;
Jambū trees that always rained down sweet fruits; and
Utpala blossoms and *padma* blossoms that adorned the ponds.[94]

正體字

時善財童子。見彼仙人在栴檀樹
345b06‖ 下。敷草而坐。領徒一萬。或著鹿皮。或著樹
345b07‖ 皮。或復編草。以為衣服。髻環垂鬢。前後圍
345b08‖ 遶。善財見已。往詣其所。五體投地。作如是
345b09‖ 言。我今得遇真善知識。善知識者。則是趣
345b10‖ 向一切智門。令我得入真實道故。善知識者。
345b11‖ 則是趣向一切智乘。令我得至如來地故。善
345b12‖ 知識者。則是趣向一切智船。令我得至智寶
345b13‖ 洲故。善知識者。則是趣向一切智炬。令我
345b14‖ 得生十力光故。善知識者。則是趣向一切智
345b15‖ 道。令我得入涅槃城故。善知識者。則是趣
345b16‖ 向一切智燈。令我得見夷險道故。善知識者。
345b17‖ 則是趣向一切智橋。令我得度險惡處故。善
345b18‖ 知識者。則是趣向一切智蓋。令我得生大慈
345b19‖ 涼故。善知識者。則是趣向一切智眼。令我
345b20‖ 得見法性門故。善知識者。則是趣向一切智
345b21‖ 潮。令我滿足大悲水故。作是語已。從地而
345b22‖ 起。遶無量匝。合掌前住。白言聖者。我已先發
345b23‖ 阿耨多羅三藐三菩提心。而未知菩薩云何
345b24‖ 學菩薩行。云何修菩薩道。

简体字

时，善财童子见彼仙人在栴檀树下敷草而坐，领徒一万，或著鹿皮，或著树皮，或复编草以为衣服，髻环垂鬓，前后围绕。善财见已，往诣其所，五体投地，作如是言：“我今得遇真善知识。善知识者，则是趣向一切智门，令我得入真实道故；善知识者，则是趣向一切智乘，令我得至如来地故；善知识者，则是趣向一切智船，令我得至智宝洲故；善知识者，则是趣向一切智炬，令我得生十力光故；善知识者，则是趣向一切智道，令我得入涅槃城故；善知识者，则是趣向一切智灯，令我得见夷险道故；善知识者，则是趣向一切智桥，令我得度险恶处故；善知识者，则是趣向一切智盖，令我得生大慈凉故；善知识者，则是趣向一切智眼，令我得见法性门故；善知识者，则是趣向一切智潮，令我满足大悲水故。”

作是语已，从地而起，绕无量匝，合掌前住，白言：“圣者，我已先发阿耨多罗三藐三菩提心，而未知菩萨云何学菩萨行？云何修菩萨道？

Sudhana the Youth then saw that rishi beneath a sandalwood tree, sitting on a grass mat, leading a group of a myriad disciples, some of whom wore deer skins, some of whom wore clothing made of tree bark, and some of whom wore robes made of woven grasses. Wearing headbands and having hair that hung down, they completely surrounded that rishi.

Having seen him, Sudhana went up to him to pay his respects, made full reverential prostrations, and spoke in this way:

I have now succeeded in meeting a true good spiritual guide:

The good spiritual guide is the gateway to all-knowledge, for he enables me to enter the true path;

The good spiritual guide is the vehicle leading to all-knowledge, for he enables me to reach the ground of the Tathāgata;

The good spiritual guide is the ship that sails toward all-knowledge, for he enables me to arrive at the jeweled isle of wisdom;

The good spiritual guide is the torch that lights the way to all-knowledge, for he enables me to produce the light of the ten powers;

The good spiritual guide is the path that leads to all-knowledge, for he enables me to enter the city of nirvāṇa;

The good spiritual guide is the lamp that illuminates the way to all-knowledge, for he enables me to recognize the safe and dangerous paths;

The good spiritual guide is the bridge that leads to all-knowledge, for he enables me to cross over dangerous and evil places;

The good spiritual guide is the parasol on the way to all-knowledge, for he enables me to bring forth the coolness of the great kindness;

The good spiritual guide is the eye that sees the way to all-knowledge, for he enables me to see the gateway of the nature of dharmas; and

The good spiritual guide is the tide that transports me to all-knowledge, for he enables me to become completely filled with the waters of the great compassion.

Having spoken in this way, he got up, circumambulated him countless times, stood before him with palms pressed together, and addressed him, saying, "O Ārya, I am one who has already resolved to attain *anuttara-samyak-saṃbodhi*. Still, I do not yet know how the bodhisattva should train in the bodhisattva practices and cultivate the bodhisattva path. I have heard that the Ārya is well able to offer

正體字

我聞聖者。善能誘
345b25‖ 誨。願為我說。時毘目瞿沙。顧其徒眾。而作是
345b26‖ 言。善男子。此童子已發阿耨多羅三藐三菩
345b27‖ 提心。善男子。此童子普施一切眾生無畏。此
345b28‖ 童子普[2]興一切眾生利益。此童子常觀一切
345b29‖ 諸佛智海。此童子欲飲一切甘露法雨。此童
345c01‖ 子欲測一切廣大法海。此童子欲令眾生住
345c02‖ 智海中。此童子欲普發起廣大悲雲。此童子
345c03‖ 欲普雨於廣大法雨。此童子欲以智月普照
345c04‖ 世間。此童子欲滅世間煩惱毒熱。此童子欲
345c05‖ 長含識一切善根。時諸仙眾。聞是語已。各以
345c06‖ 種種上妙香華。散善財上。投身作禮。圍遶恭
345c07‖ 敬。作如是言。今此童子。必當救護一切眾生。
345c08‖ 必當除滅諸地獄苦。必當永斷諸畜生道。必
345c09‖ 當轉去閻羅王界。必當關閉諸難處門。

简体字

我闻圣者善能诱诲，愿为我说！”

时，毗目瞿沙顾其徒众，而作是言：“善男子，此童子已发阿耨多罗三藐三菩提心。善男子，此童子普施一切众生无畏，此童子普兴一切众生利益，此童子常观一切诸佛智海，此童子欲饮一切甘露法雨，此童子欲测一切广大法海，此童子欲令众生住智海中，此童子欲普发起广大悲云，此童子欲普雨于广大法雨，此童子欲以智月普照世间，此童子欲灭世间烦恼毒热，此童子欲长含识一切善根。”

时，诸仙众闻是语已，各以种种上妙香华散善财上，投身作礼，围绕恭敬，作如是言：“今此童子，必当救护一切众生，必当除灭诸地狱苦，必当永断诸畜生道，必当转去阎罗王界，必当关闭诸难处门，

guidance and instruction. I pray then that he will speak on these matters for my sake."

Bhīsmottaranirghoṣa then turned to look at his congregation of disciples and spoke in this way:

Sons of Good Family, this youth is one who has already resolved to attain *anuttara-samyak-saṃbodhi*. Sons of Good Family:

This youth is one who everywhere bestows fearlessness on all beings;
This youth is one who everywhere promotes the benefit of all beings;
This youth is one who always contemplates the ocean of all buddhas' wisdom;
This youth is one who wishes to drink all of the Dharma rains of the elixir of immortality;
This youth is one who wishes to fathom the entire vast ocean of Dharma;
This youth is one who wishes to cause beings to abide in the ocean of wisdom;
This youth is one who wishes to everywhere send forth vast clouds of compassion;
This youth is one who wishes to everywhere rain down the vast rain of Dharma;
This youth is one who wishes to use the moon of wisdom to illuminate the entire world;
This youth is one who wishes to extinguish the searing heat of the world's afflictions; and
This youth is one who wishes to cause the growth of all sentient beings' roots of goodness.

Having heard these words, everyone in that congregation of rishis took up many different kinds of supremely marvelous and fragrant flowers and scattered them over Sudhana. They then prostrated their bodies before him in reverence, circumambulated him respectfully, and spoke in this way:

Now, this youth:

Is certainly bound to rescue all beings;
Is certainly bound to extinguish all the sufferings of the hells;
Is certainly bound to forever cut off descent into the path of animal rebirth;
Is certainly bound to turn away from the realms of King Yama;
Is certainly bound to close the gates to the abodes beset by the [eight] difficulties;

正體字

必當
345c10║ 乾竭諸愛欲海。必令眾生永滅苦蘊。必當永
345c11║ 破無明黑闇。必當永斷貪愛繫縛。必以福德
345c12║ 大輪圍山圍遶世間。必以智慧大寶須彌顯
345c13║ 示世間。必當出現清淨智日。必當開示善根
345c14║ 法藏。必使世間明識險易。時毘目瞿沙。告群
345c15║ 仙言。善男子。若有能發阿耨多羅三藐三菩
345c16║ 提心。必當成就一切智道。此善男子已發阿
345c17║ 耨多羅三藐三菩提心。當淨一切佛功德地。
345c18║ 時毘目瞿沙。告善財童子言。善男子。我得菩
345c19║ 薩無勝幢解脫。善財白言。聖者。無勝幢解脫
345c20║ 境界云何。時毘目仙人。即申右手。摩善財
345c21║ 頂。執善財手。即時善財。自見其身。往十方十
345c22║ 佛剎微塵數世界中。到十佛剎微塵數諸佛
345c23║ 所。見彼佛剎及其眾會。諸佛相好。種種莊
345c24║ 嚴。亦聞彼佛隨諸眾生心之所樂。而演說法。
345c25║ 一文一句。皆悉通達。各別受持。無有雜亂。亦
345c26║ 知彼佛以種種解。淨治諸願。亦知彼佛以清
345c27║ 淨願。成就諸力。亦見彼佛隨眾生心。所現色
345c28║ 相。

简体字

必当干竭诸爱欲海，必令众生永灭苦蕴，必当永破无明黑暗，必当永断贪爱系缚，必以福德大轮围山围绕世间，必以智慧大宝须弥显示世间，必当出现清净智日，必当开示善根法藏，必使世间明识险易。”

时，毗目瞿沙告群仙言：“善男子，若有能发阿耨多罗三藐三菩提心，必当成就一切智道。此善男子已发阿耨多罗三藐三菩提心，当净一切佛功德地。”

时，毗目瞿沙告善财童子言：“善男子，我得菩萨无胜幢解脱。”

善财白言：“圣者，无胜幢解脱境界云何？”

时，毗目仙人即伸右手，摩善财顶，执善财手。即时，善财自见其身往十方十佛刹微尘数世界中，到十佛刹微尘数诸佛所，见彼佛刹及其众会、诸佛相好、种种庄严；亦闻彼佛随诸众生心之所乐而演说法，一文一句皆悉通达，各别受持无有杂乱；亦知彼佛以种种解净治诸愿；亦知彼佛以清净愿成就诸力；亦见彼佛随众生心所现色相；

Is certainly bound to dry up the ocean of cravings and will certainly cause beings to forever do away with the mass of sufferings;
Is certainly bound to forever dispel the darkness of ignorance;
Is certainly bound to forever sever the bonds of cravings, will certainly surround the world with a great ring of mountains of merit, and will certainly reveal to the world a Mount Sumeru of immense jewels of wisdom;
Is certainly bound to bring forth the rising sun of pure wisdom; and
Is certainly bound to open and reveal the Dharma treasury of roots of goodness and will certainly enable those in the world to clearly distinguish what is hazardous and what is easy.

Bhīsmottaranirghoṣa then told that group of rishis, "Sons of the Buddha, if there is anyone who is able to resolve to attain *anuttara-samyak-saṃbodhi,* he will certainly be bound to achieve complete success in the path to all-knowledge. Because this son of good family is one who has already resolved to attain *anuttara-samyak-saṃbodhi,* he is bound to purify the ground of meritorious qualities of all buddhas."

Bhīsmottaranirghoṣa then spoke to Sudhana the Youth, saying, "Son of Good Family, I have acquired the bodhisattva liberation known as 'the banner of invincibility.'"

Sudhana then inquired, "O Ārya, as for this 'banner of invincibility' liberation, what is its sphere of experience like?"

Bhīsmottaranirghoṣa Rishi then extended his right hand, rubbed the crown of Sudhana's head, and grasped Sudhana's hand, at which point Sudhana immediately saw himself go off and enter worlds of the ten directions as numerous as the atoms in ten buddha *kṣetras,* whereupon he arrived in the abodes of buddhas as numerous as the atoms in ten buddha *kṣetras* in which he saw those buddhas' *kṣetras,* their congregations, those buddhas' major and secondary signs, and their many different kinds of adornments, this even as he also heard those buddhas expounding on the Dharma in ways suited to whatever pleased the minds of the beings there. He completely understood every word and phrase they spoke and absorbed and retained their teachings without mixing them up or confusing them.

He gained the knowledge of those buddhas' use of all different kinds of understanding to achieve the purification of their vows, also gained the knowledge of those buddhas' use of purified vows to perfect the powers, also saw those buddhas' manifestations of forms and appearances adapted to beings' mental dispositions, also saw those

正體字

亦見彼佛大光明網。種種諸色。清淨圓
345c29║ 滿。亦知彼佛無礙智慧。大光明力。又自見身。
346a01║ 於諸佛所。經一日夜。或七日夜。半月一月。一
346a02║ 年十年。百年千年。或經億年。或阿庾多億年。
346a03║ 或那由他億年。或經半劫。或經一劫百劫千
346a04║ 劫。或百千億。乃至不可說不可說佛剎微塵
346a05║ 數劫。爾時善財童子。為菩薩無勝幢解脫智
346a06║ 光明照故。得毘盧遮那藏三昧光明。為無盡
346a07║ 智解脫三昧光明照故。得普攝諸方陀羅尼
346a08║ 光明。為金剛輪陀羅尼門光明照故。得極清
346a09║ 淨智慧心三昧光明。為普門莊嚴藏般若波
346a10║ 羅蜜光明照故。得佛虛空藏輪三昧光明。為
346a11║ 一切佛法輪三昧光明照故。得三世無盡智
346a12║ 三昧光明。時彼仙人。放善財手。善財童子。即
346a13║ 自見身。還在本處。時彼仙人。告善財言。善男
346a14║ 子。汝憶念耶。善財言唯。此是聖者。善知識
346a15║ 力。仙人言。善男子。我唯知此菩薩無勝幢解
346a16║ 脫。如諸菩薩摩訶薩。成就一切殊勝三昧。於
346a17║ 一切時。而得自在。於一念頃。出生諸佛無量
346a18║ 智慧。

简体字

亦见彼佛大光明网，种种诸色清净圆满；亦知彼佛无碍智慧大光明力；又自见身于诸佛所，经一日夜或七日夜、半月、一月、一年、十年、百年、千年，或经亿年，或阿庾多亿年，或那由他亿年，或经半劫，或经一劫、百劫、千劫，或百千亿乃至不可说不可说佛刹微尘数劫。

尔时，善财童子为菩萨无胜幢解脱智光明照故，得毗卢遮那藏三昧光明；为无尽智解脱三昧光明照故，得普摄诸方陀罗尼光明；为金刚轮陀罗尼门光明照故，得极清净智慧心三昧光明；为普门庄严藏般若波罗蜜光明照故，得佛虚空藏轮三昧光明；为一切佛法轮三昧光明照故，得三世无尽智三昧光明。

时，彼仙人放善财手，善财童子即自见身还在本处。

时，彼仙人告善财言：“善男子，汝忆念耶？”

善财言：“唯！此是圣者善知识力。”

仙人言：“善男子，我唯知此菩萨无胜幢解脱。如诸菩萨摩诃萨成就一切殊胜三昧，于一切时而得自在，于一念顷出生诸佛无量智慧，

buddhas' immense nets of light rays of many different colors that were perfectly fulfilled in their purity, also gained the knowledge of those buddhas' unimpeded power arising from their great light of wisdom, and also saw himself there in the presence of those buddhas where he remained in some cases for one day and night, in other cases, for seven days and nights, or in other cases for a half month, or a month, or a year, or ten years, or a hundred years, or a thousand years, or a *koṭī* of years, or an *ayuta* of years, or a *nayuta* of years, or for half of a kalpa, or for a whole kalpa, or for a hundred kalpas, or a thousand kalpas, or a hundred thousand *koṭīs* of kalpas, and so forth on up to his remaining in the presence of some buddhas even for kalpas as numerous as the atoms in an ineffable-ineffable number of buddha *kṣetras*.

Then, due to being illuminated by the wisdom light of the bodhisattva's "banner of invincibility" liberation, Sudhana the Youth acquired the light of the "*vairocana* treasury" samādhi;

Due to being illuminated by the light of the samādhi of the "inexhaustible knowledge" liberation, he acquired the light of the "universal integration of all regions" *dhāraṇī*;

Due to being illuminated by the light of the "vajra wheel *dhāraṇī*" gateway, he acquired the light of the "mind of ultimately pure wisdom" samādhi;

Due to being illuminated by the light of the *prajñāpāramitā* of the "universal gateway adornment treasury," he acquired the light of the "Buddha's space treasury sphere" samādhi; and

Due to being illuminated by the light of the "Dharma wheel of all buddhas" samādhi, he acquired the light of the "endless knowledge of the three periods of time" samādhi.

Bhīsmottaranirghoṣa Rishi then released Sudhana's hand, whereupon Sudhana immediately saw himself return to his original place. Then that rishi spoke to Sudhana, saying, "Son of Good Family, do you now recall this?"

Sudhana replied, "Yes, I do. This occurred due to the powers of the Ārya, the good spiritual guide."

The Rishi then said:

> Son of Good Family, I know only this bodhisattva's "banner of invincibility" liberation. As for the bodhisattva-mahāsattvas:
>
> Who have perfected all the especially excellent samādhis;
>
> Who have achieved sovereign mastery over all times;
>
> Who in but a single mind-moment bring forth the measureless wisdom of all buddhas;

正體字

以佛智燈。而為莊嚴。普照世間。一念普
346a19‖ 入三世境界。分形遍往十方國土。智身普入
346a20‖ 一切法界。隨眾生心。普現其前。觀其根行。而
346a21‖ 為利益。放淨光明。甚可愛樂。而我云何能知
346a22‖ 能說彼功德行。彼殊勝願。彼莊嚴剎。彼智
346a23‖ 境界。彼三昧所行。彼神通變化。彼解脫遊
346a24‖ 戲。彼身相差別。彼音聲清淨。彼智慧光明。善
346a25‖ 男子。於此南方。有一聚落。名伊沙那。有婆羅
346a26‖ 門。名曰勝熱。汝詣彼問。菩薩云何學菩薩行。
346a27‖ 修菩薩道。時善財童子。歡喜踊躍。頂禮其足。
346a28‖ 遶無數匝。慇懃瞻仰。辭退南行
346a29‖ 爾時善財童子。為菩薩無勝幢解脫所照故。
346b01‖ 住諸佛不思議神力。證菩薩不思議解脫神
346b02‖ 通智。

简体字

以佛智灯而为庄严普照世间，一念普入三世境界，分形遍往十方国土，智身普入一切法界，随众生心普现其前观其根行而为利益，放净光明甚可爱乐；而我云何能知能说彼功德行、彼殊胜愿、彼庄严刹、彼智境界、彼三昧所行、彼神通变化、彼解脱游戏、彼身相差别、彼音声清净、彼智慧光明？

“善男子，于此南方，有一聚落，名伊沙那；有婆罗门，名曰胜热。汝诣彼问：菩萨云何学菩萨行、修菩萨道？”

时，善财童子欢喜踊跃，顶礼其足，绕无数匝，殷勤瞻仰，辞退南行。

尔时，善财童子为菩萨无胜幢解脱所照故，住诸佛不思议神力，证菩萨不思议解脱神通智，

Who are adorned with the Buddha's lamp of wisdom with which they everywhere illuminate the world;

Who in but a single mind-moment everywhere enter the spheres of experience of all three periods of time;

Who divide their bodies and travel everywhere throughout the lands of the ten directions;

Whose wisdom bodies everywhere enter the entire Dharma realm;

Who adapt to the minds of beings and everywhere appear directly before them;

Who contemplate the faculties and actions of beings and then benefit them accordingly; and

Who emanate pure light which is so very pleasing to behold—

How could I know of or be able to speak about:

Their meritorious qualities and practices;

Their especially excellent vows;

Their adornment of the *kṣetras*;

The spheres of cognition related to their wisdom;

The range of actions in their samādhis;

The transformations produced by their spiritual superknowledges;

Their easeful mastery of the liberations;

The differences in their physical characteristics;

The purity of their voices; or

The light of their wisdom?

Son of Good Family, south of here, there is a village known as Īṣāṇa in which there is a brahman named Jayoṣmāyatana or "Supreme Heat." You should go there, pay your respects, and ask, "How should the bodhisattva train in the bodhisattva practices and how should he cultivate the bodhisattva path?"

Sudhana the Youth was then filled with joy and exultation, whereupon he bowed down in reverence at his feet, circumambulated him countless times as he continued to gaze up at him in attentive admiration. He then respectfully withdrew and traveled southward.

9 – Jayoṣmāyatana

At that time, because Sudhana the Youth had been illuminated by the bodhisattva's "banner of invincibility" liberation:

He dwelt in the inconceivable spiritual powers of all buddhas;

He realized the bodhisattva's inconceivable liberations, spiritual superknowledges, and wisdom;

正體字

得菩薩不思議三昧智光明。得一切時
346b03║ 熏修三昧智光明。得了知一切境界皆依想
346b04║ 所住三昧智光明。得一切世間殊勝智光明。
346b05║ 於一切處。悉現其身。以究竟智。說無二無分
346b06║ 別平等法。以明淨智。普照境界。凡所聞法。皆
346b07║ 能忍受。清淨信解。於法自性。決定明了。心恒
346b08║ 不捨菩薩妙行。求一切智。永無退轉。獲得十
346b09║ 力智慧光明。勤求妙法。常無厭足。以正修行。
346b10║ 入佛境界。出生菩薩無量莊嚴。無邊大願。悉
346b11║ 已清淨。以無窮盡智。知無邊世界網。以無怯
346b12║ 弱心。度無量眾生海。了無邊菩薩諸行境界。
346b13║ 見無邊世界種種差別。見無邊世界種種莊
346b14║ 嚴。入無邊世界微細境界。知無邊世界種種
346b15║ 名號。

简体字

得菩萨不思议三昧智光明，得一切时熏修三昧智光明，得了知一切境界皆依想所住三昧智光明，得一切世间殊胜智光明；于一切处悉现其身，以究竟智说无二无分别平等法，以明净智普照境界；凡所闻法皆能忍受，清净信解，于法自性决定明了；心恒不舍菩萨妙行，求一切智永无退转，获得十力智慧光明，勤求妙法常无厌足，以正修行入佛境界，出生菩萨无量庄严，无边大愿悉已清净；以无穷尽智知无边世界网，以无怯弱心度无量众生海；了无边菩萨诸行境界，见无边世界种种差别，见无边世界种种庄严，入无边世界微细境界，知无边世界种种名号，

He acquired the wisdom light of the bodhisattva's inconceivable samādhi;

He acquired the wisdom light of the perpetually imbued cultivation samādhi;

He acquired the wisdom light of the samādhi in which one completely realizes that all spheres of cognition abide in dependence on perceptions;

He acquired the light of the wisdom that is the most supreme in all worlds;

He manifested his body in all places;

He used ultimate wisdom in teaching the dharmas of non-duality, nondiscrimination, and uniform equality;

He used bright and pure wisdom to illuminate all spheres of experience;

He was able to patiently accept with pure and resolute faith whatever dharmas he heard;

He possessed a decisive and complete understanding of the nature of dharmas;

His mind never relinquished the marvelous practices of the bodhisattva;

He was forever irreversible in his quest for all-knowledge;

He acquired the light of the wisdom of the ten powers;

He was always insatiable in diligently pursuing his quest to acquire the sublime Dharma;

Through right cultivation, he entered the Buddha's spheres of cognition;

He produced the bodhisattva's measureless adornments and boundless great vows, all of which he had already purified;

Through the use of inexhaustible wisdom, he knew the boundless web of worlds; and

With a mind free of trepidation or weakness, he liberated a measureless ocean of beings.

[Moreover]:

He completely understood the bodhisattvas' boundlessly many realms of practices;

He observed the many different kinds of differences in the boundlessly many worlds;

He saw the many different kinds of adornments existing in the boundlessly many worlds;

He penetrated the very subtle sense objects in the boundlessly many worlds;

He knew the many different names of the boundlessly many worlds;

正體字

知無邊世界種種言說。知無邊眾生種
346b16 種解。見無邊眾生種種行。見無邊眾生成熟
346b17 行。見無邊眾生差別想。念善知識漸次遊行。
346b18 至伊沙那聚落。見彼[1]勝熱修諸苦行。求一切
346b19 智。四面火聚。猶如大山。中有刀山。高峻無
346b20 極。登彼山上。投身入火。時善財童子。頂禮其
346b21 足。合掌而立。作如是言。聖者。我已先發阿耨
346b22 多羅三藐三菩提心。而未知菩薩云何學菩
346b23 薩行。云何修菩薩道。我聞聖者。善能誘誨。願
346b24 為我說。婆羅門言。善男子。汝今若能上此刀
346b25 山。投身火聚。諸菩薩行。悉得清淨。時善財童
346b26 子。作如是念。得人身難。離諸難難。得無難難。
346b27 得淨法難。得值佛難。具諸根難。聞佛法難。遇
346b28 善人難。逢真善知識難。受如理正教難。得正
346b29 命難。

简体字

知无边世界种种言说，知无边众生种种解，见无边众生种种行，见无边众生成熟行，见无边众生差别想；念善知识。

渐次游行，至伊沙那聚落，见彼胜热修诸苦行求一切智。四面火聚犹如大山，中有刀山高峻无极，登彼山上投身入火。

时，善财童子顶礼其足，合掌而立，作如是言："圣者，我已先发阿耨多罗三藐三菩提心，而未知菩萨云何学菩萨行？云何修菩萨道？我闻圣者善能诱诲，愿为我说！"

婆罗门言："善男子，汝今若能上此刀山，投身火聚，诸菩萨行悉得清净。"

时，善财童子作如是念："得人身难，离诸难难，得无难难，得净法难，得值佛难，具诸根难，闻佛法难，遇善人难，逢真善知识难，受如理正教难，得正命难，

He knew the many different kinds of languages used in the boundlessly many worlds;
He knew of the many different kinds of convictions of the boundlessly many beings;
He saw the many different kinds of practices of the boundlessly many beings;
He saw the practices leading to ripening of the boundlessly many beings; and
He saw the different types of perceptions of the boundlessly many beings.

Recalling his good spiritual guides, he continued to gradually travel onward until he reached the village of Īśāna. There he saw that Jayoṣmāyatana or "Supreme Heat" who was cultivating the austerities in quest of all-knowledge. He had built a bonfire that blazed on all four sides like an immense mountain. In the middle, there was a mountain of knives that was precipitously steep, rising endlessly upward. He climbed to the top of that mountain and then cast his body down into the flames.

Sudhana the Youth then bowed down in reverence at his feet, pressed his palms together, stood before him, and spoke these words: "O Ārya, I am one who has already resolved to attain *anuttara-samyak-saṃbodhi*. Still, I do not yet know how the bodhisattva should train in the bodhisattva practices or how he should cultivate the bodhisattva path. I have heard that the Ārya is well able to provide guidance and instruction in this. Please speak about these matters for my sake."

The Brahman then said, "Son of Good Family, if you are now able to climb this mountain of knives and throw yourself down into this bonfire, all of the bodhisattva practices will be purified."

Sudhana the Youth then had this thought:

To even acquire a human body is difficult;
To abandon the [eight] difficulties is difficult;
To acquire a circumstance free of the difficulties is difficult;
To obtain the pure Dharma is difficult;
To encounter a Buddha is difficult;
To become possessed of complete faculties is difficult;
To hear the Dharma of the Buddha is difficult;
To meet good people is difficult;
To encounter a genuine good spiritual guide is difficult;
To adopt right teachings that accord with principle is difficult;
To acquire right livelihood is difficult; and

正體字

隨法行難。此將非魔。魔所使耶。將非是
346c01║ 魔險惡徒黨。詐現菩薩善知識相。而欲為我
346c02║ 作善根難。作壽命難。障我修行一切智道。牽
346c03║ 我令入諸惡道中。欲障我法門。障我佛法。作
346c04║ 是念時。十千梵天。在虛空中。作如是言善男
346c05║ 子。莫作是念。莫作是念。今此聖者。得金剛焰
346c06║ 三昧光明。發大精進。度諸眾生。心無退轉。欲
346c07║ 竭一切貪愛海。欲截一切邪見網。欲燒一切
346c08║ 煩惱薪。欲照一切惑稠林。欲斷一切老死怖。
346c09║ 欲壞一切三世障。欲放一切法光明。善男子。
346c10║ 我諸梵天。多著邪見。皆悉自謂是自在者。是
346c11║ 能作者。於世間中。我是最勝。見婆羅門。五熱
346c12║ 炙身。於自宮殿。心不樂著。於諸禪定。不得滋
346c13║ 味。皆共來詣婆羅門所。時婆羅門。以神通
346c14║ 力。示大苦行。為我說法。能令我等滅一切見。
346c15║ 除一切慢。住於大慈。行於大悲。起廣大心。
346c16║ 發菩提意。常見諸佛。恒聞妙法。於一切處。
346c17║ 心無所礙。復有十千諸魔在虛空中。以天摩
346c18║ 尼寶。散婆羅門上。告善財言。善男子。此婆羅
346c19║ 門。五熱炙身時。

简体字

随法行难。此将非魔、魔所使耶？将非是魔险恶徒党，诈现菩萨善知识相，而欲为我作善根难、作寿命难，障我修行一切智道，牵我令入诸恶道中，欲障我法门、障我佛法？”

作是念时，十千梵天，在虚空中，作如是言：“善男子，莫作是念！莫作是念！今此圣者得金刚焰三昧光明，发大精进，度诸众生，心无退转；欲竭一切贪爱海，欲截一切邪见网，欲烧一切烦恼薪，欲照一切惑稠林，欲断一切老死怖，欲坏一切三世障，欲放一切法光明。

“善男子，我诸梵天多著邪见，皆悉自谓是自在者、是能作者，于世间中我是最胜。见婆罗门五热炙身，于自宫殿心不乐著，于诸禅定不得滋味，皆共来诣婆罗门所。时，婆罗门以神通力示大苦行为我说法，能令我等，灭一切见，除一切慢，住于大慈，行于大悲，起广大心，发菩提意，常见诸佛，恒闻妙法，于一切处心无所碍。”

复有十千诸魔，在虚空中，以天摩尼宝散婆罗门上，告善财言：“善男子，此婆罗门五热炙身时，

To practice in accordance with the Dharma is difficult.

Could this not be Māra or an emissary of Māra? Could this not be a dangerous and evil minion of Māra who is falsely manifesting the appearance of a bodhisattva and a good spiritual guide, one who wants to create an obstacle to my planting roots of goodness, one who wants to create an obstacle to my continuing this life, one who aims to obstruct my cultivation of the path to all-knowledge, one who wants to drag me into the wretched destinies, one who wishes to obstruct my gateways into the Dharma, and one who aims to obstruct my acquisition of the dharmas of a buddha?

When he had this thought, a myriad Brahma Heaven devas appeared in the sky and spoke thus:

Son of Good Family, do not think in this way, do not think in this way. This *ārya* who stands before you now has acquired the light of the vajra flame samādhi. He applies immense vigor in the liberation of beings, doing so with an irreversible resolve by which he wishes to dry up the entire ocean of desire and craving, wishes to rend the entire net of false views, wishes to burn up all the fuel of the afflictions, wishes to illuminate the entire dense forest of delusions, wishes to cut off all fear of aging and death, wishes to demolish all obstacles throughout the three periods of time, and wishes to emanate the light of all dharmas.

Son of Good Family, all of us Brahma Heaven devas have been very much attached to the wrong views and all of us have considered ourselves to be possessed of sovereign mastery, to be the creators, and to be supreme beings.

We saw the Brahman subjecting his body to the five types of burning,[95] whereupon our minds no longer delighted in our palaces, and we no longer found any flavor in the *dhyāna* absorptions. We then all came together to pay our respects to the Brahman.

The Brahman then used the power of his superknowledges to reveal his great ascetic practices. He spoke the Dharma for our sakes and enabled us to extinguish all our views, to rid ourselves of all pride, to abide in great kindness, to practice great compassion, to bring forth great determination, to resolve to attain bodhi, to always see the buddhas, to constantly listen to the sublime Dharma, and to maintain unimpeded resolve in all places.

There were also a myriad *māras* up in the sky who then sprinkled down heavenly *maṇi* jewels over the Brahman and told Sudhana:

Son of Good Family, when this brahman subjected his body to the five types of burning, the light from his fires so outshone our palaces and their adornments that by comparison they resembled

正體字

其火光明。映奪於我所有宮
346c20║ 殿諸莊嚴具。皆如聚墨。令我於中不生樂著。
346c21║ 我與眷屬。來詣其所。此婆羅門。為我說法。令
346c22║ 我及餘無量天子諸天女等。皆於阿耨多羅
346c23║ 三藐三菩提。得不退轉。復有十千自在天王。
346c24║ 於虛空中。各散天華。作如是言。善男子。此婆
346c25║ 羅門。五熱炙身時。其火光明。映奪我等所有
346c26║ 宮殿諸莊嚴具。皆如聚墨。令我於中不生愛
346c27║ 著。即與眷屬。來詣其所。此婆羅門。為我說
346c28║ 法。令我於心而得自在。於煩惱中而得自在。
346c29║ 於受生中而得自在。於諸業障而得自在。於
347a01║ 諸三昧而得自在。於[1]莊嚴具而得自在。於壽
347a02║ 命中而得自在。乃至能於一切佛法而得自
347a03║ 在。復有十千化樂天王。於虛空中。作天音
347a04║ 樂。恭敬供養。作如是言。善男子。此婆羅門。
347a05║ 五熱炙身時。其火光明。照我宮殿諸莊嚴具
347a06║ 及諸采女。能令我等不受欲樂。不求欲樂。身
347a07║ 心柔軟。即與眾俱。來詣其所。時婆羅門。為我
347a08║ 說法。能令我等心得清淨。心得明潔。心得純
347a09║ 善。心得柔軟。心生歡喜。乃至令得清淨十力
347a10║ 清淨之身。

简体字

其火光明映夺于我所有宫殿诸庄严具皆如聚墨，令我于中不生乐著，我与眷属来诣其所。此婆罗门为我说法，令我及余无量天子、诸天女等，皆于阿耨多罗三藐三菩提得不退转。”

复有十千自在天王，于虚空中，各散天华，作如是言：“善男子，此婆罗门五热炙身时，其火光明映夺我等所有宫殿诸庄严具皆如聚墨，令我于中不生爱著，即与眷属来诣其所。此婆罗门为我说法，令我于心而得自在，于烦恼中而得自在，于受生中而得自在，于诸业障而得自在，于诸三昧而得自在，于庄严具而得自在，于寿命中而得自在，乃至能于一切佛法而得自在。”

复有十千化乐天王，于虚空中，作天音乐，恭敬供养，作如是言：“善男子，此婆罗门五热炙身时，其火光明照我宫殿诸庄严具及诸采女，能令我等不受欲乐、不求欲乐、身心柔软，即与众俱来诣其所。时，婆罗门为我说法，能令我等心得清净、心得明洁、心得纯善、心得柔软、心生欢喜，乃至令得清净十力清净之身，

mere lumps of powdered ink. This caused us to no longer feel any delight in them, whereupon we came with our retinues to pay our respects to him. This brahman then spoke the Dharma for our sakes, thereby enabling all of us and all of the countless other devas' sons and devas' daughters to become irreversible in the quest to attain *anuttara-samyak-saṃbodhi.*

There were also a myriad Paranirmita Vaśavartin deva kings up in the sky who each scattered down heavenly flowers and spoke in this way:

Son of Good Family, when this brahman subjected his body to the five types of burning, the light from his fires so outshone our palaces and their adornments that by comparison they resembled mere lumps of powdered ink. This caused us to no longer feel any affectionate attachment to them. We then came with our retinues to pay respects to him. This brahman then spoke the Dharma for our sakes, thereby enabling us:

To gain sovereign mastery over our own minds;
To gain sovereign mastery even in the midst of the afflictions;
To gain sovereign mastery in taking on rebirths;
To gain sovereign mastery over all karmic obstacles;
To gain sovereign mastery in all samādhis;
To gain sovereign mastery over the adornments;
To gain sovereign mastery over the length of our life spans;
And so forth on up to our being able to gain sovereign mastery in all the dharmas of a buddha.

There were also a myriad Transformational Bliss deva kings up in the sky who made celestial music as respectful offerings. They spoke in this way:

Son of Good Family, when this brahman was subjecting his body to the five types of burning, the light from his fires illuminated our palaces and their adornments and our celestial nymphs. This was able to cause us to no longer derive pleasure from them. We then ceased our pursuit of the sensual pleasures, whereupon our bodies and minds reached a state of supple pliancy. We then came with our retinues to pay our respects to him. The brahman then spoke the Dharma for our sakes, thereby enabling our minds to become purified, enabling our minds to become radiantly immaculate, enabling our minds to become thoroughly suffused with goodness, enabling our minds to gain a state of pliancy, enabling our minds to become filled with delight, and so forth on up to its enabling us to acquire the purified ten powers, to acquire purified bodies, to produce

正體字

生無量身。乃至令得佛身佛語佛
347a11‖ 聲佛心。具足成就一切智智。復有十千兜率
347a12‖ 天王天子天女。無量眷屬。於虛空中。雨眾妙
347a13‖ 香。恭敬頂禮。作如是言。善男子。此婆羅門。
347a14‖ 五熱炙身時。令我等諸天。及其眷屬。於自宮
347a15‖ 殿。無有樂著。共詣其所。聞其說法。能令我等
347a16‖ 不貪境界。少欲知足。心生歡喜。心得充滿。生
347a17‖ 諸善根。發菩提心。乃至圓滿一切佛法。復有
347a18‖ 十千三十三天。并其眷屬天子天女。前後圍
347a19‖ 遶。於虛空中。雨天曼陀羅華。恭敬供養。作如
347a20‖ 是言。善男子。此婆羅門。五熱炙身時。令我等
347a21‖ 諸天。於天音樂。不生樂著。共詣其所。時婆羅
347a22‖ 門。為我等說一切諸法無常敗壞。令我捨離
347a23‖ 一切欲樂。令我斷除憍慢放逸。令我愛樂無
347a24‖ 上菩提。又善男子。我當見此婆羅門時。須彌
347a25‖ 山頂。六種震動。我等恐怖。皆發菩提心。堅固
347a26‖ 不動。復有十千龍王。所謂伊那跋羅龍王。難
347a27‖ 陀優波難陀龍王等。於虛空中。雨黑栴檀。無
347a28‖ 量龍女。奏天音樂。雨天妙華及天香水。恭
347a29‖ 敬供養。作如是言。善男子。此婆羅門。五熱
347b01‖ 炙身時。

简体字

生无量身，乃至令得佛身、佛语、佛声、佛心，具足成就一切智智。”

复有十千兜率天王、天子、天女、无量眷属，于虚空中，雨众妙香，恭敬顶礼，作如是言：“善男子，此婆罗门五热炙身时，令我等诸天及其眷属，于自宫殿无有乐著，共诣其所。闻其说法，能令我等不贪境界，少欲知足，心生欢喜，心得充满，生诸善根，发菩提心，乃至圆满一切佛法。”

复有十千三十三天并其眷属、天子、天女，前后围绕，于虚空中，雨天曼陀罗华，恭敬供养，作如是言：“善男子，此婆罗门五热炙身时，令我等诸天于天音乐不生乐著，共诣其所。时，婆罗门为我等说一切诸法无常败坏，令我舍离一切欲乐，令我断除憍慢放逸，令我爱乐无上菩提。又，善男子，我当见此婆罗门时，须弥山顶六种震动，我等恐怖，皆发菩提心坚固不动。”

复有十千龙王，所谓：伊那跋罗龙王、难陀优波难陀龙王等，于虚空中，雨黑栴檀；无量龙女奏天音乐，雨天妙华及天香水，恭敬供养，作如是言：“善男子，此婆罗门五热炙身时，

countless bodies, and so forth on up to its enabling us to acquire the buddha body, the buddha speech, the buddha voice, the buddha mind, and the complete perfection of the knowledge of all modes.

There were also a myriad Tuṣita Heaven deva kings, their deva sons, their deva daughters, and a measurelessly large retinue who rained down from the sky many different kinds of marvelous incense. They then bowed down in reverence and spoke in this way:

Son of Good Family, when this brahman was subjecting his body to the five kinds of burning, this caused us devas and our retinues to no longer delight in our palaces, whereupon we came together to pay our respects to him. We listened to him speak on the Dharma in ways that enabled us to no longer have any desire for any objects of the senses, to have but few desires and be easily satisfied, to feel delighted in mind, to feel mentally fulfilled, to produce roots of goodness, to resolve to attain bodhi, and so forth on up to its enabling us to progress toward the perfect fulfillment of all dharmas of a buddha.

There were also a myriad Trāyastriṃśa Heaven devas surrounded by their retinues, including their devas' sons and devas' daughters, all of whom rained down from the sky celestial *māndārava* flowers as respectful offerings. They then bowed down in reverence and spoke in this way:

Son of Good Family, when this brahman was subjecting his body to the five kinds of burning, this caused all of us devas to no longer delight in heavenly music, whereupon we came together to pay our respects to him. The Brahman then spoke for our sakes on the impermanence and destruction of all dharmas, thereby causing us to abandon all of the pleasures of the sense desires, to cut off our pride and neglectfulness, and to cherish unexcelled bodhi.

Moreover, Son of Good Family, when we had just seen this brahman, the summit of Mount Sumeru shook and moved in six ways, whereupon we were seized with fright and were all inspired to arouse the unshakably solid resolve to attain bodhi.

There were also a myriad dragon kings, namely Airāvana Dragon King, Nandopananda Dragon King, and others, all of whom rained down black sandalwood incense from the sky as countless dragon maidens played celestial music and rained down marvelous celestial flowers and celestial perfumes as respectful offerings. They then spoke in this way:

Son of Good Family, when this brahman was subjecting his body to the five kinds of burning, the light from his fires everywhere

正體字

其火光明。普照一切諸龍宮殿。令諸
347b02║ 龍眾。離熱沙怖。金翅鳥怖。滅除瞋恚。身得清
347b03║ 涼。心無垢濁。聞法信解。厭惡龍趣。以至誠
347b04║ 心。悔除業障。乃至發阿耨多羅三藐三菩提
347b05║ 意。住一切智。復有十千夜叉王。於虛空中。以
347b06║ 種種供具。恭敬供養此婆羅門及以善財。作
347b07║ 如是言。善男子。此婆羅門。五熱炙身[2]時。我
347b08║ 及眷屬。悉於眾生。發慈愍心。一切羅剎。鳩槃
347b09║ [3]茶等。亦生慈心。以慈心故。於諸眾生。無所
347b10║ 惱害。而來見我。我及彼等。於自宮殿。不生樂
347b11║ 著。即與共俱。來詣其所。時婆羅門。即為我
347b12║ 等。如應說法。一切皆得身心安樂。又令無量
347b13║ 夜叉羅剎鳩槃[＊]茶等。發於無上菩提之心。復
347b14║ 有十千乾闥婆王。於虛空中。作如是言。善男
347b15║ 子。此婆羅門。五熱炙身時。其火光明。照我宮
347b16║ 殿。悉令我等受不思議無量快樂。是故我等。
347b17║ 來詣其所。此婆羅門。為我說法。能令我等於
347b18║ 阿耨多羅三藐三菩提。得不退轉。復有十千
347b19║ 阿脩羅王。從大海出。住在虛空。舒右膝輪。合
347b20║ 掌前禮。作如是言。善男子。此婆羅門。五熱炙
347b21║ 身時。我阿脩羅所有宮殿大海大地。悉皆震
347b22║ 動。令我等捨憍慢放逸。

简体字

其火光明普照一切诸龙宫殿，令诸龙众离热沙怖、金翅鸟怖，灭除瞋恚，身得清凉，心无垢浊，闻法信解，厌恶龙趣，以至诚心悔除业障，乃至发阿耨多罗三藐三菩提意住一切智。”

复有十千夜叉王，于虚空中，以种种供具，恭敬供养此婆罗门及以善财，作如是言：“善男子，此婆罗门五热炙身时，我及眷属悉于众生发慈愍心，一切罗刹、鸠槃茶等亦生慈心；以慈心故，于诸众生无所恼害而来见我。我及彼等，于自宫殿不生乐著，即与共俱，来诣其所。时，婆罗门即为我等如应说法，一切皆得身心安乐，又令无量夜叉、罗刹、鸠槃茶等发于无上菩提之心。”

复有十千乾闼婆王，于虚空中，作如是言：“善男子，此婆罗门五热炙身时，其火光明照我宫殿，悉令我等受不思议无量快乐，是故我等来诣其所。此婆罗门为我说法，能令我等于阿耨多罗三藐三菩提得不退转。”

复有十千阿修罗王，从大海出，住在虚空，舒右膝轮，合掌前礼，作如是言：“善男子，此婆罗门五热炙身时，我阿修罗所有宫殿、大海、大地，悉皆震动，令我等舍憍慢放逸，

illuminated all the dragon palaces, causing the entire congregation of dragons to abandon fear of the burning sands and fear of the golden-winged *garuḍa* birds. Our anger was extinguished, our bodies felt fresh and cool, and our minds became free of defilement and turbidity. As we listened to the Dharma, we developed resolute faith and came to feel weariness and revulsion toward rebirth among the dragons. With deep sincerity, we repented of our karmic obstacles and resolved to attain *anuttara-samyak-saṃbodhi* so that we might dwell in all-knowledge.

There were also a myriad *yakṣa* kings there in the sky who presented all different kinds of gifts as respectful offerings to the Brahman and Sudhana, whereupon they spoke in this way:

Son of Good Family, when this brahman was subjecting his body to the five kinds of burning, together with our retinues, we aroused thoughts of kindness and pity for beings. All the *rākṣasas, kumbhāṇḍas,* and others also aroused thoughts of kindness. Because of those thoughts of kindness, they no longer tormented or harmed beings and then came to see us. We all then no longer felt delight in and attachment to our palaces.

We then went together to pay our respects to him. The Brahman then spoke the Dharma for our sakes in ways that were fitting, whereupon we all became peaceful and happy in body and mind. He also caused countless other *yakṣas, rākṣasas,* and *kumbhāṇḍas* to resolve to attain unexcelled bodhi.

There were also a myriad *gandharva* kings who, from up in the sky, spoke in this way:

Son of Good Family, when this brahman was subjecting his body to the five kinds of burning, the light from his fires illuminated our palaces and caused all of us to enjoy inconceivable feelings of measureless happiness. Because of this, we all came and paid our respects to him, whereupon this brahman spoke the Dharma for our sakes in a way that was able to cause us to become irreversible in our quest to attain *anuttara-samyak-saṃbodhi.*

There were also a myriad *asura* kings who emerged from the great ocean, stood there in the sky, knelt down on their right knees, pressed their palms together, bowed in reverence before them, and then spoke in this way:

Son of Good Family, when this brahman was subjecting his body to the five kinds of burning, all of our *asura* palaces, the great oceans, and the great earth all quaked and shook. This caused us to abandon our pride and neglectfulness. Consequently, we all came forth

正體字

是故我等來詣其所。
347b23║ 從其聞法。捨離諂誑。安住忍地。堅固不動。圓
347b24║ 滿十力。復有十千迦樓羅王。勇力持王。而為
347b25║ 上首。化作外道童子之形。於虛空中。[4]唱如
347b26║ 是言。善男子。此婆羅門。五熱炙身時。其火光
347b27║ 明。照我宮殿。一切震動。皆悉恐怖。是故我
347b28║ 等。來詣其所。時婆羅門。即為我等。如應說
347b29║ 法。令修習大慈。稱讚大悲。度生死海。於欲泥
347c01║ 中。拔濟眾生。歎菩提心。起方便智。隨其所
347c02║ 宜。調伏眾生。復有十千緊那羅王。於虛空中。
347c03║ 唱如是言。善男子。此婆羅門。五熱炙身時。我
347c04║ 等所住宮殿。諸多羅樹。諸寶鈴網。諸寶繒帶。
347c05║ 諸音樂樹。諸妙寶樹。及諸樂器。自然而出佛
347c06║ 聲法聲。及不退轉菩薩僧聲。願求無上菩提
347c07║ 之聲。云某方某國。有某菩薩。發菩提心。某方
347c08║ 某國。有某菩薩。修行苦行。難捨能捨。乃至清
347c09║ 淨一切智行。某方某國。有某菩薩。往詣道場。
347c10║ 乃至某方某國。有某如來。作佛事已。而般涅
347c11║ 槃。善男子。假使有人。以閻浮提。一切草木。
347c12║ 末為微塵。

简体字

是故我等来诣其所。从其闻法，舍离谄诳，安住忍地，坚固不动，圆满十力。”

复有十千迦楼罗王，勇力持王而为上首，化作外道童子之形，于虚空中唱如是言：“善男子，此婆罗门五热炙身时，其火光明照我宫殿，一切震动皆悉恐怖，是故我等来诣其所。时，婆罗门即为我等如应说法，令修习大慈，称赞大悲，度生死海，于欲泥中拔济众生，叹菩提心，起方便智，随其所宜调伏众生。”

复有十千紧那罗王，于虚空中，唱如是言：“善男子，此婆罗门五热炙身时，我等所住宫殿诸多罗树、诸宝铃网、诸宝缯带、诸音乐树、诸妙宝树及诸乐器，自然而出佛声、法声及不退转菩萨僧声、愿求无上菩提之声，云：‘某方、某国，有某菩萨，发菩提心；某方、某国，有某菩萨，修行苦行，难舍能舍，乃至清净一切智行；某方、某国，有某菩萨，往诣道场；乃至某方、某国，有某如来，作佛事已，而般涅槃。’善男子，假使有人，以阎浮提一切草木末为微尘，

to pay our respects to him. We heard teachings on Dharma from him [urging us] to relinquish flattery and deviousness, to dwell securely on the ground of patience, to acquire unshakably solid [samādhi], and to fulfill the ten powers.

There were also a myriad *garuḍa* kings headed by King Mahāvegadhāri or "Heroically Powerful Grip." Up in the sky, they transformed into the appearance of non-Buddhist youths[96] who chanted these words:

Son of Good Family, when this brahman was subjecting his body to the five kinds of burning, the light from his fires illuminated our palaces which then quaked and shook, whereupon we were all seized with terror. As a consequence, we all came here to pay our respects to him.

The brahman then spoke the Dharma for our sakes in ways that were fitting to cause us to cultivate great kindness, praise great compassion, cross beyond the ocean of *saṃsāra,* rescue beings from the mud of sensual desires, praise the resolve to attain bodhi, develop skillful means and wisdom, and train beings in ways that are fitting.

There were also a myriad *kiṃnara* kings who, from up in the sky, sang these words:

Son of Good Family, when this brahman was subjecting his body to the five kinds of burning, the palaces in which we dwell, the *tāla* trees, the jeweled bell nets, the jeweled silken streamers, the music trees, the marvelous jewel trees, and all of our musical instruments all spontaneously emanated the sounds of the Buddha's voice, the sounds of Dharma, the sounds of the irreversible bodhisattva sangha, and the sounds of vows to seek the unexcelled bodhi.

They proclaimed that, in a particular region, in a particular land, there is a particular bodhisattva who has resolved to attain bodhi. They proclaimed that, in a particular region, in a particular land, there is a particular bodhisattva who is cultivating the ascetic practices, who is relinquishing what is difficult to relinquish, and so forth until we come to "who is purifying the practices leading to all-knowledge." They proclaimed that, in a particular region, in a particular land, there is a particular bodhisattva who is proceeding to the site of enlightenment, and so forth until we come to, "in a particular region, in a particular land, there is a particular *tathāgata* who, having completed his buddha works, is entering *parinirvāṇa.*"

Son of Good Family, suppose that there was some man who ground to fine dust all the grasses and trees on the continent of Jambudvīpa. One might be able to know the full extent of the

正體字

此微塵數。可知邊際。我宮殿中寶
347c13║ 多羅樹。乃至樂器。所說菩薩名。如來名。所發
347c14║ 大願。所修行等。無有能得知其邊際。善男
347c15║ 子。我等以聞佛聲法聲。菩薩僧聲。生大歡
347c16║ 喜。來詣其所。時婆羅門。即為我等。如應說
347c17║ 法。令我及餘無量眾生。於阿耨多羅三藐三
347c18║ 菩提。得不退轉。復有無量欲界諸天。於虛空
347c19║ 中。以妙供具。恭敬供養。唱如是言。善男子。
347c20║ 此婆羅門。五熱炙身時。其火光明。照阿鼻等。
347c21║ 一切地獄。諸所受苦。悉令休息。我等見此火
347c22║ 光明故。心生淨信。以信心故。從彼命終。生於
347c23║ 天中。為知恩故。而來其所。恭敬瞻仰。無有厭
347c24║ 足。時婆羅門。為我說法。令無量眾生。發菩提
347c25║ 心。爾時善財童子。聞如是法。心大歡喜。於婆
347c26║ 羅門所。發起真實善知識心。頭頂禮敬。唱
347c27║ 如是言。我於大聖善知識所。生不善心。唯願
347c28║ 聖者。容我悔過。時婆羅門。即為善財。而說頌
347c29║ 言
348a01║ 若有諸菩薩　順善知識教
348a02║ 一切無疑懼　安住心不動

简体字

此微尘数可知边际，我宫殿中宝多罗树乃至乐器所说菩萨名、如来名、所发大愿、所修行等，无有能得知其边际。善男子，我等以闻佛声、法声、菩萨僧声，生大欢喜，来诣其所。时，婆罗门即为我等如应说法，令我及余无量众生于阿耨多罗三藐三菩提得不退转。”

复有无量欲界诸天，于虚空中，以妙供具，恭敬供养，唱如是言：“善男子，此婆罗门五热炙身时，其火光明照阿鼻等一切地狱，诸所受苦悉令休息。我等见此火光明故，心生净信；以信心故，从彼命终，生于天中；为知恩故，而来其所，恭敬瞻仰，无有厌足。时，婆罗门为我说法，令无量众生发菩提心。”

尔时，善财童子闻如是法，心大欢喜，于婆罗门所，发起真实善知识心，头顶礼敬，唱如是言：“我于大圣善知识所生不善心，唯愿圣者容我悔过！”

时，婆罗门即为善财而说颂言：

“若有诸菩萨，顺善知识教，
一切无疑惧，安住心不动。

number of these dust motes. But when it comes to the number of bodhisattva names, *tathāgata* names, the great vows they made, the practices in which they engaged, and so forth, the sounds of which emanated from our palaces' jeweled *tāla* trees and so forth, including from our musical instruments—there is no one who could ever know the full extent of their number.

Son of Good Family, due to hearing these sounds of the Buddha, sounds of the Dharma, and sounds of the bodhisattva sangha, we were filled with immense delight and were moved to come and pay our respects to him. The Brahman then spoke Dharma for our sakes in a manner that was fitting to cause us and countless other beings to become irreversible in our quest to reach *anuttara-samyak-saṃbodhi.*

There were also countless desire-realm devas up in the sky who used marvelous gifts which they presented as respectful offerings as they chanted these words:

Son of Good Family, when this brahman was subjecting his body to the five kinds of burning, the light from his fires illuminated the Avīci Hells as well as all the other hells and then caused all the sufferings being endured there to cease. Because we saw the light from these fires, our minds became filled with pure faith. Due to having minds filled with faith, once those lifetimes came to an end, we were reborn in the heavens.

Out of gratitude for his kindness, we came to see him and looked up to him with insatiable reverence and admiration. Then the Brahman spoke Dharma for our sakes in such a way that it caused countless beings to arouse the resolve to attain bodhi.

At that time, having heard Dharma such as this, Sudhana the Youth's mind was filled with immense delight. He then produced thoughts that inspired him to look upon the Brahman as a true good spiritual guide, whereupon he bowed his head down to the ground in reverence and announced: "I have produced an unwholesome thought toward the great Ārya and good spiritual guide. O Ārya, please accept my repentance of this transgression."

The Brahman then spoke these verses for Sudhana:

If there be any bodhisattva
who complies with the teaching of the good spiritual guide,
then he becomes free of all doubts and trepidation
and dwells securely in the unwavering mind.

正體字

348a03 當知如是人　必獲廣大利
348a04 坐菩提樹下　成於無上覺
348a05 爾時善財童子。即登刀山。自投火聚。未至中
348a06 間。即得菩薩善住三昧。纔觸火焰。又得菩薩
348a07 寂靜樂神通三昧。善財白言。甚奇聖者。如是
348a08 刀山。及大火聚。我身觸時。安隱快樂。時婆羅
348a09 門。告善財言。善男子。我唯得此菩薩無盡輪
348a10 解脫。如諸菩薩摩訶薩。大功德焰。能燒一
348a11 切。眾生見惑。令無有餘。必不退轉。無窮盡
348a12 心。無懈怠心。無怯弱心。發如金剛藏那羅延
348a13 心。疾修諸行。無遲緩心。願如風輪。普持一切
348a14 精進大誓。皆無退轉。而我云何能知能說彼
348a15 功德行。善男子。於此南方。有城名師子奮迅。
348a16 中有童女。名曰慈行。汝詣彼問。菩薩云何學
348a17 菩薩行。修菩薩道。時善財童子。頂禮其足。遶
348a18 無數匝。辭退而去

简体字

当知如是人，必获广大利，
坐菩提树下，成于无上觉。”

尔时，善财童子即登刀山，自投火聚；未至中间，即得菩萨善住三昧；才触火焰，又得菩萨寂静乐神通三昧。善财白言：“甚奇！圣者，如是刀山及大火聚，我身触时安隐快乐。”

时，婆罗门告善财言：“善男子，我唯得此菩萨无尽轮解脱。如诸菩萨摩诃萨大功德焰，能烧一切众生见惑令无有余，必不退转无穷尽心、无懈怠心、无怯弱心，发如金刚藏那罗延心，疾修诸行无迟缓心，愿如风轮普持一切精进大誓皆无退转；而我云何能知能说彼功德行？

“善男子，于此南方，有城名师子奋迅；中有童女，名曰慈行。汝诣彼问：菩萨云何学菩萨行、修菩萨道？”

时，善财童子顶礼其足，绕无数匝，辞退而去。

One should realize that such a person as this
will certainly reap the vast benefit
through which he comes to sit beneath the bodhi tree
and realize the unexcelled enlightenment.

Sudhana the Youth then climbed that mountain of knives and threw himself down into that bonfire. Before he reached the middle of it, he immediately attained the bodhisattva's fine dwelling samādhi. On first touching the flames, he also attained the bodhisattva's quiescent bliss and spiritual superknowledges samādhi.

Sudhana then addressed him, saying, "O Ārya, this is so extraordinary. Even with such a mountain of knives and such a great fiery blaze, when my body touched them, I felt peaceful, secure, and happy."

The Brahman then spoke to Sudhana, saying:

Son of Good Family, I have only acquired this bodhisattva's endless wheel liberation. As for the bodhisattva-mahāsattvas:

Whose flaming light of great meritorious qualities is able to burn up all beings' views and afflictions so completely that none remain;

Who have achieved definite irreversibility;

Whose hearts are inexhaustible;

Whose minds are free of indolence;

Whose minds are neither timid nor weak-willed;

Who bring forth resolve like that of Vajragarbha Nārāyaṇa;

Who swiftly cultivate all the practices and whose minds are never listless;

Whose vows are like a whirlwind;

Who everywhere support everyone; and

Who vigorously implement their great vows without ever retreating from any of them—

How could I know of or be able to speak about their meritorious qualities and practices?

Son of Good Family, south of here, there is a city known as Siṃhavijṛmbhita or "Lion's Sprint" in which there is a young maiden named Maitrāyaṇī. You should go there, pay your respects, and ask her, "How should the bodhisattva train in the bodhisattva practices and how should he cultivate the bodhisattva path?"

Sudhana the Youth then bowed down in reverence at his feet, circumambulated him countless times, and then respectfully withdrew and departed.

正體字

348a22 大方廣佛華嚴經卷第六十五
348a25 入法界品第三十九之六
348a26 爾時善財童子。於善知識所。起最極尊重心。
348a27 生廣大清淨解。常念大乘。專求佛智。願見諸
348a28 佛。觀法境界無障礙智。常現在前。決定了知
348a29 諸法實際常住際。一切三世諸剎那際。如虛
348b01 空際。無二際。一切法無分別際。一切義無障
348b02 礙際。一切劫無失壞際。一切如來無際之際。
348b03 於一切佛。心無分別。破眾想網。離諸執著。不
348b04 取諸佛眾會道場。亦不取佛清淨國土。知諸
348b05 眾生皆無有我。知一切聲悉皆如響。知一切
348b06 色悉皆如影。漸次南行。至師子奮迅城。周遍
348b07 推求慈行童女。聞此童女是師子幢王女。五
348b08 百童女。以為侍從。住毘盧遮那藏殿。於龍勝
348b09 栴檀足金線網天衣座上。而說妙法。善財聞
348b10 已。詣王宮門。求見彼女。見無量眾。來入宮
348b11 中。善財問言。諸人今者何所往詣。咸報之言。
348b12 我等欲詣慈行童女聽受妙法。

简体字

大方广佛华严经卷第六十五

入法界品第三十九之六

尔时，善财童子于善知识所，起最极尊重心，生广大清净解，常念大乘，专求佛智，愿见诸佛，观法境界，无障碍智常现在前，决定了知诸法实际、常住际、一切三世诸刹那际、如虚空际、无二际、一切法无分别际、一切义无障碍际、一切劫无失坏际、一切如来无际之际；于一切佛心无分别，破众想网，离诸执著，不取诸佛众会道场，亦不取佛清净国土；知诸众生皆无有我，知一切声悉皆如响，知一切色悉皆如影。

渐次南行，至师子奋迅城，周遍推求慈行童女。闻此童女是师子幢王女，五百童女以为侍从，住毗卢遮那藏殿，于龙胜栴檀足金线网天衣座上而说妙法。善财闻已，诣王宫门，求见彼女。见无量众来入宫中，善财问言：“诸人今者何所往诣？”咸报之言：“我等欲诣慈行童女听受妙法。”

10 – Maitrāyaṇī

At that time, Sudhana the Youth aroused thoughts of the highest esteem toward the good spiritual guide, developed a vast and pure conviction, always remained mindful of the Great Vehicle, focused on seeking the Buddha's wisdom, and yearned to see the buddhas. The sphere of cognition that contemplates dharmas and unimpeded wisdom always manifested directly before him. He decisively and completely knew:

The ultimate extent of the reality of all dharmas;
The ultimate extent of the eternally abiding;
The ultimate extent of all *kṣaṇas* of the three periods of time;
The ultimate extent of comparability to empty space;
The ultimate extent of non-duality;
The ultimate extent of the nondiscrimination of any dharma;
The ultimate extent of the noncontradiction among all meanings;
The ultimate extent of the nondeterioration of all kalpas; and
The ultimate extent of all *tathāgatas'* boundlessness.

His mind was free of any discriminations among all buddhas. He had destroyed the net of the many mental conceptions, had abandoned all attachments, refrained from seizing on any buddha's congregation, and also refrained from seizing on the Buddha's pure land. He realized all beings have no self, realized all sounds are like echoes, and realized all forms are like reflected images.

He then gradually traveled south until he reached the city of Siṁhavijṛmbhita where he searched all around for Maitrāyaṇī, the young maiden, and heard that this maiden was the daughter of King Siṃhaketu or "Lion Banner," that she was attended by a group of five hundred young maidens who served in her retinue, and that she dwelt in the Vairocana Treasury Hall where she taught the sublime Dharma while sitting on a seat with dragon-supremacy sandalwood legs that was covered with celestial robes made of gold-thread lace.

Having heard this, Sudhana then proceeded to the gates of the king's palace where he sought to have an audience with that maiden. He saw that a measurelessly large congregation was arriving and entering the palace. Sudhana asked those people, "What are you now going in to see?"

They all replied, "We wish to pay our respects to the young maiden, Maitrāyaṇī, and then listen to her teach the sublime Dharma."

正體字

善財童子。即
348b13 | 作是念。此王宮門。既無限礙。我亦應入。善
348b14 | 財入已。見毘盧遮那藏殿。[2]玻瓈為地。瑠璃
348b15 | 為柱。金剛為壁。閻浮檀金。以為垣牆。百千光
348b16 | 明。而為窓牖。阿僧祇摩尼寶。而莊校之。寶藏
348b17 | 摩尼鏡。周匝莊嚴。以世間最上摩尼寶。而為
348b18 | 莊飾。無數寶網羅覆其上。百千金鈴。出妙音
348b19 | 聲。有如是等不可思議眾寶嚴飾。其慈行童
348b20 | 女。皮膚金色。眼紺紫色。髮紺青色。以梵音
348b21 | 聲。而演說法。善財見已。頂禮其足。遶無數
348b22 | 匝。合掌前住。作如是言。聖者。我已先發阿耨
348b23 | 多羅三藐三菩提心。而未知菩薩。云何學菩
348b24 | 薩行。云何修菩薩道。我聞聖者。善能誘誨。願
348b25 | 為我說。時慈行童女。告善財言。善男子。汝應
348b26 | 觀我宮殿莊嚴。善財頂禮。周遍觀察。見一一
348b27 | 壁中。一一柱中。一一鏡中。一一相中。一一形
348b28 | 中。一一摩尼寶中。一一莊嚴具中。一一金鈴
348b29 | 中。一一寶樹中。一一寶形像中。一一寶瓔珞
348c01 | 中。悉見法界一切如來。從初發心。修菩薩行。
348c02 | 成滿大願。具足功德。成等正覺轉妙法輪。乃
348c03 | 至示現入於涅槃。如是影像。靡不皆現。

简体字

善财童子即作是念："此王宫门既无限碍，我亦应入。"

善财入已，见毗卢遮那藏殿，玻璃为地，琉璃为柱，金刚为壁，阎浮檀金以为垣墙，百千光明而为窗牖，阿僧祇摩尼宝而庄校之，宝藏摩尼镜周匝庄严，以世间最上摩尼宝而为庄饰，无数宝网罗覆其上，百千金铃出妙音声，有如是等不可思议众宝严饰。其慈行童女，皮肤金色，眼绀紫色，发绀青色，以梵音声而演说法。

善财见已，顶礼其足，绕无数匝，合掌前住，作如是言："圣者，我已先发阿耨多罗三藐三菩提心，而未知菩萨云何学菩萨行？云何修菩萨道？我闻圣者善能诱诲，愿为我说！"

时，慈行童女告善财言："善男子，汝应观我宫殿庄严。"

善财顶礼，周遍观察，见一一壁中、一一柱中、一一镜中、一一相中、一一形中、一一摩尼宝中、一一庄严具中、一一金铃中、一一宝树中、一一宝形像中、一一宝璎珞中，悉见法界一切如来，从初发心，修菩萨行，成满大愿，具足功德，成等正觉，转妙法轮，乃至示现入于涅槃；如是影像靡不皆现，

Sudhana the Youth then had this thought, "Since the gates of this royal palace are not blocked, I too should go ahead and enter here." Having entered, Sudhana then saw that Vairocana Treasury Hall had grounds made of crystal, pillars made of lapis lazuli, walls made of diamonds, and perimeter walls made of *jambūnada* gold. A hundred thousand lights formed its windows which were adorned with *asaṃkhyeyas* of *maṇi* jewels. Mirrors made from precious treasury *maṇi* jewels and decorated with the world's most supremely fine *maṇi* gems were arranged all around as adornments while, suspended over her, there was a net of countless jewels with a hundred thousand gold bells that rang with marvelous sounds. Such were the inconceivably many-jeweled adornments beautifying that hall.

The skin of that young maiden, Maitrāyaṇī, was the color of gold, her eyes were violet blue, and her hair was indigo colored. She expounded the Dharma with a sublimely pure voice.

Having seen her, Sudhana then bowed down in reverence at her feet, circumambulated her countless times, pressed his palms together, and stood before her. He then said, "O Ārya, I have already resolved to attain *anuttara-samyak-saṃbodhi*. Still, I do not yet know how the bodhisattva should train in the bodhisattva practices or how he should cultivate the bodhisattva path. I have heard that the Ārya is well able to offer guidance and instruction in this. Please speak about these matters for my sake."

Then that young maiden, Maitrāyaṇī, spoke to Sudhana, saying, "Son of Good Family, you should contemplate the adornments in my palace."

Sudhana then bowed down in reverence and went all around, closely contemplating those features. He saw in every wall, in every pillar, in every mirror, in every aspect, in every shape, in every *maṇi* jewel, in every adornment, in every gold bell, in every jewel tree, in every jeweled image, and in every jewel necklace, the appearance in all of them of all *tathāgatas* throughout the Dharma realm, beginning with their initial resolve and continuing on to their cultivation of the bodhisattva practices, their fulfillment of their great vows, their complete development of the meritorious qualities, their realization of the universal and right enlightenment, their turning of the Dharma wheel, and so forth on up to their manifestation of entry into nirvāṇa.

Of all these reflecting images, there were none not entirely displayed just as clearly as if one were seeing reflected on the surface of still waters the many images in space including those of the sun,

正體字

如
348c04 ‖ 淨水中普見虛空日月星宿所有眾像。如此
348c05 ‖ 皆是慈行童女。過去世中善根之力。爾時善
348c06 ‖ 財童子。憶念所見諸佛之相。合掌瞻仰慈行
348c07 ‖ 童女。爾時童女。告善財言。善男子。此是般若
348c08 ‖ 波羅蜜普莊嚴門。我於三十六恒河沙佛所。
348c09 ‖ 求得此法。彼諸如來。各以異門。令我入此般
348c10 ‖ 若波羅蜜普莊嚴門。一佛所演。餘不重說。善
348c11 ‖ 財白言。聖者。此般若波羅蜜普莊嚴門。境界
348c12 ‖ 云何。童女答言。善男子。我入此般若波羅蜜
348c13 ‖ 普莊嚴門。隨順趣向。思惟觀察。憶持分別。時
348c14 ‖ 得普門陀羅尼。百萬阿僧祇陀羅尼門。皆悉
348c15 ‖ 現前。所謂佛剎陀羅尼門。佛陀羅尼門。法
348c16 ‖ 陀羅尼門。眾生陀羅尼門。過去陀羅尼門。未
348c17 ‖ 來陀羅尼門。現在陀羅尼門。常住際陀羅尼
348c18 ‖ 門。福德陀羅尼門。福德助道具陀羅尼門。智
348c19 ‖ 慧陀羅尼門。智慧助道具陀羅尼門。諸願陀
348c20 ‖ 羅尼門。分別諸願陀羅尼門。集諸行陀羅尼
348c21 ‖ 門。清淨行陀羅尼門。[3]圓滿行陀羅尼門。業
348c22 ‖ 陀羅尼門。業不失壞陀羅尼門。業流注陀羅
348c23 ‖ 尼門。

简体字

如净水中普见虚空日月星宿所有众像，如此皆是慈行童女过去世中善根之力。

尔时，善财童子忆念所见诸佛之相，合掌瞻仰慈行童女。

尔时，童女告善财言：“善男子，此是般若波罗蜜普庄严门，我于三十六恒河沙佛所求得此法。彼诸如来各以异门，令我入此般若波罗蜜普庄严门；一佛所演，余不重说。”

善财白言：“圣者，此般若波罗蜜普庄严门境界云何？”

童女答言：“善男子，我入此般若波罗蜜普庄严门，随顺趣向，思惟观察，忆持分别时得普门陀罗尼，百万阿僧祇陀罗尼门皆悉现前。所谓：佛刹陀罗尼门、佛陀罗尼门、法陀罗尼门、众生陀罗尼门、过去陀罗尼门、未来陀罗尼门、现在陀罗尼门、常住际陀罗尼门、福德陀罗尼门、福德助道具陀罗尼门、智慧陀罗尼门、智慧助道具陀罗尼门、诸愿陀罗尼门、分别诸愿陀罗尼门、集诸行陀罗尼门、清净行陀罗尼门、圆满行陀罗尼门、业陀罗尼门、

moon, stars, and constellations. All the phenomena such as these appeared due to the power of the past lives' roots of goodness planted by the young maiden, Maitrāyaṇī.

Then Sudhana the Youth, bearing in mind those images of all buddhas that he had just seen, pressed his palms together and gazed up in admiration at the young maiden, Maitrāyaṇī. The young maiden then informed Sudhana, "Son of Good Family, this is 'the *prajñāpāramitā* universal adornment gateway.' I sought and acquired this dharma under buddhas as numerous as the sands in thirty-six Ganges Rivers during which those *tathāgatas* each caused me to enter this *prajñāpāramitā* universal adornment gateway through a different entryway. Whatever any buddha had already expounded upon was never redundantly taught by those other buddhas."

Sudhana then asked her, "O Āryā, what is this *prajñāpāramitā* universal adornment gateway's sphere of experience like?"

The maiden replied:

Son of Good Family, on entering this *prajñāpāramitā* universal adornment gateway, as I progress into it, reflectively contemplate it, and bear in mind and distinguish its aspects, I then acquire the universal gateway *dhāraṇī*, whereupon a hundred myriads of *asaṃkhyeyas* of *dhāraṇī* gateways all manifest directly before me, including the following *dhāraṇī* gateways:

The buddha *kṣetra dhāraṇī* gateway;
The buddha *dhāraṇī* gateway;
The Dharma *dhāraṇī* gateway;
The beings *dhāraṇī* gateway;
The *dhāraṇī* gateway of the past;
The *dhāraṇī* gateway of the future;
The *dhāraṇī* gateway of the present;
The ultimate extent of the eternally abiding *dhāraṇī* gateway;
The merit *dhāraṇī* gateway;
The merit-based path provision *dhāraṇī* gateway;
The wisdom *dhāraṇī* gateway;
The wisdom-based path provision *dhāraṇī* gateway;
The vows *dhāraṇī* gateway;
The distinguishing of vows *dhāraṇī* gateway;
The accumulation of practices *dhāraṇī* gateway;
The pure practices *dhāraṇī* gateway;
The perfectly fulfilled practices *dhāraṇī* gateway;
The karmic deeds *dhāraṇī* gateway;

正體字

業所作陀羅尼門。捨離惡業陀羅尼門。
348c24‖ 修習正業陀羅尼門。業自在陀羅尼門。善行
348c25‖ 陀羅尼門。持善行陀羅尼門。三昧陀羅尼門。
348c26‖ 隨順三昧陀羅尼門。觀察三昧陀羅尼門。三
348c27‖ 昧境界陀羅尼門。從三昧起陀羅尼門。神通
348c28‖ 陀羅尼門。心海陀羅尼門。種種心陀羅尼門。
348c29‖ 直心陀羅尼門。照心稠林陀羅尼門。調心清
349a01‖ 淨陀羅尼門。知眾生所從生陀羅尼門。知眾
349a02‖ 生煩惱行陀羅尼門。知煩惱習氣陀羅尼門。
349a03‖ 知煩惱方便陀羅尼門。知眾生解陀羅尼門。
349a04‖ 知眾生行陀羅尼門。知眾生行不同陀羅尼
349a05‖ 門。知眾生性陀羅尼門。知眾生欲陀羅尼門。
349a06‖ 知眾生想陀羅尼門。普見十方陀羅尼門。說
349a07‖ 法陀羅尼門。大悲陀羅尼門。大慈陀羅尼門。
349a08‖ 寂靜陀羅尼門。言語道陀羅尼門。方便非方
349a09‖ 便陀羅尼門。隨順陀羅尼門。差別陀羅尼門。
349a10‖ 普入陀羅尼門。

简体字

业不失坏陀罗尼门、业流注陀罗尼门、业所作陀罗尼门、舍离恶业陀罗尼门、修习正业陀罗尼门、业自在陀罗尼门、善行陀罗尼门、持善行陀罗尼门、三昧陀罗尼门、随顺三昧陀罗尼门、观察三昧陀罗尼门、三昧境界陀罗尼门、从三昧起陀罗尼门、神通陀罗尼门、心海陀罗尼门、种种心陀罗尼门、直心陀罗尼门、照心稠林陀罗尼门、调心清净陀罗尼门、知众生所从生陀罗尼门、知众生烦恼行陀罗尼门、知烦恼习气陀罗尼门、知烦恼方便陀罗尼门、知众生解陀罗尼门、知众生行陀罗尼门、知众生行不同陀罗尼门、知众生性陀罗尼门、知众生欲陀罗尼门、知众生想陀罗尼门、普见十方陀罗尼门、说法陀罗尼门、大悲陀罗尼门、大慈陀罗尼门、寂静陀罗尼门、言语道陀罗尼门、方便非方便陀罗尼门、随顺陀罗尼门、差别陀罗尼门、普入陀罗尼门、

The nondeterioration of karmic deeds *dhāraṇī* gateway;
The flowing onward of karmic deeds *dhāraṇī* gateway;
The creation of karma *dhāraṇī* gateway;
The abandonment of evil karmic deeds *dhāraṇī* gateway;
The cultivation of correct karmic deeds *dhāraṇī* gateway;
The sovereign mastery over karmic deeds *dhāraṇī* gateway;
The good practices *dhāraṇī* gateway;
The sustaining of good practices *dhāraṇī* gateway;
The samādhi *dhāraṇī* gateway;
The samādhi-accordant *dhāraṇī* gateway;
The contemplation samādhi *dhāraṇī* gateway;
The samādhi spheres of cognition *dhāraṇī* gateway;
The emergence from samādhi *dhāraṇī* gateway;
The spiritual superknowledges *dhāraṇī* gateway;
The ocean of mind *dhāraṇī* gateway;
The various types of mind *dhāraṇī* gateway;
The straight mind *dhāraṇī* gateway;
The illumination of the mind's dense thickets *dhāraṇī* gateway;
The training of the mind in purity *dhāraṇī* gateway;
The cognition of beings' origins *dhāraṇī* gateway;
The cognition of beings' afflicted conduct *dhāraṇī* gateway;
The cognition of affliction-based habitual karmic propensities *dhāraṇī* gateway;
The cognition of affliction-related expedients *dhāraṇī* gateway;
The cognition of beings' resolute convictions *dhāraṇī* gateway;
The cognition of beings' practices *dhāraṇī* gateway;
The cognition of the differences in beings' practices *dhāraṇī* gateway;
The cognition of beings' natures *dhāraṇī* gateway;
The cognition of beings' inclinations *dhāraṇī* gateway;
The cognition of beings' perceptions *dhāraṇī* gateway;
The universal vision of the ten directions *dhāraṇī* gateway;
The speaking on Dharma *dhāraṇī* gateway;
The great compassion *dhāraṇī* gateway;
The great kindness *dhāraṇī* gateway;
The quiescence *dhāraṇī* gateway;
The path of speech *dhāraṇī* gateway;
The expedience or nonexpedience *dhāraṇī* gateway;
The adaptation *dhāraṇī* gateway;
The differentiation *dhāraṇī* gateway;
The universal entry *dhāraṇī* gateway;

正體字

無礙際陀羅尼門。普遍陀羅
349a11║ 尼門。佛法陀羅尼門。菩薩法陀羅尼門。聲
349a12║ 聞法陀羅尼門。獨覺法陀羅尼門。世間法陀
349a13║ 羅尼門。世界成陀羅尼門。世界壞陀羅尼門。
349a14║ 世界住陀羅尼門。淨世界陀羅尼門。垢世界
349a15║ 陀羅尼門。於垢世界現淨陀羅尼門。於淨世
349a16║ 界現垢陀羅尼門。純垢世界陀羅尼門。純淨
349a17║ 世界陀羅尼門。平坦世界陀羅尼門。不平坦
349a18║ 世界陀羅尼門。覆世界陀羅尼門。因陀羅網
349a19║ 世界陀羅尼門。世界轉陀羅尼門。知依想住
349a20║ 陀羅尼門。細入麁陀羅尼門。麁入細陀羅尼
349a21║ 門。見諸佛陀羅尼門。分別佛身陀羅尼門。佛
349a22║ 光明莊嚴網陀羅尼門。佛圓滿音陀羅尼門。
349a23║ 佛法輪陀羅尼門。成就佛法輪陀羅尼門。差
349a24║ 別佛法輪陀羅尼門。無差別佛法輪陀羅尼
349a25║ 門。解釋佛法輪陀羅尼門。轉佛法輪陀羅尼
349a26║ 門。能作佛事陀羅尼門。分別佛眾會陀羅尼
349a27║ 門。入佛眾會海陀羅尼門。

简体字

无碍际陀罗尼门、普遍陀罗尼门、佛法陀罗尼门、菩萨法陀罗尼门、声闻法陀罗尼门、独觉法陀罗尼门、世间法陀罗尼门、世界成陀罗尼门、世界坏陀罗尼门、世界住陀罗尼门、净世界陀罗尼门、垢世界陀罗尼门、于垢世界现净陀罗尼门、于净世界现垢陀罗尼门、纯垢世界陀罗尼门、纯净世界陀罗尼门、平坦世界陀罗尼门、不平坦世界陀罗尼门、覆世界陀罗尼门、因陀罗网世界陀罗尼门、世界转陀罗尼门、知依想住陀罗尼门、细入粗陀罗尼门、粗入细陀罗尼门、见诸佛陀罗尼门、分别佛身陀罗尼门、佛光明庄严网陀罗尼门、佛圆满音陀罗尼门、佛法轮陀罗尼门、成就佛法轮陀罗尼门、差别佛法轮陀罗尼门、无差别佛法轮陀罗尼门、解释佛法轮陀罗尼门、转佛法轮陀罗尼门、能作佛事陀罗尼门、分别佛众会陀罗尼门、入佛众会海陀罗尼门、

The apex of the unimpeded *dhāraṇī* gateway;
The universally pervasive *dhāraṇī* gateway;
The buddha dharmas *dhāraṇī* gateway;
The bodhisattva dharmas *dhāraṇī* gateway;
The *śrāvaka*-disciple dharmas *dhāraṇī* gateway;
The *pratyekabuddha* dharmas *dhāraṇī* gateway;
The worldly dharmas *dhāraṇī* gateway;
The world creation *dhāraṇī* gateway;
The world destruction *dhāraṇī* gateway;
The world abiding *dhāraṇī* gateway;
The pure world *dhāraṇī* gateway;
The defiled world *dhāraṇī* gateway;
The manifestation of purity in defiled worlds *dhāraṇī* gateway;
The manifestation of defilement in pure worlds *dhāraṇī* gateway;
The entirely defiled world *dhāraṇī* gateway;
The entirely pure world *dhāraṇī* gateway;
The level world *dhāraṇī* gateway;
The non-level world *dhāraṇī* gateway;
The inverted world *dhāraṇī* gateway;
The Indra's net world *dhāraṇī* gateway;
The world-transformation *dhāraṇī* gateway;
The cognition of thought-dependent abiding *dhāraṇī* gateway;
The entry of the subtle into the coarse *dhāraṇī* gateway;
The entry of the coarse into the subtle *dhāraṇī* gateway;
The vision of all buddhas *dhāraṇī* gateway;
The differentiation among the Buddha's bodies *dhāraṇī* gateway;
The Buddha's adornment with a net of light rays *dhāraṇī* gateway;
The Buddha's perfectly complete sound *dhāraṇī* gateway;
The Buddha's Dharma wheel *dhāraṇī* gateway;
The complete development of the Buddha's Dharma wheel *dhāraṇī* gateway;
The differentiated Dharma wheel of the Buddha *dhāraṇī* gateway;
The undifferentiated Dharma wheel of the Buddha *dhāraṇī* gateway;
The explanation of the Buddha's Dharma wheel *dhāraṇī* gateway;
The turning of the Buddha's Dharma wheel *dhāraṇī* gateway;
The ability to do the Buddha's works *dhāraṇī* gateway;
The distinguishing the Buddha's congregations *dhāraṇī* gateway;
The entry into the ocean of the Buddha's congregations *dhāraṇī* gateway;

正體字

普照佛力陀羅尼
349a28║ 門。諸佛三昧陀羅尼門。諸佛三昧自在用陀
349a29║ 羅尼門。諸佛所住陀羅尼門。諸佛所持陀羅
349b01║ 尼門。諸佛變化陀羅尼門。佛知眾生心行陀
349b02║ 羅尼門。諸佛神通變現陀羅尼門。住兜率天
349b03║ 宮乃至示現入于涅槃陀羅尼門。利益無量
349b04║ 眾生陀羅尼門。入甚深法陀羅尼門。入微妙
349b05║ 法陀羅尼門。菩提心陀羅尼門。起菩提心陀
349b06║ 羅尼門。助菩提心陀羅尼門。諸願陀羅尼門。
349b07║ 諸行陀羅尼門。神通陀羅尼門。出離陀羅尼
349b08║ 門。總持清淨陀羅尼門。智輪清淨陀羅尼門。
349b09║ 智慧清淨陀羅尼門。菩提無量陀羅尼門。自
349b10║ 心清淨陀羅尼門。善男子。我唯知此般若波
349b11║ 羅蜜普莊嚴門。如諸菩薩摩訶薩。其心廣大。
349b12║ 等虛空界。入於法界。福德成滿。住出世法。遠
349b13║ 世間行。智眼無[1]瞖。普觀法界。慧心廣大。猶
349b14║ 如虛空。一切境界。悉皆明見。獲無礙地大光
349b15║ 明藏。

简体字

普照佛力陀罗尼门、诸佛三昧陀罗尼门、诸佛三昧自在用陀罗尼门、诸佛所住陀罗尼门、诸佛所持陀罗尼门、诸佛变化陀罗尼门、佛知众生心行陀罗尼门、诸佛神通变现陀罗尼门、住兜率天宫乃至示现入于涅槃陀罗尼门、利益无量众生陀罗尼门、入甚深法陀罗尼门、入微妙法陀罗尼门、菩提心陀罗尼门、起菩提心陀罗尼门、助菩提心陀罗尼门、诸愿陀罗尼门、诸行陀罗尼门、神通陀罗尼门、出离陀罗尼门、总持清净陀罗尼门、智轮清净陀罗尼门、智慧清净陀罗尼门、菩提无量陀罗尼门、自心清净陀罗尼门。

“善男子，我唯知此般若波罗蜜普庄严门。如诸菩萨摩诃萨，其心广大，等虚空界，入于法界，福德成满，住出世法，远世间行，智眼无瞖，普观法界，慧心广大犹如虚空，一切境界悉皆明见，获无碍地大光明藏，

The universal illumination of the Buddha's powers *dhāraṇī* gateway;
The buddhas' samādhis *dhāraṇī* gateway;
The buddhas' transformational uses of samādhi *dhāraṇī* gateway;[97]
The buddhas' abodes *dhāraṇī* gateway;
The buddhas' empowerment *dhāraṇī* gateway;
The buddhas' transformations *dhāraṇī* gateway;
The buddhas' cognition of beings' mental actions *dhāraṇī* gateway;
The transformations manifested by the buddhas' spiritual superknowledges *dhāraṇī* gateway;
The abiding in the Tuṣita Heaven Palace and so forth on through to manifesting entry into nirvāṇa *dhāraṇī* gateway;
The benefiting of countless beings *dhāraṇī* gateway;
The entry into extremely profound Dharma *dhāraṇī* gateway;
The entry into the sublime Dharma *dhāraṇī* gateway;
The bodhi resolve *dhāraṇī* gateway;
The arousing of bodhi resolve *dhāraṇī* gateway;
The factors supporting the bodhi resolve *dhāraṇī* gateway;
The vows *dhāraṇī* gateway;
The practices *dhāraṇī* gateway;
The spiritual superknowledges *dhāraṇī* gateway;
The final emancipation *dhāraṇī* gateway;
The purity of the complete-retention *dhāraṇī* gateway;
The purity of the circle of knowledge *dhāraṇī* gateway;
The purification of wisdom *dhāraṇī* gateway;
The immeasurability of bodhi *dhāraṇī* gateway; and
The purity of one's own mind *dhāraṇī* gateway.

Son of Good Family, I know only this *prajñāpāramitā* universal adornment gateway. As for the bodhisattva-mahāsattvas:

Whose minds are as vast as the realm of empty space;
Who enter into the Dharma realm;
Whose merit has become fulfilled;
Who dwell in the world-transcending dharmas;
Who remain distant from worldly practices;
Whose wisdom eyes have no obscurations;
Who everywhere contemplate the Dharma realm;
Whose wise minds are as vast as empty space;
Who clearly perceive all spheres of objective experience;
Who have acquired the treasury of great light of the unimpeded ground;

正體字

善能分別一切法義。行於世行。不染世
349b16‖ 法。能益於世非世所壞。普作一切世間依止。
349b17‖ 普知一切眾生心行。隨其所應。而為說法。於
349b18‖ 一切時。恒得自在。而我云何能知能說彼功
349b19‖ 德行。善男子。於此南方。有一國土。名為三
349b20‖ 眼。彼有比丘。名曰善見。汝詣彼問。菩薩云何
349b21‖ 學菩薩行。修菩薩道。時善財童子。頂禮其足。
349b22‖ 遶無數匝。戀慕瞻仰。辭退而行
349b23‖ 爾時善財童子。思惟菩薩所住行甚深。思惟
349b24‖ 菩薩所證法甚深。思惟菩薩所入處甚深。思
349b25‖ 惟眾生微細智甚深。思惟世間依想住甚深。
349b26‖ 思惟眾生所作行甚深。思惟眾生心流注甚
349b27‖ 深。思惟眾生如光影甚深。思惟眾生名號甚
349b28‖ 深。

简体字

善能分别一切法义，行于世行不染世法，能益于世非世所坏，普作一切世间依止，普知一切众生心行，随其所应而为说法，于一切时恒得自在；而我云何能知能说彼功德行？

“善男子，于此南方，有一国土，名为三眼；彼有比丘，名曰善见。汝诣彼问：菩萨云何学菩萨行、修菩萨道？”

时，善财童子顶礼其足，绕无数匝，恋慕瞻仰，辞退而行。

尔时，善财童子思惟菩萨所住行甚深，思惟菩萨所证法甚深，思惟菩萨所入处甚深，思惟众生微细智甚深，思惟世间依想住甚深，思惟众生所作行甚深，思惟众生心流注甚深，思惟众生如光影甚深，思惟众生名号甚深，

Who are well able to distinguish the meaning of all dharmas;

Who may engage in worldly practices and yet not be defiled by worldly dharmas;

Who are able to benefit the world without being harmed by the world;

Who everywhere serve as refuges for the entire world;

Who everywhere know all beings' mental actions;

Who adapt to what is suitable for others when speaking Dharma for their sakes; and

Who at all times are constant in their sovereign mastery—

How could I know of or be able to speak about their meritorious qualities and practices?

Son of Good Family, south of here there is a country known as Trinayana or "Three Eyes" in which there is a bhikshu known as Sudarśana or "Good to Behold." You should go there, pay your respects to him, and ask, "How should a bodhisattva train in the bodhisattva practices and how should he cultivate the bodhisattva path?"

Sudhana the Youth then bowed down in reverence at her feet, circumambulated her countless times as he gazed up at her in fond admiration, respectfully withdrew, and departed.

11 – Sudarśana

At that time, Sudhana the Youth reflected as follows:

He reflected on the extreme profundity of the practices in which a bodhisattva dwells;

He reflected on the extreme profundity of the dharmas a bodhisattva realizes;

He reflected on the extreme profundity of the stations a bodhisattva enters;

He reflected on the extreme profundity of the subtle knowledge regarding beings;

He reflected on the extreme profundity of the world's dwelling in dependence on perceptions;

He reflected on the extreme profundity of the practices in which beings engage;

He reflected on the extreme profundity of beings' mental streams;

He reflected on the extreme profundity of beings' similarity to mere reflections;

He reflected on the extreme profundity of beings' names;

正體字

思惟眾生言說甚深。思惟莊嚴法界甚深。
349b29║ 思惟種植業行甚深。思惟業莊飾世間甚深。
349c01║ 漸次遊行。至三眼國。於城邑聚落村隣市肆。
349c02║ 川原山谷一切諸處。周遍求覓善見比丘。見
349c03║ 在林中。經行往返。壯年美貌。端正可喜。其髮
349c04║ 紺青。右旋不亂。頂有肉髻。皮膚金色。頸文三
349c05║ 道。額廣平正。眼目修廣。如青蓮華。脣口丹潔
349c06║ 如頻婆果。胸摽卍字。七處平滿。其臂纖長。其
349c07║ 指網縵。手足掌中。有金剛輪。其身殊妙。如淨
349c08║ 居天。上下端直。如尼拘陀樹。諸相隨好。悉皆
349c09║ 圓滿。如雪山王。種種嚴飾。目視不瞬。圓光一
349c10║ 尋。智慧廣博。猶如大海。於諸境界。心無所
349c11║ 動。若沈若舉。若智非智。動轉戲論。一切皆
349c12║ 息。得佛所行平等境界。大悲教化一切眾生。
349c13║ 心無暫捨。為欲利樂一切眾生。為欲開示如
349c14║ 來法眼。為踐如來所行之道。

简体字

思惟众生言说甚深，思惟庄严法界甚深，思惟种植业行甚深，思惟业庄饰世间甚深。

渐次游行，至三眼国，于城邑聚落、村邻市肆、川原山谷、一切诸处，周遍求觅善见比丘。

见在林中，经行往返，壮年美貌，端正可喜。其发绀青，右旋不乱，顶有肉髻，皮肤金色，颈文三道，额广平正，眼目修广如青莲华，唇口丹洁如频婆果，胸摽卍字，七处平满，其臂纤长，其指网缦，手足掌中有金刚轮。其身殊妙如净居天，上下端直如尼拘陀树，诸相随好，悉皆圆满，如雪山王种种严饰，目视不瞬，圆光一寻。智慧广博犹如大海，于诸境界心无所动，若沉若举，若智非智，动转戏论，一切皆息。得佛所行平等境界，大悲教化一切众生，心无暂舍。为欲利乐一切众生，为欲开示如来法眼，为践如来所行之道，

He reflected on the extreme profundity of beings' languages;
He reflected on the extreme profundity of the adornments of the Dharma realm;
He reflected on the extreme profundity of the planting of causes that occurs through karmic actions; and
He reflected on the extreme profundity of karmic deeds as adornments of the world.

He then traveled onward until he arrived in the country known as Trinayana where he searched all over in its cities, villages, hamlets, neighborhoods, markets, rivers, plateaus, mountains, and valleys, looking everywhere for Bhikshu Sudarśana. Finally, he saw him in a forest where he was engaged in back-and-forth walking meditation.

He was in the prime of his life and was possessed of a splendid appearance and a delightfully handsome physical presence. His hair was indigo colored, coiled in an orderly rightward swirl, and, on the crown of his head, he had the fleshy *uṣṇīṣa* prominence. His skin was the color of gold. His neck had the three horizontal creases. His forehead was broad, flat, and evenly proportioned. His eyes were long in their lateral proportions and widely set, like blue lotus flowers. His lips and mouth had the immaculately red hue of the *bimba* fruit.

His chest had the mark of the *svastika* emblem. His body had the seven prominences. His arms were slender and long. His fingers had the proximal webbing. There were vajra wheel emblems on his palms and soles. His body was especially marvelous and was like that of a deva from the Pure Abode Heaven. He was as vertically erect and straight as the trunk of the *nyagrodha* tree. His body was completely endowed with all of the major marks and secondary signs. It was like the king of mountains in the Himalayas and it was graced with various adornments.

His gaze was unblinking. His aura was two meters wide. His wisdom was as vast as a great ocean. His mind was unmoved by any sense objects. Whether it be sunken or agitated states, application or non-application of cognition, or the various permutations of conceptual elaborations—he had laid all those things to rest, for he had acquired the even-minded sphere of cognition practiced by the Buddha.

He used the great compassion in teaching all beings. His mind never abandoned them for even a moment. He was motivated by the wish to benefit all beings and make them happy, by the wish to reveal the vision of the Tathāgata's Dharma eye, and by the wish to tread the very path traveled by the Tathāgata himself.

正體字

不遲不速。審
349c15‖ 諦經行。無量天龍夜叉乾闥婆阿脩羅迦樓
349c16‖ 羅緊那羅摩睺羅伽釋梵護世人與非人。前
349c17‖ 後圍遶。主方之神隨方迴轉引導其前。足行
349c18‖ 諸神持寶蓮華以承其足。無盡光神舒光破
349c19‖ 闇。閻浮幢林神雨眾雜華。不動藏地神現諸
349c20‖ 寶藏。普光明虛空神莊嚴虛空。成就德海神
349c21‖ 雨摩尼寶。無垢藏須彌山神頭頂禮敬曲躬
349c22‖ 合掌。無礙力風神雨妙香華。春和主夜神莊
349c23‖ 嚴其身舉體投地。常覺主晝神執普照諸方
349c24‖ 摩尼幢住在虛空。放大光明。時善財童子。詣
349c25‖ 比丘所。頂禮其足。曲躬合掌。白言。聖者。我
349c26‖ 已先發阿耨多羅三藐三菩提心。求菩薩行。
349c27‖ 我聞聖者。善能開示諸菩薩道。願為我說。菩
349c28‖ 薩云何學菩薩行。云何修菩薩道。善見答言。
349c29‖ 善男子。我年既少。出家又近。我此生中。於三
350a01‖ 十八恒河沙佛所。淨修梵行。

简体字

不迟不速，审谛经行。

无量天、龙、夜叉、乾闼婆、阿修罗、迦楼罗、紧那罗、摩睺罗伽、释、梵、护世、人与非人前后围绕，主方之神随方回转引导其前，足行诸神持宝莲华以承其足，无尽光神舒光破暗，阎浮幢林神雨众杂华，不动藏地神现诸宝藏，普光明虚空神庄严虚空，成就德海神雨摩尼宝，无垢藏须弥山神头顶礼敬曲躬合掌，无碍力风神雨妙香华，春和主夜神庄严其身举体投地，常觉主昼神执普照诸方摩尼幢住在虚空放大光明。

时，善财童子诣比丘所，顶礼其足，曲躬合掌，白言：“圣者，我已先发阿耨多罗三藐三菩提心，求菩萨行。我闻圣者善能开示诸菩萨道，愿为我说：菩萨云何学菩萨行？云何修菩萨道？”

善见答言：“善男子，我年既少，出家又近。我此生中，于三十八恒河沙佛所净修梵行，

He was neither slow nor hurried in his pace as, engaged in deep investigative contemplation, he continued his meditative walking in which he was attended and surrounded by a congregation of countless devas, dragons, *yakṣas, gandharvas, asuras, garuḍas, kiṃnaras, mahoragas,* Śakras, Brahma Heaven kings, world-protecting devas, humans, and nonhumans as:

The spirits hosting each of the directions took turns in accordance with their particular region, preceding and leading him along;

The foot-travel spirits held jeweled lotuses that supported every placement of his feet;

The spirits possessed of inexhaustible radiance emanated light that dispelled the darkness;

Jambudhvaja forest spirits scattered a sprinkling of the many different kinds of flowers;

The unmoving-treasury earth spirits displayed all the treasuries of jewels;

The universal-radiance sky spirits adorned the sky;

The perfected-virtue ocean spirits sprinkled down a rain of *maṇi* jewels;

The stainless-treasury Mount Sumeru spirits bowed down their heads in reverential prostrations and then, out of respect, bent low their bodies and held their palms pressed together;

The unimpeded-power wind spirits sprinkled down a rain of wonderfully fragrant flowers;

The springtime-harmony night spirits dressed themselves in adornments and prostrated their entire bodies in reverence; and

The constant-awareness day spirits held up universal-illumination-of-all-directions *maṇi* jewel banners and stood there in the sky, emanating great radiance.

Sudhana the Youth then approached the Bhikshu, bowed down in reverence at his feet, and, with stooped torso and pressed palms, addressed him, saying:

O Ārya, I have already resolved to attain *anuttara-samyak-saṃbodhi* and I seek the bodhisattva practices. I have heard that the Ārya is well able to provide instruction in the path of all bodhisattvas. Please teach me how the bodhisattva should train in the bodhisattva practices and how he should cultivate the bodhisattva path.

Sudarśana replied, saying:

Son of Good Family, I am young in years and have only recently left the home life. Still, in this life, I have purely cultivated the practice of *brahmacarya* under buddhas as numerous as the sands in thirty-eight Ganges Rivers, in some cases purely cultivating *brahmacarya*

正體字

或有佛所一日
350a02║ 一夜。淨修梵行。或有佛所七日七夜。淨修梵
350a03║ 行。或有佛所半月一月。一歲百歲。萬歲億歲。
350a04║ 那由他歲。乃至不可說不可說歲。或一小劫。
350a05║ 或半大劫。或一大劫。或百大劫。乃至不可說
350a06║ 不可說大劫。聽聞妙法。受行其教。莊嚴諸願。
350a07║ 入所證處。淨修諸行。滿足六種波羅蜜海。亦
350a08║ 見彼佛成道說法。各各差別。無有雜亂。住持
350a09║ 遺教。乃至滅盡。亦知彼佛本所興願。以三
350a10║ 昧願力。嚴淨一切。諸佛國[1]土。以入一切行
350a11║ 三昧力。淨修一切諸菩薩行。以普賢乘出離
350a12║ 力。清淨一切佛波羅蜜。又善男子。我經行時。
350a13║ 一念中。一切十方皆悉現前。智慧清淨故。一
350a14║ 念中。一切世界皆悉現前。經過不可說不可
350a15║ 說世界故。一念中。不可說不可說佛剎皆悉
350a16║ 嚴淨。成就大願力故。一念中。不可說不可說
350a17║ 眾生差別。行皆悉現前。滿足十力智故。一
350a18║ 念中。不可說不可說諸佛清淨身皆悉現前。
350a19║ 成就普賢行願力故。

简体字

或有佛所一日一夜净修梵行，或有佛所七日七夜净修梵行，或有佛所半月、一月、一岁、百岁、万岁、亿岁、那由他岁，乃至不可说不可说岁，或一小劫、或半大劫、或一大劫、或百大劫，乃至不可说不可说大劫，听闻妙法，受行其教，庄严诸愿，入所证处，净修诸行，满足六种波罗蜜海。亦见彼佛成道说法，各各差别，无有杂乱，住持遗教，乃至灭尽。亦知彼佛本所兴愿，以三昧愿力严净一切诸佛国土，以入一切行三昧力净修一切诸菩萨行，以普贤乘出离力清净一切佛波罗蜜。

“又，善男子，我经行时，一念中，一切十方皆悉现前，智慧清净故；一念中，一切世界皆悉现前，经过不可说不可说世界故；一念中，不可说不可说佛刹皆悉严净，成就大愿力故；一念中，不可说不可说众生差别行皆悉现前，满足十力智故；一念中，不可说不可说诸佛清净身皆悉现前，成就普贤行愿力故；

under a buddha for one day and one night, sometimes purely cultivating *brahmacarya* under a buddha for seven days and seven nights, sometimes remaining under a buddha for a half month or a month, one year, a hundred years, ten thousand years, a *koṭī* of years, a *nayuta* of years, and so forth on up to an ineffable-ineffable number of years, or one small kalpa, or half of a great kalpa, or for one great kalpa, or for a hundred great kalpas, and so forth on up to even an ineffable-ineffable number of great kalpas during which I listened to the teaching of the sublime Dharma, took on the practice of their teachings, acquired the adornment of purified vows, entered the stations they had realized, purely cultivated all the practices, and fulfilled the ocean of practices related to the six *pāramitās*.

I also observed those buddhas as they attained enlightenment, proclaimed the Dharma, each one of them in different ways. Then, without mixing them up or confusing them, I sustained and preserved their legacy teachings all the way up until the time of their [Dharma's] complete disappearance.

I also knew the vows that those buddhas originally made and used the power of vows enhanced by samādhi to purify the lands of all buddhas. Using the power of the "penetrating all practices" samādhi, I purely cultivated the practices of all bodhisattvas. Through the emancipating power of the vehicle of Samantabhadra, I achieved the purification of the *pāramitās* of all buddhas.

Furthermore, Son of Good Family, even as I am engaged in this meditative walking:

In but a single mind-moment, through the purification of wisdom, everything throughout the ten directions manifests directly before me;

In but a single mind-moment, by passing through an ineffable-ineffable number of worlds, all worlds manifest directly before me;

In but a single mind-moment, by perfecting the power of great vows, I purify an ineffable-ineffable number of buddha *kṣetras*;

In but a single mind-moment, by fulfilling the knowledge of the ten powers, all the different practices of an ineffable-ineffable number of beings manifest directly before me;

In but a single mind-moment, by perfecting the power of Samantabhadra's conduct and vows, the pure bodies of an ineffable-ineffable number of buddhas all manifest directly before me;

In but a single mind-moment, by perfecting the power of vows through which, with a pliant mind, one makes offerings to the

正體字

一念中。恭敬供養不可
350a20║ 說不可說佛刹微塵數如來。成就柔軟心。供
350a21║ 養如來願力故。一念中。領受不可說不可說
350a22║ 如來法。得證阿僧祇差別法。住持法輪陀羅
350a23║ 尼力故。一念中。不可說不可說菩薩行海。皆
350a24║ 悉現前。得能淨一切行。如因陀羅網願力故。
350a25║ 一念中。不可說不可說諸三昧海。皆悉現前。
350a26║ 得於一三昧門。入一切三昧門。皆令清淨願
350a27║ 力故。一念中。不可說不可說諸根海。皆悉
350a28║ 現前。得了知諸根際。於一根中。見一切根願
350a29║ 力故。一念中。不可說不可說佛刹微塵數時。
350b01║ 皆悉現前。得於一切時。轉法輪。眾生界盡。法
350b02║ 輪無盡願力故。一念中。不可說不可說一切
350b03║ 三世海。皆悉現前。得了知一切世界中一切
350b04║ 三世分位。智光明願力故。善男子。我唯知
350b05║ 此菩薩隨順燈解脫門。如諸菩薩摩訶薩。如
350b06║ 金剛燈。於如來家。真正受生。具足成就。不死
350b07║ 命根常然智燈。無有盡滅。其身堅固。不可沮
350b08║ 壞。現於如幻色相之身。[2]如緣起法無量差
350b09║ 別。隨眾生心。各各示現。

简体字

一念中，恭敬供养不可说不可说佛刹微尘数如来，成就柔软心供养如来愿力故；一念中，领受不可说不可说如来法，得证阿僧祇差别法住持法轮陀罗尼力故；一念中，不可说不可说菩萨行海皆悉现前，得能净一切行如因陀罗网愿力故；一念中，不可说不可说诸三昧海皆悉现前，得于一三昧门入一切三昧门皆令清净愿力故；一念中，不可说不可说诸根海皆悉现前，得了知诸根际于一根中见一切根愿力故；一念中，不可说不可说佛刹微尘数时皆悉现前，得于一切时转法轮众生界尽法轮无尽愿力故；一念中，不可说不可说一切三世海皆悉现前，得了知一切世界中一切三世分位智光明愿力故。

“善男子，我唯知此菩萨随顺灯解脱门。如诸菩萨摩诃萨如金刚灯，于如来家真正受生，具足成就不死命根，常燃智灯无有尽灭，其身坚固不可沮坏，现于如幻色相之身，如缘起法无量差别，随众生心各各示现，

tathāgatas, I pay reverence and make offerings to *tathāgatas* as numerous as the atoms in an ineffable-ineffable number of buddha *kṣetras;*

In but a single mind-moment, through the power of the Dharma wheel sustaining *dhāraṇī,* I take in the Dharma of an ineffable-ineffable number of *tathāgatas* and realize an *asaṃkhyeya* of different dharmas;

In but a single mind-moment, through the power of vows like Indra's net, an ocean of an ineffable-ineffable number of bodhisattva practices all manifests directly before me and I become able to purify all practices;

In but a single mind-moment, due to the vow power by which one enters and purifies all samādhi gateways from within but one samādhi gateway, an ocean of an ineffable-ineffable number of samādhis all manifests directly before me;

In but a single mind-moment, due to the vow power by which one completely knows the ultimate extent of all faculties and sees all faculties in one faculty, an ineffable-ineffable number of faculties all manifest directly before me;

In but a single mind-moment, due to the vow power by which one turns the Dharma wheel in all times, resolving that, even were the realms of beings to end, the turning of the Dharma wheel will never end, different times as numerous as the atoms in an ineffable-ineffable number of buddha *kṣetras* all manifest directly before me; and

In but a single mind-moment, due to the vow power by which the light of one's wisdom knows in all worlds all divisions of time throughout the three periods of time, the ocean of an ineffable-ineffable number of circumstances within all three periods of time all manifests directly before me.

Son of Good Family, I know only this bodhisattva's liberation gateway, "the lamp of compliance." As for the bodhisattva-mahāsattvas:

Who are like vajra lamps;

Who are truly and rightly born into the house of the Tathāgata;

Who have completely perfected the undying life faculty;

Who always keep lit the unextinguishable lamp of wisdom;

Whose bodies are so solid they cannot be either impeded or destroyed, yet appear in bodies with forms and appearances like illusory conjurations;

Who, in accordance with the countless variations of the dharma of conditioned origination, adapt to beings' minds and manifest for every one of them with forms and appearances unmatched

正體字

形貌色相。世無倫
350b10║ 匹。毒刃火災。所不能害。如金剛山無能壞者。
350b11║ 降伏一切諸魔外道。其身妙好。如真金山。於
350b12║ 天人中。最為殊特。名稱廣大。靡不聞知。觀諸
350b13║ 世間。咸對目前。演深法藏。如海無盡。放大光
350b14║ 明。普照十方。若有見者。必破一切障礙大山。
350b15║ 必拔一切不善根本。必令種植廣大善根。如
350b16║ 是之人。難可得見。難可出世。而我云何能知
350b17║ 能說彼功德行。善男子。於此南方。有一國土。
350b18║ 名曰名聞。於河渚中。有一童子。名自在主。汝
350b19║ 詣彼問。菩薩云何學菩薩行。修菩薩道。時
350b20║ 善財童子。為欲究竟菩薩勇猛清淨之行。欲
350b21║ 得菩薩大力光明。欲修菩薩無勝無盡諸功
350b22║ 德行欲滿菩薩堅固大願。欲成菩薩廣大深
350b23║ 心。欲持菩薩無量勝行。於菩薩法心無厭足。
350b24║ 願入一切菩薩功德。欲常攝御一切眾生。

简体字

形貌色相世无伦匹，毒刃火灾所不能害，如金刚山无能坏者，降伏一切诸魔外道；其身妙好如真金山，于天人中最为殊特，名称广大靡不闻知，观诸世间咸对目前，演深法藏如海无尽，放大光明普照十方。若有见者，必破一切障碍大山，必拔一切不善根本，必令种植广大善根。如是之人，难可得见，难可出世；而我云何能知能说彼功德行？

“善男子，于此南方，有一国土，名曰名闻；于河渚中，有一童子，名自在主。汝诣彼问：菩萨云何学菩萨行、修菩萨道？”

时，善财童子为欲究竟菩萨勇猛清净之行，欲得菩萨大力光明，欲修菩萨无胜无尽诸功德行，欲满菩萨坚固大愿，欲成菩萨广大深心，欲持菩萨无量胜行，于菩萨法心无厌足，愿入一切菩萨功德，欲常摄御一切众生，

anywhere in the world that cannot be injured by poison, knives, or fire disasters;

Who are like mountains of vajra that cannot by destroyed by anyone;

Who vanquish all the *māras* and adherents of non-Buddhist paths;

Whose bodies are marvelously fine, like mountains of real gold;

Who, among all devas and men, are the most especially exceptional;

Whose fame has spread so widely that no one does not hear and know of them;

Who, as they contemplate all worlds, they all manifest directly before their very eyes;

Who, when expounding on the treasury of profound Dharma, are as inexhaustible as the ocean;

Who emanate immensely brilliant light that everywhere illuminates the ten directions; and

Who are such that, anyone who so much as sees them will certainly crush the great mountains of all their obstacles, will certainly extricate all their roots of bad actions, and will certainly be caused to plant vast roots of goodness—

Such people are but rarely ever encountered and but rarely ever come forth into the world. This being so, how could I know of or be able to speak about their meritorious qualities and practices?

Son of Good Family, south of here, there is a country known as Sumukha, or "Renowned" where, on an island in the river, there is a youth named Indriyeśvara or "Sovereign Lord." You should go there, pay your respects to him, and ask, "How should a bodhisattva train in the bodhisattva practices and how should he cultivate the bodhisattva path?"

At that time, Sudhana the Youth:

Wished to achieve the most ultimate realization of the bodhisattva's courageous and pure practices;

Wished to acquire the light of the bodhisattva's great powers;

Wished to cultivate the practices leading to the bodhisattva's insuperable and inexhaustible meritorious qualities;

Wished to fulfill the bodhisattva's solid and great vows;

Wished to establish the bodhisattva's vast and profound resolve;

Wished to uphold the bodhisattva's countless supreme practices and maintain an insatiable resolve to acquire the bodhisattva's dharmas;

Wished to access the meritorious qualities of all bodhisattvas;

Wished to always attract and guide along all beings;

正體字

欲
350b25║ 超生死稠林曠野。於善知識。常樂見聞。承事
350b26║ 供養。無有厭倦。頂禮其足。遶無量匝。慇懃瞻
350b27║ 仰。辭退而去
350b28║ 爾時善財童子。受善見比丘教已。憶念誦持。
350b29║ 思惟修習。明了決定。於彼法門。而得悟入。天
350c01║ 龍夜叉乾闥婆眾。前後圍遶。向名聞國。周遍
350c02║ 求覓自在主童子。時有天龍乾闥婆等。於虛
350c03║ 空中。告善財言。善男子。今此童子。在河渚
350c04║ 上。爾時善財。即詣其所。見此童子。十千童
350c05║ 子。所共圍遶。聚沙為戲。善財見已。頂禮其
350c06║ 足。遶無量匝。合掌恭敬。却住一面。白言。聖
350c07║ 者。我已先發阿耨多羅三藐三菩提心。而未
350c08║ 知菩薩云何學菩薩行。云何修菩薩道。願為
350c09║ 解說。自在主言。善男子。我昔曾於文殊師利
350c10║ 童子所。修學書數算印等法。即得悟入一切
350c11║ 工巧神通智法門。善男子。我因此法門故。得
350c12║ 知世間書數算印界處等法。

简体字

欲超生死稠林旷野，于善知识常乐见闻，承事供养无有厌倦；顶礼其足，绕无量匝，殷勤瞻仰，辞退而去。

尔时，善财童子受善见比丘教已，忆念诵持，思惟修习，明了决定，于彼法门而得悟入。天、龙、夜叉、乾闼婆众前后围绕，向名闻国，周遍求觅自在主童子。

时，有天、龙、乾闼婆等，于虚空中告善财言：“善男子，今此童子在河渚上。”尔时，善财即诣其所，见此童子，十千童子所共围绕，聚沙为戏。善财见已，顶礼其足，绕无量匝，合掌恭敬，却住一面，白言：“圣者，我已先发阿耨多罗三藐三菩提心，而未知菩萨云何学菩萨行？云何修菩萨道？愿为解说！”

自在主言：“善男子，我昔曾于文殊师利童子所，修学书、数、算、印等法，即得悟入一切工巧神通智法门。善男子，我因此法门故，得知世间书、数、算、印、界、处等法，

Wished to step beyond the dense thickets and vast wilderness of *saṃsāra*; and

Always delighted in seeing and hearing the good spiritual guides and in tirelessly serving them and making offerings to them.

He then bowed down in reverence at the feet of Bhikshu Sudarśana, circumambulated him countless times as he continued to gaze up at him in attentive admiration, respectfully withdrew, and then departed.

12 – Indriyeśvara

At that time, having received Bhikshu Sudarśana's teachings, Sudhana the Youth bore them in mind, recited them, retained them, reflected on them, cultivated them, reached a completely clear and definite understanding of them, and then awakened to and entered that Dharma gateway.

Then, surrounded by a multitude of devas, dragons, *yakṣas,* and *gandharvas,* he traveled toward the country of Sumukha where he searched around everywhere for the youth Indriyeśvara. Then devas, dragons, *gandharvas,* and other such beings appeared in the sky and told Sudhana, "Son of Good Family, this youth is just now living on that river island."

Sudhana then went to where he was and saw him surrounded by ten thousand youths delighting in scooping up piles of sand. Having seen him there, Sudhana then bowed down in reverence at his feet, circumambulated him countless times, respectfully pressed his palms together, withdrew to one side, and addressed him, saying, "O Ārya, I have already resolved to attain *anuttara-samyak-saṃbodhi.* However, I do not yet know how the bodhisattva should train in the bodhisattva practices or how he should cultivate the bodhisattva path. I hope that you will explain these matters for me."

Indriyeśvara then spoke to him, saying:

Son of Good Family, in the past, under Mañjuśrī the Youth, I cultivated and trained in writing, mathematics, calculation, printing, and other such dharmas and then straightaway succeeded in awakening to and entering the Dharma gateway into knowledge of all skills, arts, and spiritual superknowledges.

Son of Good Family, because of this Dharma gateway, I was able to know the realms and foundations of the world's writing, mathematics, calculation, seal-carving, and other such dharmas. I also

正體字

亦能療治風癇
350c13‖ 消瘦鬼魅所著。如是所有一切諸病。亦能
350c14‖ 造立城邑聚落園林臺觀。宮殿屋宅種種諸
350c15‖ 處。亦善調[3]鍊種種仙藥。亦善營理田農商估
350c16‖ 一切諸業。取捨進退咸得其所。又善別知眾
350c17‖ 生身相。作善作惡。當生善趣。當生惡趣。此人
350c18‖ 應得聲聞乘道。此人應得緣覺乘道。此人應
350c19‖ 入一切智地。如是等事。皆悉能知。亦令眾
350c20‖ 生學習此法。增長決定。究竟清淨。善男子。我
350c21‖ 亦能知菩薩算法。所謂一百洛叉為一俱胝。
350c22‖ 俱胝俱胝為一阿庾多。阿庾多阿庾多為一
350c23‖ 那由他。那由他那由他為一頻婆羅。頻婆羅
350c24‖ 頻婆羅為一矜羯羅。廣說。乃至優鉢羅優鉢
350c25‖ 羅為一波頭摩。波頭摩波頭摩。為一僧祇。僧
350c26‖ 祇僧祇為一趣。趣趣為一[4]諭。[*]諭[*]諭為一無
350c27‖ 數。無數無數。為一無數轉。無數轉無數轉為
350c28‖ 一無量。無量無量為一無量轉。無量轉無量
350c29‖ 轉為一無邊。無邊無邊為一無邊轉。

简体字

亦能疗治风痫、消瘦、鬼魅所著——如是所有一切诸病，亦能造立城邑聚落、园林台观、宫殿屋宅种种诸处，亦善调炼种种仙药，亦善营理田农商贾一切诸业，取舍进退咸得其所；又善别知众生身相，作善作恶，当生善趣，当生恶趣，此人应得声闻乘道，此人应得缘觉乘道，此人应入一切智地，如是等事皆悉能知。亦令众生学习此法，增长决定究竟清净。

“善男子，我亦能知菩萨算法。所谓：一百洛叉为一俱胝，俱胝俱胝为一阿庾多，阿庾多阿庾多为一那由他，那由他那由他为一频婆罗，频婆罗频婆罗为一矜羯罗；广说乃至，优钵罗优钵罗为一波头摩，波头摩波头摩为一僧祇，僧祇僧祇为一趣，趣趣为一喻，喻喻为一无数，无数无数为一无数转，无数转无数转为一无量，无量无量为一无量转，无量转无量转为一无边，无边无边为一无边转，

became able to cure stroke, seizures, wasting disorders, possession by ghosts and *māras*, and all other sicknesses such as these.

I also became able to construct cities, villages, parks, groves, viewing towers, palaces, residential buildings, houses, and the many other kinds of places. I also became skilled in the preparation of many different kinds of life-prolonging elixirs, also became skilled in planning and management in agriculture, trade, and all kinds of livelihoods, in all of which I learned precisely what was right in taking, relinquishing, advancing, and retreating.

I also became skilled in distinguishing the characteristics of beings' physiognomy, in distinguishing whether they do what is good or do what is evil, in distinguishing whether they are bound for rebirth in good destinies or are bound for rebirth in bad rebirth destinies, and in distinguishing that this particular person should succeed in the path of the *śrāvaka*-disciple vehicle, that this other person should succeed in the path of the *pratyekabuddha* vehicle, and that this other person should succeed in entering the ground of all-knowledge. Thus I was able to know all matters such as these while also being able to enable beings to train in these dharmas and increase the certainty that they will achieve ultimate purification.

Son of Good Family, I also became able to know the bodhisattva's methods of making numerical calculations, thereby knowing for instance:

That a hundred *lakṣas* equals a *koṭī*;
That a *koṭī* times a *koṭī* equals an *ayuta*;
That an *ayuta* times an *ayuta* equals a *nayuta*;
That a *nayuta* times a *nayuta* equals a *bimbara*;
That a *vimbara* times a *vimbara* equals a *kaṅkara*;
That, extrapolating this series on forward, an *utpala* times an *utpala* equals a *padma*;
That a *padma* times a *padma* equals a *saṃkhya*;
That a *saṃkhya* times a *saṃkhya* equals a *gati*;
That a *gati* times a *gati* equals an *upaga*;
That an *upaga* times an *upaga* equals an *asaṃkhya*;
That an *asaṃkhya* times an *asaṃkhya* equals an *asaṃkhyaparivarta*;
That an *asaṃkhyaparivarta* times an *asaṃkhyaparivarta* equals an *aparimāṅa*;
That an *aparimāṇa* times an *aparimāṇa* equals an *aparimāṇaparivarta*;
That an *aparimāṇaparivarta* times an *aparimāṇaparivarta* equals an *aparyanta*;
That an *aparyanta* times an *aparyanta* equals an *aparyantaparivarta*;

正體字

無邊轉
351a01‖ 無邊轉為一無等。無等無等為一無等轉。無
351a02‖ 等轉無等轉為一不可數。不可數不可數為
351a03‖ 一不可數轉。不可數轉不可數轉為一不可
351a04‖ 稱。不可稱不可稱為一不可稱轉。不可稱轉
351a05‖ 不可稱轉為一不可思。不可思不可思為一
351a06‖ 不可思轉。不可思轉不可思轉為一不可量。
351a07‖ 不可量不可量為一不可量轉。不可量轉不
351a08‖ 可量轉為一不可說。不可說不可說為一不
351a09‖ 可說轉。不可說轉不可說轉為一不可說不
351a10‖ 可說。此又不可說不可說為一不可說不可
351a11‖ 說轉。善男子。我以此菩薩算法。算無量由旬
351a12‖ 廣大沙聚。悉知其內顆粒多少。亦能算知東
351a13‖ 方所有一切世界種種差別。次第安住。南西
351a14‖ 北方。四維上下。亦復如是。亦能算知十方
351a15‖ 所有一切世界廣狹大小。及以名字。其中所
351a16‖ 有一切劫名。一切佛名。一切法名。一切眾生
351a17‖ 名。一切業名。一切菩薩名。一切諦名。皆悉了
351a18‖ 知。善男子。我唯知此一切工巧大神通智光
351a19‖ 明法門。如諸菩薩摩訶薩。能知一切諸眾生
351a20‖ 數。能知一切諸法品類數。能知一切諸法差
351a21‖ 別數。

简体字

无边转无边转为一无等，无等无等为一无等转，无等转无等转为一不可数，不可数不可数为一不可数转，不可数转不可数转为一不可称，不可称不可称为一不可称转，不可称转不可称转为一不可思，不可思不可思为一不可思转，不可思转不可思转为一不可量，不可量不可量为一不可量转，不可量转不可量转为一不可说，不可说不可说为一不可说转，不可说转不可说转为一不可说不可说，此又不可说不可说为一不可说不可说转。

“善男子，我以此菩萨算法，算无量由旬广大沙聚，悉知其内颗粒多少；亦能算知东方所有一切世界种种差别次第安住，南西北方、四维上下亦复如是；亦能算知十方所有一切世界广狭大小及以名字，其中所有一切劫名、一切佛名、一切法名、一切众生名、一切业名、一切菩萨名、一切谛名，皆悉了知。

“善男子，我唯知此一切工巧大神通智光明法门。如诸菩萨摩诃萨，能知一切诸众生数，能知一切诸法品类数，能知一切诸法差别数，

That an *aparyantaparivarta* times an *aparyantaparivarta* equals an *asamanta;*

That an *asamanta* times an *asamanta* equals an *asamantaparivarta;*

That an *asamantaparivarta* times an *asamantaparivarta* equals an *agaṇeya;*

That an *agaṇaneya* times an *agaṇaneya* equals an *agaṇaneyaparivarta;*

That an *agaṇanīyaparivarta* times an *agaṇanīyaparivarta* equals an *atulya;*

That an *atulya* times an *atulya* equals an *atulyaparivarta;*

That an *atulyaparivarta* times an *atulyaparivarta* equals an *acintya;*

That an *acintya* times an *acintya* equals an *acintyaparivarta;*

That an *acintyaparivarta* times an *acintyaparivarta* equals an *ameya;*

That an *ameya* times an *ameya* equals an *ameyaparivarta;*

That an *ameyaparivarta* times an *ameyaparivarta* equals an *anabhilāpya;*

That an *anabhilāpya* times an *anabhilāpya* equals an *anabhilāpyaparivarta;*

That an *anabhilāpyaparivarta* times an *anabhilāpyaparivarta* equals an *anabhilāpya-anabhilāpya;* and

That an *anabhilāpya-anabhilāpya* times an *anabhilāpya-anabhilāpya* equals an *anabhilāpya-anabhilāpya-parivarta.*

Son of Good Family, I have used these bodhisattva calculation methods to calculate and know the number of grains of sand in vast accumulations of sand that stretch across a distance of countless *yojanas.* I have also thereby been able to calculate and know with regard to all worlds in the east their many different distinctions and their sequential establishment while also being able to do so in the same way with regard to all worlds in the south, the west, the north, the four midpoints, the zenith, and the nadir.

I have also been able to calculate the breadth and size of all worlds throughout the ten directions along with all their names, the names of all their kalpas, the names of all their buddhas, the names of all their dharmas, the names of all their beings, the names of all their karmic works, the names of all their bodhisattvas, and the names of all their truths, thereby completely knowing all these things.

Son of Good Family, I know only this Dharma gateway into the light of knowledge of all skills, arts, and great spiritual superknowledges. As for the bodhisattva-mahāsattvas:

Who are able to know the number of all beings;

Who are able to know the number of types of all dharmas;

Who are able to know the number of differences in all dharmas;

正體字

能知一切三世數。能知一切眾生名數。
351a22║ 能知一切諸法名數。能知一切諸如來數。能
351a23║ 知一切諸佛名數。能知一切諸菩薩數。能知
351a24║ 一切菩薩名數。而我[1]何能說其功德。示其
351a25║ 所行。顯其境界。讚其勝力。[2]辨其樂欲。宣其
351a26║ 助道。彰其大願。歎其妙行。闡其諸度。演其清
351a27║ 淨。發其殊勝。智慧光明。善男子。於此南方。
351a28║ 有一大城。名曰海住。有優婆夷。名為具足。汝
351a29║ 詣彼問。菩薩云何學菩薩行。修菩薩道。時善
351b01║ 財童子。聞是語已。舉身毛豎。歡喜踊躍。獲得
351b02║ 希有信樂寶心。成就廣大利眾生心。悉能明
351b03║ 見一切諸佛出興次第。悉能通達甚深智慧
351b04║ 清淨法輪。於一切趣。皆隨現身。了知三世平
351b05║ 等境界。出生無盡功德大海。放大智慧自在
351b06║ 光明。開三有城。所有關鑰。頂禮其足。遶無量
351b07║ 匝。慇懃瞻仰。辭退而去

简体字

能知一切三世数，能知一切众生名数，能知一切诸法名数，能知一切诸如来数，能知一切诸佛名数，能知一切诸菩萨数，能知一切菩萨名数；而我何能说其功德，示其所行，显其境界，赞其胜力，辩其乐欲，宣其助道，彰其大愿，叹其妙行，阐其诸度，演其清净，发其殊胜智慧光明？

“善男子，于此南方，有一大城，名曰海住；有优婆夷，名为具足。汝诣彼问：菩萨云何学菩萨行、修菩萨道？”

时，善财童子闻是语已，举身毛竖，欢喜踊跃，获得希有信乐宝心，成就广大利众生心，悉能明见一切诸佛出兴次第，悉能通达甚深智慧清净法轮，于一切趣皆随现身，了知三世平等境界，出生无尽功德大海，放大智慧自在光明，开三有城所有关钥；顶礼其足，绕无量匝，殷勤瞻仰，辞退而去。

Who are able to know the numbers of all three periods of time;
Who are able to know the number of all beings' names;
Who are able to know the number of all dharmas' names;
Who are able to know the number of all *tathāgatas;*
Who are able to know the number of all buddhas' names;
Who are able to know the number of all bodhisattvas; and
Who are able to know the number of all bodhisattvas' names—

How could I be able to describe their meritorious qualities, explain what they practice, reveal their spheres of cognition, praise their supreme powers, distinguish their inclinations, proclaim their possession of the provisions for the path, show their great vows, praise their marvelous practices, explain their practice of the perfections, expound on their purity, or reveal the light of their extraordinarily superior wisdom?

Son of Good Family, south of here, there is a great city known as Samudrapratiṣṭhāna or "Ocean Dwelling" in which there is an *upāsikā* known as Prabhūtā or "Fully Endowed." You should go there, pay your respects, and ask her, "How should the bodhisattva train in the bodhisattva practices and how should he cultivate the bodhisattva path?"

When Sudhana the Youth heard these words:

All the hairs on his body stood on end and he was filled with joyous delight;
He acquired a faith-filled resolve that was like a rare and precious jewel;[98]
He developed the resolve to bestow vast benefit on beings;
He became able to clearly see the sequence of all buddhas' appearances in the world;
He became able to comprehend extremely profound wisdom and purify the sphere of Dharma;[99]
He manifested his bodies in all the rebirth destinies in ways adapted to each of them;
He came to completely know the sphere of cognition that perceives the uniform equality of the three periods of time;
He developed a great ocean of inexhaustible meritorious qualities;
He emanated the light of the sovereign mastery of great wisdom; and
He opened the locks on all the gates leading out of the city of the three realms of existence.

He then bowed down in reverence at his feet, circumambulated him countless times as he attentively gazed up at him in admiration, and then respectfully withdrew and departed.

正體字

351b08║ 爾時善財童子。觀察思惟善知識教。猶如巨
351b09║ 海受大雲雨。無有厭足。作是念言。善知識教。
351b10║ 猶如春日生長一切善法根苗。善知識教。猶
351b11║ 如滿月。凡所照及。皆使清涼。善知識教。如夏
351b12║ 雪山。能除一切諸獸熱渴。善知識教。如芳池
351b13║ 日。能開一切善心蓮華。善知識教。如大寶洲。
351b14║ 種種法寶。充滿其心。善知識教。如閻浮樹。積
351b15║ 集一切福智華果。善知識教。如大龍王。於虛
351b16║ 空中。遊戲自在。善知識教。如須彌山。無量善
351b17║ 法。三十三天。於中止住。善知識教。猶如帝
351b18║ 釋。眾會圍遶。無能映蔽。能伏異道脩羅軍眾。
351b19║ 如是思惟。漸次遊行。至海住城。處處尋覓此
351b20║ 優婆夷。時彼眾人。咸告之言。善男子。此優婆
351b21║ 夷。在此城中所住宅內。善財聞已。即詣其門。
351b22║ 合掌而立。其宅廣博。

简体字

尔时，善财童子观察思惟善知识教，犹如巨海受大云雨无有厌足，作是念言：“善知识教，犹如春日，生长一切善法根苗；善知识教，犹如满月，凡所照及皆使清凉；善知识教，如夏雪山，能除一切诸兽热渴；善知识教，如芳池日，能开一切善心莲华；善知识教，如大宝洲，种种法宝充满其心；善知识教，如阎浮树，积集一切福智华果；善知识教，如大龙王，于虚空中游戏自在；善知识教，如须弥山无量善法，三十三天于中止住；善知识教，犹如帝释，众会围绕，无能映蔽，能伏异道、修罗军众。”如是思惟。

渐次游行，至海住城，处处寻觅此优婆夷。时，彼众人咸告之言：“善男子，此优婆夷在此城中所住宅内。”善财闻已，即诣其门，合掌而立。

其宅广博，

13 – Prabhūtā

At that time, as he contemplated and reflected on the teachings of the good spiritual guides, Sudhana the Youth was like a great ocean that insatiably takes in all the rain from the immense clouds. He then had these thoughts:

The teachings of the good spiritual guides are like the spring sun, for they are able to spur growth in the sprouts and roots of all good dharmas;

The teachings of the good spiritual guides are like the full moon, for they cause everything they illuminate to become clear and cool;

The teachings of the good spiritual guides are like the Himalaya mountains in the summer, for they are able to rid all creatures of their burning thirst;

The teachings of the good spiritual guides are like the sun shining on a fragrant flower pond, for they are able to cause the lotus flowers of all good thoughts to blossom;

The teachings of the good spiritual guides are like an immense isle of jewels, for they enable the many different jewels of Dharma to completely fill one's mind;

The teachings of the good spiritual guides are like the *jambū* tree, for they enable one to gather together all the flowers and fruit of merit and wisdom;

The teachings of the good spiritual guides are like the great dragon king, for they enable one to act with easeful mastery in the spiritual powers;

The teachings of the good spiritual guides are like Mount Sumeru for they are the dwelling place of countless good dharmas, just as that mountain is the dwelling place of the Trāyastriṃśa Heaven devas; and

The teachings of the good spiritual guides are like Śakra, ruler of the devas, for they are surrounded by a congregation that none can outshine and are able to vanquish the *asura* armies of the heterodox paths.

Reflecting in this way, he then gradually traveled onward until he reached the city of Samudrapratiṣṭhāna where he searched in place after place for this *upāsikā*. Then the many people there all told him: "Son of Good Family, this *upāsikā* lives in this city in a house where she dwells."

Having heard this, he then went to pay his respects and stood at her door with palms pressed together. Her house was vast, decorated

正體字

種種莊嚴。眾寶垣牆。周
351b23‖ 匝圍遶。四面皆有寶莊嚴門。善財入已。見
351b24‖ 優婆夷。處於寶座。盛年好色。端正可喜。素服
351b25‖ 垂髮。身無瓔珞。其身色相。威德光明。除佛菩
351b26‖ 薩。餘無能及。於其宅內。敷十億座。超出人天
351b27‖ 一切所有。皆是菩薩業力成就。宅中無有衣
351b28‖ 服飲食及餘一切資生之物。但於其前。置一
351b29‖ 小器。復有一萬童女圍遶。威儀色相。如天
351c01‖ 采女。妙寶嚴具。莊飾其身。言音美妙。聞者喜
351c02‖ 悅。常在左右。親近瞻仰。思惟觀察。曲躬低
351c03‖ 首。應其教命。彼諸童女。身出妙香。普熏一
351c04‖ 切。若有眾生。遇斯香者。皆不退轉。無怒害
351c05‖ 心。無怨結心。無慳嫉心。無諂誑心。無險曲
351c06‖ 心。無憎愛心。無瞋恚心。無下劣心。無高慢
351c07‖ 心。生平等心。起大慈心。發利益心。住律儀
351c08‖ 心。離貪求心。聞其音者。歡喜踊躍。見其身
351c09‖ 者。悉離貪染。爾時善財。既見具足優婆夷已。
351c10‖ 頂禮其足。恭敬圍遶。合掌而立。白言。聖者。

简体字

种种庄严，众宝垣墙周匝围绕，四面皆有宝庄严门。善财入已，见优婆夷处于宝座，盛年好色，端正可喜，素服垂发，身无璎珞，其身色相威德光明，除佛菩萨余无能及。于其宅内，敷十亿座，超出人、天一切所有，皆是菩萨业力成就。宅中无有衣服、饮食及余一切资生之物，但于其前置一小器。复有一万童女围绕，威仪色相如天采女，妙宝严具庄饰其身，言音美妙，闻者喜悦，常在左右，亲近瞻仰，思惟观察，曲躬低首，应其教命。彼诸童女，身出妙香，普熏一切；若有众生遇斯香者，皆不退转，无怒害心，无怨结心，无悭嫉心，无谄诳心，无险曲心，无憎爱心，无瞋恚心，无下劣心，无高慢心，生平等心，起大慈心，发利益心，住律仪心，离贪求心。闻其音者，欢喜踊跃；见其身者，悉离贪染。

尔时，善财既见具足优婆夷已，顶礼其足，恭敬围绕，合掌而立，白言：“圣者，

with many different kinds of adornments, and was surrounded by a perimeter wall made of many kinds of jewels. All four sides had doors adorned with jewels.

Having entered, Sudhana saw the Upāsikā seated there on a jeweled seat. She was in in the prime of her youth, of fine appearance, and delightfully beautiful. She was dressed in white, had flowing hair, and wore no necklaces at all. With the exception of the buddhas and bodhisattvas, no one else could match her physical appearance or the radiance of her awesome virtue.

She had arranged within her house ten *koṭīs* of seats that surpassed anything possessed by either humans or gods. All of these things had been brought about through the power of that bodhisattva's karmic works. There were no robes, food, drink, or any other kinds of life-sustaining things within her house. There was only a small bowl that had been placed in front of her.

She was also surrounded by a myriad young maidens who were awe-inspiring in their deportment and physical appearance and who were like celestial nymphs. Marvelous jeweled ornaments adorned their bodies. Their voices were beautiful and marvelous, such that whoever heard them felt pleased. They constantly served her to the left and right, drawing close and gazing up at her in admiration as they observed her with bodies respectfully stooped and heads held down, responding as appropriate to her instructions

Those maidens' bodies emitted a marvelous perfume that everywhere imbued everything with its scent. If any being so much as encountered this scent, they would all achieve irreversibility, become free of thoughts of anger or injuriousness, become free of thoughts of enmity, become free of jealous or miserly thoughts, become free of thoughts of flattery or deviousness, become free of treacherous or devious thoughts, become free of thoughts of loathing or affection, become free of thoughts of hatred, become free of base or inferior thoughts, and become free of arrogant thoughts. They would produce thoughts of equal regard for all, arouse thoughts of great kindness, generate thoughts to benefit others, dwell in thoughts consistent with the moral codes, and abandon thoughts of desire or covetousness.

When others heard their voices, they became filled with abundant joyous delight. When others saw their bodies, they all abandoned the defilement of lust.

Having seen the Upāsikā Prabhūtā, Sudhana then bowed down in reverence at her feet, respectfully circumambulated her, pressed his palms together, stood before her, and addressed her, saying, "O Āryā,

正體字

351c11‖ 我已先發阿耨多羅三藐三菩提心。而未知
351c12‖ 菩薩云何學菩薩行。云何修菩薩道。我聞聖
351c13‖ 者。善能誘誨。願為我說。彼即告言。善男子。
351c14‖ 我得菩薩無盡福德藏解脫門。能於如是一
351c15‖ 小器中。隨諸眾生種種欲樂。出生種種美味
351c16‖ 飲食。悉令充滿。假使百眾生。千眾生。百千眾
351c17‖ 生。億眾生。百億眾生。千億眾生。百千億那由
351c18‖ 他眾生。乃至不可說不可說眾生。假使閻浮
351c19‖ 提微塵數眾生。一四天下微塵數眾生。小千
351c20‖ 世界中千世界大千世界。乃至不可說不可
351c21‖ 說佛剎微塵數眾生。假使十方世界一切眾
351c22‖ 生。隨其欲樂悉令充滿。而其飲食無有窮盡。
351c23‖ 亦不減少。[3]如飲食。如是種種上味。種種床
351c24‖ 座。種種衣服。種種臥具。種種車乘。種種華。
351c25‖ 種種鬘。種種香。種種塗香。種種燒香。種種末
351c26‖ 香。種種珍寶。種種瓔珞。種種幢。種種幡。種
351c27‖ 種蓋。種種上妙資生之具。隨意所樂悉令充
351c28‖ 足。

简体字

我已先发阿耨多罗三藐三菩提心，而未知菩萨云何学菩萨行？云何修菩萨道？我闻圣者善能诱诲，愿为我说！”

彼即告言：“善男子，我得菩萨无尽福德藏解脱门，能于如是一小器中，随诸众生种种欲乐，出生种种美味饮食，悉令充满。假使百众生、千众生、百千众生、亿众生、百亿众生、千亿众生、百千亿那由他众生，乃至不可说不可说众生；假使阎浮提微尘数众生、一四天下微尘数众生，小千世界、中千世界、大千世界，乃至不可说不可说佛刹微尘数众生；假使十方世界一切众生，随其欲乐悉令充满，而其饮食无有穷尽亦不减少。如是饮食，如是种种上味、种种床座、种种衣服、种种卧具、种种车乘、种种华、种种鬘、种种香、种种涂香、种种烧香、种种末香、种种珍宝、种种瓔珞、种种幢、种种幡、种种盖、种种上妙资生之具，随意所乐悉令充足。

I am one who has already resolved to attain *anuttara-samyak-saṃbodhi.* Still, I do not yet know how the bodhisattva should train in the bodhisattva practices and how he should cultivate the bodhisattva path. I have heard that the Āryā is well able to offer guidance and instruction. Please speak about these matters for my sake."

She then spoke to him, saying:

Son of Good Family, I have acquired the bodhisattva's liberation gateway of the treasury of endless merit whereby, with such a small bowl as this, I am able to adapt to the many different kinds of desires and delights of all beings and produce many different kinds of delectably flavored food and drink and enable them all to be filled to satisfaction.

This is so no matter whether it be for a hundred beings, a thousand beings, a hundred thousand beings, a *koṭī* of beings, a hundred *koṭīs* of beings, a thousand *koṭīs* of beings, a hundred thousand *koṭīs* of *nayutas* of beings, and so forth on up to an ineffable-ineffable number of beings. Even if there were beings as numerous as the atoms in the entire continent of Jambudvīpa, beings as numerous as the atoms in all four continents, beings as numerous as the atoms in a small chiliocosm's worlds, a mid-sized chiliocosm's worlds, a great chiliocosm's worlds, and so forth on up to beings as numerous as the atoms in an ineffable-ineffable number of buddha *kṣetras,* or even if there were all beings in all worlds of the ten directions—still, I could adapt to their individual desires and delights and thereby enable them all to be completely filled to satisfaction, and yet their food and drink would be inexhaustible and would not even be diminished in quantity at all.

And just as this would be so with regard to food and drink, so too would this be so with regard to the many different kinds of supremely flavored delicacies, the many different kinds of seats, the many different kinds of robes, the many different kinds of bedding, the many different kinds of carriages, the many different kinds of flowers, the many different kinds of garlands, the many different kinds of incense, the many different kinds of perfumes, the many different kinds of burning incense, the many different kinds of powdered incense, the many different kinds of precious jewels, the many different kinds of necklaces, the many different kinds of banners, the many different kinds of pennants, the many different kinds of canopies, and the many different supremely marvelous means of subsistence. In all such cases, in accordance with whatever their minds find delightful, I enable them all to become completely satisfied.

正體字

又善男子。假使東方一世界中。聲聞獨
351c29 ‖ 覺。食我食已。皆證聲聞辟支佛果。住最後
352a01 ‖ 身。如一世界中。如是百世界。千世界。百千世
352a02 ‖ 界。億世界。百億世界。千億世界。百千億世
352a03 ‖ 界。百千億那由他世界。閻浮提微塵數世界。
352a04 ‖ 一四天下微塵數世界。小千國土微塵數世
352a05 ‖ 界。中千國土微塵數世界。三千大千國土微
352a06 ‖ 塵數世界。乃至不可說不可說佛剎微塵數
352a07 ‖ 世界中。所有一切聲聞獨覺。食我食已。皆證
352a08 ‖ 聲聞辟支佛果。住最後身。如於東方。南西
352a09 ‖ 北方。四維上下。亦復如是。又善男子。東方一
352a10 ‖ 世界。乃至不可說不可說佛剎微塵數世界
352a11 ‖ 中。所有一生所繫菩薩。食我食已。皆菩提樹
352a12 ‖ 下。坐於道場。降伏魔軍。成阿耨多羅三藐三
352a13 ‖ 菩提。如東方。南西北方。四維上下。亦復如
352a14 ‖ 是。善男子。汝見我此十千童女眷屬[1]以不。
352a15 ‖ 答言已見。優婆夷言。善男子。此十千童女。而
352a16 ‖ 為上首。如是眷屬百萬阿僧祇。皆悉與我同
352a17 ‖ 行同願。

简体字

“又，善男子，假使东方一世界中，声闻、独觉食我食已，皆证声闻、辟支佛果，住最后身；如一世界中，如是百世界、千世界、百千世界、亿世界、百亿世界、千亿世界、百千亿世界、百千亿那由他世界、阎浮提微尘数世界、一四天下微尘数世界、小千国土微尘数世界、中千国土微尘数世界、三千大千国土微尘数世界，乃至不可说不可说佛刹微尘数世界中，所有一切声闻、独觉食我食已，皆证声闻、辟支佛果，住最后身。如于东方，南、西、北方，四维、上、下，亦复如是。

“又，善男子，东方一世界，乃至不可说不可说佛刹微尘数世界中，所有一生所系菩萨食我食已，皆菩提树下坐于道场，降伏魔军，成阿耨多罗三藐三菩提；如东方，南、西、北方，四维、上、下，亦复如是。

“善男子，汝见我此十千童女眷属已不？”

答言：“已见。”

优婆夷言：“善男子，此十千童女而为上首，如是眷属百万阿僧祇，皆悉与我同行、同愿、

Son of Good Family, if the adherents of the *śrāvaka*-disciple or *pratyekabuddha* paths in a world off to the east were to eat the food I provide them, then they would all attain the corresponding fruits of their *śrāvaka*-disciple and *pratyekabuddha* paths, and would thus abide then in their very last physical body.

Just as this would be so in that single world, so too would this also be the case for a hundred worlds, a thousand worlds, a hundred thousand worlds, a *koṭī* of worlds, a hundred *koṭīs* of worlds, a thousand *koṭīs* of worlds, a hundred thousand *koṭīs* of worlds, a hundred thousand *koṭīs* of *nayutas* of worlds, worlds as numerous as the atoms in the continent of Jambudvīpa, worlds as numerous as the atoms in all four continents, worlds as numerous as the atoms in a small chiliocosm, worlds as numerous as the atoms in a mid-sized chiliocosm, worlds as numerous as the atoms in a great trichiliocosm, and so forth on up to all the *śrāvaka*-disciple and *pratyekabuddha* adherents in worlds as numerous as the atoms in an ineffable-ineffable number of worlds—even in all those cases, once they had eaten my food, they would all attain the corresponding fruits of their *śrāvaka*-disciple and *pratyekabuddha* paths and would thus abide then in their very last physical body.

And just as this would be so with respect to the east, so too would this also be so with respect to the south, the west, the north, the four midpoints, the zenith, and the nadir.

So too, Son of Good Family, is this also true of all of the bodhisattvas with but one remaining lifetime in one world to the east and so forth on up to a number of worlds to the east as numerous as the atoms in an ineffable-ineffable number of buddha *kṣetras*, for by merely having eaten this food of mine, they will all sit in the site of enlightenment beneath the bodhi tree, will vanquish Māra's armies, and will attain *anuttara-samyak-saṃbodhi*.

And just as this is the case with east, so too is it also so with regard to the south, the west, the north, the four midpoints, the zenith, and the nadir.

Son of Good Family, do you or do you not now see this retinue of mine consisting of a myriad maidens?

Sudhana replied, "Yes, I see them."

The Upāsikā then said:

Son of Good Family, these myriad maidens are but those who serve at the head of just such a retinue that altogether is a hundred myriads of *asaṃkhyeyas* in number. All of them share with me:

The same practices;

The same vows;

正體字

同善根。同出離道。同清淨解。同清淨
352a18‖ 念。同清淨趣。同無量覺。同得諸根。同廣大
352a19‖ 心。同所行境。同理同義。同明了法。同淨色
352a20‖ 相。同無量力。同最精進。同正法音。同隨類
352a21‖ 音。同清淨第一音。同讚無量清淨功德。同清
352a22‖ 淨業。同清淨報。同大慈周普救護一切。同大
352a23‖ 悲周普成熟眾生。同清淨身業隨緣集起令
352a24‖ 見者欣悅。同清淨口業隨世語言宣布法化。
352a25‖ 同往詣一切諸佛眾會道場。同往詣一切佛
352a26‖ 剎供養諸佛。同能現見一切法門。同住菩薩
352a27‖ 清淨行地。善男子。是十千童女。能於此器。取
352a28‖ 上飲食。一剎那頃。遍至十方。供養一切後
352a29‖ 身菩薩聲聞獨覺。乃至遍及諸餓鬼趣。皆令
352b01‖ 充足。

简体字

同善根、同出离道、同清净解、同清净念、同清净趣、同无量觉、同得诸根、同广大心、同所行境、同理、同义、同明了法、同净色相、同无量力、同最精进、同正法音、同随类音、同清净第一音、同赞无量清净功德、同清净业、同清净报、同大慈周普救护一切、同大悲周普成熟众生、同清净身业随缘集起令见者欣悦、同清净口业随世语言宣布法化、同往诣一切诸佛众会道场、同往诣一切佛刹供养诸佛、同能现见一切法门、同住菩萨清净行地。

"善男子，是十千童女，能于此器取上饮食，一刹那顷遍至十方，供养一切后身菩萨、声闻、独觉，乃至遍及诸饿鬼趣，皆令充足。

The same roots of goodness;
The same path of emancipation;[100]
The same pure resolute convictions;[101]
The same pure mindfulness;
The same pure tendencies;
The same measureless awakening;[102]
The same attainment of faculties;
The same vast resolve;[103]
The same sphere of practice;
The same principles;
The same meanings;
The same clear understanding of dharmas;
The same pure forms and appearances;
The same measureless powers;
The same supreme vigor;
The same right Dharma sound;
The same adaptation of their voices to the types of beings;
The same voice that is foremost in its purity;
The same praise of the countless pure meritorious qualities;
The same pure karmic works;
The same pure karmic rewards;
The same great kindness that everywhere rescues everyone;
The same great compassion that everywhere ripens all beings;
The same pure physical karmic deeds that adapt to the conjunction and arising of conditions and please those who see them;
The same pure verbal karmic deeds that adapt to worldly discourse in proclaiming the Dharma's transformative teaching;
The same going to pay respects in all buddhas' congregations;
The same going to pay our respects and make offerings to all buddhas in all buddha *kṣetras*;
The same ability to directly see all Dharma gateways; and
The same abiding on the bodhisattva's grounds of pure practice.

Son of Good Family, these myriad maidens are able to take such superior food and drink from this bowl, whereupon, in the instant of but a single *kṣaṇa*, they go everywhere throughout the ten directions to make offerings to all those bodhisattvas, *śrāvaka* disciples, and *pratyekabuddhas* abiding in their very last physical body while also going to all the other rebirth destinies including even the rebirth destiny of the hungry ghosts where they enable them all to become completely satisfied.

正體字

善男子。此十千女。以我此器。能於天中
352b02║ 充足天食。乃至人中充足人食。善男子。且待
352b03║ 須臾。汝當自見。說是語時。善財則見無量眾
352b04║ 生。從四門入。皆優婆夷。本願所請。既來集已。
352b05║ 敷座令坐。隨其所須。給施飲食。悉使充足。告
352b06║ 善財言。善男子。我唯知此無盡福德藏解脫
352b07║ 門。如諸菩薩摩訶薩一切功德。猶如大海甚
352b08║ 深無盡。猶如虛空廣大無際。如如意珠滿眾
352b09║ 生願。如大聚落所求皆得。如須彌山普集眾
352b10║ 寶。猶如奧藏常貯法財。猶如明燈破諸黑闇。
352b11║ 猶如高蓋普蔭群生。而我云何能知能說彼
352b12║ 功德行。善男子。南方有城。名曰大興。彼有居
352b13║ 士。名曰明智。汝詣彼問。菩薩云何學菩薩行。
352b14║ 修菩薩道。

简体字

善男子，此十千女以我此器，能于天中充足天食，乃至人中充足人食。善男子，且待须臾，汝当自见。”

说是语时，善财则见无量众生从四门入，皆优婆夷本愿所请。既来集已，敷座令坐，随其所须，给施饮食，悉使充足。告善财言：“善男子，我唯知此无尽福德藏解脱门。如诸菩萨摩诃萨一切功德，犹如大海甚深无尽，犹如虚空广大无际，如如意珠满众生愿，如大聚落所求皆得，如须弥山普集众宝，犹如奥藏常贮法财，犹如明灯破诸黑暗，犹如高盖普荫群生；而我云何能知能说彼功德行？

“善男子，南方有城，名曰大兴；彼有居士，名曰明智。汝诣彼问：菩萨云何学菩萨行、修菩萨道？”

Son of Good Family, using this bowl of mine, these myriad maidens are able to cause those in the heavens to become completely satisfied with heavenly food while also being able to cause those in the human realm to become completely satisfied with the food that humans consume.

Son of Good Family, wait a moment. You should see this for yourself.

After she said this, Sudhana then saw countless beings enter from the four doors. They were all those whom the Upāsikā had invited to come through the power of her original vows. After they had all come and gathered, they were shown to their seats, whereupon they were provided with food and drink in accordance with their needs so that they were all caused to become completely satisfied. She then informed Sudhana:

Son of Good Family, I know only this liberation gateway of the treasury of endless merit. As for all the meritorious qualities of the bodhisattva-mahāsattvas:

Who are like a great ocean in that they are extremely deep and inexhaustible;

Who are like empty space in that they are boundlessly vast;

Who are like wish-fulfilling jewels in that they fulfill beings' wishes;

Who are like a large city in that one may obtain whatever one seeks to acquire from them;

Who are like Mount Sumeru in that the many different kinds of precious jewels are all completely collected together there;

Who are like a hidden treasury in that they always store up the wealth of Dharma;

Who are like a bright lamp in that they dispel all darkness; and

Who are like a lofty canopy in that they everywhere shade the many kinds of beings—

How could I know of or be able to speak about their meritorious qualities and practices?

Son of Good Family, south of here, there is a city known as Mahāsaṃbhava or "Great Flourishing." There is a householder there known as Vidvān or "Clear Knowledge." You should go there, pay your respects, and ask him, "How should the bodhisattva train in the bodhisattva practices and how should he cultivate the bodhisattva path?"

正體字

時善財童子。頂禮其足。遶無量匝。
352b15║ 瞻仰無厭。辭退而去。爾時善財童子。得無盡
352b16║ 莊嚴福德藏解脫光明已。思惟彼福德大海。
352b17║ 觀察彼福德虛空。趣彼福德聚。登彼福德山。
352b18║ 攝彼福德藏。入彼福德淵。遊彼福德池。淨
352b19║ 彼福德輪。見彼福德藏。入彼福德門。行彼福
352b20║ 德道。修彼福德種。漸次而行。至大興城。周遍
352b21║ 推求明智[2]長者。於善知識。心生渴仰。以善
352b22║ 知識。熏習其心。於善知識。志欲堅固。方便求
352b23║ 見諸善知識。心不退轉。願得承事諸善知識。
352b24║ 心無懈倦。知由依止善知識故。能滿眾善。知
352b25║ 由依止善知識故。能生眾福。知由依止善知
352b26║ 識故。能長眾行。知由依止善知識故。不由他
352b27║ 教。自能承事一切善友。

简体字

时，善财童子顶礼其足，绕无量匝，瞻仰无厌，辞退而去。

尔时，善财童子得无尽庄严福德藏解脱光明已，思惟彼福德大海，观察彼福德虚空，趣彼福德聚，登彼福德山，摄彼福德藏，入彼福德渊，游彼福德池，净彼福德轮，见彼福德藏，入彼福德门，行彼福德道，修彼福德种。

渐次而行，至大兴城，周遍推求明智居士。于善知识心生渴仰，以善知识熏习其心，于善知识志欲坚固，方便求见诸善知识心不退转，愿得承事诸善知识心无懈倦；知由依止善知识故，能满众善；知由依止善知识故，能生众福；知由依止善知识故，能长众行；知由依止善知识故，不由他教，自能承事一切善友。

Sudhana the Youth then bowed down in reverence at her feet and circumambulated her countless times while continuing to gaze up at her in tireless admiration, after which he respectfully withdrew and departed.

14 – Vidvān

At that time, after Sudhana the Youth had acquired the light of the liberation of the treasury of endless adornment and merit:

He reflected upon that great ocean of merit;
He contemplated that sky of merit;
He progressed into that aggregation of merit;
He climbed up that mountain of merit;
He gathered together that treasury of merit;
He entered that deep pool of merit;
He roamed about on that lake of merit;
He purified that wheel of merit;
He saw that treasury of merit;
He entered that gateway of merit;
He traveled along that path of merit; and
He cultivated those seeds of merit.

He then gradually traveled on to that city of Mahāsaṃbhava in which he searched all around for that elder, Vidvān.[104] As he did so:

His mind felt longing and admiration for the good spiritual guides;
Because the influence of the good spiritual guides permeated his mind, his resolute aspiration to encounter the good spiritual guides was firm;[105]
His mind never retreated in its efforts to search for and see the good spiritual guides;
His mind was tireless in pursuing his aspiration to tirelessly serve the good spiritual guides;
He realized that it is due to relying on the good spiritual guides that one is able to fulfill the many kinds of goodness;
He realized that it is due to relying on the good spiritual guides that one is able to produce the many varieties of merit;
He realized that it is due to relying on the good spiritual guides that one is able to produce growth in the many practices;
He realized that it is due to relying on the good spiritual guides that, without further reliance on teachings provided by others, one is able to serve all one's good spiritual friends.

正體字

如是思惟時。長其
352b28 善根。淨其深心。增其根性。益其德本。加其大
352b29 願。廣其大悲。近一切智。具普賢道。照明一切
352c01 諸佛正法。增長如來十力光明。爾時善財。見
352c02 彼居士在其城內市四衢道七寶臺上。處無
352c03 數寶莊嚴之座。其座妙好。清淨摩尼。以為
352c04 其身。金剛帝青。以為其足。寶繩交絡。五百妙
352c05 寶。而為校飾。敷天寶衣。建天幢幡。張大寶
352c06 網。施大寶帳。閻浮檀金。以為其蓋。毘瑠璃
352c07 寶。以為其竿。令人執持。以覆其上。鵝王羽
352c08 翮。清淨嚴潔。以為其扇。熏眾妙香。雨眾天
352c09 華。左右常奏五百樂音。其音美妙。過於天樂。
352c10 眾生聞者。無不悅豫。十千眷屬。前後圍遶。色
352c11 相端嚴。人所喜見。天莊嚴具。以為嚴飾。於天
352c12 人中。最勝無比。悉已成就菩薩志欲。皆與
352c13 居士。同昔善根。侍立瞻對。承其教命。爾時善
352c14 財。頂禮其足。遶無量匝。合掌而立。白言。聖
352c15 者。我為利益一切眾生故。

简体字

如是思惟时，长其善根，净其深心，增其根性，益其德本，加其大愿，广其大悲，近一切智，具普贤道，照明一切诸佛正法，增长如来十力光明。

尔时，善财见彼居士在其城内市四衢道七宝台上，处无数宝庄严之座。其座妙好，清净摩尼以为其身，金刚帝青以为其足，宝绳交络，五百妙宝而为校饰；敷天宝衣，建天幢幡，张大宝网，施大宝帐；阎浮檀金以为其盖，毗琉璃宝以为其竿，令人执持以覆其上；鹅王羽翮清净严洁以为其扇；熏众妙香，雨众天华；左右常奏五百乐音，其音美妙过于天乐，众生闻者无不悦豫。十千眷属前后围绕，色相端严，人所喜见，天庄严具以为严饰，于天人中最胜无比，悉已成就菩萨志欲，皆与居士同昔善根，侍立瞻对，承其教命。

尔时，善财顶礼其足，绕无量匝，合掌而立，白言：“圣者，我为利益一切众生故，

As he reflected in this way, he increased his roots of goodness, purified his deep resolve, enhanced the nature of his faculties, increased his foundation in virtue, augmented his great vows, broadened his great compassion, drew closer to all-knowledge, equipped himself with the path of Samantabhadra, brightly illuminated the right Dharma of all buddhas, and increased [his illumination by] the light of the Tathāgata's ten powers.

Sudhana then saw that householder on a seven-jeweled stage in the market at the city's crossroads where he was sitting on a throne adorned with countless jewels. That throne was marvelously fine, with its main structure composed of pristine *maṇi* jewels, and its feet made of vajra and *indranīla* sapphires. It was crisscrossed with jeweled cords, decorated with five hundred kinds of marvelous jewels, and it was covered with jeweled celestial robes.

Celestial banners and pennants were erected there and an immense net made of jewels was stretched over the area. A grand tent decorated with jewels had been set up there. He was sheltered by a canopy made of *jambūnada* gold supported by *vaiḍūrya* poles held up by his assistants. He was being fanned with immaculate decorated fans made from the feathers of royal geese.

Many marvelous perfumes scented the air and a rain of the many kinds of celestial flowers sprinkled down as, to his left and right, there was the constant playing of five hundred varieties of music, the beautifully sublime sounds of which surpassed even the music of the heavens. Whenever beings heard this music, none of them did not feel pleased and contented by it.

He was surrounded by a retinue of ten thousand followers. Their physical appearances were so splendidly handsome that, on seeing them, people felt joyful. They wore heavenly adornments that were the most incomparably excellent of all those found among either gods or humans. All of them had already perfected the aspirations of the bodhisattva and, in past lives, all of them had developed roots of goodness together with that householder. They stood there serving him and gazing up at him as they received his teachings and instructions.

Sudhana then bowed down in reverence at his feet, circumambulated him countless times, pressed his palms together, stood before him, and addressed him, saying:

O Ārya:

In order to benefit all beings;

正體字

為令一切眾生出
352c16‖ 諸苦難故。為令一切眾生究竟安樂故。為令
352c17‖ 一切眾生出生死海故。為令一切眾生住法
352c18‖ 寶洲故。為令一切眾生枯竭愛河故。為令一
352c19‖ 切眾生起大慈悲故。為令一切眾生捨離欲
352c20‖ 愛故。為令一切眾生渴仰佛智故。為令一切
352c21‖ 眾生出生死曠野故。為令一切眾生樂諸佛
352c22‖ 功德故。為令一切眾生出三界城故。為令一
352c23‖ 切眾生入一切智城故。發阿耨多羅三藐三
352c24‖ 菩提心。而未知菩薩云何學菩薩行。云何修
352c25‖ 菩薩道。能為一切眾生。作依止處。長者告言。
352c26‖ 善哉善哉。善男子。汝乃能發阿耨多羅三藐
352c27‖ 三菩提心。善男子。發阿耨多羅三藐三菩提
352c28‖ 心。是人難得。若能發心。是人則能求菩薩行。
352c29‖ 值遇善知識恒無厭足。親近善知識恒無勞
353a01‖ 倦。供養善知識恒不疲懈。給侍善知識不生
353a02‖ 憂慼。求覓善知識終不退轉。愛念善知識終
353a03‖ 不放捨。

简体字

为令一切众生出诸苦难故，为令一切众生究竟安乐故，为令一切众生出生死海故，为令一切众生住法宝洲故，为令一切众生枯竭爱河故，为令一切众生起大慈悲故，为令一切众生舍离欲爱故，为令一切众生渴仰佛智故，为令一切众生出生死旷野故，为令一切众生乐诸佛功德故，为令一切众生出三界城故，为令一切众生入一切智城故，发阿耨多罗三藐三菩提心，而未知菩萨云何学菩萨行，云何修菩萨道，能为一切众生作依止处？”

长者告言：“善哉！善哉！善男子，汝乃能发阿耨多罗三藐三菩提心。

“善男子，发阿耨多罗三藐三菩提心，是人难得。若能发心，是人则能求菩萨行，值遇善知识恒无厌足，亲近善知识恒无劳倦，供养善知识恒不疲懈，给侍善知识不生忧戚，求觅善知识终不退转，爱念善知识终不放舍，

In order to enable all beings to escape from sufferings and difficulties;
In order to enable all beings to find ultimate happiness;
In order to enable all beings to escape the ocean of *saṃsāra;*
In order to cause all beings to abide on the isle of Dharma jewels;
In order to enable all beings to dry up the river of cravings;
In order to enable all beings to produce great kindness and compassion;
In order to enable all beings to abandon sensual craving;
In order to enable all beings to long for and admire the Buddha's wisdom;
In order to enable all beings to escape the vast wilderness of *saṃsāra;*
In order to enable all beings to delight in the Buddha's meritorious qualities;
In order to enable all beings to escape the city of the three realms of existence; and
In order to enable all beings to enter the city of all-knowledge—

For reasons such as these, I have already resolved to attain *anuttara-samyak-saṃbodhi.* Still, I do not yet know how the bodhisattva should train in the bodhisattva practices, how he should cultivate the bodhisattva path, or how he can serve as a support for all beings.

The Elder then spoke to him, saying:

It is good indeed, good indeed, Son of Good Family, that you have now been able to resolve to attain *anuttara-samyak-saṃbodhi.*

Son of Good Family, a person who resolves to attain *anuttara-samyak-saṃbodhi* is only rarely encountered. If someone is able to arouse that resolve, then such a person becomes able to pursue the bodhisattva practices and, in doing so:

He is constantly insatiable in seeking encounters with the good spiritual guides;
He never grows weary of drawing near to the good spiritual guides;
He is always tireless in making offerings to the good spiritual guides;
He never becomes troubled or distressed in serving the good spiritual guides;
He never retreats from searching for the good spiritual guides;
He is unremitting in his fond mindfulness of the good spiritual guides;

正體字

承事善知識無暫休息。瞻仰善知識
353a04║ 無時憩止。行善知識教未曾怠惰。稟善知識
353a05║ 心無有誤失。善男子。汝見我此眾會人不。善
353a06║ 財答言。唯然已見。居士言。善男子。我已令其
353a07║ 發阿耨多羅三藐三菩提心。生如來家。增長
353a08║ 白法。安住無量諸波羅蜜。學佛十力。離世
353a09║ 間種。住如來種。棄生死輪。轉正法輪。滅三惡
353a10║ 趣。住正法趣。如諸菩薩悉能救護一切眾生。
353a11║ 善男子。我得隨意出生福德藏解脫門。凡有
353a12║ 所須。悉滿其願。所謂衣服瓔珞。象馬車乘。華
353a13║ 香幢蓋。飲食湯藥。房舍屋宅。床座燈炬。奴婢
353a14║ 牛羊。及諸侍使。如是一切資生之物。諸有所
353a15║ 須。悉令充滿。乃至為說真實妙法。善男子。且
353a16║ 待須臾。汝當自見。

简体字

承事善知识无暂休息，瞻仰善知识无时憩止，行善知识教未曾怠惰，禀善知识心无有误失。

“善男子，汝见我此众会人不？”

善财答言：“唯然！已见。”

居士言：“善男子，我已令其发阿耨多罗三藐三菩提心，生如来家，增长白法，安住无量诸波罗蜜，学佛十力，离世间种，住如来种，弃生死轮，转正法轮，灭三恶趣，住正法趣，如诸菩萨悉能救护一切众生。

“善男子，我得随意出生福德藏解脱门，凡有所须，悉满其愿。所谓：衣服、瓔珞、象马、车乘、华香、幢盖、饮食、汤药、房舍、屋宅、床座、灯炬、奴婢、牛羊及诸侍使，如是一切资生之物，诸有所须，悉令充满，乃至为说真实妙法。善男子，且待须臾，汝当自见。”

He never even briefly desists from serving the good spiritual guides;
He never desists from looking up in admiration to the good spiritual guides;
He is never indolent in carrying out the teachings of the good spiritual guides; and
He never errs or fails in carrying out the intentions of the good spiritual guides.

Son of Good Family, have you seen those in this congregation of mine, or not?

Sudhana replied, "Yes, I have seen them."

The Householder then said:

Son of Good Family, I have already caused them:

To resolve to attain *anuttara-samyak-saṃbodhi;*
To be born into the clan of the Tathāgata;
To increase in the white dharmas of pristine purity;
To abide securely in the countless *pāramitās;*
To train in the ten powers of the Buddha;
To abandon worldly lineages and instead abide in the lineage of the Tathāgata;
To cast off the wheel of *saṃsāra* and instead turn the wheel of right Dharma;
To extinguish the three wretched destinies and abide in the right Dharma destinies; and
To be able to rescue all beings just as the bodhisattvas do.

Son of Good Family, I have acquired the liberation gateway of producing at will a treasury of merit by which I completely fulfill anyone's wishes for whatever they may need, including:

Clothing and necklaces;
Elephants, horses, and carriages;
Flowers, scents, banners, and canopies;
Food, drink, and medicinal decoctions;
Shelters and residences;
Beds, seating, lamps, and torches;
Servants, cattle, and sheep; and
All kinds of assistants and messengers.

In this way, I completely satisfy beings with all essential life-supporting provisions up to and including the teaching of the true and sublime Dharma for their benefit. Son of Good Family, wait a moment. You should observe this for yourself.

正體字

說是語時。無量眾生。從種
353a17‖ 種方所。種種世界。種種國土。種種城邑。形類
353a18‖ 各別。愛欲不同。皆以菩薩。往昔願力。其數無
353a19‖ 邊。俱來集會。各隨所欲。而有求請。爾時居
353a20‖ 士。知眾普集。須臾繫念。仰視虛空。如其所
353a21‖ 須。悉從空下。一切眾會。普皆滿足。然後復為
353a22‖ 說種種法。所謂為得美食而充足者。與說種
353a23‖ 種集福德行。離貧窮行。知諸法行。成就法喜
353a24‖ 禪悅食行。修習具足諸相好行。增長成就難
353a25‖ 屈伏行。善能了達無上食行。成就無盡大威
353a26‖ 德力降魔怨行。為得好飲而充足者。與其說
353a27‖ 法。令於生死。捨離愛著。入佛法味。為得種種
353a28‖ 諸上味者。與其說法。皆令獲得諸佛如來上
353a29‖ 味之相。

简体字

说是语时，无量众生从种种方所、种种世界、种种国土、种种城邑，形类各别，爱欲不同，皆以菩萨往昔愿力，其数无边俱来集会，各随所欲而有求请。

尔时，居士知众普集，须臾系念，仰视虚空；如其所须，悉从空下，一切众会普皆满足。然后复为说种种法。所谓：为得美食而充足者，与说种种集福德行、离贫穷行、知诸法行、成就法喜禅悦食行、修习具足诸相好行、增长成就难屈伏行、善能了达无上食行、成就无尽大威德力降魔冤行；为得好饮而充足者，与其说法，令于生死，舍离爱著，入佛法味；为得种种诸上味者，与其说法，皆令获得诸佛如来上味之相；

Just as he said this, countless beings came from all the many different regions, from all the many different worlds, from all the many different countries, and from all the many different cities and towns. Of all different appearances and types and possessed of all different kinds of desires, they all came due to the power of the bodhisattva's past vows. Boundlessly numerous, they all came and congregated there, each with their particular requests corresponding to each of their individual desires.

Then the Householder, knowing that the congregation was assembled, focused his thought for but an instant and then looked up to the sky, whereupon whatever they all required then descended from the sky. Everyone in that congregation was thus entirely satisfied, after which he also taught the many different dharmas for their sakes, in particular:

For those who had become satisfied in their wishes to acquire fine food, he taught them:

- The many different kinds of merit-gathering practices;
- The practices for leaving behind their poverty;
- The practices for knowing all dharmas;
- The practices for perfecting Dharma joy and finding sustenance in the bliss of *dhyāna* meditation;
- The practices by which one cultivates and becomes completely equipped with the major marks and secondary signs;
- The practices by which one increases and perfects one's invincibility;
- The practices by which one becomes well able to completely comprehend what constitutes the unexcelled form of sustenance; and
- The practices by which one perfects the power of inexhaustible and immense awesome virtue and vanquishes Māra's armies.

For those who had become satisfied in their wishes to acquire exquisite things to drink, he spoke Dharma for them that enabled them to abandon their thirsting attachment for existence in *saṃsāra* and then penetrate the flavor of the Buddha's Dharma.

For those who sought to acquire the many different kinds of superior flavors, he spoke Dharma for them that enabled them all to experience the characteristically superior flavor known by the buddhas, the *tathāgatas*.

正體字

為得車乘而充足者。與其宜說種種
353b01║ 法門。皆令得載摩訶衍乘。為得衣服而充足
353b02║ 者。與其說法。令得清淨慚愧之衣。乃至如來
353b03║ 清淨妙色。如是一切。靡不周贍。然後悉為如
353b04║ 應說法。既聞法已還歸本處。爾時居士。為善
353b05║ 財童子。示現菩薩不可思議解脫境界已。告
353b06║ 言。善男子。我唯知此隨意出生福德藏解脫
353b07║ 門。如諸菩薩摩訶薩。成就寶手。遍覆一切十
353b08║ 方國土。以自在力。普雨一切資生之具。所謂
353b09║ 雨種種色寶。種種色瓔珞。種種色寶冠。種種
353b10║ 色衣服。種種色音樂。種種色華。種種色香。種
353b11║ 種色末香。種種色燒香。種種色寶蓋。種種色
353b12║ 幢幡。遍滿一切眾生住處。及諸如來眾會道
353b13║ 場。或以成熟一切眾生。或以供養一切諸佛。
353b14║ 而我云何能知能說彼諸功德自在神力。善
353b15║ 男子。於此南方。有一大城。名師子宮。彼有長
353b16║ 者。名法寶髻。汝可往問。菩薩云何學菩薩行。
353b17║ 修菩薩道。

简体字

为得车乘而充足者，与其宜说种种法门，皆令得载摩诃衍乘；为得衣服而充足者，与其说法，令得清净惭愧之衣，乃至如来清净妙色。如是一切靡不周赡，然后悉为如应说法。既闻法已，还归本处。

尔时，居士为善财童子示现菩萨不可思议解脱境界已，告言："善男子，我唯知此随意出生福德藏解脱门。如诸菩萨摩诃萨成就宝手，遍覆一切十方国土，以自在力普雨一切资生之具，所谓：雨种种色宝、种种色璎珞、种种色宝冠、种种色衣服、种种色音乐、种种色华、种种色香、种种色末香、种种色烧香、种种色宝盖、种种色幢幡，遍满一切众生住处，及诸如来众会道场，或以成熟一切众生，或以供养一切诸佛；而我云何能知能说彼诸功德自在神力？

"善男子，于此南方，有一大城，名师子宫；彼有长者，名法宝髻。汝可往问：菩萨云何学菩萨行、修菩萨道？"

For those who had become satisfied in their wishes to acquire carriages, he taught them the many different Dharma gateways and enabled them all to board the vehicle of the Mahāyāna.

For those who had become satisfied in their wishes to acquire clothing, he spoke Dharma for them in a way that allowed them to acquire the pristine robes of the sense of shame and dread of blame and then eventually acquire the pristine and marvelous form of the Tathāgata.

In this way, there was no one who was not completely satisfied, after which he spoke Dharma for them in accordance with what was appropriate for them. Then, having heard his teachings on Dharma, they all returned to their original places from which they had come.

Then, having shown Sudhana this inconceivable realm of the bodhisattva's liberation, the Householder spoke to him, saying:

Son of Good Family, I know only this liberation gateway of producing at will a treasury of merit. As for the bodhisattva-mahāsattvas' perfection of the jeweled hand that reaches everywhere to cover all lands of the ten directions and then, with the power of sovereign mastery, everywhere rains down all different kinds of life-supporting provisions with which they everywhere fill up the dwelling places of all beings as well as the congregations of all *tathāgatas,* in some cases using these as means to promote the ripening of beings and in some cases using them as offerings to all buddhas, in particular raining down:

The many different colored jewels,
The many different colored necklaces,
The many different colored jeweled crowns,
The many different colored robes,
The many different colorations of music,
The many different colored flowers,
The many different colors of incense,
The many different colors of powdered incense,
The many different colors of burning incense,
The many different colors of jeweled canopies,
And the many different colors of banners and pennants—

How could I know of or be able to speak about their meritorious qualities and their sovereign mastery in using the spiritual powers?

Son of Good Family, south of here, there is a great city known as Siṁhapota or "Lion Temple" in which there is an elder known as Ratnacūḍa or "Dharma Jewel Crest." You could go there and ask him, "How should a bodhisattva train in the bodhisattva practices and how should he cultivate the bodhisattva path?"

正體字

時善財童子。歡喜踊躍。恭敬尊重。
353b18║ 如弟子禮。作如是念。由此居士護念於我。令
353b19║ 我得見一切智道。不斷愛念善知識見。不壞
353b20║ 尊重善知識心。常能隨順善知識教。決定深
353b21║ 信善知識語。恒發深心。事善知識。頂禮其足。
353b22║ 遶無量匝。慇懃瞻仰。辭退而去
353c02║ 大方廣佛華嚴經卷第六十六
353c05║ 入法界品第三十九之七
353c06║ 爾時善財童子。於明智居士所。聞此解脫已。
353c07║ [1]遊彼福德海。治彼福德田。仰彼福德山。趣
353c08║ 彼福德津。開彼福德藏。觀彼福德法。淨彼福
353c09║ 德輪。味彼福德聚。生彼福德力。增彼福德勢。
353c10║ 漸次而行。向師子城。周遍推求寶髻長者。見
353c11║ 此長者在於市中。遽即往詣。頂禮其足。遶無
353c12║ 數匝。合掌而立。白言。聖者。我已先發阿耨多
353c13║ 羅三藐三菩提心。而未知菩薩。云何學菩薩
353c14║ 行。云何修菩薩道。善哉聖者。願為我說諸菩
353c15║ 薩道。我乘此道。趣一切智。爾時長者。執善財
353c16║ 手。將詣所居示其舍宅。作如是言。善男子。且
353c17║ 觀我家。爾時善財。見其舍宅。清淨光明。真金
353c18║ 所成。白銀為牆。

简体字

时，善财童子欢喜踊跃，恭敬尊重，如弟子礼，作如是念："由此居士护念于我，令我得见一切智道，不断爱念善知识见，不坏尊重善知识心，常能随顺善知识教，决定深信善知识语，恒发深心事善知识。"顶礼其足，绕无量匝，殷勤瞻仰，辞退而去。

大方广佛华严经卷第六十六

入法界品第三十九之七

尔时，善财童子于明智居士所，闻此解脱已，游彼福德海，治彼福德田，仰彼福德山，趣彼福德津，开彼福德藏，观彼福德法，净彼福德轮，味彼福德聚，生彼福德力，增彼福德势。

渐次而行，向师子城，周遍推求宝髻长者。见此长者在于市中，遽即往诣，顶礼其足，绕无数匝，合掌而立，白言："圣者，我已先发阿耨多罗三藐三菩提心，而未知菩萨云何学菩萨行？云何修菩萨道？善哉圣者，愿为我说诸菩萨道，我乘此道趣一切智！"

尔时，长者执善财手，将诣所居，示其舍宅，作如是言："善男子，且观我家。"

尔时，善财见其舍宅，清净光明，真金所成，白银为墙，

Then Sudhana the Youth, feeling joyous exultation, expressed respect and veneration for the Householder and bowed in reverence to him after the manner of a disciple. He then reflected in this way:

> It is because of this householder's protective mindfulness for me that I have been enabled to see the path to all-knowledge, that I never cease to fondly recollect the views of the good spiritual guides, that I never relinquish the mind that feels reverence for the good spiritual guides, that I am always able to comply with the good spiritual guides' teachings, that I possess a resolute and deep faith in the good spiritual guides' words, and that I constantly produce the deep resolve to serve the good spiritual guides.

He then bowed down in reverence at his feet and circumambulated him countless times as he gazed up at him in attentive admiration. He then respectfully withdrew and departed.

15 – Ratnacūḍa

At that time, after Sudhana the Youth had heard of this liberation from Vidvān the Householder, he roamed in his ocean of merit, cultivated his field of merit, gazed up at his mountain of merit, proceeded across his ford of merit, opened up his treasury of merit, contemplated his merit dharma,[106] purified his wheel of merit, tasted of his aggregation of merit, generated his merit power, and grew in his merit's strength.

He then gradually traveled onward until he reached Siṁhapota or "Lion City" where he searched all around for Ratnacūda, the Elder, until he saw this elder in the marketplace. He then immediately went up to him to pay his respects. He bowed down in reverence at his feet, circumambulated him countless times, pressed his palms together, stood before him, and addressed him, saying:

> O Ārya, I am one who has already resolved to attain *anuttara-samyak-saṃbodhi*. Still, I do not yet know how the bodhisattva should train in the bodhisattva practices or how he should cultivate the bodhisattva path. It would be good indeed, O Ārya, if you would please teach me about the path of the bodhisattvas so that I may ascend to this path and progress toward all-knowledge.

The Elder then took Sudhana's hand, led him to where he lived to show him his dwelling, and said, "Son of Good Family, you should also look at my house."

Sudhana then saw that his house emanated pure light, that it was made of real gold, that its walls were made of white silver, its hall

正體字

[2]玻瓈為殿。紺瑠璃寶。以為
353c19 樓閣。硨磲妙寶。而作其柱。百千種寶。周遍莊
353c20 嚴。赤珠摩尼。為師子座。摩尼為帳。真珠為
353c21 網。彌覆其上。[3]碼碯寶池。香水盈滿。無量寶
353c22 樹。周遍行列。其宅廣博。十層八門。善財入
353c23 已。次第觀察。見最下層。施諸飲食。見第二
353c24 層。施諸寶衣。見第三層。布施一切寶莊嚴具。
353c25 見第四層。施諸采女并及一切上妙珍寶。見
353c26 第五層。乃至五地菩薩雲集。演說諸法。利益
353c27 世間。成就一切陀羅尼門。諸三昧印。諸三昧
353c28 行。智慧光明。見第六層。有諸菩薩。皆已成就
353c29 甚深智慧。於諸法性。明了通達。成就廣大總
354a01 持三昧。無障礙門。所行無礙。不住二法。在不
354a02 可說妙莊嚴道場中。而共集會。分別顯示般
354a03 若波羅蜜門。所謂寂靜藏般若波羅蜜門。善
354a04 分別諸眾生智般若波羅蜜門。不可動轉般
354a05 若波羅蜜門。離欲光明般若波羅蜜門。不可
354a06 降伏藏般若波羅蜜門。照眾生輪般若波羅
354a07 蜜門。海藏般若波羅蜜門。普眼捨得般若波
354a08 羅蜜門。入無盡藏般若波羅蜜門。一切方便
354a09 海般若波羅蜜門。入一切世間海般若波羅
354a10 蜜門。

简体字

玻璃为殿，绀琉璃宝以为楼阁，砗磲妙宝而作其柱，百千种宝周遍庄严；赤珠摩尼为师子座；摩尼为帐，真珠为网，弥覆其上；玛瑙宝池香水盈满，无量宝树周遍行列；其宅广博，十层八门。

善财入已，次第观察。见最下层，施诸饮食。见第二层，施诸宝衣。见第三层，布施一切宝庄严具。见第四层，施诸采女并及一切上妙珍宝。见第五层，乃至五地菩萨云集，演说诸法利益世间，成就一切陀罗尼门、诸三昧印、诸三昧行智慧光明。见第六层，有诸菩萨皆已成就甚深智慧，于诸法性明了通达，成就广大总持三昧无障碍门，所行无碍，不住二法，在不可说妙庄严道场中而共集会，分别显示般若波罗蜜门，所谓：寂静藏般若波罗蜜门、善分别诸众生智般若波罗蜜门、不可动转般若波罗蜜门、离欲光明般若波罗蜜门、不可降伏藏般若波罗蜜门、照众生轮般若波罗蜜门、海藏般若波罗蜜门、普眼舍得般若波罗蜜门、入无尽藏般若波罗蜜门、一切方便海般若波罗蜜门、入一切世间海般若波罗蜜门、

was made of crystal, its tower was made of purple *vaiḍūrya*, its pillars were made of carnelian and fine gems, and a hundred thousand kinds of precious jewels everywhere served as adornments. It had a lion throne made of red pearls and *maṇi* jewels. It had a canopy of *maṇi* jewels and was covered by a suspended net of true pearls. It had a pool lined with emerald gems that was filled with fragrant waters and was surrounded all around by rows of countless jeweled trees. The house itself was vast and had ten levels and eight doors.

After he entered it, Sudhana, looked around it in an orderly manner and saw that, on its lowest level, all kinds of food and drink were provided, on the second level, all kinds of jeweled robes were provided, on the third level, all kinds of jewel adornments were distributed, and on the fourth level, palace maidens and marvelous precious jewels were provided.

He saw that, on the fifth level, bodhisattvas abiding on grounds up to the fifth ground had gathered there like clouds where they expounded on various dharmas, engaged in benefiting those in the world, and perfected the *dhāraṇī* gateways, the seals of samādhi, the samādhi practices, and the light of wisdom.

He saw that, on the sixth level, there were all kinds of bodhisattvas who had already perfected the extremely profound wisdom by which one clearly comprehends the nature of all dharmas. They had perfected the unimpeded gateways of the vast complete-retention *dhāraṇī* samādhis, had become unimpeded in whatever they practiced, and refrained from abiding in dualistic dharmas. They had gathered in an ineffable number of marvelously adorned congregations and were analyzing and elucidating the gateways to *prajñāpāramitā*, in particular:

The treasury of quiescence *prajñāpāramitā* gateway;
The wisdom that skillfully distinguishes beings *prajñāpāramitā* gateway;
The unshakable and irreversible *prajñāpāramitā* gateway;
The light of dispassion *prajñāpāramitā* gateway;
The matrix of invincibility *prajñāpāramitā* gateway;
The illumination of the sphere of beings *prajñāpāramitā* gateway;
The oceanic matrix *prajñāpāramitā* gateway;
The *prajñāpāramitā* gateway acquired through the universal eye's equanimity;
The entry into the inexhaustible treasury *prajñāpāramitā* gateway;
The ocean of all skillful means *prajñāpāramitā* gateway;
The entry into the ocean of all worlds *prajñāpāramitā* gateway;

正體字

無礙辯才般若波羅蜜門。隨順眾生般
354a11‖ 若波羅蜜門。無礙光明般若波羅蜜門。常觀
354a12‖ 宿緣而布法雲般若波羅蜜門。說如是等百
354a13‖ 萬阿僧祇般若波羅蜜門。見第七層。有諸菩
354a14‖ 薩。得如響忍。以方便智。分別觀察。而得出
354a15‖ 離。悉能聞持諸佛正法。見第八層。無量菩薩。
354a16‖ 共集其中。皆得神通。無有退墮。能以一音。遍
354a17‖ 十方剎。其身普現一切道場。盡于法界。靡不
354a18‖ 周遍。普入佛境。普見佛身。普於一切佛眾會
354a19‖ 中。而為上首。演說於法。見第九層。一生所繫
354a20‖ 諸菩薩眾。於中集會。見第十層。一切如來。充
354a21‖ 滿其中。從初發心。修菩薩行。超出生死。成滿
354a22‖ 大願及神通力。淨佛國土道場眾會。轉正法
354a23‖ 輪。調伏眾生。如是一切。悉使明見。爾時善
354a24‖ 財。見是事已。白言。聖者。何緣致此清淨眾
354a25‖ 會。種何善根。獲如是報。長者告言。善男子。
354a26‖ 我念過去。過佛剎微塵數劫。

简体字

无碍辩才般若波罗蜜门、随顺众生般若波罗蜜门、无碍光明般若波罗蜜门、常观宿缘而布法云般若波罗蜜门，说如是等百万阿僧祇般若波罗蜜门。见第七层，有诸菩萨得如响忍，以方便智分别观察而得出离，悉能闻持诸佛正法。见第八层，无量菩萨共集其中，皆得神通无有退堕，能以一音遍十方刹，其身普现一切道场，尽于法界靡不周遍，普入佛境，普见佛身，普于一切佛众会中而为上首演说于法。见第九层，一生所系诸菩萨众于中集会。见第十层，一切如来充满其中，从初发心，修菩萨行，超出生死，成满大愿及神通力，净佛国土道场众会，转正法轮，调伏众生。如是一切，悉使明见。

尔时，善财见是事已，白言：“圣者，何缘致此清净众会？种何善根获如是报？”

长者告言：“善男子，我念过去，过佛刹微尘数劫，

The unimpeded eloquence *prajñāpāramitā* gateway;
The adaptation to beings *prajñāpāramitā* gateway;
The unimpeded light *prajñāpāramitā* gateway; and
The constant contemplation of previous-life conditions in spreading forth the clouds of Dharma *prajñāpāramitā* gateway.

They discussed hundreds of myriads of *asaṃkhyeyas* of *prajñāpāramitā* gateways such as these.

He saw that, on the seventh level, there were bodhisattvas who had acquired the patience that perceives phenomena as like mere echoes and who used skillful means and wisdom to contemplate and transcend them. They were all able to hear and retain the right Dharma of all buddhas.

He saw that, on the eighth level, there were countless bodhisattvas who had assembled together there, all of whom had acquired the spiritual superknowledges from which they could never fall away. They were able with but one sound to pervade all the *kṣetras* of the ten directions. Their bodies manifested everywhere in all congregations throughout the entire Dharma realm, having none in which they were not everywhere present. They everywhere entered the realms of the buddhas, everywhere saw the bodies of the buddhas, and everywhere served at the head of all buddhas' congregations in which capacity they expounded on the Dharma.

He saw that, on the ninth level, all the bodhisattvas bound to but one more physical life prior to buddhahood were gathered together there.

He saw that, on the tenth level, it was completely filled with all *tathāgatas* who appeared there from the time when they first produced the resolve to when they cultivated the bodhisattva practices, achieved emancipation from birth and death, completely fulfilled their great vows, acquired the power of the spiritual superknowledges, purified their buddha lands, acquired their congregations, turned the wheel of right Dharma, and trained beings.

It was in this way that he was enabled to clearly see all these things.

Having seen all these phenomena, Sudhana then addressed the Elder, saying, "O Ārya, what are the conditions that have brought about the gathering of this pure congregation? The planting of which sort of roots of goodness have led to acquiring rewards such as these?"

The Elder then told him:

Son of Good Family, I recall that, in the past, beyond a period of kalpas as numerous as the atoms in a buddha *kṣetra*, there was a

正體字

有世界。名圓滿
354a27║ 莊嚴。佛號無邊光明法界普莊嚴王如來應正
354a28║ 等覺。十號圓滿。彼佛入城。我奏樂音。并燒一
354a29║ 丸香。而以供養。以此功德。迴向三處。謂永離
354b01║ 一切貧窮困苦。常見諸佛及善知識。恒聞正
354b02║ 法故獲斯報。善男子。我唯知此菩薩無量福
354b03║ 德寶藏解脫門。如諸菩薩摩訶薩。得不思議
354b04║ 功德寶藏。入無分別如來身海。受無分別無
354b05║ 上法雲。修無分別功德道具。起無分別普賢
354b06║ 行網。入無分別三昧境界。等無分別菩薩善
354b07║ 根。住無分別如來所住。證無分別三世平等。
354b08║ 住無分別普眼境界。住一切劫。無有疲厭。而
354b09║ 我云何能知能說彼功德行。善男子。於此南
354b10║ 方。有一國土。名曰藤根。其土有城。名曰普
354b11║ 門。中有長者。名為普眼。汝詣彼問。菩薩云何
354b12║ 學菩薩行。修菩薩道。

简体字

有世界，名圆满庄严，佛号无边光明法界普庄严王如来、应、正等觉，十号圆满。彼佛入城，我奏乐音，并烧一丸香而以供养，以此功德回向三处，谓：永离一切贫穷困苦、常见诸佛及善知识、恒闻正法，故获斯报。

“善男子，我唯知此菩萨无量福德宝藏解脱门。如诸菩萨摩诃萨，得不思议功德宝藏，入无分别如来身海，受无分别无上法云，修无分别功德道具，起无分别普贤行网，入无分别三昧境界，等无分别菩萨善根，住无分别如来所住，证无分别三世平等，住无分别普眼境界，住一切劫无有疲厌；而我云何能知能说彼功德行？

“善男子，于此南方，有一国土，名曰藤根；其土有城，名曰普门；中有长者，名为普眼。汝诣彼问：菩萨云何学菩萨行、修菩萨道？”

world named Completely Fulfilled Adornment in which there was a Buddha named Universally Adorned King of the Dharma Realm of Boundless Light Tathāgata, Arhat, the One of Right and Universal Enlightenment who was complete with all ten titles.

When that buddha entered the city, I played music and burned a lump of incense as offerings to him. It was due to then dedicating the merit from this to attaining three objectives that I have acquired these karmic rewards, namely: [dedicating it] to forever abandoning all difficulties and sufferings arising from poverty; [dedicating it] to always being able to see all buddhas and good spiritual guides; and [dedicating it] to always being able to hear right Dharma.

Son of Good Family, I know only this bodhisattva's liberation gateway of the jewel treasury of measureless merit. As for the bodhisattva-mahāsattvas:

Who have acquired the jewel treasury of inconceivable meritorious qualities;
Who have entered the undifferentiated ocean of *tathāgata*'s bodies;
Who have received the undifferentiated cloud of the unexcelled Dharma;
Who have cultivated the undifferentiated meritorious qualities as provisions for the path;
Who have raised up the undifferentiated net of Samantabhadra's practices;
Who have entered the undifferentiated realms of samādhi;
Who possess identical and undifferentiated bodhisattva roots of goodness;
Who abide in the undifferentiated abodes of the *tathāgatas*;
Who realize the undifferentiated uniform equality of the three periods of time;
Who abide in the undifferentiated spheres of experience of the universal eye; and
Who tirelessly remain throughout all kalpas—

How could I know of or be able to speak about their practice of these meritorious qualities?

Son of Good Family, south of here, there is a land known as Vetramūlaka or "Cane Root" in which there is a city known as Samantamukha or "Universal Gateway" in which there is an elder known as Samantanetra or "Universal Eye." You should go there, pay your respects, and ask him, "How should a bodhisattva train in the bodhisattva practices and how should he cultivate the bodhisattva path?"

正體字

時善財童子。頂禮其足。
354b13║ 遶無數匝。慇懃瞻仰。辭退而去
354b14║ 爾時善財童子。於寶髻長者所。聞此解脫已。
354b15║ 深入諸佛無量知見。安住菩薩無量勝行。了
354b16║ 達菩薩無量方便。希求菩薩無量法門。清淨
354b17║ 菩薩無量信解。明利菩薩無量諸根。成就菩
354b18║ 薩無量欲樂。通達菩薩無量行門。增長菩薩
354b19║ 無量願力。建立菩薩無能勝幢。起菩薩智照
354b20║ 菩薩法。漸次而行。至藤根國。推問求覓彼城
354b21║ 所在。雖歷艱難不憚勞苦。但唯正念善知識
354b22║ 教。願常親近承事供養。遍策諸根。離眾放逸。
354b23║ 然後乃得見普門城。百千聚落。周匝圍遶。雉
354b24║ 堞崇[1][山/陵]。衢路寬平。見彼長者。往詣其所。於
354b25║ 前頂禮。合掌而立。白言。聖者。我已先發阿耨
354b26║ 多羅三藐三菩提心。而未知菩薩云何學菩
354b27║ 薩行。云何修菩薩道。長者告言。善哉善哉。善
354b28║ 男子。汝已能發阿耨多羅三藐三菩提心。

简体字

时，善财童子顶礼其足，绕无数匝，殷勤瞻仰，辞退而去。

尔时，善财童子于宝髻长者所，闻此解脱已，深入诸佛无量知见，安住菩萨无量胜行，了达菩萨无量方便，希求菩萨无量法门，清净菩萨无量信解，明利菩萨无量诸根，成就菩萨无量欲乐，通达菩萨无量行门，增长菩萨无量愿力，建立菩萨无能胜幢，起菩萨智照菩萨法。

渐次而行，至藤根国，推问求觅彼城所在。虽历艰难，不惮劳苦，但唯正念善知识教，愿常亲近承事供养，遍策诸根离众放逸。然后乃得见普门城，百千聚落周匝围绕，雉堞崇峻，衢路宽平。见彼长者，往诣其所，于前顶礼，合掌而立，白言："圣者，我已先发阿耨多罗三藐三菩提心，而未知菩萨云何学菩萨行？云何修菩萨道？"

长者告言："善哉！善哉！善男子，汝已能发阿耨多罗三藐三菩提心。

Sudhana the Youth then bowed down in reverence at his feet and circumambulated him countless times as he gazed up at him in attentive admiration. He then respectfully withdrew and departed.

16 – Samantanetra

At that time, having heard of this liberation from Ratnacūda the Elder, Sudhana the Youth then:

Deeply entered all buddhas' measureless knowledge and vision;
Became established in the bodhisattva's countless supreme practices;
Fully comprehended the bodhisattva's countless skillful means;
Sought to acquire the bodhisattva's countless Dharma gateways;
Purified the bodhisattva's measureless resolute faith;
Brightened and sharpened the bodhisattva's measureless faculties;
Perfected the bodhisattva's measureless aspirations;
Gained a penetrating comprehension of the bodhisattva's measureless gateways of practice;
Grew in the bodhisattva's measureless power of vows;
Erected the bodhisattva's banner of invincibility;
Produced the bodhisattva's knowledge; and
Illuminated the bodhisattva's Dharma.

He then gradually traveled onward until he reached the country of Vetramūlaka in which he searched for the location of that city. Even though he endured hardships in this, he did not fear weariness or suffering, but rather only remained intent on right mindfulness of the good spiritual guides' teachings while yearning to always be able to draw near to, serve, and make offerings to them. He urged on all of his faculties to abandon the many kinds of negligence. After that, he was then able to gain sight of the city of Samantamukha which was surrounded all around by a hundred thousand villages. It had parapets which rose steeply upward and its avenues and streets were broad and level.

He saw that elder and went up to him to pay his respects. He then bowed down in reverence before him, stood with palms pressed together, and addressed him, saying, "O Ārya, I am one who has already resolved to attain *anuttara-samyak-saṃbodhi*. Still, I do not yet know how the bodhisattva should train in the bodhisattva practices or how he should cultivate the bodhisattva path."

The Elder then spoke to him, saying:

It is good indeed, good indeed, Son of Good Family, that you have already been able to resolve to attain *anuttara-samyak-saṃbodhi*. Son

正體字

善
354b29‖ 男子。我知一切眾生諸病。風黃[2]痰熱。鬼魅
354c01‖ 蠱毒。乃至水火之所傷害。如是一切所生諸
354c02‖ 疾。我悉能以方便救療。善男子。十方眾生。諸
354c03‖ 有病者。咸來我所。我皆療治。令其得差。復以
354c04‖ 香湯。沐浴其身。香華瓔珞。名衣上服。種種莊
354c05‖ 嚴。施諸飲食及以財寶。悉令充足。無所乏短。
354c06‖ 然後各為如應說法。為貪欲多者教不淨觀。
354c07‖ 瞋恚多者教慈悲觀。愚癡多者教其分別種
354c08‖ 種法相。等分行者為其顯示殊勝法門。為欲
354c09‖ 令其發菩提心。稱揚一切諸佛功德。為欲
354c10‖ 令其起大悲意。顯示生死無量苦惱。為欲令
354c11‖ 其增長功德。讚歎修集無量福智。為欲令其
354c12‖ 發大誓願。稱讚調伏一切眾生。為欲令其修
354c13‖ 普賢行。說諸菩薩於一切剎。一切劫住。修諸
354c14‖ 行網。為欲令其具佛相好。稱揚讚歎檀波羅
354c15‖ 蜜。為欲令其得佛淨身悉能遍至一切處故。
354c16‖ 稱揚讚歎尸波羅蜜。為欲令其得佛清淨不
354c17‖ 思議身。稱揚讚歎忍波羅蜜。

简体字

“善男子，我知一切众生诸病：风黄、痰热、鬼魅、蛊毒，乃至水火之所伤害。如是一切所生诸疾，我悉能以方便救疗。

“善男子，十方众生诸有病者咸来我所，我皆疗治，令其得差；复以香汤沐浴其身，香华、璎珞、名衣、上服、种种庄严，施诸饮食及以财宝，悉令充足无所乏短。然后各为如应说法：为贪欲多者，教不净观；瞋恚多者，教慈悲观；愚痴多者，教其分别种种法相；等分行者，为其显示殊胜法门。为欲令其发菩提心，称扬一切诸佛功德；为欲令其起大悲意，显示生死无量苦恼；为欲令其增长功德，赞叹修习无量福智；为欲令其发大誓愿，称赞调伏一切众生；为欲令其修普贤行，说诸菩萨于一切刹、一切劫住，修诸行网；为欲令其具佛相好，称扬赞叹檀波罗蜜；为欲令其得佛净身，悉能遍至一切处故，称扬赞叹尸波罗蜜；为欲令其得佛清净不思议身，称扬赞叹忍波罗蜜；

of Good Family, I recognize all the sicknesses that afflict beings, including those caused by wind, bile, phlegm, or fever and those caused by possession by demonic ghosts or poisoning, and so forth, including all of the injuries due to fire or water. By various means, I can cure all illnesses such as these.

Son of Good Family, all beings of the ten directions who fall ill come to me and I treat them and cure them. I then have them bathed in perfumed waters and dressed in fragrant flower garlands, fine clothes, superior robes, and many different kinds of adornments, after which I see to their being provided with food and drink as well as wealth and jewels so that they are all completely satisfied and do not want for anything.

After that, I then teach the Dharma for each of them in accordance with what is fitting. For those beset by an abundance of sensual lust, I teach them the contemplation of the unlovely. For those beset by an abundance of hatred, I teach them the kindness and compassion contemplations. For those beset by an abundance of delusion, I teach them to distinguish the many different characteristics of dharmas. And for those coursing in an equal measure of all of these afflictions, I reveal to them especially superior Dharma gateways. [Furthermore, for yet others]:

Wishing to enable them to resolve to attain bodhi, I praise the meritorious qualities of all buddhas;

Wishing to enable them to develop the greatly compassionate mind, I reveal the measureless bitter torments of the realms of *saṃsāra;*

Wishing to enable them to increase in their meritorious qualities, I praise the cultivation and accumulation of measureless merit and wisdom;

Wishing to enable them to make the great vows, I praise the training of all beings;

Wishing to enable them to cultivate the practices of Samantabhadra, I speak about the bodhisattvas' cultivation of the web of practices in all *kṣetras* and throughout all kalpas;

Wishing to enable them to possess the Buddha's major marks and secondary signs, I proclaim the praises of *dāna pāramitā;*

Wishing to enable them to acquire the Buddha's pure body that is able to travel everywhere to all places, I proclaim the praises of *śīla pāramitā;*

Wishing to enable them to acquire the Buddha's inconceivably pure body, I proclaim the praises of *kṣānti pāramitā;*

正體字

為欲令其獲於
354c18 | 如來無能勝身。稱揚讚歎精進波羅蜜。為欲
354c19 | 令其得於清淨無與等身。稱揚讚歎禪波羅
354c20 | 蜜。為欲令其顯現如來清淨法身。稱揚讚歎
354c21 | 般若波羅蜜。為欲令其現佛世尊清淨色身。
354c22 | 稱揚讚歎方便波羅蜜。為欲令其為諸眾生
354c23 | 住一切劫。稱揚讚歎願波羅蜜。為欲令其現
354c24 | 清淨身。悉過一切諸佛剎土。稱揚讚歎力波
354c25 | 羅蜜。為欲令其現清淨身隨眾生心悉使歡
354c26 | 喜。稱揚讚歎智波羅蜜。為欲令其獲於究竟
354c27 | 淨妙之身。稱揚讚歎永離一切諸不善法。如
354c28 | 是施已。各令還去。善男子。我又善知和合一
354c29 | 切諸香要法。所謂無等香。辛頭波羅香。無勝
355a01 | 香。覺悟香。阿盧那跋底香。堅黑栴檀香。烏洛
355a02 | 迦栴檀香。沈水香。不動諸根香。如是等香。悉
355a03 | 知調理和合之法。又善男子。我持此香。以為
355a04 | 供養。普見諸佛。所願皆滿。所謂救護一切眾
355a05 | 生願。嚴淨一切佛剎願。供養一切如來願。又
355a06 | 善男子。然此香時。一一香中。出無量香。遍至
355a07 | 十方一切法界。一切諸佛眾會道場。或為香
355a08 | 宮。或為香殿。如是香欄檻。香垣牆。香却敵。
355a09 | 香戶牖。香重閣。香半月。香蓋香幢。香幡香
355a10 | 帳。香羅網。香形像。

简体字

为欲令其获于如来无能胜身，称扬赞叹精进波罗蜜；为欲令其得于清净无与等身，称扬赞叹禅波罗蜜；为欲令其显现如来清净法身，称扬赞叹般若波罗蜜；为欲令其现佛世尊清净色身，称扬赞叹方便波罗蜜；为欲令其为诸众生住一切劫，称扬赞叹愿波罗蜜；为欲令其现清净身，悉过一切诸佛刹土，称扬赞叹力波罗蜜；为欲令其现清净身，随众生心悉使欢喜，称扬赞叹智波罗蜜；为欲令其获于究竟净妙之身，称扬赞叹永离一切诸不善法。如是施已，各令还去。

“善男子，我又善知和合一切诸香要法，所谓：无等香、辛头波罗香、无胜香、觉悟香、阿卢那跋底香、坚黑栴檀香、乌洛迦栴檀香、沉水香、不动诸根香，如是等香，悉知调理和合之法。

“又，善男子，我持此香以为供养，普见诸佛，所愿皆满，所谓：救护一切众生愿、严净一切佛刹愿、供养一切如来愿。

“又，善男子，燃此香时，一一香中出无量香，遍至十方一切法界一切诸佛众会道场，或为香宫，或为香殿，如是香栏槛、香垣墙、香却敌、香户牖、香重阁、香半月、香盖、香幢、香幡、香帐、香罗网、香形像、

Wishing to enable them to acquire the Tathāgata's invincible body, I proclaim the praises of the vigor *pāramitā;*

Wishing to enable them to acquire the incomparably pure body, I proclaim the praises of the *dhyāna pāramitā;*

Wishing to enable them to manifest the Tathāgata's pure Dharma body, I proclaim the praises of the *prajñāpāramitā;*

Wishing to enable them to manifest the pure form body of the Buddha, the Bhagavat, I proclaim the praises of the skillful means *pāramitā;*

Wishing to enable them to abide for the benefit of beings throughout all kalpas, I proclaim the praises of the vows *pāramitā;*

Wishing to enable them to manifest the pure body that passes through all buddha *kṣetras,* I proclaim the praises of the powers *pāramitā;*

Wishing to enable them to manifest the pure body that adapts to beings' minds and thereby pleases them, I proclaim the praises of the knowledge *pāramitā;* and

Wishing to enable them to acquire the most ultimately pure and marvelous of bodies, I proclaim the praises of forever abandoning all bad dharmas.

Then, having engaged in all the forms of giving such as these, they are each sent back [to their abodes].

Son of Good Family, I also know the methods for blending all the essential fragrances, in particular peerless incense, *sindhuvārita* incense, insuperable incense, awakening incense, *aruṇavati* incense, *kālānusāri* sandalwood incense, *uragasāra* sandalwood incense, *meghāgaru* incense, and unshakable faculties incense. I know the methods for the blending of all kinds of incense such as these.

Furthermore, Son of Good Family, when I hold up these types of incense and use them to make offerings, I then everywhere see the fulfillment of all buddhas' vows, namely the vow to rescue all beings, the vow to purify all buddha *kṣetras,* and the vow to make offerings to all *tathāgatas.*

Furthermore, Son of Good Family, when I burn this incense, every one of these types of incense sends forth countless kinds of incense that everywhere reach the congregations of all buddhas throughout the ten directions of the entire Dharma realm. Some form incense palaces and some form incense halls. In this same way, they then form the incense railings, incense walls, incense battlements, incense doors and windows, incense multistoried pavilions, incense half-moon adornments, incense canopies, incense banners, incense pennants, incense curtains, incense nets, incense images,

正體字

香莊嚴具。香光明。香雲
355a11║ 雨。處處充滿。以為莊嚴。善男子。我唯知此令
355a12║ 一切眾生普見諸佛歡喜法門。如諸菩薩摩
355a13║ 訶薩。如大藥王。若見若聞。若憶念若同住。若
355a14║ 隨行往。若稱名號。皆獲利益。無空過者。若有
355a15║ 眾生。暫得值遇。必令[1]銷滅一切煩惱。入於
355a16║ 佛法。離諸苦蘊。永息一切生死怖畏。到無所
355a17║ 畏一切智處。摧壞一切老死大山。安住平等
355a18║ 寂滅之樂。而我云何能知能說彼功德行。善
355a19║ 男子。於此南方。有一大城。名多羅幢。彼中有
355a20║ 王。名無厭足。汝[2]詣彼問。菩薩云何。學菩薩
355a21║ 行。修菩薩道。時善財童子。禮普眼足。遶無量
355a22║ 匝。慇懃瞻仰。辭退而去
355a23║ 爾時善財童子。憶念思惟善知識教。念善知
355a24║ 識。能攝受我。能守護我。令我於阿耨多羅三
355a25║ 藐三菩提。無有退轉。如是思惟。生歡喜心。淨
355a26║ 信心。廣大心。怡暢心。踊躍心。欣慶心。勝妙
355a27║ 心。寂靜心。莊嚴心。無著心。無礙心。平等心。
355a28║ 自在心。住法心。

简体字

香庄严具、香光明、香云雨，处处充满以为庄严。

“善男子，我唯知此令一切众生普见诸佛欢喜法门。如诸菩萨摩诃萨如大药王，若见、若闻、若忆念、若同住、若随行往、若称名号，皆获利益，无空过者；若有众生暂得值遇，必令消灭一切烦恼，入于佛法，离诸苦蕴，永息一切生死怖畏，到无所畏一切智处，摧坏一切老死大山，安住平等寂灭之乐。而我云何能知能说彼功德行？

“善男子，于此南方，有一大城，名多罗幢；彼中有王，名无厌足。汝诣彼问：菩萨云何学菩萨行、修菩萨道？”

时，善财童子礼普眼足，绕无量匝，殷勤瞻仰，辞退而去。

尔时，善财童子忆念思惟善知识教，念善知识：“能摄受我，能守护我，令我于阿耨多罗三藐三菩提无有退转。”如是思惟，生欢喜心、净信心、广大心、怡畅心、踊跃心、欣庆心、胜妙心、寂静心、庄严心、无著心、无碍心、平等心、自在心、住法心、

incense adornments, incense light, and incense clouds and rain that completely fill up place after place as adornments.

Son of Good Family, I know only this Dharma gateway of delighting all beings by enabling them to everywhere see all buddhas. As for the bodhisattva-mahāsattvas:

Who are like great physician kings who, if one but merely sees them, hears them, bears them in mind, dwells together with them, follows along with them in their travels, or utters their names, one will always benefit from that and will not have done so in vain; and

Who, if any being merely briefly encounters them, he will certainly be enabled to have all his afflictions melt away, will enter the Buddha's Dharma, will leave behind his entire accumulation of sufferings, will forever put to rest all fear of *saṃsāra*, will arrive at the fearless place of all-knowledge, will entirely crush all the great mountains of aging and death, and will come to securely abide in the bliss of uniform quiescence—

How could I know of or be able to speak about their meritorious qualities and practices?

Son of Good Family, south of here, there is a great city known as Tāladhvaja or "Tāla Banner" in which there is a king named Anala. You should go there, pay your respects, and then ask him, "How should the bodhisattva train in the bodhisattva practices and how should he cultivate the bodhisattva path?"

Sudhana the Youth then bowed down in reverence at the feet of Samantanetra and circumambulated him countless times as he gazed up at him in attentive admiration. He then respectfully withdrew and departed.

17 – Anala

At that time, Sudhana the Youth then brought to mind and reflected upon the teachings of the good spiritual guides, thinking, "The good spiritual guides are the ones who are able to draw me forth, are the ones who are able to protect me, and are the ones who enable me to gain irreversibility in my quest to realize *anuttara-samyak-saṃbodhi*."

As he reflected in this manner, his mind was filled with joyous thought, thoughts of pure faith, vast thoughts, contented thoughts, thoughts of exultation, thoughts of rejoicing, supremely sublime thoughts, peaceful thoughts, thoughts of adornment, thoughts of non-attachment, unimpeded thoughts, thoughts of equal regard for all, thoughts of sovereign mastery, thoughts of abiding in the Dharma,

正體字

遍往佛剎心。見佛莊嚴心。不
355a29‖ 捨十力心。漸次遊行。經歷國土村邑聚落。至
355b01‖ 多羅幢城。問無厭足王所在之處。諸人答言。
355b02‖ 此王今者在於正殿。坐師子座。宣布法化。調
355b03‖ 御眾生。可治者治。可攝者攝。罰其罪惡。決其
355b04‖ 諍訟。撫其孤弱。皆令永斷殺盜邪婬。亦令禁
355b05‖ 止妄言兩舌惡口綺語。又使遠離貪瞋邪見。
355b06‖ 時善財童子。依眾人語。尋即往詣遙見彼王
355b07‖ 坐那羅延金剛之座。阿僧祇寶。以為其足。無
355b08‖ 量寶像。以為莊嚴。金繩為網彌覆其上。如
355b09‖ 意摩尼以為寶冠。莊嚴其首。閻浮檀金以為
355b10‖ 半月。莊嚴其額。帝青摩尼以為耳璫。相對垂
355b11‖ 下。無價摩尼以為瓔珞。莊嚴其頸。天妙摩
355b12‖ 尼以為印釧。莊嚴其臂。閻浮檀金以為其蓋。
355b13‖ 眾寶間錯以為輪輻。大瑠璃寶以為其竿。光
355b14‖ 味摩尼以為其齎。雜寶為鈴。恒出妙音。放
355b15‖ 大光明。周遍十方。如是寶蓋。而覆其上。阿那
355b16‖ 羅王。有大力勢。能伏他眾。無能與敵。以離垢
355b17‖ 繒。而繫其頂。十千大臣。前後圍遶。共理王
355b18‖ 事。其前復有十萬猛卒。形貌醜惡。衣服褊陋。
355b19‖ 執持器仗。

简体字

遍往佛刹心、见佛庄严心、不舍十力心。

渐次游行，经历国土、村邑、聚落，至多罗幢城，问无厌足王所在之处，诸人答言："此王今者在于正殿，坐师子座，宣布法化，调御众生，可治者治，可摄者摄，罚其罪恶，决其诤讼，抚其孤弱，皆令永断杀、盗、邪淫，亦令禁止妄言、两舌、恶口、绮语，又使远离贪、瞋、邪见。"时，善财童子依众人语，寻即往诣。

遥见彼王坐那罗延金刚之座，阿僧祇宝以为其足，无量宝像以为庄严，金绳为网弥覆其上；如意摩尼以为宝冠庄严其首，阎浮檀金以为半月庄严其额，帝青摩尼以为耳珰相对垂下，无价摩尼以为璎珞庄严其颈，天妙摩尼以为印钏庄严其臂；阎浮檀金以为其盖，众宝间错以为轮辐，大琉璃宝以为其竿，光味摩尼以为其脐，杂宝为铃恒出妙音，放大光明周遍十方，如是宝盖而覆其上。

阿那罗王有大力势，能伏他众，无能与敌；以离垢缯而系其顶，十千大臣前后围绕共理王事。其前复有十万猛卒，形貌丑恶，衣服褊陋，执持器仗，

thoughts of pervading all buddha *kṣetras*, thoughts adorned with the sight of the buddhas, and thoughts of never forsaking [the development of] the ten powers.

He then gradually traveled onward, passing through countries, villages, and towns until he reached the city of Tāladhvaja where he inquired about the location of King Anala's abode. Everyone replied, "This king is now in the main hall, seated on a lion throne, proclaiming and spreading the transformative influence of the Dharma, ruling over and governing beings, restraining those who should be restrained, drawing forth those who can be drawn forth, punishing their crimes, issuing decisions on their disputes, comforting those who have become orphaned or who are weak, in all cases causing them to forever cease killing, stealing, and sexual misconduct while also forbidding lying, divisive speech, harsh speech, and frivolous or lewd speech. He is also persuading his subjects to abandon greed, hatred, and wrong views."

Relying on what all those people had reported, Sudhana the Youth, continuing his search, straightaway went to pay his respects. From a distance, he saw that king sitting on a throne of *nārāyaṇa* vajra with feet made of an *asaṃkhyeya* of jewels. It was adorned with countless jeweled images and was covered with netting woven from gold cord. He had a crown of wish-fulfilling *maṇi* jewels adorning his head, a *jambūnada* gold crescent adorning his forehead, matching hanging earrings made of *indranīla* sapphires, a necklace of priceless *maṇi* jewels adorning his neck, and engraved bracelets made of marvelous celestial *maṇi* jewels that adorned his arms. He had a canopy made of *jambūnada* gold with a central hub inlaid with the many kinds of precious jewels. Its support poles were made of immense lapis lazuli gems, lustrous *maṇi* jewels formed its accessories, various jewels formed the bells that constantly resounded with marvelous sounds and emanated a bright radiance that everywhere pervaded the ten directions. It was just such a jeweled canopy that sheltered him from above.

King Anala possessed great power with which he was able to subdue the masses. He had no enemies able to engage him. The topknot atop his head was secured with an immaculate silk headband. He was surrounded by ten thousand great officials who together managed the king's affairs. Before him were arrayed ten myriads of fierce shock troops with fearsomely threatening forms and countenances who were dressed in rough looking uniforms, and who held weapons

正體字

攘臂瞋目。眾生見者。無不恐怖。無
355b20 ‖ 量眾生。犯王教勅。或盜他物。或害他命。或侵
355b21 ‖ 他妻。或生邪見。或起瞋恨。或懷貪嫉。作如是
355b22 ‖ 等種種惡業。身被五縛。將詣王所。隨其所犯。
355b23 ‖ 而治罰之。或斷手足。或截耳鼻。或挑其目。或
355b24 ‖ 斬其首。或剝其皮。或解其體。或以湯煮。或以
355b25 ‖ 火焚。或驅上高山推令墮落。有如是等無量
355b26 ‖ 楚毒。發聲號叫。譬如眾合大地獄中。善財
355b27 ‖ 見已。作如是念。我為利益一切眾生。求菩
355b28 ‖ 薩行。修菩薩道。今者此王滅諸善法。作大罪
355b29 ‖ 業。逼惱眾生。乃至斷命。曾不顧懼未來惡道。
355c01 ‖ 云何於此而欲求法。發大悲心。救護眾生。作
355c02 ‖ 是念時。空中有天。而告之言。善男子。汝當憶
355c03 ‖ 念普眼長者善知識教。善財仰視。而白之曰。
355c04 ‖ 我常憶念。初不敢忘。天曰。善男子。汝莫厭離
355c05 ‖ 善知識語。善知識者。能引導汝。至無險難安
355c06 ‖ 隱之處。善男子。菩薩善巧方便智不可思議。
355c07 ‖ 攝受眾生智不可思議。護念眾生智不可思
355c08 ‖ 議。成熟眾生智不可思議。

简体字

攘臂瞋目，众生见者无不恐怖。无量众生犯王教敕，或盗他物，或害他命，或侵他妻，或生邪见，或起瞋恨，或怀贪嫉，作如是等种种恶业，身被五缚，将诣王所，随其所犯而治罚之。或断手足，或截耳鼻，或挑其目，或斩其首，或剥其皮，或解其体，或以汤煮，或以火焚，或驱上高山推令堕落，有如是等无量楚毒；发声号叫，譬如众合大地狱中。

善财见已，作如是念：“我为利益一切众生，求菩萨行，修菩萨道。今者，此王灭诸善法，作大罪业，逼恼众生，乃至断命，曾不顾惧未来恶道。云何于此而欲求法，发大悲心救护众生？”

作是念时，空中有天而告之言：“善男子，汝当忆念普眼长者善知识教。”

善财仰视而白之曰：“我常忆念，初不敢忘。”

天曰：“善男子，汝莫厌离善知识语，善知识者能引导汝至无险难安隐之处。善男子，菩萨善巧方便智不可思议，摄受众生智不可思议，护念众生智不可思议，成熟众生智不可思议，

in their bared arms as they glared with such hate-filled gazes that any being seeing them could not fail to be struck with terror.

There were countless beings there who had transgressed against the king's edicts, whether through stealing others' possessions, injuring or killing them, violating their wives, promoting wrong views, generating hatred or grudges, cherishing covetous jealousy, or otherwise engaging in many other kinds of evil deeds. They had been tied up with bonds restraining all five parts of their bodies and dragged up to the king who meted out punishment in accordance with the nature of their transgressions. Their hands or feet were cut off, or their ears and noses were sliced away, or their eyes were plucked out, or they were beheaded or skinned alive, or their bodies were sliced open, or they were boiled or burned alive, or they were driven up a high mountain and pushed off a steep precipice. There were countless cruelties such as these that were inflicted on them so that they screamed and howled like the denizens of the Great Unification Hells.[107]

After Sudhana saw all this, he thought, "It is for the sake of benefiting all beings that I seek to follow the bodhisattva practices and cultivate the bodhisattva path. But now this king destroys good dharmas, creates great karmic transgressions, and even torments and afflicts beings to the point of taking their lives, doing so without having any regard for or fear of future rebirths in the wretched destinies. How could I hope to acquire from him the Dharma by which one produces the mind of great compassion and strives to rescue beings?"

When he had this thought, a deva[108] appeared in the sky and told him, "Son of Good Family, you should recall the teachings of the good spiritual guide, Samantanetra, the Elder."

Sudhana then looked up at him and said, "I always bear them in mind and, from the very first, I have never dared to forget them."

The deva replied:

Son of Good Family, you must not depart from the instructions of the good spiritual guides. The good spiritual guides are able to lead you to the safe and secure place free of danger and difficulty.

Son of Good Family, as for the bodhisattva:

His knowledge of how to use skillful means is inconceivable;

His knowledge of how to gather in beings is inconceivable;

His knowledge of how to protect and care for beings is inconceivable;

His knowledge of how to ripen beings is inconceivable;

正體字

守護眾生智不可
355c09‖ 思議。度脫眾生智不可思議。調伏眾生智不
355c10‖ 可思議。時善財童子。聞此語已。即詣王所。頂
355c11‖ 禮其足。白言。聖者。我已先發阿耨多羅三藐
355c12‖ 三菩提心。而未知菩薩云何學菩薩行。云何
355c13‖ 修菩薩道。我聞聖者。善能教誨。願為我說。時
355c14‖ 阿那羅王。理王事已。執善財手。將入宮中。命
355c15‖ 之同坐。告言。善男子。汝應觀我所住宮殿。善
355c16‖ 財如語。即遍觀察。見其宮殿。廣大無比。皆以
355c17‖ 妙寶之所合成。七寶為牆。周匝圍遶。百千眾
355c18‖ 寶。以為樓閣。種種莊嚴。悉皆妙好。不思議摩
355c19‖ 尼寶網。羅覆其上。十億侍女。端正殊絕。威儀
355c20‖ 進止。皆悉可觀。凡所施為無非巧妙。先起後
355c21‖ 臥。軟意承旨。時阿那羅王。告善財言。善男子。
355c22‖ 於意云何。我若實作如是惡業。云何而得如
355c23‖ 是果報。如是色身。如是眷屬。如是富贍。如是
355c24‖ 自在。善男子。我得菩薩如幻解脫。善男子。我
355c25‖ 此國土。所有眾生。多行殺盜乃至邪見。作餘
355c26‖ 方便。不能令其捨離惡業。善男子。我為調伏
355c27‖ 彼眾生故。化作惡人。

简体字

守护众生智不可思议，度脱众生智不可思议，调伏众生智不可思议。”

时，善财童子闻此语已，即诣王所，顶礼其足，白言：“圣者，我已先发阿耨多罗三藐三菩提心，而未知菩萨云何学菩萨行？云何修菩萨道？我闻圣者善能教诲，愿为我说！”

时，阿那罗王理王事已，执善财手，将入宫中，命之同坐，告言：“善男子，汝应观我所住宫殿。”

善财如语即遍观察，见其宫殿广大无比，皆以妙宝之所合成，七宝为墙周匝围绕，百千众宝以为楼阁，种种庄严悉皆妙好，不思议摩尼宝网罗覆其上；十亿侍女端正殊绝，威仪进止皆悉可观，凡所施为无非巧妙，先起后卧软意承旨。

时，阿那罗王告善财言：“善男子，于意云何？我若实作如是恶业，云何而得如是果报、如是色身、如是眷属、如是富赡、如是自在？

“善男子，我得菩萨如幻解脱。善男子，我此国土所有众生，多行杀、盗乃至邪见，作余方便不能令其舍离恶业。善男子，我为调伏彼众生故，化作恶人

His knowledge of how to guard beings is inconceivable;
His knowledge of how to liberate beings is inconceivable; and
His knowledge of how to train beings is inconceivable.

Then, having heard these words, Sudhana the Youth immediately went to pay his respects to the king. He bowed down in reverence at his feet and then addressed him, saying:

O Ārya, I am one who has resolved to attain *anuttara-samyak-saṃbodhi*. Still, I do not yet know how the bodhisattva should train in the bodhisattva practices or how he should cultivate the bodhisattva path. I have heard that the Ārya is well able to provide guidance and instruction. Please speak about these matters for my sake.

Then, after finishing his management of royal matters, King Anala took Sudhana by the hand, led him into his palace, and ordered him to sit down with him, whereupon he told him, "Son of Good Family, take a look around the palace where I live."

As instructed, Sudhana then looked all around and saw that his palace was incomparably large and was made entirely of combinations of marvelous jewels. It was completely surrounded by walls made of the seven types of jewels and it had a tower made of a hundred thousand kinds of gems as well as many different kinds of adornments, all of which were marvelously fine.

It had a net of inconceivable *maṇi* jewels that stretched over the top of it. There were ten *koṭīs* of incomparably beautiful female attendants, all of whom were so impressively lovely in their deportment and manners that, whatever they did, nothing was not splendidly marvelous. They were first to arise and last to take their rest and had pliant minds receptive to instruction.

King Anala then spoke to Sudhana, saying:

Son of Good Family, what do you think? If I was one who truly committed evil deeds such as these, how could I acquire karmic rewards such as these, a physical body such as this, a retinue such as this, an endowment of wealth such as this, and sovereignty such as this?

Son of Good Family, I have acquired the bodhisattva's illusion-like liberation. Son of Good Family, all the beings in this land are for the most part inclined to commit everything from killing and stealing to the holding of wrong views. If I were to resort to other methods, I would be unable to cause them to relinquish their evil deeds.

Son of Good Family, in order to train those beings, I have transformationally created evil people who commit all kinds of karmic

正體字

造諸罪業。受種種苦。令
355c28 其一切作惡眾生。見是事已。心生惶怖。心生
355c29 厭離。心生怯弱。斷其所作一切惡業。發阿耨
356a01 多羅三藐三菩提意。善男子。我以如是巧方
356a02 便故。令諸眾生。捨十惡業。住十善道。究竟快
356a03 樂。究竟安隱。究竟住於一切智地。善男子。我
356a04 身語意。未曾惱害於一眾生。善男子。如我心
356a05 者。寧於未來。受無間苦。終不發生一念之意。
356a06 與一蚊一蟻。而作苦事。況復人耶。人是福田。
356a07 能生一切諸善法故。善男子。我唯得此如幻
356a08 解脫。如諸菩薩摩訶薩。得無生忍。知諸有
356a09 趣悉皆如幻。菩薩諸行悉皆如化。一切世間
356a10 悉皆如影。一切諸法悉皆如夢。入真實相無
356a11 礙法門。修行帝網。一切諸行。以無礙智。行於
356a12 境界。普入一切平等三昧。於陀羅尼。已得自
356a13 在。而我云何能知能說彼功德行。

简体字

造诸罪业受种种苦，令其一切作恶众生见是事已，心生惶怖，心生厌离，心生怯弱，断其所作一切恶业，发阿耨多罗三藐三菩提意。善男子，我以如是巧方便故，令诸众生，舍十恶业，住十善道，究竟快乐，究竟安隐，究竟住于一切智地。善男子，我身、语、意未曾恼害于一众生。善男子，如我心者，宁于未来受无间苦，终不发生一念之意与一蚊一蚁而作苦事，况复人耶！人是福田，能生一切诸善法故。

“善男子，我唯得此如幻解脱。如诸菩萨摩诃萨得无生忍，知诸有趣悉皆如幻，菩萨诸行悉皆如化，一切世间悉皆如影，一切诸法悉皆如梦，入真实相无碍法门，修行帝网一切诸行，以无碍智行于境界，普入一切平等三昧，于陀罗尼已得自在；而我云何能知能说彼功德行？

offenses and then undergo all different kinds of excruciating punishments, doing this in order to cause all those beings who commit evil deeds to witness these things and then have thoughts of terror, thoughts inclined to renounce such deeds, and thoughts inclined to trepidation on account of which they will cease all of the evil deeds they do and then resolve to attain *anuttara-samyak-saṃbodhi.*

Son of Good Family, through the use of these kinds of skillful expedients, I cause beings to relinquish the ten courses of evil karmic actions and abide instead in the ten courses of good karmic action so that they will attain ultimate happiness, ultimate peace and security, and then ultimately dwell on the ground of all-knowledge.

Son of Good Family, I have never tormented or injured even one being through any of my actions of body, speech, or mind.

Son of Good Family, anyone possessed of a mind like mine would rather endure the sufferings of the non-intermittent hells throughout the course of the future than ever produce so much as a single thought intending to inflict any suffering on even one mosquito or one ant, how much the less on a human being, for people are fields for the planting of merit because they are able to bring forth all good dharmas.

Son of Good Family, I know only this illusion-like liberation. As for the bodhisattva-mahāsattvas:

Who have realized the unproduced-dharmas patience;
Who have realized that all rebirth destinies in the realms of existence are like mere conjured illusions;
Who have realized that all bodhisattva practices are like mere magical transformations;
Who have realized that all worlds are like mere reflected images;
Who have realized that all dharmas are like mere dreams;
Who have entered the unimpeded Dharma gateway of the true character of dharmas;
Who have cultivated all the practices as symbolized by Indra's net;
Who use unimpeded wisdom in their practice throughout all realms;
Who have everywhere entered the samādhi of the uniform equality of everything; and
Who have already attained sovereign mastery of the *dhāraṇīs*—

How could I know of or be able to speak about their meritorious qualities and practices?

正體字

善男子。於
356a14 此南方。有城。名妙光。王名大光。汝詣彼問。
356a15 菩薩云何學菩薩行。修菩薩道。時善財童子。
356a16 頂禮王足。遶無數匝。辭退而去
356a17 爾時善財童子。一心正念彼王所得幻智法
356a18 門。思惟彼王如幻解脫。觀察彼王如幻法性。
356a19 發如幻願。淨如幻法。普於一切如幻三世。起
356a20 於種種如幻變化。如是思惟。漸次遊行。或至
356a21 人間城邑聚落。或經曠野巖谷險難。無有疲
356a22 懈。未曾休息。然後乃至妙光大城。而問人言。
356a23 妙光大城。在於何所。人咸報言。妙光城者。今
356a24 此城是。是大光王之所住處。時善財童子。歡
356a25 喜踊躍。作如是念。我善知識。在此城中。我今
356a26 必當親得奉見。聞諸菩薩所行之行。聞諸菩
356a27 薩出要之門。聞諸菩薩所證之法。聞諸菩薩
356a28 不思議功德。聞諸菩薩不思議自在。聞諸菩
356a29 薩不思議平等。聞諸菩薩不思議勇猛。聞諸
356b01 菩薩不思議境界廣大清淨。

简体字

“善男子，于此南方，有城名妙光；王名大光。汝诣彼问：菩萨云何学菩萨行、修菩萨道？”

时，善财童子顶礼王足，绕无数匝，辞退而去。

尔时，善财童子一心正念彼王所得幻智法门，思惟彼王如幻解脱，观察彼王如幻法性，发如幻愿，净如幻法，普于一切如幻三世起于种种如幻变化，如是思惟。

渐次游行，或至人间城邑、聚落，或经旷野、岩谷、险难，无有疲懈，未曾休息。然后乃至妙光大城，而问人言：“妙光大城在于何所？”人咸报言：“妙光城者，今此城是，是大光王之所住处。”

时，善财童子欢喜踊跃，作如是念：“我善知识在此城中，我今必当亲得奉见，闻诸菩萨所行之行，闻诸菩萨出要之门，闻诸菩萨所证之法，闻诸菩萨不思议功德，闻诸菩萨不思议自在，闻诸菩萨不思议平等，闻诸菩萨不思议勇猛，闻诸菩萨不思议境界广大清净。”

> Son of Good Family, south of here, there is a city known as Suprabha or "Marvelous Radiance" that is ruled by a king known as Mahāprabha or "Great Radiance." You should go there, pay your respects, and ask him, "How should a bodhisattva train in the bodhisattva practices and how should he cultivate the bodhisattva path?"

Sudhana the Youth then bowed down in reverence at the feet of the king and circumambulated him countless times. He then respectfully withdrew and departed.

18 – Mahāprabha

At that time, Sudhana the Youth then single-mindedly recollected the Dharma gateway of the cognition of illusion which that king had acquired. He reflected on that king's illusion-like liberation, contemplated that king's illusion-like nature of dharmas, made illusion-like vows, purified illusion-like dharmas, and produced many different kinds of illusion-like transformations everywhere throughout all three illusion-like periods of time.

Reflecting in this manner, he then gradually traveled onward, sometimes arriving at inhabited cities or towns, sometimes passing through the dangers and difficulties of desolate wildernesses, canyons, and gorges, doing so tirelessly and without ever resting. Finally, he reached the great city of Suprabha and inquired of the people there, "Where is the great city of Suprabha?"

The people there replied, "This is indeed the city of Suprabha and it is the abode of King Mahāprabha."

Feeling joyous exultation, Sudhana the Youth then reflected in this way:

> My good spiritual guide is in this very city. Now I will certainly be able to serve him, see him, and:
>
> Hear of the practices practiced by the bodhisattvas;
> Hear of the bodhisattvas' essential gateways of emancipation;
> Hear of the dharmas realized by the bodhisattvas;
> Hear of the bodhisattvas' inconceivable meritorious qualities;
> Hear of the inconceivable sovereign mastery of the bodhisattvas;
> Hear of the inconceivable uniform equality of the bodhisattvas;
> Hear of the inconceivable courage of the bodhisattvas; and
> Hear of the vast purity of the bodhisattvas' inconceivable spheres of experience.

正體字

作是念已。入妙
356b02 光城。見此大城。以金銀瑠璃[＊]玻瓈真珠硨磲
356b03 [＊]碼碯七寶所成。七寶深塹。七重圍遶。八功
356b04 德水。盈滿其中。底布金沙。優鉢羅華。波頭摩
356b05 華。拘物頭華。芬陀利華。遍布其上。寶多羅
356b06 樹。七重行列。七種金剛。以為其垣。各各圍
356b07 遶。所謂師子光明金剛垣。無能超勝金剛垣。
356b08 不可沮壞金剛垣。不可毀缺金剛垣。堅固無
356b09 礙金剛垣。勝妙網藏金剛垣。離塵清淨金剛
356b10 垣。悉以無數摩尼妙寶。間錯莊嚴。種種眾寶
356b11 而為埤堄。其城縱廣。一十由旬。周迴八方。面
356b12 開八門。皆以七寶。周遍嚴飾。毘瑠璃寶。以為
356b13 其地。種種莊嚴。甚可愛樂。其城之內。十億衢
356b14 道。一一道間。皆有無量萬億眾生。於中止住。
356b15 有無數閻浮檀金樓閣。毘瑠璃摩尼網。羅覆
356b16 其上。無數銀樓閣。赤真珠摩尼網。羅覆其上。
356b17 無數毘瑠璃樓閣。妙藏摩尼網。羅覆其上。無
356b18 數[＊]玻瓈樓閣。無垢藏摩尼王網。羅覆其上。
356b19 無數光照世間。摩尼寶樓閣。日藏摩尼王網。
356b20 羅覆其上。無數帝青摩尼寶樓閣。妙光摩尼
356b21 王網。羅覆其上。無數眾生海摩尼王樓閣。焰
356b22 光明摩尼王網。羅覆其上。無數金剛寶樓閣。
356b23 無能勝幢摩尼王網。羅覆其上。無數黑栴檀
356b24 樓閣。天曼陀羅華網。羅覆其上。

简体字

作是念已，入妙光城。

见此大城，以金、银、琉璃、玻璃、真珠、砗磲、玛瑙七宝所成，七宝深堑，七重围绕；八功德水盈满其中，底布金沙，优钵罗华、波头摩华、拘物头华、芬陀利华遍布其上；宝多罗树七重行列，七种金刚以为其垣各各围绕，所谓：师子光明金刚垣、无能超胜金刚垣、不可沮坏金刚垣、不可毁缺金刚垣、坚固无碍金刚垣、胜妙网藏金刚垣、离尘清净金刚垣，悉以无数摩尼妙宝间错庄严，种种众宝而为埤堄。其城纵广一十由旬，周回八方，面开八门，皆以七宝周遍严饰，毗琉璃宝以为其地，种种庄严甚可爱乐。

其城之内，十亿衢道，一一道间，皆有无量万亿众生于中止住。有无数阎浮檀金楼阁，毗琉璃摩尼网罗覆其上；无数银楼阁，赤真珠摩尼网罗覆其上；无数毗琉璃楼阁，妙藏摩尼网罗覆其上；无数玻璃楼阁，无垢藏摩尼王网罗覆其上；无数光照世间摩尼宝楼阁，日藏摩尼王网罗覆其上；无数帝青摩尼宝楼阁，妙光摩尼王网罗覆其上；无数众生海摩尼王楼阁，焰光明摩尼王网罗覆其上；无数金刚宝楼阁，无能胜幢摩尼王网罗覆其上；无数黑栴檀楼阁，天曼陀罗华网罗覆其上；

Having had these thoughts, he then entered the city of Suprabha where he saw that this great city was made of the seven precious things, namely gold, silver, lapis lazuli, crystal, pearls, carnelian, and emeralds. It was encircled by seven concentric deep moats made of the seven precious things that were filled with waters possessed of the eight qualities. The bottoms of the moats were carpeted with gold sand and their waters were everywhere covered with *udumbara* blossoms, *padma* blossoms, *kumuda* blossoms, and *puṇḍarīka* blossoms. The moats were surrounded by seven concentric rows of jeweled *tāla* trees, and seven kinds of vajra formed each of their perimeter walls. In particular, there was a perimeter wall made of lion light vajra, a perimeter wall made of insurmountable vajra, a perimeter wall made of indestructible vajra, a perimeter wall made of unbreachable vajra, a perimeter wall made of solid and unimpeded vajra, a perimeter wall made of supremely marvelous net treasury vajra, and a perimeter wall made of immaculate purity vajra. All of them were inlaid with adornments consisting of countless marvelous *maṇi* jewels.

It had viewing ports in its parapets made from the many different kinds of jewels. The city was in the shape of an octagon that was ten *yojanas* across. It had eight gates, one of which opened on each of its sides. They were each everywhere adorned with decorations made of the seven precious things. Its grounds were made of *vaiḍūrya* and its many different adornments were especially delightful.

Within that city, there were ten *koṭīs* of avenues and countless myriads of *koṭīs* of beings resided on each of its avenues. There were countless towers made of *jambūnada* gold with nets made of *vaiḍūrya* and *maṇi* jewels suspended overhead, countless silver towers with nets made of true red pearls and *maṇi* jewels suspended overhead, countless *vaiḍūrya* towers with nets made of marvelous-core *maṇi* jewels suspended overhead, countless crystal towers with nets made of immaculate-core *maṇi* jewels suspended overhead, countless world-illuminating *maṇi* jewel towers with nets made of solar-core sovereign *maṇi* jewels suspended overhead, countless sapphire and *maṇi* jewel towers with nets made of wondrous-light sovereign *maṇi* jewels suspended overhead, countless sea-of-beings sovereign *maṇi* jewel towers with nets made of flaming-light sovereign *maṇi* jewels suspended overhead, countless vajra jeweled towers with nets made of banner-of-invincibility sovereign *maṇi* jewels suspended overhead, countless black sandalwood towers with nets made of heavenly *māndārava* flowers suspended overhead, and countless incomparable

正體字

無數無等
356b25 香王樓閣。種種華網。羅覆其上。其城復有無
356b26 數摩尼網。無數寶鈴網。無數天香網。無數天
356b27 華網。無數寶形像網。無數寶衣帳。無數寶蓋
356b28 帳。無數寶樓閣帳。無數寶華鬘帳之所彌覆。
356b29 處處建立寶蓋幢幡。當此城中。有一樓閣。名
356c01 正法藏。阿僧祇寶。以為莊嚴。光[朋>明]赫奕。最勝
356c02 無比。眾生見者。心無厭足。彼大光王。常處其
356c03 中。爾時善財童子。於此一切珍寶妙物。乃至
356c04 男女。六塵境界。皆無愛著。但正思惟究竟之
356c05 法。一心願樂見善知識。漸次遊行。見大光王。
356c06 去於所住樓閣。不遠四衢道中。坐如意摩尼
356c07 寶蓮華藏廣大莊嚴師子之座。紺瑠璃寶。以
356c08 為其足。金繒為帳。眾寶為網。上妙天衣。以為
356c09 茵蓐。其王於上。結[1]跏趺坐。二十八種大人
356c10 之相。八十隨好。而以嚴身。如真金山光色熾
356c11 盛。如淨空日威光赫奕。如盛滿月見者清涼。
356c12 如梵天王處於梵眾。亦如大海功德法寶。無
356c13 有邊際。

简体字

无数无等香王楼阁，种种华网罗覆其上。

其城复有无数摩尼网、无数宝铃网、无数天香网、无数天华网、无数宝形像网，无数宝衣帐、无数宝盖帐、无数宝楼阁帐、无数宝华鬘帐之所弥覆，处处建立宝盖、幢、幡。

当此城中，有一楼阁，名正法藏，阿僧祇宝以为庄严，光明赫奕最胜无比，众生见者心无厌足，彼大光王常处其中。

尔时，善财童子于此一切珍宝妙物，乃至男女、六尘境界，皆无爱著，但正思惟究竟之法，一心愿乐见善知识。

渐次游行，见大光王去于所住楼阁不远四衢道中，坐如意摩尼宝莲华藏广大庄严师子之座，绀琉璃宝以为其足，金缯为帐，众宝为网，上妙天衣以为茵褥。其王于上结跏趺坐，二十八种大人之相、八十随好而以严身；如真金山，光色炽盛；如净空日，威光赫奕；如盛满月，见者清凉；如梵天王，处于梵众；亦如大海，功德法宝无有边际；

sovereign incense towers with nets made of all different kinds of flowers suspended overhead.

That city also had countless *maṇi* jewel nets, countless jeweled bell nets, countless heavenly incense nets, countless heavenly flower nets, countless nets of jeweled images, countless jeweled robe curtains, countless jeweled canopy curtains, countless jeweled tower curtains, and countless jeweled flower garland curtains spread across it. In place after place there were erected jeweled canopies, banners, and pennants.

Right in the very center of this city, there was one tower known as "Right Dharma Treasury" that was adorned with *asaṃkhyeyas* of jewels, the resplendently beautiful radiance of which was of the most incomparably excellent sort. Beings never grew weary of looking at it. That King Mahāprabha always dwelt within it.

At that time, Sudhana the Youth had become free of any affectionate attachment for any of these marvelous jeweled phenomena, the men or women, or any of the spheres of experience associated with the objects of the six senses. Rather, he only pursued right meditative reflection on the most ultimate Dharma and single-mindedly yearned to see the good spiritual guide.

He gradually traveled onward until he saw King Mahāprabha in the intersection of the four avenues, not far from the tower in which he dwelt. He was seated on an extensively adorned lotus flower dais lion throne that was made of wish-fulfilling *maṇi* jewels and which had legs made of purple lapis lazuli gems. There were banners made of gold-embroidered silks and a net made of the many kinds of jewels. It had cushions made from marvelous celestial robes on which the king sat in the lotus posture, his body adorned with twenty-eight of the major marks of a great man as well as with the eighty secondary signs. As he sat there:

He was like a mountain of gold emanating brilliantly flaming colored light;

He was like the sun in a clear sky resplendently beautiful with its awesome shining radiance;

He was like the full moon that brings clarity and coolness to all who view it;

He was like the Brahma Heaven King dwelling in the midst of his congregation of Brahma Heaven devas;

He was also like the great ocean, boundless in his possession of meritorious qualities and Dharma jewels;

正體字

亦如雪山相好樹林。以為嚴飾。亦如
356c14‖ 大雲能震法雷。啟悟群品。亦如虛空顯現種
356c15‖ 種法門星[2]象。如須彌山四色普現眾生心海。
356c16‖ 亦如寶洲種種智寶。充滿其中。於王座前。有
356c17‖ 金銀瑠璃摩尼真珠珊瑚琥珀珂貝璧玉。諸
356c18‖ 珍寶聚。衣服瓔珞。及諸飲食。無量無邊。種種
356c19‖ 充滿。復見無量百千萬億上妙寶車。百千萬
356c20‖ 億諸天[3]妓樂。百千萬億天諸妙香。百千萬
356c21‖ 億病緣湯藥。資生之具。如是一切悉皆珍好。
356c22‖ 無量乳牛。蹄角金色。無量千億端正女人上
356c23‖ 妙栴檀。以塗其體。天衣瓔珞。種種莊嚴。六十
356c24‖ 四能。靡不該練。世情禮則。悉皆善解。隨眾生
356c25‖ 心。而以給施。城邑聚落。四衢道側。悉置一切
356c26‖ 資生之具。一一道傍。皆有二十億菩薩。以
356c27‖ 此諸物。給施眾生。為欲普攝眾生故。為令眾
356c28‖ 生歡喜故。為令眾生踊躍故。為令眾生心淨
356c29‖ 故。為令眾生清涼故。為滅眾生煩惱故。

简体字

亦如雪山，相好树林以为严饰；亦如大云，能震法雷，启悟群品；亦如虚空，显现种种法门星象；如须弥山，四色普现众生心海；亦如宝洲，种种智宝充满其中。

于王座前，有金、银、琉璃、摩尼、真珠、珊瑚、琥珀、珂贝、璧玉诸珍宝聚，衣服、璎珞及诸饮食无量无边种种充满。复见无量百千万亿上妙宝车、百千万亿诸天妓乐、百千万亿天诸妙香、百千万亿病缘汤药资生之具，如是一切悉皆珍好。无量乳牛，蹄角金色；无量千亿端正女人，上妙栴檀以涂其体，天衣、璎珞种种庄严，六十四能靡不该练，世情礼则悉皆善解，随众生心而以给施。

城邑、聚落、四衢道侧，悉置一切资生之具。一一道傍皆有二十亿菩萨，以此诸物给施众生，为欲普摄众生故，为令众生欢喜故，为令众生踊跃故，为令众生心净故，为令众生清凉故，为灭众生烦恼故，

He was also like the Himalaya Mountains, adorned with his forest of major marks and secondary signs;
He was also like an immense cloud in his ability to awaken the many kinds of beings with the quaking of his Dharma thunder;
He was also like the realm of empty space in his revealing the many different constellations of Dharma gateways;
He was like Mount Sumeru's fourfold reflection in that he was everywhere reflected in the mind seas of all beings; and
He was also like an isle of jewels due to his being filled with the many different kinds of wisdom jewels.

In front of the king's throne there were heaps of every kind of precious jewel, including gold, silver, lapis lazuli, *maṇi* jewels, pearls, coral, amber, quartz, cowries, and jade, these as well as robes, necklaces, food and drink, all of these in measureless and boundless abundance in their many different varieties.

He also saw countless hundreds of thousands of myriads of *koṭīs* of marvelous jeweled carriages, heard hundreds of thousands of myriads of *koṭīs* of all kinds of heavenly music being played, saw hundreds of thousands of myriads of *koṭīs* of all kinds of exquisite celestial incense, and saw hundreds of thousands of myriads of *koṭīs* of medicinal decoctions and life-sustaining necessities. All of these kinds of things such as these were of the rarest and finest varieties.

There were countless milk cows with gold-colored hooves and horns, countless thousands of *koṭīs* of beautiful women whose bodies had been made fragrant with the application of superior sandalwood perfumes, who were dressed in celestial robes, jewel necklaces, and various other kinds of adornments, who had none of the sixty-four types of abilities in which they were not thoroughly skilled, who well understood the protocols of worldly sentiments and thus provided for the needs of beings in ways which suited their intentions.

Alongside the intersection of the four avenues of the city and its surrounding towns there were arrayed all of the types of life-sustaining provisions, and alongside every one of those roads there were twenty *koṭīs* of bodhisattvas bestowing all these things on the beings there, doing so:

Wishing to everywhere attract and sustain beings;
Wishing to cause beings to be delighted;
Wishing to cause beings to feel joyous exultation;
Wishing to cause beings' minds to become purified;
Wishing to cause beings to feel clear and cool;
Wishing to extinguish beings' afflictions;

正體字

為
357a01‖ 令眾生知一切義理故。為令眾生入一切智
357a02‖ 道故。為令眾生捨怨敵心故。為令眾生離身
357a03‖ 語惡故。為令眾生拔諸邪見故。為令眾生淨
357a04‖ 諸業道故。時善財童子。五體投地。頂禮其足。
357a05‖ 恭敬右遶。經無量匝。合掌而住。白言。聖者。
357a06‖ 我已先發阿耨多羅三藐三菩提心。而未知
357a07‖ 菩薩云何學菩薩行。云何修菩薩道。我聞聖
357a08‖ 者。善能誘誨。願為我說。時王告言。善男子。
357a09‖ 我淨修菩薩大慈幢行。我滿足菩薩大慈幢
357a10‖ 行。善男子。我於無量百千萬億。乃至不可
357a11‖ 說不可說佛所。問難此法。思惟觀察。修習莊
357a12‖ 嚴。善男子。我以此法為王。以此法教勅。以此
357a13‖ 法攝受。以此法隨逐世間。以此法引導眾生。
357a14‖ 以此法令眾生修行。以此法令眾生趣入。以
357a15‖ 此法與眾生方便。以此法令眾生熏習。以此
357a16‖ 法令眾生起行。

简体字

为令众生知一切义理故，为令众生入一切智道故，为令众生舍冤敌心故，为令众生离身、语恶故，为令众生拔诸邪见故，为令众生净诸业道故。

时，善财童子五体投地，顶礼其足，恭敬右绕，经无量匝，合掌而住，白言：“圣者，我已先发阿耨多罗三藐三菩提心，而未知菩萨云何学菩萨行？云何修菩萨道？我闻圣者善能诱诲，愿为我说！”

时，王告言：“善男子，我净修菩萨大慈幢行，我满足菩萨大慈幢行。善男子，我于无量百千万亿乃至不可说不可说佛所，问难此法，思惟观察，修习庄严。

“善男子，我以此法为王，以此法教敕，以此法摄受，以此法随逐世间，以此法引导众生，以此法令众生修行，以此法令众生趣入，以此法与众生方便，以此法令众生熏习，以此法令众生起行，

Wishing to enable beings to understand all meaningful principles;
Wishing to induce beings to enter the path to all-knowledge;
Wishing to induce beings to relinquish hostile thoughts;
Wishing to induce beings to abandon physical and verbal misconduct;
Wishing to cause beings to rid themselves of all kinds of wrong views; and
Wishing to cause beings to purify their courses of karmic action.

Sudhana the Youth then prostrated himself in reverence at the feet of the king and respectfully circumambulated him countless times to his right. He then stood before him with palms pressed together and addressed him, saying:

O Ārya, I am one who has already resolved to attain *anuttara-samyak-saṃbodhi*. Still, I do not yet know how the bodhisattva should train in the bodhisattva practices or how he should cultivate the bodhisattva path. I have heard that the Ārya is well able to offer guidance and instruction in this. Please speak about these matters for my sake."

The king then spoke to him, saying:

Son of Good Family, I have purified the bodhisattva practice of the banner of great kindness and I have fulfilled the bodhisattva practice of the banner of great kindness.

Son of Good Family, I have posed difficult questions on this dharma to countless hundreds of thousands of myriads of *koṭīs* of buddhas, even to as many as an ineffable-ineffable number of buddhas, and I have also reflected on it, contemplated it, and cultivated its adornment.

Son of Good Family:

I use this dharma in ruling as a king;
I use this dharma in providing instruction and issuing edicts;
I use this dharma in attracting and assisting beings;
I use this dharma in adapting to the world;
I use this dharma in guiding beings;
I use this dharma in causing beings to cultivate;
I use this dharma in enabling beings to progress along and enter the path;
I use this dharma to provide beings with skillful means;
I use this dharma to enable beings to become imbued with the practices;
I use this dharma to enable beings to develop the practices;

正體字

以此法令眾生安住思惟諸
357a17 ‖ 法自性。以此法令眾生安住慈心。以慈為主。
357a18 ‖ 具足慈力。如是令住利益心。安樂心。哀愍
357a19 ‖ 心。攝受心。守護眾生不捨離心。拔眾生苦無
357a20 ‖ 休息心。我以此法。令一切眾生。畢竟快樂。恒
357a21 ‖ 自悅豫。身無諸苦。心得清涼。斷生死愛。樂正
357a22 ‖ 法樂。滌煩惱垢。破惡業障。絕生死流。入真法
357a23 ‖ 海。斷諸有趣。求一切智。淨諸心海。生不壞
357a24 ‖ 信。善男子。我已住此大慈幢行。能以正法。教
357a25 ‖ 化世間。善男子。我國土中。一切眾生。皆於我
357a26 ‖ 所。無有恐怖。善男子。若有眾生。貧窮困乏。
357a27 ‖ 來至我所。而有求索。我開庫藏。恣其所取。而
357a28 ‖ 語之言。莫造諸惡。莫害眾生。莫起諸見。莫生
357a29 ‖ 執著。汝等貧乏。若有所須。當來我所。及四衢
357b01 ‖ 道。一切諸物。種種具足。隨意而取。勿生疑
357b02 ‖ 難。善男子。此妙光城。所住眾生。皆是菩薩發
357b03 ‖ 大乘意。隨心所欲。所見不同。或見此城其量
357b04 ‖ 狹小。或見此城其量廣大。

简体字

以此法令众生安住思惟诸法自性，以此法令众生安住慈心，以慈为主，具足慈力；如是，令住利益心、安乐心、哀愍心、摄受心、守护众生不舍离心、拔众生苦无休息心。我以此法令一切众生毕竟快乐，恒自悦豫，身无诸苦，心得清凉，断生死爱，乐正法乐，涤烦恼垢，破恶业障，绝生死流，入真法海，断诸有趣，求一切智，净诸心海，生不坏信。善男子，我已住此大慈幢行，能以正法教化世间。

“善男子，我国土中一切众生，皆于我所无有恐怖。善男子，若有众生贫穷困乏，来至我所而有求索。我开库藏，恣其所取，而语之言：‘莫造诸恶，莫害众生，莫起诸见，莫生执著。汝等贫乏，若有所须，当来我所及四衢道，一切诸物种种具足，随意而取勿生疑难。’

“善男子，此妙光城所住众生，皆是菩萨发大乘意，随心所欲，所见不同，或见此城其量狭小，或见此城其量广大；

I use this dharma to establish beings in meditative reflection on the nature of all dharmas;

I use this dharma to establish beings in the mind of kindness; and

I take kindness as primary in perfecting the power of kindness.

In this way, I get them to abide in the mind motivated to benefit others, in the mind that bestows happiness, in the mind that is motivated by deep sympathy, in the mind inclined to attract and support others, in the mind inclined to protect beings and never abandon them, and in the mind ceaselessly determined to extricate beings from their sufferings.

I use this dharma to induce all beings to attain the most ultimate sort of happiness, to constantly abide in blissful contentment, to remain free of all physical sufferings, to acquire clarity and coolness of mind, to cut off *saṃsāra's* cravings, to delight in the happiness of right Dharma, to rinse away the filth of the afflictions, to demolish the obstacles created by evil karmic deeds, to interrupt the stream of *saṃsāra,* to enter the ocean of true Dharma, to sever their continuance in the rebirth destinies of the realms of existence, to strive for the attainment of all-knowledge, to purify the ocean of thoughts, and to develop indestructible faith.

Son of Good Family, having already come to dwell in this practice of the banner of great kindness, I am able to use right Dharma to teach and transform the world.

Son of Good Family, all beings in this land of mine are free of any fear of me. Son of Good Family, if there are any beings who are poor, destitute, beset with difficulties, or otherwise in need who come to me with a request for anything they might seek, I open up the storehouses and allow them to freely take whatever they want whereupon I also tell them this: "You must not engage in any sort of evil, you must not injure any being, you must not adopt any of the wrong views, and you must not become attached to anything. You who are so poor and destitute—If you have anything you need, then you should come to me or to the crossroads where all kinds of things are abundantly available for you to take as you will. Have no doubts with regard to any of this."

Son of Good Family, the beings dwelling in this city of Suprabha are all bodhisattvas who have aroused the Great Vehicle practitioner's resolve and who, in accordance with their inclinations, see it in different ways:

They may see this city as but narrow and small or they may instead see this city as immensely vast;

正體字

或見土沙以為其
357b05║ 地。或見眾寶而以莊嚴。或見聚土以為垣牆。
357b06║ 或見寶牆周匝圍遶。或見其地多諸瓦石。高
357b07║ 下不平。或見無量大摩尼寶。間錯莊嚴。平
357b08║ 坦如掌。或見屋宅土木所成。或見殿堂及諸
357b09║ 樓閣。階墀窓闥。軒檻戶牖。如是一切無非妙
357b10║ 寶。善男子。若有眾生。其心清淨。曾種善根。
357b11║ 供養諸佛。發心趣向一切智道。以一切智。為
357b12║ 究竟處。及我昔時。修菩薩行。曾所攝受。則見
357b13║ 此城眾寶嚴淨。餘皆見穢。善男子。此國土中
357b14║ 一切眾生。五濁世時。樂作諸惡。我心哀愍。而
357b15║ 欲救護。入於菩薩大慈為首隨順世間三昧
357b16║ 之門。入此三昧時。彼諸眾生。所有怖畏心。惱
357b17║ 害心。怨敵心。諍論心。如是諸心。悉自消滅。
357b18║ 何以故。入於菩薩大慈為首順世三昧。法如
357b19║ 是故。善男子。且待須臾。自當現見。時大光
357b20║ 王。即入此定。其城內外。六種震動。諸寶地寶
357b21║ 牆。寶堂寶殿。臺觀樓閣。階砌戶牖。如是一切
357b22║ 咸出妙音。悉向於王。曲躬敬禮。妙光城內。所
357b23║ 有居人。靡不同時。歡喜踊躍。

简体字

或见土沙以为其地，或见众宝而以庄严；或见聚土以为垣墙，或见宝墙周匝围绕；或见其地多诸瓦石高下不平，或见无量大摩尼宝间错庄严平坦如掌；或见屋宅土木所成，或见殿堂及诸楼阁、阶墀、窗闼、轩槛、户牖——如是一切无非妙宝。

“善男子，若有众生其心清净，曾种善根供养诸佛，发心趣向一切智道，以一切智为究竟处，及我昔时修菩萨行曾所摄受，则见此城众宝严净；余皆见秽。

“善男子，此国土中一切众生，五浊世时乐作诸恶。我心哀愍而欲救护，入于菩萨大慈为首随顺世间三昧之门。入此三昧时，彼诸众生所有怖畏心、恼害心、冤敌心、诤论心，如是诸心，悉自消灭。何以故？入于菩萨大慈为首顺世三昧，法如是故。善男子，且待须臾，自当现见。”

时，大光王即入此定。其城内外六种震动，诸宝地、宝墙、宝堂、宝殿、台观、楼阁、阶砌、户牖，如是一切咸出妙音，悉向于王曲躬敬礼。妙光城内所有居人，靡不同时欢喜踊跃，

They may see its grounds as composed of dirt and sand or they may instead see it as adorned with many kinds of jewels;
They may see the perimeter walls as made of amassed dirt or they may instead see encircling walls made of jewels;
They may see its soils as containing an abundance of tiles and stones, as uneven with elevations and depressions, or they may instead see it to be as level as one's palm and adorned with inlaid patterns of countless immense *maṇi* jewels; and
They may see its buildings and homes as made of soil and wood or may instead see it as having halls and all kinds of towers with stairs, portholes, gates, railed balconies, doors, and windows, none of which are not composed of marvelous jewels.

Son of Good Family, if there are any beings whose minds are pure, who have planted roots of goodness, who have made offerings to buddhas, who have resolved to progress along the path to all-knowledge, who have taken all-knowledge as the ultimate station, and who were attracted and assisted by me in the past when I was cultivating the bodhisattva practices, then they will see this city as consisting of the many kinds of jewels and as adorned and pure. Anyone else will see it as dirty.

Son of Good Family, all the beings in this land, living in the world in an age beset by the five turbidities,[109] delight in engaging in all kinds of evil deeds. Feeling deep pity for them and wishing to rescue them, I enter this bodhisattva's samādhi gateway known as "taking great kindness as foremost in adapting to the world." When I enter this samādhi, all of those beings' fearful thoughts, tormenting and injurious thoughts, hostile thoughts, and disputatious thoughts—all such thoughts as these then naturally disappear.

And why does this occur? It is in the very nature of this dharma that this occurs when one enters this bodhisattva's samādhi known as "taking great kindness as foremost in adapting to the world."

Son of Good Family, wait a moment. You should see this directly for yourself.

Then King Mahāprabha immediately entered this meditative absorption, whereupon his city, both within and without, quaked and shook in six ways and all the jeweled grounds, jeweled walls, jeweled halls, jeweled palaces, viewing terraces, towers, steps, doors, and windows then emanated marvelous sounds as all of them leaned toward the king, bending themselves in reverential respect. Then, of all the people living there within the city of Suprabha, there were none who did not simultaneously become filled with joyous delight and exultation.

正體字

俱向王所。舉身
357b24║ 投地。村營城邑。一切人眾。咸來見王。歡喜敬
357b25║ 禮。近王所住。鳥獸之屬。互相瞻視。起慈悲
357b26║ 心。咸向王前。恭敬禮拜。一切山原。及諸草
357b27║ 樹。莫不迴轉向王敬禮。陂池泉井。及以河海。
357b28║ 悉皆騰溢。流注王前。十千龍王。起大香雲。激
357b29║ 電震雷。注微細雨。有十千天王。所謂忉利天
357c01║ 王。夜摩天王。兜率陀天王。善變化天王。他
357c02║ 化自在天王。如是等而為上首。於虛空中。
357c03║ 作眾[*]妓樂。無數天女。歌詠讚歎。雨無數華
357c04║ 雲。無數香雲。無數寶鬘雲。無數寶衣雲。無
357c05║ 數寶蓋雲。無數寶幢雲。無數寶幡雲。於虛
357c06║ 空中。而為莊嚴。供養其王。伊羅婆拏大象
357c07║ 王。以自在力。於虛空中。敷布無數大寶蓮華。
357c08║ 垂無數寶瓔珞。無數寶繒帶。無數寶鬘。無
357c09║ 數寶嚴具。無數寶華。無數寶香。種種奇妙。以
357c10║ 為嚴飾。無數采女。種種歌讚。閻浮提內。復有
357c11║ 無量百千萬億諸羅刹王。諸夜叉王鳩槃[*]荼
357c12║ 王。毘舍闍王。或住大海。或居陸地。飲血噉
357c13║ 肉。殘害眾生。皆起慈心。願行利益。明識後
357c14║ 世。

简体字

俱向王所举身投地。村营、城邑一切人众，咸来见王，欢喜敬礼。

近王所住，鸟兽之属，互相瞻视，起慈悲心，咸向王前恭敬礼拜。一切山原及诸草树，莫不回转向王敬礼。陂池、泉井及以河海，悉皆腾溢，流注王前。十千龙王起大香云，激电震雷，注微细雨。有十千天王，所谓：忉利天王、夜摩天王、兜率陀天王、善变化天王、他化自在天王，如是等而为上首，于虚空中作众妓乐。无数天女歌咏赞叹，雨无数华云、无数香云、无数宝鬘云、无数宝衣云、无数宝盖云、无数宝幢云、无数宝幡云，于虚空中而为庄严，供养其王。伊罗婆拏大象王，以自在力，于虚空中敷布无数大宝莲华，垂无数宝璎珞、无数宝缯带、无数宝鬘、无数宝严具、无数宝华、无数宝香，种种奇妙以为严饰，无数采女种种歌赞。

阎浮提内复有无量百千万亿诸罗刹王、诸夜叉王、鸠槃荼王、毗舍阇王，或住大海，或居陆地，饮血啖肉，残害众生；皆起慈心，愿行利益，明识后世，

They all then faced the king and bowed down in full reverential prostration. The entire population of the villages, encampments, the city, and its surrounding areas all then came to see the king and bowed to him in joyful reverential respect. Close to the king's residence, even the birds and animals gazed at each other with thoughts of kindness and compassion and then went directly before the king and bowed to him in reverential respect.

Of all the mountains and plateaus as well as the grasses and trees, there were none that did not then turn in the direction of the king and incline themselves in reverential respect. The ponds, springs, and wells as well as the rivers and seas all gushed forth leaping waterspouts and sent waters flowing before the king. A myriad dragon kings produced immense incense clouds that sent out lightning bolts and quaking thunder and then sprinkled down a fine misty rain. Ten thousand deva kings headed by the Trāyastriṃśa Heaven King, the Yāma Heaven King, the Tuṣita Heaven King, the Enjoyment of Transformations Heaven King, the Paranirmita Vaśavartin Heaven King, and other such deva kings appeared in the sky and played many different kinds of music. Countless heavenly maidens sang praises and rained down countless flower clouds, countless incense clouds, countless jeweled garland clouds, countless jeweled robe clouds, countless jeweled canopy clouds, countless jeweled banner clouds, and countless jeweled pennant clouds which appeared in space as adornments and offerings to the king.

The great elephant king, Airāvaṇa, used his masterful spiritual powers to spread out in space countless immense jeweled lotus flowers that trailed down countless jeweled necklaces, countless jeweled silken sashes, countless jeweled garlands, countless jeweled adornments, countless jeweled flowers, countless types of precious incense, and all different kinds of other extraordinarily marvelous phenomena such as these which he presented as adornments. There were countless palace maidens who sang all different kinds of praise songs.

On that continent of Jambudvīpa, there were also countless hundreds of thousands of myriads of *koṭīs* of *rākṣasa* kings, *yakṣa* kings, *kumbhāṇḍa* kings, and *piśāca* kings, some of whom dwelt in the great oceans and some of whom dwelt on land, all of whom drank blood, ate flesh, or inflicted cruel injuries on the beings there. All of these then produced thoughts of kindness, vowed to practice whatever is beneficial, clearly recognized what would unfold in later lives, refrained

正體字

不造諸惡。恭敬合掌。頂禮於王。如閻浮
357c15‖ 提。餘三天下。乃至三千大千世界。乃至十方
357c16‖ 百千萬億那由他世界中。所有一切毒惡眾
357c17‖ 生。悉亦如是。時大光王。從三昧起。告善財
357c18‖ 言。善男子。我唯知此菩薩大慈為首隨順世
357c19‖ 間三昧門。如諸菩薩摩訶薩。為高蓋。慈心普
357c20‖ 蔭諸眾生故。為修行。下中上行悉等行故。為
357c21‖ 大地。能以慈心任持一切諸眾生故。為滿月。
357c22‖ 福德光明於世間中平等現故。為淨日。以智
357c23‖ 光明照耀一切所知境故。為明燈。能破一切
357c24‖ 眾生心中諸黑闇故。為水清珠。能清一切眾
357c25‖ 生心中諂誑濁故。為如意寶。悉能滿足一切
357c26‖ 眾生心所願故。為大風。速令眾生修習三昧
357c27‖ 入一切智大城中故。而我云何能知其行能
357c28‖ 說其德。能稱量彼福德大山。能瞻仰彼功德
357c29‖ 眾星。能觀察彼大願風輪。能趣入彼甚深法
358a01‖ 門。能顯示彼莊嚴大海。

简体字

不造诸恶；恭敬合掌，顶礼于王。如阎浮提，余三天下，乃至三千大千世界，乃至十方百千万亿那由他世界中，所有一切毒恶众生悉亦如是。

时，大光王从三昧起，告善财言："善男子，我唯知此菩萨大慈为首随顺世间三昧门。如诸菩萨摩诃萨为高盖，慈心普荫诸众生故；为修行，下、中、上行悉等行故；为大地，能以慈心任持一切诸众生故；为满月，福德光明于世间中平等现故；为净日，以智光明照耀一切所知境故；为明灯，能破一切众生心中诸黑暗故；为水清珠，能清一切众生心中谄诳浊故；为如意宝，悉能满足一切众生心所愿故；为大风，速令众生修习三昧入一切智大城中故。而我云何能知其行，能说其德，能称量彼福德大山，能瞻仰彼功德众星，能观察彼大愿风轮，能趣入彼甚深法门，能显示彼庄严大海，

from committing any kinds of evil deeds, respectfully pressed their palms together, and then bowed down in reverence to the king.

And just as this was so on the continent of Jambudvīpa, so too was this so on the other three continents as well as in all the worlds of the great trichiliocosm, extending even to the hundreds of thousands of myriads of *koṭīs* of *nayutas* of worlds throughout the ten directions where all the toxic evil beings were transformed in the very same way.

King Mahāprabha then emerged from samādhi and told Sudhana:

Son of Good Family, I know only this bodhisattva's samādhi gateway that takes the great kindness as foremost in adapting to the world. As for the bodhisattva-mahāsattvas:

Who serve as lofty canopies because their minds of kindness everywhere shade all beings;

Who, in carrying out their cultivation, practice impartiality toward those whose practice is inferior, middling, or superior;

Who serve as the great earth because they are able to use the mind of kindness to support all beings;

Who serve as full moons because the light of their merit equally illuminates everyone in the world;

Who serve as suns shining in a clear sky because the dazzling radiance of their wisdom illuminates the realm of whatever can be known;

Who serve as bright lamps because they are able to dispel the darkness in all beings' minds;

Who serve as water-clarifying jewels because they are able to clarify the turbidities of flattery and deviousness in all beings' minds;

Who serve as wish-fulfilling jewels because they are able to fulfill the wishes in all beings' minds; and

Who serve as great winds because they cause beings to swiftly cultivate samādhi and enter the great city of all-knowledge—

How could I know of their practices;

How could I speak about their virtues;

How could I weigh their immense mountains of merit;

How could I gaze with admiration on their many constellations of meritorious qualities;

How could I contemplate the wind sphere of their great vows;

How could I progress into their extremely profound Dharma gateways;

How could I reveal their immense oceans of adornments;

正體字

能闡明彼普賢行門。
358a02║ 能開示彼諸三昧窟。能讚歎彼大慈悲雲。善
358a03║ 男子。於此南方。有一王都。名曰安住。有優婆
358a04║ 夷。名曰不動。汝詣彼問。菩薩云何學菩薩行。
358a05║ 修菩薩道。時善財童子。頂禮王足。遶無數匝。
358a06║ 殷懃瞻仰。辭退而去
358a07║ 爾時善財童子。出妙光城。遊行道路。正念思
358a08║ 惟。大光王教。憶念菩薩大慈幢行門。思惟菩
358a09║ 薩隨順世間三昧光明門。增長彼不思議願
358a10║ 福德自在力。堅固彼不思議成熟眾生智。觀
358a11║ 察彼不思議不共受用大威德。憶念彼不思
358a12║ 議差別相。思惟彼不思議清淨眷屬。思惟彼
358a13║ 不思議所作業。生歡喜心。生淨信心。生猛利
358a14║ 心。生欣悅心。生踊躍心。生慶幸心。生無濁
358a15║ 心。生清淨心。生堅固心。生廣大心。生無盡
358a16║ 心。如是思惟。悲泣流淚。念善知識。實為希
358a17║ 有。出生一切諸功德處。出生一切諸菩薩行。

简体字

能阐明彼普贤行门，能开示彼诸三昧窟，能赞叹彼大慈悲云？

“善男子，于此南方，有一王都，名曰安住；有优婆夷，名曰不动。汝诣彼问：菩萨云何学菩萨行、修菩萨道？”

时，善财童子顶礼王足，绕无数匝，殷勤瞻仰，辞退而去。

尔时，善财童子出妙光城，游行道路，正念思惟大光王教，忆念菩萨大慈幢行门，思惟菩萨随顺世间三昧光明门，增长彼不思议愿福德自在力，坚固彼不思议成熟众生智，观察彼不思议不共受用大威德，忆念彼不思议差别相，思惟彼不思议清净眷属，思惟彼不思议所作业；生欢喜心，生净信心，生猛利心，生欣悦心，生踊跃心，生庆幸心，生无浊心，生清净心，生坚固心，生广大心，生无尽心。如是思惟，悲泣流泪，念善知识实为希有，出生一切诸功德处，出生一切诸菩萨行，

How could I explicate their gateways of Samantabhadra's practices;
How could I open up and reveal the caves of all of their samādhis; and
How could I praise their clouds of the great kindness and great compassion?

Son of Good Family, south of here there is a royal capital known as Sthirā or "Peaceful Abiding" in which there is an *upāsikā* named Acalā. You should go there, pay your respects, and ask her, "How should a bodhisattva train in the bodhisattva practices and how should he cultivate the bodhisattva path?"

Sudhana the Youth then bowed down in reverence at the feet of the king and circumambulated him countless times as he gazed up at him in attentive admiration. He then respectfully withdrew and departed.

19 – Acalā

At that time, Sudhana the Youth then left that city of Suprabha and traveled on along the road as he:

Mindfully reflected on King Mahāprabha's teaching;
Recalled the bodhisattvas' practice gateway of the banner of great kindness;
Reflected on the radiant gateway of the bodhisattvas' adaptation to the world samādhi;
Increased in their inconceivable power of sovereign mastery of vows and merit;
Strengthened their inconceivable knowledge of ripening beings;
Contemplated their inconceivable exclusive experiences and great awesome virtue;
Recalled their inconceivable different signs;
Reflected on their inconceivable pure retinues; and
Reflected on the inconceivable deeds they have done.

He then developed a happy mind, a mind of pure faith, an intensely sharp mind, a joyful mind, an exultant mind, a rejoicing mind, a mind free of turbidity, a pure mind, a solid mind, a vast mind, and an inexhaustible mind. Having reflected in ways such as these, he was moved to tears of sadness. He then brought to mind how truly rare it is to encounter good spiritual guides and how it is that:

They produce all the bases of the meritorious qualities;[110]
They produce all the bodhisattva practices;

正體字

358a18║ 出生一切菩薩淨念。出生一切陀羅尼輪。出
358a19║ 生一切三昧光明。出生一切諸佛知見。普雨
358a20║ 一切諸佛法雨。顯示一切菩薩願門。出生難
358a21║ 思智慧光明。增長一切菩薩根[1]芽。又作是
358a22║ 念。善知識者。能普救護一切惡道。能普演說
358a23║ 諸平等法。能普顯示諸夷險道。能普開闡大
358a24║ 乘奧義。能普勸發普賢諸行。能普引到一切
358a25║ 智城。能普令入法界大海。能普令見三世法
358a26║ 海。能普授與眾聖道場。能普增長一切白法。
358a27║ 善財童子。如是悲哀。思念之時。彼常隨逐。覺
358a28║ 悟菩薩。如來使天。於虛空中。而告之言。善男
358a29║ 子。其有修行善知識教。諸佛世尊。悉皆歡
358b01║ 喜。其有隨順善知識語。則得近於一切智地。
358b02║ 其有能於善知識語無疑惑者。則常值遇一
358b03║ 切善友。

简体字

出生一切菩萨净念，出生一切陀罗尼轮，出生一切三昧光明，出生一切诸佛知见，普雨一切诸佛法雨，显示一切菩萨愿门，出生难思智慧光明，增长一切菩萨根芽。又作是念："善知识者，能普救护一切恶道，能普演说诸平等法，能普显示诸夷险道，能普开阐大乘奥义，能普劝发普贤诸行，能普引到一切智城，能普令入法界大海，能普令见三世法海，能普授与众圣道场，能普增长一切白法。"

善财童子如是悲哀思念之时，彼常随逐觉悟菩萨、如来使天，于虚空中而告之言："善男子，其有修行善知识教，诸佛世尊悉皆欢喜；其有随顺善知识语，则得近于一切智地；其有能于善知识语无疑惑者，则常值遇一切善友；

They produce all bodhisattvas' pure thoughts;
They produce the sphere of all *dhāraṇīs;*
They produce the light of all samādhis;
They produce the knowledge and vision of all buddhas;
They everywhere rain down the Dharma rain of all buddhas;
They reveal the gateway of the vows of all bodhisattvas;
They produce the inconceivable light of wisdom; and
They increase the sprouting of all bodhisattvas' faculties.

He also had this thought:

As for the good spiritual guides:

They are able to everywhere rescue one from all the wretched destinies;
They are able to everywhere expound on the dharma of equality;
They are able to everywhere reveal which paths are smooth and which paths are dangerous;
They are able to everywhere elucidate the abstruse meaning of the Great Vehicle;
They are able to everywhere encourage beginning to take up Samantabhadra's practices;
They are able to everywhere guide one to the city of all-knowledge;
They are able to everywhere enable beings to enter the great ocean of the Dharma realm;
They are able to everywhere enable one to see the ocean of Dharma of the three periods of time;
They are able to everywhere introduce one to the sites of enlightenment of the many *āryas;* and
They are able to everywhere bring about the growth of all the white dharmas of pristine purity.

Just when Sudhana the Youth was reflecting in these ways with such deep sadness, the Tathāgata's emissary devas who always follow along and awaken bodhisattvas then spoke to Sudhana from up in the sky, telling him:

Son of Good Family:

Whoever cultivates in accordance with the good spiritual guide's instructions delights all the buddhas, the *bhagavats;*
Whoever complies with the instructions of the good spiritual guide is then able to draw near to the ground of all-knowledge;
Whoever is able to remain free of doubts regarding the instructions of the good spiritual guide then becomes forever bound to encounter all good spiritual friends; and

正體字

其有發心願常不離善知識者。則得
358b04║ 具足一切義利。善男子。汝可往詣安住王都。
358b05║ 即當得見不動優婆夷大善知識。時善財童
358b06║ 子。從彼三昧智光明起。漸次遊行。至安住
358b07║ 城。周遍推求不動優婆夷。今在何所。無量人
358b08║ 眾。咸告之言。善男子。不動優婆夷。身是童女
358b09║ 在其家內。父母守護。與自親屬無量人眾。演
358b10║ 說妙法。善財童子。聞是語已。其心歡喜。如見
358b11║ 父母。即詣不動優婆夷舍。入其宅內。見彼堂
358b12║ 宇。金色光明。普皆照[2]耀遇斯光者。身意清
358b13║ 涼。善財童子。光明觸身。即時獲得五百三昧
358b14║ 門。所謂了一切希有相三昧門。入寂靜三昧
358b15║ 門。遠離一切世間三昧門。普眼捨得三昧門。
358b16║ 如來藏三昧門。得如是等五百三昧門。以此
358b17║ 三昧門故。身心柔軟。如七日胎。又聞妙香。非
358b18║ 諸天龍乾闥婆等。人與非人之所能有。善財
358b19║ 童子。前詣其所。恭敬合掌。一心觀察。見其形
358b20║ 色。端正殊妙。十方世界一切女人。無有能及。
358b21║ 況其過者。唯除如來及以一切灌頂菩薩。口
358b22║ 出妙香。宮殿莊嚴。并其眷屬。悉無與等。況復
358b23║ 過者。

简体字

其有发心愿常不离善知识者，则得具足一切义利。善男子，汝可往诣安住王都，即当得见不动优婆夷大善知识。”

时，善财童子从彼三昧智光明起，渐次游行，至安住城，周遍推求不动优婆夷今在何所？无量人众咸告之言：“善男子，不动优婆夷身是童女，在其家内，父母守护，与自亲属无量人众演说妙法。”善财童子闻是语已，其心欢喜，如见父母，即诣不动优婆夷舍。

入其宅内，见彼堂宇，金色光明普皆照耀，遇斯光者身意清凉。善财童子光明触身，即时获得五百三昧门，所谓：了一切希有相三昧门、入寂静三昧门、远离一切世间三昧门、普眼舍得三昧门、如来藏三昧门，得如是等五百三昧门；以此三昧门故，身心柔软，如七日胎。又闻妙香，非诸天、龙、乾闼婆等人与非人之所能有。

善财童子前诣其所，恭敬合掌，一心观察，见其形色端正殊妙，十方世界一切女人无有能及，况其过者？唯除如来及以一切灌顶菩萨。口出妙香，宫殿庄严，并其眷属悉无与等，况复过者？

Whoever vows to never abandon the good spiritual guide is then able to completely fulfill every form of meaningful benefit.

Son of Good Family, you may continue on to the royal capital of Sthirā or "Peaceful Abiding" where you should then go to see the *upāsikā* Acalā, a great good spiritual guide.

Sudhana the Youth then arose from his wisdom light samādhi and gradually traveled onward until he reached the city of Sthirā where he searched about everywhere, looking for the present location of Upāsikā Acalā. Countless people there all told him, "Son of Good Family, Upāsikā Acalā is a young maiden living at home under the protection of her father and mother, together with a group of countless relatives. It is there that she expounds on the sublime Dharma."

On hearing this, Sudhana the Youth was as filled with joy as one would be on seeing his own parents. He immediately went to the home of Upāsikā Acalā where, having entered her household, he saw that their main hall everywhere emanated dazzling golden light. Whoever encountered this light felt clarity and coolness in body and mind. When that light touched Sudhana the Youth, he immediately acquired five hundred samādhi gateways, in particular:

The understanding of all rare signs samādhi gateway;
The penetration of quiescence samādhi gateway;
The renunciation of all worlds samādhi gateway;
The samādhi gateway acquired through the universal eye's equanimity; and
The *tathāgatagarbha* samādhi gateway.

He acquired five hundred samādhi gateways such as these. Because of these samādhi gateways, his body and mind became as supple and soft as a seven-day-old embryo and he also then smelled a marvelous fragrance that not even any sort of deva, dragon, *gandharva*, human, or nonhuman would ever be able to possess.

Sudhana the Youth then went before her, paid his respects, respectfully pressed his palms together, and single-mindedly contemplated her. He then saw that, physically, she possessed such extraordinary and marvelously beauty that no woman in any of the worlds of the ten directions could ever match it, how much the less might they ever surpass it.

The marvelous fragrance issuing from her mouth as well as the adornments of her palace and retinue were such that, with the exception of a *tathāgata* or the bodhisattvas who have received the crown-anointing consecration, they could never even be equaled by anyone, how much less could they be surpassed.

正體字

十方世界。一切眾生。無有於此優婆夷
358b24║ 所。起染著心。若得暫見。所有煩惱。悉自[3]消
358b25║ 滅。譬如百萬大梵天王。決定不生欲界煩惱。
358b26║ 其有見此優婆夷者。所有煩惱應知亦然。十
358b27║ 方眾生。觀此女人。皆無厭足。唯除具足大智
358b28║ 慧者。爾時善財童子。曲躬合掌。正念觀察。見
358b29║ 此女人。其身自在。不可思議。色相顏容。世無
358c01║ 與等。光明洞徹。物無能障。普為眾生。而作利
358c02║ 益。其身毛孔。恒出妙香。眷屬無邊。宮殿第
358c03║ 一。功德深廣。莫知涯際。心生歡喜。以頌讚曰
358c04║ 守護清淨戒　修行廣大忍
358c05║ 精進不退轉　光明照世間
358c06║ 爾時善財童子。說此頌已。白言。聖者。我已先
358c07║ 發阿耨多羅三藐三菩提心。而未知菩薩云
358c08║ 何學菩薩行。云何修菩薩道。我聞聖者。善能
358c09║ 誘誨。願為我說。時不動優婆夷。以菩薩柔軟
358c10║ 語悅意語。慰諭善財。而告之言。

简体字

十方世界一切众生，无有于此优婆夷所起染著心；若得暂见，所有烦恼悉自消灭。譬如百万大梵天王，决定不生欲界烦恼；其有见此优婆夷者，所有烦恼应知亦然。十方众生观此女人皆无厌足，唯除具足大智慧者。

尔时，善财童子曲躬合掌，正念观察，见此女人，其身自在不可思议，色相颜容世无与等，光明洞彻物无能障，普为众生而作利益，其身毛孔恒出妙香，眷属无边，宫殿第一，功德深广莫知涯际；心生欢喜，以颂赞曰：

“守护清净戒，修行广大忍，精进不退转，光明照世间。”

尔时，善财童子说此颂已，白言：“圣者，我已先发阿耨多罗三藐三菩提心，而未知菩萨云何学菩萨行？云何修菩萨道？我闻圣者善能诱诲，愿为我说！”

时，不动优婆夷以菩萨柔软语、悦意语，慰喻善财，而告之言：

Still, of all the beings throughout the worlds of the ten directions, there were none who conceived any thoughts of defiled attachment for this *upāsikā*. Rather, if they merely saw her for but a moment, all their afflictions would then naturally disappear. Just as the hundred myriad Great Brahma Heaven kings could never produce any of the afflictions typical of desire-realm beings, so too, one should realize that all the afflictions of whoever saw this *upāsikā* would also similarly subside. Still, whenever any of the beings throughout the ten directions looked at this woman, they would all gaze at her insatiably with the sole exception of those who were already replete in great wisdom.

Sudhana the Youth then respectfully bent low his torso and pressed his palms together as he contemplated her with right mindfulness. He saw:

That this woman possessed an inconceivable physical majesty;
That her physical features and countenance were unequaled anywhere in the world;
That her radiance was so penetrating, no physical object could block it;
That it everywhere benefited beings;
That her body's pores constantly emanated a sublime fragrance;
That her retinue was boundless;
That her palace was of the most superior sort; and
That her meritorious qualities were so deep and vast that no one could know their bounds.

His mind was filled with delight and he then uttered a verse in praise, saying:

Through guarding the purity of precepts,
cultivating vast patience,
and practicing irreversible vigor,
your radiance illuminates the world.

Having spoken this verse, Sudhana the Youth then addressed her, saying:

O Āryā, I am one who has already resolved to attain *anuttara-samyak-saṃbodhi*. Still, I do not yet know how the bodhisattva should train in the bodhisattva practices or how he should cultivate the bodhisattva path. I have heard that the Āryā is well able to offer guidance and instruction in this. Please speak about these matters for my sake.

With a bodhisattva's gentle and mind-pleasing words, Upāsikā Acalā comforted Sudhana and said to him:

正體字

善哉善哉。善
358c11‖ 男子。汝已能發阿耨多羅三藐三菩提心。善
358c12‖ 男子。我得菩薩難摧伏智慧藏解脫門。我得
358c13‖ 菩薩堅固受持行門。我得菩薩一切法平等
358c14‖ 地總持門。我得菩薩照明一切法辯才門。我
358c15‖ 得菩薩求一切法無疲厭三昧門。善財童子
358c16‖ 言。聖者。菩薩難摧伏智慧藏解脫門。乃至求
358c17‖ 一切法無疲厭三昧門。境界云何。童女言。善
358c18‖ 男子。此處難知。善財白言。唯願聖者。承佛神
358c19‖ 力。為我宣說。我當因善知識。能信能受。能知
358c20‖ 能了。趣入觀察。修習隨順。離諸分別。究竟平
358c21‖ 等。優婆夷言。善男子。過去世中有劫。名離
358c22‖ 垢。佛號脩臂。時有國王。名曰電授。唯有一
358c23‖ 女。即我身是。我於夜分。廢音樂時。父母兄
358c24‖ 弟。悉已眠寢。五百童女。亦皆昏寐。我於樓
358c25‖ 上。仰觀星宿。於虛空中。見彼如來如寶山王。
358c26‖ 無量無邊。天龍八部。諸菩薩眾。所共圍遶。

简体字

“善哉！善哉！善男子，汝已能发阿耨多罗三藐三菩提心。善男子，我得菩萨难摧伏智慧藏解脱门，我得菩萨坚固受持行门，我得菩萨一切法平等地总持门，我得菩萨照明一切法辩才门，我得菩萨求一切法无疲厌三昧门。”

善财童子言：“圣者，菩萨难摧伏智慧藏解脱门，乃至求一切法无疲厌三昧门，境界云何？”

童女言：“善男子，此处难知。”

善财白言：“唯愿圣者，承佛神力，为我宣说！我当因善知识，能信能受，能知能了，趣入观察，修习随顺，离诸分别，究竟平等。”

优婆夷言：“善男子，过去世中有劫，名离垢，佛号修臂。时，有国王名曰电授，唯有一女，即我身是。我于夜分废音乐时，父母兄弟悉已眠寝，五百童女亦皆昏寐。我于楼上仰观星宿，于虚空中见彼如来如宝山王，无量无边天龙八部、诸菩萨众所共围绕，

It is good indeed, good indeed, Son of Good Family, that you have already been able to bring forth the resolve to attain *anuttara-samyak-saṃbodhi*. Son of Good Family:

I have acquired the bodhisattva's liberation gateway, "the treasury of invincible wisdom";

I have acquired the bodhisattva's practice gateway, "firm determination";

I have acquired the bodhisattva's complete-retention *dhāraṇī* gateway, "the ground of the uniform equality of all dharmas";

I have acquired the bodhisattva's eloquence gateway, "the illumination of all dharmas"; and

I have acquired the bodhisattva's samādhi gateway, "the tireless quest for all dharmas."

Sudhana the Youth then asked:

O Āryā, as for this bodhisattva's liberation gateway, "the treasury of invincible wisdom" and all those other gateways up to and including the samādhi gateway, "the tireless quest for all dharmas," what are their spheres of experience like?

That maiden then replied, "Son of Good Family, these matters would be difficult for you to understand."

Sudhana responded:

I only wish that, aided by the Buddha's spiritual powers, the Āryā would explain these matters for me. Through the assistance of the Good Spiritual Guide, I will be able to have faith in it, will be able to accept it, will be able to know it, and will be able to completely understand it, enter into it, contemplate it, cultivate it, comply with it, abandon all discriminations about it, and realize ultimate equality.

The Upāsikā then replied:

Son of Good Family, in the past, there was a kalpa known as "the immaculate kalpa" in which there was a Buddha known as Long Arms. At that time, there was a king named Bestower of Lightning who had but one daughter who was none other than myself. It happened that, one night after the music had ceased, when my parents and siblings had gone to bed and my five hundred female attendants had also all gone to sleep, I went up to the top of that building to gaze up at the stars and constellations. There, up in the sky, I saw that *tathāgata* who appeared like the king of jeweled mountains. He was surrounded by countlessly and boundlessly many devas, dragons, and the rest of the eight classes of spiritual beings[111] in addition to his congregation of bodhisattvas.

正體字

佛
358c27 身普放大光明網。周遍十方。無所障礙。佛身
358c28 毛孔。皆出妙香。我聞是香。身體柔軟。心生歡
358c29 喜。便從樓下。至於地上。合十指爪。頂禮於
359a01 佛。又觀彼佛。不見頂相。觀身左右。莫知邊
359a02 際。思惟彼佛諸相隨好。無有厭足。竊自念言。
359a03 此佛世尊。作何等業。獲於如是上妙之身。相
359a04 好圓滿。光明具足。眷屬成就。宮殿嚴好。福德
359a05 智慧。悉皆清淨。總持三昧。不可思議神通自
359a06 在。辯才無礙。善男子。爾時如來。知我心念。
359a07 即告我言。汝應發不可壞心滅諸煩惱。應發
359a08 無能勝心破諸取著。應發無退怯心入深法
359a09 門。應發能堪耐心救惡眾生。應發無迷惑心
359a10 普於一切諸趣受生。應發無厭足心。求見諸
359a11 佛無有休息。應發無知足心。悉受一切如來
359a12 法雨。應發正思惟心。普生一切佛法光明。應
359a13 發大住持心。普轉一切諸佛法輪。

简体字

佛身普放大光明网周遍十方无所障碍，佛身毛孔皆出妙香。我闻是香，身体柔软，心生欢喜；便从楼下至于地上，合十指爪，顶礼于佛。又观彼佛不见顶相，观身左右莫知边际。思惟彼佛诸相随好无有厌足，窃自念言：‘此佛世尊作何等业，获于如是上妙之身，相好圆满，光明具足，眷属成就，宫殿严好，福德智慧悉皆清净，总持三昧不可思议，神通自在，辩才无碍？’

“善男子，尔时，如来知我心念，即告我言：‘汝应发不可坏心，灭诸烦恼；应发无能胜心，破诸取著；应发无退怯心，入深法门；应发能堪耐心，救恶众生；应发无迷惑心，普于一切诸趣受生；应发无厌足心，求见诸佛无有休息；应发无知足心，悉受一切如来法雨；应发正思惟心，普生一切佛法光明；应发大住持心，普转一切诸佛法轮；

That buddha's body everywhere emanated an immense net of light rays that were unimpeded in reaching everywhere throughout the ten directions. That buddha's pores all exuded a marvelous fragrance. When I smelled this fragrance, my body relaxed into a state of pliancy and my mind was filled with joyous delight, whereupon I descended from the building down to the ground where I pressed my palms together and bowed down in reverence to that buddha.

I also saw that buddha's summit mark, the peak of which can never be seen, while also seeing that the lateral dimensions of his body were such that no one could ever know their bounds. Insatiably contemplating that buddha's major marks and secondary signs, I thought to myself, "What kinds of karmic works must this buddha, this *bhagavat,* have done that now: he has acquired such a supremely marvelous body as this; he has so perfectly fulfilled the major marks and secondary signs; he is so fully developed in his radiance; he is attended by such a complete retinue; he has such a finely adorned palace; he has become so entirely pure in his merit and wisdom; he has become so inconceivable in his complete-retention *dhāraṇīs* and samādhis; he has such sovereign mastery of the spiritual superknowledges; and he is so unimpeded in his eloquence?"

Son of Good Family, having known my thoughts, that Tathāgata then spoke to me, saying:

You should arouse the indestructible resolve to extinguish all afflictions;

You should arouse the invincible resolve to destroy all attachments;

You should arouse the irreversible and fearless resolve to enter the gates of the profound Dharma;

You should arouse the patiently enduring resolve to rescue evil beings;

You should arouse the undeluded resolve to everywhere take on rebirths in all the rebirth destinies;

You should arouse the insatiable resolve to ceaselessly seek to see all buddhas;

You should arouse the unquenchable resolve to take in the Dharma rain of all *tathāgatas;*

You should arouse the resolve to pursue right meditative reflection and everywhere produce the light of the Dharma of all buddhas;

You should arouse the vast sustaining resolve to everywhere turn the Dharma wheel of all buddhas; and

正體字

應發廣流
359a14‖ 通心。隨眾生欲施其法寶。善男子。我於彼佛
359a15‖ 所。聞如是法。求一切智。求佛十力。求佛辯
359a16‖ 才。求佛光明。求佛色身。求佛相好。求佛眾
359a17‖ 會。求佛國土。求佛威儀。求佛壽命。發是心
359a18‖ 已。其心堅固。猶如金剛。一切煩惱。及以二
359a19‖ 乘。悉不能壞。善男子。我發是心已來。經閻浮
359a20‖ 提微塵數劫。尚不生於念欲之心。況行其事。
359a21‖ 爾所劫中。於自親屬。不起瞋心。況他眾生。爾
359a22‖ 所劫中。於其自身。不生我見。況於眾具。而計
359a23‖ 我所。爾所劫中。死時生時。及住胎藏。未曾迷
359a24‖ 惑。起眾生想。及無記心。況於餘時。爾所劫
359a25‖ 中。乃至夢中。隨見一佛。未曾忘失。何況菩薩
359a26‖ 十眼所見。爾所劫中。受持一切如來正法。未
359a27‖ 曾忘失一文一句。乃至世俗所有言[1]辭。尚
359a28‖ 不忘失。何況如來金口所說。爾所劫中。受
359a29‖ 持一切如來法海。一文一句。無不思惟。無
359b01‖ 不觀察。乃至一切世俗之法。亦復如是。

简体字

应发广流通心，随众生欲施其法宝。’

“善男子，我于彼佛所闻如是法，求一切智，求佛十力，求佛辩才，求佛光明，求佛色身，求佛相好，求佛众会，求佛国土，求佛威仪，求佛寿命。发是心已，其心坚固犹如金刚，一切烦恼及以二乘悉不能坏。

“善男子，我发是心已来，经阎浮提微尘数劫，尚不生于念欲之心，况行其事？尔所劫中，于自亲属不起瞋心，况他众生？尔所劫中，于其自身不生我见，况于众具而计我所？尔所劫中，死时、生时及住胎藏，未曾迷惑起众生想及无记心，况于余时？尔所劫中，乃至梦中随见一佛未曾忘失，何况菩萨十眼所见？尔所劫中，受持一切如来正法，未曾忘失一文一句，乃至世俗所有言辞尚不忘失，何况如来金口所说？尔所劫中，受持一切如来法海，一文一句无不思惟、无不观察，乃至一切世俗之法亦复如是。

You should arouse the vast resolve to distribute the teachings with which to adapt to beings' aspirations in giving them the jewels of the Dharma.

Son of Good Family, when I had heard this Dharma from that buddha, I then sought the realization of all-knowledge, sought a buddha's ten powers, sought a buddha's eloquence, sought a buddha's light, sought a buddha's physical body, sought a buddha's major marks and secondary signs, sought a buddha's congregations, sought a buddha's lands, sought a buddha's awesome deportment, and sought a buddha's life span.

After I produced these types of resolve, they all became as solid as vajra and became such that none of the afflictions or any of the adherents of the two vehicles could ever destroy them.

Son of Good Family, from the time I aroused this resolve to the present, I have passed through a number of kalpas as numerous as all the atoms in Jambudvīpa and during all this time I have never aroused any thoughts of sensual desire, how much the less have I engaged in any such act. Furthermore:

During all those kalpas, I have never had an angry thought toward any of my relatives, how much the less toward any other being;

During all those kalpas, I have never advanced the view imputing the existence of any "self" in relation to one's "person,"[112] how much the less have I ever conceived of any possessions as being "mine";

During all those kalpas, even when dying, being born, or abiding in the womb, I have never become confused or deluded, have never had any thoughts imputing the existence of any being, and have never had any indeterminate thought,[113] how much the less might I have done so at any other times;

During all those kalpas, whenever I saw any particular buddha, even if only in a dream, I have never forgotten this, how much the less have I forgotten any whom I have seen with the bodhisattva's ten eyes;[114]

During all those kalpas, I absorbed and retained the right Dharma of all *tathāgatas* and then never forgot so much as a single passage or sentence of it. I did not even forget so much as any mundane worldly discourse, how much the less might I have forgotten anything uttered by a *tathāgata*'s golden mouth;

During all those kalpas, I took in and retained[115] the ocean of Dharma of all *tathāgatas*. Of all of its passages and sentences, there were none that I failed to reflect upon and none that I failed to contemplate. So too was this so even with regard to all worldly dharmas;

正體字

爾所
359b02║ 劫中。受持如是一切法海。未曾於一法中。不
359b03║ 得三昧。乃至世間[2]技術之法。一一法中。悉
359b04║ 亦如是。爾所劫中。住持一切如來法輪。隨所
359b05║ 住持。未曾廢捨一文一句。乃至不曾生於世
359b06║ 智。唯除為欲調眾生故。爾所劫中。見諸佛
359b07║ 海。未曾於一佛所。不得成就清淨大願。乃至
359b08║ 於諸化佛之所。悉亦如是。爾所劫中。見諸菩
359b09║ 薩修行妙行。無有一行我不成就。爾所劫中。
359b10║ 所見眾生。無一眾生我不勸發阿耨多羅三
359b11║ 藐三菩提心。未曾勸一眾生發於聲聞辟支
359b12║ 佛意。爾所劫中。於一切佛法乃至一文一句。
359b13║ 不生疑惑。不生二想。不生分別想。不生種種
359b14║ 想。不生執著想。不生勝劣想。不生愛憎想。善
359b15║ 男子。我從是來。常見諸佛。常見菩薩。常見真
359b16║ 實善知識。常聞諸佛願。常聞菩薩行。常聞菩
359b17║ 薩波羅蜜門。常聞菩薩地智光明門。

简体字

尔所劫中，受持如是一切法海，未曾于一法中不得三昧，乃至世间技术之法，一一法中悉亦如是。尔所劫中，住持一切如来法轮，随所住持，未曾废舍一文一句，乃至不曾生于世智，唯除为欲调众生故。尔所劫中，见诸佛海，未曾于一佛所不得成就清净大愿，乃至于诸化佛之所悉亦如是。尔所劫中，见诸菩萨修行妙行，无有一行我不成就。尔所劫中，所有众生，无一众生我不劝发阿耨多罗三藐三菩提心，未曾劝一众生发于声闻、辟支佛意。尔所劫中，于一切佛法，乃至一文一句，不生疑惑，不生二想，不生分别想，不生种种想，不生执著想，不生胜劣想，不生爱憎想。

“善男子，我从是来，常见诸佛，常见菩萨，常见真实善知识，常闻诸佛愿，常闻菩萨行，常闻菩萨波罗蜜门，常闻菩萨地智光明门，

During all those kalpas, I took in and retained the ocean of all dharmas in this way and yet never failed to achieve samādhi with regard to any one of those dharmas. This was also so with regard even to every other dharma up to and including the dharmas of all of the world's skills and arts;

During all those kalpas, I sustained and preserved the turning of the Dharma wheel of all *tathāgatas*, and, no matter what I was sustaining and preserving, I never lost even one passage or sentence of it. This was also so even to the point that I never brought forth merely worldly knowledge except when I wished to provide guidance to beings;

During all those kalpas in which I saw the ocean of all buddhas, I never failed to fulfill pure and vast vows under even one of those buddhas. In this very same way, I never failed to also do so even in the presence of all of their transformation buddhas;

During all those kalpas when I observed the bodhisattvas cultivating marvelous practices, I never had even one of those practices which I did not perfect;

During all those kalpas, of all the beings I saw, there was not one being that I did not encourage to resolve to attain *anuttara-samyak-saṃbodhi*, and, during all that time, I never encouraged even one being to produce the resolve of a *śrāvaka*-disciple or *pratyekabuddha* practitioner; and

During all those kalpas, with respect to all those dharmas of the buddhas, there was never even one passage or one sentence about which I ever had any doubt, about which I ever had any duality-based thought, about which I ever had any discriminating thought, about which I ever had differentiating thought, about which I ever had any thoughts of attachment, about which I ever had any thoughts ascribing relative superiority or inferiority, or about which I ever had any thought of fondness or dislike.

Son of Good Family, from that point onward:

I have always met all buddhas;

I have always met bodhisattvas;

I have always met genuine good spiritual guides;

I have always learned of all buddhas' vows;

I have always learned of the bodhisattva practices;

I have always learned of the gateways into the bodhisattva's *pāramitā* gateways;

I have always learned of the gateways into the wisdom light of the bodhisattva grounds;

正體字

常聞菩
359b18 薩無盡藏門。常聞入無邊世界網門。常聞出
359b19 生無邊眾生界因門。常以清淨智慧光明。除
359b20 滅一切眾生煩惱。常以智慧。生長一切眾生
359b21 善根。常隨一切眾生所樂。示現其身。常以
359b22 清淨上妙言音。開悟法界一切眾生。善男子。
359b23 我得菩薩求一切法無厭足莊嚴門。我得一
359b24 切法平等地總持門。現不思議自在神變。汝
359b25 欲見不。善財言唯。我心願見。爾時不動優婆
359b26 夷。坐於龍藏師子之座。入求一切法無厭足
359b27 莊嚴三昧門。不空輪莊嚴三昧門。十力智輪
359b28 現前三昧門。佛種無盡藏三昧門。入如是等
359b29 一萬三昧門。入此三昧門時。十方各有不可
359c01 說佛剎微塵數世界。六種震動。皆悉清淨瑠
359c02 璃所成。一一世界中。有百億四天下。百億如
359c03 來。或住兜率天。乃至般涅槃。一一如來。放光
359c04 明網。周遍法界道場眾會。清淨圍遶。轉妙
359c05 法輪。開悟群生。

简体字

常闻菩萨无尽藏门，常闻入无边世界网门，常闻出生无边众生界因门，常以清净智慧光明除灭一切众生烦恼，常以智慧生长一切众生善根，常随一切众生所乐示现其身，常以清净上妙言音开悟法界一切众生。

“善男子，我得菩萨求一切法无厌足庄严门，我得一切法平等地总持门，现不思议自在神变。汝欲见不？”

善财言：“唯！我心愿见。”

尔时，不动优婆夷坐于龙藏师子之座，入求一切法无厌足庄严三昧门、不空轮庄严三昧门、十力智轮现前三昧门、佛种无尽藏三昧门，入如是等一万三昧门。入此三昧门时，十方各有不可说佛刹微尘数世界六种震动，皆悉清净琉璃所成；一一世界中，有百亿四天下，百亿如来或住兜率天乃至般涅槃；一一如来放光明网，周遍法界道场众会，清净围绕，转妙法轮，开悟群生。

I have always learned of the gateways into the bodhisattva's inexhaustible treasuries;
I have always learned of and entered the gateways into the boundless net of worlds;
I have always learned of the causal gateway for taking birth in the boundlessly many realms of beings;
I have always used the light of pure wisdom to extinguish the afflictions of all beings;
I have always used wisdom to promote the growth of all beings' roots of goodness;
I have always manifested bodies adapted to whatever all beings find pleasing;[116] and
I have always used pure and supremely marvelous speech to awaken all beings throughout the Dharma realm.

Son of Good Family, I have acquired the bodhisattva's adornment gateway called "the insatiable quest for all dharmas" and I have acquired the complete-retention *dhāraṇī* gateway called "the ground of all dharmas' equality." So it is that I manifest inconceivable sovereign mastery of spiritual transformations. Do you wish to see these, or not?

Sudhana replied, "Indeed, I do wish to see them."

Upāsikā Acalā then sat on her dragon treasury lion throne and entered the bodhisattva's adornment samādhi gateway called "the insatiable quest for all dharmas," the adornment samādhi gateway called "the sphere of efficaciousness," the samādhi gateway called "the manifestation of the wheel of the wisdom of the ten powers," and the samādhi gateway called "the treasury of the endlessness of the Buddha's lineage." She then proceeded to enter a myriad samādhi gateways such as these.

When she entered these samādhi gateways,[117] in each of the ten directions there were worlds as numerous as the atoms in an ineffable number of buddha *kṣetras* that quaked and moved in six ways. They were all composed of pure lapis lazuli. In every one of those worlds, there were a hundred *koṭīs* of fourfold continents and a hundred *koṭīs* of *tathāgatas* who in some cases dwelt in the Tuṣita Heavens [and in some cases manifested in the other stages of a buddha's life] up to and including their entry into *parinirvāṇa*. Every one of those *tathāgatas* emanated a net of light rays that everywhere pervaded the pure sites of enlightenment and their surrounding congregations throughout the Dharma realm where they turned the wheel of the sublime Dharma and awakened the many kinds of beings.

正體字

時不動優婆夷。從三昧起。告
359c06║ 善財言。善男子。汝見此不。善財言唯。我皆已
359c07║ 見。優婆夷言。善男子。我唯得此求一切法無
359c08║ 厭足三昧光明。為一切眾生。說微妙法。皆
359c09║ 令歡喜。如諸菩薩摩訶薩如金翅鳥。遊行虛
359c10║ 空。無所障礙。能入一切眾生大海。見有善根
359c11║ 已成熟者。便即執取置菩提岸。又如商客入
359c12║ 大寶洲。採求如來十力智寶。又如漁師持正
359c13║ 法網。入生死海。於愛水中。漉諸眾生。如阿脩
359c14║ 羅王能遍[3]撓動三有大城諸煩惱海。又如日
359c15║ 輪出現虛空。照愛水泥。令其乾竭。又如滿月
359c16║ 出現虛空。令可化者。心華開敷。又如大地普
359c17║ 皆平等。無量眾生。於中止住。增長一切善法
359c18║ 根芽。又如大風所向無礙。能拔一切諸見大
359c19║ 樹。如轉輪王遊行世間。以四攝事。攝諸眾
359c20║ 生。而我云何能知能說彼功德行。善男子。於
359c21║ 此南方。有一大城。名無量都薩羅。

简体字

时，不动优婆夷从三昧起，告善财言："善男子，汝见此不？"

善财言："唯！我皆已见。"

优婆夷言："善男子，我唯得此求一切法无厌足三昧光明，为一切众生说微妙法，皆令欢喜。如诸菩萨摩诃萨，如金翅鸟，游行虚空无所障碍，能入一切众生大海，见有善根已成熟者，便即执取置菩提岸；又如商客，入大宝洲，采求如来十力智宝；又如渔师，持正法网，入生死海，于爱水中漉诸众生；如阿修罗王，能遍[打-丁+毛]动三有大城诸烦恼海；又如日轮，出现虚空，照爱水泥，令其干竭；又如满月，出现虚空，令可化者心华开敷；又如大地，普皆平等，无量众生于中止住，增长一切善法根芽；又如大风，所向无碍，能拔一切诸见大树；如转轮王，游行世间，以四摄事摄诸众生。而我云何能知能说彼功德行？

"善男子，于此南方，有一大城，名无量都萨罗；

Upāsikā Acalā then arose from samādhi and asked Sudhana, "Son of Good Family, did you see this, or not?"

Sudhana replied, "Indeed, I saw it all."

Upāsikā Acalā then said:

Son of Good Family, I have only acquired the light of this samādhi of the insatiable quest for all dharmas with which I speak on the sublime Dharma for the sake of all beings, thereby causing them all to feel happy. As for the bodhisattva-mahāsattvas:

Who are like the golden-winged *garuḍa* birds that roam unimpeded through the skies, for they are able to enter the great ocean of all beings and, seeing those whose roots of goodness have already ripened, they then immediately lay hold of them and place them on the shore of bodhi;

Who are also like the merchants who have gone out and entered the isles of great jewels in that they have sought for and gathered up the Tathāgata's jewels of wisdom of the ten powers;

Who are also like the fishermen in that they take the net of right Dharma out into the ocean of *saṃsāra* and use it to scoop up all beings from the waters of sensual craving;

Who are like the *asura* king in their ability to everywhere stir up the ocean of afflictions of the great city of the three realms of existence;[118]

Who are also like the sun that rises in the sky in that they shine their light on the wet mud of sensual craving and cause it to completely dry up;

Who are also like the full moon that rises in empty space in that they cause the blossoming of the flower of the mind of those who are capable of being transformed;

Who are also like the great earth in that they serve as the uniformly equal support for the countless beings who abide there and increase the growth of their roots and sprouts of all good dharmas;

Who are also like the great winds in that, wherever they go, they are unimpeded and able to uproot the great trees of all the wrong views; and

Who are also like the wheel-turning sage king in that they roam throughout the world, using the four means of attraction to gather in all beings—

How could I know of or be able to speak about their meritorious qualities and practices?

Son of Good Family, south of here, there is a great city known as Amitatosala or "Limitless Tosala" in which there is a wandering

正體字

其中有一
359c22 出家外道。名曰遍行。汝往彼問。菩薩云何學
359c23 菩薩行。修菩薩道。時善財童子。頂禮其足。遶
359c24 無量匝。慇懃瞻仰。辭退而去
360a02 大方廣佛華嚴經卷第六十七
360a05 入法界品第三十九之八
360a06 爾時善財童子。於不動優婆夷所。得聞法已。
360a07 專心憶念所有教誨。皆悉信受。思惟觀察。漸
360a08 漸遊行。經歷國邑。至都薩羅城。於日沒時。入
360a09 彼城中。鄽店隣里。四衢道側。處處尋覓遍行
360a10 外道。城東有山。名曰善[1]德。善財童子。於中
360a11 夜時。見此山頂。草樹巖巘。光明照[2]耀。如日
360a12 初出。見此事已。生大歡喜。作是念言。我必於
360a13 此。見善知識。便從城出。而登彼山。見此外道
360a14 於其山上平坦之處。徐步經行。色相圓滿。
360a15 威光照[*]耀。大梵天王。所不能及。十千梵眾
360a16 之所圍遶。往詣其所。頭頂禮足。遶無量匝。於
360a17 前合掌。而作是言。聖者。我已先發阿耨多羅
360a18 三藐三菩提心。而我未知菩薩云何學菩薩
360a19 行。云何修菩薩道。我聞聖者。善能教誨。願
360a20 為我說。遍行答言。

简体字

其中有一出家外道，名曰遍行。汝往彼问：菩萨云何学菩萨行、修菩萨道？”

时，善财童子顶礼其足，绕无量匝，殷勤瞻仰，辞退而去。

大方广佛华严经卷第六十七

入法界品第三十九之八

尔时，善财童子于不动优婆夷所得闻法已，专心忆念所有教诲，皆悉信受，思惟观察。

渐渐游行，经历国邑，至都萨罗城，于日没时入彼城中，廛店、邻里、四衢道侧，处处寻觅遍行外道。

城东有山，名曰善德。善财童子于中夜时，见此山顶草树岩巘，光明照耀如日初出；见此事已，生大欢喜，作是念言：“我必于此见善知识。”便从城出而登彼山，见此外道于其山上平坦之处徐步经行，色相圆满，威光照耀，大梵天王所不能及，十千梵众之所围绕。往诣其所，头顶礼足，绕无量匝，于前合掌而作是言：“圣者，我已先发阿耨多罗三藐三菩提心，而我未知菩萨云何学菩萨行？云何修菩萨道？我闻圣者善能教诲，愿为我说！”

遍行答言：

ascetic[119] known as Sarvagāmin or "Going Everywhere." You should go there and ask him, "How should a bodhisattva train in the bodhisattva practices and how should he cultivate the bodhisattva path?"

Sudhana the Youth then bowed down in reverence at her feet and circumambulated her countless times as he gazed up at her in attentive admiration. He then respectfully withdrew and departed.

20 – Sarvagāmin

At that time, having heard the Dharma from Upāsikā Acalā, Sudhana single-mindedly recalled all of her teachings, all of which he accepted in faith, reflected upon, and contemplated.

He gradually traveled onward, passing through countries and towns until he reached the city of Tosala. He entered that city at sunset and then searched for Sarvagāmin, the wandering ascetic, in place after place among the shops and stalls in the neighborhoods near the intersection of the four roads. To the east of the city, there was a mountain called Sulabha or "Good Gain."[120] In the middle of the night, Sudhana the Youth saw on this mountain peak amidst the grasses, trees, cliffs, and peaks, a dazzling light that was like the sunlight at sunrise.

After he saw this phenomenon, he was filled with great happiness and thought, "I will certainly encounter that good spiritual guide in this place," whereupon he left the city, climbed up that mountain, and saw this wandering ascetic engaged in slow meditative walking on a level area on the mountain. His physical appearance was perfectly complete in awesome radiance the splendor of which not even the Great Brahma Heaven King could approach. He was surrounded by a congregation of ten thousand brahmans. Sudhana then approached him to pay his respects, bowed down in reverence at his feet, circumambulated him countless times, paused before him with palms pressed together, and then said:

O Ārya, I am one who has already resolved to attain *anuttara-samyak-saṃbodhi.* Still, I do not yet know how the bodhisattva should train in the bodhisattva practices or how he should cultivate the bodhisattva path. I have heard that the Ārya is well able to offer guidance and instruction in this. Please speak about these matters for my sake.

Sarvagāmin then replied, saying:

正體字

善哉善哉。善男子。我已安
360a21 住至一切處菩薩行。已成就普觀世間三昧
360a22 門。已成就無依無作神通力。已成就普門般
360a23 若波羅蜜。善男子。我普於世間種種方所。種
360a24 種形貌。種種行解。種種沒生。一切諸趣。所謂
360a25 天趣龍趣。夜叉趣。乾闥婆阿脩羅迦樓羅緊
360a26 那羅摩睺羅伽。地獄畜生。閻羅王界。人非人
360a27 等。一切諸趣。或住諸見。或信二乘。或復信樂
360a28 大乘之道。如是一切諸眾生中。我以種種方
360a29 便。種種智門。而為利益。所謂或為演說一
360b01 切世間種種[3]技藝。令得具足一切巧術陀羅
360b02 尼智。或為演說四攝方便。令得具足一切智
360b03 道。或為演說諸波羅蜜。令其迴向一切智位。
360b04 或為稱讚大菩提心。令其不失無上道意。或
360b05 為稱讚諸菩薩行。令其滿足淨佛國土度眾生
360b06 願。或為演說造諸惡行。受地獄等種種苦報。
360b07 令於惡業。深生厭離。或為演說供養諸佛。種
360b08 諸善根。決定獲得一切智果。令其發起歡喜
360b09 之心。

简体字

“善哉！善哉！善男子，我已安住至一切处菩萨行，已成就普观世间三昧门，已成就无依无作神通力，已成就普门般若波罗蜜。善男子，我普于世间种种方所、种种形貌、种种行解、种种殁生一切诸趣。所谓：天趣、龙趣、夜叉趣、乾闼婆、阿修罗、迦楼罗、紧那罗、摩睺罗伽、地狱、畜生、阎罗王界、人非人等，一切诸趣，或住诸见，或信二乘，或复信乐大乘之道。如是一切诸众生中，我以种种方便、种种智门而为利益。所谓：或为演说一切世间种种技艺，令得具足一切巧术陀罗尼智；或为演说四摄方便，令得具足一切智道；或为演说诸波罗蜜，令其回向一切智位；或为称赞大菩提心，令其不失无上道意；或为称赞诸菩萨行，令其满足净佛国土度众生愿；或为演说造诸恶行受地狱等种种苦报，令于恶业深生厌离；或为演说供养诸佛种诸善根决定获得一切智果，令其发起欢喜之心；

This is good indeed, good indeed. Son of Good Family, I have already come to securely abide in the bodhisattva practice of going everywhere, have already perfected the samādhi gateway of universal contemplation of the world, have already perfected the power of the independent and effortless spiritual superknowledges, and have already perfected the *prajñāpāramitā* of the universal gateway.

Son of Good Family, everywhere throughout the world, including:

In the many different regions;

Among those of the various forms and appearances;

Among those of the various practices and understandings;

Among those dying and taking birth into all the various rebirth destinies, including the path of the devas, the path of the dragons, and the path of the *yakṣas*, as well as all of the rebirth destinies of the *gandharvas*, the *asuras*, the *garuḍas*, the *kiṃnaras*, the *mahoragas*, the hell-dwellers, the animals, the denizens of King Yama's realms,[121] the humans, the nonhumans, and so forth;

Among those who abide in the various kinds of views;

Among those who place their faith in the two vehicles; and

Among those who place their faith and delight in the path of the Great Vehicle—

Among all such beings as these, I use many different kinds of skillful means and many different kinds of gateways to wisdom to benefit them, for instance:

For some, I expound on all of the world's many different kinds of technical skills and arts to enable them to acquire complete knowledge of the *dhāraṇīs* related to all such technical skills;

For some, I expound on the skillful means of the four means of attraction to enable them to succeed in fulfilling the path to all-knowledge;

For some, I expound on the *pāramitās* to enable them to dedicate [their practice to reaching] the stage of all-knowledge;

For some, I praise the resolve to attain the great *bodhi* to prevent them from losing their determination to pursue the unexcelled path;

For some, I praise the bodhisattva practices to enable them to fulfill their vows to purify the buddha lands and liberate beings;

For some, I expound on undergoing many different kinds of agonizing retributions in the hells as a result of engaging in all kinds of evil actions, doing so to cause them to deeply renounce evil karmic deeds;

For some, I expound on making offerings to buddhas, on planting all kinds of roots of goodness, and on definitely gaining the fruit of all-knowledge, doing so to make them feel joyful;

正體字

或為讚說一切如來應正等覺。所有功
360b10‖ 德。令樂佛身。求一切智。或為讚說諸佛威德。
360b11‖ 令其願樂佛不壞身。或為讚說佛自在身。令
360b12‖ 求如來無能映蔽大威德體。又善男子。此都
360b13‖ 薩羅城中。一切方所。一切族類。若男若女。諸
360b14‖ 人眾中。我皆以方便。示同其形。隨其所應。而
360b15‖ 為說法。諸眾生等。悉不能知。我是何人。從何
360b16‖ 而至。唯令聞者。如實修行。善男子。如於此城
360b17‖ 利益眾生。於閻浮提城邑聚落。所有人眾。住
360b18‖ 止之處。悉亦如是。而為利益。善男子。閻浮提
360b19‖ 內九十六眾。各起異見。而生執著。我悉於中。
360b20‖ 方便調伏。令其捨離所有諸見。如閻浮提。餘
360b21‖ 四天下。亦復如是。如四天下。三千大千世界。
360b22‖ 亦復如是。如三千大千世界。如是十方無量
360b23‖ 世界。諸眾生海。我悉於中。隨諸眾生心之所
360b24‖ 樂。以種種方便。種種法門。現種種色身。以種
360b25‖ 種言音。而為說法。令得利益。善男子。我唯知
360b26‖ 此至一切處菩薩行。如諸菩薩摩訶薩。身與
360b27‖ 一切眾生數等。得與眾生無差別身。

简体字

或为赞说一切如来、应、正等觉所有功德，令乐佛身求一切智；或为赞说诸佛威德，令其愿乐佛不坏身；或为赞说佛自在身，令求如来无能映蔽大威德体。

“又，善男子，此都萨罗城中，一切方所一切族类，若男若女诸人众中，我皆以方便示同其形，随其所应而为说法。诸众生等，悉不能知我是何人、从何而至，唯令闻者如实修行。善男子，如于此城利益众生，于阎浮提城邑聚落，所有人众住止之处，悉亦如是而为利益。

“善男子，阎浮提内九十六众，各起异见而生执著，我悉于中方便调伏，令其舍离所有诸见；如阎浮提，余四天下亦复如是；如四天下，三千大千世界亦复如是；如三千大千世界，如是十方无量世界诸众生海，我悉于中，随诸众生心之所乐，以种种方便、种种法门，现种种色身，以种种言音而为说法，令得利益。

“善男子，我唯知此至一切处菩萨行。如诸菩萨摩诃萨，身与一切众生数等，得与众生无差别身，

For some, I praise all the meritorious qualities of all the Tathāgatas, the arhats, those of right and universal enlightenment, doing so to cause them to delight in the body of a buddha and seek the realization of all-knowledge;

For some, I praise the awesome virtue of all buddhas to cause them to aspire to acquire the indestructible body of a buddha; and

For some, I praise the Buddha's body possessed of sovereign mastery to cause them to seek a *tathāgata* body which possesses immensely awesome virtue that no one can outshine.

Also, Son of Good Family, within this city of Tosala, in all places, among all the classes of beings, and among the entire human population, whether male or female, using skillful means, I manifest in forms of the same sorts as theirs in which I speak the Dharma for them in accordance with whatever is fitting for them.

Among all those various kinds of beings, none of them are able to know what sort of person I am or from where I have come to them. This is done solely to cause those who are listening to me to cultivate in accordance with what is true.

Son of Good Family, just as I benefit beings here in this city, so too do I also benefit all the people on this continent of Jambudvīpa in this very same way, doing so wherever they dwell in the cities, in their outlying communities, and in the villages.

Son of Good Family, the ninety-six kinds of religious sects on the continent of Jambudvīpa each produce deviant views and thereby develop their attachments. I use skillful means to train them all, thereby causing them to relinquish all their wrong views.

And just as this is so on the continent of Jambudvīpa, so too is this so on the rest of the four continents. And just as this is so on all four continents, so too is this so in all worlds of the great trichiliocosm. And just as this is so throughout the worlds of this great trichiliocosm, so too is this so with regard to the ocean of all beings throughout the countless worlds of the ten directions. For all of them, I adapt to each of their mental dispositions by using many different kinds of skillful means and many different kinds of Dharma gateways as I manifest many different kinds of form bodies and use many different kinds of languages to speak Dharma for their sakes and thus enable them to benefit from this.

Son of Good Family, I know only this bodhisattva practice of going everywhere. As for the bodhisattva-mahāsattvas:

Whose bodies equal the number of all beings;

Who take on bodies no different than those of beings;

正體字

以變化
360b28 ‖ 身。普入諸趣。於一切處。皆現受生。普現一切
360b29 ‖ 眾生之前。清淨光明。遍照世間。以無礙願住
360c01 ‖ 一切劫。得如帝網諸無等行。常勤利益一切
360c02 ‖ 眾生。恒與共居。而無所著。普於三世。悉皆平
360c03 ‖ 等。以無我智。周遍照[*]耀。以大悲藏。一切觀
360c04 ‖ 察。而我云何能知能說彼功德行。善男子。於
360c05 ‖ 此南方。有一國土。名為廣大。有鬻香長者。名
360c06 ‖ 優鉢羅華。汝詣彼問。菩薩云何學菩薩行。修
360c07 ‖ 菩薩道。時善財童子。頂禮其足。遶無量匝。慇
360c08 ‖ 懃瞻仰。辭退而去
360c09 ‖ 爾時善財童子。因善知識教。不顧身命。不著
360c10 ‖ 財寶。不樂人眾。不耽五欲。不戀眷屬。不重王
360c11 ‖ 位。唯願化度一切眾生。唯願嚴淨諸佛國土。
360c12 ‖ 唯願供養一切諸佛。唯願證知諸法實性。唯
360c13 ‖ 願修集一切菩薩大功德海。

简体字

以变化身普入诸趣，于一切处皆现受生，普现一切众生之前，清净光明遍照世间，以无碍愿住一切劫，得如帝网诸无等行，常勤利益一切众生，恒与共居而无所著，普于三世悉皆平等，以无我智周遍照耀，以大悲藏一切观察；而我云何能知能说彼功德行？

“善男子，于此南方，有一国土，名为广大；有鬻香长者，名优钵罗华。汝诣彼问：菩萨云何学菩萨行、修菩萨道？”

时，善财童子顶礼其足，绕无量匝，殷勤瞻仰，辞退而去。

尔时，善财童子因善知识教，不顾身命，不著财宝，不乐人众，不耽五欲，不恋眷属，不重王位；唯愿化度一切众生，唯愿严净诸佛国土，唯愿供养一切诸佛，唯愿证知诸法实性，唯愿修集一切菩萨大功德海，

Who use transformation bodies to enter all the rebirth destinies;
Who manifest the taking on of births in all places;
Who everywhere manifest directly before all beings;
Whose pure light everywhere illuminates the world;
Who use unimpeded vows to abide in all kalpas;
Who acquire all the peerless practices which are [interrelated] like Indra's net;
Who are always diligent in benefiting all beings;
Who constantly dwell together with them and yet have none of them to whom they become attached;
Who maintain equal regard for everyone throughout all three periods of time;
Who use the knowledge of non-self to manifest universally pervasive illumination; and
Who use the treasury of the great compassion in all their contemplations—

How could I know of or be able to speak about their meritorious qualities and practices?

Son of Good Family, south of here, there is a land known as Pṛthurāṣṭra or "Vastness" in which there is an elder, a fragrance seller by the name of Utpalabhūti. You should go there, pay your respects, and ask him, "How should a bodhisattva train in the bodhisattva practices and how should he cultivate the bodhisattva path?"

Sudhana the Youth then bowed down in reverence at his feet and circumambulated him countless times as he gazed up at him in attentive admiration. He then respectfully withdrew and departed.

21 – Utpalabhūti

At that time, because of the teachings of the good spiritual guides, Sudhana the Youth felt no concern for his own physical life, felt no attachment to wealth or jewels, did not delight in crowds of people, did not indulge in the five types of sensual pleasures, did not long for a retinue of followers, and did not esteem the idea of becoming a monarch. Rather:

He wished only to teach and liberate all beings;
He wished only to purify all buddha lands;
He wished only to make offerings to all buddhas;
He wished only to realize the true nature of all dharmas;
He wished only to cultivate and accumulate the great ocean of all bodhisattvas' meritorious qualities;

正體字

唯願修行一切
360c14‖ 功德終無退轉。唯願恒於一切劫中以大願
360c15‖ 力修菩薩行。唯願普入一切諸佛眾會道場。
360c16‖ 唯願入一三昧門普現一切三昧門自在神
360c17‖ 力。唯願於佛一毛孔中見一切佛心無厭足。
360c18‖ 唯願得一切法智慧光明。能持一切諸佛法
360c19‖ 藏。專求此等一切諸佛菩薩功德。漸次遊行。
360c20‖ 至廣大國。詣長者所。頂禮其足。遶無量匝。合
360c21‖ 掌而立。白言。聖者。我已先發阿耨多羅三藐
360c22‖ 三菩提心。欲求一切佛平等智慧。欲滿一切
360c23‖ 佛無量大願。欲淨一切佛最上色身。欲見一
360c24‖ 切佛清淨法身。欲知一切佛廣大智身。欲淨
360c25‖ 治一切菩薩諸行。欲照明一切菩薩三昧。欲
360c26‖ 安住一切菩薩總持。欲除滅一切所有障礙。
360c27‖ 欲遊行一切十方世界。而未知菩薩云何學
360c28‖ 菩薩行。云何修菩薩道。而能出生一切智智。
360c29‖ 長者告言。善哉善哉。善男子。汝乃能發阿耨
361a01‖ 多羅三藐三菩提心。善男子。我善別知一切
361a02‖ 諸香。亦知調合一切香法。

简体字

唯愿修行一切功德终无退转，唯愿恒于一切劫中以大愿力修菩萨行，唯愿普入一切诸佛众会道场，唯愿入一三昧门普现一切三昧门自在神力，唯愿于佛一毛孔中见一切佛心无厌足，唯愿得一切法智慧光明能持一切诸佛法藏，专求此等一切诸佛菩萨功德。

漸次游行，至广大国，诣长者所，顶礼其足，绕无量匝，合掌而立，白言：“圣者，我已先发阿耨多罗三藐三菩提心，欲求一切佛平等智慧，欲满一切佛无量大愿，欲净一切佛最上色身，欲见一切佛清净法身，欲知一切佛广大智身，欲净治一切菩萨诸行，欲照明一切菩萨三昧，欲安住一切菩萨总持，欲除灭一切所有障碍，欲游行一切十方世界，而未知菩萨云何学菩萨行、云何修菩萨道，而能出生一切智智？”

长者告言：“善哉！善哉！善男子，汝乃能发阿耨多罗三藐三菩提心。

“善男子，我善别知一切诸香，亦知调合一切香法，

He wished only to cultivate all meritorious qualities and never retreat from doing so;
He wished only to constantly cultivate the bodhisattva practices in all kalpas through the power of great vows;
He wished only to enter the congregations of all buddhas;
He wished only to enter one samādhi gateway and thus everywhere manifest sovereign mastery in the spiritual powers of all samādhi gateways;
He wished only to see, with an insatiable mind, all buddhas in but one of the Buddha's pores; and
He wished only to acquire the light of wisdom with respect to all dharmas and thus be able to preserve the Dharma treasury of all buddhas.

Single-mindedly seeking such meritorious qualities of all buddhas and bodhisattvas, he then gradually traveled onward until he reached the country of Pṛthurāṣṭra. Then, having made his way to the abode of that elder, he bowed down in reverence at his feet, circumambulated him countless times, and then stood before him with palms pressed together as he addressed him, saying:

O Ārya, I am one who has already resolved to attain *anuttara-samyak-saṃbodhi*. Accordingly:

I wish to pursue the wisdom common to all buddhas;
I wish to fulfill the measureless great vows of all buddhas;
I wish to purify the supreme form body of all buddhas;
I wish to see the pure Dharma body of all buddhas;
I wish to know the vast wisdom body of all buddhas;
I wish to purify the practices of all bodhisattvas;
I wish to illuminate the samādhis of all bodhisattvas;
I wish to abide securely in the complete-retention *dhāraṇīs* of all bodhisattvas;
I wish to eliminate all obstacles; and
I wish to travel to all worlds throughout the ten directions.

Still, I do not yet know how the bodhisattva should train in the bodhisattva practices or how he should cultivate the bodhisattva path so as to be able to produce the wisdom of all-knowledge.

The Elder then spoke to him, saying:

It is good indeed, good indeed, Son of Good Family, that you were then able to resolve to attain *anuttara-samyak-saṃbodhi*. Son of Good Family, I am well able to distinguish all types of fragrances and also know the methods used in the blending and creation of all types

正體字

所謂一切香。一切
361a03║ 燒香。一切塗香。一切末香。亦知如是一切香
361a04║ 王所出之處。又善了知天香。龍香。夜叉香。乾
361a05║ 闥婆阿脩羅迦樓羅緊那羅摩睺羅伽人非人
361a06║ 等。所有諸香。又善別知治諸病香。斷諸惡
361a07║ 香。生歡喜香。增煩惱香。滅煩惱香。令於有為
361a08║ 生樂著香。令於有為生厭離香。捨諸憍逸香。
361a09║ 發心念佛香。證解法門香。聖所受用香。一切
361a10║ 菩薩差別香。一切菩薩地位香。如是等香。形
361a11║ 相生起。出現成就。清淨安隱。方便境界。威德
361a12║ 業用。及以根本。如是一切我皆了達。善男子。
361a13║ 人間有香。名曰象藏。因龍鬪生。若燒一丸。即
361a14║ 起大香雲。彌覆王都。於七日中。雨細香雨。若
361a15║ 著身者。身則金色。若著衣服。宮殿樓閣。亦皆
361a16║ 金色。若因風吹。入宮殿中。眾生嗅者。七日七
361a17║ 夜。歡喜充滿。身心快樂。無有諸病。不相侵
361a18║ 害。離諸憂苦。不驚不怖。不亂不恚。慈心相
361a19║ 向。志意清淨。我知是已。而為說法。令其決定
361a20║ 發阿耨多羅三藐三菩提心。

简体字

所谓：一切香、一切烧香、一切涂香、一切末香。亦知如是一切香王所出之处，又善了知天香、龙香、夜叉香，乾闼婆、阿修罗、迦楼罗、紧那罗、摩睺罗伽、人非人等所有诸香。又善别知治诸病香、断诸恶香、生欢喜香、增烦恼香、灭烦恼香、令于有为生乐著香、令于有为生厌离香、舍诸憍逸香、发心念佛香、证解法门香、圣所受用香、一切菩萨差别香、一切菩萨地位香，如是等香形相生起、出现成就、清净安隐、方便境界、威德业用及以根本，如是一切，我皆了达。

“善男子，人间有香，名曰象藏，因龙斗生。若烧一丸，即起大香云弥覆王都，于七日中雨细香雨。若著身者，身则金色；若著衣服、宫殿、楼阁，亦皆金色。若因风吹入宫殿中，众生嗅者，七日七夜欢喜充满，身心快乐，无有诸病，不相侵害，离诸忧苦，不惊不怖，不乱不恚，慈心相向，志意清净。我知是已而为说法，令其决定发阿耨多罗三藐三菩提心。

of scents, in particular, all types of incense, all types of burned incense, all types of perfumes, and all types of powdered incense. I also know in this same way the place of origin of all the kings of fragrances. I also thoroughly know the fragrances of the heavens, the fragrances of the dragons, the fragrances of the *yakṣas*, and all the fragrances of the *gandharvas, asuras, garuḍas, kiṃnaras, mahoragas*, humans, nonhumans, and others.

I also skillfully distinguish the fragrances used in the treatment of all diseases, the fragrances that halt the doing of evil, the fragrances that produce happiness, the fragrances that increase afflictions, the fragrances that extinguish afflictions, the fragrances that cause blissful attachment to the conditioned, the fragrances that cause one to renounce the conditioned, the fragrances that cause one to relinquish vanity and negligence, the fragrances that inspire the resolve to practice mindfulness of the Buddha, the fragrances that instigate realized understanding of the Dharma gateways, the fragrances used by the *āryas*, the different fragrances used by all bodhisattvas, the fragrances associated with all the bodhisattva grounds, and other fragrances such as these.

Also, as for their forms, their appearances, their production, their manifestation, their perfection, their purity and preservation, their sphere of application, their powers, their functions, and their origins—I possess a completely penetrating comprehension of all matters such as these.

Son of Good Family, in the human realm there is an incense known as "elephant treasury" which originates from the fighting of dragons. If one burns a lump of it, it immediately produces a great cloud of incense that spreads across the royal capital and, for a period of seven days, sprinkles down a fine rain of incense. If it touches one's body, one's body turns the color of gold. If it touches one's clothes, palaces, or towers, they too become the color of gold. If, due to being wafted in by the wind, it enters one's palace and beings smell it, then for seven days and seven nights, they are filled with delight, their bodies and minds are blissful and free of all sickness, they do not attack or harm each other, they leave behind all their worries and sufferings, they are not frightened or terrified, they are not thrown into confusion or beset by anger, and they treat each other with thoughts of kindness and pure intentions. Once I know this has come to pass, then I speak Dharma for them and cause them to make the definite resolve to attain *anuttara-samyak-saṃbodhi*.

正體字

善男子。摩羅耶
361a21‖ 山。出栴檀香。名曰牛頭。若以塗身。設入火
361a22‖ 坑。火不能燒。善男子。海中有香。名無能勝。
361a23‖ 若以塗鼓及諸螺貝。其聲發時。一切敵軍。皆
361a24‖ 自退散。善男子。阿那婆達多池邊。出沈水香。
361a25‖ 名蓮華藏。其香一丸。如麻子大。若以燒之。香
361a26‖ 氣普熏閻浮提界。眾生聞者。離一切罪。戒品
361a27‖ 清淨。善男子。雪山有香。名阿盧那。若有眾
361a28‖ 生。嗅此香者。其心決定。離諸染著。我為說
361a29‖ 法。莫不皆得離垢三昧。善男子。羅剎界中
361b01‖ 有香。名海藏。其香但為轉輪王用。若燒一丸。
361b02‖ 而以熏之。[1]王及四軍。皆騰虛空。善男子。善
361b03‖ 法天中有香。名淨莊嚴。若燒一丸。而以熏之。
361b04‖ 普使諸天。心念於佛。善男子。須夜摩天有香。
361b05‖ 名淨藏。若燒一丸。而以熏之。夜摩天眾。莫不
361b06‖ 雲集彼天王所。而共聽法。善男子。兜率天中
361b07‖ 有香。名先陀婆。於一生所繫菩薩座前。燒
361b08‖ 其一丸。興大香雲。遍覆法界。普雨一切諸
361b09‖ 供養具。供養一切諸佛菩薩。善男子。善變
361b10‖ 化天有香。名曰奪意。若燒一丸。於七日中。普
361b11‖ 雨一切諸莊嚴具。善男子。我唯知此調和香
361b12‖ 法。如諸菩薩摩訶薩。

简体字

“善男子，摩罗耶山出栴檀香，名曰牛头；若以涂身，设入火坑，火不能烧。善男子，海中有香，名无能胜；若以涂鼓及诸螺贝，其声发时，一切敌军皆自退散。善男子，阿那婆达多池边出沉水香，名莲华藏，其香一丸如麻子大；若以烧之，香气普熏阎浮提界，众生闻者，离一切罪，戒品清净。善男子，雪山有香，名阿卢那；若有众生嗅此香者，其心决定离诸染著，我为说法莫不皆得离垢三昧。善男子，罗刹界中有香，名海藏，其香但为转轮王用；若烧一丸而以熏之，王及四军皆腾虚空。善男子，善法天中有香，名净庄严；若烧一丸而以熏之，普使诸天心念于佛。善男子，须夜摩天有香，名净藏；若烧一丸而以熏之，夜摩天众莫不云集彼天王所而共听法。善男子，兜率天中有香，名先陀婆；于一生所系菩萨座前烧其一丸，兴大香云遍覆法界，普雨一切诸供养具，供养一切诸佛菩萨。善男子，善变化天有香，名曰夺意；若烧一丸，于七日中，普雨一切诸庄严具。

“善男子，我唯知此调和香法。如诸菩萨摩诃萨，

Son of Good Family, Malaya Mountain produces a sandalwood incense known as "ox-head incense." If someone applies it to his body, even if he enters a fire pit, the fire cannot burn him.

Son of Good Family, there is a fragrance in the ocean known as "invincible." If one applies it to a drum or conch shell, when sounded, all opposing armies will naturally retreat and scatter.

Son of Good Family, Lake Anavatapta produces an *agaru* incense known as "lotus flower treasury." If one burns a pellet of that incense the size of a sesame seed, the vapors from that incense will permeate the entire realm of Jambudvīpa. When beings smell it, they abandon all karmic transgressions and become pure in their observance of the moral precepts.

Son of Good Family, there is a type of incense from the Himalaya Mountains known as *aruṇavatī*. If anyone smells this fragrance, his mind becomes resolutely determined to abandon all defiling attachments. Then, when I speak the Dharma for them, none of them fail to acquire the samādhi of immaculate purity.

Son of Good Family, in the realm of the *rākṣasas* there is a type of incense known as "ocean treasury." That incense is only for the use of the wheel-turning king. If he burns a pellet of it and lets it permeate the area, then the king and his fourfold armies all rise up into the air.

Son of Good Family, in the Good Dharma Hall of the devas[122] there is a type of incense known as "pure adornment." If one burns a pellet of it and lets it permeate the area, it everywhere causes all the devas to focus their minds on mindfulness of the Buddha.

Son of Good Family, in the Suyāma Heaven there is a type of incense known as "treasury of purity." If one burns a pellet of it and lets it permeate the area, then, all of the Suyāma Heaven devas gather like a cloud around the king of that heaven to listen to the teaching of the Dharma.

Son of Good Family, in the Tuṣita Heaven there is an incense known as *sindhuvāritā*. When one pellet of that incense is burned before the throne of a bodhisattva bound to but one more incarnation, it sends forth an immense incense cloud that spreads everywhere across the Dharma realm and rains down all kinds of offerings to all buddhas and bodhisattvas.

Son of Good Family, in the Skillful Transformations Heaven there is an incense known as "mind-captivator." If one burns a pellet of it, then, for seven days, all kinds of adornments rain down everywhere.

Son of Good Family, I know only this dharma of fragrance blending. As for the bodhisattva-mahāsattvas:

正體字

遠離一切諸惡習氣。不
361b13 染世欲。永斷煩惱眾魔羂索。超諸有趣。以智
361b14 慧香。而自莊嚴。於諸世間。皆無染著。具足成
361b15 就無所著戒。淨無著智。行無著境。於一切處。
361b16 悉無有著。其心平等。無著無依。而我[2]何能
361b17 知其妙行。說其功德。顯其所有清淨戒門。示
361b18 其所作無過失業。辨其離染身語意行。善男
361b19 子。於此南方。有一大城。名曰樓閣。中有船
361b20 師。名婆施羅。汝詣彼問。菩薩云何學菩薩行。
361b21 修菩薩道。時善財童子。頂禮其足。遶無量匝。
361b22 慇懃瞻仰。辭退而去
361b23 爾時善財童子。向樓閣城。觀察道路。所謂觀
361b24 道高卑。觀道夷險。觀道淨穢。觀道曲直。漸次
361b25 遊行。作是思惟。我當親近彼善知識。善知識
361b26 者。是成就修行諸菩薩道因。是成就修行波
361b27 羅蜜道因。是成就修行攝眾生道因。

简体字

远离一切诸恶习气，不染世欲，永断烦恼众魔罥索，超诸有趣，以智慧香而自庄严，于诸世间皆无染著，具足成就无所著戒，净无著智，行无著境，于一切处悉无有著，其心平等，无著无依；而我何能知其妙行？说其功德？显其所有清净戒门？示其所作无过失业？辩其离染身、语、意行？

“善男子，于此南方，有一大城，名曰楼阁；中有船师，名婆施罗。汝诣彼问：菩萨云何学菩萨行、修菩萨道？”

时，善财童子顶礼其足，绕无量匝，殷勤瞻仰，辞退而去。

尔时，善财童子向楼阁城，观察道路。所谓：观道高卑，观道夷险，观道净秽，观道曲直。

渐次游行，作是思惟：“我当亲近彼善知识。善知识者，是成就修行诸菩萨道因，是成就修行波罗蜜道因，是成就修行摄众生道因，

Who have abandoned all the evil habitual karmic propensities;
Who remain undefiled by worldly desires;
Who forever sever the snares of the many *māras* of the afflictions;
Who have stepped beyond all the rebirth destinies;
Who adorn themselves with the incense of wisdom;
Who remain free of all defiling attachments to anything in the world;
Who completely perfect the precepts of nonattachment;
Who purify the wisdom of nonattachment;
Who course in the realm of nonattachment;
Who have no attachment to any place;
Whose minds abide in uniform equality; and
Who are attached to nothing and depend on nothing—

How could I know their marvelous practices, speak about their meritorious qualities, reveal all their gateways to pure moral precepts, show their faultless conduct, or distinguish their transcendence of defilement in the actions of body, speech, and mind?

Son of Good Family, south of here, there is a great city known as Kūṭāgāra or "Tower" in which there is a ship captain named Vaira. You should go there, pay your respects, and ask him, "How should a bodhisattva train in the bodhisattva practices and how should he cultivate the bodhisattva path?"

Sudhana the Youth then bowed down in reverence at his feet and circumambulated him countless times as he gazed up at him in attentive admiration. He then respectfully withdrew and departed.

22 – Vaira

At that time, as Sudhana the Youth traveled toward the city of Kūṭāgāra, he contemplated the path, in particular contemplating where it was high or low, contemplating where it was safe or hazardous, contemplating where it was pure or defiled, and contemplating where it was crooked or straight. As he gradually traveled along, he reflected in this way:

I should draw near to that good spiritual guide. As for the good spiritual guide:

He is the cause for successfully cultivating the path of all bodhisattvas;
He is the cause for successfully cultivating the path of the *pāramitās*;
He is the cause for successfully cultivating the path of attracting [and sustaining] beings;

正體字

是成就
361b28‖ 修行普入法界。無障礙道因。是成就修行令
361b29‖ 一切眾生除惡慧道因。是成就修行令一切
361c01‖ 眾生離憍慢道因。是成就修行令一切眾生
361c02‖ 滅煩惱道因。是成就修行令一切眾生捨諸
361c03‖ 見道因。是成就修行令一切眾生拔一切惡
361c04‖ 刺道因。是成就修行令一切眾生至一切智
361c05‖ 城道因。何以故。於善知識處。得一切善法
361c06‖ 故。依善知識力。得一切智道故。善知識者。難
361c07‖ 見難遇。如是思惟。漸次遊行。既至彼城。見其
361c08‖ 船師。在城門外海岸上住。百千商人。及餘
361c09‖ 無量大眾圍遶。說大海法。方便開示佛功德
361c10‖ 海。善財見已。往詣其所。頂禮其足。遶無量
361c11‖ 匝。於前合掌。而作是言。聖者。我已先發阿耨
361c12‖ 多羅三藐三菩提心。而未知菩薩云何學菩
361c13‖ 薩行。云何修菩薩道。我聞聖者。善能教誨。
361c14‖ 願為我說。船師告言。善哉善哉。善男子。汝已
361c15‖ 能發阿耨多羅三藐三菩提心。今復能問生
361c16‖ 大智因。斷除一切生死苦因。

简体字

是成就修行普入法界无障碍道因，是成就修行令一切众生除恶慧道因，是成就修行令一切众生离憍慢道因，是成就修行令一切众生灭烦恼道因，是成就修行令一切众生舍诸见道因，是成就修行令一切众生拔一切恶刺道因，是成就修行令一切众生至一切智城道因。何以故？于善知识处，得一切善法故；依善知识力，得一切智道故。善知识者，难见难遇。”如是思惟。

渐次游行，既至彼城，见其船师在城门外海岸上住，百千商人及余无量大众围绕，说大海法，方便开示佛功德海。善财见已，往诣其所，顶礼其足，绕无量匝，于前合掌而作是言：“圣者，我已先发阿耨多罗三藐三菩提心，而未知菩萨云何学菩萨行？云何修菩萨道？我闻圣者善能教诲，愿为我说！”

船师告言：“善哉！善哉！善男子，汝已能发阿耨多罗三藐三菩提心，今复能问生大智因、断除一切生死苦因、

He is the cause for successfully cultivating the path of unimpededly entering the Dharma realm;
He is the cause for successfully cultivating the path by which one enables all beings to rid themselves of evil mental tendencies;[123]
He is the cause for successfully cultivating the path by which one enables all beings to abandon arrogance;
He is the cause for successfully cultivating the path by which one enables all beings to extinguish the afflictions;
He is the cause for successfully cultivating the path by which one enables all beings to relinquish all wrong views;[124]
He is the cause for successfully cultivating the path by which one enables all beings to remove all the thorns of evil; and
He is the cause for successfully cultivating the path by which one enables all beings to reach the city of all-knowledge.

And how is this so? This is because it is from the abode of the good spiritual guide that one acquires all good dharmas and it is in reliance upon the powers of the good spiritual guide that one acquires the path to all-knowledge. The good spiritual guide is one who is but rarely seen and rarely encountered.

Reflecting in this manner, he gradually traveled onward until, having reached that city, he saw that ship captain outside the city gates where he was standing on the ocean shore, surrounded by an immense congregation of a hundred thousand merchants and countless others. He was speaking on dharmas related to the great ocean while skillfully offering instruction on the Buddha's ocean of meritorious qualities.

Having seen him there, Sudhana approached him to pay his respects, whereupon he bowed down in reverence at his feet, circumambulated him countless times, stood before him with palms pressed together, and said:

O Ārya, I am one who has already resolved to attain *anuttara-samyak-saṃbodhi*. Still, I do not yet know how the bodhisattva should train in the bodhisattva practices or how he should cultivate the bodhisattva path. I have heard that the Ārya is well able to offer instruction in this. Please speak about these matters for my sake.

The Ship Captain replied, saying:

It is good indeed, good indeed, Son of Good Family, that you have already been able to bring forth the resolve to attain *anuttara-samyak-saṃbodhi* and are now also able to inquire:

About the causes for the arising of great wisdom;
About the causes for cutting off all the sufferings of *saṃsāra*;

正體字

往一切智大寶
361c17‖ 洲因。成就不壞摩訶衍因。遠離二乘怖畏生
361c18‖ 死住諸寂靜三昧旋因。乘大願車。遍一切處
361c19‖ 行菩薩行無有障礙清淨道因。以菩薩行莊
361c20‖ 嚴一切無能壞智清淨道因。普觀一切十方
361c21‖ 諸法。皆無障礙清淨道因。速能趣入一切智
361c22‖ 海清淨道因。善男子。我在此城海岸路中。淨
361c23‖ 修菩薩大悲幢行。善男子。我觀閻浮提內。貧
361c24‖ 窮眾生。為饒益故。修諸苦行。隨其所願。悉令
361c25‖ 滿足。先以世物。充滿其意。復施法財。令其歡
361c26‖ 喜。令修福行。令生智道。令增善根力。令起菩
361c27‖ 提心。令淨菩提願。令[3]堅大悲力。令修能滅
361c28‖ 生死道。令生不厭生死行。令攝一切眾生海。
361c29‖ 令修一切功德海。令照一切諸法海。令見一
362a01‖ 切諸佛海。令入一切智智海。

简体字

往一切智大宝洲因、成就不坏摩诃衍因、远离二乘怖畏生死住诸寂静三昧旋因、乘大愿车遍一切处行菩萨行无有障碍清净道因、以菩萨行庄严一切无能坏智清净道因、普观一切十方诸法皆无障碍清净道因、速能趣入一切智海清净道因。

"善男子，我在此城海岸路中，净修菩萨大悲幢行。善男子，我观阎浮提内贫穷众生，为饶益故，修诸苦行，随其所愿悉令满足。先以世物，充满其意；复施法财，令其欢喜，令修福行，令生智道，令增善根力，令起菩提心，令净菩提愿，令坚大悲力，令修能灭生死道，令生不厌生死行，令摄一切众生海，令修一切功德海，令照一切诸法海，令见一切诸佛海，令入一切智智海。

About the causes for reaching the great jeweled isle of all-knowledge;

About the causes for complete success in the indestructible Mahāyāna;

About the causes for leaving behind the two vehicles practitioners' fear of *saṃsāra* by which they remain in the whirlpool of their quiescent samādhis;

About the causes of the pure path involved in boarding the vehicle of great vows and going everywhere, unimpededly practicing the bodhisattva practices;

About the causes of the pure path involved in using the bodhisattva practices to adorn the cultivation of indestructible wisdom;

About the causes of the pure path involved in the comprehensive and unimpeded contemplation of all dharmas throughout the ten directions; and

About the causes of the pure path involved in swiftly entering the ocean of all-knowledge.

Son of Good Family, on this city's seashore road I engage in the purifying cultivation of the bodhisattva's practice of the banner of great compassion.

Son of Good Family, I contemplate the poverty-stricken beings on this continent of Jambudvīpa and then, in order to benefit them, I cultivate the austerities and satisfy them in accordance with whatever they wish for. I first use worldly goods to fulfill their wishes and then also provide them with the wealth of the Dharma. In this way:

I cause them to feel joyous delight;

I cause them to cultivate meritorious practices;

I cause them to bring forth the path of wisdom;

I cause them to increase the power of their roots of goodness;

I cause them to arouse the resolve to attain bodhi;

I cause them to purify the vow to attain bodhi;

I cause them to strengthen the power of great compassion;

I cause them to cultivate the path by which they are able to extinguish *saṃsāra*;[125]

I cause them to bring forth the practices by which they do not weary of *saṃsāra*;

I cause them to attract the ocean of all beings;

I cause them to cultivate the ocean of all meritorious qualities;

I cause them to illuminate the ocean of all dharmas;

I cause them to see the ocean of all buddhas; and

I cause them to enter the ocean of the wisdom of all-knowledge.

正體字

善男子。我住於
362a02‖ 此如是思惟。如是作意。如是利益一切眾生。
362a03‖ 善男子。我知海中一切寶洲。一切寶處。一切
362a04‖ 寶類。一切寶種。我知淨一切寶。鑽一切寶。出
362a05‖ 一切寶。作一切寶。我知一切寶器。一切寶用。
362a06‖ 一切寶境界。一切寶光明。我知一切龍宮處。
362a07‖ 一切夜叉宮處。一切部多宮處。皆善迴避。免
362a08‖ 其諸難。亦善別知[1]漩澓淺深。波濤遠近。水
362a09‖ 色好惡。種種不同。亦善別知日月星宿。運行
362a10‖ 度數。晝夜晨晡。晷漏延促。亦知其船鐵木堅
362a11‖ 脆。機關澁滑。水之大小。風之逆順。如是一切
362a12‖ 安危之相。無不明了。可行則行。可止則止。善
362a13‖ 男子。我以成就如是智慧。常能利益一切眾
362a14‖ 生。善男子。我以好船。運諸商眾。行安隱道。
362a15‖ 復為說法。令其歡喜。引至寶州。與諸珍寶。咸
362a16‖ 使充足。然後將領。還閻浮提。善男子。我將大
362a17‖ 船。如是往來。未始令其一有損壞。若有眾生。
362a18‖ 得見我身。聞我法者。令其永不怖生死海。必
362a19‖ 得入於一切智海。必能[2]消竭諸愛欲海。

简体字

善男子，我住于此，如是思惟，如是作意，如是利益一切众生。

“善男子，我知海中一切宝洲、一切宝处、一切宝类、一切宝种。我知净一切宝、钻一切宝、出一切宝、作一切宝。我知一切宝器、一切宝用、一切宝境界、一切宝光明。我知一切龙宫处、一切夜叉宫处、一切部多宫处，皆善回避，免其诸难。亦善别知，漩澓浅深，波涛远近，水色好恶，种种不同。亦善别知，日月星宿运行度数，昼夜晨晡，晷漏延促。亦知其船铁木坚脆、机关涩滑，水之大小，风之逆顺；如是一切安危之相无不明了，可行则行，可止则止。善男子，我以成就如是智慧，常能利益一切众生。

“善男子，我以好船运诸商众行安隐道，复为说法令其欢喜，引至宝洲与诸珍宝咸使充足，然后将领还阎浮提。善男子，我将大船如是往来，未始令其一有损坏。若有众生得见我身、闻我法者，令其永不怖生死海，必得入于一切智海，必能消竭诸爱欲海，

Son of Good Family, as I dwell here, I engage in just such contemplation, just such reflection, and just such benefit of all beings. Son of Good Family, I know all the isles of jewels out in the sea, all the places where jewels are located, all the classes of jewels, and all the species of jewels. I know how to purify all jewels, how to drill through all jewels, how to extract all jewels, and how to make things from all types of jewels. I know all the vessels made of jewels, all the uses of jewels, the spheres of experience associated with all jewels, and the radiance of all jewels.

I know the locations of all dragon palaces, the locations of all *yakṣa* palaces, and the locations of all *bhūta* palaces while also being skilled in avoiding these beings and averting the difficulties they create. I am also skilled in distinguishing the many differences in the relative depth of whirlpools, the distance from crashing surf waves, and the good or bad colorations of the waters.

I am also well able to distinguish in accordance with the sun, moon, stars, and constellations, the speed and distance of travel, the time of the day, night, morning, or afternoon, and the amount of elapsed time, and also know the relative solidity or fragility of a ship's iron and wood structures, the state of a mechanism's lubrication, the depth of the waters, whether there are opposing or favorable winds, and all other such signs of safety or danger, having none of these matters I do not completely understand. Thus, knowing when one should proceed, I then proceed, and, knowing when one should stop, I then stop.

Son of Good Family, it is because I have perfected such wisdom as this that I am ever able to benefit all beings. Son of Good Family, using a fine ship and following a safe route, I transport groups of merchants and also speak about the Dharma for them, thereby causing them to feel delighted. I lead them to the isle of jewels, provide them with all kinds of precious jewels, ensure that they are completely satisfied and then, afterward, I take them back to Jambudvīpa.

Son of Good Family, while transporting them back and forth in this great ship in this way, I have never yet allowed even one of them to come to harm. Any beings who are able to see me and hear the Dharma that I teach:

Will be caused to remain forever free of any fear of the ocean of *saṃsāra*;
Will certainly succeed in entering the ocean of all-knowledge;
Will certainly be able to dry up the ocean of craving;

正體字

能
362a20 以智光。照三世海。能盡一切眾生苦海。能淨
362a21 一切眾生心海。速能嚴淨一切剎海。普能往
362a22 詣十方大海。普知一切眾生根海。普了一切
362a23 眾生行海。普順一切眾生心海。善男子。我
362a24 唯得此大悲幢行。若有見我。及以聞我。與
362a25 我同住。憶念我者。皆悉不空。如諸菩薩摩訶
362a26 薩。善能遊涉生死大海。不染一切諸煩惱海。
362a27 能捨一切諸妄見海。能觀一切諸法性海。能
362a28 以四攝。攝眾生海。已善安住一切智海。能
362a29 滅一切眾生著海。能平等住一切時海。能以
362b01 神通。度眾生海。能以其時。調眾生海。而我云
362b02 何能知能說彼功德行。善男子。於此南方。有
362b03 城名可樂。中有長者。名無上勝。汝詣彼問。菩
362b04 薩云何學菩薩行。修菩薩道。時善財童子。頂
362b05 禮其足。遶無量匝。慇懃瞻仰。悲泣流淚。

简体字

能以智光照三世海，能尽一切众生苦海，能净一切众生心海，速能严净一切刹海，普能往诣十方大海，普知一切众生根海，普了一切众生行海，普顺一切众生心海。

“善男子，我唯得此大悲幢行；若有见我及以闻我、与我同住、忆念我者，皆悉不空。如诸菩萨摩诃萨，善能游涉生死大海，不染一切诸烦恼海，能舍一切诸妄见海，能观一切诸法性海，能以四摄摄众生海，已善安住一切智海，能灭一切众生著海，能平等住一切时海，能以神通度众生海，能以其时调众生海；而我云何能知能说彼功德行？

“善男子，于此南方，有城名可乐；中有长者，名无上胜。汝诣彼问：菩萨云何学菩萨行、修菩萨道？”

时，善财童子顶礼其足，绕无量匝，殷勤瞻仰，悲泣流泪，

Will be able to use the light of wisdom to illuminate the ocean of the three periods of time;
Will be able to put an end to the ocean of all beings' sufferings;
Will be able to purify the ocean of all beings' minds;
Will be able to swiftly purify the ocean of all *kṣetras;*
Will be able to travel and pay their respects everywhere in the ocean of the ten directions;
Will everywhere know the ocean of all beings' faculties;
Will everywhere completely understand the ocean of all beings' actions; and
Will everywhere adapt to the ocean of all beings' minds.

Son of Good Family, I have acquired only this practice of the banner of the great compassion. If anyone so much as sees me, hears me, dwells together with me, or brings me to mind, then none of them will have done so in vain. As for the bodhisattva-mahāsattvas:

Who are well able to roam about on the great ocean of *saṃsāra;*
Who remain undefiled by the ocean of all afflictions;
Who are able to relinquish the ocean of all wrong views;
Who are able to contemplate the ocean of the nature of all dharmas;
Who are able to use the four means of attraction to attract the ocean of beings;
Who have already come to skillfully and securely dwell in the ocean of all-knowledge;
Who are able to extinguish the ocean of all beings' attachments;
Who are able to equally abide throughout the ocean of all times;
Who are able to use the spiritual superknowledges to liberate the ocean of all beings; and
Who are able to accord with the appropriate time in training the ocean of beings—

How could I know of or be able to speak about their meritorious qualities and practices?

Son of Good Family, south of here, there is a city named Nandihāraṃ or "Delightful" in which there is an elder named Jayottama or "Unsurpassed Supremacy." You should go there, pay your respects, and ask him, "How should a bodhisattva train in the bodhisattva practices and how should he cultivate the bodhisattva path?"

Sudhana the Youth then bowed down in reverence at his feet and circumambulated him countless times as he gazed up at him in attentive admiration and tears of sadness flowed down his countenance.

正體字

求善
362b06║ 知識。心無厭足。辭退而去
362b07║ 爾時善財童子。起大慈周遍心。大悲潤澤心。
362b08║ 相續不斷。福德智慧二種莊嚴。捨離一切煩
362b09║ 惱塵垢。證法平等。心無高下。拔不善刺。滅一
362b10║ 切障。堅固精進以為牆塹。甚深三昧而作園
362b11║ 苑。以慧日光破無明暗。以方便風開智慧華。
362b12║ 以無礙願充滿法界。心常現入一切智城。如
362b13║ 是而求菩薩之道。漸次經歷。到彼城內。見無
362b14║ 上勝在其城東大莊嚴幢無憂林中。無量商
362b15║ 人。百千居士之所圍遶。理斷人間種種事務。
362b16║ 因為說法。令其永拔一切我慢。離我我所。捨
362b17║ 所積聚。滅慳嫉[3]垢。心得清淨。無諸穢濁。獲
362b18║ 淨信力。常樂見佛。受持佛法。生菩薩力。起菩
362b19║ 薩行。

简体字

求善知识心无厌足，辞退而去。

尔时，善财童子起大慈周遍心、大悲润泽心相续不断，福德、智慧二种庄严，舍离一切烦恼尘垢，证法平等，心无高下，拔不善刺，灭一切障，坚固精进以为墙堑，甚深三昧而作园苑，以慧日光破无明暗，以方便风开智慧华，以无碍愿充满法界，心常现入一切智城，如是而求菩萨之道。

渐次经历，到彼城内。见无上胜在其城东大庄严幢无忧林中，无量商人、百千居士之所围绕，理断人间种种事务；因为说法，令其永拔一切我慢，离我、我所，舍所积聚，灭悭嫉垢，心得清净，无诸秽浊，获净信力，常乐见佛，受持佛法，生菩萨力，起菩萨行，

Then, with a mind that was insatiable in the search for good spiritual guides, he respectfully withdrew and departed.

23 – Jayottama

At that time, Sudhana the Youth:

Continuously and ceaselessly produced the mind of universal great kindness and the mind moistened by great compassion;
Cultivated merit and wisdom, the two types of adornment;
Abandoned the filth of all the afflictions;
Realized the uniform equality of dharmas;
Kept his mind free of any judgments as to superiority or inferiority;
Pulled out all the thorns of bad actions;
Destroyed all obstacles;
Drew strength from the practice of vigor as his city wall and moat;
Took extremely deep samādhi as his park and gardens;
Used the sunlight of wisdom to dispel the darkness of ignorance;
Used the breeze of skillful means to cause the flowers of wisdom to bloom;
Used unimpeded vows to fill the Dharma realm; and
Caused his mind to always manifest entry into the city of all-knowledge.

Continuing his quest for the bodhisattva path in this way, he gradually traveled along until, reaching the inner precincts of that city, he saw that Jayottama was east of the city at the great adornment banner in the Aśoka or "Sorrow-Free" Forest where he was surrounded by a group of countless merchants and a hundred thousand laymen for whom he adjudicated many different kinds of human affairs on account of which he spoke about the Dharma and thereby enabled them:

To forever uproot all conceit;
To abandon the concepts of a self and anything belonging to a self;
To relinquish whatever they had amassed;
To extinguish the filth of miserliness and jealousy;
To acquire purity of mind;
To become free of the turbidity of the defilements;
To gain the power of pure faith;
To always delight in seeing the Buddha;
To absorb and retain the Buddha's Dharma;
To develop the power of the bodhisattva;
To bring forth the bodhisattva practices;

正體字

入菩薩三昧。得菩薩智慧。住菩薩正念。
362b20‖ 增菩薩樂欲。爾時善財童子。觀彼長者為眾
362b21‖ 說法已。以身投地。頂禮其足。良久乃起。白
362b22‖ 言。聖者。我是善財。我是善財。我專尋求菩薩
362b23‖ 之行。菩薩云何學菩薩行。菩薩云何修菩薩
362b24‖ 道。隨修學時。常能化度一切眾生。常能現
362b25‖ 見一切諸佛。常得聽聞一切佛法。常能住持
362b26‖ 一切佛法。常能趣入一切法門。入一切剎。學
362b27‖ 菩薩行。住一切劫。修菩薩道。能知一切如
362b28‖ 來神力。能受一切如來護念。能得一切如來
362b29‖ 智慧。時彼長者。告善財言。善哉善哉。善男
362c01‖ 子。汝已能發阿耨多羅三藐三菩提心。善男
362c02‖ 子。我成就至一切處菩薩行門無依無作神
362c03‖ 通之力。善男子。云何為至一切處菩薩行門。
362c04‖ 善男子。我於此三千大千世界。欲界一切諸
362c05‖ 眾生中。所謂一切三十三天。一切須夜摩天。
362c06‖ 一切兜率陀天。一切善變化天。一切他化自
362c07‖ 在天。一切魔天。及餘一切天龍夜叉羅剎娑
362c08‖ 鳩槃[4]茶乾闥婆。阿脩羅迦樓羅緊那羅摩睺
362c09‖ 羅伽人與非人。村營城邑。

简体字

入菩萨三昧，得菩萨智慧，住菩萨正念，增菩萨乐欲。

尔时，善财童子观彼长者为众说法已，以身投地，顶礼其足，良久乃起，白言："圣者，我是善财！我是善财！我专寻求菩萨之行，菩萨云何学菩萨行？菩萨云何修菩萨道？随修学时，常能化度一切众生，常能现见一切诸佛，常得听闻一切佛法，常能住持一切佛法，常能趣入一切法门，入一切刹学菩萨行，住一切劫修菩萨道，能知一切如来神力，能受一切如来护念，能得一切如来智慧？"

时，彼长者告善财言："善哉！善哉！善男子，汝已能发阿耨多罗三藐三菩提心。

"善男子，我成就至一切处菩萨行门无依无作神通之力。善男子，云何为至一切处菩萨行门？善男子，我于此三千大千世界，欲界一切诸众生中，所谓：一切三十三天、一切须夜摩天、一切兜率陀天、一切善变化天、一切他化自在天、一切魔天，及余一切天、龙、夜叉、罗刹娑、鸠槃荼，乾闼婆、阿修罗、迦楼罗、紧那罗、摩睺罗伽、人与非人，村营、城邑、

To enter the bodhisattva samādhis;
To acquire the bodhisattva's wisdom;
To abide in the bodhisattva's right mindfulness; and
To increase in the resolute intentions of the bodhisattva.

Having seen that elder teaching the Dharma for that congregation, Sudhana the Youth then cast his body to the ground as he bowed down in reverence at his feet. After remaining in that prostration for a good while, he rose and addressed him, saying:

O Ārya, I am Sudhana. I am Sudhana. I am solely in search of the bodhisattva practices. How should a bodhisattva train in the bodhisattva practices and how should he cultivate the bodhisattva path? When one is following the course of cultivation and training:

How can one always be able to teach and liberate all beings?
How can one always directly see all buddhas?
How can one always hear the Dharma of all buddhas?
How can one always sustain and preserve all buddhas' Dharma?
How can one always enter all Dharma gateways?
How can one enter all *kṣetras* and train in the bodhisattva practices?
How can one remain throughout all kalpas, cultivating the bodhisattva path?
How can one know all *tathāgatas'* spiritual powers?
How can one receive the protection of all *tathāgatas*?
How can one gain the wisdom of all *tathāgatas*?

That elder then spoke to Sudhana, saying:

It is good indeed, good indeed, Son of Good Family, that you have been able to resolve to attain *anuttara-samyak-saṃbodhi.*

Son of Good Family, I have perfected the bodhisattva's practice gateway of going everywhere using the independent and effortless powers of the spiritual superknowledges.

Son of Good Family, of what does the bodhisattva practice gateway of going everywhere consist? Son of Good Family, taking as my focus all beings of the desire realm in this great trichiliocosm, including all devas of the Trāyastriṃśa Heaven, all devas of the Suyāma Heaven, all devas of the Tuṣita Heaven, all devas of the Skillful Transformations Heaven, all devas of the Paranirmita Vaśavartin Heaven, and all of the *māra* devas as well as all the others in the realms of the devas, dragons, *yakṣas, rākṣasas, kumbhāṇḍas, gandharvas, asuras, garuḍas, kiṃnaras, mahoragas,* humans, and nonhumans, including those in villages, encampments, cities, towns,

正體字

一切住處。諸眾
362c10‖ 生中。而為說法。令捨非法。令息諍論。令除鬪
362c11‖ 戰。令止忿競。令破怨結。令解繫縛。令出牢
362c12‖ 獄。令免怖畏。令斷殺生。乃至邪見一切惡業。
362c13‖ 不可作事。皆令禁止。令其順行一切善法。令
362c14‖ 其修學一切[*]技藝。於諸世間而作利益。為
362c15‖ 其分別種種諸論。令生歡喜。令漸成熟。隨
362c16‖ 順外道。為說勝智。令斷諸見。令入佛法。乃至
362c17‖ 色界一切梵天。我亦為其說超勝法。如於此
362c18‖ 三千大千世界。乃至十方十不可說百千億
362c19‖ 那由他佛剎微塵數世界中。我皆為說佛法。
362c20‖ 菩薩法。聲聞法。獨覺法。說地獄。說地獄眾
362c21‖ 生。說向地獄道。說畜生。說畜生差別。說畜生
362c22‖ 受苦。說向畜生道。說閻羅王世間。說閻羅
362c23‖ 王世間苦。說向閻羅王世間道。說天世間。說
362c24‖ 天世間樂。說向天世間道。說人世間。

简体字

一切住处诸众生中而为说法，令舍非法，令息诤论，令除斗战，令止忿竞，令破冤结，令解系缚，令出牢狱，令免怖畏，令断杀生乃至邪见一切恶业，不可作事皆令禁止；令其顺行一切善法，令其修学一切技艺，于诸世间而作利益；为其分别种种诸论，令生欢喜，令渐成熟；随顺外道，为说胜智，令断诸见，令入佛法。乃至色界一切梵天，我亦为其说超胜法。如于此三千大千世界，乃至十方十不可说百千亿那由他佛刹微尘数世界中，我皆为说佛法、菩萨法、声闻法、独觉法；说地狱，说地狱众生，说向地狱道；说畜生，说畜生差别，说畜生受苦，说向畜生道；说阎罗王世间，说阎罗王世间苦，说向阎罗王世间道；说天世间，说天世间乐，说向天世间道；说人世间，

and all other dwelling places—in the midst of all those beings, I teach the Dharma for their sakes, doing so:

To enable them to abandon what is non-Dharma;
To enable them to stop their disputation;
To enable them to do away with war;
To enable them to halt their angry conflicts;
To enable them to break off their grudge-ridden feuding;
To enable them to release themselves from the bonds;
To enable them to escape their imprisonment;
To enable them to avoid terrifying circumstances;
To enable them to cut off the killing of beings, and so forth up to and including cutting off the holding of wrong views;[126]
To enable them to strictly halt all bad actions and all forbidden endeavors;
To enable them to comply with all good dharmas;
To enable them to cultivate and train in all the technical skills and arts that benefit the world;
To distinguish for their sakes [the teachings of] the many different kinds of treatises so that they may be gladdened and gradually ripened; and
To adapt to the adherents of the non-Buddhist paths and teach them superior wisdom so they may be caused to cut off all their wrong views and enter the Dharma of the Buddha.

I also teach the transcendently supreme Dharma even for all the devas of the form realm's Brahma Heaven. And just as I proceed in this way in all the worlds of this great trichiliocosm, so too do I also do so even for all beings in the worlds of the ten directions that are as numerous as the atoms in ten ineffable numbers of hundreds of thousands of *koṭīs* of *nayutas* of buddha *kṣetras*. For all of them I teach the dharmas of a buddha, the dharmas of a bodhisattva, the dharmas of a *śrāvaka* disciple, and the dharmas of a *pratyekabuddha*.

I teach about the hell realms, teach about the beings in the hell realms, and teach about the paths leading to the hell realms. I teach about the animal realms, teach about the different kinds of animals, teach about the suffering experienced by animals, and teach about the paths leading into the animal realms. I teach about the worlds of King Yama, teach about the sufferings in the worlds of King Yama, and teach about the paths leading into the worlds of King Yama. I teach about the worlds of the devas, teach about the bliss of the deva worlds, and teach about the paths leading to the deva worlds. And I teach about the worlds of humans, teach about the suffering and

正體字

說人
362c25‖ 世間苦樂。說向人世間道。為欲開顯菩薩功
362c26‖ 德。為令捨離生死過患。為令知見一切智人
362c27‖ 諸妙功德。為欲令知諸有趣中迷惑受苦。為
362c28‖ 令知見無障礙法。為欲顯示一切世間生起
362c29‖ 所因。為欲顯示一切世間寂滅為樂。為令眾
363a01‖ 生捨諸想著。為令證得佛無依法。為令永滅
363a02‖ 諸煩惱輪。為令能轉如來法輪。我為眾生。說
363a03‖ 如是法。善男子。我唯知此至一切處修菩薩
363a04‖ 行清淨法門。無依無作神通之力。如諸菩薩
363a05‖ 摩訶薩。具足一切自在神通。悉能遍往一切
363a06‖ 佛剎。得普眼地。悉聞一切音聲言說。普入
363a07‖ 諸法智慧自在。無有乖諍。勇健無比。以廣長
363a08‖ 舌。出平等音。其身妙好。同諸菩薩。與諸如來
363a09‖ 究竟無二。無有差別。智身廣大普入三世。境
363a10‖ 界無際同於虛空。而我云何能知能說彼功
363a11‖ 德行。

简体字

说人世间苦乐，说向人世间道。为欲开显菩萨功德，为令舍离生死过患，为令知见一切智人诸妙功德，为欲令知诸有趣中迷惑受苦，为令知见无障碍法，为欲显示一切世间生起所因，为欲显示一切世间寂灭为乐，为令众生舍诸想著，为令证得佛无依法，为令永灭诸烦恼轮，为令能转如来法轮，我为众生说如是法。

“善男子，我唯知此至一切处修菩萨行清净法门无依无作神通之力。如诸菩萨摩诃萨，具足一切自在神通，悉能遍往一切佛刹，得普眼地；悉闻一切音声言说，普入诸法智慧自在，无有乖诤，勇健无比，以广长舌出平等音；其身妙好，同诸菩萨，与诸如来究竟无二、无有差别；智身广大，普入三世，境界无际，同于虚空。而我云何能知能说彼功德行？

pleasure of the human worlds, and teach about the paths leading to the human worlds. I do this:

Wishing to reveal the bodhisattva's meritorious qualities;
To cause beings to relinquish the faults of *saṃsāra;*
To cause beings to know and see all the marvelous meritorious qualities of those possessed of all-knowledge;
Wishing to cause beings to know of the delusion and suffering in all the rebirth destinies of existence;
To cause beings to know and see the unimpeded dharmas;
Wishing to reveal the causes of the origination of all worlds;
Wishing to reveal how nirvāṇa is the most blissful thing in all worlds;
To cause beings to relinquish all conceptual attachments;
To cause beings to realize the Buddha's non-dependent Dharma;
To cause beings to forever extinguish the cycle of all afflictions; and
To cause beings to be able to turn the Tathāgata's wheel of Dharma.

I teach dharmas such as these for the benefit of beings.

Son of Good Family, I know only this pure Dharma gateway of going everywhere to cultivate the bodhisattva practices using the independent and effortless powers of the spiritual superknowledges. As for the bodhisattva-mahāsattvas:

Who are completely possessed of sovereign mastery in all the spiritual superknowledges;
Who are all able to go everywhere to all buddha *kṣetras;*
Who have reached the ground of the universal eye;
Who all hear all voices and languages;
Who have achieved sovereign mastery of the wisdom which everywhere penetrates all dharmas;
Who are free of any disputation;
Who are incomparably brave and strong;
Who use their vast and long tongues to send forth the sound of impartial teachings;
Whose bodies are marvelously fine and identical to those of the other bodhisattvas;
Who will ultimately be no different from the Tathāgatas;
Whose wisdom bodies are so vast that they penetrate all three periods of time; and
Whose spheres of objective experience are as boundless as empty space—

How could I know of or speak about their meritorious qualities and practices?

正體字

善男子。於此南方。有一國土。名曰輸
363a12‖ 那。其國有城。名迦陵迦林。有比丘尼。名師子
363a13‖ [1]頻申。汝詣彼問。菩薩云何學菩薩行。修菩
363a14‖ 薩道。時善財童子。頂禮其足。遶無量匝。慇懃
363a15‖ 瞻仰。辭退而去
363a16‖ 爾時善財童子。漸次遊行。至彼國城。周遍推
363a17‖ 求此比丘尼。有無量人。咸告之言。善男子。此
363a18‖ 比丘尼。在勝光王之所捨施日光園中。說法
363a19‖ 利益無量眾生。時善財童子。即詣彼園。周
363a20‖ 遍觀察。見其園中。有一大樹。名為滿月。形如
363a21‖ 樓閣。放大光明。照一由旬。見一葉樹。名為普
363a22‖ 覆。其形如蓋。放毘瑠璃紺青光明。見一華樹。
363a23‖ 名曰華藏。其形高大。如雪山王。雨眾妙華。無
363a24‖ 有窮盡。如忉利天中波利質多羅樹。復見有
363a25‖ 一甘露果樹。形如金山。常放光明。種種眾果。
363a26‖ 悉皆具足。復見有一摩尼寶樹。名毘盧遮那
363a27‖ 藏。其形無比。心王摩尼寶。最在其上阿僧祇
363a28‖ 色相摩尼寶。周遍莊嚴。復有衣樹。名為清
363a29‖ 淨種種色衣。垂布嚴飾。復有音樂樹。名為
363b01‖ 歡喜。其音美妙。過諸天樂。

简体字

“善男子，于此南方，有一国土，名曰输那；其国有城，名迦陵迦林；有比丘尼，名师子嚬申。汝诣彼问：菩萨云何学菩萨行、修菩萨道？”

时，善财童子顶礼其足，绕无量匝，殷勤瞻仰，辞退而去。

尔时，善财童子渐次游行，至彼国城，周遍推求此比丘尼。有无量人咸告之言：“善男子，此比丘尼在胜光王之所舍施日光园中说法利益无量众生。”时，善财童子即诣彼园，周遍观察。

见其园中有一大树，名为满月，形如楼阁，放大光明照一由旬；见一叶树，名为普覆，其形如盖，放毗琉璃绀青光明；见一华树，名曰华藏，其形高大，如雪山王，雨众妙华无有穷尽，如忉利天中波利质多罗树。复见有一甘露果树，形如金山，常放光明，种种众果悉皆具足；复见有一摩尼宝树，名毗卢遮那藏，其形无比，心王摩尼宝最在其上，阿僧祇色相摩尼宝周遍庄严。复有衣树，名为清净，种种色衣垂布严饰；复有音乐树，名为欢喜，其音美妙，过诸天乐；

Son of Good Family, south of here, there is a land known as Śroṇāparānta. That country has a city known as Kaliṅgavana in which there is a bhikshuni named Siṃhavijṛmbhitā. You should go there, pay your respects, and ask her, "How should the bodhisattva train in the bodhisattva practices and how should he cultivate the bodhisattva path?"

Sudhana the Youth then bowed down in reverence at his feet and circumambulated him countless times as he gazed up at him in attentive admiration. He then respectfully withdrew and departed.

24 – Siṁhavijṛmbhitā

At that time, Sudhana the Youth then gradually traveled on until he reached the city in that country where he then searched all around for this bhikshuni. Countless people all told him: "Son of Good Family, this bhikshuni resides in Sunlight Park, a place donated by King Jayapraha or 'Supreme Light' where she teaches the Dharma for the benefit of countless beings."

Sudhana the Youth then went to that park where, looking all around, he saw a huge tree in that park that was known as "Full Moon" that, shaped like a tower, emanated a bright light that cast its illumination a full *yojana* all around.

He saw a leafy tree known as "Universal Shelter" that, shaped like a canopy, emanated a purple-blue lapis lazuli light.

He saw a flowering tree known as "Blossom Treasury" that, in its height and breadth, resembled the king of the Himalaya mountains. Like the *pārajātaka* tree of the Trāyastriṃśa Heaven, it endlessly sprinkled down many kinds of marvelous blossoms.

He also saw an "elixir of immortality" fruit tree shaped like a mountain of gold that always emanated light and that was abundantly laden with many different kinds of fruits.

He also saw a uniquely shaped *maṇi* jewel tree known as "Vairocana Treasury" that had mind-king *maṇi* jewels up at the very top and that was adorned all around with *maṇi* jewels appearing in infinitely many different colors.

There was also a robe tree known as "Purity" that had robes of many different colors draping down from it as decorative adornments.

There was also a music tree known as "Joyous Delight," the sounds of which were more exquisitely marvelous than the music of the heavens.

正體字

復有香樹。名普莊
363b02║ 嚴。恒出妙香。普熏十方。無所障礙。園中復有
363b03║ 泉流陂池。一切皆以七寶莊嚴。黑栴檀泥。凝
363b04║ 積其中。上妙金沙。彌布其底。八功德水。具足
363b05║ 盈滿。優鉢羅華。波頭摩華。拘物頭華。芬陀利
363b06║ 華。遍覆其上。無量寶樹。周遍行列。諸寶樹
363b07║ 下。敷師子座。種種妙寶。以為莊嚴。布以天
363b08║ 衣。熏諸妙香。垂諸寶繒。施諸寶帳。閻浮金
363b09║ 網。彌覆其上。寶鐸徐搖。出妙音聲。或有樹下
363b10║ 敷蓮華藏師子之座。或有樹下敷香王摩尼
363b11║ 藏師子之座。或有樹下敷龍莊嚴摩尼王藏
363b12║ 師子之座。或有樹下敷寶師子聚摩尼王藏
363b13║ 師子之座。或有樹下敷毘盧遮那摩尼王藏
363b14║ 師子之座。或有樹下敷十方毘盧遮那摩尼
363b15║ 王藏師子之座。其一一座。各有十萬寶師子
363b16║ 座。周匝圍遶。一一皆具無量莊嚴。此大園中。
363b17║ 眾寶遍滿。猶如大海寶洲之上。迦隣陀衣。以
363b18║ 布其地。柔軟妙好。能生樂觸。蹈則沒足。舉則
363b19║ 還復。無量諸鳥。出和雅音。

简体字

复有香树，名普庄严，恒出妙香，普熏十方，无所障碍。

园中复有泉流陂池，一切皆以七宝庄严，黑栴檀泥凝积其中，上妙金沙弥布其底，八功德水具足盈满，优钵罗华、波头摩华、拘物头华、芬陀利华遍覆其上，无量宝树周遍行列。诸宝树下敷师子座，种种妙宝以为庄严，布以天衣，熏诸妙香，垂诸宝缯，施诸宝帐，阎浮金网弥覆其上，宝铎徐摇出妙音声。或有树下敷莲华藏师子之座，或有树下敷香王摩尼藏师子之座，或有树下敷龙庄严摩尼王藏师子之座，或有树下敷宝师子聚摩尼王藏师子之座，或有树下敷毗卢遮那摩尼王藏师子之座，或有树下敷十方毗卢遮那摩尼王藏师子之座；其一一座各有十万宝师子座周匝围绕，一一皆具无量庄严。

此大园中众宝遍满，犹如大海宝洲之上。迦邻陀衣以布其地，柔软妙好，能生乐触，蹈则没足，举则还复；无量诸鸟出和雅音，

And there was also a fragrance tree known as "Universal Adornment" that always exuded marvelous fragrances that were unimpeded in everywhere suffusing the ten directions with their scents.

In that park, there were also springs, streams, and ponds, all of which were adorned with the seven precious things and had bottoms coated with *kālānusāri* sandalwood incense gum that had collected and thickened there. Spread all across their bottoms were supremely marvelous sands of gold. They were completely filled with the waters of the eight qualities that were everywhere covered with *utpala* blossoms, *padma* blossoms, *kumuda* blossoms, and *puṇḍarīka* blossoms and they were surrounded all around by rows of trees adorned with countless jewels.

Beneath those jeweled trees were lion thrones adorned with all different kinds of marvelous jewels. They were spread with celestial robes, imbued with all kinds of marvelous fragrances, hung with all kinds of jeweled silken sashes, graced by jeweled curtains, covered with suspended nets woven with *jambūnada* gold, and hung with slowly swaying jeweled bells sending forth sublime music. Moreover:

Beneath some of the trees, there were lotus dais lion thrones;

Beneath other trees, there were incense-king *maṇi* jewel lotus dais lion thrones;

Beneath other trees, there were sovereign *maṇi* jewel lotus dais lion thrones adorned with dragons;

Beneath other trees, there were sovereign *maṇi* jewel lotus dais lion thrones adorned with groups of jeweled lions;

Beneath other trees, there were *vairocana* sovereign *maṇi* jewel lotus dais lion thrones; and

Beneath other trees, there were ten directions illumining *vairocana* sovereign *maṇi* jewel lotus dais lion thrones.

Every one of those thrones was surrounded by ten myriads of jeweled lion thrones, every one of which was replete with countless varieties of adornments.

The area within this immense park was everywhere so filled with many types of jewels that it resembled a jeweled isle out on the great ocean. Its grounds were spread with *kācalindika* robes that were so soft and pliant that they caused one to feel blissful sensations as, stepping down on them, one's foot sank into them, and, when one's foot was raised, it returned to its original appearance.

There were countless varieties of birds singing harmonious and elegant sounds.

正體字

寶栴檀林。上妙莊
363b20‖ 嚴。種種妙華。常雨無盡。猶如帝釋雜華之園。
363b21‖ 無比香王普熏一切。猶如帝釋善法之堂。諸
363b22‖ 音樂樹寶多羅樹眾寶鈴網出妙音聲。如自
363b23‖ 在天善口天女所出歌音。諸如意樹種種妙
363b24‖ 衣垂布莊嚴。猶如大海有無量色百千樓閣。
363b25‖ 眾寶莊嚴。如忉利天宮善見大城。寶蓋遐張
363b26‖ 如須彌峯。光明普照如梵王宮。爾時善財童
363b27‖ 子。見此大園無量功德。種種莊嚴。皆是菩
363b28‖ 薩業報成就。出世善根之所生起。供養諸佛
363b29‖ 功德所流。一切世間無與等者。如是皆從師
363c01‖ 子[＊]頻申比丘尼了法如幻集。廣大清淨福德
363c02‖ 善業之所成就。三千大千世界。天龍八部。無
363c03‖ 量眾生。皆入此園。而不迫窄。何以故。此比丘
363c04‖ 尼。不可思議威神力故。爾時善財。見師子
363c05‖ [＊]頻申比丘尼。遍坐一切諸寶樹下大師子座。
363c06‖ 身相端嚴。威儀寂靜。

简体字

宝栴檀林上妙庄严，种种妙华常雨无尽，犹如帝释杂华之园。无比香王普熏一切，犹如帝释善法之堂。诸音乐树、宝多罗树、众宝铃网出妙音声，如自在天善口天女所出歌音。诸如意树，种种妙衣垂布庄严，犹如大海。有无量色百千楼阁，众宝庄严，如忉利天宫善见大城。宝盖遐张，如须弥峰。光明普照，如梵王宫。

尔时，善财童子见此大园无量功德、种种庄严，皆是菩萨业报成就，出世善根之所生起，供养诸佛功德所流，一切世间无与等者，如是皆从师子嚬申比丘尼了法如幻集广大清净福德善业之所成就。三千大千世界天龙八部、无量众生，皆入此园而不迫窄。何以故？此比丘尼不可思议威神力故。

尔时，善财见师子嚬申比丘尼遍坐一切诸宝树下大师子座，身相端严，威仪寂静，

The jeweled sandalwood forest was adorned with supremely marvelous adornments that constantly sprinkled down an endless rain of many kinds of exquisite flowers in a manner similar to Śakra's park full of various flowers.

Peerlessly fine imperial fragrances everywhere permeated everything just as they do in Śakra's Sudharma Hall.

All of the music trees, jeweled *pārijātaka* trees, and the nets hung with the many-jeweled bells sent forth the sounds of marvelous music comparable in its beauty to the songs sung by the heavenly nymph, Fine Mouth, in the Paranirmita Vaśavartin Heaven.

All of the wish-fulfilling trees hung with adornments consisting of many different kinds of marvelous robes created an appearance comparable to a great ocean.

There were hundreds of thousands of towers in countless colors adorned with many different kinds of jewels which created an appearance like that of the Trāyastriṃśa Heaven palace's great city of Sudarśana, "Good to Behold."

A jeweled canopy stretched far across it appeared like the profile of Sumeru's peaks and produced a universally illuminating radiance similar to that of the palace of the Brahma Heaven King.

Sudhana the Youth then saw that this immense park with its countless excellent qualities and many kinds of adornments had all been accomplished as the karmic rewards of this bodhisattva, were created by her world-transcending roots of goodness, were results flowing from the merit of the offerings she had presented to all buddhas, and were phenomena unmatched by anything else in any world. Appearances such as these had all been brought together through Siṃhavijṛmbhitā Bhikshuni's complete understanding of dharmas' similarity to mere conjured illusions and were the perfected culmination of her vast pure merit and good karmic deeds.

The devas, dragons, and others of the eight groups of spiritual beings as well as countless other beings from the worlds of the great trichiliocosm were all able to enter this park and yet they were not crowded together. How could this be so? This was possible due to this bhikshuni's inconceivable and awe-inspiring spiritual powers.

Sudhana the Youth then saw that Siṃhavijṛmbhitā Bhikshuni was seated everywhere on all the lion thrones beneath all those jeweled trees. He saw too that:

Her physical appearance was proper and dignified and her deportment was serene;

正體字

諸根調順如大象王。心
363c07 ‖ 無垢濁如清淨池。普濟所求如如意寶。不染
363c08 ‖ 世法猶如蓮華。心無所畏如師子王。護持淨
363c09 ‖ 戒不可傾動如須彌山。能令見者心得清涼
363c10 ‖ 如妙香王。能除眾生諸煩惱熱如雪山中妙
363c11 ‖ 栴檀香。眾生見者諸苦消滅如善見藥王。見
363c12 ‖ 者不空如婆樓那天。能長一切眾善根芽如
363c13 ‖ 良沃田。在一一座。眾會不同。所說法門。亦各
363c14 ‖ 差別。或見處座淨居天眾所共圍遶。大自在
363c15 ‖ 天子而為上首。此比丘尼為說法門。名無盡
363c16 ‖ 解脫。或見處座諸梵天眾所共圍遶。愛樂梵
363c17 ‖ 王而為上首。此比丘尼為說法門。名普門差
363c18 ‖ 別清淨言音輪。或見處座他化自在天天子
363c19 ‖ 天女所共圍遶。自在天王而為上首。此比丘
363c20 ‖ 尼為說法門。名菩薩清淨心。或見處座善變
363c21 ‖ 化天天子天女所共圍遶。善化天王而為上
363c22 ‖ 首。此比丘尼為說法門。名一切法善莊嚴。

简体字

诸根调顺，如大象王；心无垢浊，如清净池；普济所求，如如意宝；不染世法，犹如莲华；心无所畏，如师子王；护持净戒不可倾动，如须弥山；能令见者心得清凉，如妙香王；能除众生诸烦恼热，如雪山中妙栴檀香；众生见者，诸苦消灭，如善见药王；见者不空，如婆楼那天；能长一切众善根芽，如良沃田。

在一一座，众会不同，所说法门亦各差别；或见处座，净居天众所共围绕，大自在天子而为上首；此比丘尼为说法门，名无尽解脱。或见处座，诸梵天众所共围绕，爱乐梵王而为上首；此比丘尼为说法门，名普门差别清净言音轮。或见处座，他化自在天天子、天女所共围绕，自在天王而为上首；此比丘尼为说法门，名菩萨清净心。或见处座，善变化天天子、天女所共围绕，善化天王而为上首；此比丘尼为说法门，名一切法善庄严。

All of her faculties were as well trained and compliant as the great king of elephants;

Her mind was as free of the turbidity of the defilements as a clear lake of pure waters;

In her everywhere relieving the wants of beings, she was like a wish-fulfilling jewel;

She was as unstained by worldly dharmas as a lotus flower;

Her mind was as fearless as the king of lions;

In guarding and preserving the precepts of purity, she was as unshakable as Mount Sumeru;

In her ability to cause the minds of those seeing her to become clear and cool, she was like the marvelous king of incense;

In her ability to rid beings of the fever of their afflictions, she was like the marvelous sandalwood incense from the Himalaya Mountains;

In allaying all the sufferings of those who see her, she was like *Śudarśana* or "Good to Behold," the king of all medicines;

In benefiting all who saw her so that they did not come to her in vain, she was like the deva, Varuṇa; and

In her ability to promote the growth of all beings' roots of goodness, she was like an especially fine and fertile field.

At every one of those throne sites, the assembled congregations were different from each other and the Dharma gateways she taught were also different:

In one place, he saw her seated there, surrounded by a congregation of devas from the Pure Abodes Heaven headed by Maheśvara for whom this bhikshuni taught a Dharma gateway known as "endless liberation";

In another place, he saw her seated there, surrounded by a congregation of Brahma Heaven devas, headed by the Brahma Heaven King known as Rucira for whom this bhikshuni taught a Dharma gateway known as "universal gateway of the wheel of different pure voices";

In another place, he saw her seated there, surrounded by a congregation of Paranirmita Vaśavartin Heaven devas' sons and devas' daughters headed by the Paranirmitavaśavartin Heaven King for whom this bhikshuni taught a Dharma gateway known as "the bodhisattva's pure resolve";

In another place, he saw her seated there, surrounded by a congregation of Skillful Transformations Heaven devas' sons and devas' daughters headed by the Skillful Transformations Heaven King for whom this bhikshuni taught a Dharma gateway known as "the skillful adornment of all dharmas";

正體字

或
363c23 | 見處座兜率陀天天子天女所共圍遶。兜率
363c24 | 天王而為上首。此比丘尼為說法門。名心藏
363c25 | 旋。或見處座須夜摩天天子天女所共圍遶
363c26 | 夜摩天王而為上首。此比丘尼為說法門。名
363c27 | 無邊莊嚴。或見處座三十三天天子天女所
363c28 | 共圍遶。釋提桓因而為上首。此比丘尼為說
363c29 | 法門。名厭離門。或見處座百光明龍王難陀
364a01 | 龍王優波難陀龍王摩那斯龍王伊羅跋難陀
364a02 | 龍王阿那婆達多龍王等龍子龍女所共圍
364a03 | 遶。娑伽羅龍王而為上首。此比丘尼為說法
364a04 | 門。名佛神通境界光明莊嚴。或見處座諸夜
364a05 | 叉眾所共圍遶。毘沙門天王而為上首。此比
364a06 | 丘尼為說法門。名救護眾生藏。或見處座。乾
364a07 | 闥婆眾所共圍遶。持國乾闥婆王而為上首。
364a08 | 此比丘尼為說法門。名無盡喜。或見處座阿
364a09 | 脩羅眾所共圍遶。羅睺阿脩羅王而為上首。
364a10 | 此比丘尼為說法門。名速疾莊嚴法界智門。
364a11 | 或見處座迦樓羅眾所共圍遶。捷持迦樓羅
364a12 | 王而為上首。此比丘尼為說法門。名怖動諸
364a13 | 有海。或見處座緊那羅眾所共圍遶。大樹緊
364a14 | 那羅王而為上首。此比丘尼為說法門。名佛
364a15 | 行光明。或見處座摩睺羅伽眾所共圍遶。菴
364a16 | 羅林摩睺羅伽王而為上首。此比丘尼為說
364a17 | 法門。名生佛歡喜心。

简体字

或见处座，兜率陀天天子、天女所共围绕，兜率天王而为上首；此比丘尼为说法门，名心藏旋。或见处座，须夜摩天天子、天女所共围绕，夜摩天王而为上首；此比丘尼为说法门，名无边庄严。或见处座，三十三天天子、天女所共围绕，释提桓因而为上首；此比丘尼为说法门，名厌离门。或见处座，百光明龙王、难陀龙王、优波难陀龙王、摩那斯龙王、伊罗跋难陀龙王、阿那婆达多龙王等龙子、龙女所共围绕，娑伽罗龙王而为上首；此比丘尼为说法门，名佛神通境界光明庄严。或见处座，诸夜叉众所共围绕，毗沙门天王而为上首；此比丘尼为说法门，名救护众生藏。或见处座，乾闼婆众所共围绕，持国乾闼婆王而为上首；此比丘尼为说法门，名无尽喜。或见处座，阿修罗众所共围绕，罗睺阿修罗王而为上首；此比丘尼为说法门，名速疾庄严法界智门。或见处座，迦楼罗众所共围绕，捷持迦楼罗王而为上首；此比丘尼为说法门，名怖动诸有海。或见处座，紧那罗众所共围绕，大树紧那罗王而为上首；此比丘尼为说法门，名佛行光明。或见处座，摩睺罗伽众所共围绕，庵罗林摩睺罗伽王而为上首；此比丘尼为说法门，名生佛欢喜心。

In another place, he saw her seated there, surrounded by a congregation of Tuṣita Heaven devas' sons and devas' daughters headed by the Tuṣita Heaven King for whom this bhikshuni taught a Dharma gateway known as "the turning of the mind treasury";

In another place, he saw her seated there, surrounded by a congregation of Suyāma Heaven devas' sons and devas' daughters headed by the Suyāma Heaven King for whom this bhikshuni taught a Dharma gateway known as "boundless adornment";

In another place, he saw her seated there, surrounded by a congregation of Trāyastriṃśa Heaven devas' sons and devas' daughters headed by Śakra, lord of the devas, for whom this bhikshuni taught a Dharma gateway known as "the gateway of renunciation";

In another place, he saw her seated there, surrounded by a congregation of Hundred Light Rays Dragon King, Nanda Dragon King, Upananda Dragon King, Manasvin Dragon King, Airāvanaṇa Dragon King, Anavatapta Dragon King, and others as well as dragons' sons and dragons' daughters, all of these headed by Sāgara Dragon King for whom this bhikshuni taught a Dharma gateway known as "the radiant adornments of the realm of the Buddha's spiritual superknowledges";

In another place, he saw her seated there, surrounded by a congregation of *yakṣas* headed by Vaiśravaṇa for whom this bhikshuni taught a Dharma gateway known as "the treasury that rescues beings";

In another place, he saw her seated there, surrounded by a congregation of *gandharvas* headed by Supporter of the Country Gandharva King for whom this bhikshuni taught a Dharma gateway known as "endless joy";

In another place, he saw her seated there, surrounded by a congregation of *asuras* headed by Rāhu Asura King for whom this bhikshuni taught a Dharma gateway known as "the wisdom gateway of the Dharma realm's swift adornment";

In another place, he saw her seated there, surrounded by a congregation of *garuḍas* headed by Agile Grasp Garuḍa King for whom this bhikshuni taught a Dharma gateway known as "terrifying and shaking the ocean of all realms of existence";

In another place, he saw her seated there, surrounded by a congregation of *kiṃnaras* headed by Great Tree Kinnara King for whom this bhikshuni taught a Dharma gateway known as "the light of the Buddha's practices";

In another place, he saw her seated there, surrounded by a congregation of *mahoragas* headed by Amra Grove Kinnara King for whom this bhikshuni taught a Dharma gateway known as "arousing the Buddha's mind of joyous delight";

正體字

或見處座無量百千男
364a18 ‖ 子女人所共圍遶。此比丘尼為說法門。名殊
364a19 ‖ 勝行。或見處座諸羅剎眾所共圍遶。常奪精
364a20 ‖ 氣大樹羅剎王而為上首。此比丘尼為說法
364a21 ‖ 門。名發生悲愍心。或見處座信樂聲聞。乘
364a22 ‖ 眾生所共圍遶。此比丘尼為說法門。名勝智
364a23 ‖ 光明。或見處座信樂緣覺乘眾生所共圍遶。
364a24 ‖ 此比丘尼為說法門。名佛功德廣大光明。或
364a25 ‖ 見處座信樂大乘眾生所共圍遶。此比丘尼
364a26 ‖ 為說法門。名普門三昧智光明門。或見處座
364a27 ‖ 初發心諸菩薩所共圍遶。此比丘尼為說法
364a28 ‖ 門。名一切佛願聚。或見處座第二地諸菩薩
364a29 ‖ 所共圍遶。此比丘尼為說法門。名離垢輪。或
364b01 ‖ 見處座第三地諸菩薩所共圍遶。此比丘尼
364b02 ‖ 為說法門。名寂靜莊嚴。或見處座第四地諸
364b03 ‖ 菩薩所共圍遶。此比丘尼為說法門。名生一
364b04 ‖ 切智境界。或見處座第五地諸菩薩所共圍
364b05 ‖ 遶。此比丘尼為說法門。名妙華藏。或見處
364b06 ‖ 座第六地諸菩薩所共圍遶。此比丘尼為說
364b07 ‖ 法門。名毘盧遮那藏。

简体字

或见处座，无量百千男子、女人所共围绕；此比丘尼为说法门，名殊胜行。或见处座，诸罗刹众所共围绕，常夺精气大树罗刹王而为上首；此比丘尼为说法门，名发生悲愍心。或见处座，信乐声闻乘众生所共围绕；此比丘尼为说法门，名胜智光明。或见处座，信乐缘觉乘众生所共围绕；此比丘尼为说法门，名佛功德广大光明。或见处座，信乐大乘众生所共围绕；此比丘尼为说法门，名普门三昧智光明门。或见处座，初发心诸菩萨所共围绕；此比丘尼为说法门，名一切佛愿聚。或见处座，第二地诸菩萨所共围绕；此比丘尼为说法门，名离垢轮。或见处座，第三地诸菩萨所共围绕；此比丘尼为说法门，名寂静庄严。或见处座，第四地诸菩萨所共围绕；此比丘尼为说法门，名生一切智境界。或见处座，第五地诸菩萨所共围绕；此比丘尼为说法门，名妙华藏。或见处座，第六地诸菩萨所共围绕；此比丘尼为说法门，名毗卢遮那藏。

In another place, he saw her seated there, surrounded by a congregation of countless hundreds of thousands of men and women for whom this bhikshuni taught a Dharma gateway known as "the especially excellent practices";

In another place, he saw her seated there, surrounded by a congregation of *rākṣasas* headed by Ever Stealing Essential Energies Big Tree Rākṣasa for whom this bhikshuni taught a Dharma gateway known as "generating the mind of compassionate sympathy";

In another place, he saw her seated there, surrounded by a congregation of beings whose resolute faith was aligned with the *śrāvaka*-disciple vehicle for whom this bhikshuni taught a Dharma gateway known as "the light of supreme wisdom";

In another place, he saw her seated there, surrounded by a congregation of beings whose resolute faith was aligned with the *pratyekabuddha* vehicle for whom this bhikshuni taught a Dharma gateway known as "the vast light of the Buddha's meritorious qualities";

In another place, he saw her seated there, surrounded by a congregation of beings whose resolute faith was aligned with the Great Vehicle for whom this bhikshuni taught a Dharma gateway known as "the wisdom light gateway to the universal gateway samādhi";

In another place, he saw her seated there, surrounded by a congregation of bodhisattvas at the stage of the initial generation of the resolve for whom this bhikshuni taught a Dharma gateway known as "the accumulation of all buddhas' vows";

In another place, he saw her seated there, surrounded by a congregation of bodhisattvas on the second ground for whom this bhikshuni taught a Dharma gateway known as "the stainless wheel";

In another place, he saw her seated there, surrounded by a congregation of bodhisattvas on the third ground for whom this bhikshuni taught a Dharma gateway known as "adornment through quiescence";

In another place, he saw her seated there, surrounded by a congregation of bodhisattvas on the fourth ground for whom this bhikshuni taught a Dharma gateway known as "bringing forth the realm of all-knowledge";

In another place, he saw her seated there, surrounded by a congregation of bodhisattvas on the fifth ground for whom this bhikshuni taught a Dharma gateway known as "the treasury of marvelous flowers";

In another place, he saw her seated there, surrounded by a congregation of bodhisattvas on the sixth ground for whom this bhikshuni taught a Dharma gateway known as "the *vairocana* treasury";

正體字

或見處座第七地諸菩
364b08║ 薩所共圍遶。此比丘尼為說法門。名普莊嚴
364b09║ 地。或見處座第八地諸菩薩所共圍遶。此比
364b10║ 丘尼為說法門。名遍法界境界身。或見處座
364b11║ 第九地諸菩薩所共圍遶。此比丘尼為說法
364b12║ 門。名無所得力莊嚴。或見處座第十地諸菩
364b13║ 薩所共圍遶。此比丘尼為說法門。名無礙輪。
364b14║ 或見處座執金剛神所共圍遶。此比丘尼為
364b15║ 說法門。名金剛智那羅延莊嚴。善財童子。見
364b16║ 如是等一切諸趣所有眾生。已成熟者。已調
364b17║ 伏者。堪為法器。皆入此園。各於座下。圍遶而
364b18║ 坐。師子[＊]頻申比丘尼。隨其欲解勝劣差別。
364b19║ 而為說法。令於阿耨多羅三藐三菩提。得不
364b20║ 退轉。何以故。此比丘尼。入普眼捨得般若波
364b21║ 羅蜜門。說一切佛法般若波羅蜜門。法界差
364b22║ 別般若波羅蜜門。散壞一切障礙輪般若波
364b23║ 羅蜜門。生一切眾生善心般若波羅蜜門。殊
364b24║ 勝莊嚴般若波羅蜜門。無礙真實藏般若波
364b25║ 羅蜜門。法界圓滿般若波羅蜜門。

简体字

或见处座，第七地诸菩萨所共围绕；此比丘尼为说法门，名普庄严地。或见处座，第八地诸菩萨所共围绕；此比丘尼为说法门，名遍法界境界身。或见处座，第九地诸菩萨所共围绕；此比丘尼为说法门，名无所得力庄严。或见处座，第十地诸菩萨所共围绕；此比丘尼为说法门，名无碍轮。或见处座，执金刚神所共围绕；此比丘尼为说法门，名金刚智那罗延庄严。

善财童子见如是等一切诸趣所有众生已成熟者、已调伏者，堪为法器，皆入此园，各于座下围绕而坐。师子嚬申比丘尼，随其欲解胜劣差别而为说法，令于阿耨多罗三藐三菩提得不退转。何以故？此比丘尼入普眼舍得般若波罗蜜门、说一切佛法般若波罗蜜门、法界差别般若波罗蜜门、散坏一切障碍轮般若波罗蜜门、生一切众生善心般若波罗蜜门、殊胜庄严般若波罗蜜门、无碍真实藏般若波罗蜜门、法界圆满般若波罗蜜门、

In another place, he saw her seated there, surrounded by a congregation of bodhisattvas on the seventh ground for whom this bhikshuni taught a Dharma gateway known as "the ground of universal adornment";

In another place, he saw her seated there, surrounded by a congregation of bodhisattvas on the eighth ground for whom this bhikshuni taught a Dharma gateway known as "the body that pervades the Dharma realm's sphere of objective experience";

In another place, he saw her seated there, surrounded by a congregation of bodhisattvas on the ninth ground for whom this bhikshuni taught a Dharma gateway known as "adornment through the power of having nothing at all that is apprehensible";

In another place, he saw her seated there, surrounded by a congregation of bodhisattvas on the tenth ground for whom this bhikshuni taught a Dharma gateway known as "the unimpeded wheel"; and

In yet another place, he saw her seated there, surrounded by a congregation of vajra-wielding spirits for whom this bhikshuni taught a Dharma gateway known as "the *nārāyaṇa*'s adornment with vajra wisdom."

Sudhana the Youth saw all such beings from all of the rebirth destinies who had already become ripened, who had already become trained, and thus who were able to become vessels for retaining the Dharma. They all entered this park and sat there surrounding these Dharma thrones. Siṃhavijṛmbhitā Bhikshuni adapted to the differences in the relative superiority or inferiority of their various aspirations and understandings in teaching the Dharma for their sakes, thereby enabling them to become irreversible in their progress toward *anuttara-samyak-saṃbodhi*. And how could this be so? This bhikshuni had entered:

The *prajñāpāramitā* gateway of the universal eye acquired through equanimity;

The *prajñāpāramitā* gateway of teaching all dharmas of the Buddha;

The *prajñāpāramitā* gateway of the distinctions in the Dharma realm;

The *prajñāpāramitā* gateway of the scattering and demolishing of the sphere of all obstacles;

The *prajñāpāramitā* gateway that brings forth thoughts of goodness in all beings;

The *prajñāpāramitā* gateway of supreme adornment;

The *prajñāpāramitā* gateway of the treasury of unimpeded truth;

The *prajñāpāramitā* gateway of the perfect fulfillment of the Dharma realm;

正體字

心藏般若
364b26║ 波羅蜜門。普出生藏般若波羅蜜門。此十般
364b27║ 若波羅蜜門為首。入如是等無數百萬般若
364b28║ 波羅蜜門。此日光園中。所有菩薩。及諸眾
364b29║ 生。皆是師子[＊]頻申比丘尼。初勸發心。受持
364c01║ 正法。思惟修習。於阿耨多羅三藐三菩提。得
364c02║ 不退轉。時善財童子。見師子[＊]頻申比丘尼。
364c03║ 如是園林。如是床座。如是經行。如是眾會。如
364c04║ 是神力。如是辯才。復聞不可思議法門。廣
364c05║ 大法雲。潤澤其心。便生是念。我當右遶無量
364c06║ 百千匝。時比丘尼。放大光明。普照其園眾會
364c07║ 莊嚴。善財童子。即自見身及園林中。所有眾
364c08║ 樹。皆悉右遶此比丘尼。經於無量百千萬匝。
364c09║ 圍遶畢已。善財童子。合掌而住。白言。聖者。
364c10║ 我已先發阿耨多羅三藐三菩提心。而未知
364c11║ 菩薩云何學菩薩行。云何修菩薩道。我聞聖
364c12║ 者。善能誘誨。願為我說。比丘尼言。善男子。
364c13║ 我得解脫。名成就一切智。善財言。聖者何故。
364c14║ 名為成就一切智。比丘尼言。善男子。此智光
364c15║ 明。於一念中。普照三世一切諸法。善財白言。
364c16║ 聖者。此智光明境界云何。

简体字

心藏般若波罗蜜门、普出生藏般若波罗蜜门，此十般若波罗蜜门为首，入如是等无数百万般若波罗蜜门。此日光园中所有菩萨及诸众生，皆是师子嚬申比丘尼初劝发心，受持正法，思惟修习，于阿耨多罗三藐三菩提得不退转。

时，善财童子见师子嚬申比丘尼如是园林、如是床座、如是经行、如是众会、如是神力、如是辩才，复闻不可思议法门，广大法云润泽其心，便生是念：“我当右绕无量百千匝。”

时，比丘尼放大光明，普照其园众会庄严。善财童子即自见身，及园林中所有众树，皆悉右绕此比丘尼，经于无量百千万匝。围绕毕已，善财童子合掌而住，白言：“圣者，我已先发阿耨多罗三藐三菩提心，而未知菩萨云何学菩萨行？云何修菩萨道？我闻圣者善能诱诲，愿为我说！”

比丘尼言：“善男子，我得解脱，名成就一切智。”

善财言：“圣者，何故名为成就一切智？”

比丘尼言：“善男子，此智光明，于一念中普照三世一切诸法。”

善财白言：“圣者，此智光明境界云何？”

The *prajñāpāramitā* gateway of the mind treasury; and
The *prajñāpāramitā* gateway of the treasury of universal generation.

These ten *prajñāpāramitā* gateways were foremost among the countless hundreds of myriads of such *prajñāpāramitā* gateways that she had entered. All these bodhisattvas and other beings within this Sunlight Park were those who this Siṃhavijṛmbhitā Bhikshuni had first encouraged to bring forth the resolve, had enabled to absorb and retain right Dharma, and had encouraged to reflect upon it and cultivate it and then become irreversible in progressing toward *anuttara-samyak-saṃbodhi*.

Then, when Sudhana the Youth saw that Siṃhavijṛmbhitā Bhikshuni had a park and grove such as this, Dharma thrones such as these, meditation walkways such as these, congregations such as these, spiritual powers such as these, and eloquence such as this while also having heard her teaching of inconceivable Dharma gateways such as these, the rain from vast Dharma clouds moistened his mind and he had this thought: "With my right side facing her, I should circumambulate her countless hundreds of thousands of times."

The Bhikshuni then emanated an immense beam of light that everywhere illuminated the park, its congregations, and their adornments. Sudhana the Youth then saw his own body as well as all of the many trees in that park and its groves all circumambulating this bhikshuni in a rightward direction countless hundreds of thousands of myriads of times. When those circumambulations were finished, Sudhana the Youth then pressed his palms together, stood before her, and addressed her, saying:

> O Āryā, I am one who has already resolved to attain *anuttara-samyak-saṃbodhi*. Still, I do not yet know how the bodhisattva should train in the bodhisattva practices or how he should cultivate the bodhisattva path. I have heard that the Ārya is well able to offer guidance and instruction in this. Please speak about these matters for my sake.

The Bhikshuni replied, "I have acquired a liberation known as 'the perfection of all-knowledge.'"

Sudhana then asked, "O Āryā, why is it known as 'the perfection of all-knowledge'?"

The Bhikshuni replied, "Son of Good Family, in but a single mind-moment, this light of wisdom everywhere illuminates all dharmas of the three periods of time."

Sudhana then asked, "O Āryā, of what does the sphere of experience of this light of wisdom consist?"

正體字

比丘尼言。善男子。
364c17‖ 我入此智光明門。得出生一切法三昧王。以
364c18‖ 此三昧故。得意生身。往十方一切世界兜率
364c19‖ 天宮一生所繫菩薩所。一一菩薩前。現不可
364c20‖ 說佛剎微塵數身。一一身。作不可說佛剎微
364c21‖ 塵數供養。所謂現天王身。乃至人王身。執
364c22‖ 持華雲。執持鬘雲。燒香塗香。及以末香。衣服
364c23‖ 瓔珞。幢幡繒蓋。寶網寶帳。寶藏寶燈。如是一
364c24‖ 切諸莊嚴具。我皆執持。而以供養。如於住兜
364c25‖ 率宮菩薩所。如是於住胎出胎。在家出家。往
364c26‖ 詣道場。成等正覺。轉正法輪。入於涅槃。如是
364c27‖ 中間。或住天宮。或住龍宮。乃至或復住於人
364c28‖ 宮。於彼一一諸如來所。我皆如是而為供養。
364c29‖ 若有眾生。知我如是供養佛者。皆於阿耨多
365a01‖ 羅三藐三菩提。得不退轉。若有眾生來至我
365a02‖ 所。我即為說般若波羅蜜。善男子。我見一
365a03‖ 切眾生。不分別眾生相。智眼明見故。聽一
365a04‖ 切語言。不分別語言相。心無所著故。見一
365a05‖ 切如來。不分別如來相。了達法身故。

简体字

比丘尼言："善男子，我入此智光明门，得出生一切法三昧王；以此三昧故，得意生身，往十方一切世界兜率天宫一生所系菩萨所，一一菩萨前现不可说佛刹微尘数身，一一身作不可说佛刹微尘数供养。所谓：现天王身乃至人王身，执持华云，执持鬘云，烧香、涂香及以末香，衣服、璎珞、幢幡、缯盖、宝网、宝帐、宝藏、宝灯，如是一切诸庄严具，我皆执持而以供养。如于住兜率宫菩萨所，如是于住胎、出胎、在家、出家、往诣道场、成等正觉、转正法轮、入于涅槃，如是中间，或住天宫，或住龙宫，乃至或复住于人宫，于彼一一诸如来所，我皆如是而为供养。若有众生，知我如是供养佛者，皆于阿耨多罗三藐三菩提得不退转；若有众生来至我所，我即为说般若波罗蜜。

"善男子，我见一切众生，不分别众生相，智眼明见故；听一切语言，不分别语言相，心无所著故；见一切如来，不分别如来相，了达法身故；

The Bhikshuni then said:

When I enter this light of wisdom gateway, I am able to bring forth "the sovereign samādhi of all dharmas" and with this samādhi, I acquire mind-generated bodies which then go to the abodes of all those bodhisattvas who are bound to but one more birth where they dwell in their palaces in the Tuṣita Heavens of the worlds of the ten directions. Then, before every one of those bodhisattvas, I manifest bodies as numerous as the atoms in an ineffable number of buddha *kṣetras*. Every one of those bodies then makes offerings to them as numerous as the atoms in an ineffable number of buddha *kṣetras*. In particular, I manifest in the bodies of deva kings as well as in other ways up to and including in the bodies of human kings, all of whom hold flower clouds, garland clouds, burning incenses, perfumes, powdered incenses, robes, necklaces, banners, pennants, silken streamers, canopies, jeweled nets, jeweled curtains, jewel treasuries, and jewel lamps. I hold up all kinds of adornments such as these and present them as offerings.

And just as I present such offerings to the bodhisattvas abiding in the Tuṣita Heavens, so too do I also present such offerings to them at the stages when they abide in the womb, when they emerge from the womb, when they abide within the household, when they leave behind the householder's life, when they approach the site of enlightenment, when they realize the universal and right enlightenment, when they turn the wheel of right Dharma, and when they enter *nirvāṇa*. Thus, in all these circumstances, whether they be dwelling in a heavenly palace, a dragon palace, or in other circumstances up to and including also when they dwell in a palace among humans—in every one of those places where the Tathāgatas dwell, I present offerings in this same way.

If there is any being at all who becomes aware of my making offerings to buddhas in this way, they all attain irreversibility in their progress toward *anuttara-samyak-saṃbodhi*. If there is any being at all who comes into my presence, I immediately teach them about the *prajñāpāramitā*.

Son of Good Family:

Whenever I see any being, I do not distinguish any marks of a being. This is because I see them clearly with the wisdom eye;

Whenever I hear any speech, I do not distinguish any marks of verbal discourse. This is because my mind remains entirely free of attachment;

Whenever I see any of the *tathāgatas*, I do not distinguish any marks of a *tathāgata*. This is because I have completely comprehended the Dharma body;

正體字

住持
365a06 ‖ 一切法輪。不分別法輪相。悟法自性故。一
365a07 ‖ 念遍知一切法。不分別諸法相。知法如幻故。
365a08 ‖ 善男子。我唯知此成就一切智解脫。如諸菩
365a09 ‖ 薩摩訶薩。心無分別。普知諸法。一身端坐。充
365a10 ‖ 滿法界。於自身中現一切剎。一念悉[1]詣一
365a11 ‖ 切佛所。於自身內。普現一切諸佛神力。一
365a12 ‖ 毛遍舉不可言說諸佛世界。於其自身一毛
365a13 ‖ 孔中。現不可說世界成壞。於一念中。與不
365a14 ‖ 可說不可說眾生同住。於一念中。入不可說
365a15 ‖ 不可說一切諸劫。而我云何能知能說彼功
365a16 ‖ 德行。善男子。於此南方。有一國土。名曰險
365a17 ‖ 難。此國有城。名寶莊嚴。中有女人。名婆須蜜
365a18 ‖ 多。汝詣彼問。菩薩云何學菩薩行。修菩薩道。
365a19 ‖ 時善財童子。頂禮其足。遶無數匝。慇懃瞻仰。
365a20 ‖ 辭退而去
365a24 ‖ 大方廣佛華嚴經卷第六十八
365a27 ‖ 　　入法界品第三十九之九
365a28 ‖ 爾時善財童子。大智光明。照啟其心。

简体字

住持一切法轮，不分别法轮相，悟法自性故；一念遍知一切法，不分别诸法相，知法如幻故。

“善男子，我唯知此成就一切智解脱。如诸菩萨摩诃萨，心无分别，普知诸法，一身端坐，充满法界，于自身中现一切刹，一念悉诣一切佛所，于自身内普现一切诸佛神力，一毛遍举不可言说诸佛世界，于其自身一毛孔中现不可说世界成坏，于一念中与不可说不可说众生同住，于一念中入不可说不可说一切诸劫；而我云何能知能说彼功德行？

“善男子，于此南方，有一国土，名曰险难；此国有城，名宝庄严；中有女人，名婆须蜜多。汝诣彼问：菩萨云何学菩萨行、修菩萨道？”

时，善财童子顶礼其足，绕无数匝，殷勤瞻仰，辞退而去。

大方广佛华严经卷第六十八

入法界品第三十九之九

尔时，善财童子，大智光明照启其心，

Whenever I sustain the turning the Dharma wheel [of all buddhas],[127] I do not distinguish any marks of the wheel of Dharma. This is because I have awakened to the inherent nature of dharmas; and

When I pervasively know all dharmas in but a single mind-moment, I do not distinguish any marks of dharmas. This is because I realize that dharmas are like mere conjured illusions.

Son of Good Family, I know only this perfection of all-knowledge liberation. As for the bodhisattva-mahāsattvas:

Whose minds remain free of discriminations even as they know all dharmas;

Who sit erect in one body even as they completely fill the Dharma realm;

Who, even within their own bodies, manifest all *kṣetras*;

Who, even in but a single mind-moment, visit and pay their respects to all buddhas;

Who, even within their own bodies, manifest all the spiritual powers of all buddhas;

Who, even with but one hair, everywhere lift up the worlds of an ineffable number of buddhas;

Who, even within but one pore of their own bodies, reveal the creation and destruction of an ineffable number of worlds;

Who, even in but a single mind-moment, dwell together with an ineffable-ineffable number of beings; and

Who, even in but a single mind-moment, enter an ineffable-ineffable number of all kalpas—

How could I know of or be able to speak about their meritorious qualities and practices?

Son of Good Family, south of here, there is a land known as Durga or "Dangerous Difficulty." This country has a city known as Ratnavyūha or "Jeweled Adornment" in which there is a woman known as Vasumitrā. You should go there, pay your respects, and ask her, "How should the bodhisattva train in the bodhisattva practices and how should he cultivate the bodhisattva path?"

Sudhana the Youth then bowed down in reverence at her feet and circumambulated her countless times as he gazed up at her in attentive admiration. He then respectfully withdrew and departed.

25 – Vasumitrā

At that time, the light of great wisdom illuminated the mind of Sudhana the Youth, whereupon he then took up the meditative

正體字

思惟觀
365a29║ 察。見諸法性。得了知一切言音陀羅尼門。得
365b01║ 受持一切法輪陀羅尼門。得與一切眾生作
365b02║ 所歸依大悲力。得觀察一切法義理光明門。
365b03║ 得充滿法界清淨願。得普照十方一切法智
365b04║ 光明。得遍莊嚴一切世界自在力。得普發起
365b05║ 一切菩薩業圓滿願。漸次遊行。至險難國寶
365b06║ 莊嚴城。處處尋覓婆須蜜多女。城中有人。不
365b07║ 知此女功德智慧。作如是念。今此童子。諸根
365b08║ 寂靜。智慧明了。不迷不亂。諦視一尋。無有疲
365b09║ 懈。無所取著。目視不瞬。心無所動。甚深寬
365b10║ 廣。猶如大海。不應於此婆須蜜女。有貪愛心。
365b11║ 有顛倒心。生於淨想。生於欲想。不應為此女
365b12║ 色所攝。此童子者。不行魔行。不入魔境。不沒
365b13║ 欲泥。不被魔縛。不應作處。已能不作。有何等
365b14║ 意。而求此女。其中有人。先知此女有智慧者。
365b15║ 告善財言。

简体字

思惟观察见诸法性，得了知一切言音陀罗尼门，得受持一切法轮陀罗尼门，得与一切众生作所归依大悲力，得观察一切法义理光明门，得充满法界清净愿，得普照十方一切法智光明，得遍庄严一切世界自在力，得普发起一切菩萨业圆满愿。

漸次游行，至险难国宝庄严城，处处寻觅婆须蜜多女。

城中有人不知此女功德智慧，作如是念：“今此童子，诸根寂静，智慧明了，不迷不乱，谛视一寻，无有疲懈，无所取著，目视不瞬，心无所动，甚深宽广，犹如大海；不应于此婆须蜜女，有贪爱心，有颠倒心，生于净想，生于欲想；不应为此女色所摄。此童子者，不行魔行，不入魔境，不没欲泥，不被魔缚，不应作处已能不作，有何等意而求此女？”

其中有人先知此女有智慧者，告善财言：

reflections with which he perceived the nature of all dharmas. Consequently:

He acquired the *dhāraṇī* gateway of the complete cognition of all speech;
He acquired the *dhāraṇī* gateway of the preservation of all the wheels of Dharma;
He acquired the power of the great compassion in which all beings find refuge;
He acquired the gateway of contemplation of the light of the principles of all dharmas;
He acquired the purification of vows that completely fill the Dharma realm;
He acquired the light of wisdom that everywhere illuminates all dharmas of the ten directions;
He acquired the power of the sovereign masteries by which one everywhere adorns all worlds; and
He acquired the vows by which one everywhere brings forth the perfect fulfillment of all the deeds of a bodhisattva.

He then gradually traveled onward until he reached the city of Ratnavyūha in the country of Durga in which he searched everywhere for Lady Vasumitrā. In that city, there were people who were unaware of this woman's meritorious qualities and wisdom who thought:

This youth before us now is one whose faculties are calm, one whose wisdom is bright, one who is neither confused nor disturbed, one whose attentive gaze extends just a meter ahead of him, one who is free of weariness or indolence, one who has nothing he is attached to, one who is unblinking in his gaze, and one whose mind is unshakable and as deep and vast as the great ocean.

He should not be having thoughts of desire for this Lady Vasumitrā, should not be having thoughts about her affected by inverted views, should not be conceiving of her as lovely, should not be producing thoughts of desire for her, and should not be one who is captivated by this woman's beauty.

This youth does not engage in the actions of Māra, does not enter the realm of Māra, does not sink into the mud of desire, and does not become entrapped in Māra's snares. He is already able to refrain from doing what should not be done. What then might be his motivation be in searching for this lady?

Among the people there, there were those who were already aware that this woman was one who is wise. They told Sudhana:

正體字

善哉善哉。善男子。汝今乃能推求
365b16║ 尋覓婆須蜜女。汝已獲得廣大善利。善男子。
365b17║ 汝應決定求佛果位。決定欲為一切眾生作所
365b18║ 依怙。決定欲拔一切眾生貪愛毒箭。決定欲
365b19║ 破一切眾生於女色中所有淨想。善男子。婆
365b20║ 須蜜女。於此城內市鄽之北。自宅中住。時
365b21║ 善財童子。聞是語已。歡喜踊躍。往詣其門。見
365b22║ 其住宅。廣博嚴麗。寶牆寶樹。及以寶塹。一一
365b23║ 皆有十重圍遶。其寶塹中。香水盈滿。金沙布
365b24║ 地。諸天寶華。優鉢羅華。波頭摩華。拘物頭
365b25║ 華。[2]芬陀利華。遍覆水上。宮殿樓閣。處處分
365b26║ 布。門闥窓牖。相望間列。咸施網鐸。悉置幡
365b27║ 幢。無量珍奇。以為嚴飾。瑠璃為地。眾寶間
365b28║ 錯。燒諸沈水。塗以栴檀。懸眾寶鈴。風動成
365b29║ 音。散諸天華。遍布其地。種種嚴麗。不可稱
365c01║ 說。諸珍寶藏。其數百千。十大園林。以為莊
365c02║ 嚴。爾時善財。見此女人。顏貌端嚴。色相圓
365c03║ 滿。皮膚金色。目髮紺青。不長不短。

简体字

“善哉！善哉！善男子，汝今乃能推求寻觅婆须蜜女，汝已获得广大善利。善男子，汝应决定求佛果位，决定欲为一切众生作所依怙，决定欲拔一切众生贪爱毒箭，决定欲破一切众生于女色中所有净想。善男子，婆须蜜女于此城内市廛之北自宅中住。”

时，善财童子闻是语已，欢喜踊跃，往诣其门。见其住宅广博严丽，宝墙、宝树及以宝堑，一一皆有十重围绕；其宝堑中，香水盈满，金沙布地，诸天宝华、优钵罗华、波头摩华、拘物头华、芬陀利华遍覆水上；宫殿、楼阁处处分布，门闼、窗牖相望间列，咸施网铎，悉置幡幢，无量珍奇以为严饰；琉璃为地，众宝间错，烧诸沉水，涂以栴檀，悬众宝铃，风动成音，散诸天华遍布其地；种种严丽不可称说，诸珍宝藏其数百千，十大园林以为庄严。

尔时，善财见此女人，颜貌端严，色相圆满，皮肤金色，目发绀青，不长不短，

It is good indeed, good indeed, Son of Good Family, that you are now able to search for this Lady Vasumitrā. By this alone, you have already acquired vast and wholesome benefit. Son of Good Family:

You should be resolute in seeking the stage of the realization of the fruit of buddhahood;

You should be resolute in wishing to become a refuge for all beings;

You should be resolute in wishing to extricate the poisonous arrows of lust from all beings; and

You should be resolute in crushing all beings' perceptions of a woman's form as lovely.

Son of Good Family, Lady Vasumitrā lives in this city in her own house north of the marketplace.

Having heard these words, Sudhana the Youth was filled with joyous exultation. He then went to her gates where he saw that the house where she dwelt was vast, beautifully adorned, and surrounded by ten concentric rings of jeweled walls, jeweled trees, and jeweled moats.

Those jeweled moats were brimming with perfumed waters and their depths were carpeted with gold sand. All kinds of heavenly jeweled flowers were floating everywhere across the surface of those waters. They included jeweled *utpala* blossoms, *padma* blossoms, *kumuda* blossoms, and *puṇḍarīka* blossoms.

Palatial halls and towers were spread everywhere about. They were constructed with rows of interspersed and mutually interfacing gateways and windows, each of which was hung with nets of bells and each of which was graced with pennants and banners decorated with countless precious and extraordinary adornments.

The grounds were made of lapis lazuli inlaid with many kinds of jewels. *Agaru* incense was burning there and sandalwood incense perfume had been spread there as well. The breezes which caused strands of many-jeweled bells to sway and resound also scattered all kinds of heavenly flowers that everywhere covered the grounds. The place was so replete with all these many different kinds of beautiful adornments that it was beyond one's ability to describe it. There were treasuries full of the various kinds of precious jewels, hundreds of thousands in number, with which these ten immense parks and groves were adorned.

Sudhana then saw this woman possessed of a beautiful countenance, perfectly full physical form and features, skin the color of gold, and indigo eyes and hair. She was neither tall nor short, neither

正體字

不麁不
365c04║ 細。欲界人天。無能與比。音聲美妙。超諸梵
365c05║ 世。一切眾生。差別言音。悉皆具足。無不解
365c06║ 了。深達字義。善巧談說。得如幻智。入方便
365c07║ 門。眾寶瓔珞。及諸嚴具。莊嚴其身。如意摩尼
365c08║ 以為寶冠而冠其首。復有無量眷屬圍遶。皆
365c09║ 共善根同一行願。福德大藏。具足無盡。時婆
365c10║ 須蜜多女。從其身出廣大光明。普照宅中一
365c11║ 切宮殿。遇斯光者。身得清涼。爾時善財。前詣
365c12║ 其所。頂禮其足。合掌而住。白言。聖者。我已
365c13║ 先發阿耨多羅三藐三菩提心。而未知菩薩
365c14║ 云何學菩薩行。云何修菩薩道。我聞聖者。善
365c15║ 能教誨。願為我說。彼即告言。善男子。我得菩
365c16║ 薩解脫。名離貪欲際。隨其欲樂。而為現身。若
365c17║ 天見我。我為天女。形貌光明。殊勝無比。如是
365c18║ 乃至人非人等。而見我者。我即為現人非人
365c19║ 女。隨其樂欲。皆令得見。

简体字

不粗不细，欲界人、天无能与比；音声美妙超诸梵世，一切众生差别言音，悉皆具足，无不解了；深达字义，善巧谈说，得如幻智，入方便门；众宝璎珞及诸严具庄严其身，如意摩尼以为宝冠而冠其首；复有无量眷属围绕，皆共善根同一行愿，福德大藏具足无尽。时，婆须蜜多女从其身出广大光明，普照宅中一切宫殿；遇斯光者，身得清凉。

尔时，善财前诣其所，顶礼其足，合掌而住，白言：“圣者，我已先发阿耨多罗三藐三菩提心，而未知菩萨云何学菩萨行？云何修菩萨道？我闻圣者善能教诲，愿为我说！”

彼即告言：“善男子，我得菩萨解脱，名离贪欲际，随其欲乐而为现身。若天见我，我为天女，形貌、光明殊胜无比；如是乃至人非人等而见我者，我即为现人非人女，随其乐欲皆令得见。

heavy nor slight, and so beautiful that no human or deva from the desire-realm could even be compared to her.

Her voice, exquisitely marvelous, surpassed even those heard in the Brahma World, completely embodying all the different types of speech of all beings. There was nothing at all that she failed to completely understand. She possessed a deeply penetrating comprehension of words and their meanings. She was extremely skillful in her discourse, had acquired the wisdom that perceives phenomena as like mere conjured illusions, and had entered the gateway of skillful means.

Her body was graced with necklaces made of many kinds of jewels and other kinds of adornments and wish-fulfilling *maṇī* jewels composed the jeweled tiara crowning her head. She was also surrounded by a retinue of countless followers, all of whom shared equivalent roots of goodness and the same practices and vows. She possessed an immense treasury of inexhaustible merit.

At that time, Lady Vasumitrā emanated an immense radiance from her body that everywhere illuminated all the halls in her house. The bodies of all who were touched by this light felt sensations of clarity and coolness.

Sudhana then went before her to pay his respects and bowed down in reverence at her feet. He then stood before her with palms pressed together and addressed her, saying:

> O Āryā, I am one who has already resolved to attain *anuttara-samyak-saṃbodhi*. Still, I do not yet know how the bodhisattva should train in the bodhisattva practices or how he should cultivate the bodhisattva path. I have heard that the Āryā is well able to offer guidance and instruction in this. Please speak about these matters for my sake.

She then told him:

> Son of Good Family, I have acquired the bodhisattva's liberation known as "the pinnacle of dispassion"[128] with which I adapt to others' desires and then manifest bodies accordingly. Thus, if a deva sees me, I become a female deva possessed of an incomparably superior form, appearance, and radiance. So too for others, including those in the human realm, the nonhuman realms, and so forth for whom, adapting to whoever sees me, I then manifest in the form of just such a human female or nonhuman female in accordance with their inclinations, thereby allowing them to see me in that form. For instance:

正體字

若有眾生。欲意
365c20 ‖ 所纏。來詣我所。我為說法。彼聞法已。則離貪
365c21 ‖ 欲。得菩薩無著境界三昧。若有眾生。暫見
365c22 ‖ 於我。則離貪欲。得菩薩歡喜三昧。若有眾
365c23 ‖ 生。暫與我語。則離貪欲。得菩薩無礙音聲三
365c24 ‖ 昧。若有眾生。暫執我手。則離貪欲。得菩薩遍
365c25 ‖ 往一切佛剎三昧。若有眾生。暫昇我座。則離
365c26 ‖ 貪欲。得菩薩解脫光明三昧。若有眾生。暫觀
365c27 ‖ 於我。則離貪欲。得菩薩寂靜莊嚴三昧。若有
365c28 ‖ 眾生。見我頻[3]申。則離貪欲。得菩薩摧伏外
365c29 ‖ 道三昧。若有眾生。見我目瞬。則離貪欲。得菩
366a01 ‖ 薩佛境界光明三昧。若有眾生。抱持於我。則
366a02 ‖ 離貪欲。得菩薩攝一切眾生恒不捨離三昧。
366a03 ‖ 若有眾生。唼我脣吻。則離貪欲。得菩薩增長
366a04 ‖ 一切眾生福德藏三昧。凡有眾生。親近於我。
366a05 ‖ 一切皆得住離貪際。入菩薩一切智地現前
366a06 ‖ 無礙解脫。善財白言。聖者。種何善根。修何
366a07 ‖ 福業。而得成就如是自在。答言。善男子。我念
366a08 ‖ 過去。有佛出世。名為高行。其王都城。名曰
366a09 ‖ 妙門。

简体字

“若有众生欲意所缠来诣我所，我为说法，彼闻法已，则离贪欲，得菩萨无著境界三昧；若有众生暂见于我，则离贪欲，得菩萨欢喜三昧；若有众生暂与我语，则离贪欲，得菩萨无碍音声三昧；若有众生暂执我手，则离贪欲，得菩萨遍往一切佛刹三昧；若有众生暂升我座，则离贪欲，得菩萨解脱光明三昧；若有众生暂观于我，则离贪欲，得菩萨寂静庄严三昧；若有众生见我频申，则离贪欲，得菩萨摧伏外道三昧；若有众生见我目瞬，则离贪欲，得菩萨佛境界光明三昧；若有众生抱持于我，则离贪欲，得菩萨摄一切众生恒不舍离三昧；若有众生唼我唇吻，则离贪欲，得菩萨增长一切众生福德藏三昧。凡有众生亲近于我，一切皆得住离贪际，入菩萨一切智地现前无碍解脱。”

善财白言：“圣者种何善根、修何福业，而得成就如是自在？”

答言：“善男子，我念过去，有佛出世，名为高行；其王都城，名曰妙门。

If there are any beings entangled by the desire-ridden mind who come to see me, I teach the Dharma for them, whereupon, having heard the Dharma, they then abandon sensual desire and acquire the bodhisattva's "sphere of nonattachment" samādhi;

If there are any beings who see me only briefly, they then abandon sensual desire and acquire the bodhisattva's "joyous delight" samādhi;

If there are any beings who speak to me only briefly, they then abandon sensual desire and acquire the bodhisattva's "unimpeded voice" samādhi;

If there are any beings who only briefly grasp my hand, they then abandon sensual desire and acquire the bodhisattva's "traveling to all buddha *kṣetras*" samādhi;

If there are any beings who but briefly ascend to my throne, they then abandon sensual desire and acquire the bodhisattva's "light of liberation" samādhi;

If there are any beings who but briefly gaze at me, they then abandon sensual desire and acquire the bodhisattva's "quiescent adornment" samādhi;

If there are any beings who merely see me stretching, they then abandon sensual desire and acquire the bodhisattva's "vanquishing proponents of other traditions" samādhi;

If there are any beings who see me so much as blink an eye, they then abandon sensual desire and acquire the bodhisattva's "light of the buddha realm" samādhi;

If there are any beings who simply hug me, they then abandon sensual desire and acquire the bodhisattva's "attracting and never forsaking all beings" samādhi;

If there are any beings who merely kiss my lips, they then abandon sensual desire and acquire the bodhisattva's "increasing all beings' treasury of merit" samādhi; and

If there are any beings who so much as draw near to me, they are all established in the bodhisattva's liberation that has reached the pinnacle of dispassion and is directed toward the ground of unimpeded all-knowledge.

Sudhana then addressed her, asking, "O Āryā, through the planting of which roots of goodness and through the cultivation of which meritorious deeds have you achieved such sovereign mastery as this?"

She replied, saying:

Son of Good Family, I recall that, in the past, there was a Buddha who appeared in the world who was named Atyuccagāmī or "Lofty Practice." The king's capital city was known as Sumukhā or "Marvelous Gates."

正體字

善男子。彼高行如來。哀愍眾生。入於王
366a10‖ 城。蹈彼門閫。其城一切悉皆震動。忽然廣博。
366a11‖ 眾寶莊嚴。無量光明。遞相映徹。種種寶華散
366a12‖ 布其地。諸天音樂同時俱奏。一切諸天充滿
366a13‖ 虛空。善男子。我於彼時。為長者妻。名曰善
366a14‖ 慧。見佛神力。心生覺悟。則與其夫。往詣佛
366a15‖ 所。以一寶錢。而為供養。是時文殊師利童子。
366a16‖ 為佛侍者。為我說法。令發阿耨多羅三藐三
366a17‖ 菩提心。善男子。我唯知此菩薩離貪際解脫。
366a18‖ 如諸菩薩摩訶薩。成就無邊巧方便智。其藏
366a19‖ 廣大。境界無比。而我云何能知能說彼功德
366a20‖ 行。善男子。於此南方有城。名善度。中有居
366a21‖ 士。名鞞瑟胝羅。彼常供養栴檀座佛塔。汝
366a22‖ 詣彼問。菩薩云何學菩薩行。修菩薩道。時善
366a23‖ 財童子。頂禮其足。遶無量匝。慇懃瞻仰。辭退
366a24‖ 而去
366a25‖ 爾時善財童子。漸次遊行。至善度城。詣居士
366a26‖ 宅。頂禮其足。合掌而立。白言

简体字

善男子，彼高行如来哀愍众生，入于王城蹈彼门阃，其城一切悉皆震动，忽然广博，众宝庄严，无量光明递相映彻，种种宝华散布其地，诸天音乐同时俱奏，一切诸天充满虚空。善男子，我于彼时，为长者妻，名曰善慧；见佛神力，心生觉悟，则与其夫往诣佛所，以一宝钱而为供养。是时，文殊师利童子为佛侍者，为我说法，令发阿耨多罗三藐三菩提心。

“善男子，我唯知此菩萨离贪际解脱。如诸菩萨摩诃萨，成就无边巧方便智，其藏广大，境界无比；而我云何能知能说彼功德行？

“善男子，于此南方有城，名善度；中有居士，名鞞瑟胝罗，彼常供养栴檀座佛塔。汝诣彼问：菩萨云何学菩萨行、修菩萨道？”

时，善财童子顶礼其足，绕无量匝，殷勤瞻仰，辞退而去。

尔时，善财童子渐次游行，至善度城，诣居士宅，顶礼其足，合掌而立，白言：

Son of Good Family, that Atyuccagāmī Tathāgata was one who felt deep pity for beings. When, on entering the royal capitol, his feet stepped on the threshold of its gates, that entire city then quaked and shook, whereupon it suddenly grew immensely vast and became adorned with many kinds of jewels emanating countless beams of light that interlaced the penetrating brilliance of their rays. All different kinds of jeweled flowers scattered down and spread across its grounds and all varieties of celestial music then resounded in unison as all the devas came forth and filled the skies above.

Son of Good Family, I was then an elder's wife named Sumatī or "Fine Wisdom." On witnessing that buddha's power, my mind was aroused, whereupon I went with my husband to pay my respects to that buddha at which point I presented a precious coin to him as an offering. The buddha's attendant at that time was Mañjuśrī the Youth who then spoke Dharma for me, thereby causing me to resolve to attain *anuttara-samyak-saṃbodhi.*

Son of Good Family, I know only this bodhisattva's liberation known as "the pinnacle of dispassion." As for the bodhisattva-mahāsattvas who have perfected boundless skillful means and wisdom, who have accumulated vast treasuries of these, and whose spheres of cognition are incomparable—how could I know of or be able to speak about their meritorious qualities and practices?

Son of Good Family, south of here, there is a city known as Śubhapāraṃgama or "Beautiful Crossing" in which there is a layman named Veṣṭhila. He always makes offerings at the stupa of Candanapīṭha or "Sandalwood Throne" Buddha. You should go there, pay your respects, and ask him, "How should the bodhisattva train in the bodhisattva practices and how should he cultivate the bodhisattva path?"

Sudhana the Youth then bowed down in reverence at her feet and circumambulated her countless times as he gazed up at her in attentive admiration. He then respectfully withdrew and departed.

26 – Veṣṭhila

At that time, Sudhana the Youth then gradually traveled onward until he reached the city of Śubhapāraṃgama. When he arrived at that layman's household, he bowed down in reverence at his feet. He then stood before him with palms pressed together and addressed him, saying:

正體字

聖者。我已先發
366a27‖ 阿耨多羅三藐三菩提心。而未知菩薩云何
366a28‖ 學菩薩行。云何修菩薩道。我聞聖者。善能
366a29‖ 誘誨。願為我說。居士告言。善男子。我得菩薩
366b01‖ 解脫。名不般涅槃際。善男子。我不生心言如
366b02‖ 是如來已般涅槃。如是如來現般涅槃。如是
366b03‖ 如來當般涅槃。我知十方一切世界諸佛如
366b04‖ 來。畢竟無有般涅槃者。唯除為欲調伏眾生
366b05‖ 而示現耳。善男子。我開栴檀座如來塔門時。
366b06‖ 得三昧。名佛種無盡。善男子。我念念中。入此
366b07‖ 三昧。念念得知一切無量殊勝之事。善財白
366b08‖ 言。此三昧者。境界云何。居士答言。善男子。
366b09‖ 我入此三昧。隨其次第。見此世界一切諸佛。
366b10‖ 所謂迦葉佛。拘那含牟尼佛。拘留孫佛。尸
366b11‖ 棄佛。毘婆尸佛。提舍佛。弗沙佛。無上勝佛。
366b12‖ 無上蓮華佛。如是等而為上首。於一念頃。得
366b13‖ 見百佛。得見千佛。得見百千佛。得見億佛。千
366b14‖ 億佛。百千億佛。阿庾多億佛。那由他億佛。乃
366b15‖ 至不可說不可說世界微塵數佛。如是一切
366b16‖ 次第皆見。亦見彼佛初始發心。種諸善根。

简体字

“圣者，我已先发阿耨多罗三藐三菩提心，而未知菩萨云何学菩萨行？云何修菩萨道？我闻圣者善能诱诲，愿为我说！”

居士告言：“善男子，我得菩萨解脱，名不般涅槃际。善男子，我不生心言：‘如是如来已般涅槃，如是如来现般涅槃，如是如来当般涅槃。’我知十方一切世界诸佛如来，毕竟无有般涅槃者，唯除为欲调伏众生而示现耳。

“善男子，我开栴檀座如来塔门时，得三昧，名佛种无尽。善男子，我念念中入此三昧，念念得知一切无量殊胜之事。”

善财白言：“此三昧者，境界云何？”

居士答言：“善男子，我入此三昧，随其次第，见此世界一切诸佛，所谓：迦葉佛、拘那含牟尼佛、拘留孙佛、尸弃佛、毗婆尸佛、提舍佛、弗沙佛、无上胜佛、无上莲华佛；如是等而为上首，于一念顷，得见百佛，得见千佛，得见百千佛，得见亿佛、千亿佛、百千亿佛、阿庾多亿佛、那由他亿佛，乃至不可说不可说世界微尘数佛，如是一切，次第皆见。亦见彼佛，初始发心，种诸善根，

O Ārya, I am one who has already resolved to attain *anuttara-samyak-saṃbodhi*. Still, I do not yet know how the bodhisattva should train in the bodhisattva practices or how he should cultivate the bodhisattva path. I have heard that the Ārya is well able to offer guidance and instruction in this. Please speak about these matters for my sake.

The Layman then spoke to him, saying:

Son of Good Family, I have acquired a bodhisattva liberation known as "nonentry into the apex of *parinirvāṇa*." Son of Good Family, I have never had any thought in which I reflected: "This *tathāgata* has already entered *parinirvāṇa*, this other *tathāgata* is now entering *parinirvāṇa*, and this other *tathāgata* will be entering *parinirvāṇa* in the future." I have realized that, throughout all the worlds in the ten directions, of all the buddhas, the *tathāgatas*, there are ultimately none of them who have actually ever entered *parinirvāṇa* with the sole exception of instances where they have merely manifested that appearance for the sake of training beings.

Son of Good Family, when I opened the gate to the stupa memorializing Candanapīṭha Tathāgata, I acquired a samādhi known as "the endless lineage of the buddhas." Son of Good Family, I enter this samādhi in each successive mind-moment and, in each successive mind-moment, I acquire the knowledge of all their countless extraordinary deeds.

Sudhana then asked: "What is this samādhi's sphere of experience like?"

The Layman replied, saying:

Son of Good Family, when I enter into this samādhi, in accordance with the order of their appearance, I see all the buddhas of this world headed by Kāśyapa Buddha, Kanakamuni Buddha, Krakucchanda Buddha, Śikhin Buddha, Vipaśyin Buddha, Tiṣya Buddha, Puṣya Buddha, Puṣyayaśottara or "Unsurpassable Victory" Buddha, and Padmottara or "Unsurpassable Lotus Flower" Buddha. In but a single mind-moment, I am able to see a hundred buddhas, a thousand buddhas, a hundred thousand buddhas, a *koṭī* of buddhas, a thousand *koṭīs* of buddhas, a hundred thousand *koṭīs* of buddhas, an *ayuta* of *koṭīs* of buddhas, a *nayuta* of *koṭīs* of buddhas, and so forth until I am able to see even buddhas as numerous as the atoms in an ineffable-ineffable number of worlds. In this way, I see all of them in accordance with the order of their coming forth into the world.

I also see those buddhas when they first aroused the resolve, when they planted roots of goodness, when they acquired the

正體字

獲
366b17 | 勝神通。成就大願。修行妙行。具波羅蜜。入菩
366b18 | 薩地。得清淨忍。摧伏魔軍。成正等覺。國土清
366b19 | 淨。眾會圍遶。放大光明。轉妙法輪。神通
366b20 | 變現。種種差別。我悉能持。我悉能憶。悉能觀
366b21 | 察。分別顯示。未來彌勒佛等一切諸佛。現在
366b22 | [昆>毘]盧遮那佛等一切諸佛。悉亦如是。如此世
366b23 | 界。十方世界。所有三世。一切諸佛。聲聞獨
366b24 | 覺。諸菩薩眾。悉亦如是。善男子。我唯得此菩
366b25 | 薩所得不般涅槃際解脫。如諸菩薩摩訶薩。
366b26 | 以一念智普知三世。一念遍入一切三昧。如
366b27 | 來智日恒照其心。於一切法無有分別。了一
366b28 | 切佛悉皆平等。如來及我一切眾生。等無有
366b29 | 二。知一切法自性清淨。無有思慮。無有動轉。
366c01 | 而能普入一切世間。離諸分別。住佛法印。悉
366c02 | 能開悟法界眾生。而我云何能知能說彼功
366c03 | 德行。善男子。於此南方。有山。名補怛洛迦。
366c04 | 彼有菩薩。名觀自在。

简体字

获胜神通，成就大愿，修行妙行，具波罗蜜，入菩萨地，得清净忍，摧伏魔军，成正等觉，国土清净，众会围绕，放大光明，转妙法轮，神通变现；种种差别，我悉能持，我悉能忆，悉能观察，分别显示。未来弥勒佛等一切诸佛，现在毗卢遮那佛等一切诸佛，悉亦如是。如此世界，十方世界所有三世一切诸佛、声闻、独觉、诸菩萨众，悉亦如是。

“善男子，我唯得此菩萨所得不般涅槃际解脱。如诸菩萨摩诃萨，以一念智普知三世，一念遍入一切三昧，如来智日恒照其心，于一切法无有分别，了一切佛悉皆平等、如来及我一切众生等无有二，知一切法自性清净，无有思虑，无有动转，而能普入一切世间，离诸分别，住佛法印，悉能开悟法界众生；而我云何能知能说彼功德行？

“善男子，于此南方有山，名补怛洛迦；彼有菩萨，名观自在。

supreme spiritual superknowledges, when they achieved the realization of their great vows, when they cultivated the marvelous practices, when they acquired the *pāramitās*, when they entered the bodhisattva grounds, when they acquired the pure patiences, when they vanquished the armies of Māra, when they attained the right and universal enlightenment, when they purified the lands, when they were surrounded by congregations, when they emanated great light, when they turned the wheel of the sublime Dharma, and when, using the spiritual superknowledges, they manifested transformations.

As for all the various differences which occurred as these events occurred, I am able to retain them all, remember them all, contemplate them all, distinguish them all, and display the appearance of them all. So too is this true of Maitreya and all the buddhas of the future and Vairocana and all the buddhas of the present.

And just as this is so with respect to this world, in this same way, I am also able to see all buddhas of all the worlds of the ten directions throughout the three periods of time along with their congregations of *śrāvaka* disciples, *pratyekabuddhas,* and bodhisattvas.

Son of Good Family, I have acquired only this bodhisattva liberation known as "nonentry into the apex of *parinirvāṇa*." As for the bodhisattva-mahāsattvas:

Who, in but a single mind-moment of cognition, comprehensively know all three periods of time;
Who, in but a single mind-moment, everywhere enter all samādhis;
Whose minds are constantly illuminated by the sun of the Tathāgata's wisdom;
Who make no discriminations regarding any dharma;
Who completely understand the equality of all buddhas;
Who realize the identity and non-duality of the Tathāgata, themselves, and all beings;
Who realize the inherently pure nature of all dharmas;
Who have no reflective thought and have no movement at all even as they are still able to everywhere enter all worlds;
Who have abandoned all discriminations and dwell in the Buddha's Dharma seal; and
Who are able to awaken all beings throughout the Dharma realm—

How could I know of or be able to speak about their meritorious qualities and practices?

Son of Good Family, south of here, there is a mountain known as Potalaka where there is a bodhisattva known as Avalokiteśvara.

正體字

汝詣彼問。菩薩云何。學
366c05‖ 菩薩行。修菩薩道。即說頌曰
366c06‖ 海上有山多聖賢　眾寶所成極清淨
366c07‖ 華果樹林皆遍滿　泉流池沼悉具足
366c08‖ 勇猛丈夫觀自在　為利眾生住此山
366c09‖ 汝應往問諸功德　彼當示汝大方便
366c10‖ 時善財童子。頂禮其足。遶無量匝已。慇懃瞻
366c11‖ 仰。辭退而去
366c12‖ 爾時善財童子。一心思惟彼居士教。入彼菩
366c13‖ 薩解脫之藏。得彼菩薩能隨念力。憶彼諸佛
366c14‖ 出現次第。念彼諸佛相續次第。持彼諸佛名
366c15‖ 號次第。觀彼諸佛所說妙法。知彼諸佛具足
366c16‖ 莊嚴。見彼諸佛成正等覺。了彼諸佛不思議
366c17‖ 業。漸次遊行。至於彼山。處處求覓此大菩薩。
366c18‖ 見其西面巖谷之中。泉流[1]縈映。樹林蓊欝。
366c19‖ 香草柔軟。右旋布地。觀自在菩薩。於金剛寶
366c20‖ 石上。結[2]跏趺坐。無量菩薩。皆坐寶石。恭敬
366c21‖ 圍遶。而為宣說大慈悲法。令其攝受一切眾
366c22‖ 生。

简体字

汝诣彼问：菩萨云何学菩萨行、修菩萨道？”

即说颂曰：

“海上有山多圣贤，众宝所成极清净，
华果树林皆遍满，泉流池沼悉具足。
勇猛丈夫观自在，为利众生住此山；
汝应往问诸功德，彼当示汝大方便。”

时，善财童子顶礼其足，绕无量匝已，殷勤瞻仰，辞退而去。

尔时，善财童子一心思惟彼居士教，入彼菩萨解脱之藏，得彼菩萨能随念力，忆彼诸佛出现次第，念彼诸佛相续次第，持彼诸佛名号次第，观彼诸佛所说妙法，知彼诸佛具足庄严，见彼诸佛成正等觉，了彼诸佛不思议业。

渐次游行，至于彼山，处处求觅此大菩萨。见其西面岩谷之中，泉流萦映，树林蓊郁，香草柔软，右旋布地。观自在菩萨于金刚宝石上结跏趺坐，无量菩萨皆坐宝石恭敬围绕，而为宣说大慈悲法，令其摄受一切众生。

You should go there, pay your respects, and ask him, "How should a bodhisattva train in the bodhisattva practices and how should he cultivate the bodhisattva path?"

He then spoke these verses:

Out at sea, there is a mountain where many *āryas* and worthies abide.
Composed of the many jewels, it is the ultimate in pristine purity.
It is everywhere full of flowers, fruits, trees, and forests,
and is entirely replete with springs, creeks, lakes, and ponds.

The heroically brave man there, Avalokiteśvara,
dwells on this mountain in order to benefit beings.
You should go there and inquire about the meritorious qualities.
He will then reveal to you his great skillful means.

Sudhana the Youth then bowed down in reverence at his feet and circumambulated him countless times as he gazed up at him in attentive admiration. He then respectfully withdrew and departed.

27 – Avalokiteśvara

At that time, Sudhana the Youth then single-mindedly reflected on that layman's teachings by which:

He entered the treasury of that bodhisattva's liberation;
Acquired that bodhisattva's power of mindfulness;
Recalled the sequence of all those buddhas' appearance in the world;
Bore in mind the continual successive appearance of those buddhas;
Retained the names of those buddhas according to their sequence;
Contemplated the sublime Dharma taught by those buddhas;
Knew the complete adornments of those buddhas;
Saw those buddhas gain the right and universal enlightenment; and
Completely understood those buddhas' inconceivable works.

He then gradually traveled onward until he reached that mountain. He then searched about everywhere for this great bodhisattva until, on its western slope, he saw him in a steep-walled valley with brightly reflecting intertwined springs and creeks and with forests, densely luxuriant vegetation, and fragrant and soft grasses that carpeted the ground in rightward-radiating swirls.

Avalokiteśvara Bodhisattva was sitting there in the full-lotus posture on a vajra-jewel stone, surrounded by countless respectful bodhisattvas, all of whom sat there atop jewel stones as he taught them a Dharma discourse on the great kindness and the great compassion with which he encouraged them to devote themselves to gathering in all beings.

正體字

善財見已。歡喜踊躍。合掌諦觀。目不暫
366c23‖ 瞬。作如是念。善知識者則是如來。善知識者
366c24‖ 一切法雲。善知識者諸功德藏。善知識者難
366c25‖ 可值遇。善知識者十力寶因。善知識者無盡
366c26‖ 智炬。善知識者福德根芽。善知識者一切智
366c27‖ 門。善知識者智海導師。善知識者至一切智
366c28‖ 助道之具。便即往詣大菩薩所。爾時觀自在
366c29‖ 菩薩。遙見善財。告言善來。汝發大乘意普攝
367a01‖ 眾生。起正直心專求佛法。大悲深重救護一
367a02‖ 切。普賢妙行相續現前。大願深心圓滿清淨。
367a03‖ 勤求佛法悉能領受。積集善根恒無厭足。順
367a04‖ 善知識不違其教。從文殊師利功德智慧大
367a05‖ 海所生。其心成熟。得佛勢力。已獲廣大三昧
367a06‖ 光明。專意希求甚深妙法。常見諸佛。生大
367a07‖ 歡喜。智慧清淨。猶如虛空。

简体字

善财见已，欢喜踊跃，合掌谛观，目不暂瞬，作如是念：“善知识者，则是如来；善知识者，一切法云；善知识者，诸功德藏；善知识者，难可值遇；善知识者，十力宝因；善知识者，无尽智炬；善知识者，福德根芽；善知识者，一切智门；善知识者，智海导师；善知识者，至一切智助道之具。”便即往诣大菩萨所。

尔时，观自在菩萨遥见善财，告言：“善来！汝发大乘意普摄众生，起正直心专求佛法，大悲深重救护一切，普贤妙行相续现前，大愿深心圆满清净，勤求佛法悉能领受，积集善根恒无厌足，顺善知识不违其教；从文殊师利功德智慧大海所生，其心成熟，得佛势力；已获广大三昧光明，专意希求甚深妙法，常见诸佛生大欢喜，智慧清净犹如虚空，

Having observed this, Sudhana was overcome with joyous exultation. He then pressed his palms together and gazed attentively, eyes unblinking, at what he beheld there. He then had these thoughts:

The good spiritual guides are the Tathāgata himself;
The good spiritual guides are the cloud of all dharmas;
The good spiritual guides are the treasury of all meritorious qualities;
The good spiritual guides are only rarely encountered;
The good spiritual guides are the cause of the jewels of the ten powers;
The good spiritual guides are the endlessly burning torch of wisdom;
The good spiritual guides are the roots and sprouts of merit;
The good spiritual guides are the guides on the ocean of wisdom; and
The good spiritual guides are the provisions on the path to all-knowledge.

He then immediately went to pay his respects to that great bodhisattva. Seeing Sudhana from a distance, Avalokiteśvara Bodhisattva then spoke to him, saying, "Welcome!":

You have brought forth the Great Vehicle's resolve to everywhere gather in beings;

You have raised forth the right and straightforward mind especially intent on seeking the Buddha's Dharma;

You are one of great compassion who deeply esteems the rescue and protection of all;

The marvelous practices of Samantabhadra continuously manifest directly before you;

The deep resolve of your great vows is completely fulfilled and purified;

You diligently seek the Buddha's Dharma while being well able to take it all in;

You are insatiable in constantly collecting roots of goodness;

You comply with the good spiritual guide and never oppose his teachings;

You are one born from the great ocean of Mañjuśrī's meritorious qualities and wisdom;

As your mind becomes ripened, you will acquire the empowerment of the buddhas;

You have already acquired the light of vast samādhis;

You are especially intent on seeking the extremely profound and sublime Dharma;

You will always see all buddhas and be filled with great happiness;

Your wisdom is as pure as empty space;

正體字

既自明了。復為他
367a08‖ 說。安住如來智慧光明。爾時善財童子。頂禮
367a09‖ 觀自在菩薩足。遶無數匝。合掌而住。白言。聖
367a10‖ 者。我已先發阿耨多羅三藐三菩提心。而未
367a11‖ 知菩薩云何學菩薩行。云何修菩薩道。我聞
367a12‖ 聖者。善能教誨。願為我說。菩薩告言。善哉善
367a13‖ 哉。善男子。汝已能發阿耨多羅三藐三菩提
367a14‖ 心。善男子。我已成就菩薩大悲行解脫門。善
367a15‖ 男子。我以此菩薩大悲行門。平等教化一切
367a16‖ 眾生。相續不斷。善男子。我住此大悲行門。常
367a17‖ 在一切諸如來所。普現一切眾生之前。或以
367a18‖ 布施攝取眾生。或以愛語。或以利行。或以
367a19‖ 同事攝取眾生。或現色身。攝取眾生。或現
367a20‖ 種種不思議色淨光明網。攝取眾生。或以音
367a21‖ 聲。或以威儀。或為說法。或現神變。令其心
367a22‖ 悟。而得成熟。或為化現同類之形。與其共居。
367a23‖ 而成熟之。善男子。我修行此大悲行門。願常
367a24‖ 救護一切眾生。願一切眾生。離險道怖。離熱
367a25‖ 惱怖。離迷惑怖。離繫縛怖。離殺害怖。

简体字

既自明了复为他说，安住如来智慧光明。”

尔时，善财童子顶礼观自在菩萨足，绕无数匝，合掌而住，白言：“圣者，我已先发阿耨多罗三藐三菩提心，而未知菩萨云何学菩萨行？云何修菩萨道？我闻圣者善能教诲，愿为我说！”

菩萨告言：“善哉！善哉！善男子，汝已能发阿耨多罗三藐三菩提心。

“善男子，我已成就菩萨大悲行解脱门。善男子，我以此菩萨大悲行门，平等教化一切众生相续不断。

“善男子，我住此大悲行门，常在一切诸如来所，普现一切众生之前。或以布施，摄取众生；或以爱语，或以利行，或以同事，摄取众生；或现色身，摄取众生；或现种种不思议色净光明网，摄取众生；或以音声，或以威仪，或为说法，或现神变，令其心悟而得成熟；或为化现同类之形，与其共居而成熟之。

“善男子，我修行此大悲行门，愿常救护一切众生；愿一切众生，离险道怖，离热恼怖，离迷惑怖，离系缚怖，离杀害怖，

Having gained complete understanding yourself, you then teach this for the benefit of others; and

You are securely established in the light of the Tathāgata's wisdom.

Sudhana the Youth then bowed down in reverence at the feet of Avalokiteśvara Bodhisattva and circumambulated him countless times. He then stood before him with palms pressed together and addressed him, saying:

O Ārya, I am one who has already resolved to attain *anuttara-samyak-saṃbodhi*. Still, I do not yet know how the bodhisattva should train in the bodhisattva practices or how he should cultivate the bodhisattva path. I have heard that the Ārya is well able to offer instruction in this. Please speak about these matters for my sake.

The Bodhisattva then told him:

It is good indeed, good indeed, Son of Good Family, that you have been able to resolve to attain *anuttara-samyak-saṃbodhi*. Son of Good Family, I have already perfected the bodhisattva's liberation gateway known as "the practice of the great compassion." Son of Good Family, through this bodhisattva's gateway of the practice of the great compassion, I continuously and incessantly provide impartial teaching to all beings.

Son of Good Family, as I dwell in this gateway of the practice of the great compassion, I always remain in the presence of all *tathāgatas* while manifesting everywhere directly before all beings. I may use giving to attract beings, or I may use pleasing words, beneficial actions, or joint endeavors to attract beings. I may manifest a form body to attract beings or I may manifest nets of pure light of all different inconceivable colors to attract beings. I may use voices, the awesome deportment, the teaching of Dharma, or the manifestation of spiritual transformations to arouse the minds of beings, thereby ripening them. And, in some cases, I manifest in a form identical to theirs and then dwell together with them in order to ripen them.

Son of Good Family, in my cultivation of this gateway of the practice of the great compassion, I vow to always rescue all beings and vow as well that all beings:

Shall escape the fear of dangerous paths;
Shall escape the fear of the feverish afflictions;
Shall escape the fear of doubts and delusions;
Shall escape the fear of bondage;
Shall escape the fear of killing or injury;

正體字

離貧窮
367a26 怖。離不活怖。離惡名怖。離於死怖。離大眾
367a27 怖。離惡趣怖。離黑闇怖。離遷移怖。離愛別
367a28 怖。離怨會怖。離逼迫身怖。離逼迫心怖。離憂
367a29 悲怖。復作是願。願諸眾生若念於我。若稱我
367b01 名。若見我身。皆得免離一切怖畏。善男子。我
367b02 以此方便。令諸眾生。離怖畏已。復教令發阿
367b03 耨多羅三藐三菩提心。永不退轉。善男子。我
367b04 唯得此菩薩大悲行門。如諸菩薩摩訶薩。已
367b05 淨普賢一切願。已住普賢一切行。常行一切
367b06 諸善法。常入一切諸三昧。常住一切無邊劫。
367b07 常知一切三世法。常詣一切無邊剎。常息一
367b08 切眾生惡。常長一切眾生善。常絕眾生生死
367b09 流。而我云何能知能說彼功德行。爾時東方
367b10 有一菩薩。名曰正趣。從空中來。至娑婆世界
367b11 輪圍山頂。

简体字

离贫穷怖，离不活怖，离恶名怖，离于死怖，离大众怖，离恶趣怖，离黑暗怖，离迁移怖，离爱别怖，离冤会怖，离逼迫身怖，离逼迫心怖，离忧悲怖。复作是愿：‘愿诸众生，若念于我，若称我名，若见我身，皆得免离一切怖畏。’善男子，我以此方便，令诸众生离怖畏已，复教令发阿耨多罗三藐三菩提心永不退转。

“善男子，我唯得此菩萨大悲行门。如诸菩萨摩诃萨，已净普贤一切愿，已住普贤一切行，常行一切诸善法，常入一切诸三昧，常住一切无边劫，常知一切三世法，常诣一切无边刹，常息一切众生恶，常长一切众生善，常绝众生生死流；而我云何能知能说彼功德行？”

尔时，东方有一菩萨，名曰正趣，从空中来，至娑婆世界轮围山顶，

Shall escape the fear of poverty and destitution;
Shall escape the fear of not being able to survive;
Shall escape the fear of ill repute;
Shall escape the fear of death;
Shall escape the fear of great assemblies;
Shall escape the fear of the wretched destinies;
Shall escape the fear of darkness;
Shall escape the fear of moving;
Shall escape the fear of being separated from those one loves;
Shall escape the fear of coming together with adversaries;
Shall escape the fear of being subjected to physical torment;
Shall escape the fear of being subjected to mental torment; and
Shall escape the fear of worry and grief.

I also make this vow: "I vow that all beings who merely bring me to mind, merely call out my name, or merely see me will be able to avoid whatever frightens them."

Son of Good Family, after using these skillful means to enable beings to become free of fear, I then teach them how to arouse the resolve to attain *anuttara-samyak-saṃbodhi* and then remain forever irreversible in this resolve.

Son of Good Family, I have attained only this bodhisattva's gateway of the practice of the great compassion. As for the bodhisattva-mahāsattvas:

Who have already purified all of Samantabhadra's vows;
Who have already dwelt in all of Samantabhadra's practices;
Who always practice all good dharmas;
Who always enter all samādhis;
Who always remain throughout all the boundlessly many kalpas;
Who always know all dharmas of the three periods of time;
Who always go to pay their respects in all the boundlessly many *kṣetras*;
Who always halt all beings' evils;
Who always increase all beings' goodness; and
Who always cut short beings' drifting along in the flow of *saṃsāra*—

How could I know of or be able to speak about their meritorious qualities and practices?

At that time, a bodhisattva from the eastern direction named Ananyagāmin or "Right Progression" descended from space to the peak of the Sahā World's Iron Ring Mountains. As soon as he placed

正體字

以足按地。其娑婆世界。六種震動。
367b12║ 一切皆以眾寶莊嚴。正趣菩薩。放身光明。映
367b13║ 蔽一切日月星電。天龍八部。釋梵護世。所有
367b14║ 光明。皆如聚墨。其光普照一切地獄畜生餓
367b15║ 鬼閻羅王處。令諸惡趣。眾苦皆滅。煩惱不起。
367b16║ 憂悲悉離。又於一切諸佛國土。普雨一切華
367b17║ 香瓔珞。衣服幢蓋。如是所有諸莊嚴具。供養
367b18║ 於佛。復隨眾生心之所樂。普於一切諸宮殿
367b19║ 中。而現其身。令其見者。皆悉歡喜。然後來詣
367b20║ 觀自在所。時觀自在菩薩。告善財言。善男子。
367b21║ 汝見正趣菩薩。來此會不。白言已見。告言善
367b22║ 男子。汝可往問。菩薩云何學菩薩行。修菩薩
367b23║ 道
367b24║ 爾時善財童子。敬承其教遽。即往詣彼菩薩
367b25║ 所。頂禮其足。合掌而立。白言。聖者。我已先
367b26║ 發阿耨多羅三藐三菩提心。而未知菩薩云
367b27║ 何學菩薩行。云何修菩薩道。我聞聖者。善能
367b28║ 教誨。願為我說。正趣菩薩言。善男子。我得菩
367b29║ 薩解脫。名普門速疾行。

简体字

以足按地；其娑婆世界六种震动，一切皆以众宝庄严。正趣菩萨放身光明，映蔽一切日、月、星、电，天龙八部、释、梵、护世所有光明皆如聚墨；其光普照一切地狱、畜生、饿鬼、阎罗王处，令诸恶趣，众苦皆灭，烦恼不起，忧悲悉离。又于一切诸佛国土，普雨一切华香、璎珞、衣服、幢盖；如是所有诸庄严具，供养于佛。复随众生心之所乐，普于一切诸宫殿中而现其身，令其见者皆悉欢喜，然后来诣观自在所。

时，观自在菩萨告善财言：“善男子，汝见正趣菩萨来此会不？”

白言：“已见。”

告言：“善男子，汝可往问：菩萨云何学菩萨行、修菩萨道？”

尔时，善财童子敬承其教，遽即往诣彼菩萨所，顶礼其足，合掌而立，白言：“圣者，我已先发阿耨多罗三藐三菩提心，而未知菩萨云何学菩萨行？云何修菩萨道？我闻圣者善能教诲，愿为我说！”

正趣菩萨言：“善男子，我得菩萨解脱，名普门速疾行。”

his feet on the ground, the entire Sahā World quaked and moved in six ways and then became entirely adorned with the many kinds of jewels. Then Ananyagāmin Bodhisattva emanated rays of light from his body, the brightness of which outshone the light of the sun, moon, stars, and lightning while also diminishing to the appearance of ink blots the light of the devas, the dragons, the rest of the eight types of spiritual beings, Śakra, Brahmā, and the world-protecting kings.

His light everywhere illuminated all realms of the hells, animals, hungry ghosts, and King Yama where it extinguished the many kinds of sufferings in those wretched destinies, prevented the afflictions from arising, and also allowed those beings to escape from all worry and anguish. Further, in all buddha lands there everywhere rained down all varieties of flowers, incense, necklaces, robes, banners, canopies, and all other such adornments, all of which were presented as offerings to the buddhas.

Furthermore, in accordance with whatever delighted the minds of those beings, he everywhere manifested his body in all the palaces, gladdening all those who saw this, after which they all came and paid their respects to Avalokiteśvara.

Then Avalokiteśvara Bodhisattva spoke to Sudhana, asking, "Son of Good Family, did you see Ananyagāmin Bodhisattva arrive in this congregation, or not?"

Sudhana replied, "I did indeed see him."

Avalokiteśvara then told Sudhana: "You may go and ask him, 'How should the bodhisattva train in the bodhisattva practices and how should he cultivate the bodhisattva path?'"

28 – Ananyagāmin

At that time, having respectfully received his instruction, Sudhana the Youth quickly went to pay his respects to that bodhisattva. After bowing down in reverence at his feet, he stood before him with palms pressed together and addressed him, saying:

> O Ārya, I am one who has already resolved to attain *anuttara-samyak-saṃbodhi*. Still, I do not yet know how the bodhisattva should train in the bodhisattva practices or how he should cultivate the bodhisattva path. I have heard that the Ārya is well able to offer instruction in this. Please speak about these matters for my sake.

Ananyagāmin Bodhisattva then said, "Son of Good Family, I have acquired the bodhisattva's liberation known as 'swift travel through the universal gateway.'"

正體字

善財言。聖者。於何佛
367c01║ 所。得此法門。所從來剎。去此幾何。發來久
367c02║ 如。告言。善男子。此事難知。一切世間。天人
367c03║ 阿脩羅。沙門婆羅門等。所不能了。唯勇猛精
367c04║ 進無退無怯。諸菩薩眾。已為一切善友所攝。
367c05║ 諸佛所念。善根具足。志樂清淨。得菩薩根。有
367c06║ 智慧眼。能聞能持。能解能說。善財言。聖者。
367c07║ 我承佛神力善知識力。能信能受願為我說。
367c08║ 正趣菩薩言。善男子。我從東方妙藏世界。普
367c09║ 勝生佛所。而來此土。於彼佛所。得此法門。從
367c10║ 彼發來。已經不可說不可說佛剎微塵數劫。
367c11║ 一一念中。舉不可說不可說佛剎微塵數步。
367c12║ 一一步。過不可說不可說世界微塵數佛剎。
367c13║ 一一佛剎。我皆遍入。至其佛所。以妙供具而
367c14║ 為供養。此諸供具。皆是無上心所成。無作法
367c15║ 所印。諸如來所忍。諸菩薩所歎。善男子。我又
367c16║ 普見彼世界中。一切眾生。悉知其心。悉知其
367c17║ 根。隨其欲解。現身說法。或放光明。或施財寶。

简体字

善财言："圣者，于何佛所得此法门？所从来刹，去此几何？发来久如？"

告言："善男子，此事难知，一切世间天、人、阿修罗、沙门、婆罗门等所不能了；唯勇猛精进无退无怯诸菩萨众，已为一切善友所摄、诸佛所念，善根具足，志乐清净，得菩萨根，有智慧眼，能闻能持，能解能说。"

善财言："圣者，我承佛神力、善知识力，能信能受，愿为我说！"

正趣菩萨言："善男子，我从东方妙藏世界普胜生佛所而来此土，于彼佛所得此法门，从彼发来已经不可说不可说佛刹微尘数劫，一一念中举不可说不可说佛刹微尘数步，一一步过不可说不可说世界微尘数佛刹。一一佛刹，我皆遍入，至其佛所，以妙供具而为供养；此诸供具，皆是无上心所成，无作法所印，诸如来所忍，诸菩萨所叹。善男子，我又普见彼世界中一切众生，悉知其心，悉知其根，随其欲解，现身说法，或放光明，或施财宝，

Sudhana replied, "O Ārya, under which buddhas did you acquire this Dharma gateway? Also, how far is it from that *kṣetra* to here, and how long did it take you to come this far?"

The Bodhisattva then told him:

Son of Good Family, this is a matter that would be difficult to understand for it is something that all the world's devas, humans, *asuras*, *śramaṇas*, brahmans, and others could never completely comprehend. It is only the community of heroically brave, vigorous, irreversible, and dauntless bodhisattvas—those who have already been attracted by all the good spiritual guides, who are born in mind by all buddhas, whose roots of goodness are completely developed, whose aspirations are pure, who have acquired the faculties of the bodhisattva, and who possess the wisdom eye—it is only these who are able to hear this, able to retain this, able to understand this, and able to speak about this.

Sudhana replied, "With the assistance of the buddhas' spiritual powers and the powers of the good spiritual guides, I will be able to have faith in it and will able to receive it. Please teach me about this matter."

Ananyagāmin Bodhisattva then said:

Son of Good Family, I have come here to this land from the presence of Samantaśrīsaṃbhava or "Universally Supreme Birth" Buddha in the Śrīgarbhavati or "Marvelous Treasury" world off to the east. It is from that buddha that I acquired this Dharma gateway. It has already been kalpas as numerous as the atoms in an ineffable-ineffable number of worlds since I left that place to come here.

In every mind-moment, I take a number of footsteps as numerous as the atoms in an ineffable-ineffable number of buddha *kṣetras* and, with every footstep, I pass through buddha *kṣetras* as numerous as the atoms in an ineffable-ineffable number of worlds. I go everywhere in each of those *kṣetras* and then go to the abodes of all those buddhas to present offerings of marvelous gifts to them. All of these gifts are produced by the power of unexcelled resolve. They are gifts bearing the seal of the dharma of wishlessness, gifts in which all *tathāgatas* acquiesce, and gifts that are praised by all bodhisattvas.

Son of the Buddha, I also everywhere see all the beings in those worlds, and, knowing all their minds, knowing all their faculties, and adapting to their particular desires and understandings, I manifest bodies for them and teach the Dharma accordingly. In some cases I emanate light and in some cases I bestow wealth or jewels,

正體字

367c18‖ 種種方便。教化調伏。無有休息。如從東方。
367c19‖ 南西北方。四維上下。亦復如是。善男子。我唯
367c20‖ 得此菩薩普疾行解脫能疾周遍到一切處。
367c21‖ 如諸菩薩摩訶薩。普於十方。無所不至。智慧
367c22‖ 境界。等無差別。善布其身。悉遍法界。至一切
367c23‖ 道。入一切剎。知一切法。到一切世。平等演說
367c24‖ 一切法門。同時照[1]耀一切眾生。於諸佛所。
367c25‖ 不生分別。於一切處。無有障礙。而我云何能
367c26‖ 知能說彼功德行。善男子。於此南方有城。名
367c27‖ 墮羅鉢底。其中有神。名曰大天。汝詣彼問。菩
367c28‖ 薩云何學菩薩行。修菩薩道。時善財童子。頂
367c29‖ 禮其足。遶無數匝殷懃瞻仰。辭退而去
368a01‖ 爾時善財童子。入菩薩廣大行。求菩薩智慧
368a02‖ 境。見菩薩神通事。念菩薩勝功德。生菩薩大
368a03‖ 歡喜。

简体字

种种方便，教化调伏，无有休息。如从东方，南、西、北方，四维、上、下，亦复如是。

“善男子，我唯得此菩萨普疾行解脱，能疾周遍到一切处。如诸菩萨摩诃萨，普于十方无所不至，智慧境界等无差别，善布其身悉遍法界，至一切道，入一切刹，知一切法，到一切世，平等演说一切法门，同时照耀一切众生，于诸佛所不生分别，于一切处无有障碍；而我云何能知能说彼功德行？

“善男子，于此南方有城，名堕罗钵底；其中有神，名曰大天。汝诣彼问：菩萨云何学菩萨行、修菩萨道？”

时，善财童子顶礼其足，绕无数匝，殷勤瞻仰，辞退而去。

尔时，善财童子入菩萨广大行，求菩萨智慧境，见菩萨神通事，念菩萨胜功德，生菩萨大欢喜，

thus incessantly using all different kinds of skillful means to teach and train them.

And just as I do this in the east, so too do I also do this in the south, west, and north as well as in the directions of the midpoints, the zenith, and the nadir.

Son of Good Family, I have acquired only this bodhisattva's liberation of universal and swift travel with which I am able to swiftly go to all places everywhere. As for the bodhisattva-mahāsattvas:

Who go everywhere throughout the ten directions, having no place they do not reach;
Whose spheres of wisdom are the same and no different;
Who thoroughly spread their bodies everywhere throughout the Dharma realm;
Who go to all the rebirth destinies;
Who enter all *kṣetras;*
Who know all dharmas;
Who reach all periods of time;
Who teach all Dharma gateways impartially;
Who simultaneously illuminate all beings;
Who make no discriminations regarding any of the buddhas; and
Who are free of obstacles wherever they go—

How could I know of or be able to speak about their meritorious qualities and practices?

Son of Good Family, south of here, there is a city known as Dvāravatī in which there is a spirit known as Mahādeva. You should go there, pay your respects, and ask him, "How should the bodhisattva train in the bodhisattva practices and how should he cultivate the bodhisattva path?"

Sudhana the Youth then bowed down in reverence at his feet and circumambulated him countless times as he gazed up at him in attentive admiration. He then respectfully withdrew and departed.

29 – Mahādeva

At that time, Sudhana the Youth then:

Entered the bodhisattva's vast practice;
Sought the bodhisattva's sphere of wisdom;
Saw the bodhisattva's works accomplished with the spiritual superknowledges;
Bore in mind the bodhisattva's supreme meritorious qualities;
Experienced the bodhisattva's great happiness;

正體字

起菩薩堅精進。入菩薩不思議自在解
368a04║ 脫。行菩薩功德地。觀菩薩三昧地。住菩薩總
368a05║ 持地。入菩薩大願地。得菩薩辯才地。成菩薩
368a06║ 諸力地。漸次遊行。至於彼城。推問大天今在
368a07║ 何所。人咸告言。在此城內。現廣大身。為眾說
368a08║ 法。爾時善財。至大天所。頂禮其足。於前合
368a09║ 掌。而作是言。聖者。我已先發阿耨多羅三藐
368a10║ 三菩提心。而未知菩薩云何學菩薩行。云何
368a11║ 修菩薩道。我聞聖者。善能教誨。願為我說。爾
368a12║ 時大天。長舒四手。取四大海水。自洗其面。持
368a13║ 諸金華。以散善財。而告之言。善男子。一切菩
368a14║ 薩。難可得見。難可得聞。希出世間。於眾生
368a15║ 中。最為第一。是諸人中芬陀利華。為眾生
368a16║ 歸。為眾生救。為諸世間作安隱處。為諸世
368a17║ 間作大光明。示迷惑者安隱正道。為大導師。
368a18║ 引諸眾生入佛法門。為大法將。善能守護一
368a19║ 切智城。菩薩如是難可值遇。唯身語意無過
368a20║ 失者。然後乃得見其形像。聞其辯才。於一
368a21║ 切時。常現在前。

简体字

起菩萨坚精进，入菩萨不思议自在解脱，行菩萨功德地，观菩萨三昧地，住菩萨总持地，入菩萨大愿地，得菩萨辩才地，成菩萨诸力地。

漸次游行，至于彼城，推问大天今在何所？人咸告言：“在此城内，现广大身，为众说法。”

尔时，善财至大天所，顶礼其足，于前合掌而作是言：“圣者，我已先发阿耨多罗三藐三菩提心，而未知菩萨云何学菩萨行？云何修菩萨道？我闻圣者善能教诲，愿为我说！”

尔时，大天长舒四手，取四大海水自洗其面，持诸金华以散善财，而告之言：“善男子，一切菩萨，难可得见，难可得闻，希出世间，于众生中最为第一，是诸人中芬陀利华，为众生归，为众生救，为诸世间作安隐处，为诸世间作大光明，示迷惑者安隐正道；为大导师，引诸众生入佛法门；为大法将，善能守护一切智城。菩萨如是难可值遇，唯身、语、意无过失者，然后乃得见其形像、闻其辩才，于一切时常现在前。

Aroused the bodhisattva's steadfast vigor;
Entered the bodhisattva's inconceivable sovereign masteries and liberations;
Practiced on the ground of the bodhisattva's meritorious qualities;
Contemplated the ground of the bodhisattva's samādhis;
Dwelt on the ground of the bodhisattva's complete-retention *dhāraṇīs;*
Entered the ground of the bodhisattva's great vows;
Reached the ground of the bodhisattva's eloquence; and
Established himself on the ground of the bodhisattva's powers.

He then gradually traveled onward until he reached that city where he searched about, asking about the present location of Mahādeva. Everyone told him: "He is residing in the inner precincts of this city where he is manifesting an immensely large body as he teaches the Dharma for the masses."

Sudhana then went to where Mahādeva was and bowed down in reverence at his feet. He then stood before him with palms pressed together and said:

O Ārya, I am one who has already resolved to attain *anuttara-samyak-saṃbodhi.* Still, I do not yet know how the bodhisattva should train in the bodhisattva practices or how he should cultivate the bodhisattva path. I have heard that the Ārya is well able to offer instruction in this. Please speak about these matters for my sake.

Mahādeva then stretched out four hands and scooped up waters from the four seas with which he rinsed his face. Then he lifted up all kinds of gold-colored flowers, scattered them down over Sudhana, and spoke to him, saying:

Son of Good Family, all bodhisattvas are difficult to ever see, are difficult to ever hear, and only rarely appear in the world. They are foremost among all beings. They are the *puṇḍarīka* blossoms of all humanity, the refuge for beings, and the rescuers of beings. They serve the entire world as a place of peace and security and serve the entire world as sources of the great light that reveals the peaceful, secure, and right path to the confused and deluded. They serve as great guides who lead beings through the gates of the Buddha's Dharma and they serve as great Dharma generals who are well able to preserve and protect the city of all-knowledge.

The bodhisattvas are just so very difficult to encounter, for it is only those who become free of fault in body, speech, and mind who are then able to see their physical forms, hear their eloquence, and always dwell in their presence.

正體字

善男子。我已成就菩薩解
368a22 脫。名為雲網。善財言。聖者。雲網解脫。境界
368a23 云何。爾時大天。於善財前。示現金聚銀聚。瑠
368a24 璃聚玻瓈聚。硨磲聚碼碯聚。大焰寶聚。離垢
368a25 藏寶聚。大光明寶聚。普現十方寶聚。寶冠聚
368a26 寶印聚。寶瓔珞聚。寶璫聚寶釧聚。寶鎖聚珠
368a27 網聚。種種摩尼寶聚。一切莊嚴具聚。如意摩
368a28 尼聚。皆如大山。又復示現一切華。一切鬘。一
368a29 切香。一切燒香。一切塗香。一切衣服。一切幢
368b01 幡一切音樂。一切五欲娛樂之具。皆如山積。
368b02 及現無數百千萬億諸童女眾。而彼大天。告
368b03 善財言。善男子。可取此物供養如來。修諸福
368b04 德。并施一切。攝取眾生。令其修學檀波羅蜜
368b05 能捨難捨。善男子。如我為汝示現此物。教汝
368b06 行施。為一切眾生。悉亦如是。皆令以此善根
368b07 熏習。於三寶所。善知識所。恭敬供養。增長善
368b08 法。發於無上菩提之意。善男子。若有眾生。貪
368b09 著五欲。自放逸者。為其示現不淨境界。若有
368b10 眾生。瞋恚憍慢。多諍競者。為其示現極可怖
368b11 形如羅剎等。飲血噉肉。

简体字

“善男子，我已成就菩萨解脱，名为云网。”

善财言：“圣者，云网解脱境界云何？”

尔时，大天于善财前，示现金聚、银聚、琉璃聚、玻璃聚、砗磲聚、玛瑙聚、大焰宝聚、离垢藏宝聚、大光明宝聚、普现十方宝聚、宝冠聚、宝印聚、宝璎珞聚、宝珰聚、宝钏聚、宝锁聚、珠网聚、种种摩尼宝聚、一切庄严具聚、如意摩尼聚，皆如大山；又复示现一切华、一切鬘、一切香、一切烧香、一切涂香、一切衣服、一切幢幡、一切音乐、一切五欲娱乐之具，皆如山积；及现无数百千万亿诸童女众。而彼大天告善财言：“善男子，可取此物，供养如来，修诸福德，并施一切，摄取众生，令其修学檀波罗蜜，能舍难舍。善男子，如我为汝，示现此物，教汝行施；为一切众生悉亦如是，皆令以此善根熏习，于三宝所、善知识所，恭敬供养，增长善法，发于无上菩提之意。

“善男子，若有众生贪著五欲，自放逸者，为其示现不净境界；若有众生瞋恚、憍慢、多诤竞者，为其示现极可怖形，如罗刹等饮血啖肉；

> Son of Good Family, I have already perfected a bodhisattva's liberation known as "the net of clouds."

Sudhana then asked, "O Ārya, as for this 'net of clouds' liberation, what is its sphere of experience like?"

Mahādeva then manifested directly before Sudhana heaps of gold, heaps of silver, heaps of lapis lazuli, heaps of crystal, heaps of *musāragalva*, heaps of emeralds, heaps of great flaming-radiance jewels, heaps of stainless treasury jewels, heaps of great radiance jewels, heaps of jewels everywhere revealing the ten directions, heaps of jeweled crowns, heaps of jeweled insignia seals, heaps of jeweled necklaces, heaps of jeweled earrings, heaps of jeweled bracelets, heaps of jeweled lockets, heaps of pearl nets, heaps of all different kinds of *maṇi* jewels, heaps of all kinds of adornments, and heaps of wish-fulfilling *maṇi* jewels. All of these heaps were the size of large mountains.

He then also manifested all kinds of flowers, all kinds of garlands, all kinds of incense, all kinds of burning incense, all kinds of perfumes, all kinds of robes, all kinds of banners and pennants, all kinds of music, and all kinds of pleasure-inducing objects of the five desires, each of which appeared like heap as high as a mountain. He then also manifested countless hundreds of thousands of myriads of *koṭīs* of maidens. Mahādeva then told Sudhana:

> Son of Good Family, you may take these things and offer them to the Tathāgatas, thereby cultivating all kinds of merit, while also giving them to everyone in order to attract beings and enable them to cultivate and train in *dāna pāramitā* and the ability to relinquish what is difficult to relinquish.
>
> Son of Good Family, just as I manifest these things for you and instruct you on the practice of giving, so too and in this very same way do I also do so for all beings. So it is that I imbue them with these roots of goodness, inspire them to respectfully make offerings to the Three Jewels and to their good spiritual guides, instigate them to increase their practice of the good dharmas, and induce them to resolve to attain unexcelled bodhi.
>
> Son of Good Family, wherever there are beings who, attached to the objects of the five types of sensual desires, have become indulgently neglectful, I then show them the impurity of those sense objects. Wherever there are beings who, angry and arrogant, involve themselves in much disputation and struggle, I then manifest for them the most extremely frightful kinds of forms such as those of *rākṣasas* and others who drink blood and feast on flesh,

正體字

令其見已。驚恐惶懼。
368b12 心意調柔。捨離怨結。若有眾生。惛沈懶惰。為
368b13 其示現王賊水火。及諸重疾。令其見已。心生
368b14 惶怖。知有憂苦。而自勉策。以如是等種種方
368b15 便。令捨一切諸不善行。修行善法令除一切。
368b16 波羅蜜障。具波羅蜜。令超一切障礙險道。到
368b17 無障處。善男子。我唯知此雲網解脫。如諸菩
368b18 薩摩訶薩猶如帝釋已能摧伏一切煩惱阿脩
368b19 羅軍。猶如大水普能消滅一切眾生諸煩惱
368b20 火。猶如猛火普能乾竭一切眾生。諸愛欲水。
368b21 猶如大風普能吹倒一切眾生諸見取幢。猶
368b22 如金剛悉能摧破一切眾生諸我見山。而我
368b23 云何能知能說彼功德行。善男子。此閻浮提
368b24 摩竭提國菩提場中。有主地神。其名安住。汝
368b25 詣彼問。菩薩云何學菩薩行。修菩薩道。時善
368b26 財童子。禮大天足。遶無數匝。辭退而去

简体字

令其见已，惊恐惶惧，心意调柔，舍离冤结。若有众生惛沉、懒惰，为其示现王、贼、水、火及诸重疾；令其见已，心生惶怖，知有忧苦而自勉策。以如是等种种方便，令舍一切诸不善行，修行善法；令除一切波罗蜜障，具波罗蜜；令超一切障碍险道，到无障处。

“善男子，我唯知此云网解脱。如诸菩萨摩诃萨，犹如帝释，已能摧伏一切烦恼阿修罗军；犹如大水，普能消灭一切众生诸烦恼火；犹如猛火，普能干竭一切众生诸爱欲水；犹如大风，普能吹倒一切众生诸见取幢；犹如金刚，悉能摧破一切众生诸我见山。而我云何能知能说彼功德行？

“善男子，此阎浮提摩竭提国菩提场中，有主地神，其名安住。汝诣彼问：菩萨云何学菩萨行、修菩萨道？”

时，善财童子礼大天足，绕无数匝，辞退而去。

thereby causing them, having seen this, to be so struck with terror and agitated fright that their minds become subdued and pliant, and, as a consequence, they relinquish their animosity.

Wherever there are beings who are overcome with mental torpor and indolence, I then manifest for them the depredations of kings, thieves, floods, conflagrations, or grave illnesses which, once they have seen them, cause their minds to experience such agitated fearfulness that they realize the existence of such sorrows and sufferings and then goad themselves along.

Using all different kinds of skillful means such as these, I cause beings to relinquish all bad actions and cultivate good dharmas, cause them to do away with all obstacles to the *pāramitās* and equip themselves with the *pāramitās*, and cause them to step beyond the hazardous paths beset with all kinds of obstacles so that they may reach the place free of all obstacles.

Son of Good Family, I know only this "net of clouds" liberation. As for the bodhisattva-mahāsattvas:

Who are like Śakra in their ability to vanquish all the armies of the *asura*-like afflictions;

Who are like a great flood in their ability to everywhere extinguish the fires of all beings' afflictions;

Who are like a fierce fire in their ability to everywhere dry up the waters of all beings' cravings;

Who are like a great wind in their ability to everywhere blow down the banners of all beings' attachments to wrong views; and

Who are also like vajra in their ability to completely crush the mountains of all beings' mountains of the view of a self—

How could I know of or be able to speak about their meritorious qualities and practices?

Son of Good Family, in the site of enlightenment in Jambudvīpa's state of Magadha, there is an earth spirit known as Sthāvarā or "Peaceful Abiding." You should go there, pay your respects to her, and ask, "How should the bodhisattva train in the bodhisattva practices and how should he cultivate the bodhisattva path?"

Sudhana the Youth then bowed down in reverence at the feet of Mahādeva and circumambulated him countless times. He then respectfully withdrew and departed.

正體字

368b27 | 爾時善財童子。漸次遊行。趣摩竭[1]提國菩
368b28 | [2]薩場內安住神所。百萬地神。同在其中。更
368b29 | 相謂言。此來童子。即是佛藏。必當普為一切
368c01 | 眾生作所依處。必當普壞一切眾生無明[穀-禾+卵]
368c02 | 藏。此人已生法王種中。當以離垢無礙法繒。
368c03 | 而冠其首。當開智慧大珍寶藏。摧伏一切邪
368c04 | 論異道。時安住等百萬地神。放大光明。遍
368c05 | 照三千大千世界。普令大地同時震吼。種種
368c06 | 寶物。處處莊嚴。影潔光流。遞相鑒徹。一切葉
368c07 | 樹俱時生長。一切華樹咸共開敷。一切果樹
368c08 | 靡不成熟。一切河流遞相灌注。一切池沼悉
368c09 | 皆盈滿。雨細香雨遍灑其地。風來吹華普散
368c10 | 其上。無數音樂一時俱奏。天莊嚴具咸出美
368c11 | 音。牛王象王。師子王等。皆生歡喜。踊躍哮吼
368c12 | 猶如大山。相擊出聲。百千伏藏。自然[3]踊現。
368c13 | 時安住地神。告善財言善來童子。汝於此地。
368c14 | 曾種善根。我為汝現。汝欲見不。爾時善財。禮
368c15 | 地神足。遶無數匝。合掌而立。白言。聖者。唯
368c16 | 然欲見。

简体字

尔时，善财童子渐次游行，趣摩竭提国菩提场内安住神所，百万地神同在其中，更相谓言：“此来童子即是佛藏，必当普为一切众生作所依处，必当普坏一切众生无明[穀-禾+卵]藏。此人已生法王种中，当以离垢无碍法缯而冠其首，当开智慧大珍宝藏，摧伏一切邪论异道。”

时，安住等百万地神，放大光明，遍照三千大千世界，普令大地同时震吼，种种宝物处处庄严，影洁光流递相鉴彻；一切树叶俱时生长，一切华树咸共开敷，一切果树靡不成熟，一切河流递相灌注，一切池沼悉皆盈满；雨细香雨遍洒其地，风来吹华普散其上，无数音乐一时俱奏，天庄严具咸出美音；牛王、象王、师子王等，皆生欢喜，踊跃、哮吼，犹如大山相击出声；百千伏藏自然涌现。

时，安住地神告善财言：“善来童子！汝于此地曾种善根，我为汝现，汝欲见不？”

尔时，善财礼地神足，绕无数匝，合掌而立，白言：“圣者，唯然！欲见。”

30 – Sthāvarā

At that time, Sudhana the Youth then gradually traveled onward until he arrived at the abode of the spirit Sthāvarā at the site of enlightenment in the state of Magadha. There were a million earth spirits there who were conversing among themselves, saying:

> This youth who has come here is an embryonic *tathāgata.* He will certainly become a refuge for all beings and will certainly become one who destroys all beings' shells of ignorance.
>
> This person has already been born into the lineage of the Dharma King and thus is one who is bound to be crowned with the silken sash of stainless and unimpeded Dharma. He is bound to open the great treasury of the jewels of wisdom and vanquish all the erroneous doctrines of those adhering to deviant paths.

Then Sthāvarā and the million other earth spirits emanated a brilliant light that everywhere illuminated the worlds of the great trichiliocosm and everywhere caused the great earth to simultaneously quake and howl. The many different kinds of jeweled objects that everywhere adorned that place emanated interwoven streams of pure penetrating radiance.

All the leafy trees simultaneously produced new growth, all the flowering trees blossomed in unison, and the fruits of all the fruit trees became fully ripened. All the rivers wove together their flowing currents and all the lakes and ponds rose to abundant fullness.

A fine rain of perfume fell, everywhere soaking the ground, whereupon a breeze arose and scattered blossoms everywhere across it as countless musical phrasings simultaneously resounded and all the heavenly adornments emanated exquisite sounds. The kings of bulls, elephant kings, lion kings, and others all felt joyous delight and gamboled about, roaring and howling, producing sounds like the crashing together of mountains as the hundred thousand hidden treasures spontaneously welled up from the earth and displayed themselves.

Then Sthāvarā, the earth spirit, spoke to Sudhana, saying, "Welcome, Youth. You have previously planted roots of goodness on these very grounds. I could reveal them to you. Do you wish to see this, or not?"

Sudhana, then bowed down in reverence at the earth spirit's feet and circumambulated her countless times. He then stood before her with his palms pressed together and addressed her, saying, "O Aryā, please do so, as, indeed, I do wish to see them."

正體字

時安住地神。以足按地。百千億阿僧
368c17‖ 祇寶藏。自然[＊]踊出。告言。善男子。今此寶藏。
368c18‖ 隨逐於汝。是汝往昔善根果報。是汝福力之
368c19‖ 所攝受。汝應隨意自在受用。善男子。我得
368c20‖ 菩薩解脫。名不可壞智慧藏。常以此法。成
368c21‖ 就眾生。善男子。我憶自從然燈佛來。常隨
368c22‖ 菩薩。恭敬守護。觀察菩薩所有心行智慧境
368c23‖ 界。一切誓願。諸清淨行。一切三昧。廣大神
368c24‖ 通。大自在力。無能壞法。遍往一切諸佛國土。
368c25‖ 普[4]授一切諸如來記。轉於一切諸佛法輪。廣
368c26‖ 說一切修多羅門。大法光明普皆照[＊]耀。教化
368c27‖ 調伏一切眾生。示現一切諸佛神變。我皆能
368c28‖ 領受。皆能憶持。善男子。乃往古世。過須彌山
368c29‖ 微塵數劫。有劫名莊嚴。世界名月幢。佛號妙
369a01‖ 眼。於彼佛所。得此法門。善男子。我於此法
369a02‖ 門。若入若出。修習增長。常見諸佛。未曾捨
369a03‖ 離。始從初得。乃至賢劫。於其中間。值遇不可
369a04‖ 說不可說佛剎微塵數如來應正等覺。悉皆
369a05‖ 承事。恭敬供養。亦見彼佛詣菩提座。現大神
369a06‖ 力。亦見彼佛所有一切功德善根。

简体字

时，安住地神以足按地，百千亿阿僧祇宝藏自然涌出，告言："善男子，今此宝藏随逐于汝，是汝往昔善根果报，是汝福力之所摄受，汝应随意自在受用。

"善男子，我得菩萨解脱，名不可坏智慧藏，常以此法成就众生。

"善男子，我忆自从燃灯佛来，常随菩萨，恭敬守护，观察菩萨所有心行、智慧境界、一切誓愿、诸清净行、一切三昧、广大神通、大自在力、无能坏法，遍往一切诸佛国土，普受一切诸如来记，转于一切诸佛法轮，广说一切修多罗门，大法光明普皆照耀，教化调伏一切众生，示现一切诸佛神变，我皆能领受、皆能忆持。

"善男子，乃往古世，过须弥山微尘数劫，有劫名庄严，世界名月幢，佛号妙眼，于彼佛所得此法门。善男子，我于此法门，若入若出修习增长，常见诸佛未曾舍离，始从初得乃至贤劫，于其中间，值遇不可说不可说佛刹微尘数如来、应、正等觉，悉皆承事，恭敬供养；亦见彼佛诣菩提座，现大神力；亦见彼佛所有一切功德善根。

Sthāvarā, the earth spirit, then placed her foot on the earth, whereupon hundreds of thousands of *koṭīs* of *asaṃkhyeyas* of jewel treasuries spontaneously welled up and emerged from the earth. She then told Sudhana:

Son of Good Family, these jewel treasuries that have now appeared here follow along after you. They are the karmic fruition of the roots of goodness you planted in the distant past that have been drawn forth by the power of your karmic merit. You should freely put them to use however you wish.

Son of Good Family, I have acquired the bodhisattva liberation known as "the indestructible treasury of wisdom" and I always use this dharma to assist the development of beings. Son of Good Family, I recall that, since the time of Dīpaṃkara or "Burning Lamp" Buddha, I have always followed along after bodhisattvas, respectfully protecting them. I contemplate all the mental actions and spheres of wisdom of bodhisattvas, all their vows and pure conduct, all their samādhis and vast spiritual superknowledges, their great powers of sovereign mastery, their indestructible dharmas, their travel everywhere to all buddha lands, their everywhere receiving[129] all *tathāgatas'* predictions, their turning of all buddhas' wheel of the Dharma, their vast teaching of all the sutra gateways, their immense Dharma light which illuminates everything everywhere, their instruction and training of all beings, and their revealing of all buddhas' spiritual transformations. I am able to absorb all of this and am able to remember all of this.

Son of Good Family, long ago, in the ancient past, beyond a number of kalpas as numerous as the atoms in Mount Sumeru, there was a kalpa named "Adornment" in which there was a world named Candradhvajā or "Lunar Banner" and a Buddha named Sunetra or "Wondrous Eyes." It was under that Buddha that I acquired this Dharma gateway.

Son of Good Family, whether entering or emerging from this Dharma Gateway, as I cultivate and develop it, I always see all buddhas and am never apart from them. From the time I first acquired it all the way up to this Bhadra Kalpa, during this period I have encountered *tathāgatas*, arhats, those of right and universal enlightenment, equal in number to all the atoms in an ineffable-ineffable number of buddha *kṣetras*. I have served and made reverential offerings to all of them. I also saw those buddhas when they went to their bodhi thrones and when they revealed their great spiritual powers. I also saw all the meritorious qualities and roots of goodness possessed by all those buddhas.

正體字

善男子。我
369a07║ 唯知此不可壞智慧藏法門。如諸菩薩摩訶
369a08║ 薩。常隨諸佛。能持一切諸佛所說。入一切佛
369a09║ 甚深智慧。念念充遍一切法界。等如來身。生
369a10║ 諸佛心。具諸佛法。作諸佛事。而我云何能知
369a11║ 能說彼功德行。善男子。此閻浮提摩竭提國
369a12║ 迦毘羅城。有主夜神。名婆珊婆演底。汝詣彼
369a13║ 問。菩薩云何學菩薩行。修菩薩道。時善財
369a14║ 童子。禮地神足。遶無數匝。慇懃瞻仰。辭退而
369a15║ 去
369a16║ 爾時善財童子。一心思惟安住神教。憶持菩
369a17║ 薩不可沮壞智[1]藏解脫。修其三昧。學其軌
369a18║ 則。觀其遊戲。入其微妙。得其智慧。達其平
369a19║ 等。知其無邊。測其甚深。漸次遊行。至於彼
369a20║ 城。從東門入。佇立未[2]久。便見日沒。心念隨
369a21║ 順諸菩薩教。渴仰欲見彼主夜神。於善知識。
369a22║ 生如來想。復作是念。由善知識。得周遍眼。普
369a23║ 能明見十方境界。由善知識。得廣大解。普能
369a24║ 了達一切所緣。

简体字

“善男子，我唯知此不可坏智慧藏法门。如诸菩萨摩诃萨常随诸佛，能持一切诸佛所说，入一切佛甚深智慧，念念充遍一切法界，等如来身，生诸佛心，具诸佛法，作诸佛事；而我云何能知能说彼功德行？

“善男子，此阎浮提摩竭提国迦毗罗城，有主夜神，名婆珊婆演底。汝诣彼问：菩萨云何学菩萨行、修菩萨道？”

时，善财童子礼地神足，绕无数匝，殷勤瞻仰，辞退而去。

尔时，善财童子一心思惟安住神教，忆持菩萨不可沮坏智藏解脱，修其三昧，学其轨则，观其游戏，入其微妙，得其智慧，达其平等，知其无边，测其甚深。

渐次游行，至于彼城，从东门入，伫立未久，便见日没。心念随顺诸菩萨教，渴仰欲见彼主夜神，于善知识生如来想，复作是念：“由善知识得周遍眼，普能明见十方境界；由善知识得广大解，普能了达一切所缘；

Son of Good Family, I know only this Dharma gateway of the indestructible treasury of wisdom. As for the bodhisattva-mahāsattvas:

Who always follow the buddhas;
Who are able to retain whatever all buddhas teach;
Who penetrate the extremely profound wisdom of all buddhas;
Who, in each successive mind-moment, completely pervade the entire Dharma realm, the same as the body of the Tathāgata;
Who bring forth the mind of all buddhas;
Who possess the dharmas of all buddhas; and
Who carry out the deeds of all buddhas—

How could I know of or be able to speak about their meritorious qualities and practices?

Son of Good Family, on this continent of Jambudvīpa, in the state of Magadha, in the city of Kapilavastu, there is a night spirit known as Vāsantī. You should go there, pay your respects, and ask her, "How should the bodhisattva train in the bodhisattva practices and how should he cultivate the bodhisattva path?"

Sudhana the Youth then bowed down in reverence at the earth spirit's feet and circumambulated her countless times as he gazed up at her in attentive admiration. He then respectfully withdrew and departed.

31 – Vāsantī

At that time, Sudhana the Youth single-mindedly reflected on the teachings of Sthāvarā and recalled the bodhisattva's liberation of the indestructible treasury of wisdom, cultivated her samādhis, trained in her principles, contemplated her easeful mastery,[130] penetrated her subtleties, acquired her wisdom, comprehended her impartiality, came to know her boundlessness, and fathomed her extreme profundity.

He gradually traveled onward until he reached that city and entered its eastern gates. Not long after he came to stand there, he saw that the sun was setting. Bearing in mind compliance with the teachings of all bodhisattvas, he eagerly longed to see that night spirit. Thinking of the good spiritual guides as he would the *tathāgatas,* he further reflected:

It is because of the good spiritual guides that one acquires the universal eye that is everywhere able to clearly see the realms of the ten directions.

It is because of the good spiritual guides that one acquires the vast understanding by which one is everywhere able to completely comprehend all objective conditions.

正體字

由善知識。得三昧眼。普能觀
369a25 | 察一切法門。由善知識。得智慧眼。普能明照
369a26 | 十方剎海。作是念時。見彼夜神於虛空中。處
369a27 | 寶樓閣香蓮華藏師子之座。身真金色。目髮
369a28 | 紺青。形貌端嚴。見者歡喜。眾寶瓔珞。以為嚴
369a29 | 飾。身服朱衣。首戴梵冠。一切星宿。炳然在
369b01 | 體。於其身上一一毛孔。皆現化度無量無數
369b02 | 惡道眾生。令其免離險難之像。是諸眾生。或
369b03 | 生人中。或生天上。或有趣向二乘菩提。或有
369b04 | 修行一切智道。又彼一一諸毛孔中。示現種
369b05 | 種教化方便。或為現身。或為說法。或為示現
369b06 | 聲聞乘道。或為示現獨覺乘道。或為示現諸
369b07 | 菩薩行。菩薩勇猛。菩薩三昧。菩薩自在。菩薩
369b08 | 住處。菩薩觀察。菩薩師子[3]頻[4]申。菩薩解脫
369b09 | 遊戲。如是種種成熟眾生。善財童子。見聞
369b10 | 此已。心大歡喜。以身投地。禮夜神足。遶無數
369b11 | 匝。於前合掌。而作是言。聖者。我已先發阿耨
369b12 | 多羅三藐三菩提心。我心冀望。依善知識。獲
369b13 | 諸如來功德法藏。

简体字

由善知识得三昧眼，普能观察一切法门；由善知识得智慧眼，普能明照十方刹海。”

作是念时，见彼夜神于虚空中，处宝楼阁香莲华藏师子之座，身真金色，目发绀青，形貌端严，见者欢喜，众宝璎珞以为严饰，身服朱衣，首戴梵冠，一切星宿炳然在体。于其身上一一毛孔，皆现化度无量无数恶道众生，令其免离险难之像；是诸众生，或生人中，或生天上，或有趣向二乘菩提，或有修行一切智道。又彼一一诸毛孔中，示现种种教化方便，或为现身，或为说法，或为示现声闻乘道，或为示现独觉乘道，或为示现诸菩萨行、菩萨勇猛、菩萨三昧、菩萨自在、菩萨住处、菩萨观察、菩萨师子频申、菩萨解脱游戏，如是种种成熟众生。

善财童子见闻此已，心大欢喜，以身投地，礼夜神足，绕无数匝，于前合掌而作是言：“圣者，我已先发阿耨多罗三藐三菩提心，我心冀望依善知识获诸如来功德法藏。

It is because of the good spiritual guides that one acquires the eye of samādhi that is everywhere able to contemplate all Dharma gateways.

And it is because of the good spiritual guides that one acquires the wisdom eye with which one is everywhere able to clearly illuminate the ocean of *kṣetras* throughout the ten directions.

While he was reflecting in this way, he saw that night spirit up in the sky, in a jeweled tower, sitting on a fragrant lotus dais lion throne. Her body was the color of gold, her eyes and hair were indigo colored, and her physical form was beautiful and well adorned, delighting those who saw her. She was adorned with a necklace composed of the many kinds of jewels, her robe was vermillion red, and her head was crested with a brahman crown.

All the stars and constellations shone forth brightly from within her body. Every pore of her body revealed images of the measurelessly and numberlessly many beings of the wretched destinies who had been liberated by her and thereby spared difficult and dangerous ordeals. Of these beings, some were born in the human realm, some were born in the heavens, some progressed toward the bodhi of the two vehicles, and some cultivated the path to all-knowledge.

Moreover, in every one of her pores, there appeared all different kinds of skillful means she used in teaching, in some cases manifesting bodies for them, in some cases speaking Dharma for them, in some cases revealing the path of the *śrāvaka*-disciple vehicle for them, in some cases revealing the path of the *pratyekabuddha* vehicle for them, and in some cases revealing the practices of the bodhisattvas for them. These included the bodhisattvas' heroic bravery, the bodhisattvas' samādhis, the bodhisattvas' sovereign masteries, the bodhisattvas' abodes, the bodhisattvas' contemplations, the bodhisattvas' swiftness, and the bodhisattvas' easeful mastery in the liberations, the many different ways such as these in which she ripened beings.

On seeing and hearing this, Sudhana the Youth was filled with joyous delight. He then cast his body to the ground and prostrated in reverence at the feet of the night spirit, after which he circumambulated her countless times. He then stood before her with his palms pressed together, and addressed her, saying:

O Ārya, I am one who has already resolved to attain *anuttara-samyaksaṃbodhi*. I hope that, by relying on the good spiritual guides, I might acquire the *tathāgatas'* Dharma treasury of meritorious qualities.

正體字

唯願示我一切智道。我行
369b14‖ 於中。至十力地。時彼夜神。告善財言。善哉善
369b15‖ 哉。善男子。汝能深心敬善知識。樂聞其語。修
369b16‖ 行其教。以修行故。決定當得阿耨多羅三藐
369b17‖ 三菩提。善男子。我得菩薩破一切眾生癡暗
369b18‖ 法光明解脫。善男子。我於惡慧眾生。起大
369b19‖ 慈心。於不善業眾生。起大悲心。於作善業眾
369b20‖ 生。起於喜心。於善惡二行眾生。起不二心。於
369b21‖ 雜染眾生。起令生清淨心。於邪道眾生。起令
369b22‖ 生正行心。於劣解眾生。起令興大解心。於樂
369b23‖ 生死眾生。起令捨輪轉心。於住二乘道眾生。
369b24‖ 起令住一切智心。善男子。我以得此解脫故。
369b25‖ 常與如是心共相應。善男子。我於夜闇人靜。
369b26‖ 鬼神盜賊。諸惡眾生。所遊行時。密雲重霧。惡
369b27‖ 風暴雨。日月星宿。並皆昏蔽。不見色時。見諸
369b28‖ 眾生。若入於海。若行於陸。山林曠野。諸險難
369b29‖ 處。或遭盜賊。

简体字

唯愿示我一切智道，我行于中，至十力地！”

时，彼夜神告善财言：“善哉！善哉！善男子，汝能深心敬善知识，乐闻其语，修行其教；以修行故，决定当得阿耨多罗三藐三菩提。

“善男子，我得菩萨破一切众生痴暗法光明解脱。善男子，我于恶慧众生，起大慈心；于不善业众生，起大悲心；于作善业众生，起于喜心；于善恶二行众生，起不二心；于杂染众生，起令生清净心；于邪道众生，起令生正行心；于劣解众生，起令兴大解心；于乐生死众生，起令舍轮转心；于住二乘道众生，起令住一切智心。善男子，我以得此解脱故，常与如是心共相应。

“善男子，我于夜暗人静，鬼、神、盗贼、诸恶众生所游行时，密云重雾、恶风暴雨、日月星宿并皆昏蔽不见色时，见诸众生，若入于海，若行于陆，山林、旷野、诸险难处，或遭盗贼，

Please show me the path to all-knowledge that, when I practice in accordance with it, will lead to the ground of the ten powers.

That night spirit then told Sudhana:

It is good indeed, good indeed, Son of Good Family, that you have been able to arouse the deep resolve to revere the good spiritual guides, delight in their words, and cultivate in accordance with their teachings, for it is through just such cultivation that you will be certain to attain *anuttara-samyak-saṃbodhi.*

Son of Good Family, I have acquired the bodhisattva's liberation known as "the Dharma light that dispels the darkness of all beings' delusions." Son of Good Family:

For beings of evil intelligence, I bring forth the mind of great kindness;
For beings who engage in bad karmic deeds, I bring forth the mind of great compassion;
For beings who engage in good karmic deeds, I bring forth the mind of sympathetic joy;
For beings who engage in both good and bad actions, I bring forth the impartial mind;
For defiled beings, I bring forth the mind that causes them to become pure;
For beings who follow wrong paths, I bring forth the mind that induces them to develop right practice;
For beings with inferior beliefs, I bring forth the mind that induces them to develop great beliefs;[131]
For beings who delight in *saṃsāra,* I bring forth the mind that enables them to renounce cyclic existence; and
For beings who abide in the paths of the two vehicles, I bring forth the mind that induces them to establish themselves in the path to all-knowledge.[132]

Son of Good Family, because I have acquired this liberation, I am always accompanied by modes of thought such as these.

Son of Good Family, in the darkness of the night, when the activities of people have quieted down and the ghosts, spirits, thieves, and all kinds of evil beings are roaming about, when there are dense clouds, heavy fog, vicious winds, crashing rains, and the sun, moon, stars, and constellations are all so obscured that one cannot even see any forms—I see all these beings, whether they have gone to sea, or are traveling on land, through the mountains, in the forests, or through desolate wildernesses or other hazardous and difficult circumstances where they may encounter thieves, may run

正體字

或乏資糧。或迷惑方隅。或忘失
369c01 道路。憧惶憂怖。不能自出。我時即以種種方
369c02 便。而救濟之。為海難者。示作船師。魚王馬
369c03 王。龜王象王。阿脩羅王。及以海神。為彼眾
369c04 生。止惡風雨。息大波浪。引其道路。示其洲
369c05 岸。令免怖畏。悉得安隱。復作是念。以此善
369c06 根。迴施眾生。願令捨離一切諸苦。為在陸
369c07 地一切眾生。於夜暗中。遭恐怖者。現作日
369c08 月及諸星宿。[5]晨霞夕電。種種光明。或作屋
369c09 宅。或為人眾。令其得免恐怖之厄。復作是念。
369c10 以此善根。迴施眾生。悉令除滅諸煩惱暗。一
369c11 切眾生。有惜壽命。有愛名聞。有貪財寶。有重
369c12 官位。有著男女。有戀妻妾。未稱所求。多生憂
369c13 怖。我皆救濟。令其離苦。為行山險而留難者。
369c14 為作善神。現形親近。為作好鳥發音慰悅。為
369c15 作靈藥舒光照[＊]耀。示其[界>果]樹。示其泉井。示
369c16 正直道。示平坦地。令其免離一切憂厄。為行
369c17 曠野稠林險道。

简体字

或乏资粮，或迷惑方隅，或忘失道路，憧惶忧怖不能自出；我时即以种种方便而救济之。

“为海难者，示作船师、鱼王、马王、龟王、象王、阿修罗王及以海神；为彼众生，止恶风雨，息大波浪，引其道路，示其洲岸，令免怖畏，悉得安隐。复作是念：‘以此善根，回施众生，愿令舍离一切诸苦。’

“为在陆地一切众生于夜暗中遭恐怖者，现作日月及诸星宿、晨霞、夕电种种光明，或作屋宅，或为人众，令其得免恐怖之厄。复作是念：‘以此善根，回施众生，悉令除灭诸烦恼暗。’一切众生，有惜寿命，有爱名闻，有贪财宝，有重官位，有著男女，有恋妻妾，未称所求，多生忧怖；我皆救济，令其离苦。

“为行山险而留难者，为作善神，现形亲近；为作好鸟，发音慰悦；为作灵药，舒光照耀；示其果树，示其泉井，示正直道，示平坦地，令其免离一切忧厄。

“为行旷野、稠林、险道，

short of supplies, may become confused and disoriented, may forget and lose their way on the roads, and may become full of dread, agitated, worried, or frightened in straits from which they cannot escape on their own—for all of them, I immediately use all different kinds of skillful means to rescue them from their respective plights.

For those who have encountered difficulties at sea, I may manifest as a ship captain, or else as some king of the fishes, king of the horses, king of the turtles, king of the elephants, king of the *asuras*, or some ocean spirit who, for the sake of those beings, stops the vicious winds and rain, stills the immense waves, and leads them on a route by which they are shown the shores of land, thereby allowing them to avoid the cause of their terror and find safety and security. I also think: "I dedicate these roots of goodness to beings, wishing to enable them to leave behind all their sufferings."

For all those beings on land who encounter fearsome situations at night, I may manifest as many different kinds of illumination—as the light of the sun, the moon, or the stars and constellations, as the rose-colored sky at dawn, or as lightning in late evening. Or else I may appear as a building providing shelter or as a group of people, thereby enabling them to avoid the danger of fearsome circumstances. I also think: "I dedicate these roots of goodness to beings so that they may all be able to extinguish the darkness of their afflictions."

Wherever there are any beings who hope for long life, who are fond of a fine reputation, who desire wealth and jewels, who esteem the holding of state office, who are attached to sons or daughters, or who are enamored of wives or consorts, and, so long as those aspirations are not yet realized, are very much prone to being bothered by worries and fears on these accounts—for all of these, I rescue them from their plights so that they are allowed to leave behind their sufferings.

For those traveling in hazardous situations in the mountains who become stranded in difficult circumstances, I appear for them in the form of a good spirit who draws near to provide assistance, appear for them as a fine bird that sings comforting and pleasing songs, appear for them as magical shrubs that stream forth illuminating radiance, or manifest fruit trees for them, manifest springs or wells for them, show them a straight and direct road, or show them level ground, thereby enabling them to avoid and escape all their worries and dangers.

For those traveling through desolate wilderness, dense forests, or dangerous roads in which they become so entrapped in entangling

正體字

藤蘿所羂。雲霧所暗。而恐
369c18║ 怖者。示其正道。令得出離。作是念言。願一切
369c19║ 眾生。伐見稠林。截愛羅網。出生死野。滅煩惱
369c20║ 暗。入一切智平坦正道。到無畏處。畢竟安
369c21║ 樂。善男子。若有眾生。樂著國土。而憂苦者。
369c22║ 我以方便。令生厭離。作是念言。願一切眾生。
369c23║ 不著諸蘊。住一切佛薩婆若境。善男子。若有
369c24║ 眾生。樂著聚落貪愛宅舍。常處黑暗。受諸
369c25║ 苦者。我為說法。令生厭離。令法滿足。令依法
369c26║ 住。作是念言。願一切眾生。悉不貪樂六處聚
369c27║ 落。速得出離生死境界。究竟安住一切智城。
369c28║ 善男子。若有眾生。行暗夜中。迷惑十方。於平
369c29║ 坦路生險難想。於險難道起平坦想。以高為
370a01║ 下。以下為高。其心迷惑。生大苦惱。我以方
370a02║ 便。舒光照及。若欲出者示其門戶。若欲行者
370a03║ 示其道路。欲度溝洫示其橋梁。欲涉河海與
370a04║ 其船筏。樂觀方者示其險易安危之處。欲休
370a05║ 息者示其城邑水樹之所。作是念言。如我於
370a06║ 此照除夜暗。令諸世事悉得宣敘。

简体字

藤萝所罥、云雾所暗而恐怖者，示其正道，令得出离。作是念言：'愿一切众生，伐见稠林，截爱罗网，出生死野，灭烦恼暗，入一切智平坦正道，到无畏处毕竟安乐。'

"善男子，若有众生，乐著国土而忧苦者；我以方便，令生厌离。作是念言：'愿一切众生不著诸蕴，住一切佛萨婆若境。'

"善男子，若有众生，乐著聚落，贪爱宅舍，常处黑暗，受诸苦者；我为说法，令生厌离，令法满足，令依法住。作是念言：'愿一切众生，悉不贪乐六处聚落，速得出离生死境界，究竟安住一切智城。'

"善男子，若有众生行暗夜中，迷惑十方，于平坦路生险难想，于险难道起平坦想，以高为下，以下为高，其心迷惑，生大苦恼。我以方便舒光照及，若欲出者，示其门户；若欲行者，示其道路；欲度沟洫，示其桥梁；欲涉河海，与其船筏；乐观方者，示其险易安危之处；欲休息者，示其城邑、水、树之所。作是念言：'如我于此照除夜暗，令诸世事悉得宣叙；

vines or so immersed in the darkness of clouds and fog that they are overcome with fear, I show them the right road and thereby enable them to escape their plight. I also think, "May all beings chop their way out of their dense jungle of views, rend their entangling net of cravings, escape from the wilderness of *saṃsāra*, extinguish the darkness of the afflictions, enter the level and right road to all-knowledge, and reach the ultimate happiness of the fearless state."

Son of Good Family, wherever there are any beings who, due to a fond attachment to their country, are beset by distress and worry on that account, I use skillful means to cause them to renounce their attachment. I then think, "May all beings refrain from any attachment to the aggregates and then come to dwell in the realm of the all-knowledge of all buddhas."

Son of Good Family, wherever there are any beings who always dwell in darkness and undergo all kinds of suffering due to a fond attachment to the village or due to a covetous affection for a house, I speak Dharma for them to induce them to develop the renunciation, find fulfillment in the Dharma, and dwell in reliance on the Dharma. I then think, "May all beings refrain from any attachment to the village of the six sense bases, swiftly gain emancipation from the realm of *saṃsāra*, and ultimately dwell securely in the city of all-knowledge."

Son of Good Family, wherever there are any beings who, while traveling along on a dark night, become so confused and disoriented about the ten directions that they mistake a level path for one that is dangerous and difficult, mistake a dangerous and difficult path for one that is level, mistake one that ascends for one that descends, or mistake one that descends for one that ascends so that, because of their confusion, they experience great suffering and torment—I then use skillful means to illuminate their location.

For those who wish to find a way out, I show them a door. For those wishing to travel on, I show them the road. For those wishing to cross over a canal, I show them a bridge. For those wishing to ford a river or go beyond the sea, I provide them with a ship or a raft. For those who delight in seeing the sights of some region, I make them aware of which areas are treacherous, which are easy, which are safe, and which are dangerous. For those who wish to find a place to rest, I show them a place with a city, a village, a water source, or a tree. I then think:

> Just as I provide illumination in these situations to dispel the darkness of the night, thereby causing such worldly circumstances to be clearly seen, may I also use the light of wisdom to everywhere

正體字

願我普於
370a07║ 一切眾生生死長夜。無明暗處。以智慧光。普
370a08║ 皆照了。是諸眾生。無有智眼。想心見倒之所
370a09║ 覆翳。無常常想。無樂樂想。無我我想。不淨淨
370a10║ 想。堅固執著。我人眾生。蘊界處法。迷惑因
370a11║ 果。不識善惡。殺害眾生。乃至邪見。不孝父
370a12║ 母。不敬沙門及婆羅門。不知惡人。不識善
370a13║ 人。貪著惡事。安住邪法。毀謗如來。壞正法
370a14║ 輪。於諸菩薩。呰辱傷害。輕大乘道。斷菩提
370a15║ 心。於有恩人反加殺害。於無恩處常懷怨結。
370a16║ 毀謗賢聖。親近惡伴。盜塔寺物。作五逆罪。不
370a17║ 久當墮三惡道處。願我速以大智光明。破彼
370a18║ 眾生無明黑暗。令其疾發阿耨多羅三藐三
370a19║ 菩提心。既發心已。示普賢乘。

简体字

愿我普于一切众生生死长夜、无明暗处，以智慧光普皆照了。是诸众生无有智眼，想心见倒之所覆翳，无常常想，无乐乐想，无我我想，不净净想，坚固执著我人众生、蕴界处法，迷惑因果，不识善恶，杀害众生，乃至邪见，不孝父母，不敬沙门及婆罗门，不知恶人，不识善人，贪著恶事，安住邪法，毁谤如来，坏正法轮，于诸菩萨呰辱伤害，轻大乘道，断菩提心，于有恩人反加杀害，于无恩处常怀冤结，毁谤贤圣，亲近恶伴，盗塔寺物，作五逆罪，不久当堕三恶道处。愿我速以大智光明，破彼众生无明黑暗，令其疾发阿耨多罗三藐三菩提心。’既发心已，示普贤乘，

illuminate all beings' circumstances as they are enveloped in the darkness of ignorance during their long night of travel through the realm of *saṃsāra.* These beings do not possess the eye of wisdom. Their vision is obscured by the cataracts of inverted views regarding perceptions, thought, and views. Because of this:

They impute permanence to what is impermanent;
They impute blissfulness to what is not blissful;
They impute selfhood to what is entirely devoid of a self;
They impute loveliness to what is unlovely;
They rigidly cling to concepts of self, persons, and beings as well as to the dharmas of the aggregates, the sense realms, and the sense bases;
They are deluded with regard to cause and effect;
They do not distinguish between good and evil;
They kill beings and so forth, up to and including holding wrong views;[133]
They do not practice filial devotion to their parents;
They do not revere *śramaṇas* or brahmans;
They do not know those who are evil;
They do not recognize those who are good;
They are covetously attached to evil endeavors;
They abide in wrong dharmas;
They slander the Tathāgata;
They interfere with turning the wheel of right Dharma;
They disparage, insult, and injure bodhisattvas;
They slight the Great Vehicle path;
They cut off the resolve to attain bodhi;
They turn against and even kill those who have been kind to them;
They constantly cherish grudges against those who do not treat them with kindness;
They slander the worthies and *āryas;*
They draw near to bad companions;
They steal things from stupas and temples;
They engage in the five nefarious karmic offenses;[134] and
They are bound before long to descend into the three wretched destinies.

May I swiftly bring forth the light of great wisdom to dispel the darkness of these beings' ignorance, thereby inducing them to quickly resolve to attain *anuttara-samyak-saṃbodhi.* Once they have brought forth that resolve, may I show them the vehicle of

正體字

開十力道。亦示
370a20║ 如來法王境界。亦示諸佛一切智城。諸佛所
370a21║ 行。諸佛自在。諸佛成就。諸佛總持。一切諸
370a22║ 佛。共同一身。一切諸佛平等之處。令其安住。
370a23║ 善男子。一切眾生。或病所纏。或老所侵。或苦
370a24║ 貧窮。或遭禍難。或犯王法。臨當受刑。無所依
370a25║ 怙。生大怖畏。我皆救濟。使得安隱。復作是
370a26║ 念。願我以法。普攝眾生。令其解脫一切煩惱。
370a27║ 生老病死。憂悲苦患。近善知識。常行法施。勤
370a28║ 行善業。速得如來。清淨法身。住於究竟無變
370a29║ 易處。善男子。一切眾生。入見稠林。住於邪
370b01║ 道。於諸境界。起邪分別。常行不善。身語意
370b02║ 業。妄作種種諸邪苦行。於非正覺生正覺想。
370b03║ 於正覺所非正覺想。為惡知識之所攝受。以
370b04║ 起惡見。將墮惡道。我以種種諸方便門。而為
370b05║ 救護。令住正見。生人天中。復作是念。

简体字

开十力道，亦示如来法王境界，亦示诸佛一切智城、诸佛所行、诸佛自在、诸佛成就、诸佛总持、一切诸佛共同一身、一切诸佛平等之处，令其安住。

“善男子，一切众生，或病所缠，或老所侵，或苦贫穷，或遭祸难，或犯王法，临当被刑，无所依怙，生大怖畏；我皆救济，使得安隐。复作是念：‘愿我以法普摄众生，令其解脱一切烦恼、生老病死、忧悲苦患，近善知识，常行法施，勤行善业，速得如来清净法身，住于究竟无变易处。’

“善男子，一切众生入见稠林，住于邪道，于诸境界起邪分别，常行不善身、语、意业，妄作种种诸邪苦行，于非正觉生正觉想，于正觉所非正觉想，为恶知识之所摄受，以起恶见，将堕恶道；我以种种诸方便门而为救护，令住正见，生人天中。复作是念：

> Samantabhadra and open the path of the ten powers for them while also showing them the sphere of action of the Tathāgata, the Dharma King. May I also show them all buddhas' city of all-knowledge, all buddhas' practices, all buddhas' sovereign masteries, all buddhas' perfect accomplishments, all buddhas' complete-retention *dhāraṇīs*, and all buddhas' sharing of a single identical body, while also causing them to dwell securely in all buddhas' station of uniform equality.

Son of Good Family, as for all those beings who may be bound up by disease, who have been beset by the effects of old age, who may suffer from poverty, who may have encountered disastrous difficulties, who may be on the verge of undergoing torture for violating the king's law, who may have no one to rely on, or who have become filled with terror, I rescue all of them and enable them to find peace and security. I also think:

> May I use the Dharma to everywhere attract beings, thereby enabling them to become liberated from all the afflictions, from birth, aging, sickness, and death, and from worry, lamentation, suffering, and distress. May I lead them to draw near to good spiritual guides, to always practice the giving of Dharma, to diligently practice good karmic deeds, to swiftly acquire the Tathāgata's pure Dharma body, and to dwell in the ultimate and changeless state.

Son of Good Family, for all beings:

> Who have entered the dense forest of the various [wrong] views;
> Who dwell in wrong paths;
> Who make erroneous discriminations regarding their spheres of cognition;
> Who always practice bad karmic actions of body, speech, and mind;
> Who mistakenly engage in many different kinds of wrongly conceived ascetic practices;
> Who regard as having reached right enlightenment those who have not reached right enlightenment;
> Who regard as not having reached right enlightenment those who have reached right enlightenment;
> Who are taken in by evil spiritual guides; or
> Who, due to developing wrong views, become bound to fall into the wretched destinies—

I use all different kinds of skillful means to rescue them, to cause them to abide in right views, and to enable them to achieve rebirth among humans and devas. I also think:

正體字

如我救
370b06 | 此將墜惡道諸眾生等。願我普救一切眾生。
370b07 | 悉令解脫一切諸苦。住波羅蜜。出世聖道。於
370b08 | 一切智。得不退轉。具普賢願。近一切智。而不
370b09 | 捨離諸菩薩行。常勤教化一切眾生。爾時婆
370b10 | 珊婆演底主夜神。欲重宣此解脫義。承佛神
370b11 | 力。觀察十方。為善財童子。而說頌[1]曰
370b12 | 我此解脫門　生淨法光明
370b13 | 能破愚癡暗　待時而演說
370b14 | 我昔無邊劫　勤行廣大慈
370b15 | 普覆諸世間　佛子應修學
370b16 | 寂靜大悲海　出生三世佛
370b17 | 能滅眾生苦　汝應入此門
370b18 | 能生世間樂　亦生出世樂
370b19 | 令我心歡喜　汝應入此門
370b20 | 既捨有為患　亦遠聲聞果
370b21 | 淨修諸佛力　汝應入此門
370b22 | 我目甚清淨　普見十方剎
370b23 | 亦見其中佛　菩提樹下坐
370b24 | 相好莊嚴身　無量眾圍遶
370b25 | 一一毛孔內　種種光明出

简体字

‘如我救此将坠恶道诸众生等，愿我普救一切众生，悉令解脱一切诸苦，住波罗蜜出世圣道，于一切智得不退转，具普贤愿，近一切智，而不舍离诸菩萨行，常勤教化一切众生。’”

尔时，婆珊婆演底主夜神，欲重宣此解脱义，承佛神力，观察十方，为善财童子而说颂曰：

“我此解脱门，生净法光明，
能破愚痴暗，待时而演说。
我昔无边劫，勤行广大慈，
普覆诸世间，佛子应修学。
寂静大悲海，出生三世佛，
能灭众生苦，汝应入此门。
能生世间乐，亦生出世乐，
令我心欢喜，汝应入此门。
既舍有为患，亦远声闻果，
净修诸佛力，汝应入此门。
我目甚清净，普见十方刹，
亦见其中佛，菩提树下坐，
相好庄严身，无量众围绕，
一一毛孔内，种种光明出；

> Just as I rescue these beings who are bound to fall into the wretched destinies, may I everywhere rescue all beings. May I enable them all to be liberated from all their sufferings and abide in the *pāramitās* and the world-transcending path of the *āryas*. May they achieve irreversibility in their progress toward all-knowledge. May they equip themselves with the vows of Samantabhadra, draw close to all-knowledge, and yet still not abandon the bodhisattva practices or their constant diligence in teaching and transforming all beings.

At that time, wishing to once again proclaim the meaning of this liberation, Vāsantī Night Spirit, aided by the Buddha's spiritual powers, surveyed the ten directions and spoke these verses for Sudhana the Youth:

This gate of liberation I have acquired
produces the light of pure Dharma.
It is able to dispel the darkness of delusion
when one awaits the right time and then expounds it.

Beginning boundlessly many kalpas ago,
I diligently practiced the vast practice of great kindness
that extends everywhere to cover all worlds.
Son of the Buddha, you should cultivate and train in this.

The quiescent ocean of the great compassion
gives birth to the buddhas of the three periods of time
and is able to extinguish the sufferings of beings.
You should enter this gateway.

It is able to produce worldly bliss
and also produces world-transcending bliss
even as it causes joyous delight in one's own mind.
You should enter this gateway.

Having left behind the ills of conditioned existence
and having avoided as well the fruits of the *śrāvaka*'s path,
I cultivate the purification of the powers of all buddhas.
You should enter this gateway.

With my eyes extremely well purified
I see everywhere throughout the *kṣetras* of the ten directions
and also see the buddhas there within them,
sitting beneath their bodhi trees,

their bodies adorned with the marks and signs,
as, surrounded by measureless congregations,
from every one of their pores,
there stream forth the many different kinds of light rays.

正體字

370b26 | 見諸群生類　死此而生彼
370b27 | 輪迴五趣中　常受無量苦
370b28 | 我耳甚清淨　聽之無不及
370b29 | 一切語言海　悉聞能憶持
370c01 | 諸佛轉法輪　其聲妙無比
370c02 | 所有諸文字　悉皆能憶持
370c03 | 我鼻甚清淨　於法無所礙
370c04 | 一切皆自在　汝應入此門
370c05 | 我舌甚廣大　淨好能言說
370c06 | 隨應演妙法　汝應入此門
370c07 | 我身甚清淨　三世等如如
370c08 | 隨諸眾生心　一切悉皆現
370c09 | 我心淨無礙　如空含萬[2]像
370c10 | 普念諸如來　而亦不分別
370c11 | 了知無量剎　一切諸心海
370c12 | 諸根及欲樂　而亦不分別
370c13 | 我以大神通　震動無量剎
370c14 | 其身悉遍往　調彼難調眾
370c15 | 我福甚廣大　如空無有盡
370c16 | 供養諸如來　饒益一切眾

简体字

见诸群生类，死此而生彼，
轮回五趣中，常受无量苦。
我耳甚清净，听之无不及，
一切语言海，悉闻能忆持；
诸佛转法轮，其声妙无比，
所有诸文字，悉皆能忆持。
我鼻甚清净，于法无所碍，
一切皆自在，汝应入此门。
我舌甚广大，净好能言说，
随应演妙法，汝应入此门。
我身甚清净，三世等如如，
随诸众生心，一切悉皆现。
我心净无碍，如空含万像，
普念诸如来，而亦不分别。
了知无量刹，一切诸心海，
诸根及欲乐，而亦不分别。
我以大神通，震动无量刹，
其身悉遍往，调彼难调众。
我福甚广大，如空无有尽，
供养诸如来，饶益一切众。

I see the many different types of beings
dying in this place and taking rebirth in that place
as they travel in cycles in the five destinies of rebirth
and always undergo countless sufferings.

With my ears so extremely well purified
that their hearing has no place it does not reach,
the ocean of all verbal discourse
is completely heard and I am able to remember it all.

As all buddhas turn the wheel of Dharma
with voices which are incomparably sublime,
all of those passages and words they speak,
I am able to retain them all in memory.

With my sense of smell extremely well purified,
there are no dharmas it is impeded in sensing.
It has sovereign mastery in all things.
You should enter this gateway.

My tongue is extremely wide and large[135]
and it is pure, fine, and articulate in speech.
I expound the sublime Dharma in ways that are fitting.
You should enter this gateway.

With my body so extremely well purified,
in all three periods of time, it equally abides in suchness.
Adapting to what is fitting for the minds of beings,
it thus manifests there for all of them.

My mind has become so pure and unimpeded
that, like space, it embraces the myriad appearances.
It everywhere bears in mind all *tathāgatas*
and yet it still does not make any discriminations.

It completely knows [the beings in] the countless *kṣetras,*
the ocean of all their minds,
all their faculties, and all their mental dispositions,
and yet it still does not make any discriminations.

I use the great spiritual superknowledges
to cause countless *kṣetras* to quake
as my bodies all travel everywhere
to train those many beings who are difficult to train.

My merit has become so extremely vast that,
like space, it has become inexhaustible.
I use it to make offerings to all *tathāgatas*
and to bestow abundant benefit on all beings.

正體字

370c17 我智廣清淨　了知諸法海
370c18 除滅眾生惑　汝應入此門
370c19 我知三世佛　及以一切法
370c20 亦了彼方便　此門遍無等
370c21 一一塵中見　三世一切剎
370c22 亦見彼諸佛　此是普門力
370c23 十方剎塵內　悉見盧舍那
370c24 菩提樹下坐　成道演妙法
370c25 爾時善財童子。白夜神言。汝發阿耨多羅三
370c26 藐三菩提心。為幾時耶。得此解脫。其已久如。
370c27 乃能如是饒益眾生。其神答言。善男子。乃往
370c28 古世。過如須彌山微塵數劫。有劫名寂靜光。
370c29 世界名出生妙寶。有五億佛於中出現。彼世
371a01 界中有四天下。名寶月燈光。有城名蓮華光。
371a02 王名善法度。以法施化。成就七寶。王四天下。
371a03 王有夫人名法慧月。夜久眠寐。時彼城東有
371a04 一大林。名為寂住。林中有一大菩提樹。名一
371a05 切光摩尼王莊嚴身出生一切佛神力光明
371a06 爾時有佛。名一切法雷音王。於此樹下。成等
371a07 正覺。放無量色廣大光明。遍照出生妙寶世
371a08 界。蓮[1]華光城內。有主夜神。名為淨月。

简体字

我智广清净，了知诸法海，
除灭众生惑，汝应入此门。
我知三世佛，及以一切法，
亦了彼方便，此门遍无等。
一一尘中见，三世一切刹，
亦见彼诸佛，此是普门力。
十方刹尘内，悉见卢舍那，
菩提树下坐，成道演妙法。”

尔时，善财童子白夜神言：“汝发阿耨多罗三藐三菩提心为几时耶？得此解脱其已久如，乃能如是饶益众生？”

其神答言：“善男子，乃往古世，过如须弥山微尘数劫，有劫名寂静光，世界名出生妙宝，有五亿佛于中出现。彼世界中有四天下，名宝月灯光，有城，名莲华光，王名善法度，以法施化，成就七宝，王四天下。王有夫人，名法慧月，夜久眠寐。时，彼城东有一大林，名为寂住，林中有一大菩提树，名一切光摩尼王庄严身出生一切佛神力光明。尔时，有佛名一切法雷音王，于此树下成等正觉，放无量色广大光明，遍照出生妙宝世界。莲华城内有主夜神，名为净月，

My wisdom has become so vast and pure
that it completely knows the ocean of all dharmas
and extinguishes the delusions of beings.
You should enter this gateway.

I know the buddhas of all three periods of time
as well as all their dharmas
and also completely understand their skillful means.
This gateway is completely pervasive and peerless.

In every mote of dust, I see
all *kṣetras* throughout the three periods of time
and I also see all their buddhas.
This is the power of the universal gateway.

In the atoms of the *kṣetras* of the ten directions,
I see Vairocana within them all,
sitting beneath the bodhi tree, attaining buddhahood,
and expounding on the sublime Dharma.

Sudhana the Youth then addressed the night spirit, inquiring, "How long has it been since you resolved to attain *anuttara-samyak-saṃbodhi*? And how long has it been now since you acquired this liberation that enables you to bestow such abundant benefit on beings?"

That spirit then replied, saying:

Son of Good Family, that was in ancient times, back beyond a number of kalpas equal in number to the atoms in Mount Sumeru. It was in a kalpa named "Quiescent Light," in a world named "Producer of Marvelous Jewels" in which there were five *koṭīs* of buddhas who appeared within it. Within that world, there was a set of four continents named "Lamplight of the Jeweled Moon" in which there was a city named "Lotus Flower Radiance" with a king named "Good Dharma Bridge"[136] who used the Dharma to bestow his transformative influence. Fully endowed with the seven precious things, he ruled over the four continents. That king had a wife, "Dharma Wisdom Moon," who, as the night wore on, fell fast asleep.

At that time, east of that city, there was a great forest named "Peaceful Dwelling" in which there was an immense bodhi tree known as "the body emanating the light of all buddhas' spiritual powers that is adorned with omni-radiant sovereign *maṇi* jewels."[137] At that time, there was a buddha named "King Who Thunders All Dharmas" who attained right enlightenment as he sat beneath this tree and emanated a vast radiance of countless colors that everywhere illuminated that "Producer of Marvelous Jewels" world.

In the city of "Lotus Flower Radiance," there was a night spirit named "Pure Moon" who then went to the Queen, "Dharma

正體字

詣王
371a09| 夫人法慧月所。動身瓔珞。以覺夫人。而告
371a10| 之言。夫人當知一切法雷音王如來。於寂住
371a11| 林。成無上覺。及廣為說諸佛功德自在神力。
371a12| 普賢菩薩所有行願。令王夫人。發阿耨多羅
371a13| 三藐三菩提意。供養彼佛及諸菩薩聲聞僧
371a14| 眾。善男子。時王夫人。法慧月者。豈異人乎。
371a15| 我身是也。我於彼佛所。發菩提心。種善根故。
371a16| 於須彌山微塵數劫。不生地獄餓鬼畜生。諸
371a17| 惡趣中。亦不生於下賤之家。諸根具足。無
371a18| 有眾苦。於天人中。福德殊勝。不生惡世。恒不
371a19| 離佛及諸菩薩。大善知識。常於其所。種植
371a20| 善根。經八十須彌山微塵數劫。常受安樂。而
371a21| 未滿足菩薩諸根。過此劫已。復過萬劫。於
371a22| 賢劫前。有劫名無憂遍照。世界名離垢妙光。
371a23| 其世界中。淨穢相雜。有五百佛於中出現。其
371a24| 第一佛。名須彌幢寂靜妙眼如來應正等覺。
371a25| 我為名稱長者。女名妙慧光明。端正殊妙。彼
371a26| 淨月夜神。以願力故。於離垢世界一四天下
371a27| 妙幢王城中生。作主夜神。名清淨眼。

简体字

诣王夫人法慧月所，动身璎珞以觉夫人，而告之言：‘夫人当知，一切法雷音王如来，于寂住林成无上觉，及广为说诸佛功德自在神力、普贤菩萨所有行愿。’令王夫人发阿耨多罗三藐三菩提意，供养彼佛及诸菩萨、声闻、僧众。

“善男子，时王夫人法慧月者，岂异人乎？我身是也！

“我于彼佛所发菩提心种善根故，于须弥山微尘数劫，不生地狱、饿鬼、畜生诸恶趣中，亦不生于下贱之家，诸根具足，无有众苦，于天人中福德殊胜，不生恶世，恒不离佛及诸菩萨、大善知识，常于其所种植善根，经八十须弥山微尘数劫常受安乐，而未满足菩萨诸根。

“过此劫已，复过万劫，于贤劫前，有劫名无忧遍照，世界名离垢妙光。其世界中净秽相杂，有五百佛于中出现。其第一佛，名须弥幢寂静妙眼如来、应、正等觉；我为：名称长者；女名妙慧光明，端正殊妙。彼净月夜神，以愿力故，于离垢世界一四天下妙幢王城中生，作主夜神，名清净眼。

Wisdom Moon," and awakened her by shaking the necklace she was wearing. She then told her: "The Lady should know that, within the Peaceful Dwelling Forest, King of All Dharmas' Thunder Tathāgata has just attained the unexcelled enlightenment." She then extensively described the buddhas' meritorious qualities and sovereign mastery of the spiritual powers as well as all the practices and vows of Samantabhadra Bodhisattva, thereby inspiring the Queen to resolve to attain *anuttara-samyak-saṃbodhi.* She then presented offerings to that buddha and his sangha assemblies of bodhisattvas and *śrāvaka* disciples.

Son of Good Family, who else might the Queen, "Dharma Wisdom Moon," have been? She was none other than myself. Because I resolved to attain bodhi and planted roots of goodness under that buddha, during subsequent kalpas as numerous as the atoms in Mount Sumeru, I was never reborn in any of the wretched destinies—the hell realms, the hungry ghost realms, or the animal realms—nor was I ever born into a family of inferior social station. I have possessed complete faculties, have remained free of the many kinds of sufferings, and have had an especially excellent endowment of merit as I have continued to reside in the celestial and human realms. Nor have I ever been born into bad times. I have never been separated from buddhas, bodhisattvas, or great good spiritual guides and I have always planted roots of goodness under them.

I have passed through kalpas as numerous as the atoms in eighty Mount Sumerus during which I have always enjoyed peace and happiness. Still, I have not yet completely developed all the faculties of a bodhisattva. Having passed through all those kalpas, I then passed through a myriad more kalpas prior to the beginning of this Bhadra Kalpa, at which point there was a kalpa known as "Worry Free Pervasive Illumination" in which there was a world known as "Immaculate Sublime Light." That world was characterized by a mixture of purity and defilement and there were five hundred buddhas who appeared in it. The first of those buddhas was named Sumeru Banner Quiescent and Marvelous Eyes Tathāgata, Arhat, One of Right and Universal Enlightenment. I was born there as a daughter of a well-known elder. I was named "Light of Sublime Wisdom" and was possessed of especially marvelous beauty.

Due to the power of her vows, that "Pure Moon" night spirit was reborn as a night spirit called "Pure Eyes" in King Marvelous Banner's royal capital in the "Stainless" four-continent world.

正體字

我於
371a28| 一時。在父母邊。夜久眠息。彼清淨眼。來詣我
371a29| 所。震動我宅。放大光明。出現其身。讚佛功
371b01| 德言。妙眼如來。坐菩提座。始成正覺。勸[2]諭
371b02| 於我及以父母。并諸眷屬。令速見佛。自為
371b03| 前導。引至佛所。廣興供養。我纔見佛。即得三
371b04| 昧。名出生見佛調伏眾生三世智光明輪。獲
371b05| 此三昧故。能憶念須彌山微塵數劫。亦見其
371b06| 中諸佛出現。於彼佛所。聽聞妙法。以聞法故。
371b07| 即得此破一切眾生暗法光明解脫。得此解
371b08| 脫已。即見其身。遍往佛剎微塵數世界。亦見
371b09| 彼世界所有諸佛。又見自身在其佛所。亦見
371b10| 彼世界一切眾生。解其言音。識其根性。知其
371b11| 往昔曾為善友之所攝受。隨其所樂。而為現
371b12| 身。令生歡喜。我時於彼所。得解脫。念念增
371b13| 長。此心無間。又見自身。遍往百佛剎微塵數
371b14| 世界。此心無間。又見自身。遍往千佛剎微
371b15| 塵數世界。此心無間。又見自身。遍往百千佛
371b16| 剎微塵數世界。如是念念。乃至不可說不可
371b17| 說佛剎微塵數世界。亦見彼世界中一切如
371b18| 來。

简体字

我于一时，在父母边，夜久眠息。彼清净眼来诣我所，震动我宅，放大光明，出现其身，赞佛功德言：‘妙眼如来坐菩提座，始成正觉。’劝喻于我及以父母并诸眷属，令速见佛；自为前导，引至佛所，广兴供养。

“我才见佛，即得三昧，名出生见佛调伏众生三世智光明轮。获此三昧故，能忆念须弥山微尘数劫，亦见其中诸佛出现，于彼佛所听闻妙法；以闻法故，即得此破一切众生暗法光明解脱。得此解脱已，即见其身遍往佛刹微尘数世界，亦见彼世界所有诸佛，又见自身在其佛所；亦见彼世界一切众生，解其言音，识其根性，知其往昔曾为善友之所摄受，随其所乐而为现身，令生欢喜。

“我时于彼所得解脱，念念增长，此心无间；又见自身遍往百佛刹微尘数世界，此心无间；又见自身遍往千佛刹微尘数世界，此心无间；又见自身遍往百千佛刹微尘数世界。如是，念念乃至不可说不可说佛刹微尘数世界，亦见彼世界中一切如来；

One night, when I had fallen fast asleep alongside my parents, "Pure Eyes" came to me. She made our house tremble, emanated a bright light, and manifested her body, whereupon she praised the Buddha's meritorious qualities, saying, "Marvelous Eyes Tathāgata is sitting on the bodhi seat where he has just attained right enlightenment."

She then urged me and my parents as well as our relatives to quickly go and see the Buddha. She then served as our guide in leading us to see the Buddha to whom we then presented an abundance of offerings. When I saw the Buddha, I immediately acquired a samādhi known as "the manifestation of the wheel of wisdom light by which one sees the buddhas training beings throughout the three periods of time."

Due to having acquired this samādhi, I could recall kalpas as numerous as Mount Sumeru's atoms, could see the emergence of all the buddhas within them, and could hear those buddhas teaching the sublime Dharma wherever they were. Due to hearing their Dharma teachings, I immediately acquired this liberation known as "the Dharma light that dispels the darkness of all beings' [delusions]."

Having acquired this liberation, I immediately saw my own body traveling everywhere to worlds as numerous as the atoms in a buddha *kṣetra*. I also saw all the buddhas in those worlds, saw my own body in the presence of those buddhas, saw all the beings of those worlds, understood their languages, recognized the nature of their faculties, and knew how in their past lives they had been attracted and sustained by good spiritual guides. Then, in accordance with their inclinations, I manifested bodies for them in ways that pleased them.

Having acquired this liberation there, it continued to develop in each successive mind-moment with no interruption in this mind state. I then also saw my body traveling everywhere to worlds as numerous as the atoms in a hundred buddha *kṣetras* without any interruption in this mind state. I then also saw my body traveling everywhere to worlds as numerous as the atoms in a thousand buddha *kṣetras* without any interruption in this mind state. I then also saw my body traveling everywhere to worlds as numerous as the atoms in a hundred thousand buddha *kṣetras*. And so it was that this continued in this way in each successive mind-moment until the scope of this vision comprised worlds as numerous as the atoms in an ineffable-ineffable number of buddha *kṣetras* in which I also saw all the *tathāgatas* in those worlds and saw my body in

正體字

亦自見身。在彼佛所。聽聞妙法。受持憶
371b19 ‖ 念。觀察決了。亦知彼佛諸本事海。諸大願海。
371b20 ‖ 彼諸如來嚴淨佛刹。我亦嚴淨。亦見彼世界
371b21 ‖ 一切眾生。隨其所應。而為現身。教化調伏。此
371b22 ‖ 解脫門。念念增長。如是乃至充滿法界。善男
371b23 ‖ 子。我唯知此菩薩破一切眾生暗法光明解
371b24 ‖ 脫。如諸菩薩摩訶薩。成就普賢無邊行願。普
371b25 ‖ 入一切諸法界海。得諸菩薩金剛智幢自在
371b26 ‖ 三昧。出生大願。住持佛種。於念念中。成滿一
371b27 ‖ 切大功德海。嚴淨一切廣大世界。以自在智。
371b28 ‖ 教化成熟一切眾生。以智慧日。滅除一切世
371b29 ‖ 間暗障。以勇猛智。覺悟一切眾生惛睡。以智
371c01 ‖ 慧月。決了一切眾生疑惑。以清淨音。斷除
371c02 ‖ 一切諸有執著。於一切法界一一塵中。示現
371c03 ‖ 一切自在神力。智眼明淨。等見三世。而我
371c04 ‖ [3]何能知其妙行。說其功德。入其境界。示其
371c05 ‖ 自在。善男子。此閻浮提摩竭提國菩提場內。
371c06 ‖ 有主夜神。名普德淨光。

简体字

亦自见身在彼佛所，听闻妙法，受持忆念，观察决了；亦知彼佛诸本事海、诸大愿海，彼诸如来严净佛刹，我亦严净；亦见彼世界一切众生，随其所应而为现身教化调伏。此解脱门，念念增长，如是乃至充满法界。

“善男子，我唯知此菩萨破一切众生暗法光明解脱。如诸菩萨摩诃萨，成就普贤无边行愿，普入一切诸法界海，得诸菩萨金刚智幢自在三昧，出生大愿，住持佛种；于念念中，成满一切大功德海，严净一切广大世界；以自在智，教化成熟一切众生；以智慧日，灭除一切世间暗障；以勇猛智，觉悟一切众生惛睡；以智慧月，决了一切众生疑惑；以清净音，断除一切诸有执著；于一切法界一一尘中，示现一切自在神力，智眼明净，等见三世。而我何能知其妙行、说其功德、入其境界、示其自在？

“善男子，此阎浮提摩竭提国菩提场内，有主夜神，名普德净光。

the presence of those buddhas, listening to their teachings on the sublime Dharma, absorbing and remembering them, contemplating them, and definitely understanding them. I also knew the ocean of the past deeds of those buddhas as well as the ocean of their great vows.

Just as those *tathāgatas* purified buddha *kṣetras*, so too did I also purify them. I also saw all the beings in those worlds and, adapting to whatever was suitable for them, I manifested bodies for them with which I taught and trained them. This liberation gateway continued to develop in this way in each successive mind-moment until it filled the entire Dharma realm.

Son of Good Family, I know only this bodhisattva's liberation known as "the Dharma light that dispels the darkness of all beings' [delusions]." As for the bodhisattva-mahāsattvas:

Who fulfill Samantabhadra's boundless conduct and vows;
Who everywhere enter the ocean of the entire Dharma realm;
Who acquire all bodhisattvas' vajra wisdom banner sovereign mastery samādhi;
Who make the great vows through which they sustain and preserve the lineage of the buddhas;
Who completely fulfill in each successive mind-moment the ocean of all immense meritorious qualities as they purify all the vast world systems;
Who use their freely invoked wisdom to teach and ripen all beings;
Who use their suns of wisdom to extinguish the darkness of all worlds;
Who use their heroic wisdom to awaken all beings from their slumber;
Who use their moon of wisdom to resolve the doubts of all beings;
Who use their pure voices to cut off all attachments to all stations of existence;
Who manifest all forms of sovereign mastery of the spiritual powers in every atom throughout the entire Dharma realm; and
Who use the radiantly pure eye of wisdom to equally see the three periods of time—

How could I be able to know about their marvelous practices, speak about their meritorious qualities, penetrate their spheres of cognition, or show their command of the sovereign masteries?

Son of Good Family, on the continent of Jambudvīpa, at the site of enlightenment in the state of Magadha, there is a night spirit known as § Samantagambhīraśrīvimalaprabhā or "Pure Light of Universal Virtue." It was due to her that I originally resolved to attain

正體字

我本從其。發阿耨多
371c07 羅三藐三菩提心。常以妙法。開悟於我。汝詣
371c08 彼問。菩薩云何學菩薩行。修菩薩道。爾時善
371c09 財童子。向婆珊婆演底神。而說頌曰
371c10 見汝清淨身　相好超世間
371c11 如文殊師利　亦如寶山王
371c12 汝法身清淨　三世悉平等
371c13 世界悉入中　成壞無所礙
371c14 我觀一切趣　悉見汝形像
371c15 一一毛孔中　星月各分布
371c16 汝心極廣大　如空遍十方
371c17 諸佛悉入中　清淨無分別
371c18 一一毛孔內　悉放無數光
371c19 十方諸佛所　普雨莊嚴具
371c20 一一毛孔內　各現無數身
371c21 十方諸國土　方便度眾生
371c22 一一毛孔內　示現無量剎
371c23 隨諸眾生欲　種種令清淨
371c24 若有諸眾生　聞名及見身
371c25 悉獲功德利　成就菩提道
371c26 多劫在惡趣　始得見聞汝

简体字

我本从其发阿耨多罗三藐三菩提心，常以妙法开悟于我。汝诣彼问：菩萨云何学菩萨行、修菩萨道。”

尔时，善财童子向婆珊婆演底神而说颂曰：

“见汝清净身，相好超世间，
如文殊师利，亦如宝山王。
汝法身清净，三世悉平等，
世界悉入中，成坏无所碍。
我观一切趣，悉见汝形像，
一一毛孔中，星月各分布。
汝心极广大，如空遍十方，
诸佛悉入中，清净无分别。
一一毛孔内，悉放无数光，
十方诸佛所，普雨庄严具。
一一毛孔内，各现无数身，
十方诸国土，方便度众生。
一一毛孔内，示现无量刹，
随诸众生欲，种种令清净。
若有诸众生，闻名及见身，
悉获功德利，成就菩提道。
多劫在恶趣，始得见闻汝，

> *anuttara-samyak-saṃbodhi*. She has always used the sublime Dharma to awaken me. You should go there, pay your respects, and ask her, "How should the bodhisattva train in the bodhisattva practices and how should he cultivate the bodhisattva path?"

Sudhana the Youth then spoke these verses addressed to Vāsantī, the night spirit:

I see your pure body with its marks and signs
surpassing those of anyone in the world,
like that of Mañjuśrī,
and also like the king of jeweled mountains.

Your Dharma body is pure
and it equally pervades all three periods of time.
The worlds all enter into it
and it is unimpeded by their creation and destruction.

I contemplate all the destinies of rebirth
and see your appearances in all of them.
In each and every pore,
even the stars and moons are arrayed there.

Your mind is the epitome of vastness.
Like space itself, it pervades the ten directions.
All buddhas enter into it
and yet it remains pure and free of discriminations.

From every one of your pores,
there emanate countless rays of light
that everywhere rain down ornaments
over all buddhas of the ten directions.

In each and every pore,
there appear countless bodies
that, throughout the lands of the ten directions,
use skillful means to liberate beings.

In each and every pore
there appear countless *kṣetras*
in which, adapting to the aspirations of their beings,
you use many different means to purify them.

Wherever there are any beings
who hear your name or see your body,
they all acquire the benefit of meritorious qualities
and perfect the path to bodhi.

If beings had to live for many kalpas in the wretched destinies
before they were first able to see or hear you,

正體字

371c27 亦應歡喜受　以滅煩惱故
371c28 千剎微塵劫　歎汝一毛德
371c29 劫數猶可窮　功德終無盡
372a01 時善財童子。說此頌已。頂禮其足。遶無量匝。
372a02 慇懃瞻仰。辭退而去
372a06 大方廣佛華嚴經卷第六十九
372a09 入法界品第三十九之十
372a10 爾時善財童子。了知彼婆珊婆演底夜神。初
372a11 發菩提心。所生菩薩藏。所發菩薩願。所淨菩
372a12 薩度。所入菩薩地。所修菩薩行。所行出離道
372a13 一切智光海。普救眾生心。普遍大悲雲。於一
372a14 切佛剎。盡未來際。常能出生普賢行願。漸次
372a15 遊行。至普德淨光夜神所。頂禮其足。遶無
372a16 數匝。於前合掌。而作是言。聖者。我已先發阿
372a17 耨多羅三藐三菩提心。而我未知菩薩云何
372a18 修行菩薩地。云何出生菩薩地。云何成就菩
372a19 薩地。夜神答言。善哉善哉。善男子。汝已能發
372a20 阿耨多羅三藐三菩提心。今復問於菩薩地
372a21 修行出生。及以成就。

简体字

亦应欢喜受，以灭烦恼故。
千刹微尘劫，叹汝一毛德，
劫数犹可穷，功德终无尽。”

时，善财童子说此颂已，顶礼其足，绕无量匝，殷勤瞻仰，辞退而去。

大方广佛华严经卷第六十九

入法界品第三十九之十

尔时，善财童子了知彼婆珊婆演底夜神初发菩提心所生菩萨藏、所发菩萨愿、所净菩萨度、所入菩萨地、所修菩萨行、所行出离道、一切智光海、普救众生心、普遍大悲云、于一切佛刹尽未来际常能出生普贤行愿。

渐次游行，至普德净光夜神所，顶礼其足，绕无数匝，于前合掌而作是言：“圣者，我已先发阿耨多罗三藐三菩提心，而我未知菩萨云何修行菩萨地？云何出生菩萨地？云何成就菩萨地？”

夜神答言：“善哉！善哉！善男子，汝已能发阿耨多罗三藐三菩提心，今复问于菩萨地修行、出生及以成就。

they should still be happy to endure this,
for you would then extinguish their afflictions.

One could praise the qualities associated with but one of your hairs
for kalpas as numerous as the atoms in a thousand *kṣetras*.
One could completely exhaust the sum of all kalpas in this way
and yet still never come to the end of your meritorious qualities.

When Sudhana the Youth had finished speaking these verses, he bowed down in reverence at her feet and circumambulated her countless times as he gazed up at her in attentive admiration. He then respectfully withdrew and departed.

32 – Samantagambhīraśrīvimalaprabhā

At that time, Sudhana the Youth completely understood with regard to the night spirit Vāsantī's initial resolve to attain bodhi:

The bodhisattva treasury she had produced;
The bodhisattva vows she had made;
The bodhisattva perfections she had purified;
The bodhisattva grounds she had entered;
The bodhisattva practices she had cultivated;
The path of emancipation she had traveled;
Her luminous ocean of all-knowledge;
Her resolve to rescue all beings;
Her universally pervasive cloud of great compassion; and
Her ability to forever manifest the conduct and vows of Samantabhadra in all buddha *kṣetras* until the very end of future time.

He gradually traveled along until he met that night spirit, Samantagambhīraśrīvimalaprabhā, or "Pure Light of Universal Virtue," whereupon he bowed down in reverence at her feet and circumambulated her countless times. He then stood before her with palms pressed together and spoke these words:

O Ārya, I am one who has already resolved to attain *anuttara-samyak-saṃbodhi*. Still, I do not yet know just how a bodhisattva should cultivate the bodhisattva grounds, how he should produce the bodhisattva grounds, or how he should perfect the bodhisattva grounds.

The Night Spirit then replied by saying:

It is good indeed, good indeed, Son of Good Family, that you have already been able to resolve to attain *anuttara-samyak-saṃbodhi* and now also ask about the cultivation, generation, and perfection of the bodhisattva grounds.

正體字

善男子。菩薩成就十法。
372a22 能圓滿菩薩行。何者為十。一者得清淨三昧。
372a23 常見一切佛。二者得清淨眼。常觀一切佛。相
372a24 好莊嚴。三者知一切如來無量無邊。功德大
372a25 海。四者知等法界無量諸佛。法光明海。五
372a26 者知一切如來。一一毛孔。放等眾生數大光
372a27 明海。利益無量一切眾生。六者見一切如來。
372a28 一一毛孔。出一切寶色光明焰海。七者於念
372a29 念中。出現一切佛變化海。充滿法界。究竟
372b01 一切諸佛境界。調伏眾生。八者得佛音聲同
372b02 一切眾生言音海轉三世一切佛法輪。九者
372b03 知一切佛無邊名號海。十者知一切佛調伏
372b04 眾生不思議自在力。善男子。菩薩成就此十
372b05 種法。則能圓滿菩薩諸行。善男子。我得菩
372b06 薩解脫。名寂靜禪定樂普遊步。普見三世一
372b07 切諸佛。亦見彼佛清淨國土道場眾會。神通
372b08 名號。說法壽命。言音身相。種種不同。悉皆明
372b09 覩。而無取著。何以故。知諸如來。非去。世趣
372b10 永滅故。

简体字

“善男子，菩萨成就十法，能圆满菩萨行。何者为十？一者、得清净三昧，常见一切佛；二者、得清净眼，常观一切佛相好庄严；三者、知一切如来无量无边功德大海；四者、知等法界无量诸佛法光明海；五者、知一切如来，一一毛孔放等众生数大光明海，利益无量一切众生；六者、见一切如来，一一毛孔出一切宝色光明焰海；七者、于念念中出现一切佛变化海充满法界，究竟一切诸佛境界调伏众生；八者、得佛音声同一切众生言音海，转三世一切佛法轮；九者、知一切佛无边名号海；十者、知一切佛调伏众生不思议自在力。善男子，菩萨成就此十种法，则能圆满菩萨诸行。

“善男子，我得菩萨解脱，名寂静禅定乐普游步。普见三世一切诸佛，亦见彼佛清净国土、道场、众会、神通、名号、说法、寿命、言音、身相，种种不同，悉皆明睹而无取著。何以故？知诸如来非去，世趣永灭故；

Son of Good Family, the bodhisattva perfects ten types of dharmas by which he is able to perfectly fulfill the bodhisattva practices. What then are those ten? They are as follows:

First, he acquires pure samādhis by which he always sees all buddhas;

Second, he acquires the pure eyes by which he always contemplates all buddhas' adornment with the major marks and secondary signs;

Third, he knows the ocean of all *tathāgatas'* measureless and boundless meritorious qualities;

Fourth, he knows the countless buddhas' ocean of Dharma light commensurate with the Dharma realm;

Fifth, he knows that all *tathāgatas* emit from every one of their pores an immense ocean of light rays as numerous as all beings, rays that then flow forth to benefit all the countless beings;

Sixth, he sees all *tathāgatas* sending forth from every one of their pores an ocean of flaming light with the colors of all jewels;

Seventh, in every mind-moment, he manifests an ocean of all buddhas' transformations that completely fills the Dharma realm and ultimately fathoms the realm of all buddhas and their training of beings;

Eighth, he acquires the voice of the Buddha that speaks the ocean of all beings' languages and turns the Dharma wheel of all buddhas of the three periods of time;

Ninth, he knows the ocean of all buddhas' countless names; and

Tenth, he knows all buddhas' inconceivable powers of sovereign mastery in training beings.

Son of Good Family, if the bodhisattva perfects these ten kinds of dharmas, he will be able to completely fulfill all bodhisattva practices.

Son of Good Family, I have acquired a bodhisattva liberation known as "roaming everywhere in the bliss of quiescent *dhyāna* absorption" with which I everywhere see all buddhas of the three periods of time and also see all the many different variations in those buddhas' pure lands, sites of enlightenment, congregations, spiritual superknowledges, names, discourses on Dharma, life spans, languages, and physical marks, all of which I clearly observe while remaining free of any attachment to them.

And how is this so? This is because I realize with regard to all *tathāgatas* that:

They go nowhere because their migration in the world has been forever extinguished;

正體字

非來。體性無生故。非生。法身平等
372b11║ 故。非滅。無有生相故。非實。住如幻法故。非
372b12║ 妄。利益眾生故。非遷。超過生死故。非壞。性
372b13║ 常不變故一相。言語悉離故。無相。性相本空
372b14║ 故。善男子。我如是了知一切如來時。於菩
372b15║ 薩寂靜禪定樂普遊步解脫門。分明了達。成
372b16║ 就增長。思惟觀察。堅固莊嚴。不起一切妄想
372b17║ 分別。大悲救護一切眾生。一心不動。修習
372b18║ 初禪。息一切意業。攝一切眾生。智力勇猛。喜
372b19║ 心悅豫。修第二禪。思惟一切眾生自性。厭離
372b20║ 生死。修第三禪。悉能息滅一切眾生眾苦熱
372b21║ 惱。修第四禪。增長圓滿一切智願。出生一
372b22║ 切諸三昧海。入諸菩薩解脫海門。遊戲一切
372b23║ 神通。成就一切變化。以清淨智普入法界。善
372b24║ 男子。我修此解脫時。以種種方便。成就眾生。
372b25║ 所謂於在家放逸眾生。令生不淨想。可厭想。

简体字

非来，体性无生故；非生，法身平等故；非灭，无有生相故；非实，住如幻法故；非妄，利益众生故；非迁，超过生死故；非坏，性常不变故；一相，言语悉离故；无相，性相本空故。

“善男子，我如是了知一切如来时，于菩萨寂静禅定乐普游步解脱门，分明了达，成就增长，思惟观察，坚固庄严，不起一切妄想分别，大悲救护一切众生。一心不动，修习初禅，息一切意业，摄一切众生，智力勇猛，喜心悦豫；修第二禅，思惟一切众生自性，厌离生死；修第三禅，悉能息灭一切众生众苦热恼；修第四禅，增长圆满一切智愿，出生一切诸三昧海，入诸菩萨解脱海门，游戏一切神通，成就一切变化，以清净智普入法界。

“善男子，我修此解脱时，以种种方便成就众生。所谓：于在家放逸众生，令生不净想、可厌想、

They come from nowhere because their essential nature has no arising;
They have no arising because they are identical with the Dharma body;
They have no extinction because they have no characteristics of arising;
They have no reality because they abide in the dharma of the illusory nature of all things;
They are not false because they benefit beings;
They do not move at all because they have gone beyond birth and death;
They do not perish because their nature is one of eternal absence of any transformations;
They have one sign that lies entirely beyond the reach of any verbal description; and
They are signless because of the fundamental emptiness of their nature and signs.

Son of Good Family, when, in this way, I entirely know all *tathāgatas*, I clearly and completely comprehend, perfect, develop, meditatively reflect upon, stabilize, and adorn this bodhisattva's liberation gateway of roaming everywhere in the bliss of quiescent *dhyāna* absorption.

Not giving rise to any discursive thinking or discriminations, to use the great compassion to rescue all beings and achieve single-minded stillness, I cultivate the first *dhyāna*.

To put to rest all mental activity, to attract all beings, to manifest the courageous application of the power of wisdom, and to develop a mind of joyous contentment, I cultivate the second *dhyāna*.

To meditate on the inherent nature of all beings and renounce *saṃsāra*, I cultivate the third *dhyāna*.

To be able to entirely extinguish all beings' many sufferings and feverish afflictions, I cultivate the fourth *dhyāna*.

I nurture and bring to fulfillment the vow to attain all-knowledge, bring forth the ocean of all samādhis, enter the gateway of all bodhisattvas' ocean of liberations, achieve easeful mastery of all spiritual superknowledges, perfect all miraculous transformations, and use pure wisdom to everywhere enter the Dharma realm.

Son of Good Family, when I cultivate this liberation, I use all different kinds of skillful means to ripen beings. For instance, for neglectful beings living as householders, I cause them to bring forth:

The reflection on unloveliness;
The reflection on renunciation;

正體字

372b26‖ 疲勞想。逼迫想。繫縛想。羅剎想。無常想。苦
372b27‖ 想。無我想。空想。無生想。不自在想。老病死
372b28‖ 想。自於五欲。不生樂著。亦勸眾生。不著欲
372b29‖ 樂。唯住法樂。出離於家。入於非家。若有眾
372c01‖ 生。住於空閑。我為止息諸惡音聲。於靜夜時。
372c02‖ 為說深法。與順行緣。開出家門。示正道路。為
372c03‖ 作光明。除其闇障。滅其怖畏。讚出家業。歎佛
372c04‖ 法僧及善知識。具諸功德。亦歎親近善知識
372c05‖ 行。復次善男子。我修解脫時。令諸眾生。不
372c06‖ 生非法貪。不起邪分別不作諸罪業。若已作
372c07‖ 者皆令止息。若未生善法。未修波羅蜜行。未
372c08‖ 求一切智。未起大慈悲。未造人天業。皆令其
372c09‖ 生。若已生者令其增長。

简体字

疲劳想、逼迫想、系缚想、罗刹想、无常想、苦想、无我想、空想、无生想、不自在想、老病死想。自于五欲不生乐著，亦劝众生不著欲乐，唯住法乐，出离于家，入于非家。若有众生住于空闲，我为止息诸恶音声，于静夜时为说深法，与顺行缘，开出家门，示正道路，为作光明，除其暗障，灭其怖畏，赞出家业，叹佛、法、僧及善知识具诸功德，亦叹亲近善知识行。

“复次，善男子，我修解脱时，令诸众生，不生非法贪，不起邪分别，不作诸罪业。若已作者，皆令止息；若未生善法，未修波罗蜜行，未求一切智，未起大慈悲，未造人天业，皆令其生；若已生者，令其增长。

The reflection on wearisomeness;
The reflection on oppressiveness;
The reflection on bondage;
The reflection on *rākṣasī* she-demons;[138]
The reflection on impermanence;
The reflection on suffering;
The reflection on non-self;
The reflection on emptiness;
The reflection on nonproduction;
The reflection on the absence of inherent existence; and
The reflection on aging, sickness, and death.

They then naturally refrain from producing pleasure-driven attachments to the five objects of sensual pleasure. I also exhort beings to refrain from attachments to sensual pleasures, to dwell solely in Dharma bliss, to leave behind the householder's life, and to enter into the homeless state.

Where there are beings dwelling at leisure in a vacant place:
I assist them by causing the cessation of all disturbing noises;
In the quiet of the night, I teach them profound Dharma;
I provide them with conditions conducive to practicing;
I open the gateway to leaving behind the household life;
I show them the right path;
I create a light for them;
I dispel all their darkness-induced obstacles;
I extinguish their fears;
I praise the act of leaving behind the householder's life;
I praise the meritorious qualities possessed by the Buddha, the Dharma, the Sangha, and the good spiritual guides; and
I also praise the practice of drawing near to good spiritual guides.

Further, Son of Good Family, when I cultivate this liberation, I enable beings to refrain from bringing forth desires contrary to the Dharma, to refrain from generating wrong discriminations, and to not commit any karmic transgressions. If they have already committed them, I cause them to stop all of them.

If they have not yet produced the good dharmas, have not yet cultivated the practice of the *pāramitās*, have not yet begun the quest for all-knowledge, have not yet developed the great kindness and compassion, or have not yet engaged in the karmic actions resulting in birth among humans or devas—in all such cases, I induce them to engage in these actions. If they have already begun practicing them, I enable them to increase them.

正體字

我與如是順道因緣。
372c10 乃至令成一切智智。善男子。我唯得此菩薩
372c11 寂靜禪定樂普遊步解脫門。如諸菩薩摩訶
372c12 薩。具足普賢所有行願。了達一切無邊法界。
372c13 常能增長一切善根。照見一切如來[1]十力。住
372c14 於一切如來境界。恒處生死。心無障礙。疾能
372c15 滿足一切智願。普能往詣一切世界。悉能觀
372c16 見一切諸佛。遍能聽受一切佛法。能破一切
372c17 眾生癡闇。能於生死大夜之中。出生一切智
372c18 慧光明。而我云何能知能說彼功德行。善男
372c19 子。去此不遠。於菩提場右邊。有一夜神。名喜
372c20 目觀察眾生。汝詣彼問。菩薩云何學菩薩行。
372c21 修菩薩道。爾時普德淨光夜神。欲重宣此解
372c22 脫義。為善財童子。而說頌曰
372c23 若有信解心　盡見三世佛
372c24 彼人眼清淨　能入諸佛海
372c25 汝觀諸佛身　清淨相莊嚴
372c26 一念神通力　法界悉充滿

简体字

我与如是顺道因缘，乃至令成一切智智。

“善男子，我唯得此菩萨寂静禅定乐普游步解脱门。如诸菩萨摩诃萨，具足普贤所有行愿，了达一切无边法界，常能增长一切善根，照见一切如来智力，住于一切如来境界，恒处生死，心无障碍，疾能满足一切智愿，普能往诣一切世界，悉能观见一切诸佛，遍能听受一切佛法，能破一切众生痴暗，能于生死大夜之中出生一切智慧光明；而我云何能知能说彼功德行？

“善男子，去此不远，于菩提场右边，有一夜神，名喜目观察众生。汝诣彼问：菩萨云何学菩萨行、修菩萨道？”

尔时，普德净光夜神，欲重宣此解脱义，为善财童子而说颂曰：

“若有信解心，尽见三世佛；
彼人眼清净，能入诸佛海。
汝观诸佛身，清净相庄严，
一念神通力，法界悉充满。

So it is that I bestow such path-facilitating causes and conditions on them, even to the point that I may eventually cause them to acquire the wisdom of all-knowledge.

Son of Good Family, I have acquired only this bodhisattva liberation gateway of roaming everywhere in the bliss of quiescent *dhyāna* absorption. As for the bodhisattva-mahāsattvas:

Who have completely acquired all of Samantabhadra's practices and vows;

Who possess a complete comprehension of the entire boundless Dharma realm;

Who are ever able to increase all roots of goodness;

Who illuminate and perceive the ten powers of all *tathāgatas*;

Who abide in all *tathāgatas'* spheres of cognition;

Who constantly abide in *saṃsāra* with unimpeded minds;

Who are able to swiftly fulfill their vow to attain all-knowledge;

Who are everywhere able to travel and pay their respects in all worlds;

Who are able to contemplate and see all buddhas;

Who are everywhere able to listen to and take on the Dharma of all buddhas;

Who are able to dispel all beings' darkness of delusion; and

Who are able in the great night of *saṃsāra* to manifest the light of all-knowledge—

How could I know of or be able to speak about their meritorious qualities and practices?

Son of Good Family, not far from here, off to the right of the site of enlightenment, there is a night spirit known as Pramuditanayanajagadvirocanā or "Observing Beings with Delighted Eyes." You should go there, pay your respects, and ask her, "How should the bodhisattva train in the bodhisattva practices and how should he cultivate the bodhisattva path?"

Then the night spirit Samantagambhīraśrīvimalaprabhā, wishing to once again proclaim the meaning of this liberation, spoke these verses for Sudhana the Youth:

Those who possess the mind of resolute faith
may see all buddhas of the three periods of time.
Once the eyes of those people have thus become purified,
they become able to enter the ocean of all buddhas.

You should contemplate the bodies of all buddhas
adorned with their pure characteristic signs
as well as the power of their spiritual superknowledges that,
in but a single mind-moment, fill the entire Dharma realm.

正體字

372c27	盧舍那如來	道場成正覺
372c28	一切法界中	轉於淨法輪
372c29	如來知法性	寂滅無有二
373a01	清淨相嚴身	遍示諸世間
373a02	佛身不思議	法界悉充滿
373a03	普現一切剎	一切無不見
373a04	佛身常光明	一切剎塵等
373a05	種種清淨色	念念遍法界
373a06	如來一毛孔	放不思議光
373a07	普照諸群生	令其煩惱滅
373a08	如來一毛孔	出生無盡化
373a09	充遍於法界	除滅眾生苦
373a10	佛演一妙音	隨類皆令解
373a11	普雨廣大法	使發菩提意
373a12	佛昔修諸行	已曾攝受我
373a13	故得見如來	普現一切剎
373a14	諸佛出世間	量等眾生數
373a15	種種解脫境	非我所能知
373a16	一切諸菩薩	入佛一毛孔
373a17	如是妙解脫	非我所能知

简体字

卢舍那如来，道场成正觉，
一切法界中，转于净法轮。
如来知法性，寂灭无有二，
清净相严身，遍示诸世间。
佛身不思议，法界悉充满，
普现一切刹，一切无不见。
佛身常光明，一切刹尘等，
种种清净色，念念遍法界。
如来一毛孔，放不思议光，
普照诸群生，令其烦恼灭。
如来一毛孔，出生无尽化，
充遍于法界，除灭众生苦。
佛演一妙音，随类皆令解，
普雨广大法，使发菩提意。
佛昔修诸行，已曾摄受我，
故得见如来，普现一切刹。
诸佛出世间，量等众生数，
种种解脱境，非我所能知。
一切诸菩萨，入佛一毛孔，
如是妙解脱，非我所能知。

In the site of enlightenment, Vairocana Tathāgata
has realized the right enlightenment
and, throughout the entire Dharma realm,
turns the wheel of the pure Dharma.

The Tathāgata knows the nature of dharmas
as quiescent and non-dual.
His pure body adorned with the characteristic signs
is everywhere revealed in all worlds.

The inconceivable body of the Buddha
fills the entire Dharma realm.
It everywhere appears in all *kṣetras*
so that there are none in which it is not seen.

The ever-radiant light rays emitted by the Buddha's body
are equal in number to the atoms in all *kṣetras*.
Their many different pure colors
pervade the Dharma realm in each successive mind-moment.

A single pore of the Tathāgata
streams forth an inconceivable number of light rays
that everywhere illuminate all beings
and cause their afflictions to be extinguished.

A single pore of the Tathāgata
sends forth endless transformations
that completely pervade the Dharma realm
and extinguish the sufferings of beings.

The Buddha expounds with one marvelous voice
that adapts to all types of beings and causes them all to understand.
It everywhere sends down the vast rain of Dharma
and causes them to resolve to attain bodhi.

In the past, when cultivating the practices,
the Buddha had already attracted and accepted me.
As a consequence, I was able to see the Tathāgata,
manifesting everywhere in all *kṣetras*.

Buddhas appear in the world
on a scale commensurate with the number of beings.
Their many different spheres of liberation
are not such as I am able to know.

All bodhisattvas enter into
but a single pore of the Buddha's body.
Such marvelous liberations as these
are not such as I am able to know.

正體字

373a18 ‖ 此近有夜神　名喜目觀察
373a19 ‖ 汝應往詣彼　問修菩薩行
373a20 ‖ 時善財童子。頂禮其足。遶無數匝。慇懃瞻仰。
373a21 ‖ 辭退而去
373a22 ‖ 爾時善財童子。敬善知識教。行善知識語。作
373a23 ‖ 如是念。善知識者難見難遇。見善知識令心
373a24 ‖ 不散亂。見善知識破障礙山。見善知識入大
373a25 ‖ 悲海。救護眾生。見善知識得智慧光。普照法
373a26 ‖ 界。見善知識悉能修行一切智道。見善知識
373a27 ‖ 普能覩見十方佛海。見善知識得見諸佛。轉
373a28 ‖ 於法輪。憶持不忘。作是念已。發意欲詣喜目
373a29 ‖ 觀察眾生夜神所。時喜目神。加善財童子。令
373b01 ‖ 知親近善知識。能生諸善根。增長成熟。所謂
373b02 ‖ 令知親近善知識能修助道具。令知親近善
373b03 ‖ 知識能起勇猛心。令知親近善知識能作難
373b04 ‖ 壞業。

简体字

此近有夜神，名喜目观察，
汝应往诣彼，问修菩萨行。”

时，善财童子顶礼其足，绕无数匝，殷勤瞻仰，辞退而去。

尔时，善财童子敬善知识教，行善知识语，作如是念：“善知识者，难见难遇；见善知识，令心不散乱；见善知识，破障碍山；见善知识，入大悲海救护众生；见善知识，得智慧光普照法界；见善知识，悉能修行一切智道；见善知识，普能睹见十方佛海；见善知识，得见诸佛转于法轮忆持不忘。”作是念已，发意欲诣喜目观察众生夜神所。

时，喜目神加善财童子，令知亲近善知识，能生诸善根，增长成熟，所谓：令知亲近善知识，能修助道具；令知亲近善知识，能起勇猛心；令知亲近善知识，能作难坏业；

Near here, there is a night spirit
by the name of "Observing with Delighted Eyes."
You should go and pay your respects to her,
and then ask her how to cultivate the bodhisattva practices.

At that time, Sudhana the Youth bowed down in reverence at her feet and circumambulated her countless times as he gazed up at her in attentive admiration. He then respectfully withdrew and departed.

33 – Pramuditanayanajagadvirocanā

At that time, Sudhana the Youth, revering the teaching of the good spiritual guides and practicing in accordance with the words of the good spiritual guides, reflected in these ways:

Good spiritual guides are difficult to see and difficult to encounter;
It is through seeing good spiritual guides that one's mind becomes able to no longer be scattered;
It is through seeing good spiritual guides that one destroys the mountain of obstacles;
It is through seeing good spiritual guides that one enters the ocean of the great compassion and rescues beings;
It is through seeing good spiritual guides that one acquires the light of wisdom that everywhere illuminates the Dharma realm;
It is through seeing good spiritual guides that one is able to cultivate the path leading to all-knowledge;
It is through seeing good spiritual guides that one is everywhere able to see the ocean of the buddhas of the ten directions; and
It is through seeing good spiritual guides that one is able to see the buddhas turning the wheel of Dharma and then remembers [their teachings] without ever forgetting them.

After reflecting in this way, he wished to go and pay his respects to the night spirit known as Pramuditanayanajagadvirocanā or "Observing Beings with Delighted Eyes." At that very moment, that spirit, "Delighted Eyes," came to the aid of Sudhana the Youth, causing him to realize that it is by drawing near to good spiritual guides that one is able to produce all the roots of goodness and then cause them to grow and become fully ripened, [doing so in these ways]:

By making him realize that, by drawing near to good spiritual guides, one can cultivate the provisions essential to the path;
By making him realize that, by drawing near to good spiritual guides, one can marshal courageous resolve;
By making him realize that, by drawing near to good spiritual guides, one can perform indestructible karmic deeds;

正體字

令知親近善知識能得難伏力。令知親
373b05‖ 近善知識能入無邊方。令知親近善知識能
373b06‖ 久遠修行。令知親近善知識能[1]辨無邊業。令
373b07‖ 知親近善知識能行無量道。令知親近善知
373b08‖ 識能得速疾力普詣諸剎。令知親近善知識
373b09‖ 能不離本處遍至十方。時善財童子。遽發是
373b10‖ 念。由親近善知識能勇猛勤修一切智道。由
373b11‖ 親近善知識能速疾出生諸大願海。由親近
373b12‖ 善知識。能為一切眾生。盡未來劫。受無邊
373b13‖ 苦。由親近善知識。能被大精進甲。於一微塵
373b14‖ 中。說法聲遍法界。由親近善知識。能速往詣
373b15‖ 一切方海。由親近善知識。於一毛道。盡未來
373b16‖ 劫。修菩薩行。由親近善知識。於念念中。行菩
373b17‖ 薩行。究竟安住一切智地。由親近善知識。能
373b18‖ 入三世一切如來。自在神力諸莊嚴道。由親
373b19‖ 近善知識。能常遍入諸法界門。由親近善知
373b20‖ 識。常緣法界

简体字

令知亲近善知识，能得难伏力；令知亲近善知识，能入无边方；令知亲近善知识，能久远修行；令知亲近善知识，能办无边业；令知亲近善知识，能行无量道；令知亲近善知识，能得速疾力普诣诸刹；令知亲近善知识，能不离本处遍至十方。

时，善财童子遽发是念："由亲近善知识，能勇猛勤修一切智道；由亲近善知识，能速疾出生诸大愿海；由亲近善知识，能为一切众生，尽未来劫受无边苦；由亲近善知识，能被大精进甲，于一微尘中说法声遍法界；由亲近善知识，能速往诣一切方海；由亲近善知识，于一毛道，尽未来劫修菩萨行；由亲近善知识，于念念中行菩萨行，究竟安住一切智地；由亲近善知识，能入三世一切如来自在神力诸庄严道；由亲近善知识，能常遍入诸法界门；由亲近善知识，常缘法界

By making him realize that, by drawing near to good spiritual guides, one can acquire invincible power;

By making him realize that, by drawing near to good spiritual guides, one can enter boundlessly many realms;

By making him realize that, by drawing near to good spiritual guides, one can continue one's cultivation forever;

By making him realize that, by drawing near to good spiritual guides, one can accomplish boundless karmic works;

By making him realize that, by drawing near to good spiritual guides, one can travel along a measurelessly vast path;

By making him realize that, by drawing near to good spiritual guides, one can acquire the power of swiftly traveling everywhere to pay one's respects in all *kṣetras*; and

By making him realize that, by drawing near to good spiritual guides, one can go everywhere throughout the ten directions without ever leaving one's original place.

Sudhana the Youth then suddenly had these thoughts:

By drawing near to good spiritual guides, one can courageously and diligently cultivate the path to all-knowledge;

By drawing near to good spiritual guides, one can swiftly bring forth an ocean of great vows;

By drawing near to good spiritual guides, one can undergo boundless suffering on behalf of all beings, doing so to the very end of all future kalpas;

By drawing near to good spiritual guides, one can don the armor of great vigor and, even as one teaches the Dharma within but a single dust mote, one's voice will pervade the Dharma realm;

By drawing near to good spiritual guides, one can swiftly go and pay one's respects in the ocean of all regions;

By drawing near to good spiritual guides, within but a single pore, one can cultivate the bodhisattva practices until the very end of all future kalpas;

By drawing near to good spiritual guides, in each successive mind-moment, one can engage in the bodhisattva practices and ultimately dwell securely on the ground of all-knowledge;

By drawing near to good spiritual guides, one can enter the path of all *tathāgatas* of the three periods of time replete with the miraculous spiritual powers and all manner of adornments;

By drawing near to good spiritual guides, one can always pervasively enter all the gateways into the Dharma realm; and

By drawing near to good spiritual guides, while always keeping the Dharma realm as one's objective focus, without ever moving from

正體字

未曾動出。而能遍往十方國土
373b21‖ 爾時善財童子。發是念已。即詣喜目觀察眾
373b22‖ 生夜神所。見彼夜神。在於如來眾會道場。坐
373b23‖ 蓮華藏師子之座。入大勢力普喜幢解脫。於
373b24‖ 其身上一一毛孔。出無量種變化身雲。隨其
373b25‖ 所應。以妙言音。而為說法。普攝無量一切眾
373b26‖ 生。皆令歡喜而得利益。所謂出無量化身雲。
373b27‖ 充滿十方一切世界。說諸菩薩行檀波羅蜜。
373b28‖ 於一切事。皆無戀著。於一切眾生。普皆施與。
373b29‖ 其心平等。無有輕慢。內外悉施。難捨能捨。
373c01‖ [2]又出等眾生數無量化身雲。充滿法界。普
373c02‖ 現一切眾生之前。說持淨戒無有缺犯。修諸
373c03‖ 苦行。皆悉具足。於諸世間無有所依。於諸境
373c04‖ 界無所愛著說在生死。輪迴往返。說諸人天
373c05‖ 盛衰苦樂。說諸境界皆是不淨。說一切法皆
373c06‖ 是無常。說一切行悉苦無味。令諸世間捨離
373c07‖ 顛倒。住諸佛境。持如來戒。如是演說種種戒
373c08‖ 行戒香普熏。令諸眾生。悉得成熟。

简体字

未曾动出，而能遍往十方国土。”

尔时，善财童子发是念已，即诣喜目观察众生夜神所。

见彼夜神在于如来众会道场，坐莲华藏师子之座，入大势力普喜幢解脱，于其身上一一毛孔，出无量种变化身云，随其所应，以妙言音而为说法，普摄无量一切众生，皆令欢喜而得利益，所谓：出无量化身云，充满十方一切世界，说诸菩萨行檀波罗蜜，于一切事皆无恋著，于一切众生普皆施与；其心平等，无有轻慢，内外悉施，难舍能舍。

出等众生数无量化身云，充满法界，普现一切众生之前，说持净戒无有缺犯，修诸苦行皆悉具足，于诸世间无有所依，于诸境界无所爱著，说在生死轮回往返，说诸人天盛衰苦乐，说诸境界皆是不净，说一切法皆是无常，说一切行悉苦无味，令诸世间舍离颠倒，住诸佛境持如来戒。如是演说种种戒行，戒香普熏，令诸众生悉得成熟。

one's place, one can travel everywhere to all the lands of the ten directions.

At that very time when Sudhana the Youth had these thoughts, he suddenly came upon the night spirit Pramuditanayanajagadvirocanā by seeing that night spirit in the Tathāgata's congregation, sitting on a lotus flower dais lion seat where she had entered "the immensely powerful banner of universal joy liberation." From every one of the pores of her body, she sent forth countless kinds of clouds of transformation bodies which, in accordance with whatever was fitting for beings, used marvelous voices to teach the Dharma for them. Thus she everywhere gathered in countless beings, all of whom she caused to rejoice and receive benefit from this. For instance:

She emanated clouds of countless transformation bodies that filled all worlds of the ten directions and spoke on the bodhisattvas' practice of *dāna pāramitā* in which, in all their endeavors, they remain free of sentimental attachments, everywhere practice giving to all beings with an impartial mind free of any slighting condescension, give away all of their inward and outward possessions, and are able to relinquish what is difficult to relinquish.

She also emanated clouds of countless transformation bodies equal in number to all beings, transformation bodies that filled the Dharma realm and everywhere appeared directly before beings where they:

Spoke to them about observing the pure moral precepts without omissions or transgressions, completely cultivating all the austerities, not depending on anything in the world, and not having any attachment to any of the sense fields;

Spoke to them about going and coming in cyclic existence within *saṃsāra;*

Spoke to them about the alternations between success and failure and suffering and happiness to which all humans and devas are prone;

Spoke to them about the pervasive impurity of all the sense fields;

Spoke to them about the impermanence of all dharmas; and

Spoke to them about all conditioned things being characterized by suffering and flavorlessness, thus enabling those in the world to relinquish inverted views, dwell in the realm of the buddhas, and uphold the Tathāgata's moral precepts.

As they expounded in this way on the many different precept practices, the incense fragrance of moral virtue became everywhere pervasive, thus enabling all beings to become ripened.

正體字

又出等眾
373c09║ 生數種種身雲。說能忍受一切眾苦。所謂割
373c10║ 截捶楚。訶罵欺辱。其心泰然不動不亂。於
373c11║ 一切行不卑不高。於諸眾生不起我慢。於諸
373c12║ 法性安住忍受。說菩提心。無有窮盡。心無盡
373c13║ 故。智亦無盡。普斷一切眾生煩惱。說諸眾生
373c14║ 卑賤醜陋。不具足身。令生厭離。讚諸如來清
373c15║ 淨妙色無上之身。令生欣樂。如是方便。成熟
373c16║ 眾生。又出等眾生界種種身雲。隨諸眾生心
373c17║ 之所樂。說勇猛精進。修一切智助道之法。勇
373c18║ 猛精進。降伏魔怨。勇猛精進。發菩提心。不動
373c19║ 不退。勇猛精進。度一切眾生。出生死海。勇猛
373c20║ 精進。除滅一切惡道諸難。勇猛精進。壞無智
373c21║ 山。勇猛精進供養一切諸佛如來。不生疲厭。
373c22║ 勇猛精進。受持一切諸佛法輪。勇猛精進。壞
373c23║ 散一切諸障礙山。勇猛精進。教化成熟一切
373c24║ 眾生。勇猛精進。嚴淨一切諸佛國土。如是方
373c25║ 便成熟眾生。

简体字

又出等众生数种种身云，说能忍受一切众苦，所谓：割截、捶楚、诃骂、欺辱，其心泰然，不动不乱；于一切行不卑不高，于诸众生不起我慢，于诸法性安住忍受；说菩提心无有穷尽，心无尽故智亦无尽，普断一切众生烦恼；说诸众生卑贱丑陋不具足身，令生厌离；赞诸如来清净妙色无上之身，令生欣乐。如是方便，成熟众生。

又出等众生界种种身云，随诸众生心之所乐，说勇猛精进，修一切智助道之法；勇猛精进，降伏魔冤；勇猛精进，发菩提心，不动不退；勇猛精进，度一切众生，出生死海；勇猛精进，除灭一切恶道诸难；勇猛精进，坏无智山；勇猛精进，供养一切诸佛如来不生疲厌；勇猛精进，受持一切诸佛法轮；勇猛精进，坏散一切诸障碍山；勇猛精进，教化成熟一切众生；勇猛精进，严净一切诸佛国土。如是方便，成熟众生。

She also emanated clouds of many different kinds of transformation bodies equal in number to all beings that spoke on the ability to maintain patience when enduring all the many kinds of sufferings, for instance:

They spoke about maintaining a calm, unmoving, and undisturbed mind even when being dismembered, brutally beaten, loudly cursed, or bullied and humiliated, about being neither servile nor aloof in all one's actions, about never acting with arrogance toward any being, and about abiding peacefully in the patient acquiescence in the nature of dharmas;

They spoke on the inexhaustibility of the resolve to attain bodhi and the fact that, because one's resolve is inexhaustible, one's wisdom is also inexhaustible;

They spoke about the severance of all beings' afflictions;

They spoke on how beings can come to be of low social station, ugly, or possessed of incompletely formed bodies, thereby causing those who were listening to develop renunciation; and

They praised all *tathāgatas*' pure, marvelous, and unexcelled form bodies, thereby gladdening those who were listening.

So it was that, using skillful means such as these, she brought about the ripening of beings.

She also emanated clouds of many different kinds of transformation bodies equal in number to all beings that, adapting to beings' inclinations, spoke about:

Heroic vigor in cultivating the dharmas of the provisions for the path to all-knowledge;

Heroic vigor in vanquishing of Māra, the Adversary;

Heroic vigor in producing the unshakable and irreversible resolve to attain bodhi;

Heroic vigor in liberating all beings from the ocean of *saṃsāra*;

Heroic vigor in extinguishing all the wretched destinies and all the difficulties;[139]

Heroic vigor in destroying the mountain of ignorance;

Heroic vigor in tirelessly making offerings to all buddhas, the *tathāgatas*;

Heroic vigor in receiving and preserving the teachings of the wheel of Dharma of all buddhas;

Heroic vigor in demolishing the mountain of all obstacles;

Heroic vigor in the teaching and ripening of all beings; and

Heroic vigor in purifying all buddha lands.

So it was that she used skillful means such as these in ripening beings.

正體字

又出種種無量身雲。以種種方
373c26‖ 便。令諸眾生。心生歡喜。捨離惡意。厭一切
373c27‖ 欲。為說慚愧。令諸眾生。藏護諸根。為說無上
373c28‖ 清淨梵行。為說欲界是魔境界令生恐怖。為
373c29‖ 現不樂世間欲樂。住於法樂。隨其次第。入
374a01‖ 諸禪定諸三昧樂。令思惟觀察。除滅一切所
374a02‖ 有煩惱。又為演說一切菩薩諸三昧海。神力
374a03‖ 變現。自在遊戲。令諸眾生歡喜適悅。離諸憂
374a04‖ 怖。其心清淨。諸根猛利。愛重於法。修習增
374a05‖ 長。又出等眾生界種種身雲。為說往詣十方
374a06‖ 國土。供養諸佛及以師長真善知識。受持一
374a07‖ 切諸佛法輪。精勤不懈。又為演說稱讚一切
374a08‖ 諸如來海。觀察一切諸法門海。顯示一切諸
374a09‖ 法性相。開闡一切諸三昧門。開智慧境界。竭
374a10‖ 一切眾生疑海。示智慧金剛壞一切眾生見
374a11‖ 山。昇智慧日輪破一切眾生癡闇。

简体字

又出种种无量身云，以种种方便，令诸众生，心生欢喜，舍离恶意，厌一切欲；为说惭愧，令诸众生藏护诸根；为说无上清净梵行；为说欲界是魔境界，令生恐怖；为现不乐世间欲乐，住于法乐，随其次第，入诸禅定诸三昧乐，令思惟观察，除灭一切所有烦恼；又为演说一切菩萨诸三昧海神力变现自在游戏，令诸众生欢喜适悦，离诸忧怖，其心清净，诸根猛利，爱重于法，修习增长。

又出等众生界种种身云，为说往诣十方国土，供养诸佛及以师长、真善知识，受持一切诸佛法轮精勤不懈；又为演说、称赞一切诸如来海，观察一切诸法门海，显示一切诸法性相，开阐一切诸三昧门，开智慧境界，竭一切众生疑海；示智慧金刚，坏一切众生见山；升智慧日轮，破一切众生痴暗。

She also emanated clouds of many different kinds of transformation bodies, measureless in number, that used many different kinds of skillful means to cause beings to feel happy, relinquish evil intentions, and renounce all desires, doing so in ways such as these:

They spoke to them about having a sense of shame and dread of blame, thereby causing beings to preserve and guard their faculties;

They spoke to them about the unexcelled practice of pure *brahmacarya;*

They spoke to them about the desire realm as the realm of Māra, causing them to fear it;

They showed them that they should not delight in the worlds' sensual bliss, but rather should dwell in Dharma bliss by entering in order each of the *dhyāna* absorptions and experiencing the bliss of their samādhis, thereby causing them to engage in the meditative contemplations by which one extinguishes all afflictions; and

They also expounded for them on the ocean of all bodhisattvas' samādhis and on their freely invoked easeful mastery of transformations produced by their spiritual powers.

So it was that she caused beings to be delighted, to turn toward happiness, to turn away from sorrows and fears, to purify their minds, to sharpen their faculties, to deeply cherish the Dharma, and to increase their cultivation.

She also emanated clouds of transformation bodies equal in number to the realms of all beings:

They taught them to travel and pay their respects in the lands of the ten directions, to make offerings to all buddhas, teachers, elders, and genuine good spiritual guides, and to be intensely diligent and unremitting in receiving and preserving the teachings of the wheel of Dharma of all buddhas;

They also expounded on praising the ocean of all *tathāgatas* and on contemplating the ocean of all Dharma gateways;

They revealed the nature and characteristics of all dharmas;

They opened and explained the gateways of all samādhis;

They opened up the realms of wisdom and dried up the ocean of all beings' doubts;

They revealed the vajra pestle of wisdom that demolishes the mountain of all beings' various views; and

They raised up the sun of wisdom that dispels the darkness of all beings' delusions.

正體字

皆令歡喜
374a12║ 成一切智。又出等眾生界種種身雲。普詣一
374a13║ 切眾生之前。隨其所應。以種種言[1]辭。而為
374a14║ 說法。或說世間神通福力。或說三界皆是可
374a15║ 怖。令其不作世[門>間]業行。離三界處。出見稠
374a16║ 林。或為稱讚一切智道。令其超越二乘之地。
374a17║ 或為演說不住生死不住涅槃。令其不著有
374a18║ 為無為。或為演說住於天宮乃至道場。令其
374a19║ 欣樂發菩提意。如是方便。教化眾生。皆令究
374a20║ 竟得一切智。又出一切世界微塵數身雲。普
374a21║ 詣一切眾生之前。念念中。示普賢菩薩一切
374a22║ 行願。念念中。示清淨大願充滿法界。念念中。
374a23║ 示嚴淨一切世界海。念念中。示供養一切如
374a24║ 來海。念念中。示入一切法門海。念念中。示入
374a25║ 一切世界海微塵數世界海。

简体字

皆令欢喜，成一切智。

又出等众生界种种身云，普诣一切众生之前，随其所应，以种种言辞而为说法：或说世间神通福力；或说三界皆是可怖，令其不作世间业行，离三界处，出见稠林；或为称赞一切智道，令其超越二乘之地；或为演说不住生死、不住涅槃，令其不著有为、无为；或为演说住于天宫乃至道场，令其欣乐发菩提意。如是方便，教化众生，皆令究竟得一切智。

又出一切世界微尘数身云，普诣一切众生之前，念念中，示普贤菩萨一切行愿；念念中，示清净大愿充满法界；念念中，示严净一切世界海；念念中，示供养一切如来海；念念中，示入一切法门海；念念中，示入一切世界海、微尘数世界海；

So it was that she filled them with joyous delight at [the prospect of] realizing all-knowledge.

She also emanated clouds of many different kinds of transformation bodies equal in number to the realms of all beings that everywhere appeared directly before all beings and, in accordance with what was fitting for them, used all different kinds of words and phrases to speak Dharma for them:

For some of them, they spoke about the powers of worldly spiritual superknowledges and merit;

For some, they spoke of the fearsomeness of the three realms of existence, thereby convincing them to avoid worldly karmic actions, to abandon the stations of existence within the three realms, and to escape from the dense thickets of the various views;

For some, they praised the path to all-knowledge, thereby causing them to step beyond the grounds of the two vehicles;

For some, they expounded on not residing in either *saṃsāra* or nirvāṇa, thereby causing them to avoid attachment to either the conditioned or the unconditioned; and

For some, they expounded on dwelling in the celestial palace, and so forth up to an including arriving at the site of enlightenment, thereby causing them to delight in the resolve to attain bodhi.

So it was that she used skillful means such as these to instruct beings and thereby cause them to ultimately attain the realization of all-knowledge.

She also emanated clouds of transformation bodies equal in number to the atoms in all worlds that traveled everywhere, appeared directly before all beings, and instructed them in these ways:

In each successive mind-moment, they provided instruction in all the practices and vows of Samantabhadra Bodhisattva;

In each successive mind-moment, they provided instruction in pure and great vows that completely fill the Dharma realm;

In each successive mind-moment, they provided instruction in the purification of the ocean of all worlds;

In each successive mind-moment, they provided instruction in making offerings to the ocean of all *tathāgatas;*

In each successive mind-moment, they provided instruction in entering the ocean of all Dharma gateways;

In each successive mind-moment, they provided instruction in entering the ocean of worlds as numerous as the atoms in all oceans of all worlds;

正體字

念念中。示於一
374a26‖ 切剎盡未來劫清淨修行一切智道。念念中。
374a27‖ 示入如來力。念念中。示入一切三世方便海。
374a28‖ 念念中。示往一切剎現種種神通變化。念念
374a29‖ 中。示諸菩薩一切行願。令一切眾生住一切
374b01‖ 智。如是所作恒無休息。又出等一切眾生心
374b02‖ 數身雲。普詣一切眾生之前。說諸菩薩集一
374b03‖ 切智助道之法無邊際力。求一切智不破壞
374b04‖ 力。無窮盡力。修無上行不退轉力。無間斷力。
374b05‖ 於生死法無染著力。能破一切諸魔眾力。遠
374b06‖ 離一切煩惱垢力。能破一切業障山力。住一
374b07‖ 切劫修大悲行無疲倦力。震動一切諸佛國
374b08‖ 土令一切眾生生歡喜力。能破一切諸外道
374b09‖ 力。普於世間轉法輪力。以如是等方便成熟。
374b10‖ 令諸眾生至一切智。

简体字

念念中，示于一切刹尽未来劫清净修行一切智道；念念中，示入如来力；念念中，示入一切三世方便海；念念中，示往一切刹现种种神通变化；念念中，示诸菩萨一切行愿，令一切众生住一切智。如是所作，恒无休息。

又出等一切众生心数身云，普诣一切众生之前，说诸菩萨集一切智助道之法无边际力、求一切智不破坏力、无穷尽力、修无上行不退转力、无间断力、于生死法无染著力、能破一切诸魔众力、远离一切烦恼垢力、能破一切业障山力、住一切劫修大悲行无疲倦力、震动一切诸佛国土令一切众生生欢喜力、能破一切诸外道力、普于世间转法轮力。以如是等方便成熟，令诸众生至一切智。

In each successive mind-moment, they provided instruction in purely cultivating the path to all-knowledge in all *kṣetras* to the very end of all future kalpas;

In each successive mind-moment, they provided instruction in entering the powers of the Tathāgata;

In each successive mind-moment, they provided instruction in entering the ocean of all skillful means throughout the three periods of time;

In each successive mind-moment, they provided instruction in traveling to all *kṣetras* and manifesting many different kinds of transformations with the spiritual superknowledges; and

In each successive mind-moment, they provided instruction in all the practices and vows of all bodhisattvas.

So it was that she induced all beings to dwell in all-knowledge as they constantly and incessantly engaged in endeavors such as these.

She also emanated clouds of transformation bodies equal in number to the thoughts of all beings that traveled everywhere and appeared directly before all beings to teach them about these capacities of all bodhisattvas:

Their boundless power to accumulate the provisions for the path to all-knowledge;

Their indestructible power to pursue the realization of all-knowledge;

Their inexhaustible powers;

Their power of irreversibility in cultivating the unexcelled practices;

Their power to continue on without interruption;

Their power to avoid defiling attachment to any of the dharmas of *saṃsāra*;

Their power by which they are able to overcome all the hordes of Māra;

Their power to separate from all affliction-related defilements;

Their power to destroy the mountain of all karmic obstacles;

Their power to tirelessly dwell in all kalpas, cultivating the practice of the great compassion;

Their power to cause all buddha lands to quake and shake and thus gladden all beings;

Their power to demolish all non-Buddhist paths; and

Their power to turn the wheel of Dharma everywhere throughout the worlds.

So it was that she used skillful means such as these to ripen beings and enable them to reach all-knowledge.

正體字

又出等一切眾生心數
374b11‖ 無量變化色身雲。普詣十方無量世界。隨眾
374b12‖ 生心。演說一切菩薩智行。所謂說入一切眾
374b13‖ 生界海智。說入一切眾生心海智。說入一切
374b14‖ 眾生根海智。說入一切眾生行海智。說度一
374b15‖ 切眾生未曾失時智。說出一切法界音聲智。
374b16‖ 說念念遍一切法界海智。說念念知一切世
374b17‖ 界海壞智。說念念知一切世界海成住莊嚴
374b18‖ 差別智。說念念自在親近供養一切如來聽
374b19‖ 受法輪智。示現如是智波羅蜜。令諸眾生。皆
374b20‖ 大歡喜。調暢適悅。其心清淨。生決定解。求一
374b21‖ 切智。無有退轉。如說菩薩諸波羅蜜成熟眾
374b22‖ 生。如是宣說一切菩薩種種行法。而為利益。
374b23‖ 復於一一諸毛孔中。出無量種眾生身雲。所
374b24‖ 謂

简体字

又出等一切众生心数无量变化色身云，普诣十方无量世界，随众生心，演说一切菩萨智行。所谓：说入一切众生界海智，说入一切众生心海智，说入一切众生根海智，说入一切众生行海智，说度一切众生未曾失时智，说出一切法界音声智，说念念遍一切法界海智，说念念知一切世界海坏智，说念念知一切世界海成住庄严差别智，说念念自在亲近供养一切如来听受法轮智。示现如是智波罗蜜，令诸众生，皆大欢喜，调畅适悦，其心清净，生决定解，求一切智无有退转。如说菩萨诸波罗蜜成熟众生，如是宣说一切菩萨种种行法而为利益。

复于一一诸毛孔中，出无量种众生身云。所谓：

She also emanated clouds of countless transformation form bodies equal in number to the thoughts of all beings that traveled everywhere to countless worlds throughout the ten directions and, adapting to the minds of beings, expounded on all the wisdom and conduct of the bodhisattva, for instance:

They spoke about the knowledge that penetrates all realms of beings;

They spoke about the knowledge that penetrates the ocean of all beings' thoughts;

They spoke about the knowledge that penetrates the ocean of all beings' faculties;

They spoke about the knowledge that penetrates the ocean of all beings' actions;

They spoke about the knowledge that facilitates the liberation of all beings without ever missing the right time in doing so;

They spoke about the knowledge that is able to send forth all types of speech throughout the entire Dharma realm;

They spoke about the knowledge that, in each successive mind-moment, reaches everywhere throughout the ocean of the entire Dharma realm;

They spoke about the knowledge that, in each successive mind-moment, knows the destruction of the ocean of all worlds;

They spoke about the knowledge that, in each successive mind-moment, knows the variations in the formation, abiding, and adornment of the ocean of all worlds; and

They spoke about the knowledge by which, in each successive mind-moment, one may assume various forms[140] as one draws near to all *tathāgatas,* makes offerings to them, and then listens to and receives the teachings arising from their turning of the Dharma wheel.

So it was that, in these ways, she revealed the *pāramitā* of knowledge and thereby inspired in beings immense joy, delighted them, suitably pleased them, purified their minds, and engendered in them the decisive resolve by which they irreversibly pursued the attainment of all-knowledge.

And just as she had spoken about the bodhisattvas' *pāramitās,* thereby bringing about the ripening of beings, in this same way, she benefited them by expounding on all bodhisattvas' many different kinds of practice dharmas.

Moreover, from every one of her pores, she emanated clouds of countless kinds of beings' bodies, doing so in these ways:

正體字

出[2]與色究竟天善現天善見天無熱天無
374b25║ 煩天相似身雲。出少廣廣果福生無雲天相
374b26║ 似身雲。出遍淨無量淨少淨天相似身雲。出
374b27║ 光音無量光少光天相似身雲。出大梵梵輔
374b28║ 梵眾天相似身雲。出自在天化樂天兜率陀
374b29║ 天須夜摩天忉利天及其采女諸天子眾相似
374c01║ 身雲。出提頭賴吒乾闥婆王乾闥婆子乾闥
374c02║ 婆女相似身雲。出毘樓勒叉鳩槃[3]茶王鳩槃
374c03║ [*]茶子鳩槃[*]茶女相似身雲。出毘樓博叉龍
374c04║ 王龍子龍女相似身雲。出毘沙門夜叉王夜
374c05║ 叉子夜叉女相似身雲。出大樹緊那羅王善
374c06║ 慧摩睺羅伽王大速疾力迦樓羅王羅睺阿脩
374c07║ 羅王閻羅法王及其子其女相似身雲。出諸
374c08║ 人[4]主及其子其女相似身雲。出聲聞獨覺及
374c09║ 諸佛眾相似身雲。

简体字

出与色究竟天、善现天、善见天、无热天、无烦天相似身云，出少广、广果、福生、无云天相似身云，出遍净、无量净、少净天相似身云，出光音、无量光、少光天相似身云，出大梵、梵辅、梵众天相似身云，出自在天、化乐天、兜率陀天、须夜摩天、忉利天及其采女、诸天子众相似身云，出提头赖吒乾闼婆王、乾闼婆子、乾闼婆女相似身云，出毗楼勒叉、鸠槃荼王、鸠槃荼子、鸠槃荼女相似身云，出毗楼博叉龙王、龙子、龙女相似身云，出毗沙门夜叉王、夜叉子、夜叉女相似身云，出大树紧那罗王、善慧摩睺罗伽王、大速疾力迦楼罗王、罗睺阿修罗王、阎罗法王及其子、其女相似身云，出诸人王及其子、其女相似身云，出声闻、独觉及诸佛众相似身云，

She emanated clouds of transformation bodies in the form of Akaniṣṭha Heaven devas, Sudarśana Heaven devas, Sudṛśa Heaven devas, Atapa Heaven devas, and Avṛha Heaven devas;

She emanated clouds of transformation bodies in the form of Lesser Vastness Heaven devas,[141] Bṛhatphala Heaven devas, Puṇyaprasava Heaven devas, and Anabhraka Heaven devas;

She emanated clouds of transformation bodies in the form of Śubhakṛtsna Heaven devas, Apramāṇāśubha Heaven devas, and Pārīttaśubha Heaven devas;

She emanated clouds of transformation bodies in the form of Ābhāsvara Heaven devas, Apramāṇābha Heaven devas, and Parīttābha Heaven devas;

She emanated clouds of transformation bodies in the form of Mahābrahma Heaven devas, Brahma-purohita Heaven devas, and Brahma-pāriṣadya Heaven devas;

She emanated clouds of transformation bodies in the form of Paranirmita-vaśavartin Heaven devas, Nirmāṇa-rati Heaven devas, Tuṣita Heaven devas, Suyāma Heaven devas, and Trāyastriṃśa Heaven devas along with transformation bodies in the form of their consorts and deva sons;

She emanated clouds of transformation bodies in the form of Dhṛtarāṣṭra, the king of the *gandharvas,* along with transformation bodies in the form of *gandharva* sons and *gandharva* daughters;

She emanated clouds of transformation bodies in the form of Virūḍhaka, the king of the *kumbhāṇḍas,* along with transformation bodies in the form of *kumbhāṇḍa* sons and *kumbhāṇḍa* daughters;

She emanated clouds of transformation bodies in the form of Virūpākṣa, the king of the dragons, along with transformation bodies in the form of dragon sons and dragon daughters;

She emanated clouds of transformation bodies in the form of Vaiśravaṇa, the king of the *yakṣas,* along with transformation bodies in the form of *yakṣa* sons and *yakṣa* daughters;

She emanated clouds of transformation bodies in the form of Mahādruma, the king of the *kiṃnaras,* Sumati, the king of the *mahoragas,* Mahābalavegasthāma, the king of the *garuḍas,* Rāhu, the king of the *asuras,* and Yama, the Dharma king, along with transformation bodies in the form of their sons and daughters;

She emanated clouds of transformation bodies in the form of the human rulers together with their sons and daughters;

She emanated clouds of transformation bodies in the form of the *śrāvaka* disciples, *pratyekabuddhas,* and other congregations of the Buddha; and

正體字

出地神水神火神風神河
374c10║ 神海神山神樹神乃至晝夜主方神等相似身
374c11║ 雲。周遍十方。充滿法界。於彼一切眾生之前。
374c12║ 現種種聲。所謂風輪聲水輪聲。火焰聲海潮
374c13║ 聲。地震聲。大山相擊聲。天城震動聲。摩尼相
374c14║ 擊聲。天王聲。龍王聲。夜叉王聲。乾闥婆王
374c15║ 聲。阿脩羅王聲。迦樓羅王聲。緊那羅王聲。摩
374c16║ 睺羅伽王聲。人王聲。梵王聲。天女歌詠聲。諸
374c17║ 天音樂聲。摩尼寶王聲。以如是等種種音聲。
374c18║ 說喜目觀察眾生夜神。從初發心。所集功德。
374c19║ 所謂承事一切諸善知識。親近諸佛。修行善
374c20║ 法。行檀波羅蜜。難捨能捨。行尸波羅蜜。棄捨
374c21║ 王位宮殿眷屬。出家學道。行羼提波羅蜜。能
374c22║ 忍世間一切苦事。及以菩薩所修苦行。所持
374c23║ 正法。皆悉堅固。其心不動。亦能忍受一切
374c24║ 眾生。於己身心。惡作惡說。忍一切業。皆不
374c25║ 失壞。忍一切法。生決定解。忍諸法性。能諦
374c26║ 思惟。

简体字

出地神、水神、火神、风神、河神、海神、山神、树神乃至昼、夜、主方神等相似身云。周遍十方，充满法界。

于彼一切众生之前，现种种声。所谓：风轮声、水轮声、火焰声、海潮声、地震声、大山相击声、天城震动声、摩尼相击声、天王声、龙王声、夜叉王声、乾闼婆王声、阿修罗王声、迦楼罗王声、紧那罗王声、摩睺罗伽王声、人王声、梵王声、天女歌咏声、诸天音乐声、摩尼宝王声。

以如是等种种音声，说喜目观察众生夜神从初发心所集功德。所谓：承事一切诸善知识，亲近诸佛，修行善法；行檀波罗蜜，难舍能舍；行尸波罗蜜，弃舍王位、宫殿、眷属，出家学道；行羼提波罗蜜，能忍世间一切苦事，及以菩萨所修苦行、所持正法，皆悉坚固，其心不动，亦能忍受一切众生于己身心恶作恶说，忍一切业皆不失坏，忍一切法生决定解，忍诸法性能谛思惟；

She emanated clouds of transformation bodies in the form of earth spirits, water spirits, fire spirits, wind spirits, river spirits, ocean spirits, mountain spirits, tree spirits, and the rest up to the day and night spirits, regional spirits, and so forth.

These clouds everywhere pervaded the ten directions and completely filled the Dharma realm.

They manifested all different kinds of sounds in the presence of all beings, including the sounds of the wheel of wind, the sound of the wheel of water, the sounds of blazing flames, the sounds of the ocean surf, the sounds of earthquakes, the sounds of immense mountains crashing together, the sounds of the quaking and shaking of celestial cities, the sounds of *maṇi* jewels knocking into each other, the sounds of deva kings, the sounds of dragon kings, the sounds of *yakṣa* kings, the sounds of *gandharva* kings, the sounds of *asura* kings, the sounds of *garuḍa* kings, the sounds of *kiṃnara* kings, the sounds of *mahoraga* kings, the sounds of human kings, the sounds of Brahma Heaven kings, the sounds of singing deva maidens, the sounds of all different kinds of celestial music, and the sounds of the kings of *maṇi* jewels.

With all these many different kinds of sounds, they expounded on the meritorious qualities accumulated by that night spirit known as Pramuditanayanajagadvirocanā or "Observing Beings with Delighted Eyes" beginning with that time in the past when she first aroused the initial resolve. For instance:

They described her service to all good spiritual guides, her drawing near to the buddhas, and her cultivation of the good dharmas;

They described her past practice of the *dāna pāramitā* by which she could relinquish what is difficult to relinquish;

They described her past practice of the *śīla pāramitā* by which she had cast aside the royal throne, the palace, and the retinue in order to leave behind the home life and train in the path;

They described her past practice of the *kṣānti pāramitā* by which she was able to endure all circumstances of worldly suffering and the austere practices cultivated by the bodhisattva, by which she remained solidly persistent with unshakable resolve in the right Dharma she upheld, by which she was also able to endure all the evil actions and evil speech inflicted on her body and mind by all beings, by which she maintained patience with all her karma without ever being destroyed by it, by which she maintained patience with all dharmas and developed a decisive understanding of them, and by which she maintained patience with the nature of dharmas and reflected on it in a manner consistent with truth;

正體字

行精進波羅蜜。起一切智行。成一切
374c27‖ 佛法。行禪波羅蜜。其禪波羅蜜。所有資具
374c28‖ 所有修習。所有成就。所有清淨。所有起三
374c29‖ 昧神通。所有入三昧海門。皆悉顯示。行般
375a01‖ 若波羅蜜。其般若波羅蜜。所有資具。所有
375a02‖ 清淨。大智慧日。大智慧雲。大智慧藏。大智慧
375a03‖ 門。皆悉顯示。行方便波羅蜜。其方便波羅蜜。
375a04‖ 所有資具。所有修行。所有體性。所有理趣。所
375a05‖ 有清淨。所有相應事。皆悉顯示。行願波羅
375a06‖ [1]蜜。其願波羅[*]蜜。所有體性。所有成就。所有
375a07‖ 修習。所有相應事。皆悉顯示。行力波羅[*]蜜。
375a08‖ 其力波羅[*]蜜。所有資具。所有因緣。所有理
375a09‖ 趣。所有演說。所有相應事。皆悉顯示。行智波
375a10‖ 羅[*]蜜。其智波羅[*]蜜。所有資具。所有體性。所
375a11‖ 有成就。所有清淨。所有處所。所有增長。所有
375a12‖ 深入。所有光明。所有顯示。所有理趣。所有相
375a13‖ 應事。所有[2]揀擇。所有行相。所有相應法。所
375a14‖ 有所攝法。所知法。所知業。所知剎。所知劫。
375a15‖ 所知世。所知佛出現。所知佛。所知菩薩。所知
375a16‖ 菩薩心。菩薩位。菩薩資具。菩薩發趣。菩薩迴
375a17‖ 向。菩薩大願。菩薩法輪。菩薩[*]揀擇法。菩薩
375a18‖ 法海。菩薩法門海。

简体字

行精进波罗蜜，起一切智行，成一切佛法；行禅波罗蜜，其禅波罗蜜所有资具、所有修习、所有成就、所有清净、所有起三昧神通、所有入三昧海门，皆悉显示；行般若波罗蜜，其般若波罗蜜所有资具，所有清净、大智慧日、大智慧云、大智慧藏、大智慧门，皆悉显示；行方便波罗蜜，其方便波罗蜜所有资具、所有修行、所有体性、所有理趣、所有清净、所有相应事，皆悉显示；行愿波罗蜜，其愿波罗蜜所有体性、所有成就、所有修习、所有相应事，皆悉显示；行力波罗蜜，其力波罗蜜所有资具、所有因缘、所有理趣、所有演说、所有相应事，皆悉显示；行智波罗蜜，其智波罗蜜所有资具、所有体性、所有成就、所有清净、所有处所、所有增长、所有深入、所有光明、所有显示、所有理趣、所有相应事、所有简择、所有行相、所有相应法，所有所摄法、所知法、所知业、所知刹、所知劫、所知世、所知佛出现、所知佛、所知菩萨，所知菩萨心、菩萨位、菩萨资具、菩萨发趣、菩萨回向、菩萨大愿、菩萨法轮、菩萨简择法、菩萨法海、菩萨法门海、

They described her past practice of the vigor *pāramitā* by which she began the practices leading to all-knowledge and achieved success in all the dharmas of the Buddha;

They described her past practice of the *dhyāna pāramitā* and entirely revealed with regard to her practice of the *dhyāna pāramitā* her fulfillment of its essential provisions, her cultivation, her achievements, her purification, her production of samādhis and spiritual superknowledges, and her ways of entering the gateways to the ocean of samādhis;

They described her past practice of the *prajñā pāramitā* and entirely revealed with regard to her practice of the *prajñā pāramitā* her fulfillment of its essential provisions, her purification, her sun of great wisdom, her clouds of great wisdom, her treasury of great wisdom, and her gateways into great wisdom;

They described her past practice of the skillful means *pāramitā*, entirely revealing with regard to her practice of the skillful means *pāramitā* her fulfillment of its essential provisions, her cultivation, its essential nature, its principles and import, her purification, and her associated works;

They described her past practice of the vows *pāramitā*, entirely revealing with regard to her practice of the vows *pāramitā* its essential nature, her accomplishments, her cultivation, and her associated works;

They described her past practice of the powers *pāramitā*, entirely revealing with regard to her practice of the powers *pāramitā* her fulfillment of its essential provisions, its associated causes and conditions, its principles and their import, her expositions of it, and her associated works; and

They described her past practice of the knowledge *pāramitā*, entirely revealing with regard to her practice of the knowledge *pāramitā* her fulfillment of its essential provisions, its essential nature, her accomplishments, her purification, its locations, its growth, its deep penetration, its radiance, its manifestations, its principles and their import, its associated works, its selectivity, its practice characteristics, its associated dharmas, its dharmas of attraction, the dharmas it knows, the karmic works it knows, the *kṣetras* it knows, the kalpas it knows, the periods of time it knows, the emergence of buddhas it knows, the buddhas it knows, the bodhisattvas it knows, the bodhisattva minds it knows, the bodhisattva's stations on the path, the bodhisattva's provisions, the bodhisattva's commencement and progression, the bodhisattva's dedications, the bodhisattva's great vows, the bodhisattva's turning of the Dharma wheel, the bodhisattva's dharma selection, the bodhisattva's ocean of dharmas, the bodhisattva's ocean of Dharma gateways, the bodhisattva's Dharma

正體字

菩薩法旋流。菩薩法理趣。
375a19║ 如是等智波羅[＊]蜜。相應境界。皆悉顯示。成
375a20║ 熟眾生。又說此神從初發心所集功德。相續
375a21║ 次第。所習善根。相續次第。所修無量諸波羅
375a22║ [＊]蜜相續次第。死此生彼。及其名號相續次
375a23║ 第。親近善友。承事諸佛。受持正法。修菩薩
375a24║ 行。入諸三昧。以三昧力。普見諸佛。普見諸
375a25║ 剎。普知諸劫。深入法界。觀察眾生。入法界
375a26║ 海。知諸眾生死此生彼。得淨天耳聞一切聲。
375a27║ 得淨天眼見一切色。得他心智知眾生心。得
375a28║ 宿住智知前際事。得無依無作神足智通。自
375a29║ 在遊行遍十方剎。如是所有相續次第。得菩
375b01║ 薩解脫。入菩薩解脫海。得菩薩自在。得菩
375b02║ 薩勇猛。得菩薩遊步。住菩薩想。入菩薩道。如
375b03║ 是一切所有功德。相續次第。皆悉演說。分別
375b04║ 顯示。成熟眾生。如是說時。於念念中。十方各
375b05║ 嚴淨不可說不可說諸佛國土。度脫無量惡
375b06║ 趣眾生。令無量眾生。生天人中。富貴自在。令
375b07║ 無量眾生。出生死海。

简体字

菩萨法旋流、菩萨法理趣，如是等智波罗蜜相应境界，皆悉显示，成熟众生。

又说此神从初发心所集功德相续次第；所习善根相续次第；所修无量诸波罗蜜相续次第；死此生彼及其名号相续次第；亲近善友，承事诸佛，受持正法，修菩萨行，入诸三昧，以三昧力，普见诸佛，普见诸刹，普知诸劫，深入法界，观察众生，入法界海，知诸众生死此生彼，得净天耳闻一切声，得净天眼见一切色，得他心智知众生心，得宿住智知前际事，得无依无作神足智通自在游行遍十方刹，如是所有相续次第；得菩萨解脱，入菩萨解脱海，得菩萨自在，得菩萨勇猛，得菩萨游步，住菩萨想，入菩萨道，如是一切所有功德相续次第。皆悉演说，分别显示，成熟众生。

如是说时，于念念中，十方各严净不可说不可说诸佛国土，度脱无量恶趣众生，令无量众生生天人中富贵自在，令无量众生出生死海，

whirlpools, and the principles and import of the bodhisattva's Dharma. So it was that they revealed all such spheres of cognition related to the knowledge *pāramitā*, thereby bringing about the ripening of beings.

They also spoke about what has transpired since this spirit first aroused the initial resolve, including:

The continuity and sequence of the meritorious qualities she accumulated;

The continuity and sequence of the roots of goodness she practiced;

The continuity and sequence of the countless *pāramitās* she cultivated;

The continuity and sequence of her dying in this place, being reborn in that place, and her corresponding names;

The continuity and sequence of her drawing near to good spiritual guides, serving buddhas, receiving and upholding right Dharma, cultivating the bodhisattva practices, entering samādhis, using the powers of samādhis to everywhere see all buddhas, see all *kṣetras*, and know all kalpas, her deep entry into the Dharma realm, her contemplation of beings, her entry into the ocean of the Dharma realm, her knowing beings' deaths here and rebirths there, her attainment of the purified heavenly ear to hear all sounds, her attainment of the purified heavenly eye to see all forms, her attainment of the knowledge of others' thoughts to know beings' thoughts, her attainment of the knowledge of past existences to know past events, and her attainment of the independent and effortless use of the spiritual superknowledges to freely travel to *kṣetras* everywhere throughout the ten directions—the continuity and sequence of all matters such as these; and

The continuity and sequence of her attainment of the bodhisattva's liberations, her entry into the bodhisattva's ocean of liberations, her attainment of the bodhisattva's sovereign masteries, her attainment of the bodhisattva's heroic courage, her attainment of the bodhisattva's stride, her dwelling in the bodhisattva's thought, and her entry into the bodhisattva path.

They expounded on the continuity and sequence of her attainment of all the meritorious qualities such as these, distinguishing and revealing them, thereby bringing about the ripening of beings.

As they spoke in these ways, in each successive mind-moment and in each of the ten directions, they purified an ineffable-ineffable number of buddha lands, thereby liberating countless beings from the wretched destinies, enabling countless beings to be reborn among devas and humans with wealth, noble station, and sovereign freedom, enabling countless beings to escape from the ocean of *saṃsāra*,

正體字

令無量眾生。安住聲聞
375b08‖ 辟支佛地。令無量眾生。住如來地。爾時善財
375b09‖ 童子。見聞如上所現一切諸希有事。念念觀
375b10‖ 察思惟解了。深入安住。承佛威力及解脫力。
375b11‖ 則得菩薩不思議大勢力。普喜[憧>幢]自在力解
375b12‖ 脫。何以故。與喜目夜神。於往昔時。同修行
375b13‖ 故。如來神力所加持故。不思議善根所祐助
375b14‖ 故。得菩薩諸根故。生如來種中故。得善友力
375b15‖ 所攝受故。受諸如來所護念故。毘盧遮那如
375b16‖ 來曾所化故。彼分善根已成熟故。堪修普賢
375b17‖ 菩薩行故。爾時善財童子。得此解脫已。心
375b18‖ 生歡喜。合掌向喜目觀察眾生夜神。以偈讚
375b19‖ 曰
375b20‖ 無量無數劫　學佛甚深法
375b21‖ 隨其所應化　顯現妙色身
375b22‖ 了知諸眾生　沈迷嬰妄想
375b23‖ 種種身皆現　隨應悉調伏
375b24‖ 法身恒寂靜　清淨無二相

简体字

令无量众生安住声闻、辟支佛地，令无量众生住如来地。

尔时，善财童子见闻如上所现一切诸希有事，念念观察，思惟解了，深入安住，承佛威力及解脱力，则得菩萨不思议大势力普喜幢自在力解脱。何以故？与喜目夜神于往昔时同修行故，如来神力所加持故，不思议善根所祐助故，得菩萨诸根故，生如来种中故，得善友力所摄受故，受诸如来所护念故，毗卢遮那如来曾所化故，彼分善根已成熟故，堪修普贤菩萨行故。

尔时，善财童子得此解脱已，心生欢喜，合掌向喜目观察众生夜神，以偈赞曰：

“无量无数劫，学佛甚深法，
随其所应化，显现妙色身。
了知诸众生，沉迷婴妄想，
种种身皆现，随应悉调伏。
法身恒寂静，清净无二相，

enabling countless beings to become securely established on the grounds of *śrāvaka* disciples and *pratyekabuddhas*, and enabling countless beings to become established on the ground of the Tathāgata.

At that time, as Sudhana the Youth saw and heard all these rare phenomena such as were revealed above, in each successive mind-moment, he contemplated them, reflected on them, completely understood them, deeply penetrated them, and came to securely abide in them. Then, aided by the awesome power of the Buddha and the power of the liberations, he acquired the bodhisattva's inconceivable liberation known as "the immensely powerful banner of universal joy" that is possessed of miraculous powers.

And why was this so? It was:

Because, in the past, he had cultivated together with the night spirit, Pramuditanayanajagadvirocanā;

Because he was aided by the Tathāgata's spiritual powers;

Because he was assisted by his inconceivable roots of goodness;

Because he had acquired the bodhisattva's faculties;

Because he had been born into the lineage of the Tathāgatas;

Because he had been able to be attracted and supported by the power of the good spiritual guides;

Because he was the beneficiary of all *tathāgatas'* protective mindfulness;

Because, in the past, he had been taught by Vairocana Tathāgata;

Because his roots of goodness had already become completely ripened; and

Because he was capable of cultivating the practices of Samantabhadra Bodhisattva.

Then, having acquired this liberation, Sudhana the Youth, feeling delighted in mind, pressed his palms together and spoke these verses in praise of the night spirit, Pramuditanayanajagadvirocanā:

For measureless numberless kalpas,
you trained in the Buddha's extremely profound Dharma
and then, adapting to those who should be taught,
you manifested marvelous form bodies.

Fully understanding how all beings
are immersed in confusion and entangled in erroneous thinking,
your many different types of bodies appear to all of them
and then, adapting to what is appropriate, train them all.

The Dharma body is forever quiescent
and characterized by purity and non-duality,

正體字

375b25 | 為化眾生故　示現種種形
375b26 | 於諸蘊界處　未曾有所著
375b27 | 示行及色身　調伏一切眾
375b28 | 不著內外法　已度生死海
375b29 | 而現種種身　住於諸有界
375c01 | 遠離諸分別　戲論所不動
375c02 | 為著妄想者　弘宣十力法
375c03 | 一心住三昧　無量劫不動
375c04 | 毛孔出化雲　供養十方佛
375c05 | 得佛方便力　念念無邊際
375c06 | 示現種種身　普攝諸群生
375c07 | 了知諸有海　種種業莊嚴
375c08 | 為說無礙法　令其悉清淨
375c09 | 色身妙無比　清淨如普賢
375c10 | 隨諸眾生心　示現世間相
375c11 | 爾時善財童子。說此頌已。白言。天神。汝發阿
375c12 | 耨多羅三藐三菩提心。為幾時耶。得此解脫。
375c13 | 身已久如。爾時喜目觀察眾生主夜神。以頌
375c14 | 答曰
375c15 | 我念過去世　過於剎塵劫
375c16 | 剎號摩尼光　劫名寂靜音

简体字

为化众生故，示现种种形。
于诸蕴界处，未曾有所著，
示行及色身，调伏一切众。
不著内外法，已度生死海，
而现种种身，住于诸有界。
远离诸分别，戏论所不动，
为著妄想者，弘宣十力法。
一心住三昧，无量劫不动，
毛孔出化云，供养十方佛。
得佛方便力，念念无边际，
示现种种身，普摄诸群生。
了知诸有海，种种业庄严，
为说无碍法，令其悉清净。
色身妙无比，清净如普贤，
随诸众生心，示现世间相。”

尔时，善财童子说此颂已，白言：“天神，汝发阿耨多罗三藐三菩提心，为几时耶？得此解脱，身已久如？”

尔时，喜目观察众生主夜神以颂答曰：

“我念过去世，过于刹尘劫，
刹号摩尼光，劫名寂静音。

yet, in order to carry on the transformative teaching of beings,
you appear in many different forms.

You have never had any attachment at all
to the aggregates, sense realms, or sense bases,
yet you manifest actions and form bodies
in order to train all beings.

Having no attachment for any inward or outward dharmas,
you have already crossed beyond the ocean of *saṃsāra,*
yet you manifest many different kinds of bodies
that abide within all the realms of existence.

You have left all discriminations far behind
and are one unmoved by any conceptual proliferation,
yet for the sake of those attached to erroneous thinking,
you broadly proclaim the Dharma of the One with Ten Powers.[142]

You abide single-mindedly in samādhi
and remain unmoving for countless kalpas.
Yet your pores emit clouds of transformation bodies
that present offerings to the buddhas of the ten directions.

You have acquired the Buddha's power of skillful means
and, in each successive mind-moment, boundlessly
manifest the many different kinds of bodies
that everywhere gather in the many kinds of beings.

Fully comprehending the ocean of all the stations of existence,
you adorn it with the many different kinds of karmic works.
You teach the unimpeded Dharma for those within it
and enable them all to become purified.

Your form body is incomparably marvelous
and as pure as that of Samantabhadra.
Adapting to the minds of beings,
you manifest as possessed of worldly characteristics.

At that time, having spoken these verses, Sudhana the Youth addressed her, saying, "O Celestial Spirit, how long has it been now since you resolved to attain *anuttara-samyak-saṃbodhi*? And how long has it been since you acquired this liberation?"

Then the night spirit Pramuditanayanajagadvirocanā replied by speaking these verses:

I recall that, in the past,
back beyond kalpas as numerous as the atoms in a *kṣetra,*
there was a *kṣetra* known as "Maṇi Jewel Light"
and a kalpa named "Quiescent Sound."

正體字	375c17 百萬那由他　俱胝四天下 375c18 其王數亦爾　各各自臨馭 375c19 中有一王都　號曰香幢寶 375c20 莊嚴最殊妙　見者皆欣悅 375c21 中有轉輪王　其身甚微妙 375c22 三十二種相　隨好以莊嚴 375c23 蓮華中化生　金色光明身 375c24 騰空照遠近　普及閻浮界 375c25 其王有千子　勇猛身端正 375c26 臣佐滿一億　智慧善方便 375c27 嬪御有十億　顏容狀天女 375c28 利益調柔意　慈心給侍王 375c29 其王以法化　普及四天下 376a01 輪圍大地中　一切皆豐盛 376a02 我時為寶女　具足梵音聲 376a03 身出金色光　照及千由旬 376a04 日光既已沒　音樂咸寂然 376a05 大王及侍御　一切皆安寢 376a06 彼時德海佛　出興於世間 376a07 顯現神通力　充滿十方界
简体字	百万那由他，俱胝四天下， 其王数亦尔，各各自临驭。 中有一王都，号曰香幢宝， 庄严最殊妙，见者皆欣悦。 中有转轮王，其身甚微妙， 三十二种相，随好以庄严； 莲华中化生，金色光明身， 腾空照远近，普及阎浮界。 其王有千子，勇猛身端正； 臣佐满一亿，智慧善方便； 嫔御有十亿，颜容状天女， 利益调柔意，慈心给侍王。 其王以法化，普及四天下， 轮围大地中，一切皆丰盛。 我时为宝女，具足梵音声， 身出金色光，照及千由旬。 日光既已没，音乐咸寂然， 大王及侍御，一切皆安寝。 彼时德海佛，出兴于世间， 显现神通力，充满十方界；

It had a hundred myriads of *nayutas*
of *koṭīs* of four-continent lands.
The kings within them were equally numerous
and every one of them exercised his rule.

Among them, there was a royal capital
named Jewel of Fragrant Banners.
Its adornments were most extraordinarily marvelous,
filling with happiness whoever saw them.

Within it, there was a wheel-turning king
whose body was especially marvelous.
He was adorned with the thirty-two major marks
as well as the secondary signs.

He was transformationally born from within a lotus flower
and had a body that emanated golden light.
It soared up into space and illuminated whatever was far and near
with light that reached throughout the realm of Jambudvīpa.

That king had a thousand sons
who were courageous and handsome.
His ministers and retainers, a full *koṭī* in number,
were wise and skillful in expedient means.

He had a retinue of ten *koṭīs* of consorts and palace ladies
whose appearances resembled those of celestial maidens.
With beneficent and gentle minds,
they served the king with thoughts of kindness.

That king used the Dharma as the basis of his rule
that extended everywhere throughout the four continents
so that the immense lands within the surrounding mountains
all flourished with abundance.

At that time, I was one of the precious maidens.
I had a voice possessed of the brahman sounds
and a body that emanated golden light
with illumination that reached a thousand *yojanas*.

When the light of the sun had already set,
when the sounds of the music had grown silent,
and when the great king as well as his attendants
had all then fallen fast asleep—

At that very time, Ocean of Virtue Buddha
then came forth into the world
and manifested the power of his spiritual superknowledges
that completely filled the realms of the ten directions.

正體字

376a08 | 放大光明海　一切剎塵數
376a09 | 種種自在身　遍滿於十方
376a10 | 地震出妙音　普告佛興世
376a11 | 天人龍神眾　一切皆歡喜
376a12 | 一一毛孔中　出佛化身海
376a13 | 十方皆遍滿　隨應說妙法
376a14 | 我時於夢中　見佛諸神變
376a15 | 亦聞深妙法　心生大歡喜
376a16 | 一萬主夜神　共在空中住
376a17 | 讚歎佛興世　同時覺悟我
376a18 | 賢慧汝應起　佛已現汝國
376a19 | 劫海難值遇　見者得清淨
376a20 | 我時便寤寤　即覩清淨光
376a21 | 觀此從何來　見佛樹王下
376a22 | 諸相莊嚴體　猶如寶山王
376a23 | 一切毛孔中　放大光明海
376a24 | 見已心歡喜　便生此念言
376a25 | 願我得如佛　廣大神通力
376a26 | 我時尋覺[1]寤　大王并眷屬
376a27 | 令見佛光明　一切皆欣慶

简体字

放大光明海，一切刹尘数，
种种自在身，遍满于十方。
地震出妙音，普告佛兴世；
天人龙神众，一切皆欢喜。
一一毛孔中，出佛化身海，
十方皆遍满，随应说妙法。
我时于梦中，见佛诸神变，
亦闻深妙法，心生大欢喜。
一万主夜神，共在空中住，
赞叹佛兴世，同时觉悟我：
贤慧汝应起，佛已现汝国，
劫海难值遇，见者得清净。
我时便寤寤，即睹清净光。
观此从何来？见佛树王下，
诸相庄严体，犹如宝山王；
一切毛孔中，放大光明海。
见已心欢喜，便生此念言：
愿我得如佛，广大神通力。
我时寻觉悟，大王并眷属，
令见佛光明，一切皆欣庆。

He emanated an ocean of great radiance
and many different kinds of supernaturally created bodies
as numerous as the atoms in all *kṣetras*
that completely filled the ten directions.

The earth then quaked and sent forth a wondrous voice
that everywhere told of the Buddha's appearing in the world.
The congregations of devas, humans, dragons, and spirits
all then experienced joyous delight.

From every pore, he sent forth
oceans of Buddha's transformation bodies
that everywhere filled all ten directions,
and taught the sublime Dharma in ways that were fitting.

At that time, in the midst of a dream,
I saw the spiritual transformations of the Buddha
and also heard his profound and marvelous Dharma,
whereupon my mind was filled with great delight.

Then a myriad night spirits
stood together in space,
praising the Buddha's appearing in the world,
all at once awakening me from sleep,

saying, "O Worthy and Wise One, you should arise,
for the Buddha has already appeared here in your land.
He is rarely met with, even in an ocean of kalpas.
Whoever sees him is thereby purified."

I then awakened from sleep,
and at once saw a pure light.
Looking to see from where this was coming,
I saw the Buddha sitting beneath the king of trees.

His body adorned with all of the marks
was then like the king of jeweled mountains.
From within all his pores,
there streamed forth an immense ocean of light.

Having seen this, my mind was filled with delight,
whereupon I had this thought:
"May I be able, like the Buddha,
to gain the power of vast spiritual superknowledges."

I then searched out and awakened
the great king and his retinue.
I directed them to see the Buddha's light,
whereupon they were all elated and rejoiced.

正體字

376a28 | 我時與大王　騎從千萬億
376a29 | 眾生亦無量　俱行詣佛所
376b01 | 我於二萬歲　供養彼如來
376b02 | 七寶四天下　一切皆奉施
376b03 | 時彼如來說　功德普雲經
376b04 | 普應群生心　莊嚴諸願海
376b05 | 夜神覺悟我　令我得利益
376b06 | 我願作是身　覺諸放逸者
376b07 | 我從此初發　最上菩提願
376b08 | 往來諸有中　其心無忘失
376b09 | 從此後供養　十億那由佛
376b10 | 恒受人天樂　饒益諸群生
376b11 | 初佛功德海　第二功德燈
376b12 | 第三妙寶幢　第四虛空智
376b13 | 第五蓮華藏　第六無礙慧
376b14 | 第七法[2]月王　第八智燈輪
376b15 | 第九兩足尊　寶焰山燈王
376b16 | 第十調御師　三世華光音
376b17 | 如是等諸佛　我悉曾供養
376b18 | 然未得慧眼　入於解脫海

简体字

我时与大王，骑从千万亿，
众生亦无量，俱行诣佛所。
我于二万岁，供养彼如来，
七宝四天下，一切皆奉施。
时彼如来说，功德普云经，
普应群生心，庄严诸愿海。
夜神觉悟我，令我得利益，
我愿作是身，觉诸放逸者。
我从此初发，最上菩提愿，
往来诸有中，其心无忘失。
从此后供养，十亿那由佛，
恒受人天乐，饶益诸群生。
初佛功德海；第二功德灯；
第三妙宝幢；第四虚空智；
第五莲华藏；第六无碍慧；
第七法月王；第八智灯轮；
第九两足尊，宝焰山灯王；
第十调御师，三世华光音。
如是等诸佛，我悉曾供养，
然未得慧眼，入于解脱海。

Then I went together with the great king's
retinue of millions of *koṭīs* of followers
and countless other beings,
all of whom went to see the Buddha.

Then, for a period of twenty thousand years,
I made offerings to that *tathāgata*.
During that time I offered up to him as gifts
all of the seven precious things from the four continents.

That *tathāgata* then taught
the Universal Cloud of Meritorious Qualities Sutra.
Everywhere adapting to the minds of the many beings,
it adorned the ocean of all vows.

Just as those night spirits had then awakened me
and enabled me to acquire such benefit,
I then vowed to take on just such a body
so that I too might awaken the heedless.

From the time when I first made the vow
to attain supreme bodhi,
even while going and coming in all the stations of existence,
I have never forgotten that resolve.

From this point onward, I made offerings
to ten *koṭīs* of *nayutas* of buddhas
and constantly enjoyed the bliss of both humans and devas
as I have abundantly benefited the many kinds of beings.

The first of those buddhas was Ocean of Meritorious Qualities.
The Second was Meritorious Qualities Lamp.
The third was Marvelous Bejeweled Banner.
The fourth was Wisdom of Empty Space.

The fifth was Lotus Dais.
The sixth was Unimpeded Wisdom.
The seventh was Dharma Moon King.
The eighth was Wisdom Lamp Wheel.

The ninth of those most revered among two-footed beings
was Jewel Flame Mountain Lamp King
and the tenth of those guiding teachers
was Floral Light Sound of the Three Periods of Time.

To buddhas such as these,
I had already presented offerings,
but still had not yet acquired the wisdom eye
or entered the ocean of liberations.

正體字

376b19 從此次第有　一切寶光剎
376b20 其劫名天勝　五百佛興世
376b21 最初月光輪　第二名日燈
376b22 第三名光幢　第四寶須彌
376b23 第五名華焰　第六號燈海
376b24 第七熾然佛　第八天藏佛
376b25 九光明王幢　十普智光王
376b26 如是等諸佛　我悉曾供養
376b27 尚於諸法中　無而計為有
376b28 從此復有劫　名曰梵光明
376b29 世界蓮華燈　莊嚴極殊妙
376c01 彼有無量佛　一一無量眾
376c02 我悉曾供養　尊重聽聞法
376c03 初寶須彌佛　二功德海佛
376c04 三法界音佛　四法震雷佛
376c05 五名法幢佛　六名地光佛
376c06 七名法力光　八名虛空覺
376c07 第九須彌光　第十功德雲
376c08 如是等如來　我悉曾供養
376c09 未能明了法　而入諸佛海

简体字

从此次第有，一切宝光刹，
其劫名天胜，五百佛兴世。
最初月光轮；第二名日灯；
第三名光幢；第四宝须弥；
第五名华焰；第六号灯海；
第七炽然佛；第八天藏佛；
九光明王幢；十普智光王。
如是等诸佛，我悉曾供养，
尚于诸法中，无而计为有。
从此复有劫，名曰梵光明；
世界莲华灯，庄严极殊妙。
彼有无量佛，一一无量众，
我悉曾供养，尊重听闻法。
初宝须弥佛；二功德海佛；
三法界音佛；四法震雷佛；
五名法幢佛；六名地光佛；
七名法力光；八名虚空觉；
第九须弥光；第十功德云。
如是等如来，我悉曾供养，
未能明了法，而入诸佛海。

After this, the next one was
the *kṣetra* known as "Light of All Jewels" in which,
in a kalpa known as "Celestial Supremacy,"
five hundred buddhas appeared in the world.

The first of them was Moonlight Orb.
The second was named Solar Lamp.
The third was named Radiant Banner.
The fourth was Jeweled Sumeru.

The fifth was named Floral Flaming Light.
The sixth was called Ocean of Lanterns.
The seventh was Blazing Flames Buddha.
The eighth was Celestial Treasury Buddha.

The ninth was Radiant Royal Banner.
The tenth was Universal Wisdom Light King.
To buddhas such as these
I had already presented offerings,

yet still, with regard to all dharmas,
I had not yet acquired anything even though I assumed I had.
After this, there was yet another kalpa
known as Brahman Radiance.

There, in a world known as Lotus Flower Lamp
whose adornments were the most extraordinarily marvelous,
there came forth countless buddhas,
every one of whom had a measureless congregation.

I had already presented offerings to them,
revered them, and listened to their teaching of the Dharma.
The first of them was Jeweled Sumeru Buddha.
The second was Ocean of Meritorious Qualities Buddha.

The third was Dharma Realm Sound Buddha.
The fourth was Dharma's Quaking Thunder Buddha.
The fifth was named Dharma Banner Buddha.
The sixth was named Light of the Grounds Buddha.

The seventh was named Dharma Powers Radiance.
The eighth was named Spacious Awakening.
The ninth was Sumeru Light.
The tenth was Cloud of Meritorious Qualities.

To *tathāgatas* such as these,
I had already presented offerings,
yet I was still unable to completely comprehend the Dharma
or enter the ocean of all buddhas.

正體字

376c10 | 次後復有劫　名為功德月
376c11 | 爾時有世界　其名功德幢
376c12 | 彼中有諸佛　八十那由他
376c13 | 我皆以妙供　深心而敬奉
376c14 | 初乾闥婆王　二名大樹王
376c15 | 三功德須彌　第四寶眼佛
376c16 | 第五盧舍那　第六光莊嚴
376c17 | 第七法海佛　第八光勝佛
376c18 | 九名賢勝佛　第十法王佛
376c19 | 如是等諸佛　我悉曾供養
376c20 | 然未得深智　入於諸法海
376c21 | 此後復有劫　名為寂靜慧
376c22 | 刹號金剛寶　莊嚴悉殊妙
376c23 | 於中有千佛　次第而出興
376c24 | 眾生少煩惱　眾會悉清淨
376c25 | 初金剛臍佛　二無礙力佛
376c26 | 三名法界影　四號十方燈
376c27 | 第五名悲光　第六名戒海
376c28 | 第七忍燈輪　第八法輪光
376c29 | 九名光莊嚴　十名寂靜光

简体字

次后复有劫，名为功德月；
尔时有世界，其名功德幢。
彼中有诸佛，八十那由他，
我皆以妙供，深心而敬奉。
初乾闼婆王；二名大树王；
三功德须弥；第四宝眼佛；
第五卢舍那；第六光庄严；
第七法海佛；第八光胜佛；
九名贤胜佛；第十法王佛。
如是等诸佛，我悉曾供养，
然未得深智，入于诸法海。
此后复有劫，名为寂静慧，
刹号金刚宝，庄严悉殊妙。
于中有千佛，次第而出兴，
众生少烦恼，众会悉清净。
初金刚脐佛；二无碍力佛；
三名法界影；四号十方灯；
第五名悲光；第六名戒海；
第七忍灯轮；第八法轮光；
九名光庄严；十名寂静光。

After that there was a kalpa
named Meritorious Qualities Moon.
There was a world at that time
named Meritorious Qualities Banner.

There were buddhas therein
numbering eighty *nayutas*,
to all of whom I presented marvelous offerings
as, with deep resolve, I revered and served them.

The first among them was Gandharva King.
The second was named Great Tree King.
The third was Meritorious Qualities Sumeru.
The fourth was Jewel Eyes Buddha.

The fifth was Vairocana.
The sixth was Radiance Adornment.
The seventh was Dharma Ocean Buddha.
The eighth was Radiant Supremacy Buddha.

The ninth was named Worthy Supremacy Buddha.
And the tenth was Dharma King Buddha.
To buddhas such as these,
I had already presented offerings,

yet I still had not acquired deep wisdom
or entered into the ocean of the Dharma.
After this, there was yet another kalpa
by the name of Quiescent Wisdom

in which, in a *kṣetra* known as Vajra Jewel,
the adornments of which were all extraordinarily marvelous,
there were a thousand buddhas
who one after another appeared in the world.

The beings there had but few afflictions
and those congregations were all pure.
The first of those was Vajra Navel Buddha.
The second was Unimpeded Powers Buddha.

The third was named Dharma Realm Reflections.
The fourth was called Ten Directions' Lamp.
The fifth was named Light of Compassion.
The sixth was named Ocean of Moral Virtue.

The seventh was Patience Lamp Wheel.
The eighth was Dharma Wheel Radiance.
The ninth was named Light Adornment.
And the tenth was named Quiescent Light.

正體字

377a01 | 如是等諸佛　我悉曾供養
377a02 | 猶未能深悟　如空清淨法
377a03 | 遊行一切剎　於彼修諸行
377a04 | 次第復有劫　名為善出現
377a05 | 剎號香燈雲　淨穢所共成
377a06 | 億佛於中現　莊嚴剎及劫
377a07 | 所說種種法　我皆能憶持
377a08 | 初名廣稱佛　次名法海佛
377a09 | 三名自在王　四名功德雲
377a10 | 第五法勝佛　第六天冠佛
377a11 | 第七智焰佛　第八虛空音
377a12 | 第九兩足尊　名普生殊勝
377a13 | 第十無上士　眉間勝光明
377a14 | 如是一切佛　我悉曾供養
377a15 | 然猶未能淨　離諸障礙道
377a16 | 次第復有劫　名集堅固王
377a17 | 剎號寶幢王　一切善分布
377a18 | 有五百諸佛　於中而出現
377a19 | 我恭敬供養　求無礙解脫
377a20 | 最初功德輪　其次寂靜音

简体字

如是等诸佛，我悉曾供养，
犹未能深悟，如空清净法。
游行一切刹，于彼修诸行。
次第复有劫，名为善出现，
刹号香灯云，净秽所共成。
亿佛于中现，庄严刹及劫，
所说种种法，我皆能忆持。
初名广称佛；次名法海佛；
三名自在王；四名功德云；
第五法胜佛；第六天冠佛；
第七智焰佛；第八虚空音；
第九两足尊，名普生殊胜；
第十无上士，眉间胜光明。
如是一切佛，我悉曾供养，
然犹未能净，离诸障碍道。
次第复有劫，名集坚固王，
刹号宝幢王，一切善分布。
有五百诸佛，于中而出现；
我恭敬供养，求无碍解脱。
最初功德轮；其次寂静音；

To buddhas such as these,
I had already presented offerings,
yet I was still unable to gain a profound awakening
to the Dharma as pure as space.

I roamed to all *kṣetras,*
and cultivated the practices within them.
Next, there was a kalpa
known as Fine Manifestation

and a *kṣetra* named Fragrant Lamp Cloud
that consisted of a combination of purity and defilement.
A *koṭī* of buddhas appeared in it,
adorning that *kṣetra* as well as that kalpa.

I am able to recall and retain in mind
the many different dharmas they taught.
The first of them was named Vast Fame Buddha.
The next was named Dharma Ocean Buddha.

The third was named Sovereign Mastery King.
The fourth was named Cloud of Meritorious Qualities.
The fifth was Dharma Supremacy Buddha.
The sixth was Celestial Crown Buddha.

The seventh was Flaming Light of Wisdom Buddha.
The eighth was Voice of Empty Space.
The ninth was the one most revered of all two-legged beings
named Universally Superior Birth.

The tenth was the unexcelled teacher
known as Supreme Mid-brow Radiance.
To all such buddhas as these,
I had already presented offerings.

Even so, I still could not yet purify
the path to the transcendence of obstacles.
Next, there was yet another kalpa
named Solid Accumulation King

and a *kṣetra* called Jeweled Banner King
in which there were, all well distributed,
five hundred buddhas
who came forth and appeared in the world.

I respectfully made offerings to them
and sought the unimpeded liberations.
The very first of them was Wheel of Meritorious Qualities.
The next was Quiescent Voice.

正體字

377a21 次名功德海　次名日光王
377a22 第五功德王　第六須彌相
377a23 次名法自在　次佛功德王
377a24 第九福須彌　第十光明王
377a25 如是等諸佛　我悉曾供養
377a26 所有清淨道　普入盡無餘
377a27 然於所入門　未能成就忍
377a28 次第復有劫　名為妙勝[1]主
377a29 剎號寂靜音　眾生煩惱薄
377b01 於中有佛現　八十那由他
377b02 我悉曾供養　修行最勝道
377b03 初佛名華聚　次佛名海藏
377b04 次名功德生　次號天王髻
377b05 第五摩尼藏　第六真金山
377b06 第七寶聚尊　第八法幢佛
377b07 第九名勝財　第十名智慧
377b08 此十為上首　供養無不盡
377b09 次第復有劫　名曰千功德
377b10 爾時有世界　號善化幢燈
377b11 六十億那由　諸佛興於世

简体字

次名功德海；次名日光王；
第五功德王；第六须弥相；
次名法自在；次佛功德王；
第九福须弥；第十光明王。
如是等诸佛，我悉曾供养，
所有清净道，普入尽无余，
然于所入门，未能成就忍。
次第复有劫，名为妙胜主，
刹号寂静音，众生烦恼薄。
于中有佛现，八十那由他；
我悉曾供养，修行最胜道。
初佛名华聚；次佛名海藏；
次名功德生；次号天王髻；
第五摩尼藏；第六真金山；
第七宝聚尊；第八法幢佛；
第九名胜财；第十名智慧。
此十为上首，供养无不尽。
次第复有劫，名曰千功德；
尔时有世界，号善化幢灯；
六十亿那由，诸佛兴于世。

The next was named Ocean of Meritorious Qualities.
The next was named Solar Radiance King.
The fifth was named King of Meritorious Qualities.
The sixth was Sumeru Signs.

The next was named Sovereign Mastery of Dharma.
The next was King of a Buddha's Meritorious Qualities.
The ninth was Sumeru of Merit.
The tenth was Radiance King.

To buddhas such as these,
I had already presented offerings
and then everywhere completely entered
all the pure paths without exception.

However, in those gateways I had entered,
I was still unable to perfect patience.
Next, there was yet another kalpa
known as Wondrously Supreme Ruler,

and a *kṣetra* called Quiescent Voice
in which the beings' afflictions were only slight.
The buddhas who appeared within it
were eighty *nayutas* in number.

I had already made offerings to them
and cultivated the most supreme of paths.
The first buddha was named Floral Accumulation.
The next buddha was named Ocean Treasury.

The next was named Born of Meritorious Qualities.
The next was called Celestial King Topknot.
The fifth was Maṇi Jewel Treasury.
The sixth was Real Gold Mountain.

The seventh was Revered Accumulation of Jewels.
The eighth was Dharma Banner Buddha.
The ninth was named Supreme Wealth.
The tenth was named Mind of Wisdom.

These ten were foremost among them.
I exhaustively made offerings to all of them.
Next, there was yet another kalpa
named Thousandfold Meritorious Qualities.

At that time, there was a world
called Lamp of the Banner of Fine Transformations.
There were sixty *koṭīs* of *nayutas*
of buddhas who came forth into that world.

正體字

377b12 最初寂靜幢　其次奢摩他
377b13 第三百燈王　第四寂靜光
377b14 第五雲密陰　第六日大明
377b15 七號法燈光　八名殊勝焰
377b16 九名天勝藏　十名大吼音
377b17 如是等諸佛　我悉常供養
377b18 未得清淨忍　深入諸法海
377b19 次第復有劫　名無著莊嚴
377b20 爾時有世界　名曰無邊光
377b21 中有三十六　那由他佛現
377b22 初功德須彌　第二虛空心
377b23 第三具莊嚴　第四法雷音
377b24 第五法界聲　第六妙音雲
377b25 第七照十方　第八法海音
377b26 第九功德海　第十功德幢
377b27 如是等諸佛　我悉曾供養
377b28 次有佛出現　名為功德幢
377b29 我為月面天　供養人中主
377c01 時佛為我說　無依妙法門
377c02 我聞專念持　出生諸願海

简体字

最初寂静幢；其次奢摩他；
第三百灯王；第四寂静光；
第五云密阴；第六日大明；
七号法灯光；八名殊胜焰；
九名天胜藏；十名大吼音。
如是等诸佛，我悉常供养，
未得清净忍，深入诸法海。
次第复有劫，名无著庄严；
尔时有世界，名曰无边光；
中有三十六，那由他佛现。
初功德须弥；第二虚空心；
第三具庄严；第四法雷音；
第五法界声；第六妙音云；
第七照十方；第八法海音；
第九功德海；第十功德幢。
如是等诸佛，我悉曾供养。
次有佛出现，名为功德幢；
我为月面天，供养人中主。
时佛为我说，无依妙法门；
我闻专念持，出生诸愿海。

The very first among them was Quiescent Banner.
The next was Śamatha.
The third was Hundred Lamps King.
The fourth was Quiescent Light.

The fifth was Dense Shade of Clouds.
The sixth was Great Light of the Sun.
The seventh was Lamp Light of Dharma.
The eighth was named Extraordinarily Supreme Flaming Light.

The ninth was named Celestial Supremacy Treasury.
And the tenth was named Great Roaring Voice.
To all buddhas such as these,
I was always devoted to making offerings.

Still, I had not yet purified patience
or deeply entered the ocean of all dharmas.
Next, there was yet another kalpa
known as Adorned with Nonattachment.

There was a world at that time
known as Boundless Radiance
in which there were thirty-six *nayutas*
of buddhas who appeared there.

The first among them was Sumeru of Meritorious Qualities.
The second was Spacious Mind.
The third was Perfect Adornments.
The fourth was Voice of Dharma Thunder.

The fifth was Sound of the Dharma Realm.
The sixth was Cloud of Sublime Voices.
The seventh was Illuminator of the Ten Directions.
The eighth was Voice of the Ocean of Dharma.

The ninth was Ocean of Meritorious Qualities.
And the tenth was Banner of Meritorious Qualities.
To buddhas such as these,
I had already presented offerings.

When next the buddha appeared
who was named Banner of Meritorious Qualities,
I was a goddess named Lunar Countenance,
one who made offerings to that lord among men.

At that time, the Buddha taught for my sake
the gateway of the non-dependent sublime Dharma.
When I heard this, I single-mindedly retained it
and then made an ocean of vows.

正體字

377c03 我得清淨眼　寂滅定總持
377c04 能於念念中　悉見諸佛海
377c05 我得大悲藏　普明方便眼
377c06 增長菩提心　成就如來力
377c07 見眾生顛倒　執常樂我淨
377c08 愚癡暗所覆　妄想起煩惱
377c09 行止見稠林　往來貪欲海
377c10 集於諸惡趣　無量種種業
377c11 一切諸趣中　隨業而受身
377c12 生老死眾患　無量苦逼迫
377c13 為彼眾生故　我發無上心
377c14 願得如十方　一切十力尊
377c15 緣佛及眾生　起於大願雲
377c16 從是修功德　趣入方便道
377c17 願雲悉彌覆　普入一切道
377c18 具足波羅蜜　充滿於法界
377c19 速入於諸地　三世方便海
377c20 一念修諸佛　一切無礙行
377c21 佛子我爾時　得入普賢道
377c22 了知十法界　一切差別門

简体字

我得清净眼，寂灭定总持，
能于念念中，悉见诸佛海。
我得大悲藏，普明方便眼，
增长菩提心，成就如来力。
见众生颠倒，执常乐我净，
愚痴暗所覆，妄想起烦恼。
行止见稠林，往来贪欲海，
集于诸恶趣，无量种种业。
一切诸趣中，随业而受身，
生老死众患，无量苦逼迫。
为彼众生故，我发无上心，
愿得如十方，一切十力尊。
缘佛及众生，起于大愿云，
从是修功德，趣入方便道。
愿云悉弥覆，普入一切道，
具足波罗蜜，充满于法界。
速入于诸地，三世方便海，
一念修诸佛，一切无碍行。
佛子我尔时，得入普贤道，
了知十法界，一切差别门。

I then acquired the purified eye,
quiescent absorption, and complete-retention *dhāraṇīs*
with which I was able in each successive mind-moment
to see the entire ocean of all buddhas.

I acquired the treasury of great compassion,
obtained the universally bright eye of skillful means,
strengthened my bodhi resolve,
and developed the Tathāgata's powers.

I then perceived beings' inverted views
by which they cling to permanence, bliss, self, and purity,
remain covered by the darkness of delusion,
and, through erroneous perceptions, produce afflictions.

Whether moving or stopping, it is in a dense forest of views.
Whether going or coming, it is in an ocean of desires.
So it is that they accumulate countless different karmic deeds
leading to rebirth in all the wretched destinies.

In all of the destinies of rebirth,
they take on bodies in accordance with their karmic deeds
and are driven along and tormented by the countless sufferings
arising from the many misfortunes of birth, aging, and death.

For the sake of all those beings,
I then aroused the unexcelled resolve,
vowing to be like all the Honored Ones possessed of ten powers
who reside throughout the ten directions.

Because of the Buddha and beings,
I made a cloud of great vows.
Due to the meritorious qualities of this cultivation,
I then progressed into the path of skillful means.

Due to this cloud of vows that covers all,
I everywhere entered all the paths,
fulfilled the practice of the *pāramitās*,
and completely filled the Dharma realm.

I swiftly entered all the grounds
and the ocean of skillful means in all three periods of time.
In but a single mind-moment,
I cultivated all the unimpeded practices of all buddhas.

Son of the Buddha, it was at that very time
that I was able to enter the path of Samantabhadra.
I then came to completely know all the different gateways
throughout the realms of the ten directions.

正體字

377c23 善男子。於汝意云何。彼時轉輪聖王。名十方
377c24 主。能紹隆佛種者。豈異人乎。文殊師利童子
377c25 是也。爾時夜神。覺悟我者。普賢菩薩之所化
377c26 耳。我於爾時。為王寶女。蒙彼夜神覺悟於我。
377c27 令我見佛。發阿耨多羅三藐三菩提心。自從
377c28 是來。經佛刹微塵數劫。不墮惡趣。常生人天。
377c29 於一切處。常見諸佛。乃至於妙燈功德幢佛
378a01 所。得此大勢力普喜幢菩薩解脫。以此解脫。
378a02 如是利益一切眾生。善男子。我唯得此大勢
378a03 力普喜幢解脫門。如諸菩薩摩訶薩。於念念
378a04 中。普詣一切諸如來所。疾能趣入一切智海。
378a05 於念念中。以發趣門。入於一切諸大願海。於
378a06 念念中。以願海門。盡未來劫。念念出生一
378a07 切諸行。一一行中。出生一切刹微塵數身。一
378a08 一身。普入一切法界門。一一法界門。一切
378a09 佛刹中。隨眾生心說諸妙行。一切刹一一塵
378a10 中。悉見無邊諸如來海。一一如來所。悉見
378a11 遍法界諸佛神通。

简体字

“善男子，于汝意云何？彼时转轮圣王，名十方主，能绍隆佛种者，岂异人乎？文殊师利童子是也！尔时夜神觉悟我者，普贤菩萨之所化耳！我于尔时为王宝女，蒙彼夜神觉悟于我，令我见佛，发阿耨多罗三藐三菩提心。自从是来，经佛刹微尘数劫，不堕恶趣，常生人、天，于一切处常见诸佛，乃至于妙灯功德幢佛所，得此大势力普喜幢菩萨解脱，以此解脱如是利益一切众生。

“善男子，我唯得此大势力普喜幢解脱门。如诸菩萨摩诃萨，于念念中，普诣一切诸如来所，疾能趣入一切智海；于念念中，以发趣门，入于一切诸大愿海；于念念中，以愿海门，尽未来劫，念念出生一切诸行。一一行中出生一切刹微尘数身，一一身普入一切法界门；一一法界门，一切佛刹中，随众生心说诸妙行。一切刹一一尘中，悉见无边诸如来海；一一如来所，悉见遍法界诸佛神通；

Son of Good Family, what do you think? As for that wheel-turning sage king known as Lord of the Ten Directions who was able then to receive and carry on the lineage of the Buddha—could it have been anyone else? It was none other than Mañjuśrī the Youth. The night spirit who awakened me at that time was an emanation created by Samantabhadra Bodhisattva.

At that time, I was a precious maiden in the retinue of that king who was awakened by that night spirit and enabled to see the Buddha and resolve to attain *anuttara-samyak-saṃbodhi*. From that time on forward to the present, I have passed through kalpas equal in number to the atoms in a buddha *kṣetra* during which I never fell into the wretched destinies, always achieved rebirth among humans and devas, and, in all of those places, always saw the buddhas.

This continued on all the way along until the time when, under the Buddha known as Banner of the Marvelous Lamp of Meritorious Qualities, I acquired this bodhisattva liberation known as "the immensely powerful banner of universal joy." It was because of this liberation that I have been able to benefit all beings in these ways.

Son of Good Family, I have acquired only this liberation gateway known as "the immensely powerful banner of universal joy." As for the bodhisattva-mahāsattvas:

Who, in every mind-moment travel everywhere to pay their respects to all *tathāgatas* and are then quickly able to enter the ocean of all-knowledge;

Who, in every mind-moment, relying on the initial commencement gateways, enter the ocean of all great vows;

Who, in every mind-moment, rely on the gateways of the ocean of vows until the end of all future kalpas;

Who, in every mind-moment, bring forth all of the practices;

Who, in every one of the practices, bring forth bodies as numerous as the atoms in all *kṣetras*;

Who, in every one of those bodies, everywhere enter all the gateways into the Dharma realm;

Who, in every one of those Dharma realm gateways and in all *kṣetras*, adapt to beings' minds as they teach them the marvelous practices;

Who, in every dust mote in all *kṣetras*, see the entire boundless ocean of all *tathāgatas*;

Who, in the presence of every one of those *tathāgatas*, see all the spiritual superknowledges of all buddhas throughout the Dharma realm;

正體字

一一如來所。悉見往劫修
378a12║ 菩薩行。一一如來所。受持守護所有法輪。一
378a13║ 一如來所。悉見三世一切如來諸神變海。而
378a14║ 我云何能知能說彼功德行。善男子。此眾會
378a15║ 中。有一夜神。名普救眾生妙德。汝詣彼問。菩
378a16║ 薩云何入菩薩行。淨菩薩道。時善財童子。頂
378a17║ 禮其足。遶無數匝。慇懃瞻仰。辭退而去
378a21║ 大方廣佛華嚴經卷第七十
378a24║ 入法界品第三十九之十一
378a25║ 爾時善財童子。於喜目觀察眾生夜神所。聞
378a26║ 普喜幢解脫門。信解趣入。了知隨順。思惟修
378a27║ 習。念善知識所有教誨。心無暫捨。諸根不散。
378a28║ 一心願得見善知識。普於十方。勤求匪懈。願
378a29║ 常親近。生諸功德。與善知識同一善根。得善
378b01║ 知識巧方便行。依善知識。入精進海。

简体字

一一如来所，悉见往劫修菩萨行；一一如来所，受持守护所有法轮；一一如来所，悉见三世一切如来诸神变海。而我云何能知能说彼功德行？

“善男子，此众会中，有一夜神，名普救众生妙德。汝诣彼问：菩萨云何入菩萨行、净菩萨道？”

时，善财童子顶礼其足，绕无数匝，殷勤瞻仰，辞退而去。

大方广佛华严经卷第七十

入法界品第三十九之十一

尔时，善财童子于喜目观察众生夜神所，闻普喜幢解脱门，信解趣入，了知随顺，思惟修习，念善知识所有教诲，心无暂舍，诸根不散，一心愿得见善知识，普于十方勤求匪懈，愿常亲近，生诸功德，与善知识同一善根，得善知识巧方便行，依善知识入精进海，

Who, in the presence of every one of those *tathāgatas*, see all of their cultivation of the bodhisattva practices in past kalpas;
Who, in the presence of every one of those *tathāgatas*, receive, uphold, and preserve all the teachings arising from their turning of the Dharma wheel; and
Who, in the presence of every one of those *tathāgatas*, see the entire ocean of spiritual transformations created by all *tathāgatas* throughout all three periods of time—

How could I know of and be able to speak about their meritorious qualities and practices?

Son of Good Family, in this very congregation, there is a night spirit by the name of Samantasattvatrāṇojaḥśrī or "Sublime Virtue Universally Rescuing Beings." You should go to her, pay your respects, and ask, "How should the bodhisattva enter the bodhisattva practices and how should he purify the bodhisattva path?"

Sudhana the Youth then bowed down in reverence at her feet and circumambulated her countless times as he gazed up at her in attentive admiration. He then respectfully withdrew, and departed.

34 – Samantasattvatrāṇojaḥśrī

At that time, having learned of the liberation known as "the banner of universal joy" from the night spirit, Pramuditanayanajagadvirocanā, Sudhana the Youth then:

Progressed into it with resolute faith;
Completely understood and complied with it;
Reflected upon it and cultivated it;
Recalled the teachings provided by the good spiritual guides;
Never allowed his mind to relinquish them even briefly;
Ensured that his faculties were not allowed to become scattered;
Single-mindedly vowed to be able to see the good spiritual guides;
Diligently sought for them everywhere in the ten directions, never allowing himself to desist from this;
Vowed to always draw near to them and develop all the meritorious qualities;
Vowed to develop the same roots of goodness as the good spiritual guides;
Vowed to acquire the good spiritual guides' practices of skillful expedient means;
Vowed to rely upon the good spiritual guides in entering the ocean of vigor; and

正體字

於無量
378b02 劫。常不遠離。作是願已。往詣普救眾生妙德
378b03 夜神所。時彼夜神。為善財童子。示現菩薩。
378b04 調伏眾生解脫神力。以諸相好。莊嚴其身。於
378b05 兩眉間放大光明。名智燈普照清淨幢。無量
378b06 光明以為眷屬。其光普照一切世間。照世間
378b07 已。入善財頂。充滿其身。善財爾時。即得究竟
378b08 清淨輪三昧。得此三昧已。悉見二神兩處中
378b09 間。所有一切地塵水塵。及以火塵。金剛摩尼。
378b10 眾寶微塵。華香瓔珞。諸莊嚴具。如是一切所
378b11 有微塵。一一塵中。各見佛剎微塵數世界成
378b12 壞。及見一切地水火風諸大積聚。亦見一切
378b13 世界接連。皆以地輪。任持而住。種種山海。種
378b14 種河池。種種樹林。種種宮殿。所謂天宮殿。龍
378b15 宮殿。夜叉宮殿。乃至摩睺羅伽。人非人等。宮
378b16 殿屋宅。地獄畜生。閻羅王界。一切住處。諸趣
378b17 輪轉。生死往來。隨業受報。各各差別。靡不悉
378b18 見。又見一切世界差別。所謂或有世界雜穢。
378b19 或有世界清淨。

简体字

于无量劫常不远离。作是愿已，往诣普救众生妙德夜神所。

时，彼夜神为善财童子示现菩萨调伏众生解脱神力，以诸相好庄严其身，于两眉间放大光明，名智灯普照清净幢，无量光明以为眷属，其光普照一切世间。照世间已，入善财顶，充满其身。善财尔时即得究竟清净轮三昧。

得此三昧已，悉见二神两处中间，所有一切地尘、水尘及以火尘，金刚摩尼众宝微尘，华香、璎珞、诸庄严具，如是一切所有微尘，一一尘中各见佛刹微尘数世界成坏。及见一切地、水、火、风诸大积聚。亦见一切世界接连，皆以地轮任持而住。种种山海、种种河池、种种树林、种种宫殿，所谓：天宫殿、龙宫殿、夜叉宫殿，乃至摩睺罗伽、人非人等宫殿屋宅，地狱、畜生、阎罗王界一切住处，诸趣轮转，生死往来，随业受报，各各差别，靡不悉见。

又见一切世界差别，所谓：或有世界杂秽，或有世界清净，

Vowed to never part from them even throughout the course of countless kalpas.

Having made these vows, he then went to pay his respects to the night spirit known as Samantasattvatrāṇojaḥśrī, or "Sublime Virtue Universally Rescuing Beings."

Then, in order to show Sudhana the Youth the spiritual powers of "the bodhisattva's liberation for the training of beings," she adorned her body with the major marks and secondary signs. Then, from between her eyebrows, she emitted an immense beam of light with a retinue of countless light rays that was known as "banner of the wisdom lamp that everywhere illuminates purity." Its light everywhere illuminated the entire world and then, having illuminated the world, that light entered the crown of Sudhana's head and then filled his body.

Sudhana then immediately acquired "the sphere of ultimate purity" samādhi. Having acquired this samādhi, he then saw in the area between those two night spirits all the atoms of earth, water, and fire as well as the atoms of the vajra jewels, *maṇi* jewels, and many other kinds of jewels, including also all the atoms of the flowers' scents, the necklaces, the other adornments, and all the other phenomena such as these.

In every one of those atoms, he saw the creation and destruction of worlds as numerous as the atoms in a buddha *kṣetra* and also saw all their accumulations of earth, water, fire, and wind. He also saw the connections between all those worlds as well as the spheres of earth that supported their existence. He also saw their many different mountains and oceans, their many different rivers and lakes, their many different trees and groves, and their many different palaces, including the deva palaces, the dragon palaces, the *yakṣa* palaces, and so forth up to and including the palaces of the *mahoragas*, the humans, the nonhumans, and others, including as well all the buildings and houses associated with those palaces.

He saw all the dwelling places of the hell-dwellers, animals, and denizens of King Yama's realm and saw all the rebirth destinies in the wheel of cyclic existence in which these beings go and come in *saṃsāra*, undergoing retributions in accordance with their karmic deeds, each of which are different. There were none of these things that he did not see in their entirety. He also saw the differences in all worlds, namely:

Some worlds were defiled;
Some worlds were pure;

正體字

或有世界趣雜穢。或有世界
378b20║ 趣清淨。或有世界雜穢清淨。或有世界清淨
378b21║ 雜穢。或有世界一向清淨。或有世界其形平
378b22║ 正。或有覆住。或有側住。如是等一切世界。一
378b23║ 切趣中。悉見此普救眾生夜神。於一切時一
378b24║ 切處。隨諸眾生形貌[1]言辭行解差別。以方
378b25║ 便力。普現其前。隨宜化度。令地獄眾生免諸
378b26║ 苦毒。令畜生眾生不相食噉。令餓鬼眾生無
378b27║ 有飢渴。令諸龍等離一切怖。令欲界眾生離
378b28║ 欲界苦。令人趣眾生離暗夜怖。毀呰怖。惡
378b29║ 名怖。大眾怖。不活怖。死怖。惡道怖。斷善根
378c01║ 怖。退菩提心怖。遇惡知識怖。離善知識怖。墮
378c02║ 二乘地怖。種種生死怖。異類眾生同住怖。惡
378c03║ 時受生怖。惡種族中受生怖。

简体字

或有世界趣杂秽，或有世界趣清净，或有世界杂秽清净，或有世界清净杂秽，或有世界一向清净，或有世界其形平正，或有覆住，或有侧住。如是等一切世界一切趣中，悉见此普救众生夜神，于一切时一切处，随诸众生形貌、言辞、行解差别，以方便力普现其前，随宜化度，令地狱众生免诸苦毒，令畜生众生不相食啖，令饿鬼众生无有饥渴，令诸龙等离一切怖，令欲界众生离欲界苦，令人趣众生离暗夜怖、毁呰怖、恶名怖、大众怖、不活怖、死怖、恶道怖、断善根怖、退菩提心怖、遇恶知识怖、离善知识怖、堕二乘地怖、种种生死怖、异类众生同住怖、恶时受生怖、恶种族中受生怖、

Some worlds were becoming increasingly defiled;
Some worlds were becoming increasingly pure;
Some worlds were changing from defiled to pure;
Some worlds were changing from pure to defiled;
Some worlds retained their purity all along;
Some worlds were level and upward facing;
Some worlds were inverted; and
Some worlds were tipped sideways.

In all such worlds as these and in all their rebirth destinies, he saw this night spirit, Samantasattvatrāṇojaḥśrī, in all times and in all places, adapting to the differences in beings' forms, appearances, languages, actions, and understandings. Using the power of skillful means, she everywhere appeared before them and adapted to whatever was most fitting for them in order to teach and liberate them:

She enabled beings in the hell realms to avoid all their intensely painful sufferings;
She enabled beings in the animal realms to no longer eat each other;
She enabled beings in the hungry ghost realms to become free of hunger and thirst;
She enabled the dragons and other such beings to leave behind all their fears;
She enabled beings in the desire realm to leave behind the sufferings of the desire realm; and
She enabled human beings to leave behind:
The fear of darkness;
The fear of being disparaged;
The fear of having a bad reputation;
The fear of great assemblies;
The fear of being unable to survive;
The fear of death;
The fear of the wretched destinies;
The fear of severing their roots of goodness;
The fear of retreating from the resolve to attain bodhi;
The fear of falling under the influence of bad spiritual guides;
The fear of becoming separated from good spiritual guides;
The fear of falling down onto the grounds of the two vehicles;
The fear of the many different kinds of birth and death;
The fear of living together with other types of beings;[143]
The fear of being reborn in an evil age;
The fear of being reborn among bad people;

正體字

造惡業怖。業
378c04‖ 煩惱障怖。執著諸想繫縛怖。如是等怖。悉
378c05‖ 令捨離。又見一切眾生。卵生胎生。濕生化
378c06‖ 生。有色無色。有想無想。非有想非無想。普現
378c07‖ 其前。常勤救護。為成就菩薩大願力故。深入
378c08‖ 菩薩三昧力故。堅固菩薩神通力故。出生普
378c09‖ 賢行願力故。增廣菩薩大悲海故。得普覆眾
378c10‖ 生無礙大慈故。得普與眾生無量喜樂故。得
378c11‖ 普攝一切眾生智慧方便故。得菩薩廣大解
378c12‖ 脫自在神通故。嚴淨一切佛剎故。覺了一切
378c13‖ 諸法故。供養一切諸佛故。受持一切佛教故。
378c14‖ 積集一切善根修一切妙行故。入一切眾生
378c15‖ 心海而無障礙故。知一切眾生諸根教化成
378c16‖ 熟故。淨一切眾生信解除其惡障故。破一切
378c17‖ 眾生無知黑闇故。令得一切智清淨光明故。

简体字

造恶业怖、业烦恼障怖、执著诸想系缚怖，如是等怖悉令舍离。

又见一切众生，卵生、胎生、湿生、化生，有色、无色，有想、无想，非有想、非无想，普现其前，常勤救护，为成就菩萨大愿力故，深入菩萨三昧力故，坚固菩萨神通力故，出生普贤行愿力故，增广菩萨大悲海故，得普覆众生无碍大慈故，得普与众生无量喜乐故，得普摄一切众生智慧方便故，得菩萨广大解脱自在神通故，严净一切佛刹故，觉了一切诸法故，供养一切诸佛故，受持一切佛教故，积集一切善根修一切妙行故，入一切众生心海而无障碍故，知一切众生诸根教化成熟故，净一切众生信解除其恶障故，破一切众生无知黑暗故，令得一切智清净光明故。

The fear of engaging in evil karmic deeds;
The fear of karmic obstacles and affliction obstacles; and
The fear of the bondage resulting from attachment to various kinds of conceptual thought.

She enabled them all to abandon all kinds of fear such as these.

He also saw her appearing everywhere before all types of beings, whether they were egg-born, womb-born, moisture-born, or transformationally born, whether they were possessed of physical form or formless, and whether they were characterized by perception, by non-perception, or by neither perception nor non-perception. She was always diligent in rescuing and protecting all of these types of beings, doing so:

By perfecting the power of the bodhisattva's great vows;
By deeply entering the bodhisattva's power of samādhi;
By strengthening the bodhisattva's power in the spiritual superknowledges;
By manifesting the power of Samantabhadra's practices and vows;
By widening the bodhisattva's ocean of great compassion;
By acquiring the unimpeded great kindness that extends everywhere to cover all beings;
By everywhere bestowing measureless joy on all beings;
By acquiring the wisdom and skillful means that everywhere gather in all beings;
By acquiring the bodhisattva's vast liberations, sovereign masteries, and spiritual superknowledges;
By purifying all buddha *kṣetras;*
By awakening to and completely understanding all dharmas;
By making offerings to all buddhas;
By receiving and preserving the teachings of all buddhas;
By accumulating all roots of goodness and cultivating all marvelous practices;
By unimpededly fathoming the ocean of all beings' minds;
By knowing the faculties of all beings and providing them instruction in order to ripen them;
By purifying all beings' resolute convictions and ridding them of all their obstacles rooted in evil;
By dispelling all beings' darkness of ignorance; and
By enabling them to acquire the pure light of all-knowledge.

At that time, after Sudhana the Youth had observed the inconceivable and extremely profound spheres of cognition produced by spiritual

正體字

378c18 時善財童子。見此夜神如是神力不可思議
378c19 甚深境界。普現調伏一切眾生菩薩解脫已。
378c20 歡喜無量。頭面作禮。一心瞻仰。時彼夜神即
378c21 捨菩薩莊嚴之相。還復本形。而不捨其自在
378c22 神力。爾時善財童子。恭敬合掌。却住一面
378c23 以偈讚曰
378c24 我善財得見　如是大神力
378c25 其心生歡喜　說偈而讚歎
378c26 我見尊妙身　眾相以莊嚴
378c27 譬如空中星　一切悉嚴淨
378c28 所放殊勝光　無量剎塵數
378c29 種種微妙色　普照於十方
379a01 一一毛孔放　眾生心數光
379a02 一一光明端　皆出寶蓮華
379a03 華中出化身　能滅眾生苦
379a04 光中出妙香　普熏於眾生
379a05 復雨種種華　供養一切佛
379a06 兩眉放妙光　量與須彌等
379a07 普觸諸含識　令滅愚癡闇
379a08 口放清淨光　譬如無量日
379a09 普照於廣大　毘盧舍那境
379a10 眼放清淨光　譬如無量月

简体字

时，善财童子见此夜神如是神力不可思议甚深境界，普现调伏一切众生菩萨解脱已，欢喜无量，头面作礼，一心瞻仰。时，彼夜神即舍菩萨庄严之相，还复本形，而不舍其自在神力。

尔时，善财童子恭敬合掌，却住一面，以偈赞曰：

“我善财得见，如是大神力，
其心生欢喜，说偈而赞叹。
我见尊妙身，众相以庄严；
譬如空中星，一切悉严净。
所放殊胜光，无量刹尘数；
种种微妙色，普照于十方。
一一毛孔放，众生心数光；
一一光明端，皆出宝莲华；
华中出化身，能灭众生苦；
光中出妙香，普熏于众生；
复雨种种华，供养一切佛。
两眉放妙光，量与须弥等，
普触诸含识，令灭愚痴暗。
口放清净光，譬如无量日，
普照于广大，毗卢舍那境。
眼放清净光，譬如无量月，

powers such as these invoked by this night spirit as she everywhere manifested "the bodhisattva's liberation for the training of all beings," he became filled with measureless joy, whereupon he bowed down in reverence before her and gazed up at her with single-minded admiration. That night spirit then shed these adorned appearances of the bodhisattva and returned to her original form, but she did not relinquish her sovereign mastery of the spiritual powers.

Sudhana the Youth then pressed his palms together in reverential respect, stood off to the side, and then spoke these verses of praise:

I, Sudhana, having been enabled to see
such great spiritual powers as these
and have had my mind filled with joyous delight
by which I am inspired to speak these verses of praise:

I have seen the Venerable one's marvelous body
adorned with the many signs
as if by stars in the midst of space
so that everything became completely purified.

The especially excellent light rays you emanate
are as numerous as the atoms in countless *kṣetras*.
Their many different sublime colors
everywhere illuminate the ten directions.

Every one of your pores emanates
rays as numerous as the thoughts of all beings
and the tip of every ray of light
sends forth a jeweled lotus flower.
From within each flower comes forth a transformation body
able to extinguish the sufferings of beings.

From within the light rays comes a sublime perfume
that everywhere imbues those beings with its fragrance.
You also rain down all kinds of different flowers
and present them as offerings to all buddhas.

From between your brows is released a marvelous radiance
that is equal in size to Sumeru Mountain.
It everywhere touches all conscious beings
and extinguishes their darkness of delusion.

From your mouth is released a pure light
as bright as the light of countless suns.
It everywhere illuminates
the vast realm of Vairocana.

From your eyes is released a pure light
as bright as the light of countless moons.

正體字

379a11 | 普照十方剎　悉滅世癡翳
379a12 | 現化種種身　相狀等眾生
379a13 | 充滿十方界　度脫三有海
379a14 | 妙身遍十方　普現眾生前
379a15 | 滅除水火賊　王等一切怖
379a16 | 我承喜目教　今得詣尊所
379a17 | 見尊眉間相　放大清淨光
379a18 | 普照十方海　悉滅一切闇
379a19 | 顯現神通力　而來入我身
379a20 | 我遇圓滿光　心生大歡喜
379a21 | 得總持三昧　普見十方佛
379a22 | 我於所經處　悉見諸微塵
379a23 | 一一微塵中　各見塵數剎
379a24 | 或有無量剎　一切咸濁穢
379a25 | 眾生受諸苦　常悲歎號泣
379a26 | 或有染淨剎　少樂多憂苦
379a27 | 示現三乘像　往彼而救度
379a28 | 或有淨染剎　眾生所樂見
379a29 | 菩薩常充滿　住持諸佛法
379b01 | 一一微塵中　無量淨剎海

简体字

普照十方刹，悉灭世痴翳。
现化种种身，相状等众生，
充满十方界，度脱三有海。
妙身遍十方，普现众生前，
灭除水火贼，王等一切怖。
我承喜目教，今得诣尊所，
见尊眉间相，放大清净光，
普照十方海，悉灭一切暗，
显现神通力，而来入我身。
我遇圆满光，心生大欢喜，
得总持三昧，普见十方佛。
我于所经处，悉见诸微尘，
一一微尘中，各见尘数刹。
或有无量刹，一切咸浊秽，
众生受诸苦，常悲叹号泣。
或有染净刹，少乐多忧苦；
示现三乘像，往彼而救度。
或有净染刹，众生所乐见，
菩萨常充满，住持诸佛法。
一一微尘中，无量净刹海；

It everywhere illuminates the *kṣetras* of the ten directions
and removes all of the world's cataracts of delusion.

The many different kinds of bodies you manifest
possess appearances identical to that of the beings there.
They fill the realms throughout the ten directions
and liberate those in the ocean of the three realms of existence.

Your marvelous bodies pervade the ten directions
and everywhere appear in the presence of beings,
extinguishing their fears of floods, conflagrations, thieves,
kings, and other such types of misfortune.

I have received the teachings of the spirit, "Delighted Eyes,"
and thus am able now to pay my respects to you, Venerable One.
I have seen that sign between the Venerable One's brows
as it emanates an immense stream of pure light.

Having everywhere illuminated the ocean of the ten directions,
having entirely extinguished all the darkness,
and having revealed the powers of the spiritual superknowledges,
it then came and entered my very own body.

When I encountered your perfectly full radiance,
my mind was filled with immense happiness,
I acquired complete-retention *dhāraṇīs* and samādhis,
and then I everywhere saw the buddhas of the ten directions.

In those places through which I passed,
I saw all the atoms
and, in every one of those atoms,
I also saw *kṣetras* as numerous as motes of dust.

In some cases, there were countless *kṣetras*,
all of which were entirely turbid and defiled.
The beings within them were enduring many kinds of sufferings
as they constantly wailed grievously, screamed, and wept.

In some cases, there were pure *kṣetras* that had become defiled
in which there was but little bliss and much sorrow and suffering.
There you manifested the appearance of the Three Vehicles
and went there to rescue and liberate those beings.

In some cases, there were defiled *kṣetras* that had become purified
which beings delighted in seeing.
These were always filled with bodhisattvas
who sustained the Dharma of all buddhas.

In every one of those atoms,
there were oceans of countless pure *kṣetras*

正體字

379b02 | 毘盧遮那佛　往劫所嚴淨
379b03 | 佛於一切剎　悉坐菩提樹
379b04 | 成道轉法輪　度脫諸群生
379b05 | 我見普救天　於彼無量剎
379b06 | 一切諸佛所　普皆往供養
379b07 | 爾時善財童子。說此頌已。白普救眾生妙德
379b08 | 夜神言。天神。今此解脫甚深希有。其名何等。
379b09 | 得此解脫。其已久如。修何等行而得清淨。夜
379b10 | 神言。善男子。是處難知。諸天及人一切二乘。
379b11 | 所不能測。何以故。此是住普賢菩薩行者境
379b12 | 界故。住大悲藏者境界故。救護一切眾生
379b13 | 者境界故。能淨一切三惡八難者境界故。能
379b14 | 於一切佛剎中紹隆佛種不斷者境界故。能
379b15 | 住持一切佛法者境界故。能於一切劫修菩
379b16 | 薩行成滿大願海者境界故。能於一切法界
379b17 | 海以清淨智光滅無明闇障者境界故。能以
379b18 | 一念智慧光明普照一切三世方便海者境界
379b19 | 故。我承佛力。今為汝說。

简体字

毗卢遮那佛，往劫所严净。
佛于一切刹，悉坐菩提树，
成道转法轮，度脱诸群生。
我见普救天，于彼无量刹，
一切诸佛所，普皆往供养。”

尔时，善财童子说此颂已，白普救众生妙德夜神言：“天神！今此解脱甚深希有！其名何等？得此解脱其已久如？修何等行而得清净？”

夜神言：“善男子，是处难知，诸天及人、一切二乘所不能测。何以故？此是住普贤菩萨行者境界故，住大悲藏者境界故，救护一切众生者境界故，能净一切三恶八难者境界故，能于一切佛刹中绍隆佛种不断者境界故，能住持一切佛法者境界故，能于一切劫修菩萨行成满大愿海者境界故，能于一切法界海以清净智光灭无明暗障者境界故，能以一念智慧光明普照一切三世方便海者境界故。我承佛力，今为汝说。

that had been purified by Vairocana Buddha
during the kalpas of the distant past.

In all those *kṣetras*, the buddhas
sat beneath their bodhi trees,
gained enlightenment, turned the wheel of the Dharma,
and liberated the many kinds of beings.

I saw you, the universally rescuing goddess,
in all those countless *kṣetras*,
where, under all those buddhas,
you everywhere went and made offerings to them.

Having spoken these verses, Sudhana the Youth then addressed that night spirit, Samantasattvatrānojahśrī, saying, "O Celestial Spirit, this liberation that you have now revealed is so very profound and rare. By what name is it known? How long has it been now since you first acquired this liberation? And, through which practices might one be able to purify it?"

The Night Spirit then replied, saying:

Son of Good Family, this matter would be difficult to comprehend, for no deva, human, or practitioner of the two vehicles would ever be able to fathom it. Why is this so? It is:

Because it is the sphere of those who abide in the practices of Samantabhadra Bodhisattva;

Because it is the sphere of those who abide in the matrix of the great compassion;

Because it is the sphere of those who rescue all beings;

Because it is the sphere of those who are able to purify the three wretched destinies and the eight difficulties;

Because it is the sphere of those who are able to incessantly sustain the lineage of the buddhas in all buddha *kṣetras*;

Because it is the sphere of those who are able to maintain the Dharma of all buddhas;

Because it is the sphere of those who are able in all kalpas to cultivate the bodhisattva practices and fulfill the ocean of great vows;

Because it is the sphere of those who are able to use the light of pure wisdom to extinguish the obstacles of the darkness of delusion throughout the ocean of the Dharma realm; and

Because it is the sphere of those who are able to use the light of a single mind-moment of wisdom to everywhere illuminate the ocean of all skillful means throughout all three periods of time.

It is with the aid of the Buddha's powers that I shall now describe this for you:

正體字

善男子。乃往古世。
379b20║ 過佛剎微塵數劫。爾時有劫。名圓滿清淨。世
379b21║ 界名毘盧遮那大威德。有須彌山微塵數如
379b22║ 來。於中出現。其佛世界。以一切香王摩尼
379b23║ 寶為體。眾寶莊嚴。住無垢光明摩尼王海上。
379b24║ 其形正圓。淨穢合成。一切嚴具帳雲。而覆
379b25║ 其上。一切莊嚴摩尼輪山。千匝圍遶。有十
379b26║ 萬億那由他四天下。皆妙莊嚴。或有四天下
379b27║ 惡業眾生。於中止住。或有四天下雜業眾生。
379b28║ 於中止住。或有四天下善根眾生。於中止住。
379b29║ 或有四天下一向清淨諸大菩薩之所止住。
379c01║ 此界東際輪圍山側。有四天下。名寶燈華幢。
379c02║ 國界清淨。飲食豐足。不藉耕耘而生稻粱。宮
379c03║ 殿樓閣。悉皆奇妙。諸如意樹。處處行列。種種
379c04║ 香樹恒出香雲。種種鬘樹恒出鬘雲。種種華
379c05║ 樹常雨妙華。種種寶樹出諸奇寶。無量色光
379c06║ 周匝照耀。諸音樂樹出諸音樂。隨風吹動演
379c07║ 妙音聲。

简体字

"善男子，乃往古世，过佛刹微尘数劫，尔时有劫，名圆满清净，世界名毗卢遮那大威德，有须弥山微尘数如来于中出现。其佛世界，以一切香王摩尼宝为体，众宝庄严，住无垢光明摩尼王海上。其形正圆，净秽合成，一切严具帐云而覆其上，一切庄严摩尼轮山千匝围绕。有十万亿那由他四天下皆妙庄严，或有四天下恶业众生于中止住，或有四天下杂业众生于中止住，或有四天下善根众生于中止住，或有四天下一向清净诸大菩萨之所止住。

"此界东际轮围山侧，有四天下，名宝灯华幢。国界清净，饮食丰足，不藉耕耘而生稻粱；宫殿楼阁悉皆奇妙；诸如意树处处行列，种种香树恒出香云，种种鬘树恒出鬘云，种种华树常雨妙华；种种宝树出诸奇宝，无量色光周匝照耀；诸音乐树出诸音乐，随风吹动演妙音声；

Son of Good Family, once, long ago in the ancient past, back beyond a number of kalpas as numerous as the atoms in a buddha *kṣetra,* there was a kalpa known as "Sphere of Purity" and a world named "Vairocana's Great Awesome Virtue" in which there appeared *tathāgatas* as numerous as the atoms in Mount Sumeru.

That buddha's world took as its substance every kind of fragrant sovereign *maṇi* jewel and it was adorned with the many kinds of precious jewels. It dwelt on an ocean of stainless radiance sovereign *maṇi* jewels, was perfectly round in shape, and consisted of a combination of pure and defiled aspects. It was covered by a canopy cloud consisting of all kinds of adornments and it was surrounded by a thousand concentric rings of mountains adorned with all sorts of *maṇi* jewels. It had ten myriads of *koṭīs* of *nayutas* of four-continent lands, all of which were marvelously adorned:

Some of those four-continent lands were inhabited by beings inclined toward evil karmic deeds;

Some of those four-continent lands were inhabited by beings inclined toward mixed karmic deeds;

Some of those four-continent lands were inhabited by beings who possessed roots of goodness; and

Some of those four-continent lands were inhabited by bodhisattvas whose actions had always been consistently pure.

On this realm's eastern borderlands, on the slopes of its surrounding mountains, there was a four-continent land known as "Jeweled Lamp's Floral Banner." That realm was pure and was possessed of a flourishing abundance of food and drink. Even without cultivating the soil, the cereal grains grew spontaneously. In addition:

It was graced with palaces and towers, all of which were extraordinarily marvelous;

All kinds of wish-fulfilling trees grew in rows in place after place;

Many different varieties of incense trees constantly sent forth clouds of incense;

Many different kinds of garland trees constantly sent forth clouds of garlands;

Many different kinds of flowering trees always sent down rains of exquisite blossoms;

Many different types of jewel trees sent forth all kinds of extraordinary gems that produced a dazzling illumination all around them consisting of countless hues of light;

All kinds of music trees sent forth every variety of music as, in response to the movement of the breeze, they resounded with marvelously beautiful musical sounds;

正體字

日月光明摩尼寶王。普照一切。晝
379c08║ 夜受樂。無時間斷。此四天下。有百萬億那
379c09║ 由他諸王國土。一一國土。有千大河周匝圍
379c10║ 遶。一一皆以妙華覆上。隨流漂動。出天樂音。
379c11║ 一切寶樹列植其岸。種種珍奇以為嚴飾。舟
379c12║ 船來往。稱情戲樂。一一河間有百萬億城。一
379c13║ 一城有百萬億那由他聚落。如是一切城邑
379c14║ 聚落。各有無量百千億那由他宮殿園林。周
379c15║ 匝圍遶。此四天下閻浮提內。有一國土。名
379c16║ 寶華燈。安隱豐樂。人民熾盛。其中眾生。具行
379c17║ 十善。有轉輪王。於中出現。名毘盧遮那妙寶
379c18║ 蓮華髻。於蓮華中。忽然化生。三十二相以為
379c19║ 嚴好。七寶具足王四天下。恒以正法教導群
379c20║ 生。王有千子。端正勇健。能伏怨敵。百萬億那
379c21║ 由他宮人[1]采女。皆悉與王同種善根。同修
379c22║ 諸行。同時誕生。端正姝妙。猶如天女。身真金
379c23║ 色。常放光明。諸毛孔中。恒出妙香。良臣猛
379c24║ 將。具足十億。王有正妃。名圓滿面。是王女
379c25║ 寶。端正殊特。皮膚金色。目髮紺青。

简体字

日月光明摩尼宝王普照一切，昼夜受乐无时间断。

“此四天下有百万亿那由他诸王国土，一一国土有千大河周匝围绕，一一皆以妙华覆上，随流漂动，出天乐音，一切宝树列植其岸，种种珍奇以为严饰，舟船来往称情戏乐。一一河间有百万亿城，一一城有百万亿那由他聚落；如是一切城邑、聚落，各有无量百千亿那由他宫殿园林周匝围绕。

“此四天下阎浮提内，有一国土，名宝华灯，安隐丰乐，人民炽盛；其中众生，具行十善。有转轮王于中出现，名毗卢遮那妙宝莲华髻，于莲华中忽然化生，三十二相以为严好，七宝具足，王四天下，恒以正法教导群生。王有千子，端正勇健，能伏冤敌；百万亿那由他宫人、采女，皆悉与王同种善根、同修诸行、同时诞生，端正姝妙犹如天女，身真金色常放光明，诸毛孔中恒出妙香；良臣、猛将，具足十亿。王有正妃，名圆满面，是王女宝，端正殊特，皮肤金色，目发绀青，

Solar and lunar radiance sovereign *maṇi* jewels everywhere illuminated all things; and
Both day and night, those beings experienced uninterrupted bliss.

This four-continent land had a hundred myriads of *koṭīs* of *nayutas* of countries overseen by kings. Every one of those countries was surrounded by a thousand immense rivers, every one of which was covered by marvelous flowers that sent forth the sounds of celestial music as they bobbed along, following the currents of the rivers.

All kinds of jewel trees planted in rows along their shores were arrayed with many different types of precious and rare adornments. Boats and ships came and went with passengers enjoying pleasures perfectly suited to their inclinations. Between every one of those rivers, there were a hundred myriads of *koṭīs* of cities, and every one of those cities had a hundred myriads of *koṭīs* of *nayutas* of surrounding villages. All of the cities and villages such as these each had countless hundreds of thousands of *koṭīs* of *nayutas* of palaces, parks, and groves surrounding them.

Within this four-continent land, on the continent of Jambudvīpa, there was a country known as Jeweled Flower Lamp. Its peoples flourished in an atmosphere of peace and abundant happiness and the beings who lived there fully practiced the ten courses of good karmic action.

There was a wheel-turning king who appeared there who was known as Vairocana's Marvelous Bejeweled Lotus Topknot. He was suddenly transformationally born from within a lotus flower and was adorned with the thirty-two major marks. He was fully possessed of the seven treasures, and, in reigning over that four-continent land, he constantly relied on right Dharma for the instruction and guidance of the many types of beings there.

That king had a thousand sons who, handsome, brave, and strong, were well able to vanquish all adversaries. He had a hundred myriads of *koṭīs* of *nayutas* of palace retainers and female attendants, all of whom had in the past planted roots of goodness together with that king, had cultivated the various practices with him, had been born at the same time as he was, and who, in their especially marvelous beauty, were like celestial maidens. Their bodies were the color of gold, always emitted light, and constantly exuded a marvelous perfume from all their pores.

The good officials and brave generals were a full ten *koṭīs* in number. The king had a wife known as Perfectly Full Countenance who was this king's female treasure. Her beauty was extraordinary. Her skin was the color of gold and her eyes and hair were indigo colored.

正體字

言同梵
379c26 音。身有天香。常放光明。照千由旬。其有一女。
379c27 名普智焰妙德眼。形體端嚴。色相殊美。眾生
379c28 見者。情無厭足。爾時眾生。壽命無量。或有不
379c29 定而中夭者。種種形色。種種音聲。種種名字。
380a01 種種族姓。愚智勇怯。貧富苦樂。無量品類。皆
380a02 悉不同。時或有人。語餘人言。我身端正。汝形
380a03 鄙陋。作是語已。遞相毀辱。集不善業。以是業
380a04 故。壽命色力。一切樂事。悉皆損減。時彼城北
380a05 有菩提樹。名普光法雲音幢。以念念出現一
380a06 切如來道場莊嚴堅固摩尼王。而為其根。一
380a07 切摩尼。以為其幹。眾雜妙寶。以為其葉。次第
380a08 分布。並相稱可。四方上下。圓滿莊嚴。放寶光
380a09 明。出妙音聲。說一切如來甚深境界。於彼
380a10 樹前。有一香池。名寶華光明。演法雷音。妙寶
380a11 為岸。百萬億那由他寶樹圍遶。一一樹形。如
380a12 菩提樹。眾寶瓔珞。周匝垂下。無量樓閣。皆寶
380a13 所成。周遍道場。以為嚴飾。

简体字

言同梵音，身有天香，常放光明照千由旬。其有一女，名普智焰妙德眼，形体端严，色相殊美，众生见者情无厌足。尔时，众生寿命无量，或有不定而中夭者；种种形色、种种音声、种种名字、种种族姓，愚、智、勇、怯、贫、富、苦、乐，无量品类皆悉不同。时，或有人语余人言：‘我身端正，汝形鄙陋。’作是语已，递相毁辱，集不善业；以是业故，寿命、色力、一切乐事悉皆损减。

“时，彼城北有菩提树，名普光法云音幢，以念念出现一切如来道场庄严坚固摩尼王而为其根，一切摩尼以为其干，众杂妙宝以为其叶，次第分布，并相称可，四方上下，圆满庄严；放宝光明，出妙音声，说一切如来甚深境界。于彼树前，有一香池，名宝华光明，演法雷音；妙宝为岸，百万亿那由他宝树围绕，一一树形如菩提树，众宝璎珞周匝垂下，无量楼阁皆宝所成，周遍道场以为严饰。

Her voice was like that of the king of the Brahma Heaven. Her body had a heavenly fragrance and constantly emanated a radiance that illuminated all things to a distance of a thousand *yojanas*.

She had a daughter known as Eyes of Universal Wisdom's Flaming Radiance and Marvelous Virtue. Her body was so beautiful and her physical features were so extraordinarily lovely that all beings who saw her were insatiably captivated by her appearance.

The life span of the beings at that time, though measurelessly long, was sometimes unfixed and subject to sudden death when still young. Those beings were possessed of many different physical forms, many different voices, many different names, and many different clans. Among them, there were those who were foolish or wise, brave or timid, poor or wealthy, suffering or blissful. They were of countless sorts, and so were all different from each other.

At that time, there sometimes were those who, in speaking to someone else, would say, "My body is beautiful whereas your physical form is ugly." Then, having spoken these words, they would disparage one another and accumulate bad karmic actions. Consequently, because of these karmic actions, their life spans, physical strength, and all their sources of happiness would all deteriorate.

At that time, north of that city, there was a bodhi tree known as "banner of universally radiant Dharma cloud sounds." In each successive mind-moment, it manifested the adornments of all *tathāgatas'* sites of enlightenment. Its roots were composed of solid sovereign *maṇi* jewels. All kinds of *maṇi* jewels formed its trunk and the many varieties of marvelous gems composed its leaves, all of which were evenly distributed in their spacing and complementary in their symmetry. On all four sides, above, and below, it was perfectly full in its adornments. It emanated a jeweled radiance and emitted the sounds of voices that expounded on all *tathāgata*'s extremely profound spheres of experience.

In front of that tree, there was a perfumed pond known as "jeweled floral radiance" that emanated thunderous sounds of Dharma. It had banks composed of marvelous jewels and it was surrounded by hundreds of myriads of *koṭīs* of *nayutas* of jewel trees, every one of which was similar in shape to the bodhi tree. Necklaces of the many kinds of jewels were draped all around on the branches of each one of them.

There were countless towers there, all of which were composed of precious gems. Encircling that site of enlightenment, they served there as its adornments. Within that perfumed pond, there grew an

正體字

彼香池內出大
380a14‖ 蓮華。名普現三世一切如來莊嚴境界雲。須
380a15‖ 彌山微塵數佛。於中出現。其第一佛。名普
380a16‖ 智寶焰妙德幢。於此華上。最初得阿耨多羅
380a17‖ 三藐三菩提。無量千歲。演說正法。成熟眾生。
380a18‖ 其彼如來。未成佛時。十千年前。此大蓮華。放
380a19‖ 淨光明。名現諸神通成熟眾生。若有眾生。遇
380a20‖ 斯光者。心自開悟。無所不了。知十千年後。佛
380a21‖ 當出現。九千年前。放淨光明。名一切眾生
380a22‖ 離垢燈。若有眾生。遇斯光者。得清淨眼。見一
380a23‖ 切色。知九千年後。佛當出現。八千年前。放大
380a24‖ 光明。名一切眾生業果音。若有眾生。遇斯
380a25‖ 光者。悉得自知諸業果報。知八千年後。佛
380a26‖ 當出現。七千年前。放大光明。名生一切善
380a27‖ 根音。若有眾生遇斯光者。一切諸根。悉得圓
380a28‖ 滿。知七千年後。佛當出現。六千年前。放大光
380a29‖ 明。名佛不思議境界音。若有眾生。遇斯光
380b01‖ 者。其心廣大。普得自在。知六千年後。佛當出
380b02‖ 現。五千年前。放大光明。名嚴淨一切佛剎音。
380b03‖ 若有眾生。遇斯光者。悉見一切清淨佛土。知
380b04‖ 五千年後。佛當出現。

简体字

彼香池内出大莲华，名普现三世一切如来庄严境界云，须弥山微尘数佛于中出现。其第一佛，名普智宝焰妙德幢，于此华上，最初得阿耨多罗三藐三菩提，无量千岁演说正法成熟众生。

“其彼如来未成佛时，十千年前，此大莲华放净光明，名现诸神通成熟众生；若有众生遇斯光者，心自开悟，无所不了，知十千年后佛当出现。九千年前，放净光明，名一切众生离垢灯；若有众生遇斯光者，得清净眼，见一切色，知九千年后佛当出现。八千年前，放大光明，名一切众生业果音；若有众生遇斯光者，悉得自知诸业果报，知八千年后佛当出现。七千年前，放大光明，名生一切善根音；若有众生遇斯光者，一切诸根悉得圆满，知七千年后佛当出现。六千年前，放大光明，名佛不思议境界音；若有众生遇斯光者，其心广大，普得自在，知六千年后佛当出现。五千年前，放大光明，名严净一切佛刹音；若有众生遇斯光者，悉见一切清净佛土，知五千年后佛当出现。

immense lotus flower known as "everywhere manifesting clouds of the adorned realms of all *tathāgatas* of the three times." Buddhas as numerous as the atoms in Mount Sumeru emerged and appeared in it.

The first of those buddhas was named Banner of the Universal Wisdom Jewel's Flaming Radiance and Marvelous Qualities. He was the first of those to realize *anuttara-samyak-saṃbodhi* atop that flower. He expounded on right Dharma for countless thousands of years during which he ripened beings. Ten thousand years before that *tathāgata* attained buddhahood, this immense lotus flower emanated a pure light known as "manifesting spiritual super-knowledges for the ripening of beings." Whenever any beings were touched by this light, they spontaneously awakened and had nothing they did not completely understand. They then knew that, after ten thousand more years, a buddha would appear.

Then, nine thousand years before that was to happen, it emanated a pure light known as "all beings' lamp of immaculate purity." Whenever any beings were touched by this light, they acquired the purified eye that allowed them to see all forms and know that, after another nine thousand more years, a buddha would appear.

Then, eight thousand years beforehand, it emanated a great light known as "the sound of all beings' karmic rewards." Whenever any beings were touched by this light, they were all able to know the karmic rewards and retributions resulting from their own karmic actions and they also knew that, after eight thousand more years, a buddha would appear.

Then, seven thousand years beforehand, it emanated a great light known as "producing the sound of all roots of goodness." Whenever any beings were touched by this light, all their faculties became perfectly complete and they knew that, after seven thousand more years, a buddha would appear.

Then, six thousand years beforehand, it emanated a great light known as "the sound of the inconceivable realm of the Buddha." Whenever any beings were touched by this light, their minds became vast, they everywhere acquired the sovereign masteries, and they knew that, after six thousand more years, a buddha would appear.

Then, five thousand years beforehand, it emanated a great light known as "the sound of the purification of all buddha *kṣetras*." Whenever any beings were touched by this light, they saw all the pure buddha lands and knew that, after five thousand more years, a buddha would appear.

正體字

四千年前。放大光明。名
380b05 ‖ 一切如來境界無差別燈。若有眾生。遇斯光
380b06 ‖ 者。悉能往覲一切諸佛。知四千年後。佛當
380b07 ‖ 出現。三千年前。放大光明。名三世明燈。若有
380b08 ‖ 眾生。遇斯光者。悉能現見一切如來諸本事
380b09 ‖ 海。知三千年後。佛當出現。二千年前。放大光
380b10 ‖ 明。名如來離翳智慧燈。若有眾生。遇斯光
380b11 ‖ 者。則得普眼見一切如來神變。一切諸佛國
380b12 ‖ 土。一切世界眾生。知二千年後。佛當出現。一
380b13 ‖ 千年前。放大光明。名令一切眾生見佛集諸
380b14 ‖ 善根。若有眾生。遇斯光者。則得成就見佛三
380b15 ‖ 昧。知一千年後。佛當出現。次七日前。放大光
380b16 ‖ 明。名一切眾生歡喜音。若有眾生。遇斯光者。
380b17 ‖ 得普見諸佛生大歡喜。知七日後。佛當出現。
380b18 ‖ 滿七日已。一切世界。悉皆震動。純淨無染。念
380b19 ‖ 念普現十方一切清淨佛剎。亦現彼剎種種
380b20 ‖ 莊嚴。若有眾生。根性淳熟。應見佛者。咸詣道
380b21 ‖ 場。爾時彼世界中。一切輪圍。一切須彌。一切
380b22 ‖ 諸山。一切大海。一切地。一切城。一切垣牆。
380b23 ‖ 一切宮殿。一切音樂。一切語言。皆出音聲。讚
380b24 ‖ 說一切諸佛如來神力境界。

简体字

四千年前，放大光明，名一切如来境界无差别灯；若有众生遇斯光者，悉能往觐一切诸佛，知四千年后佛当出现。三千年前，放大光明，名三世明灯；若有众生遇斯光者，悉能现见一切如来诸本事海，知三千年后佛当出现。二千年前，放大光明，名如来离翳智慧灯；若有众生遇斯光者，则得普眼见一切如来神变、一切诸佛国土、一切世界众生，知二千年后佛当出现。一千年前，放大光明，名令一切众生见佛集诸善根；若有众生遇斯光者，则得成就见佛三昧，知一千年后佛当出现。次七日前，放大光明，名一切众生欢喜音；若有众生遇斯光者，得普见诸佛生大欢喜，知七日后佛当出现。满七日已，一切世界悉皆震动，纯净无染，念念普现十方一切清净佛刹，亦现彼刹种种庄严；若有众生根性淳熟，应见佛者，咸诣道场。

“尔时，彼世界中一切轮围、一切须弥、一切诸山、一切大海、一切地、一切城、一切垣墙、一切宫殿、一切音乐、一切语言，皆出音声，赞说一切诸佛如来神力境界；

Then, four thousand years beforehand, it emanated a great light known as "the lamp of the undifferentiated realm of all *tathāgatas*." Whenever any beings were touched by this light, they became able to travel and see all buddhas and knew that, after four thousand more years, a buddha would appear.

Then, three thousand years beforehand, it emanated a great light known as "bright lamp of the three periods of time." Whenever any beings were touched by this light, they were able to directly see the ocean of all past deeds of all *tathāgatas* and knew that, after three thousand more years, a buddha would appear.

Then, two thousand years beforehand, it emanated a great light known as "lamp of the *tathāgatas'* wisdom that removes all obscurations." Whenever any beings were touched by this light, they acquired the universally seeing eye, saw the spiritual transformations of all *tathāgatas*, all buddha lands, and all beings in all worlds, and also knew that, after two thousand more years, a buddha would appear.

Then, one thousand years beforehand, it emanated a great light known as "enabling all beings to see the buddhas' accumulation of all roots of goodness." Whenever any beings were touched by this light, they perfected the "seeing the buddhas" samādhi and knew that, after one thousand more years, a buddha would appear.

Then, seven days beforehand, it emanated a great light known as "the sound of all beings' joyous delight." Whenever any beings were touched by this light, they were able to see all buddhas and were filled with joyous delight. They then knew that, after seven more days, a buddha would appear.

After those seven days had passed, that entire world quaked and shook and it became entirely pure and free of defilements. In each successive mind-moment, all of the pure buddha *kṣetras* of the ten directions were revealed. The many different kinds of adornments in those *kṣetras* were also revealed. Wherever there were beings whose faculties and natures had become so completely ripened that they should be able to see a buddha, they all proceeded to that site of enlightenment.

Then, throughout that land, from all the encircling mountains, from all the Sumeru Mountains, from all the other mountains, from all the great oceans, from all those lands, from all those cities, from all their city walls, from all their palaces, from all their music, and from all their spoken languages, there then came forth sounds praising the sphere of action of the spiritual powers of all the buddhas, the *tathāgatas*. There also came forth clouds of all kinds of

正體字

又出一切香雲。
380b25 | 一切燒香雲。一切末香雲。一切香摩尼形
380b26 | 像雲。一切寶焰雲。一切焰藏雲。一切摩尼衣
380b27 | 雲。一切瓔珞雲。一切妙華雲。一切如來光明
380b28 | 雲。一切如來圓光雲。一切音樂雲。一切如來
380b29 | 願聲雲。一切如來言音海雲。一切如來相好
380c01 | 雲。顯示如來出現世間不思議相。善男子。此
380c02 | 普照三世一切如來莊嚴境界大寶蓮華王。
380c03 | 有十佛剎微塵數蓮華周匝圍遶。諸蓮華內。
380c04 | 悉有摩尼寶藏師子之座。一一座上。皆有菩
380c05 | 薩。結[1]跏趺坐。善男子。彼普智寶焰妙德幢
380c06 | 王如來。於此。成阿耨多羅三藐三菩提時。即
380c07 | 於十方一切世界中。成阿耨多羅三藐三菩
380c08 | 提。隨眾生心。悉現其前。為轉法輪。於一一世
380c09 | 界。令無量眾生。離惡道苦。令無量眾生。得生
380c10 | 天中。令無量眾生。住於聲聞辟支佛地。令
380c11 | 無量眾生。成就出離菩提之行。令無量眾生。
380c12 | 成就勇猛幢菩提之行。令無量眾生。成就法
380c13 | 光明菩提之行。令無量眾生。成就清淨根菩
380c14 | 提之行。令無量眾生。成就平等力菩提之行。

简体字

又出一切香云、一切烧香云、一切末香云、一切香摩尼形像云、一切宝焰云、一切焰藏云、一切摩尼衣云、一切璎珞云、一切妙华云、一切如来光明云、一切如来圆光云、一切音乐云、一切如来愿声云、一切如来言音海云、一切如来相好云，显示如来出现世间不思议相。

“善男子，此普照三世一切如来庄严境界大宝莲华王，有十佛刹微尘数莲华周匝围绕，诸莲华内悉有摩尼宝藏师子之座，一一座上皆有菩萨结跏趺坐。

“善男子，彼普智宝焰妙德幢王如来，于此成阿耨多罗三藐三菩提时，即于十方一切世界中成阿耨多罗三藐三菩提；随众生心，悉现其前为转法轮。于一一世界，令无量众生离恶道苦，令无量众生得生天中，令无量众生住于声闻、辟支佛地，令无量众生成就出离菩提之行，令无量众生成就勇猛幢菩提之行，令无量众生成就法光明菩提之行，令无量众生成就清净根菩提之行，令无量众生成就平等力菩提之行，

perfumes, clouds of all kinds of burning incense, clouds of all kinds of powdered incense, clouds of all kinds of images made of *maṇi* jewels, clouds of all kinds of flaming-radiance jewels, clouds of all kinds of flaming-radiance treasuries, clouds of all kinds of *maṇi* jewel-adorned robes, clouds of all kinds of necklaces, clouds of all kinds of marvelous flowers, clouds of all kinds of light emanated by *tathāgatas*, clouds of all kinds of auras emanated by *tathāgatas*, clouds of all kinds of music, clouds of the sounds of all vows made by *tathāgatas*, clouds of the oceans of *tathāgatas'* sayings, and clouds of all *tathāgatas'* major marks and secondary signs, all of these revealing there the inconceivable signs that a *tathāgata* was about to appear in the world.

Son of Good Family, this immense jeweled king of lotus flowers known as "everywhere illuminating clouds of the adorned realms of all *tathāgatas* of the three times," had a retinue of lotus flowers surrounding it that were as numerous as the motes of dust in ten buddha *kṣetras*. In all those lotus flowers, there were *maṇi* jewel lotus dais lion king thrones, and atop every one of those thrones, there was a bodhisattva sitting in the lotus posture.

Son of Good Family, when, in this place, that *tathāgata*, Banner King of the Universal Wisdom Jewel's Flaming Radiance and Marvelous Qualities, attained *anuttara-samyak-saṃbodhi*, he immediately attained *anuttara-samyak-saṃbodhi* in the worlds of the ten directions where, adapting to beings' mental dispositions, he appeared before them all in order to turn the wheel of the Dharma, doing so in every one of those worlds, thereby:

Enabling countless beings to leave behind the sufferings of the wretched destinies;

Enabling countless beings to succeed in being reborn in the heavens;

Enabling countless beings to abide on the grounds of *śrāvaka* disciples or *pratyekabuddhas*;

Enabling countless beings to perfect the bodhi practices by which one achieves emancipation;

Enabling countless beings to perfect the bodhi practices by which one raises the banner of courage;

Enabling countless beings to perfect the bodhi practices by which one manifests the light of Dharma;

Enabling countless beings to perfect the bodhi practices by which one purifies the faculties;

Enabling countless beings to perfect the bodhi practices by which one develops equal command of all the powers;

正體字

380c15 ‖ 令無量眾生。成就入法城菩提之行。令無量
380c16 ‖ 眾生。成就遍至一切處不可壞神通力菩提
380c17 ‖ 之行。令無量眾生。入普門方便道菩提之行。
380c18 ‖ 令無量眾生。安住三昧門菩提之行。令無量
380c19 ‖ 眾生。成就緣一切清淨境界菩提之行。令無
380c20 ‖ 量眾生。發菩提心。令無量眾生。住菩薩道。令
380c21 ‖ 無量眾生。安住清淨波羅蜜道。令無量眾生。
380c22 ‖ 住菩薩初地。令無量眾生。住菩薩二地乃至
380c23 ‖ 十地。令無量眾生。入於菩薩殊勝行願。令
380c24 ‖ 無量眾生。安住普賢清淨行願。善男子。彼
380c25 ‖ 普智寶焰妙德幢如來。現如是不思議自在
380c26 ‖ 神力。轉法輪時。於彼一一諸世界中。隨其
380c27 ‖ 所應。念念調伏無量眾生。時普賢菩薩。知
380c28 ‖ 寶華燈王城中眾生。自恃色貌及諸境界。而
380c29 ‖ 生憍慢。陵蔑他人。化現妙身。端正殊特。往詣
381a01 ‖ 彼城。放大光明。普照一切。令彼聖王及諸妙
381a02 ‖ 寶。日月星宿。眾生身等。一切光明。悉皆不
381a03 ‖ 現。

简体字

令无量众生成就入法城菩提之行，令无量众生成就遍至一切处不可坏神通力菩提之行，令无量众生入普门方便道菩提之行，令无量众生安住三昧门菩提之行，令无量众生成就缘一切清净境界菩提之行，令无量众生发菩提心，令无量众生住菩萨道，令无量众生安住清净波罗蜜道，令无量众生住菩萨初地，令无量众生住菩萨二地乃至十地，令无量众生入于菩萨殊胜行愿，令无量众生安住普贤清净行愿。

"善男子，彼普智宝焰妙德幢如来，现如是不思议自在神力转法轮时，于彼一一诸世界中，随其所应，念念调伏无量众生。

"时，普贤菩萨知宝华灯王城中众生，自恃色貌及诸境界，而生憍慢陵蔑他人；化现妙身，端正殊特，往诣彼城，放大光明，普照一切，令彼圣王及诸妙宝、日月星宿、众生身等一切光明悉皆不现，

- Enabling countless beings to perfect the bodhi practices by which one enters the city of the Dharma;
- Enabling countless beings to perfect the bodhi practices by which one pervades all places with the indestructible power of the spiritual superknowledges;
- Enabling countless beings to perfect the bodhi practices by which one enters the path of the universal gateway's skillful means;
- Enabling countless beings to perfect the bodhi practices by which one becomes established in the gateways of samādhi;
- Enabling countless beings to perfect the bodhi practices by which one takes pure realms as one's objective focus;
- Enabling countless beings to resolve to attain bodhi;
- Enabling countless beings to abide in the bodhisattva path;
- Enabling countless beings to become established in the path of purifying the *pāramitās*;
- Enabling countless beings to abide on the first bodhisattva ground;
- Enabling countless beings to abide on the second through the tenth bodhisattva grounds;
- Enabling countless beings to enter the bodhisattva's extraordinarily excellent conduct and vows; and
- Enabling countless beings to become established in Samantabhadra's pure conduct and vows.

Son of Good Family, when that *tathāgata* known as Banner of the Universal Wisdom Jewel's Flaming Radiance and Marvelous Qualities manifested such inconceivable sovereign mastery of the spiritual powers and turned the wheel of the Dharma, in each successive mind-moment, he trained countless beings in every one of those worlds, doing so in accordance with what was most fitting for them.

At that time, Samantabhadra Bodhisattva realized with regard to the beings in the royal capital of that Jewel Flower Lamp land that, based on their own physical appearance and the realms in which they dwelt, they had developed an arrogant attitude and had become inclined to humiliate and belittle others. Transformationally manifesting a marvelous body that was extraordinarily beautiful, he went to visit that city and emanated a great light that illuminated everything. It was so brilliant that it outshone all the light of that sage king, his marvelous jewels, the sun and moon, the stars and constellations, those beings' bodies, and everything else, thereby causing all of their radiance to completely disappear. It was just as when the sun rises and the many other radiant things are all robbed

正體字

譬如日出眾景奪曜。亦如聚墨對閻浮金。
381a04║ 時諸眾生。咸作是言。此為是誰。為天為梵。今
381a05║ 放此光。令我等身所有光色。皆不顯現。種
381a06║ 種思惟無能解了。爾時普賢菩薩。在彼輪王
381a07║ 寶宮殿上虛空中住。而告之言。大王當知今
381a08║ 汝國中。有佛興世。在普光明法雲音幢菩提
381a09║ 樹下。時聖王女。蓮華妙眼。見普賢菩薩所
381a10║ 現色身光明自在。及聞身上諸莊嚴具所出
381a11║ 妙音。心生歡喜。作如是念。願我所有一切
381a12║ 善根。得如是身。如是莊嚴。如是相好。如是威
381a13║ 儀。如是自在。今此大聖。能於眾生生死長
381a14║ 夜黑闇之中。放大光明。開示如來出興於世。
381a15║ 願令於我亦得如是。為諸眾生作智光明。破
381a16║ 彼所有無知黑闇。願我所在受生之處。常得
381a17║ 不離此善知識。善男子。時轉輪王。與其寶
381a18║ 女千子眷屬。大臣輔佐。四種兵眾。及其城內。
381a19║ 無量人民。前後圍遶。以王神力。俱昇虛空。高
381a20║ 一由旬。放大光明。照四天下。普使一切。咸得
381a21║ 瞻仰。欲令眾生俱往見佛。以偈讚曰
381a22║ 如來出世間　普救諸群生
381a23║ 汝等應速起　往詣導師所
381a24║ 無量無數劫　乃有佛興世

简体字

譬如日出众景夺曜，亦如聚墨对阎浮金。时，诸众生咸作是言：‘此为是谁？为天？为梵？今放此光，令我等身所有光色皆不显现。’种种思惟，无能解了。

“尔时，普贤菩萨在彼轮王宝宫殿上虚空中住，而告之言：‘大王当知，今汝国中，有佛兴世，在普光明法云音幢菩提树下。’时，圣王女——莲华妙眼，见普贤菩萨所现色身光明自在，及闻身上诸庄严具所出妙音，心生欢喜，作如是念：‘愿我所有一切善根，得如是身、如是庄严、如是相好、如是威仪、如是自在。今此大圣，能于众生生死长夜黑暗之中放大光明，开示如来出兴于世；愿令于我亦得如是，为诸众生作智光明，破彼所有无知黑暗。愿我所在受生之处，常得不离此善知识。’

“善男子，时，转轮王与其宝女、千子、眷属、大臣、辅佐、四种兵众，及其城内无量人民，前后围绕；以王神力，俱升虚空，高一由旬，放大光明照四天下，普使一切咸得瞻仰，欲令众生俱往见佛，以偈赞曰：

“‘如来出世间，普救诸群生，
汝等应速起，往诣导师所。
无量无数劫，乃有佛兴世，

of their dazzling brilliance. It was also as if they were all but heaps of charcoal placed near a mass of *jambūnada* gold.

Then the beings there all exclaimed, "Who is this? Is it a deva or a brahma heaven king who, by emanating such radiance, causes all the light from our bodies to completely disappear?" They reflected in various ways, but none of them could understand this.

Samantabhadra Bodhisattva then stood in the sky above that wheel-turning king's jeweled palace and told them: "O Great King, you should realize that a buddha has just now appeared in the world in your very own country. He is dwelling at the foot of the bodhi tree known as 'Banner of Universally Radiant Dharma Cloud Sounds.'"

When that sage king's daughter known as Wondrous Lotus Eyes saw the miraculous display of light cast by the body of Samantabhadra Bodhisattva and also heard the marvelous sounds emanating from his body's adornments, her mind was filled with joy and she thought:

> By virtue of all my roots of goodness, may I be able to acquire a body like this, one that is possessed of adornments like these, major marks and secondary signs like these, awesome deportment such as this, and miraculous powers such as these.
>
> Now, for beings in the darkness of the long night of *saṃsāra*, this great *ārya* is able to emanate a great light revealing that a *tathāgata* has come into the world. May I too be able to develop a light of wisdom for all beings with which I can dispel all the darkness of their ignorance. Wherever I am reborn, may I never be separated from this good spiritual guide.

Son of Good Family, that wheel-turning king then used his spiritual powers to rise a *yojana* high in the sky, surrounded by his precious maidens, his thousand sons, his retinue, his great officials and retainers, his fourfold army, and all the countless people in his city. He then emanated a brilliant light that illuminated that entire four-continent land and caused everyone to gaze up in admiration. Then, wishing to encourage all those beings to go and see the Buddha, he spoke these verses of praise:

The Tathāgata has appeared into the world
to everywhere rescue all the many kinds of beings.
You should all swiftly arise and go forth
to pay your respects to the Guiding Teacher.

Only with the passage of measureless and countless kalpas
does one then have a Buddha appear in the world,

正體字

381a25 ‖ 演說深妙法　饒益一切眾
381a26 ‖ 佛觀諸世間　顛倒常癡惑
381a27 ‖ 輪迴生死苦　而起大悲心
381a28 ‖ 無數億千劫　修習菩提行
381a29 ‖ 為欲度眾生　斯由大悲力
381b01 ‖ 頭目手足等　一切悉能捨
381b02 ‖ 為求菩提故　如是無量劫
381b03 ‖ 無量億千劫　導師難可遇
381b04 ‖ 見聞若承事　一切無空過
381b05 ‖ 今當共汝等　往觀調御尊
381b06 ‖ 坐於如來座　降魔成正覺
381b07 ‖ 瞻仰如來身　放演無量光
381b08 ‖ 種種微妙色　除滅一切暗
381b09 ‖ 一一毛孔中　放光不思議
381b10 ‖ 普照諸群生　咸令大歡喜
381b11 ‖ 汝等咸應發　廣大精進心
381b12 ‖ 詣彼如來所　恭敬而供養
381b13 ‖ 爾時轉輪聖王。說偈讚佛。開悟一切眾生已。
381b14 ‖ 從輪王善根。出十千種大供養雲。往詣道場。
381b15 ‖ 向如來所。所謂一切寶蓋雲。一切華帳雲。

简体字

演说深妙法，饶益一切众。
佛观诸世间，颠倒常痴惑，
轮回生死苦，而起大悲心。
无数亿千劫，修习菩提行，
为欲度众生，斯由大悲力。
头目手足等，一切悉能舍，
为求菩提故，如是无量劫。
无量亿千劫，导师难可遇；
见闻若承事，一切无空过。
今当共汝等，往观调御尊，
坐于如来座，降魔成正觉。
瞻仰如来身，放演无量光，
种种微妙色，除灭一切暗。
一一毛孔中，放光不思议，
普照诸群生，咸令大欢喜。
汝等咸应发，广大精进心，
诣彼如来所，恭敬而供养。’

“尔时，转轮圣王说偈赞佛，开悟一切众生已，从轮王善根，出十千种大供养云，往诣道场，向如来所。所谓：一切宝盖云、一切华帐云、

expounding on the profound and sublime Dharma,
and thereby bestowing benefit on all beings.

Having contemplated everyone in the world
as holding inverted views and being forever deluded
as they undergo the sufferings of cyclic existence in *saṃsāra,*
the Buddha has aroused the mind of great compassion.

For countless thousands of *koṭīs* of kalpas,
he cultivated the practices leading to bodhi,
doing so out of the wish to liberate beings.
This was due to the power of the great compassion.

His head, eyes, hands, feet, and the rest—
he was able to sacrifice all of these
for the sake of his quest to realize bodhi,
doing so in this way for countless kalpas.

Even throughout countless thousands of *koṭīs* of kalpas,
the Guiding Teacher is still difficult to ever encounter.
If one sees and hears him and if one serves him,
none of those efforts will have been expended in vain.

I shall now join with all of you
in going to see the Venerable Tamer[144]
who sits there on the Tathāgata's throne,
having vanquished Māra and attained the right enlightenment.

Gaze up in admiration at the body of the Tathāgata
that is emanating measureless radiance
of many different sublime colors
that extinguish all darkness.

From within every one of his pores,
he emanates inconceivably many light rays
that everywhere illuminate the many kinds of beings
and fills them all with joyous delight.

You should all arouse
the vast and vigorous resolve
and go pay your respects to that *tathāgata,*
revering him and presenting offerings to him.

Then, after the wheel-turning sage king had spoken these verses in praise of the Buddha to rouse all those beings, through the roots of the goodness possessed by a wheel-turning king, he produced a myriad kinds of immense offering clouds that then went along to the site of enlightenment where the Tathāgata dwelt. These included:

Clouds of all kinds of jeweled canopies;
Clouds of all kinds of floral curtains;

正體字

一
381b16 切寶衣雲。一切寶鈴網雲。一切香海雲。一切
381b17 寶座雲。一切寶幢雲。一切宮殿雲。一切妙華
381b18 雲。一切諸莊嚴具雲。於虛空中。周遍嚴飾。到
381b19 已頂禮普智寶焰妙德幢王如來足。遶無量
381b20 百千匝。即於佛前坐普照十方寶蓮華座。時
381b21 轉輪王女。普智焰妙德眼。即解身上諸莊嚴
381b22 具。持以散佛。時莊嚴具。於虛空中。變成寶
381b23 蓋。寶網垂下。龍王執持。一切宮殿。於中間列。
381b24 十種寶蓋。周匝圍遶。形如樓閣。內外清淨。諸
381b25 瓔珞雲。及諸寶樹。香海摩尼。以為莊嚴。於此
381b26 蓋中。有菩提樹。枝葉榮茂。普覆法界。念念示
381b27 現無量莊嚴。毘盧遮那如來。坐此樹下。有不
381b28 可說佛剎微塵數菩薩。前後圍遶。皆從普賢
381b29 行願出生。住諸菩薩無差別住。亦見有一切
381c01 諸世間主。亦見如來自在神力。又見一切諸
381c02 劫次第世界成壞。又亦見彼一切世界。一切
381c03 諸佛。出興次第。又亦見彼一切世界一一皆
381c04 有普賢菩薩。供養於佛。調伏眾生。

简体字

一切宝衣云、一切宝铃网云、一切香海云、一切宝座云、一切宝幢云、一切宫殿云、一切妙华云、一切诸庄严具云，于虚空中周遍严饰。到已，顶礼普智宝焰妙德幢王如来足，绕无量百千匝，即于佛前坐普照十方宝莲华座。

“时，转轮王女普智焰妙德眼，即解身上诸庄严具，持以散佛。时，庄严具于虚空中变成宝盖，宝网垂下，龙王执持，一切宫殿于中间列；十种宝盖周匝围绕，形如楼阁，内外清净，诸璎珞云及诸宝树、香海摩尼以为庄严。于此盖中，有菩提树，枝叶荣茂，普覆法界，念念示现无量庄严。毗卢遮那如来坐此树下，有不可说佛刹微尘数菩萨前后围绕，皆从普贤行愿出生，住诸菩萨无差别住，亦见有一切诸世间主，亦见如来自在神力，又见一切诸劫次第世界成坏，又亦见彼一切世界一切诸佛出兴次第，又亦见彼一切世界一一皆有普贤菩萨供养于佛、调伏众生，

Clouds of all kinds of jeweled robes;
Clouds of all kinds of jewel-adorned bell nets;
Clouds of all kinds of seas of perfumes;
Clouds of all kinds of jeweled thrones;
Clouds of all kinds of jeweled banners;
Clouds of all kinds of palaces;
Clouds of all kinds of marvelous flowers; and
Clouds of all kinds of adornments.

These all floated up in the sky and displayed their adornments all around. After he had arrived, he bowed down in reverence at the feet of the Tathāgata, Banner King of the Universal Wisdom Jewel's Flaming Radiance and Marvelous Qualities, circumambulated him countless hundreds of thousands of times, and then sat before the Buddha on a jeweled lotus flower throne that everywhere illuminated the ten directions.

Then the wheel-turning king's daughter, Eyes of Universal Wisdom's Flaming Radiance and Marvelous Qualities, immediately removed all the jewelry adorning her body and then took them to scatter as offerings over the buddha. As she did so, right there in the sky, those adornments transformed into a jeweled canopy with a jeweled curtain net that was held aloft by the dragon king. All the palaces were arrayed within it and it was in turn surrounded by ten other kinds of jeweled canopies that took the shape of a tower. They were immaculate within and without and were adorned with a cloud of jewel necklaces, jeweled trees, and *maṇi* jewels from the ocean of perfumes.

Within the area covered by this canopy was a bodhi tree with luxuriantly lush branches and leaves that stretched all across the Dharma realm and in which, in each successive mind-moment, there were displayed countless kinds of adornments. Vairocana Tathāgata was sitting beneath this tree surrounded by bodhisattvas as numerous as the atoms in an ineffable number of buddha *kṣetras*, all of whom had been born from the conduct and vows of Samantabhadra and all of whom dwelt in the undifferentiated abode of all bodhisattvas. Furthermore:

She also saw there all the world leaders;
She also witnessed the Tathāgata's miraculous spiritual powers;
She also saw in all kalpas the sequential formation and destruction of worlds;
She also saw in all of those worlds all buddhas appearing in order in the world;
She also saw that, in each one of all those worlds, Samantabhadra Bodhisattva was making offerings to those buddhas and training beings;

正體字

又亦見
381c05║ 彼一切菩薩。莫不皆在普賢身中。亦見自
381c06║ 身在其身內。亦見其身在一切如來前。一切
381c07║ 普賢前。一切菩薩前。一切眾生前。又亦見彼
381c08║ 一切世界。一一各有佛剎微塵數世界。種種
381c09║ 際畔。種種任持。種種形狀。種種體性。種種安
381c10║ 布。種種莊嚴。種種清淨。種種莊嚴雲。而覆其
381c11║ 上。種種劫名。種種佛興。種種三世。種種方
381c12║ 處。種種住法界。種種入法界。種種住虛空。種
381c13║ 種如來菩提場。種種如來神通力。種種如來
381c14║ 師子座。種種如來大眾海。種種如來眾差別。
381c15║ 種種如來巧方便。種種如來轉法輪。種種如
381c16║ 來妙音聲。種種如來言說海。種種如來契經
381c17║ 雲。既見是已。其心清淨。生大歡喜。普智寶焰
381c18║ 妙德幢王如來。為說修多羅。名一切如來轉
381c19║ 法輪。十佛剎微塵數修多羅。而為眷屬。

简体字

又亦见彼一切菩萨莫不皆在普贤身中，亦见自身在其身内，亦见其身在一切如来前、一切普贤前、一切菩萨前、一切众生前，又亦见彼一切世界一一各有佛刹微尘数世界种种际畔、种种任持、种种形状、种种体性、种种安布、种种庄严、种种清净、种种庄严云而覆其上、种种劫名、种种佛兴、种种三世、种种方处、种种住法界、种种入法界、种种住虚空、种种如来菩提场、种种如来神通力、种种如来师子座、种种如来大众海、种种如来众差别、种种如来巧方便、种种如来转法轮、种种如来妙音声、种种如来言说海、种种如来契经云；既见是已，其心清净，生大欢喜。普智宝焰妙德幢王如来，为说修多罗，名一切如来转法轮，十佛刹微尘数修多罗而为眷属。

She also saw that, of all those bodhisattvas, none were not visible within the body of Samantabhadra;

She also saw her own body within his body;

She also saw her own body there directly before all *tathāgatas*, before all Samantabhadras, before all bodhisattvas, and before all beings; and

She also saw that, in each one of all those worlds, there were worlds as numerous as the atoms in a buddha *kṣetra* with:

Many different kinds of boundaries;
Many different kinds of foundations;
Many different kinds of appearances;
Many different kinds of essential natures;
Many different kinds of arrangements;
Many different kinds of adornments;
Many different kinds of purity;
Many different kinds of adornment clouds above them;
Many different kinds of kalpa names;
Many different ways in which the buddhas arose;
Many different ways the three periods of time occurred;
Many different kinds of regions;
Many different ways of abiding in the Dharma realm;
Many different ways of entering the Dharma realm;
Many different ways of abiding in space;
Many different kinds of sites of enlightenment of *tathāgatas*;
Many different kinds of powers of a *tathāgata*'s spiritual superknowledges;
Many different kinds of lion thrones of *tathāgatas*;
Many different kinds of oceans of great assemblies of *tathāgatas*;
Many different kinds of variations in *tathāgatas'* assemblies;
Many different kinds of skillful means of *tathāgatas*;
Many different ways *tathāgatas* turned the Dharma wheel;
Many different kinds of sublime voices of *tathāgatas*;
Many different kinds of seas of *tathāgatas'* discourse; and
Many different kinds of clouds of *tathāgatas'* sutras.

Having seen all this, her mind became purified and she was filled with joyous delight. The Tathāgata, "Banner King of the Universal Wisdom Jewel's Flaming Radiance and Marvelous Qualities," then spoke a sutra for her benefit known as All Tathāgatas' Turning of the Dharma Wheel that had a retinue of sutras as numerous as the atoms in ten buddha *kṣetras*. Then, once that maiden heard this

正體字

時
381c20‖ 彼女人。聞此經已。則得成就十千三昧門。其
381c21‖ 心柔軟。無有麁彊。如初受胎。如始誕生。如娑
381c22‖ 羅樹初始生芽。彼三昧心。亦復如是。所謂
381c23‖ 現見一切佛三昧。普照一切剎三昧。入一切
381c24‖ 三世門三昧。說一切佛法輪三昧。知一切
381c25‖ 佛願海三昧。開悟一切眾生令出生死苦三
381c26‖ 昧。常願破一切眾生闇三昧。常願滅一切眾
381c27‖ 生苦三昧。常願生一切眾生樂三昧。教化一
381c28‖ 切眾生不生疲厭三昧。一切菩薩無障礙幢
381c29‖ 三昧。普詣一切清淨佛剎三昧。得如是等十
382a01‖ 千三昧已。復得妙定心。不動心。歡喜心。安慰
382a02‖ 心。廣大心。順善知識心。緣甚深一切智心。住
382a03‖ 廣大方便海心。捨離一切執著心。不住一切
382a04‖ 世間境界心。入如來境界心。普照一切色海
382a05‖ 心。無惱害心。無高倨心。無疲倦心。無退轉
382a06‖ 心。無懈怠心。

简体字

“时，彼女人闻此经已，则得成就十千三昧门，其心柔软，无有粗强，如初受胎，如始诞生，如娑罗树初始生芽。彼三昧心亦复如是，所谓：现见一切佛三昧、普照一切刹三昧、入一切三世门三昧、说一切佛法轮三昧、知一切佛愿海三昧、开悟一切众生令出生死苦三昧、常愿破一切众生暗三昧、常愿灭一切众生苦三昧、常愿生一切众生乐三昧、教化一切众生不生疲厌三昧、一切菩萨无障碍幢三昧、普诣一切清净佛刹三昧。得如是等十千三昧已，复得妙定心、不动心、欢喜心、安慰心、广大心、顺善知识心、缘甚深一切智心、住广大方便海心、舍离一切执著心、不住一切世间境界心、入如来境界心、普照一切色海心、无恼害心，无高倨心、无疲倦心、无退转心、无懈怠心、

sutra, she attained ten thousand samādhi gateways, whereupon her mind became pliant, free of coarseness or rigidity, just like one newly conceived in the womb, like one who has just been born, or like the newly emerging sprout of a *śāla* tree. Her samādhi mind state was just like this. For instance, she acquired:

The samādhi of the directly present vision of all buddhas;
The samādhi of the universal illumination of all *kṣetras;*
The samādhi of the gateway to entering all three periods of time;
The samādhi of the proclamation of the turning of the Dharma wheel by all buddhas;
The samādhi of the awareness of the ocean of all buddhas' vows;
The samādhi of rousing all beings and enabling them to escape the sufferings of *saṃsāra;*
The samādhi of always vowing to dispel the darkness of all beings;
The samādhi of always vowing to extinguish the sufferings of all beings;
The samādhi of always vowing to bring happiness to all beings;
The samādhi of tirelessly teaching all beings;
The samādhi of the banner of all bodhisattvas' freedom from obstacles; and
The samādhi of traveling everywhere to pay one's respects in all the pure buddha *kṣetras.*

After having acquired ten thousand samādhis such as these, she further acquired:

The mind of subtle meditative absorption;
The unmoving mind;
The joyous mind;
The comforting mind;
The vast mind;
The mind that complies with good spiritual guides;
The mind that takes extremely profound all-knowledge as its aim;
The mind that dwells in the vast ocean of skillful means;
The mind that relinquishes all attachments;
The mind that does not dwell in any worldly spheres of experience;
The mind that penetrates the Tathāgata's sphere of action;
The mind that everywhere illuminates the ocean of all forms;
The mind that is free of maliciousness;
The mind that is free of arrogance;
The mind that is tireless;
The mind that is irreversible;
The mind that is free of indolence;

正體字

思惟諸法自性心。安住一切法
382a07║ 門海心。觀察一切法門海心。了知一切眾生
382a08║ 海心。救護一切眾生海心。普照一切世界海
382a09║ 心。普生一切佛願海心。悉破一切障山心。積
382a10║ 集福德助道心。現見諸佛十力心。普照菩薩
382a11║ 境界心。增長菩薩助道心。遍緣一切方海心。
382a12║ 一心思惟普賢大願。發一切如來十佛剎微
382a13║ 塵數願海。願嚴淨一切佛國。願調伏一切
382a14║ 眾生。願遍知一切法界。願普入一切法界海。
382a15║ 願於一切佛剎。盡未來際劫。修菩薩行。願
382a16║ 盡未來際劫。不捨一切菩薩行。願得親近一
382a17║ 切如來。願得承事一切善友。願得供養一切
382a18║ 諸佛。願於念念中。修菩薩行。增一切智。無有
382a19║ 間斷。發如是等十佛剎微塵數願海。成就普
382a20║ 賢所有大願。時彼如來。復為其女。開示演說
382a21║ 發心已來所集善根。所修妙行。所得大果。

简体字

思惟诸法自性心、安住一切法门海心、观察一切法门海心、了知一切众生海心、救护一切众生海心、普照一切世界海心、普生一切佛愿海心、悉破一切障山心、积集福德助道心、现见诸佛十力心、普照菩萨境界心、增长菩萨助道心、遍缘一切方海心。一心思惟普贤大愿，发一切如来十佛刹微尘数愿海：愿严净一切佛国，愿调伏一切众生，愿遍知一切法界，愿普入一切法界海，愿于一切佛刹尽未来际劫修菩萨行，愿尽未来际劫不舍一切菩萨行，愿得亲近一切如来，愿得承事一切善友，愿得供养一切诸佛，愿于念念中修菩萨行增一切智无有间断。发如是等十佛刹微尘数愿海，成就普贤所有大愿。

"时，彼如来复为其女开示演说发心已来所集善根、所修妙行、所得大果，

The mind that contemplates the nature of all dharmas;
The mind that is established in the ocean of all Dharma gateways;
The mind that contemplates the ocean of all Dharma gateways;
The mind that completely knows the ocean of all beings;
The mind that rescues the ocean of all beings;
The mind that everywhere illuminates the ocean of all worlds;
The mind that everywhere makes the ocean of all buddhas' vows;
The mind that completely shatters the mountain of all obstacles;
The mind that accumulates the merit provision for the path to enlightenment;
The mind that directly observes the ten powers of the buddhas;
The mind that everywhere illuminates the bodhisattva's spheres of cognition;
The mind that increases the bodhisattva's provisions for the path to enlightenment; and
The mind that pervades the ocean of all directions.

She single-mindedly contemplated the great vows of Samantabhadra and then made an ocean of vows as numerous as the atoms in ten buddha *kṣetras*, vows that included:

I vow to purify all buddha *kṣetras;*
I vow to train all beings;
I vow to completely know the entire Dharma realm;
I vow to everywhere enter the entire ocean of the Dharma realm;
I vow to cultivate the bodhisattva practices in all buddha *kṣetras* to the very end of all future kalpas;
I vow to never abandon any of the bodhisattva practices even to the very end of all future kalpas;
I vow to be able to draw near to all *tathāgatas;*
I vow to be able to serve all good spiritual guides;
I vow to be able to make offerings to all buddhas; and
I vow that, in each successive mind-moment, I will incessantly cultivate the bodhisattva practices and progress toward all-knowledge.

So it was that she made an ocean of such vows as numerous as the atoms in ten buddha *kṣetras* and perfected all the great vows of Samantabhadra.

Then, for the sake of that maiden, the Tathāgata further revealed and expounded upon the roots of goodness he had accumulated, the marvelous practices he had cultivated, and the great stages of fruition he had acquired from the time when he made his initial resolve up until the present. So it was that he inspired her to establish the

正體字

令
382a22 其開悟成就如來所有願海。一心趣向一切
382a23 智位。善男子。復於此前。過十大劫。有世界。
382a24 名日輪光摩尼。佛號因陀羅幢妙相。此妙眼
382a25 女。於彼如來遺法之中。普賢菩薩。勸其修補
382a26 蓮華座上。故壞佛像。既修補已。而復彩畫。既
382a27 彩畫已。復寶莊嚴。發阿耨多羅三藐三菩提
382a28 心。善男子。我念過去。由普賢菩薩善知識故。
382a29 種此善根。從是已來。不墮惡趣。常於一切天
382b01 王人王種族中生。端正可喜。眾相圓滿。令
382b02 人樂見。常見於佛。常得親近普賢菩薩。乃
382b03 至於今。示導開悟。成熟於我。令生歡喜。善男
382b04 子。於意云何。爾時毘盧遮那藏妙寶蓮華髻
382b05 轉輪聖王者。豈異人乎。今彌勒菩薩是。時王
382b06 妃圓滿面者。寂靜音海夜神是。今所住處。去
382b07 此不遠。時妙德眼童女者。即我身是我於彼
382b08 時身為童女。普賢菩薩。勸我修補蓮華座像。
382b09 以為無上菩提因緣。令我發於阿耨多羅三
382b10 藐三菩提心。我於彼時。初始發心。次復引導。
382b11 令我得見妙德幢佛。解身瓔珞。散佛供養。見
382b12 佛神力。聞佛說法。即得菩薩普現一切世間
382b13 調伏眾生解脫門。於念念中。

简体字

令其开悟成就如来所有愿海，一心趣向一切智位。

“善男子，复于此前，过十大劫，有世界，名日轮光摩尼，佛号因陀罗幢妙相。此妙眼女，于彼如来遗法之中，普贤菩萨劝其修补莲华座上故坏佛像；既修补已而复彩画，既彩画已复宝庄严，发阿耨多罗三藐三菩提心。

“善男子，我念过去，由普贤菩萨善知识故，种此善根。从是已来，不堕恶趣，常于一切天王、人王种族中生，端正可喜，众相圆满，令人乐见，常见于佛，常得亲近普贤菩萨；乃至于今，示导开悟，成熟于我，令生欢喜。

“善男子，于意云何？尔时毗卢遮那藏妙宝莲华髻转轮圣王者，岂异人乎？今弥勒菩萨是。时王妃圆满面者，寂静音海夜神是，今所住处去此不远。时妙德眼童女者，即我身是。我于彼时，身为童女，普贤菩萨劝我修补莲华座像，以为无上菩提因缘，令我发于阿耨多罗三藐三菩提心。我于彼时，初始发心；次复引导，令我得见妙德幢佛，解身璎珞，散佛供养，见佛神力，闻佛说法，即得菩萨普现一切世间调伏众生解脱门。于念念中，

entire ocean of the Tathāgata's vows and single-mindedly progress toward the station of all-knowledge.

Son of Good Family, back another ten great kalpas before that time, there was a world known as Sunlight Maṇi Jewel in which there was a buddha named Marvelous Signs of Indra's Banner. This maiden, Marvelous Eyes, lived during the time when this buddha's Dharma legacy was still extant. At that time, Samantabhadra Bodhisattva encouraged her to repair a buddha image on a lotus throne that was damaged by age. Having repaired it, she then painted it and, having painted it, she also adorned it with jewels, whereupon she resolved to attain *anuttara-samyak-saṃbodhi*.

Son of Good Family, I recall that, in the past, it was due to Samantabhadra Bodhisattva's acting as a good spiritual guide that I planted these roots of goodness. From this point on, I never again fell into the wretched destinies. I was always reborn into the clans of all kinds of heavenly kings and human kings and was born so delightfully beautiful and perfectly well developed in all my features that this caused people to find me pleasing to behold. I always saw buddhas and was always able to draw near to Samantabhadra Bodhisattva so that, all the way up to the present time, he has guided, awakened, and ripened me, thereby causing me to be filled with joyous delight.

Son of Good Family, what do you think? Could that wheel-turning king known as Vairocana's Marvelous Jewel Lotus Topknot have been anyone else? He was none other than our present Maitreya Bodhisattva. As for that king's wife, Perfectly Full Countenance, she is the night spirit known as Sea of Serene Sounds who now lives not far from here.

That youthful maiden, Eyes of Marvelous Virtue was none other than myself. Then, when I had the body of a youthful maiden, Samantabhadra Bodhisattva encouraged me to repair that image seated on a lotus as a means of providing me with the causes and conditions for attaining unexcelled bodhi. He thereby caused me to resolve to attain *anuttara-samyak-saṃbodhi*.

It was at that very time that I first aroused the resolve. He next guided me onward and enabled me to see Banner of Marvelous Virtue Buddha. It was there that I unfastened my jeweled necklace, scattered its jewels over that Buddha as an offering to him, witnessed the Buddha's spiritual powers, heard the Buddha teach the Dharma, and then immediately acquired the bodhisattva's liberation gateway called "appearing everywhere in all worlds to train beings." In each successive mind-moment, I saw buddhas as

正體字

見須彌山微塵
382b14 數佛。亦見彼佛道場眾會清淨國土。我皆尊
382b15 重。恭敬供養。聽聞說法。依教修行。善男子。
382b16 過彼毘盧遮那大威德世界圓滿清淨劫已。
382b17 次有世界。名寶輪妙莊嚴。劫名大光。有五百
382b18 佛。於中出現。我皆承事恭敬供養。其最初佛。
382b19 名大悲幢。初出家時。我為夜神。恭敬供養。次
382b20 有佛出。名金剛那羅延幢。我為轉輪王。恭
382b21 敬供養。其佛為我。說修多羅。名一切佛出
382b22 現。十佛刹微塵數修多羅。以為眷屬。次有佛
382b23 出。名金剛無礙德。我於彼時。為轉輪王。恭敬
382b24 供養。其佛為我。說修多羅。名普照一切眾生
382b25 根。須彌山微塵數修多羅。而為眷屬。我皆受
382b26 持。次有佛出。名火焰山妙莊嚴。我於彼時。為
382b27 長者女。其佛為我。說修多羅。名普照三世藏。
382b28 閻浮提微塵數修多羅。而為眷屬。我皆聽聞。
382b29 如法受持。次有佛出。名一切法海高勝王。我
382c01 為阿脩羅王。恭敬供養。其佛為我。說修多羅。
382c02 名分別一切法界。五百修多羅。而為眷屬。我
382c03 皆聽聞。如法受持。次有佛出。名海嶽法光明。
382c04 我為龍王女。

简体字

见须弥山微尘数佛，亦见彼佛道场、众会、清净国土；我皆尊重，恭敬供养，听闻说法，依教修行。

“善男子，过彼毗卢遮那大威德世界圆满清净劫已，次有世界，名宝轮妙庄严，劫名大光，有五百佛于中出现，我皆承事恭敬供养。其最初佛，名大悲幢；初出家时，我为夜神，恭敬供养。次有佛出，名金刚那罗延幢；我为转轮王，恭敬供养；其佛为我说修多罗，名一切佛出现，十佛刹微尘数修多罗以为眷属。次有佛出，名金刚无碍德；我于彼时为转轮王，恭敬供养；其佛为我说修多罗，名普照一切众生根，须弥山微尘数修多罗而为眷属；我皆受持。次有佛出，名火焰山妙庄严；我于彼时为长者女；其佛为我说修多罗，名普照三世藏，阎浮提微尘数修多罗而为眷属；我皆听闻，如法受持。次有佛出，名一切法海高胜王；我为阿修罗王，恭敬供养；其佛为我说修多罗，名分别一切法界，五百修多罗而为眷属；我皆听闻，如法受持。次有佛出，名海岳法光明；我为龙王女，

numerous as the atoms in Mount Sumeru and also saw that buddha's site of enlightenment, his congregation, and his pure land. I revered them all, respectfully made offerings to them, listened to the Dharma teachings, and then relied on those teachings in my cultivation.

Son of Good Family, following upon that world known as Vairocana's Immense Awesome Virtue and that kalpa known as Perfectly Fulfilled Purity, there was next a world known as Marvelous Adornment of the Bejeweled Wheel and a kalpa known as Great Radiance in which five hundred buddhas appeared, all of whom I served and revered and presented with offerings.

The very first of those buddhas was known as Great Compassion Banner. When he first left the householder's life, I was a night spirit who respectfully presented offerings to him.

The next of those buddhas to appear was known as Vajra Nārāyaṇa Banner. I was then a wheel-turning king who respectfully made offerings to him. That buddha then taught a sutra for my sake that was known as The Manifestation of All Buddhas, one that had a retinue of sutras as numerous as the atoms in ten buddha *kṣetras*.

The next of those buddhas to appear was known as Unimpeded Vajra Virtue. At that time, I was a wheel-turning king who respectfully made offerings to him. That buddha then taught a sutra for my sake that was known as Universal Illumination of the Faculties of All Beings, one that had a retinue of sutras as numerous as the atoms in Mount Sumeru, all of which I received and retained.

The next of those buddhas to appear was known as Wondrous Adornment of the Mountain of Flaming Radiance. At that time, I was the daughter of an elder. That Buddha taught a sutra for my sake that was known as Universal Illumination of the Treasury of the Three Times, one that had a retinue of sutras as numerous as the atoms in Jambudvīpa. I listened to all of them and received and retained them in accordance with the Dharma.

The next of those buddhas to appear was known as Lofty and Supreme King of the Ocean of All Dharmas. At that time, I was an *asura* king who respectfully made offerings to him. That buddha then taught a sutra for my sake that was known as Distinguishing the Entire Dharma Realm, one that had a retinue of five hundred sutras. I listened to all of them and received and retained them in accordance with the Dharma.

The next of those buddhas to appear was known as Oceanic and Mountainous Light of Dharma. At that time, I was a dragon king's daughter who rained down clouds of wish-fulfilling *maṇi* jewels

正體字

雨如意摩尼寶雲。而為供養。其
382c05‖ 佛為我。說修多羅。名增長歡喜海。百萬億
382c06‖ 修多羅。而為眷屬。我皆聽聞。如法受持。次有
382c07‖ 佛出。名寶焰山燈。我為海神。雨寶蓮華雲。恭
382c08‖ 敬供養。其佛為我。說修多羅。名法界方便海
382c09‖ 光明佛剎微塵數修多羅。而為眷屬。我皆聽
382c10‖ 聞。如法受持次有佛出。名功德海光明輪。我
382c11‖ 於彼時為五通仙。現大神通六萬諸仙。前後
382c12‖ 圍遶。雨香華雲而為供養。其佛為我。說修
382c13‖ 多羅。名無著法燈。六萬修多羅。而為眷屬。我
382c14‖ 皆聽聞。如法受持。次有佛出。名毘盧遮那功
382c15‖ 德藏。我於彼時。為主地神。名出生平等義。與
382c16‖ 無量地神俱。雨一切寶樹。一切摩尼藏。一
382c17‖ 切寶瓔珞雲。而為供養。其佛為我。說修多羅。
382c18‖ 名出生一切如來智藏。無量修多羅。而為眷
382c19‖ 屬。我皆聽聞。受持不忘。善男子。如是次第。
382c20‖ 其最後佛。名充滿虛空法界妙德燈。我為[1]妓
382c21‖ 女。名曰美顏。見佛入城。歌舞供養。承佛神
382c22‖ 力。踊在空中。以千偈頌。讚歎於佛。佛為於
382c23‖ 我。放眉間光。名莊嚴法界大光明。遍觸我身。

简体字

雨如意摩尼宝云而为供养；其佛为我说修多罗，名增长欢喜海，百万亿修多罗而为眷属；我皆听闻，如法受持。次有佛出，名宝焰山灯；我为海神，雨宝莲华云恭敬供养；其佛为我说修多罗，名法界方便海光明，佛刹微尘数修多罗而为眷属；我皆听闻，如法受持。次有佛出，名功德海光明轮；我于彼时为五通仙，现大神通，六万诸仙前后围绕，雨香华云而为供养；其佛为我说修多罗，名无著法灯，六万修多罗而为眷属；我皆听闻，如法受持。次有佛出，名毗卢遮那功德藏；我于彼时，为主地神，名出生平等义，与无量地神俱，雨一切宝树、一切摩尼藏、一切宝璎珞云而为供养；其佛为我说修多罗，名出生一切如来智藏，无量修多罗而为眷属；我皆听闻，受持不忘。善男子，如是次第，其最后佛，名充满虚空法界妙德灯；我为妓女，名曰美颜，见佛入城，歌舞供养；承佛神力，踊在空中，以千偈颂赞叹于佛；佛为于我，放眉间光，名庄严法界大光明，遍触我身；

as offerings to him. That buddha then taught a sutra for my sake that was known as Increasing the Ocean of Joyous Delight, one that had a retinue of a hundred myriads of *koṭīs* of sutras. I listened to all of them and received and retained them in accordance with the Dharma.

The next of those buddhas to appear was known as Lamp of the Mountain of Jewels' Flaming Radiance. At that time, I was an ocean spirit who rained down clouds of jeweled lotus flowers that I respectfully presented to him as offerings. That buddha then taught a sutra for my sake that was known as Light of the Dharma Realm's Ocean of Skillful Means, one that had a retinue of sutras as numerous as the atoms in a buddha *kṣetra.* I listened to all of them and received and retained them in accordance with the Dharma.

The next of those buddhas to appear was known as Radiant Sphere of the Ocean of Meritorious Qualities. At that time, I was a rishi possessed of the five superknowledges who manifested great spiritual superknowledges and was surrounded by six myriads of rishis. I rained down clouds of incense and flowers as offerings to him. That buddha then taught a sutra for my sake that was known as Lamp of the Dharma of Nonattachment, one that had a retinue of sixty thousand sutras. I listened to all of them and then received and retained them in accordance with the Dharma.

The next of those buddhas to appear was known as Treasury of Vairocana's Meritorious Qualities. At that time, I was an earth spirit named Originator of the Meaning of Impartiality, one who was attended by a community of countless other earth spirits. I rained down clouds of all kinds of jewel trees, all kinds of *maṇi* jewel treasuries, and all kinds of jeweled necklaces as offerings to him. That buddha then taught a sutra for my sake that was known as Bringing Forth the Treasury of All Tathāgatas' Wisdom, one that had a retinue of countless sutras. I listened to all of them and received and retained them in accordance with the Dharma.

Son of Good Family, so it was that they sequentially appeared in this way. The very last of those buddhas was named Lamp of Marvelous Virtue Filling the Empty Space of the Dharma Realm. At that time, I was a female performer named Lovely Countenance who, on seeing that buddha enter the city, sang and danced as an offering to him and then, through the aid of that buddha's spiritual powers, ascended into the air and spoke a thousand verses in praise of the Buddha. Then, for my sake, that buddha emanated a light from between his brows known as Grand Radiance Adorning the Dharma Realm that touched my entire body. After I was illuminated

正體字

382c24║ 我蒙光已。即得解脫門。名法界方便不退藏。
382c25║ 善男子。此世界中。有如是等佛剎微塵數劫。
382c26║ 一切如來。於中出現。我皆承事。恭敬供養。彼
382c27║ 諸如來。所說正法。我皆憶念。乃至不忘一文
382c28║ 一句。於彼一一諸如來所。稱揚讚歎一切佛
382c29║ 法。為無量眾生。廣作利益。於彼一一諸如
383a01║ 來所。得一切智光明。現三世法界海。入一切
383a02║ 普賢行。善男子。我依一切智光明故於念念
383a03║ 中。見無量佛。既見佛已。先所未得。先所未
383a04║ 見。普賢諸行。悉得成滿。何以故。以得一切智
383a05║ 光明故。爾時普救眾生夜神欲重明此解脫
383a06║ 義。承佛神力。為善財童子。而說頌言
383a07║ 善財聽我說 甚深難見法
383a08║ 普照於三世 一切差別門
383a09║ 如我初發心 專求佛功德
383a10║ 所入諸解脫 汝今應諦聽
383a11║ 我念過去世 過剎微塵劫
383a12║ 次前有一劫 名圓滿清淨
383a13║ 是時有世界 名為遍照燈
383a14║ 須彌塵數佛 於中出興世

简体字

我蒙光已，即得解脱门，名法界方便不退藏。

“善男子，此世界中，有如是等佛刹微尘数劫，一切如来于中出现；我皆承事，恭敬供养；彼诸如来所说正法，我皆忆念，乃至不忘一文一句。于彼一一诸如来所，称扬赞叹一切佛法，为无量众生广作利益；于彼一一诸如来所，得一切智光明，现三世法界海，入一切普贤行。

“善男子，我依一切智光明故，于念念中见无量佛；既见佛已，先所未得、先所未见普贤诸行，悉得成满。何以故？以得一切智光明故。”

尔时，普救众生夜神，欲重明此解脱义，承佛神力，为善财童子而说颂言：

“善财听我说，甚深难见法，
普照于三世，一切差别门。
如我初发心，专求佛功德，
所入诸解脱，汝今应谛听。
我念过去世，过刹微尘劫，
次前有一劫，名圆满清净。
是时有世界，名为遍照灯，
须弥尘数佛，于中出兴世：

by this light, I immediately acquired a liberation gateway known as Undiminishing Treasury of the Dharma Realm's Expedients.

Son of Good Family, this world had kalpas such as these as numerous as the atoms in a buddha *kṣetra* in all of which *tathāgatas* appeared. I served them all and respectfully presented offerings to them. I so well recall and bear in mind all of the right Dharma proclaimed by all those *tathāgatas* that I never forgot so much as one passage or one sentence of it.

I proclaimed the praises of the Dharma of all buddhas in the abodes of every one of those *tathāgatas* and extensively benefited countless beings there. In the abodes of every one of those *tathāgatas,* I acquired the light of all-knowledge, revealed the ocean of the Dharma realm throughout all three periods of time, and entered all of Samantabhadra's practices.

Son of Good Family, relying on the light of all-knowledge, I saw countless buddhas in each successive mind-moment. Then, having seen those buddhas, I was able to fulfill the practices of Samantabhadra to an extent I had never before achieved and had never before witnessed. And why did this occur? This was due to having acquired the light of all-knowledge.

At that time, wishing to restate and clarify the meaning of this liberation, aided by the Buddha's spiritual powers, the Night Spirit, Universal Rescuer of Beings, then spoke these verses for Sudhana the Youth:

Sudhana, listen to me as I speak
of the extremely profound and difficult to perceive Dharma
that everywhere illuminates all three periods of time
and all of its different gateways.

You should now listen closely as I describe
how, from the time of my initial resolve,
I single-mindedly sought the Buddha's meritorious qualities.
Listen, too, as I tell you of the liberations that I entered.

I recall that in the past, back beyond kalpas
as numerous as the atoms in a *kṣetra,*
there was a kalpa just before that
known as Perfectly Fulfilled Purity.

At that time, there was a world
known as Universally Illuminating Lamp
in which the buddhas who appeared in the world
were as numerous as Mount Sumeru's atoms.

正體字

383a15 | 初佛名智焰　次佛名法幢
383a16 | 第三法須彌　第四德師子
383a17 | 第五寂靜王　第六滅諸見
383a18 | 第七高名稱　第八大功德
383a19 | 第九名勝日　第十名月面
383a20 | 於此十佛所　最初悟法門
383a21 | 從此後次第　復有十佛出
383a22 | 初名虛空處　第二名普光
383a23 | 三名住諸方　四名正念海
383a24 | 五名高勝光　六名須彌雲
383a25 | 七名法焰佛　八名山勝佛
383a26 | 九名大悲華　十名法界華
383a27 | 此十出現時　第二悟法門
383a28 | 從此後次第　復有十佛出
383a29 | 第一光幢佛　第二智慧佛
383b01 | 第三心義佛　第四德主佛
383b02 | 第五天慧佛　第六慧王佛
383b03 | 第七勝智佛　第八光王佛
383b04 | 第九勇猛佛　第十蓮華佛
383b05 | 於此十佛所　第三悟法門

简体字

初佛名智焰，次佛名法幢，
第三法须弥，第四德师子，
第五寂静王，第六灭诸见，
第七高名称，第八大功德，
第九名胜日，第十名月面。
于此十佛所，最初悟法门。
从此后次第，复有十佛出：
初名虚空处，第二名普光，
三名住诸方，四名正念海，
五名高胜光，六名须弥云，
七名法焰佛，八名山胜佛，
九名大悲华，十名法界华。
此十出现时，第二悟法门。
从此后次第，复有十佛出：
第一光幢佛，第二智慧佛，
第三心义佛，第四德主佛，
第五天慧佛，第六慧王佛，
第七胜智佛，第八光王佛，
第九勇猛佛，第十莲华佛。
于此十佛所，第三悟法门。

The first Buddha was named Wisdom's Flaming Radiance.
The next buddha was named Dharma Banner.
The third was Dharma Sumeru,
and the fourth was Lion of Virtue.

The fifth was Quiescence King,
the sixth was Destroyer of Views,
the seventh was Lofty Fame,
and the eighth was Great Meritorious Qualities.

The ninth was Supreme Sun,
and the tenth was named Lunar Countenance.
It was under these ten buddhas
that I first awakened to the Dharma gateways.

From that point forward, there came the sequential
appearance of yet another ten buddhas.
The first was named Abiding in Space,
the second was named Universal Radiance,

the third was named Abiding in all Regions,
the fourth was named Sea of Right Mindfulness,
the fifth was named Lofty and Supreme Radiance,
the sixth was named Sumeru Cloud,

the seventh was named Flaming Radiance of Dharma Buddha,
the eighth was named Mountain Supremacy Buddha,
the ninth was named Great Compassion Flower,
and the tenth was named Dharma Realm Flower.

It was when these ten appeared,
that I experienced my second awakening to the Dharma gateways.
From that point forward, there came the sequential
appearance of yet another ten buddhas

of whom the first was Radiance Banner Buddha.
The second was Wisdom Buddha,
the third was Mind Meaning Buddha,
the fourth was Virtue Ruler Buddha,

the fifth was Celestial Wisdom Buddha,
the sixth was Wisdom King Buddha,
the seventh was Supreme Wisdom Buddha,
the eighth was Light King Buddha,

the ninth was Heroic Bravery Buddha,
and the tenth was Lotus Flower Buddha.
It was under those ten buddhas
that I had my third awakening to the Dharma gateways.

正體字

383b06 ‖ 從此後次第　復有十佛出
383b07 ‖ 第一寶焰山　第二功德海
383b08 ‖ 第三法光明　第四蓮華藏
383b09 ‖ 第五眾生眼　第六香光寶
383b10 ‖ 七須彌功德　八乾闥婆王
383b11 ‖ 第九摩尼藏　第十寂靜色
383b12 ‖ 從此後次第　復有十佛出
383b13 ‖ 初佛廣大智　次佛寶光明
383b14 ‖ 第三虛空雲　第四殊勝相
383b15 ‖ 第五圓滿戒　第六那羅延
383b16 ‖ 第七須彌德　第八功德輪
383b17 ‖ 第九無勝幢　第十大樹山
383b18 ‖ 從此後次第　復有十佛出
383b19 ‖ 第一[1]娑羅藏　第二世主身
383b20 ‖ 第三高顯光　第四金剛照
383b21 ‖ 第五地威力　第六甚深法
383b22 ‖ 第七法慧音　第八須彌幢
383b23 ‖ 第九勝光明　第十妙寶光
383b24 ‖ 從此後次第　復有十佛出
383b25 ‖ 第一梵光明　第二虛空音

简体字

从此后次第，复有十佛出：
第一宝焰山，第二功德海，
第三法光明，第四莲华藏，
第五众生眼，第六香光宝，
七须弥功德，八乾闼婆王，
第九摩尼藏，第十寂静色。
从此后次第，复有十佛出：
初佛广大智，次佛宝光明，
第三虚空云，第四殊胜相，
第五圆满戒，第六那罗延，
第七须弥德，第八功德轮，
第九无胜幢，第十大树山。
从此后次第，复有十佛出：
第一娑罗藏，第二世主身，
第三高显光，第四金刚照，
第五地威力，第六甚深法，
第七法慧音，第八须弥幢，
第九胜光明，第十妙宝光。
从此后次第，复有十佛出：
第一梵光明，第二虚空音，

From that point forward, there then came the sequential
appearance of yet another ten buddhas.
The first was Mountain of Flaming Radiance Jewels,
the second was Sea of Meritorious Qualities,

the third was Dharma Radiance,
the fourth was Lotus Flower Treasury,
the fifth was Eye of Beings,
the sixth was Jewel of Incense Radiance,

the seventh was Sumeru of Meritorious Qualities,
the eighth was Gandharva King,
the ninth was Maṇi Treasury,
and the tenth was Quiescent Form.

From that point forward, there came the sequential
appearance of yet another ten buddhas.
The first buddha was Vast Wisdom,
the next buddha was Jewel Light,

The third was Space Cloud,
the fourth was Excellent Signs,
the fifth was Perfect Moral Precepts,
the sixth was Nārāyaṇa,

the seventh was Sumeru Qualities,
the eighth was Sphere of Meritorious Qualities,
the ninth was Invincible Banner,
and the tenth was Great Tree Mountain.

From that point forward, there came the sequential
appearance of yet another ten buddhas.
The first was Śāla Treasury,
the second was World Leader's Body,

the third was Light Appearing on High,
the fourth was Vajra Illumination
the fifth was Awesome Earthly Powers,
the sixth was Extremely Profound Dharma,

the seventh was Dharma Wisdom Sound,
the eighth was Sumeru Banner,
the ninth was Victorious Radiance,
and the tenth was Marvelous Jewel Light.

From that point forward, there came the sequential
appearance of yet another ten buddhas.
The first was Brahman Radiance,
the second was Empty Space Sound,

正體字

383b26 第三法界身　第四光明輪
383b27 第五智慧幢　第六虛空燈
383b28 第七微妙德　第八遍照光
383b29 第九勝福光　第十大悲雲
383c01 從此後次第　復有十佛出
383c02 第一力光慧　第二普現前
383c03 第三高顯光　第四光明身
383c04 第五法起佛　第六寶相佛
383c05 第七速疾風　第八勇猛幢
383c06 第九妙寶蓋　第十照三世
383c07 從此後次第　復有十佛出
383c08 第一願海光　第二金剛身
383c09 第三須彌德　第四念幢王
383c10 第五功德慧　第六智慧燈
383c11 第七光明幢　第八廣大智
383c12 第九法界智　第十法海智
383c13 從此後次第　復有十佛出
383c14 初名布施法　次名功德輪
383c15 三名勝妙雲　四名忍智燈
383c16 五名寂靜音　六名寂靜幢

简体字

第三法界身，第四光明轮，
第五智慧幢，第六虚空灯，
第七微妙德，第八遍照光，
第九胜福光，第十大悲云。
从此后次第，复有十佛出：
第一力光慧，第二普现前，
第三高显光，第四光明身，
第五法起佛，第六宝相佛，
第七速疾风，第八勇猛幢，
第九妙宝盖，第十照三世。
从此后次第，复有十佛出：
第一愿海光，第二金刚身，
第三须弥德，第四念幢王，
第五功德慧，第六智慧灯，
第七光明幢，第八广大智，
第九法界智，第十法海智。
从此后次第，复有十佛出：
初名布施法，次名功德轮，
三名胜妙云，四名忍智灯，
五名寂静音，六名寂静幢，

the third was Dharma Realm Body,
the fourth was Radiant Sphere,
the fifth was Wisdom Banner,
the sixth was Empty Space Lamp,

the seventh was Subtle Virtue,
the eighth was Universally Illuminating Radiance,
the ninth was Light of Supreme Merit,
and the tenth was Great Compassion Cloud.

From that point forward, there came the sequential
appearance of yet another ten buddhas.
The first was Power Light Wisdom,
the second was Universal Direct Appearance,

the third was Radiance Appearing on High,
the fourth was Radiant Body,
the fifth was Dharma Generation Buddha,
the sixth was Bejeweled Signs Buddha,

the seventh was Swift Wind,
the eighth was Banner of Courage,
the ninth was Marvelous Jewel Canopy,
and the tenth was Illuminating the Three Times.

From that point forward, there came the sequential
appearance of yet another ten buddhas.
The first was Light of an Ocean of Vows,
the second was Vajra Body,

the third was Sumeru Virtue,
the fourth was Mindfulness Banner King,
the fifth was Meritorious Qualities Wisdom,
the sixth was Wisdom Lamp,

the seventh was Radiant Banner,
the eighth was Vast Wisdom,
the ninth was Dharma Realm Wisdom,
and the tenth was Dharma Ocean Wisdom.

From that point forward, there came the sequential
appearance of yet another ten buddhas.
The first was named Giving Dharma.
The next was named Sphere of Meritorious Qualities,

the third was named Supremely Marvelous Cloud,
the fourth was named Lamp of Patience and Wisdom,
the fifth was named Quiescent Sound,
the sixth was named Banner of Quiescence,

正體字

383c17 七名世間燈　八名深大願
383c18 九名無勝幢　十名智焰海
383c19 從此後次第　復有十佛出
383c20 初佛法自在　二佛無礙慧
383c21 三名意海慧　四名[2]眾妙音
383c22 五名自在施　六名普現前
383c23 七名隨樂身　八名住勝德
383c24 第九本性佛　第十賢德佛
383c25 須彌塵數劫　此中所有佛
383c26 普作世間燈　我悉曾供養
383c27 佛剎微塵劫　所有佛出現
383c28 我皆曾供養　入此解脫門
383c29 我於無量劫　修行得此道
384a01 汝若能修行　不久亦當得
384a02 善男子。我唯知此菩薩普現一切世間調伏
384a03 眾生解脫。如諸菩薩摩訶薩。集無邊行。生種
384a04 種解。現種種身。具種種根。滿種種願。入種種
384a05 三昧。起種種神變。能種種觀察法。

简体字

七名世间灯，八名深大愿，
九名无胜幢，十名智焰海。
从此后次第，复有十佛出：
初佛法自在，二佛无碍慧，
三名意海慧，四名众妙音，
五名自在施，六名普现前，
七名随乐身，八名住胜德，
第九本性佛，第十贤德佛。
须弥尘数劫，此中所有佛，
普作世间灯，我悉曾供养。
佛刹微尘劫，所有佛出现，
我皆曾供养，入此解脱门。
我于无量劫，修行得此道；
汝若能修行，不久亦当得。

“善男子，我唯知此菩萨普现一切世间调伏众生解脱。如诸菩萨摩诃萨，集无边行，生种种解，现种种身，具种种根，满种种愿，入种种三昧，起种种神变，能种种观察法，

the seventh was named World Lamp,
the eighth was named Profound Great Vows,
the ninth was named Invincible Banner,
and the tenth was named Ocean of Fiery Wisdom.

From that point forward, there came the sequential
appearance of yet another ten buddhas.
The first buddha was Sovereign Mastery of Dharma,
the second buddha was Unimpeded Wisdom,

the third was named Mind Sea's Wisdom,
the fourth was named Manifold Marvelous Sounds,
the fifth was named Freely Bestowed Giving,
the sixth was named Universal Present Manifestation,

the seventh was named Body Adapted to Dispositions,
the eighth was named Abiding in Supreme Virtue,
the ninth was Original Nature Buddha,
and the tenth was Worthy Virtue Buddha.

I have presented offerings
to all of these buddhas who appeared
throughout kalpas as numerous as Sumeru's atoms
and everywhere served as lamps for the world,

For kalpas as numerous as a buddha *kṣetra*'s atoms,
when all of those buddhas appeared,
I made offerings to them all
and then entered this gateway of liberation.

It was across the course of countless kalpas
that I cultivated and achieved success in this path.
If you are able to pursue such cultivation,
then, before long, you too will succeed in this.

Son of Good Family, I know only this bodhisattva's liberation by which one appears everywhere in all worlds to train beings.

As for the bodhisattva-mahāsattvas:

Who have accumulated countless practices;
Who have developed many different kinds of understandings;
Who have manifested many different kinds of bodies;
Who have perfected many different kinds of faculties;
Who have fulfilled many different kinds of vows;
Who have entered many different kinds of samādhis;
Who have produced many different kinds of spiritual transformations;
Who have been able to master many different methods of contemplation;

正體字

入種種智
384a06║ 慧門。得種種法光明。而我云何能知能說彼
384a07║ 功德行。善男子。去此不遠。有主夜神。名寂靜
384a08║ 音海。坐摩尼光幢莊嚴蓮華座。百萬阿僧祇
384a09║ 主夜神。前後圍遶。汝詣彼問。菩薩云何學菩
384a10║ 薩行。修菩薩道。時善財童子。頂禮其足。遶
384a11║ 無數匝。殷懃瞻仰。辭退而去
384a15║ 大方廣佛華嚴經卷[1]第七十一
384a18║ 入法界品第三十九之十二
384a19║ 爾時善財童子。於普救眾生妙德夜神所。聞
384a20║ 菩薩普現一切世間調伏眾生解脫門。了知
384a21║ 信解。自在安住。而往寂靜音海夜神所。頂禮
384a22║ 其足。遶無數匝。於前合掌。而作是言。聖者。
384a23║ 我已先發阿耨多羅三藐三菩提心。我欲依
384a24║ 善知識。學菩薩行。入菩薩行。修菩薩行。住菩
384a25║ 薩行。唯願慈哀。為我宣說。菩薩云何學菩薩
384a26║ 行。云何修菩薩道。時彼夜神。告善財言。善哉
384a27║ 善哉。善男子。汝能依善知識。求菩薩行。善男
384a28║ 子。我得菩薩念念出生廣大喜莊嚴解脫門。
384a29║ 善財言。大聖。此解脫門。為何事業。

简体字

入种种智慧门，得种种法光明；而我云何能知能说彼功德行？

“善男子，去此不远，有主夜神，名寂静音海，坐摩尼光幢庄严莲华座，百万阿僧祇主夜神前后围绕。汝诣彼问：菩萨云何学菩萨行、修菩萨道？”

时，善财童子顶礼其足，绕无数匝，殷勤瞻仰，辞退而去。

大方广佛华严经卷第七十一

入法界品第三十九之十二

尔时，善财童子于普救众生妙德夜神所，闻菩萨普现一切世间调伏众生解脱门，了知信解，自在安住；而往寂静音海夜神所，顶礼其足，绕无数匝，于前合掌而作是言：“圣者，我已先发阿耨多罗三藐三菩提心，我欲依善知识，学菩萨行，入菩萨行，修菩萨行，住菩萨行。唯愿慈哀，为我宣说：菩萨云何学菩萨行？云何修菩萨道？”

时，彼夜神告善财言：“善哉！善哉！善男子，汝能依善知识求菩萨行。善男子，我得菩萨念念出生广大喜庄严解脱门。”

善财言：“大圣，此解脱门为何事业？

Who have entered many different kinds of wisdom gateways; and
Who have acquired the light of many different kinds of dharmas—

How could I know of or be able to speak about their meritorious qualities and practices?

Son of Good Family, not far from here, there is a night spirit by the name of Sea of Serene Sounds who sits on a lotus flower throne adorned by *maṇi* jewel radiance banners and is surrounded by a following of hundreds of myriads of *asaṃkhyeyas* of night spirits. You should go there, pay your respects, and ask, "How should the bodhisattva train in the bodhisattva practices and how should he cultivate the bodhisattva path?"

Sudhana the Youth then bowed down in reverence at her feet and circumambulated her countless times as he gazed up at her in attentive admiration. He then respectfully withdrew and departed.

35 – Praśāntarutasāgaravatī

At that time, after Sudhana the Youth had heard from the night spirit Samantasattvatrāṇojaḥśrī the explanation of the bodhisattva's liberation gateway called "appearing everywhere in all worlds to train beings," he completely comprehended it, developed resolute faith in it, and established himself in it with sovereign mastery. He then went to the night spirit known as Praśāntarutasāgaravatī or "Sea of Serene Sounds," where he bowed down in reverence at her feet and circumambulated her countless times after which he stood before her with palms pressed together, and addressed her, saying:

O Āryā, I am one who has already resolved to attain *anuttara-samyaksaṃbodhi*. I wish to rely on the good spiritual guides as I train in the bodhisattva practices, enter the bodhisattva practices, cultivate the bodhisattva practices, and abide in the bodhisattva practices. Please bestow your deep kindness on me and teach me how the bodhisattva should train in the bodhisattva practices and how he should cultivate the bodhisattva path.

That night spirit then told Sudhana, "It is good indeed, good indeed, Son of Good Family, that you are able to rely on the good spiritual guides as you seek to acquire the bodhisattva practices. Son of Good Family, I have acquired the bodhisattva's 'liberation that produces the adornment of vast joy in every mind-moment.'"

Sudhana then asked, "O Great Āryā, what sort of endeavors constitute the practice of this liberation gateway? What is its realm of

正體字

行何境
384b01║ 界。起何方便。作何觀察。夜神言。善男子。我
384b02║ 發起清淨平等樂欲心。我發起離一切世間塵
384b03║ 垢清淨堅固莊嚴不可壞樂欲心。我發起攀
384b04║ 緣不退轉位永不退轉心。我發起莊嚴功德
384b05║ 寶山不動心。我發起無住處心。我發起普現
384b06║ 一切眾生前救護心。我發起見一切佛海無
384b07║ 厭足心。我發起求一切菩薩清淨願力心。我
384b08║ 發起住大智光明海心。我發起令一切眾生
384b09║ 超過憂惱曠野心。我發起令一切眾生捨離
384b10║ 愁憂苦惱心。我發起令一切眾生捨離不可
384b11║ 意色聲香味觸法心。我發起令一切眾生捨
384b12║ 離愛別離苦[5]怨憎會苦心。我發起令一切眾
384b13║ 生捨離惡緣愚癡等苦心。我發起與一切險
384b14║ 難眾生作依怙心。我發起令一切眾生出生
384b15║ 死苦處心。我發起令一切眾生捨離生老病
384b16║ 死等苦心。我發起令一切眾生成就如來無
384b17║ 上法樂心。我發起令一切眾生皆受喜樂心。
384b18║ 發是心已。復為說法。令其漸至一切智地。所
384b19║ 謂

简体字

行何境界？起何方便？作何观察？”

夜神言：“善男子，我发起清净平等乐欲心，我发起离一切世间尘垢清净坚固庄严不可坏乐欲心，我发起攀缘不退转位永不退转心，我发起庄严功德宝山不动心，我发起无住处心，我发起普现一切众生前救护心，我发起见一切佛海无厌足心，我发起求一切菩萨清净愿力心，我发起住大智光明海心，我发起令一切众生超过忧恼旷野心，我发起令一切众生舍离愁忧苦恼心，我发起令一切众生舍离不可意色、声、香、味、触、法心，我发起令一切众生舍离爱别离苦、冤憎会苦心，我发起令一切众生舍离恶缘、愚痴等苦心，我发起与一切险难众生作依怙心，我发起令一切众生出生死苦处心，我发起令一切众生舍离生、老、病、死等苦心，我发起令一切众生成就如来无上法乐心，我发起令一切众生皆受喜乐心。

“发是心已，复为说法，令其渐至一切智地。所谓：

practice? Which skillful means does one produce in this practice? And in which kinds of contemplations does one engage?"

The Night Spirit replied:

Son of Good Family:

I have produced a pure and impartial aspiring resolve;

I have produced an indestructible aspiring resolve adorned with steadfast purity to abandon the world's defilements;

I have produced an irreversible resolve to reach the station of irreversibility;

I have produced an unshakable resolve to create a mountain of the adorning jewels of the meritorious qualities;

I have resolved to have no place in which I abide;

I have resolved to appear everywhere before all beings to rescue them;

I have produced the insatiable resolve to see the ocean of all buddhas;

I have resolved to seek the power of all bodhisattvas' pure vows;

I have resolved to abide in the ocean of the light of great wisdom;

I have resolved to enable all beings to step beyond the desolate wilderness of sorrow and afflictions;

I have resolved to enable all beings to leave behind the suffering and torment of sorrows and worries;

I have resolved to enable all beings to abandon disagreeable forms, sounds, smells, tastes, touchables, and dharmas;

I have resolved to enable all beings to abandon the suffering of separation from what is loved and the suffering of encountering what one detests;

I have resolved to enable all beings to abandon the sufferings arising from evil conditions, delusion, and so forth;

I have resolved to become a refuge for all beings beset with dangers and difficulties;

I have resolved to enable all beings to escape from the stations of existence beset by the sufferings of *saṃsāra*;

I have resolved to enable all beings to abandon the sufferings of birth, aging, sickness, death, and so forth;

I have resolved to enable all beings to perfect the Tathāgata's unexcelled Dharma bliss; and

I have resolved to enable all beings to experience joy and bliss.

Having produced these types of resolve, I then also teach the Dharma for their benefit and enable them to gradually reach the ground of all-knowledge, doing so in ways such as these:

正體字

若見眾生。樂著所住宮殿屋宅。我為說法。
384b20 令其了達諸法自性。離諸執著。若見眾生戀
384b21 著父母兄弟姊妹。我為說法。令其得預諸佛
384b22 菩薩清淨眾會。若見眾生戀著妻子。我為說
384b23 法。令其捨離生死愛染。起大悲心。於一切
384b24 眾生。平等無二。若見眾生住於王宮。[6]采女
384b25 侍奉。我為說法。令其得與眾聖集會。入如來
384b26 教。若見眾生染著境界。我為說法。令其得入
384b27 如來境界。若見眾生多瞋恚者。我為說法。令
384b28 住如來忍波羅蜜。若見眾生其心懈怠。我為
384b29 說法。令得清淨精進波羅蜜。若見眾生其心
384c01 散亂。我為說法。令得如來禪波羅蜜。若見眾
384c02 生入見稠林無明暗障。我為說法。令得出離
384c03 稠林黑暗。若見眾生無智慧者。我為說法。令
384c04 得般若波羅蜜。若見眾生染著三界。我為說
384c05 法。令出生死。若見眾生志意下劣。我為說法。
384c06 令其圓滿佛菩提願。若見眾生住自利行。我
384c07 為說法。令其發起利益一切諸眾生願。若見
384c08 眾生志力微弱。我為說法。令得菩薩力波羅
384c09 蜜。若見眾生愚癡闇心。我為說法。令得菩薩
384c10 智波羅蜜。

简体字

若见众生乐著所住宫殿、屋宅，我为说法，令其了达诸法自性，离诸执著；若见众生恋著父母、兄弟、姊妹，我为说法，令其得预诸佛菩萨清净众会；若见众生恋著妻子，我为说法，令其舍离生死爱染，起大悲心，于一切众生平等无二；若见众生住于王宫，采女侍奉，我为说法，令其得与众圣集会，入如来教；若见众生染著境界，我为说法，令其得入如来境界；若见众生多瞋恚者，我为说法，令住如来忍波罗蜜；若见众生其心懈怠，我为说法，令得清净精进波罗蜜；若见众生其心散乱，我为说法，令得如来禅波罗蜜；若见众生入见稠林无明暗障，我为说法，令得出离稠林黑暗；若见众生无智慧者，我为说法，令得般若波罗蜜；若见众生染著三界，我为说法，令出生死；若见众生志意下劣，我为说法，令其圆满佛菩提愿；若见众生住自利行，我为说法，令其发起利益一切诸众生愿；若见众生志力微弱，我为说法，令得菩萨力波罗蜜；若见众生愚痴暗心，我为说法，令得菩萨智波罗蜜；

If I see beings blissfully attached to the palaces or residences in which they dwell, I teach the Dharma for them to enable them to fully comprehend the inherent nature of dharmas and thus abandon their attachments;

If I see beings dotingly attached to parents, brothers, or sisters, I teach the Dharma for them to enable them to join the pure congregations of buddhas and bodhisattvas;

If I see beings affectionately attached to wives and sons, I teach the Dharma for them to enable them to abandon the craving and defilement of *saṃsāra* and develop the mind of great compassion and impartial, non-discriminating regard for all beings;

If I see beings abiding in royal palaces where they are served by female attendants, I teach the Dharma for them to enable them to gather together with the community of *āryas* and penetrate the Tathāgata's teachings;

If I see beings with defiling attachments to the sense realms, I teach the Dharma for them to enable them to enter the realm of the Tathāgata;

If I see beings much inclined to anger, I teach the Dharma for them to enable them to abide in the Tathāgata's *pāramitā* of patience;

If I see beings with indolent minds, I teach the Dharma for them to enable them to purify the *pāramitā* of vigor;

If I see beings with scattered minds, I teach the Dharma for them to enable them to acquire the Tathāgata's *dhyāna pāramitā;*

If I see beings who have entered the dense forest of views and the darkness of ignorance, I teach the Dharma for them to enable them to gain emancipation from that dense forest and darkness;

If I see beings who have no wisdom, I teach the Dharma for them to enable them to acquire the *prajñāpāramitā;*

If I see beings who have developed a defiling attachment for the three realms of existence, I teach the Dharma for them to enable them to escape from *saṃsāra;*

If I see beings with inferior aspirations, I teach the Dharma for them to enable them to fulfill the vow to attain the Buddha's bodhi;

If I see beings who are devoted to self-benefiting actions, I teach the Dharma for them to enable them to vow to benefit all beings;

If I see beings possessed of only weak will power, I teach the Dharma for them to enable them to acquire the bodhisattva's *pāramitā* of the powers;

If I see beings with minds overshadowed by the darkness of delusion, I teach the Dharma for them to enable them to acquire the bodhisattva's *pāramitā* of knowledge;

正體字

若見眾生色相不具。我為說法。令
384c11║ 得如來清淨色身。若見眾生形容醜陋。我為
384c12║ 說法。令得無上清淨法身。若見眾生色相麤
384c13║ 惡。我為說法令得如來微妙色身。若見眾生
384c14║ 情多憂惱。我為說法。令得如來畢竟安樂。若
384c15║ 見眾生貧窮所苦。我為說法。令得菩薩功德
384c16║ 寶藏。若見眾生住止園林。我為說法。令彼
384c17║ 勤求佛法因緣。若見眾生行於道路。我為說
384c18║ 法。令其趣向一切智道。若見眾生在聚落中。
384c19║ 我為說法。令出三界。若見眾生住止人間。我
384c20║ 為說法。令其超越二乘之道。住如來地。若見
384c21║ 眾生居住城廓。我為說法。令其得住法王城
384c22║ 中若見眾生住於四隅。我為說法。令得三世
384c23║ 平等智慧。若見眾生住於諸方。我為說法。令
384c24║ 得智慧見一切法。若見眾生貪行多者。我為
384c25║ 彼說不淨觀門。令其捨離生死愛染。若見眾
384c26║ 生瞋行多者。我為彼說大慈觀門。令其得入
384c27║ 勤加修習。若見眾生癡行多者。我為說法。令
384c28║ 得明智觀諸法海。

简体字

若见众生色相不具，我为说法，令得如来清净色身；若见众生形容丑陋，我为说法，令得无上清净法身；若见众生色相粗恶，我为说法，令得如来微妙色身；若见众生情多忧恼，我为说法，令得如来毕竟安乐；若见众生贫穷所苦，我为说法，令得菩萨功德宝藏；若见众生住止园林，我为说法，令彼勤求佛法因缘；若见众生行于道路，我为说法，令其趣向一切智道；若见众生在聚落中，我为说法，令出三界；若见众生住止人间，我为说法，令其超越二乘之道，住如来地；若见众生居住城郭，我为说法，令其得住法王城中；若见众生住于四隅，我为说法，令得三世平等智慧；若见众生住于诸方，我为说法，令得智慧见一切法；若见众生贪行多者，我为彼说不净观门，令其舍离生死爱染；若见众生瞋行多者，我为彼说大慈观门，令其得入勤加修习；若见众生痴行多者，我为说法，令得明智观诸法海；

If I see beings whose physical features are imperfect, I teach the Dharma for them to enable them to acquire the Tathāgata's pure form body;

If I see beings whose appearance is ugly, I teach the Dharma for them to enable them to acquire the unexcelled pure Dharma body;

If I see beings whose physical form and features are coarse and loathsome, I teach the Dharma for them to enable them to acquire the Tathāgata's subtle form body;

If I see beings beset by much sorrow and affliction, I teach the Dharma for them to enable them to acquire the Tathāgata's ultimate bliss;

If I see beings experiencing the sufferings of poverty, I teach the Dharma for them to enable them to acquire the jewel treasury of the bodhisattva's meritorious qualities;

If I see beings who dwell in parks and forests, I teach the Dharma for them to enable them to acquire the causes and conditions for diligently seeking the Buddha's Dharma;

If I see beings traveling along a road, I teach the Dharma for them to enable them to travel along the road to all-knowledge;

If I see beings dwelling in villages, I teach the Dharma for them to enable them to escape from the three realms of existence;

If I see beings dwelling among people, I teach the Dharma for them to enable them to step beyond the paths of the two vehicles and then dwell on the ground of the Tathāgata;

If I see beings dwelling within the walls of the city, I teach the Dharma for them to enable them to dwell in the city of the Dharma King;

If I see beings abiding in the four quarters, I teach the Dharma for them to enable them to acquire the wisdom that equally knows all three periods of time;

If I see beings abiding in all the other directions, I teach the Dharma for them to enable them to acquire the wisdom that perceives all dharmas;

If I see beings with a predominantly lustful temperament, I teach them the gateway of the unloveliness contemplation to enable them to abandon the craving and defilement of *saṃsāra;*

If I see beings with a predominantly hateful temperament, I teach them the gateway of the great kindness contemplation to enable them to enter it and diligently cultivate it;

If I see beings with a predominantly deluded temperament, I teach the Dharma for them to enable them to acquire bright wisdom with which to contemplate the ocean of all dharmas;

正體字

若見眾生等分行者。我為
384c29║ 說法。令其得入諸乘願海。若見眾生樂生死
385a01║ 樂。我為說法。令其厭離。若見眾生厭生死苦。
385a02║ 應為如來所化度者。我為說法。令能方便示
385a03║ 現受生。若見眾生愛著五蘊。我為說法。令其
385a04║ 得住無依境界。若見眾生其心下劣。我為顯
385a05║ 示勝莊嚴道。若見眾生心生憍慢。我為其說
385a06║ 平等法忍。若見眾生其心諂曲。我為其說菩
385a07║ 薩直心。善男子。我以此等無量法施。攝諸眾
385a08║ 生。種種方便。教化調伏。令離惡道受人天樂。
385a09║ 脫三界縛住一切智。我時便得廣大歡喜法
385a10║ 光明海。其心怡暢。安隱適悅。復次善男子。我
385a11║ 常觀察一切菩薩道場眾會。修種種願行。現
385a12║ 種種淨身。有種種常光。放種種光明。以種種
385a13║ 方便。入一切智門。入種種三昧。現種種神變。
385a14║ 出種種音聲海。具種種莊嚴身。入種種如來
385a15║ 門。詣種種國土海。

简体字

若见众生等分行者，我为说法，令其得入诸乘愿海；若见众生乐生死乐，我为说法，令其厌离；若见众生厌生死苦，应为如来所化度者，我为说法，令能方便示现受生；若见众生爱著五蕴，我为说法，令其得住无依境界；若见众生其心下劣，我为显示胜庄严道；若见众生心生憍慢，我为其说平等法忍；若见众生其心谄曲，我为其说菩萨直心。善男子，我以此等无量法施摄诸众生，种种方便教化调伏，令离恶道，受人天乐，脱三界缚，住一切智；我时便得广大欢喜法光明海，其心怡畅，安隐适悦。

“复次，善男子，我常观察一切菩萨道场众会，修种种愿行，现种种净身，有种种常光，放种种光明；以种种方便，入一切智门，入种种三昧，现种种神变，出种种音声海，具种种庄严身，入种种如来门，诣种种国土海，

If I see beings who are equally subject to all of these afflictions, I teach the Dharma for them to enable them to succeed in entering the ocean of all vehicles' vows;

If I see beings who delight in the pleasures of *saṃsāra,* I teach the Dharma for them to enable them to develop renunciation;

If I see beings who have come to detest the sufferings of *saṃsāra* who should be taught and liberated by a *tathāgata,* I teach the Dharma for them to enable them to expediently manifest as taking on births;

If I see beings who have become attached to the five aggregates, I teach the Dharma for them to enable them to be able to dwell in the sphere of non-dependence;

If I see beings whose minds are inferior, I show them the path of supreme adornments;

If I see beings who have developed arrogant minds, I teach them the patience that acquiesces in the equality of dharmas; and

If I see beings whose minds have become inclined toward flattery and deceptiveness, I teach them about the straightforward mind of a bodhisattva.

Son of Good Family, I use countless types of Dharma giving such as these to attract beings. Then I use many different kinds of skillful means to teach and train them and enable them to part from the wretched destinies, enjoy the bliss of humans and devas, become liberated from the bonds of the three realms of existence, and abide in all-knowledge. I then acquire a vast ocean of joyous delight in the light of Dharma in which my mind feels elated, at peace, and pleased.

Furthermore, Son of Good Family, I always contemplate the congregations of all bodhisattvas:

Who cultivate the many different kinds of vows and practices;

Who manifest many different kinds of pure bodies;

Who have many different kinds of auras;

Who emanate many different kinds of light;

Who use many different kinds of skillful means;

Who enter the gateways to all-knowledge;

Who enter many different kinds of samādhis;

Who manifest many different kinds of spiritual transformations;

Who send forth oceans of many different kinds of sounds;

Who possess many different kinds of adorned bodies;

Who enter the many different kinds of gateways of the Tathāgata;

Who go to pay their respects in the oceans of the many different kinds of lands;

正體字

見種種諸佛海。得種種辯
385a16║ 才海。照種種解脫境。得種種智光海。入種種
385a17║ 三昧海。遊戲種種諸解脫門。以種種門趣一
385a18║ 切智。種種莊嚴。虛空法界。以種種莊嚴雲遍
385a19║ 覆虛空。觀察種種道場眾會。集種種世界。入
385a20║ 種種佛剎。詣種種方海。受種種如來命。從種
385a21║ 種如來所。與種種菩薩俱。雨種種莊嚴雲。入
385a22║ 如來種種方便。觀如來種種法海。入種種智
385a23║ 慧海。坐種種莊嚴座。善男子。我觀察此道場
385a24║ 眾會。知佛神力無量無邊。生大歡喜。善男子。
385a25║ 我觀毘盧遮那如來念念出現不可思議清淨
385a26║ 色身。既見是已。生大歡喜。又觀如來於念
385a27║ 念中放大光明充滿法界。既見是已。生大歡
385a28║ 喜。

简体字

见种种诸佛海，得种种辩才海，照种种解脱境，得种种智光海，入种种三昧海，游戏种种诸解脱门，以种种门趣一切智，种种庄严虚空法界，以种种庄严云遍覆虚空，观察种种道场众会，集种种世界，入种种佛刹，诣种种方海，受种种如来命，从种种如来所，与种种菩萨俱，雨种种庄严云，入如来种种方便，观如来种种法海，入种种智慧海，坐种种庄严座。善男子，我观察此道场众会，知佛神力无量无边，生大欢喜。

“善男子，我观毗卢遮那如来，念念出现不可思议清净色身；既见是已，生大欢喜。又观如来于念念中，放大光明充满法界；既见是已，生大欢喜。

Who see oceans of many different buddhas;
Who acquire oceans of the many different kinds of eloquence;
Who illuminate the realms of the many different kinds of liberations;
Who acquire oceans of the many different kinds of wisdom light;
Who enter oceans of the many different kinds of samādhis;
Who demonstrate easeful mastery of the many different kinds of liberation gateways;
Who use the many different kinds of gateways to progress toward all-knowledge;
Who adorn empty space and the Dharma realm with many different kinds of adornments;
Who everywhere cover empty space with many different kinds of adornment clouds;
Who contemplate the many different kinds of congregations;
Who gather together in the many different kinds of worlds;
Who enter the many different kinds of buddha *kṣetras;*
Who visit the ocean of many different kinds of regions;
Who take on the many different kinds of directives issued by the Tathāgata;
Who go forth from the presence of the many different *tathāgatas;*
Who come together with the many different kinds of bodhisattvas;
Who rain down the many different kinds of clouds of adornments;
Who enter the many different kinds of skillful means of the Tathāgata;
Who contemplate the ocean of the Tathāgata's many different kinds of dharmas;
Who enter the ocean of many different kinds of wisdom; and
Who sit on thrones graced with many different kinds of adornments.

Son of Good Family, as I contemplate these congregations, realizing that the Buddha has countlessly and boundlessly many spiritual powers, I am filled with immense joyous delight.

Son of Good Family, as I contemplate Vairocana Tathāgata manifesting inconceivably many pure form bodies in each successive mind-moment, having seen this, I am filled with immense joyous delight.

Also, as I contemplate the Tathāgata emanating in each successive mind-moment light that completely fills the Dharma realm, having seen this, I am filled with immense joyous delight.

正體字

又見如來一一毛孔。念念出現無量佛刹
385a29 微塵數光明海。一一光明。以無量佛刹微塵
385b01 數光明。而為眷屬。一一周遍一切法界。消滅
385b02 一切諸眾生苦。既見是已。生大歡喜。又善男
385b03 子。我觀如來頂及兩肩。念念出現一切佛刹
385b04 微塵數寶焰山雲。充滿十方一切法界。既見
385b05 是已。生大歡喜。又善男子。我觀如來一一毛
385b06 孔。於念念中。出一切佛刹微塵數香光明雲。
385b07 充滿十方一切佛刹。既見是已。生大歡喜。又
385b08 善男子。我觀如來一一相。念念出一切佛刹
385b09 微塵數諸相莊嚴如來身雲。遍往十方一切
385b10 世界。既見是已。生大歡喜。又善男子。我觀如
385b11 來一一毛孔。於念念中出不可說佛刹微塵
385b12 數佛變化雲。示現如來從初發心修波羅蜜
385b13 具莊嚴道入菩薩地。既見是已。生大歡喜。又
385b14 善男子。我觀如來一一毛孔。念念出現不可
385b15 說不可說佛刹微塵數天王身雲。及以天王
385b16 自在神變。充遍一切十方法界。

简体字

又见如来一一毛孔，念念出现无量佛刹微尘数光明海，一一光明以无量佛刹微尘数光明而为眷属，一一周遍一切法界，消灭一切诸众生苦；既见是已，生大欢喜。又，善男子，我观如来顶及两肩，念念出现一切佛刹微尘数宝焰山云，充满十方一切法界；既见是已，生大欢喜。又，善男子，我观如来一一毛孔，于念念中，出一切佛刹微尘数香光明云，充满十方一切佛刹；既见是已，生大欢喜。又，善男子，我观如来一一相，念念出一切佛刹微尘数诸相庄严如来身云，遍往十方一切世界；既见是已，生大欢喜。又，善男子，我观如来一一毛孔，于念念中，出不可说佛刹微尘数佛变化云，示现如来从初发心、修波罗蜜、具庄严道、入菩萨地；既见是已，生大欢喜。又，善男子，我观如来一一毛孔，念念出现不可说不可说佛刹微尘数天王身云，及以天王自在神变，充遍一切十方法界，

Moreover, as I see the Tathāgata manifesting in each successive mind-moment from every one of his pores an ocean of light rays as numerous as the atoms in countless buddha *kṣetras,* I see that every light ray has a retinue of light rays as numerous as the atoms in countless buddha *kṣetras* and every one of them in turn everywhere pervades the entire Dharma realm where they put an end to the sufferings of all beings. Having seen this, I am filled with immense joyous delight.

Again, Son of Good Family, as I contemplate the crown of the Tathāgata's head and his two shoulders sending forth in each successive mind-moment clouds of mountains of flaming-radiance jewels as numerous as the atoms in all buddha *kṣetras* that fill the ten directions of the Dharma realm, having seen this, I am filled with immense joyous delight.

Also, Son of Good Family, as I contemplate every pore of the Tathāgata sending forth in each successive mind-moment clouds of fragrant radiance as numerous as the atoms in all buddha *kṣetras* that fill all the buddha *kṣetras* of the ten directions, having seen this, I am filled with immense joyous delight.

Moreover, Son of Good Family, as I contemplate every one of the Tathāgata's [major] marks sending forth in each successive mind-moment clouds of *tathāgata* bodies adorned with the marks as numerous as the atoms in all buddha *kṣetras* that then go everywhere throughout all worlds of the ten directions, having seen this, I am filled with immense joyous delight.

Again, Son of Good Family, as I contemplate every one of the Tathāgata's pores sending forth in each successive mind-moment clouds of buddhas' transformations as numerous as the atoms in an ineffable number of buddha *kṣetras* in which these clouds reveal the events occurring from the time of the initial resolve on through to the cultivation of the *pāramitās,* the complete acquisition of the path of adornments, and the entry into the bodhisattva grounds, having seen this, I am filled with immense joyous delight.

Also, Son of Good Family, as I contemplate every pore of the Tathāgata manifesting in each successive mind-moment clouds of the bodies of heavenly kings as well as the miraculous transformations created by those heavenly kings that are as numerous as the atoms in an ineffable number of buddha *kṣetras,* and as I contemplate their complete pervasion of the ten directions of the Dharma realm, their immediate appearance directly before those who should achieve liberation through encountering the body of a heavenly

正體字

應以天王身
385b17‖ 而得度者。即現其前。而為說法。既見是已。生
385b18‖ 大歡喜。如天王身雲。其龍王夜叉王。乾闥婆
385b19‖ 王。阿脩羅王。迦樓羅王。緊那羅王。摩睺羅伽
385b20‖ 王。人王梵王身雲。莫不皆於一一毛孔如是
385b21‖ 出現如是說法。我見是已。於念念中。生大歡
385b22‖ 喜。生大信樂。量與法界薩婆若等。昔所未得
385b23‖ 而今始得。昔所未證而今始證。昔所未入而
385b24‖ 今始入。昔所未滿而今始滿。昔所未見而今
385b25‖ 始見。昔所未聞而今始聞。何以故。以能了知
385b26‖ 法界相故。知一切法唯一相故。能平等入三
385b27‖ 世道故。能說一切無邊法故。善男子。我入此
385b28‖ 菩薩念念出生廣大喜莊嚴解脫光明海。又
385b29‖ 善男子。此解脫無邊。普入一切法界門故。此
385c01‖ 解脫無盡。等發一切智性心故。此解脫無際。
385c02‖ 入無際畔一切眾生心想中故。此解脫甚深。
385c03‖ 寂靜智慧所知境故。此解脫廣大周遍一切
385c04‖ 如來境故。此解脫無壞。菩薩智眼之所知故。
385c05‖ 此解脫無底。盡於法界之源底故。此解脫者
385c06‖ 即是普門。於一事中。普見一切諸神變故。

简体字

应以天王身而得度者，即现其前而为说法；既见是已，生大欢喜。如天王身云，其龙王、夜叉王、乾闼婆王、阿修罗王、迦楼罗王、紧那罗王、摩睺罗伽王、人王、梵王身云，莫不皆于一一毛孔，如是出现，如是说法；我见是已，于念念中，生大欢喜，生大信乐，量与法界萨婆若等。昔所未得而今始得，昔所未证而今始证，昔所未入而今始入，昔所未满而今始满，昔所未见而今始见，昔所未闻而今始闻。何以故？以能了知法界相故，知一切法唯一相故，能平等入三世道故，能说一切无边法故。

“善男子，我入此菩萨念念出生广大喜庄严解脱光明海。又，善男子，此解脱无边，普入一切法界门故；此解脱无尽，等发一切智性心故；此解脱无际，入无际畔一切众生心想中故；此解脱甚深，寂静智慧所知境故；此解脱广大，周遍一切如来境故；此解脱无坏，菩萨智眼之所知故；此解脱无底，尽于法界之源底故。此解脱者即是普门，于一事中普见一切诸神变故；

king, and their subsequent teaching of the Dharma for their sakes—having seen this, I am filled with immense joyous delight.

And just as this is so with the clouds of the bodies of heavenly kings, so too is this so with clouds of transformation bodies appearing as dragon kings, *yakṣa* kings, *gandharva* kings, *asura* kings, *garuḍa* kings, *kiṃnara* kings, *mahoraga* kings, human kings, and brahma heaven kings, all of which are sent forth from every pore in this same way whereupon they manifest just such teaching of Dharma as this. Having seen this, in each successive mind-moment, I am filled with immense joyous delight and am filled with immense faith and bliss are are commensurate with the Dharma realm and all-knowledge.

So it was that, whatever was not gained in the past is now gained, whatever realizations were not achieved in the past are now realized, whatever had not been penetrated in the past is now penetrated, whatever had not been fulfilled in the past is now fulfilled, whatever had not been seen in the past is now seen, and whatever was never heard in the past is now heard.

And why is this so? This is due to being able to completely know the signs of the Dharma realm, due to realizing that all dharmas are of but one sign, due to being able to equally enter the paths of the three periods of time, and due to being able to teach all of the boundless dharmas.

Son of Good Family, I have entered the ocean of light of the bodhisattva's "liberation that produces the adornment of vast joy in every mind-moment." Further, Son of Good Family:

This liberation is boundless, for it enters all gateways into the Dharma realm;

This liberation is inexhaustible, for it is commensurate with the mind that resolves to attain all-knowledge;

This liberation has no boundaries, for it enters the boundless realm of the thoughts in all beings' minds;

This liberation is extremely profound, for it is the objective domain known by quiescent wisdom;

This liberation is vast, for it pervades the objective domain of all *tathāgatas*;

This liberation is indestructible, for it is what is cognized by the bodhisattva's wisdom eye;

This liberation is bottomless, for it reaches all the way to the very source of the Dharma realm;

This liberation is just the universal gateway for, in but a single phenomenon, one sees all spiritual transformations everywhere;

正體字

此
385c07║ 解脫者終不可取。一切法身等無二故。此解
385c08║ 脫者終無有[1]生。以能了知如幻法故。此解脫
385c09║ 者猶如影像。一切智願光所生故。此解脫者
385c10║ 猶如變化。化生菩薩諸勝行故。此解脫者猶
385c11║ 如大地。為一切眾生。所依處故。此解脫者猶
385c12║ 如大水。能以大悲潤一切故。此解脫者猶如
385c13║ 大火。乾竭眾生貪愛水故。此解脫者猶如大
385c14║ 風。令諸眾生速疾趣於一切智故。此解脫者
385c15║ 猶如大海。種種功德莊嚴一切諸眾生故。此
385c16║ 解脫者如須彌山。出一切智法寶海故。此解
385c17║ 脫者如大城廓。一切妙法所莊嚴故。此解脫
385c18║ 者猶如虛空。普容三世佛神力故。此解脫者
385c19║ 猶如大雲。普為眾生雨法雨故。此解脫者猶
385c20║ 如淨日。能破眾生無知暗故。此解脫者猶如
385c21║ 滿月。滿足廣大福德海故。此解脫者猶如真
385c22║ 如。悉能周遍一切處故。此解脫者猶如自影。
385c23║ 從自善業所化出故。此解脫者猶如呼響。隨
385c24║ 其所應為說法故。此解脫者猶如影像。隨眾
385c25║ 生心而照現故。此解脫者如大樹王。開敷一
385c26║ 切神通華故。此解脫者猶如金剛。從本已來
385c27║ 不可壞故。

简体字

此解脱者终不可取，一切法身等无二故；此解脱者终无有生，以能了知如幻法故；此解脱者犹如影像，一切智愿光所生故；此解脱者犹如变化，化生菩萨诸胜行故；此解脱者犹如大地，为一切众生所依处故；此解脱者犹如大水，能以大悲润一切故；此解脱者犹如大火，干竭众生贪爱水故；此解脱者犹如大风，令诸众生速疾趣于一切智故；此解脱者犹如大海，种种功德庄严一切诸众生故；此解脱者如须弥山，出一切智法宝海故；此解脱者如大城郭，一切妙法所庄严故；此解脱者犹如虚空，普容三世佛神力故；此解脱者犹如大云，普为众生雨法雨故；此解脱者犹如净日，能破众生无知暗故；此解脱者犹如满月，满足广大福德海故；此解脱者犹如真如，悉能周遍一切处故；此解脱者犹如自影，从自善业所化出故；此解脱者犹如呼响，随其所应为说法故；此解脱者犹如影像，随众生心而照现故；此解脱者如大树王，开敷一切神通华故；此解脱者犹如金刚，从本已来不可坏故；

This liberation can never be grasped, for it is identical with and no different from the entire Dharma body;
This liberation is ultimately unproduced, for it is able to completely know all dharmas as like magical conjurations;
This liberation is like a reflected image, for it is produced by the light of the vow to attain all-knowledge;
This liberation is comparable to a supernatural transformation, for it transformationally produces all of the bodhisattva's supreme practices;
This liberation is like the great earth, for it is the place upon which all beings can rely;
This liberation is like a great flood, for it is able to moisten everyone with the waters of the great compassion;
This liberation is like an immense fire, for it is able to dry up the waters of beings' desires;
This liberation is like a great wind, for it enables all beings to swiftly progress toward all-knowledge;
This liberation is comparable to a great ocean, for its many different meritorious qualities adorn all beings;
This liberation is like Mount Sumeru, for it produces an ocean of the Dharma jewels of all-knowledge;
This liberation is like the ramparts of a great city, for it is adorned with all sublime dharmas;
This liberation is like empty space, for it completely includes the spiritual powers of all buddhas of the three periods of time;
This liberation is like a great cloud, for it everywhere rains down the Dharma rain for the sake of beings;
This liberation is like a brightly shining sun, for it is able to dispel the darkness of beings' ignorance;
This liberation is like a full moon, for it completely fills up the ocean of vast merit;
This liberation is like true suchness, for it is able to completely pervade all places;
This liberation is like one's own shadow, for it is transformationally produced from one's own good karmic works;
This liberation is like an echo, for it adapts to what is fitting for beings when speaking Dharma for them;
This liberation is like a reflected image, for its illumination appears in accordance with the minds of beings;
This liberation is like a great king of trees, for it blossoms with the flowers of the spiritual superknowledges;
This liberation is like vajra for, from its origin up to the present, it has remained indestructible;

正體字

此解脫者如如意珠。出生無量自
385c28‖ 在力故。此解脫者如離垢藏。摩尼寶王示現
385c29‖ 一切三世如來諸神力故。此解脫者如喜幢
386a01‖ 摩尼寶。能平等出一切諸佛法輪聲故。善男
386a02‖ 子。我今為汝。說此譬[1]諭。汝應思惟。隨順悟
386a03‖ 入。爾時善財童子。白寂靜音海夜神言。大聖。
386a04‖ 云何修行。得此解脫。夜神言。善男子。菩薩修
386a05‖ 行十大法藏。得此解脫。何等為十。一修布施
386a06‖ 廣大法藏。隨眾生心悉令滿足。二修淨戒廣
386a07‖ 大法藏。普入一切佛功德海。三修堪忍廣大
386a08‖ 法藏。能遍思惟一切法性。四修精進廣大法
386a09‖ 藏。趣一切智恒不退轉。五修禪定廣大法藏。
386a10‖ 能滅一切眾生熱惱。六修般若廣大法藏。能
386a11‖ 遍了知一切法海。七修方便廣大法藏。能遍
386a12‖ 成熟諸眾生海。八修諸願廣大法藏。遍一切
386a13‖ 佛刹一切[2]諸眾生海盡未來劫修菩薩行。

简体字

此解脱者如如意珠，出生无量自在力故；此解脱者如离垢藏，摩尼宝王示现一切三世如来诸神力故；此解脱者如喜幢摩尼宝，能平等出一切诸佛法轮声故。善男子，我今为汝说此譬喻，汝应思惟，随顺悟入。”

尔时，善财童子白寂静音海夜神言：“大圣，云何修行，得此解脱？”

夜神言：“善男子，菩萨修行十大法藏，得此解脱。何等为十？一修布施广大法藏，随众生心悉令满足；二修净戒广大法藏，普入一切佛功德海；三修堪忍广大法藏，能遍思惟一切法性；四修精进广大法藏，趣一切智恒不退转；五修禅定广大法藏，能灭一切众生热恼；六修般若广大法藏，能遍了知一切法海；七修方便广大法藏，能遍成熟诸众生海；八修诸愿广大法藏，遍一切佛刹、一切众生海，尽未来劫修菩萨行；

This liberation is like a wish-fulfilling jewel, for it produces supernatural powers;

This liberation is like a sovereign immaculate-core *maṇi* jewel, for it reveals the spiritual powers of all *tathāgatas* of the three periods of time; and

This liberation is like a banner-of-joyfulness *maṇi* jewel, for it is able to impartially bestow the sounds of all buddhas turning the wheel of the Dharma.

Son of Good Family, you should meditate on these analogies I have just taught you and thus achieve awakened entry in accordance with them.

Sudhana the Youth then addressed the Night Spirit, Praśāntarutasāgaravatī, saying, "O Great Āryā, how does one go about cultivating and acquiring this liberation?"

The Night Spirit replied:

Son of Good Family, it is through the practice of ten great Dharma treasuries that a bodhisattva acquires this liberation. What then are those ten? They are as follows:

First, it is through cultivating the vast Dharma treasury of giving that, adapting to beings' mental dispositions, one is able to satisfy them all;

Second, it is through cultivating the vast Dharma treasury of purity in the moral precepts that one everywhere enters the ocean of all buddhas' meritorious qualities;

Third, it is through cultivating the vast Dharma treasury of patience that one is able to everywhere contemplate the nature of all dharmas;

Fourth, it is through cultivating the vast Dharma treasury of vigor that one becomes irreversible in progressing toward all-knowledge;

Fifth, it is through cultivating the vast Dharma treasury of *dhyāna* absorption that one is able to extinguish the fever of all beings' afflictions;

Sixth, it is through cultivating the vast Dharma treasury of *prajñā* that one is everywhere able to know the ocean of all dharmas;

Seventh, it is through cultivating the vast Dharma treasury of skillful means that one is everywhere able to ripen the ocean of all beings;

Eighth, it is through cultivating the vast Dharma treasury of vows that, to the very end of all future kalpas, one cultivates the bodhisattva practices throughout all buddha *kṣetras* and everywhere in the ocean of all beings;

正體字

九
386a14 修諸力廣大法藏。念念現於一切法界海一
386a15 切佛國土成等正覺常不休息。十修淨智廣
386a16 大法藏。得如來智遍知三世一切諸法無有
386a17 障礙。善男子。若諸菩薩。安住如是十大法藏。
386a18 則能獲得如是解脫。清淨增長積集堅固。安
386a19 住圓滿。善財童子言。聖者。汝發阿耨多羅三
386a20 藐三菩提心。其已久如。夜神言。善男子。此華
386a21 藏莊嚴世界海東。過十世界海。有世界海。名
386a22 一切淨光寶。此世界海中。有世界種。名一
386a23 切如來願光明音。中有世界。名清淨光金莊
386a24 嚴。一切香金剛摩尼王為體。形如樓閣。眾妙
386a25 寶雲。以為其際。住於一切寶[3]瓔珞海。妙宮
386a26 殿雲。而覆其上。淨穢相雜。此世界中。乃往古
386a27 世。有劫名普光幢。國名普滿妙藏。道場名一
386a28 切寶藏妙月光明。有佛名不退轉法界音。於
386a29 此成阿耨多羅三藐三菩提。我於爾時。作菩
386b01 提樹神。名具足福德燈光明幢。守護道場。我
386b02 見彼佛成等正覺。示現神力。發阿耨多羅三
386b03 藐三菩提心。即於此時。獲得三昧。名普照如
386b04 來功德海。此道場中。次有如來。出興於世。

简体字

九修诸力广大法藏，念念现于一切法界海、一切佛国土，成等正觉常不休息；十修净智广大法藏，得如来智，遍知三世一切诸法无有障碍。善男子，若诸菩萨安住如是十大法藏，则能获得如是解脱，清净增长，积集坚固，安住圆满。”

善财童子言：“圣者，汝发阿耨多罗三藐三菩提心，其已久如？”

夜神言：“善男子，此华藏庄严世界海东，过十世界海，有世界海，名一切净光宝；此世界海中，有世界种，名一切如来愿光明音；中有世界，名清净光金庄严，一切香金刚摩尼王为体，形如楼阁，众妙宝云以为其际，住于一切宝璎珞海，妙宫殿云而覆其上，净秽相杂。

“此世界中，乃往古世，有劫名普光幢，国名普满妙藏，道场名一切宝藏妙月光明，有佛名不退转法界音，于此成阿耨多罗三藐三菩提；我于尔时，作菩提树神，名具足福德灯光明幢，守护道场；我见彼佛成等正觉、示现神力、发阿耨多罗三藐三菩提心，即于此时，获得三昧，名普照如来功德海。此道场中，次有如来出兴于世，

Ninth, it is through cultivating the vast Dharma treasury of the powers that, in each successive mind-moment, one appears in all buddha lands throughout the ocean of the Dharma realm, never resting as one everywhere attains the universal and right enlightenment; and

Tenth, it is through cultivating the vast Dharma treasury of pure knowledge that one acquires the Tathāgata's knowledge that pervasively and unimpededly knows all dharmas of the three periods of time.

Son of Good Family, if bodhisattvas establish themselves in the ten Dharma treasuries such as these, then they will be able to acquire liberations such as these and then purify them, increase them, accumulate them, strengthen them, secure them, and fulfill them.

Sudhana the Youth then asked, "O Āryā, how long has it now been since you first resolved to attain *anuttara-samyak-saṃbodhi*?"

The Night Spirit replied:

Son of Good Family, east of this Lotus Dais Adornment ocean of worlds, beyond ten oceans of worlds, there is an ocean of worlds known as Radiant Jewel of Complete Purity. In this ocean of worlds, there is a world system known as Light and Sound of All Tathāgatas' Vows in which there is a particular world known as Adorned with Pure Golden Light the substance of which is composed of all kinds of incense, vajra, and sovereign *maṇi* jewels. It is shaped like a tower, has boundaries consisting of clouds of the many kinds of marvelous jewels, and dwells on an ocean of all kinds of jeweled necklaces. It is sheltered by a cloud of exquisite palaces and is characterized by the blending of both pure and defiled aspects.

In this world, long ago in the ancient past, there was a kalpa known as Universal Light Banner in which there was a country known as Universally Full Treasury of Marvels. It had a site of enlightenment known as Marvelous Moonlight of the Treasury of All Jewels in which a buddha named Voice of the Irreversibly Turning Wheel of Dharma attained *anuttara-samyak-saṃbodhi*.

At that time, I was a bodhi tree spirit named Banner of Perfectly Fulfilled Merit Lamplight who guarded that site of enlightenment. I witnessed that buddha's realization of the universal and right enlightenment and his manifestation of the spiritual powers, whereupon I resolved to attain *anuttara-samyak-saṃbodhi*. I then immediately acquired a samādhi known as "universal illumination of the Tathāgata's ocean of meritorious qualities."

In this very site of enlightenment, the next *tathāgata* to appear in the world was named Tree of Dharma and Mountain of Awesome

正體字

名
386b05‖ 法樹威德山。我時命終。還生此中。為道場
386b06‖ 主夜神。名殊妙福智光。見彼如來轉正法輪。
386b07‖ 現大神通。即得三昧。名普照一切離貪境界。
386b08‖ 次有如來。出興於世。名一切法海音聲王。我
386b09‖ 於彼時。身為夜神。因得見佛承事供養。即獲
386b10‖ 三昧。名生長一切善法地。次有如來。出興於
386b11‖ 世。名寶光明燈幢王。我於彼時。身為夜神。因
386b12‖ 得見佛。承事供養。即獲三昧。名普現神通光
386b13‖ 明雲。次有如來。出興於世。名功德須彌光。我
386b14‖ 於彼時。身為夜神。因得見佛。承事供養。即獲
386b15‖ 三昧。名普照諸佛海。次有如來。出興於世。名
386b16‖ 法雲音聲王。我於彼時。身為夜神。因得見佛。
386b17‖ 承事供養。即獲三昧。名一切法海燈。次有如
386b18‖ 來。出興於世。名智燈照[4]耀王。我於彼時。身
386b19‖ 為夜神。因得見佛。承事供養。即獲三昧。名滅
386b20‖ 一切眾生苦清淨光明燈。次有如來。出興於
386b21‖ 世。名法勇妙德幢。我於彼時。身為夜神。因得
386b22‖ 見佛。承事供養。即獲三昧。名三世如來光明
386b23‖ 藏。次有如來。出興於世。名師子勇猛法智燈。
386b24‖ 我於彼時。身為夜神。因得見佛。承事供養。即
386b25‖ 獲三昧。名一切世間無障礙智慧輪。

简体字

名法树威德山；我时命终，还生此中，为道场主夜神，名殊妙福智光，见彼如来转正法轮、现大神通，即得三昧，名普照一切离贪境界。次有如来出兴于世，名一切法海音声王；我于彼时，身为夜神，因得见佛承事供养，即获三昧，名生长一切善法地。次有如来出兴于世，名宝光明灯幢王；我于彼时，身为夜神，因得见佛承事供养，即获三昧，名普现神通光明云。次有如来，出兴于世，名功德须弥光；我于彼时，身为夜神，因得见佛承事供养，即获三昧，名普照诸佛海。次有如来出兴于世，名法云音声王；我于彼时，身为夜神，因得见佛承事供养，即获三昧，名一切法海灯。次有如来出兴于世，名智灯照耀王；我于彼时，身为夜神，因得见佛承事供养，即获三昧，名灭一切众生苦清净光明灯。次有如来出兴于世，名法勇妙德幢；我于彼时，身为夜神，因得见佛承事供养，即获三昧，名三世如来光明藏。次有如来出兴于世，名师子勇猛法智灯；我于彼时，身为夜神，因得见佛承事供养，即获三昧，名一切世间无障碍智慧轮。

Virtue. My life then came to an end, whereupon I returned to be born there as a *bodhimaṇḍa* night spirit named Especially Marvelous Light of Merit and Wisdom. I saw that *tathāgata* turning the wheel of right Dharma and manifesting the great spiritual superknowledges, whereupon I acquired a samādhi known as "universal illumination of all spheres of dispassion."

Next, there was a *tathāgata* who appeared in the world who was named King of the Voice of the Ocean of All Dharmas. At that time, I was a night spirit who, due to seeing that Buddha, serving him, and making offerings to him, then acquired a samādhi known as "the ground that grows all good dharmas."

Next, there was a *tathāgata* who appeared in the world who was named Jewel Light Lamp Banner King. At that time, I was a night spirit who, due to seeing that buddha, serving him, and making offerings to him, then acquired a samādhi known as "universal manifestation of radiant clouds of spiritual superknowledges."

Next, there was a *tathāgata* who appeared in the world who was named Light of a Sumeru of Meritorious Qualities. At that time, I was a night spirit who, due to seeing that buddha, serving him, and making offerings to him, then acquired a samādhi known as "universal illumination of the ocean of all buddhas."

Next, there was a *tathāgata* who appeared in the world who was named Dharma Cloud Sound King. At that time, I was a night spirit who, due to seeing that buddha, serving him, and making offerings to him, then acquired a samādhi known as "lamp of the ocean of all dharmas."

Next, there was a *tathāgata* who appeared in the world who was named Dazzling Illumination of the Wisdom Lamp King. At that time, I was a night spirit who, due to seeing that buddha, serving him, and making offerings to him, then acquired a samādhi known as "lamp of pure light that extinguishes the sufferings of all beings."

Next, there was a *tathāgata* who appeared in the world who was named "Dharma Bravery's Banner of Marvelous Virtue." At that time, I was a night spirit who, due to seeing that buddha, serving him, and making offerings to him, then acquired a samādhi known as "treasury of the light of all tathāgatas of the three periods of time."

Next, there was a *tathāgata* who appeared in the world who was named Lion Bravery's Dharma Wisdom Lamp. At that time, I was a night spirit who, due to seeing that buddha, serving him, and making offerings to him, then acquired a samādhi known as "the wheel of unimpeded wisdom of all worlds."

正體字

次有如
386b26 來。出興於世。名智力山王。我於彼時。身為夜
386b27 神。因得見佛。承事供養。即獲三昧。名普照三
386b28 世眾生諸根行。善男子。清淨光金莊嚴世界。
386b29 普光明幢劫中。有如是等佛刹微塵數如來。
386c01 出興於世。我於彼時。或為天王。或為龍王。或
386c02 為夜叉王。或為乾闥婆王。或為阿脩羅王。或
386c03 為迦樓羅王。或為緊那羅王。或為摩睺羅伽
386c04 王。或為人王。或為梵王。或為天身。或為人
386c05 身。或為男子身。或為女人身。或為童男身。或
386c06 為童女身。悉以種種諸供養具。供養於彼一
386c07 切如來。亦聞其佛所說諸法。從此命終。還即
386c08 於此世界中生。經佛刹微塵數劫。修菩薩行。
386c09 然後命終。生此華藏莊嚴世界海娑婆世界。
386c10 值迦羅鳩孫[5]馱如來。承事供養。得三昧。名
386c11 離一切塵垢光明。次值拘那含牟尼如來。承
386c12 事供養。得三昧。名普現一切諸刹海。次值迦
386c13 葉如來。承事供養。得三昧。名演一切眾生言
386c14 音海。次值毘盧遮那如來於此道場。成正等
386c15 覺。念念示現大神通力。我時得見。即獲此念
386c16 念出生廣大喜莊嚴解脫。

简体字

次有如来出兴于世，名智力山王；我于彼时，身为夜神，因得见佛承事供养，即获三昧，名普照三世众生诸根行。

“善男子，清净光金庄严世界普光明幢劫中，有如是等佛刹微尘数如来出兴于世。我于彼时，或为天王，或为龙王，或为夜叉王，或为乾闼婆王，或为阿修罗王，或为迦楼罗王，或为紧那罗王，或为摩睺罗伽王，或为人王，或为梵王，或为天身，或为人身，或为男子身，或为女人身，或为童男身，或为童女身，悉以种种诸供养具，供养于彼一切如来，亦闻其佛所说诸法。从此命终，还即于此世界中生，经佛刹微尘数劫修菩萨行；然后命终，生此华藏庄严世界海娑婆世界，值迦罗鸠孙驮如来，承事供养，得三昧，名离一切尘垢光明。次值拘那含牟尼如来，承事供养，得三昧，名普现一切诸刹海。次值迦叶如来，承事供养，得三昧，名演一切众生言音海。次值毗卢遮那如来，于此道场成正等觉，念念示现大神通力；我时得见，即获此念念出生广大喜庄严解脱。

Next, there was a *tathāgata* who appeared in the world who was named King of the Mountain of Wisdom Power. At that time, I was a night spirit who, due to seeing that buddha, serving him, and making offerings to him, then acquired a samādhi known as "universal illumination of the faculties and practices of the beings of the three periods of time."

Son of Good Family, in that Pristinely Radiant Gold Adornments World, in the Universal Light Banner Kalpa, there were *tathāgatas* such as these who appeared in the world who were as numerous as the atoms in a buddha *kṣetra*.

During that time, I was sometimes a heavenly king, sometimes a dragon king, sometimes a *yakṣa* king, sometimes a *gandharva* king, sometimes an *asura* king, sometimes a *garuḍa* king, sometimes a *kiṃnara* king, sometimes a *mahoraga* king, sometimes a human king, and sometimes a brahma heaven king. I sometimes appeared in a deva body, sometimes appeared in a human body, sometimes appeared in a male body, sometimes appeared in a female body, sometimes appeared in the body of a young boy, and sometimes appeared in the body of a young maiden. In all those circumstances, I made all kinds of offerings to all those *tathāgatas* and also listened to the teaching of all the dharmas those buddhas taught.

When that lifetime came to an end, I was immediately reborn in this world where I then passed through kalpas as numerous as the atoms in a buddha *kṣetra* during which I cultivated the bodhisattva practices.

Then, after those lifetimes had ended, I was next born into this Flower Dais Adornment Ocean of Worlds within the Sahā World in which I met Krakucchanda Tathāgata, served him, made offerings to him, and then acquired a samādhi known as "the light from transcending all defilements."

I next met Kanakamuni Tathāgata, served him, made offerings to him, and then acquired a samādhi known as "appearing everywhere in the ocean of all *kṣetras*."

I next met Kāśyapa Tathāgata, served him, made offerings to him, and then acquired a samādhi known as "proclamation in the ocean of all beings' languages."

I next met Vairocana Tathāgata who attained the right and universal enlightenment in this very site of enlightenment and then, in each successive mind-moment, manifested the powers of the great spiritual superknowledges. Having witnessed this at that time, I then acquired "the liberation that produces the adornment of vast joy in every mind-moment."

正體字

得此解脫已。能入
386c17║ 十不可說不可說佛剎微塵數法界安立海。
386c18║ 見彼一切法界安立海一切佛剎所有微塵。
386c19║ 一一塵中。有十不可說不可說佛剎微塵數
386c20║ 佛國土。一一佛土。皆有毘盧遮那如來。坐於
386c21║ 道場。於念念中。成正等覺。現諸神變。所現神
386c22║ 變。一一皆遍一切法界海。亦見自身在彼
386c23║ 一切諸如來所。又亦聞其所說妙法。又亦
386c24║ 見彼一切諸佛一一毛孔。出變化海。現神
386c25║ 通力。於一切法界海。一切世界海。一切世界
386c26║ 種。一切世界中。隨眾生心。轉正法輪。我
386c27║ 得速疾陀羅尼力。受持思惟一切文義。以明
386c28║ 了智。普入一切清淨法藏。以自在智。普遊
386c29║ 一切甚深法海。以周遍智。普知三世諸廣大
387a01║ 義。以平等智。普達諸佛無差別法。如是悟解
387a02║ 一切法門。一一法門中。悟解一切修多羅雲。
387a03║ 一一修多羅雲中。悟解一切法海。一一法海
387a04║ 中。悟解一切法品。一一法品中。悟解一切法
387a05║ 雲。一一法雲中。悟解一切法流。一一法流中。
387a06║ 出生一切大喜海。

简体字

“得此解脱已，能入十不可说不可说佛刹微尘数法界安立海，见彼一切法界安立海一切佛刹所有微尘，一一尘中有十不可说不可说佛刹微尘数佛国土。一一佛土皆有毗卢遮那如来坐于道场，于念念中，成正等觉，现诸神变；所现神变，一一皆遍一切法界海。亦见自身在彼一切诸如来所，又亦闻其所说妙法；又亦见彼一切诸佛一一毛孔，出变化海，现神通力，于一切法界海、一切世界海、一切世界种、一切世界中，随众生心，转正法轮。我得速疾陀罗尼力，受持思惟一切文义；以明了智，普入一切清净法藏；以自在智，普游一切甚深法海；以周遍智，普知三世诸广大义；以平等智，普达诸佛无差别法。如是悟解一切法门；一一法门中，悟解一切修多罗云；一一修多罗云中，悟解一切法海；一一法海中，悟解一切法品；一一法品中，悟解一切法云；一一法云中，悟解一切法流；一一法流中，出生一切大喜海；

Having acquired that liberation, I was then able to enter an ocean of Dharma realm arrangement arrays as numerous as the atoms in ten ineffable-ineffables of buddha *kṣetras*. I see all the atoms in all the buddha *kṣetras* in that ocean of all Dharma realm arrangement arrays. I see within every atom buddha lands as numerous as the atoms in ten ineffable-ineffables of buddha *kṣetras*. I see within every one of those buddha lands Vairocana Tathāgata seated in a site of enlightenment in which, in each successive mind-moment, he manifests all kinds of spiritual transformations. Every one of the spiritual transformations that he manifests pervade the entire ocean of the Dharma realm.

I also see my own body in the presence of all those *tathāgatas* and also listen to the sublime Dharma they all proclaim. I also see all those buddhas emanating an ocean of transformations from every one of their pores that then each manifest the powers of the super-knowledges with which, in the ocean of all Dharma realms, in the ocean of all oceans of worlds, in all the world systems, and in all worlds, they adapt to the minds of beings as they then turn the wheel of the right Dharma. I have acquired the power of the "swiftness *dhāraṇī*" through which I absorb, retain, and reflect upon the meanings of all of those textual passages that they spoke.

Then, using the wisdom of complete clarity, I everywhere enter the treasury of all pure dharmas. Using masterful wisdom, I everywhere roam throughout the ocean of all extremely profound dharmas. Using the universally pervasive wisdom, I everywhere know all the vast meanings throughout all three periods of time. And, using the wisdom of uniform equality, I everywhere possess a penetrating comprehension of the unvarying Dharma of all buddhas.

So it is that I have acquired an awakened understanding of all gateways into the Dharma with which:

In every Dharma gateway, I awakened to and understood a cloud of all sutras;

In every cloud of sutras, I awakened to and understood an ocean of all dharmas;

In every ocean of dharmas, I awakened to and understood all categories of dharmas;

In every category of dharmas, I awakened to and understood a cloud of all dharmas;

In every cloud of dharmas, I awakened to and understood the stream of all dharmas;

In every stream of dharmas, I produced an ocean of all types of immense joy;

正體字

一一大喜海。出生一切地。
387a07‖ 一一地。出生一切三昧海。一一三昧海。得一
387a08‖ 切見佛海。一一見佛海。得一切智光海。一一
387a09‖ 智光海。普照三世。遍入十方。知無量如來
387a10‖ 往昔諸行海。知無量如來所有本事海。知無
387a11‖ 量如來難捨能施海。知無量如來清淨戒輪
387a12‖ 海。知無量如來清淨堪忍海。知無量如來廣
387a13‖ 大精進海。知無量如來甚深禪定海。知無量
387a14‖ 如來般若波羅蜜海。知無量如來方便波羅
387a15‖ 蜜海。知無量如來願波羅蜜海。知無量如來
387a16‖ 力波羅蜜海。知無量如來智波羅蜜海。知無
387a17‖ 量如來往昔超菩薩地。知無量如來往昔住
387a18‖ 菩薩地無量劫海現神通力。知無量如來往
387a19‖ 昔入菩薩地。知無量如來往昔修菩薩地。知
387a20‖ 無量如來往昔治菩薩地。知無量如來往昔觀
387a21‖ 菩薩地。知無量如來昔為菩薩時常見諸佛。

简体字

一一大喜海，出生一切地；一一地，出生一切三昧海；一一三昧海，得一切见佛海；一一见佛海，得一切智光海；一一智光海，普照三世，遍入十方。

“知无量如来往昔诸行海；知无量如来所有本事海；知无量如来难舍能施海；知无量如来清净戒轮海；知无量如来清净堪忍海；知无量如来广大精进海；知无量如来甚深禅定海；知无量如来般若波罗蜜海；知无量如来方便波罗蜜海；知无量如来愿波罗蜜海；知无量如来力波罗蜜海；知无量如来智波罗蜜海；知无量如来往昔超菩萨地；知无量如来往昔住菩萨地无量劫海，现神通力；知无量如来往昔入菩萨地；知无量如来往昔修菩萨地；知无量如来往昔治菩萨地；知无量如来往昔观菩萨地；知无量如来昔为菩萨时，常见诸佛；

In every ocean of all types of immense joy, I produced all the grounds;
In every ground, I produced an ocean of all samādhis;
In every ocean of samādhis, I acquired an ocean of all visions of the buddhas;
In every ocean of visions of the buddhas, I acquired an ocean of the light of all-knowledge;
In every ocean of the light of knowledge, I everywhere illuminated the three periods of time and pervasively entered the ten directions;
I knew the ocean of past practices of countless *tathāgatas*;
I knew the ocean of past endeavors of countless *tathāgatas*;
I knew the ocean of instances of countless *tathāgatas'* being able to give what is difficult to relinquish;
I knew the ocean of the spheres of pure moral conduct of countless *tathāgatas*;
I knew the ocean of the pure patience of countless *tathāgatas*;
I knew the ocean of the vast vigor of countless *tathāgatas*;
I knew the ocean of extremely deep *dhyāna* concentrations of countless *tathāgatas*;
I knew the ocean of the *prajñāpāramitā* of countless *tathāgatas*;
I knew the ocean of the skillful means *pāramitā* of countless *tathāgatas*;
I knew the ocean of the *pāramitā* of vows of countless *tathāgatas*;
I knew the ocean of the *pāramitā* of powers of countless *tathāgatas*;
I knew the ocean of the *pāramitā* of knowledge of countless *tathāgatas*;
I knew how in the past countless *tathāgatas* passed beyond the bodhisattva grounds;
I knew how in the past countless *tathāgatas* dwelt on the bodhisattva grounds for an ocean of countless kalpas, manifesting the powers of the spiritual superknowledges;
I knew how in the past countless *tathāgatas* entered the bodhisattva grounds;
I knew how in the past countless *tathāgatas* cultivated the bodhisattva grounds;
I knew how in the past countless *tathāgatas* purified the bodhisattva grounds;
I knew how in the past countless *tathāgatas* contemplated the bodhisattva grounds;
I knew how in the past countless *tathāgatas*, even while still bodhisattvas, always saw the buddhas;

正體字

387a22 ‖ 知無量如來昔為菩薩時。盡見佛海劫海同
387a23 ‖ 住。知無量如來昔為菩薩時。以無量身遍生
387a24 ‖ 剎海。知無量如來昔為菩薩時。周遍法界修
387a25 ‖ 廣大行。知無量如來昔為菩薩時。示現種種
387a26 ‖ 諸方便門調伏成熟一切眾生知無量如來放
387a27 ‖ 大光明。普照十方一切剎海。知無量如來現
387a28 ‖ 大神力。普現一切諸眾生前。知無量如來廣
387a29 ‖ 大智地。知無量如來轉正法輪。知無量如來
387b01 ‖ 示現相海。知無量如來示現身海。知無量如
387b02 ‖ 來廣大力海。彼諸如來。從初發心。乃至法滅。
387b03 ‖ 我於念念。悉得知見。善男子。汝問我言。汝發
387b04 ‖ 心來。其已久如。善男子。我於往昔過二佛剎
387b05 ‖ 微塵數劫。如上所說。於清淨光金莊嚴世界
387b06 ‖ 中。為菩提樹神。聞不退轉法界音如來說法。
387b07 ‖ 發阿耨多羅三藐三菩提心。於二佛剎微塵
387b08 ‖ 數劫中。修菩薩行。然後乃生此娑婆世界賢
387b09 ‖ 劫之中。從迦羅鳩孫[*]馱佛。至釋迦牟尼佛。
387b10 ‖ 及此劫中。未來所有一切諸佛。我皆如是。親
387b11 ‖ 近供養。

简体字

知无量如来昔为菩萨时，尽见佛海、劫海同住；知无量如来昔为菩萨时，以无量身遍生刹海；知无量如来昔为菩萨时，周遍法界修广大行；知无量如来昔为菩萨时，示现种种诸方便门，调伏成熟一切众生；知无量如来放大光明，普照十方一切刹海；知无量如来现大神力，普现一切诸众生前；知无量如来广大智地；知无量如来转正法轮；知无量如来示现相海；知无量如来示现身海；知无量如来广大力海。彼诸如来，从初发心，乃至法灭；我于念念，悉得知见。

“善男子，汝问我言：‘汝发心来，其已久如？’善男子，我于往昔，过二佛刹微尘数劫，如上所说，于清净光金庄严世界中，为菩提树神，闻不退转法界音如来说法，发阿耨多罗三藐三菩提心；于二佛刹微尘数劫中修菩萨行，然后乃生此娑婆世界贤劫之中。从迦罗鸠孙驮佛至释迦牟尼佛，及此劫中未来所有一切诸佛，我皆如是亲近供养。

I knew how in the past countless *tathāgatas*, even while still bodhisattvas, saw the entire ocean of buddhas and dwelt together with them for an ocean of kalpas;

I knew how in the past countless *tathāgatas*, even while still bodhisattvas, took birth in countless bodies everywhere throughout the ocean of *kṣetras*;

I knew how in the past countless *tathāgatas*, even while still bodhisattvas, cultivated vast practices everywhere throughout the Dharma realm;

I knew how in the past countless *tathāgatas*, even while still bodhisattvas, manifested many different kinds of skillful means gateways in training and ripening all beings;

I knew how countless *tathāgatas* emanated vast radiance that everywhere illuminated the ocean of all *kṣetras* throughout the ten directions;

I knew how countless *tathāgatas* manifested great spiritual powers with which they appeared everywhere directly before all beings;

I knew the vast wisdom grounds of countless *tathāgatas*;

I knew the turning of the wheel of right Dharma by countless *tathāgatas*;

I knew the manifestation of an ocean of signs by countless *tathāgatas*;

I knew the manifestation of an ocean of bodies by countless *tathāgatas*; and

I knew an ocean of vast powers of countless *tathāgatas*.

In each successive mind-moment, I was able to know of and see all those *tathāgatas* from the time they produced their initial resolve until the time when their Dharma finally disappeared.

Son of Good Family, you asked me, "How long has it now been since you first produced the resolve?"

Son of Good Family, as described above, in the long distant past, back beyond kalpas as numerous as the atoms in two buddha *kṣetras*, I was a bodhi tree spirit in that Adorned with Pure Golden Light world. When I heard that *tathāgata* known as Voice of the Irreversibly Turning Wheel of Dharma teach the Dharma, I resolved to attain *anuttara-samyak-saṃbodhi.*

Then, in kalpas as numerous as the atoms in two buddha *kṣetras*, I cultivated the bodhisattva practices, after which I was reborn in this Sahā World. In this Worthy Kalpa, I have drawn near to and made offerings to all the buddhas from Krakucchanda Buddha up to Śākyamuni Buddha. In the same way, I shall also do so with all future buddhas of this kalpa.

正體字

如於此世界賢劫之中供養未來一
387b12 ‖ 切諸佛。一切世界。一切劫中。所有未來一切
387b13 ‖ 諸佛。悉亦如是。親近供養。善男子。彼清淨光
387b14 ‖ 金莊嚴世界。今猶現在。諸佛出現。相續不斷。
387b15 ‖ 汝當一心修此菩薩大勇猛門。爾時寂靜音
387b16 ‖ 海主夜神。欲重宣此解脫義。為善財童子。而
387b17 ‖ 說頌言
387b18 ‖ 善財聽我說　清淨解脫門
387b19 ‖ 聞已生歡喜　勤修令究竟
387b20 ‖ 我昔於劫海　生大信樂心
387b21 ‖ 清淨如虛空　常觀一切智
387b22 ‖ 我於三世佛　皆生信樂心
387b23 ‖ 并及其眾會　悉願常親近
387b24 ‖ 我昔曾見佛　為眾生供養
387b25 ‖ 得聞清淨法　其心大歡喜
387b26 ‖ 常尊重父母　恭敬而供養
387b27 ‖ 如是無休懈　入此解脫門
387b28 ‖ 老病貧窮人　諸根不具足
387b29 ‖ 一切皆愍濟　令其得安隱
387c01 ‖ 水火及王賊　海中諸恐怖
387c02 ‖ 我昔修諸行　為救彼眾生
387c03 ‖ 煩惱恒熾然　業障所纏覆

简体字

如于此世界贤劫之中，供养未来一切诸佛；一切世界一切劫中，所有未来一切诸佛，悉亦如是亲近供养。善男子，彼清净光金庄严世界，今犹现在，诸佛出现相续不断。汝当一心修此菩萨大勇猛门。”

尔时，寂静音海主夜神，欲重宣此解脱义，为善财童子而说颂言：

“善财听我说，清净解脱门，
闻已生欢喜，勤修令究竟。
我昔于劫海，生大信乐心，
清净如虚空，常观一切智。
我于三世佛，皆生信乐心；
并及其众会，悉愿常亲近。
我昔曾见佛，为众生供养，
得闻清净法，其心大欢喜。
常尊重父母，恭敬而供养；
如是无休懈，入此解脱门。
老病贫穷人，诸根不具足；
一切皆愍济，令其得安隐。
水火及王贼，海中诸恐怖；
我昔修诸行，为救彼众生。
烦恼恒炽然，业障所缠覆，

And just as, in this Worthy Kalpa, I shall make offerings to all future buddhas of this world, so too shall I draw near to and make offerings to all those who become buddhas in all future worlds and kalpas.

Son of Good Family, within that Adorned with Pure Golden Light world, there are now still buddhas who are appearing continuously and uninterruptedly. You should single-mindedly cultivate this bodhisattva's gateway of immense courage.

At that time, wishing to once again proclaim the meaning of this liberation, the Night Spirit, Praśāntarutasāgaravatī, spoke these verses for Sudhana the Youth:

Sudhana, listen to me as I describe
this gateway of pure liberation.
Having heard this, be filled with joyous delight,
diligently cultivate it, and make it achieve its ultimate ends.

In the past, beyond an ocean of kalpas,
I developed a mind of great faithful aspiration
which was as pure as empty space
with which I always contemplated all-knowledge.

I produced a mind of faith-filled aspiration
in all buddhas of the three periods of time
and in their congregations
and then vowed to always draw near to them all.

In the past, I once saw a buddha
who was receiving the offerings of beings
and thus was able to hear his teaching of the pure Dharma,
whereupon my mind was filled with immense joyous delight.

I always revered my parents,
respected them, and presented them with offerings.
Acting in this way without rest or indolence,
I then entered this gateway of liberation.

Those people afflicted by aging, sickness, poverty,
or incompletely developed faculties—
for all of them I felt pity and came to their rescue,
thereby enabling them to gain peace and security.

For those who were victims of fearsome perils
of floods, fires, kings, thieves, or troubles out at sea,
I cultivated those practices with which
I was then able to rescue those beings.

For those constantly burned by the afflictions,
for those bound up and overcome by karmic obstacles,

正體字

387c04 | 墮於諸險道　我救彼眾生
387c05 | 一切諸惡趣　無量楚毒苦
387c06 | 生老病死等　我當悉除滅
387c07 | 願盡未來劫　普為諸群生
387c08 | 滅除生死苦　得佛究竟樂
387c09 | 善男子。我唯知此念念[1]生廣大喜莊嚴解脫。
387c10 | 如諸菩薩摩訶薩。深入一切法界海。悉知一
387c11 | 切諸劫數。普見一切剎成壞。而我云何能知
387c12 | 能說彼功德行。善男子。此菩提場如來會中。
387c13 | 有主夜神。名守護一切城增長威力。汝詣彼
387c14 | 問。菩薩云何學菩薩行。修菩薩道。爾時善財
387c15 | 童子。一心觀察寂靜音海主夜神身。而說頌
387c16 | 言
387c17 | 我因善友教　來詣天神所
387c18 | 見神處寶座　身量無有邊
387c19 | 非是著色相　計有於諸法
387c20 | 劣智淺識人　能知尊境界
387c21 | 世間天及人　無量劫觀察
387c22 | 亦不能測度　色相無邊故
387c23 | 遠離於五蘊　亦不住於處
387c24 | 永斷世間疑　顯現自在力

简体字

墮于诸险道，我救彼众生。
一切诸恶趣，无量楚毒苦，
生老病死等，我当悉除灭。
愿尽未来劫，普为诸群生，
灭除生死苦，得佛究竟乐。

“善男子，我唯知此念念生广大喜庄严解脱。如诸菩萨摩诃萨，深入一切法界海，悉知一切诸劫数，普见一切刹成坏；而我云何能知能说彼功德行？

“善男子，此菩提场如来会中，有主夜神，名守护一切城增长威力。汝诣彼问：菩萨云何学菩萨行、修菩萨道？”

尔时，善财童子一心观察寂静音海主夜神身，而说颂言：

“我因善友教，来诣天神所，
见神处宝座，身量无有边。
非是著色相，计有于诸法，
劣智浅识人，能知尊境界。
世间天及人，无量劫观察，
亦不能测度，色相无边故。
远离于五蕴，亦不住于处，
永断世间疑，显现自在力。

and for those who have fallen into the dangerous destinies—
I have come to the rescue of those beings.

The countless intensely cruel sufferings
of the wretched rebirth destinies
and of birth, aging, sickness, death, and such—
I shall extinguish them all.

I vow that, to the very end of all future kalpas,
for the sake of the many kinds of beings, I will everywhere
extinguish the sufferings of *saṃsāra*
and enable them to gain the Buddha's ultimate bliss.

Son of Good Family, I know only this "liberation that produces the adornment of vast joy in every mind-moment." As for the bodhisattva-mahāsattvas who have deeply entered the ocean of all Dharma realms, who entirely know the enumerations of all kalpas, and who everywhere see the creation and destruction of all the *kṣetras*, how could I know of or be able to speak about their meritorious qualities and practices?

Son of Good Family, within this very congregation of the Tathāgata at this site of enlightenment, there is a night spirit known as Sarva nagararaksāsambhavatejahśrī or "Increaser of Awesome Powers for the Protection of all Cities." You should go there, pay your respects, and ask her, "How should the bodhisattva train in the bodhisattva practices and how should he cultivate the bodhisattva path?"

Sudhana the Youth then single-mindedly contemplated the Night Spirit, Praśāntarutasāgaravatī, and then spoke these verses:

It was due to the instructions of the good spiritual guide
that I came to pay my respects to the Goddess
and then saw that spirit sitting on the jeweled throne
with a body of boundless dimensions.

No one who is attached to forms or their signs,
who conceives of dharmas as existent,
or who is of inferior wisdom or merely shallow awareness—
none of these could ever know the realm of the Venerable One.

The world's devas and humans
might contemplate it for countless kalpas,
but they would still be unable to fathom it,
for your form and signs are boundless.

You have left the five aggregates far behind
and do not abide in the sense bases, either.
You have forever severed the worldling's doubts
and manifest the powers of miraculous transformation.

正體字

387c25║ 不取內外法　無動無所礙
387c26║ 清淨智慧眼　見佛神通力
387c27║ 身為正法藏　心是無礙智
387c28║ 既得智光照　復照諸群生
387c29║ 心集無邊業　莊嚴諸世間
388a01║ 了世皆是心　現身等眾生
388a02║ 知世悉如夢　一切佛如影
388a03║ 諸法皆如響　令眾無所著
388a04║ 為三世眾生　念念示現身
388a05║ 而心無所住　十方遍說法
388a06║ 無邊諸剎海　佛海眾生海
388a07║ 悉在一塵中　此尊解脫力
388a08║ 時善財童子。說此偈已。頂禮其足。遶無量匝。
388a09║ 慇懃瞻仰。辭退而去
388a10║ 爾時善財童子。隨順寂靜音海夜神教。思惟
388a11║ 觀察所說法門。一一文句。皆無忘失。於無量
388a12║ 深心。無量法性。一切方便。神通智慧。憶念思
388a13║ 擇。相續不斷。其心廣大。證入安住。行詣守護
388a14║ 一切城夜神所。

简体字

不取内外法，无动无所碍，
清净智慧眼，见佛神通力。
身为正法藏，心是无碍智，
既得智光照，复照诸群生。
心集无边业，庄严诸世间，
了世皆是心，现身等众生。
知世悉如梦，一切佛如影，
诸法皆如响，令众无所著。
为三世众生，念念示现身，
而心无所住，十方遍说法。
无边诸刹海，佛海众生海，
悉在一尘中，此尊解脱力。”

时，善财童子说此偈已，顶礼其足，绕无量匝，殷勤瞻仰，辞退而去。

尔时，善财童子随顺寂静音海夜神教，思惟观察所说法门，一一文句皆无忘失，于无量深心、无量法性、一切方便神通智慧，忆念思择，相续不断；其心广大，证入安住。

行诣守护一切城夜神所，

You do not seize on any inward or outward dharmas
and are unshakable and unimpeded.
With your purified eye of wisdom, you see
the powers of the Buddha's spiritual superknowledges.

Your body is a treasury of right Dharma
and your mind is possessed of unimpeded wisdom.
Having acquired the illumination of wisdom's light,
you then also illuminate the many kinds of beings.

Your mind has accumulated boundless karmic works
with which you adorn all worlds.
You have completely understood that the world is merely mind
and manifest in bodies that are the same as beings.

Knowing that the world is entirely like a dream,
that all buddhas are like reflections,
and that dharmas are all like echoes,
you enable the multitude to become free of attachments.

For the beings of all three periods of time,
you manifest your bodies in every mind-moment,
and yet your mind has no place in which it abides
even as you proclaim the Dharma throughout the ten directions.

The boundless ocean of all *kṣetras*,
the ocean of buddhas, and the ocean of beings
all reside within a single mote of dust.
This is the power of the Venerable One's liberation.

Having spoken these verses, Sudhana the Youth then bowed down in reverence at her feet and circumambulated her countless times as he gazed up at her in admiration. He then respectfully withdrew and departed.

36 – Sarvanagararaksāsambhavatejahśrī

At that time, Sudhana the Youth then complied with the teachings provided by the Night Spirit, Praśāntarutasāgaravatī, meditated on and contemplated every passage of the Dharma gateways she had described, and thenceforth never forgot any of them. He continuously and uninterruptedly bore in mind and contemplatively examined all of their countless profound thoughts, the nature of their countless dharmas, their skillful means, their spiritual superknowledges, and their wisdom. His mind became so expansive that he penetrated them with realization and became established in them.

Intent on paying his respects to her, he then went to the night spirit known as Sarvanagararakṣāsaṁbhavatejaḥśrī or "Protector of All

正體字

見彼夜神。坐一切寶光明摩
388a15 | 尼王師子之座。無數夜神所共圍遶。現一切
388a16 | 眾生色相身。現普對一切眾生身。現不染一
388a17 | 切世間身。現一切眾生身數身。現超過一切
388a18 | 世間身。現成熟一切眾生身。現速往一切十
388a19 | 方身。現遍攝一切十方身。現究竟如來體性
388a20 | 身。現究竟調伏眾生身。善財見已。歡喜踊躍。
388a21 | 頂禮其足。遶無量匝。於前合掌。而作是言。聖
388a22 | 者。我已先發阿耨多羅三藐三菩提心。而未
388a23 | 知菩薩。修菩薩行時。云何饒益眾生。云何
388a24 | 以無上攝而攝眾生。云何順諸佛教。云何近
388a25 | 法王位。唯願慈哀。為我宣說。時彼夜神。告善
388a26 | 財言。善男子。汝為救護一切眾生故。汝為嚴
388a27 | 淨一切佛剎故。汝為供養一切如來故。汝欲
388a28 | 住一切劫救眾生故。汝欲守護一切佛種性
388a29 | 故。汝欲普入十方修諸行故。

简体字

见彼夜神坐一切宝光明摩尼王师子之座，无数夜神所共围绕，现一切众生色相身，现普对一切众生身，现不染一切世间身，现一切众生身数身，现超过一切世间身，现成熟一切众生身，现速往一切十方身，现遍摄一切十方身，现究竟如来体性身，现究竟调伏众生身。

善财见已，欢喜踊跃，顶礼其足，绕无量匝，于前合掌而作是言：“圣者，我已先发阿耨多罗三藐三菩提心，而未知菩萨修菩萨行时，云何饶益众生？云何以无上摄而摄众生？云何顺诸佛教？云何近法王位？唯愿慈哀，为我宣说！”

时，彼夜神告善财言：“善男子，汝为救护一切众生故，汝为严净一切佛刹故，汝为供养一切如来故，汝欲住一切劫救众生故，汝欲守护一切佛种性故，汝欲普入十方修诸行故，

Cities." He saw that night spirit sitting on a lion throne adorned with all kinds of jewels and radiant sovereign *maṇi* jewels. She was surrounded there by countless night spirits in the midst of whom:

She manifested bodies with the forms and features of all types of beings;
She manifested bodies everywhere in the direct presence of all beings;
She manifested bodies undefiled by any aspects of the world;
She manifested bodies as numerous as those of all beings;
She manifested bodies that transcended all aspects of the world;
She manifested bodies that ripened all beings;
She manifested bodies that traveled swiftly throughout the ten directions;
She manifested bodies that everywhere attracted beings from throughout the ten directions;
She manifested bodies with ultimately the same essential nature as the Tathāgata; and
She manifested bodies that ultimately trained all beings.

Having seen this, Sudhana was filled with joyous exultation, whereupon he bowed down in reverence at her feet and circumambulated her countless times. He then stood before her with palms pressed together and addressed her, saying:

O Āryā, I am one who has already resolved to attain *anuttara-samyak-saṃbodhi*. Still, I do not yet understand, when the bodhisattva is cultivating the bodhisattva practices, how he benefits beings, how he uses the unexcelled means of attraction to attract beings, how he complies with all teachings of the Buddha, and how he approaches the position of the Dharma King. I hope you will bring forth your kind concern and speak about these matters for my sake.

That night spirit then told Sudhana:

Son of Good Family, as you now inquire into the bodhisattva's gateways of cultivation:

You do so to rescue all beings;
You do so to purify all buddha *kṣetras*;
You do so to make offerings to all *tathāgatas*;
You do so wishing to remain throughout all kalpas, rescuing beings;
You do so wishing to preserve and protect the lineage of all buddhas;
You do so wishing to everywhere enter the ten directions, cultivating all the practices;

正體字

汝欲普入一切
388b01║ 法門海故。汝欲以平等心遍一切故。汝欲普
388b02║ 受一切佛法輪故。汝欲普隨一切眾生心之
388b03║ 所樂雨法雨故。問諸菩薩所修行門。善男子。
388b04║ 我得菩薩甚深自在妙音解脫。為大法師。無
388b05║ 所罣礙。善能開示諸佛法藏故。具大誓願。大
388b06║ 慈悲力。令一切眾生。住菩提心故。能作一切
388b07║ 利眾生事。積集善根。無有休息故。為一切
388b08║ 眾生調御之師。令一切眾生。住薩婆若道故。
388b09║ 為一切世間清淨法日。普照世間。令生善根
388b10║ 故。於一切世間其心平等。普令眾生。增長善
388b11║ 法故。於諸境界其心清淨。除滅一切諸不善
388b12║ 業故。誓願利益一切眾生。身恒普現一切國
388b13║ 土故。示現一切本事因緣。令諸眾生。安住
388b14║ 善行故。恒事一切諸善知識。為令眾生安住
388b15║ 佛教故。佛子。我以此等法施眾生。令生白法。
388b16║ 求一切智。其心堅固。猶如金剛那羅延藏。善
388b17║ 能觀察佛力魔力。

简体字

汝欲普入一切法门海故，汝欲以平等心遍一切故，汝欲普受一切佛法轮故，汝欲普随一切众生心之所乐雨法雨故，问诸菩萨所修行门。

“善男子，我得菩萨甚深自在妙音解脱，为大法师，无所挂碍，善能开示诸佛法藏故；具大誓愿、大慈悲力，令一切众生住菩提心故；能作一切利众生事，积集善根无有休息故；为一切众生调御之师，令一切众生住萨婆若道故；为一切世间清净法日，普照世间，令生善根故；于一切世间其心平等，普令众生增长善法故；于诸境界其心清净，除灭一切诸不善业故；誓愿利益一切众生，身恒普现一切国土故；示现一切本事因缘，令诸众生安住善行故；恒事一切诸善知识，为令众生安住佛教故。

“佛子，我以此等法施众生，令生白法，求一切智，其心坚固犹如金刚那罗延藏，善能观察佛力、魔力，

You do so wishing to everywhere enter the ocean of all Dharma gateways;
You do so wishing to use the impartial mind everywhere and in all things;
You do so wishing to receive all buddhas' turnings of the Dharma wheel; and
You do so wishing to everywhere rain down the rain of Dharma in accordance with the dispositions of all beings' minds.

Son of Good Family, I have acquired the "the extremely profound and miraculous sublime sound" bodhisattva liberation by which:

I serve as a great master of the Dharma who is unimpeded in being well able to explain the Dharma treasury of all buddhas;
I perfect the great vows and the power of great kindness and compassion and thus enable all beings to dwell in the resolve to attain bodhi;
I am able to engage in all kinds of endeavors that benefit beings while incessantly accumulating roots of goodness;
I serve as a training and guiding teacher for all beings and thus enable all beings to abide in the path to omniscience;
I serve the entire world as a sun of pure Dharma that everywhere illuminates the world and stimulates the growth of roots of goodness;
With an impartial mind toward the entire world, I everywhere enable beings to increase their practice of good dharmas;
With a mind that remains pure in all spheres of experience, I extinguish all unwholesome karma;
Vowing to benefit all beings, my bodies constantly appear everywhere in all lands;
By revealing all the causes and conditions of their previous lifetimes, I enable all beings to establish themselves in good conduct; and
I constantly serve all good spiritual guides to enable beings to establish themselves in the Buddha's teachings.

Son of the Buddha, I bestow dharmas such as these on beings and thus enable them:

To develop the white dharmas of pristine purity;
To pursue the realization of all-knowledge;
To develop strengths of resolve as solid as the vajras in the treasury of the Nārāyaṇas;
To become well able to contemplate the powers of the Buddha and the powers of Māra;

正體字

常得親近諸善知識。摧破
388b18‖ 一切業惑障山。集一切智助道之法。心恒不
388b19‖ 捨一切智地。善男子。我以如是淨法光明。饒
388b20‖ 益一切眾生。集善根助道法時。作十種觀察
388b21‖ 法界。何者為十。所謂我知法界無量。獲得
388b22‖ 廣大智光明故。我知法界無邊。見一切佛所
388b23‖ 知見故。我知法界無限。普入一切諸佛國土
388b24‖ 恭敬供養諸如來故。我知法界無畔。普於一
388b25‖ 切法界海中示現修行菩薩行故。我知法界
388b26‖ 無斷。入於如來不斷智故。我知法界一性。如
388b27‖ 來一音一切眾生無不了故。我知法界性淨。
388b28‖ 了如來願普度一切諸眾生故。我知法界遍
388b29‖ 眾生。普賢妙行悉周遍故。我知法界一莊嚴。
388c01‖ 普賢妙行善莊嚴故。我知法界不可壞。一切
388c02‖ 智善根充滿法界不可壞故。善男子。我作此
388c03‖ 十種觀察法界。集諸善根辦助道法。了知諸
388c04‖ 佛廣大威德。深入如來難思境界。

简体字

常得亲近诸善知识，摧破一切业惑障山，集一切智助道之法，心恒不舍一切智地。

“善男子，我以如是净法光明饶益一切众生，集善根助道法时，作十种观察法界。何者为十？所谓：我知法界无量，获得广大智光明故；我知法界无边，见一切佛所知见故；我知法界无限，普入一切诸佛国土，恭敬供养诸如来故；我知法界无畔，普于一切法界海中，示现修行菩萨行故；我知法界无断，入于如来不断智故；我知法界一性，如来一音，一切众生无不了故；我知法界性净，了如来愿普度一切诸众生故；我知法界遍众生，普贤妙行悉周遍故；我知法界一庄严，普贤妙行善庄严故；我知法界不可坏，一切智善根充满法界不可坏故。善男子，我作此十种观察法界，集诸善根办助道法，了知诸佛广大威德，深入如来难思境界。

To always succeed in drawing near to good spiritual guides;
To smash the mountain of all obstacles of karma and the afflictions;
To accumulate the provisions essential to realization of the path to all-knowledge; and
To maintain the resolve that never abandons [the intention to reach] the ground of all-knowledge.

Son of Good Family, as I use the light of pure Dharma such as this to benefit all beings, thereby accumulating roots of goodness and establishing the provisions for the path, I engage in ten kinds of contemplation of the Dharma realm. What are those ten? They are:

I realize the measurelessness of the Dharma realm in order to acquire the light of vast wisdom;
I realize the boundlessness of the Dharma realm in order to see what is known and seen by all buddhas;
I realize the limitlessness of the Dharma realm in order to everywhere enter all buddha lands to revere and make offerings to all *tathāgatas;*
I realize the Dharma realm's absence of any boundaries in order to manifest the cultivation of the bodhisattva practices throughout the ocean of the entire Dharma realm;
I realize that the Dharma realm is uninterrupted in order to enter the Tathāgata's uninterrupted wisdom;
I realize that the Dharma realm has one nature because no being fails to understand the singular voice of the Tathāgata;
I realize that the Dharma realm's nature is pure in order to completely understand the Tathāgata's vow to liberate all beings;
I realize that the Dharma realm extends everywhere to all beings because Samantabhadra's marvelous practices are universally pervasive;
I realize that the Dharma realm has a singular adornment because of the excellent adornments of Samantabhadra's marvelous practices; and
I realize that the Dharma realm is indestructible because of the indestructibility of the roots of goodness of all-knowledge that fill the Dharma realm.

Son of Good Family, as I engage in these ten kinds of contemplation of the Dharma realm, thereby accumulating roots of goodness and establishing the provisions for the path, I come to completely realize all buddhas' vast awesome virtue and deeply enter the inconceivable realm of the Tathāgata.

正體字

又善男子。
388c05║ 我如是正念思惟。得如來十種大威德陀羅
388c06║ 尼輪。何者為十。所謂普入一切法陀羅尼輪。
388c07║ 普持一切法陀羅尼輪。普說一切法陀羅尼
388c08║ 輪。普念十方一切佛陀羅尼輪。普說一切佛
388c09║ 名號陀羅尼輪。普入三世諸佛願海陀羅尼
388c10║ 輪。普入一切諸乘海陀羅尼輪。普入一切眾
388c11║ 生業海陀羅尼輪。疾轉一切業陀羅尼輪。疾
388c12║ 生一切智陀羅尼輪。善男子。此十陀羅尼輪。
388c13║ 以十千陀羅尼輪。而為眷屬。恒為眾生。演
388c14║ 說妙法。善男子。我或為眾生說聞慧法。或
388c15║ 為眾生說思慧法。或為眾生說修慧法。或為
388c16║ 眾生說一有法。或為眾生說一切有法。或為
388c17║ 說一如來名海法。或為說一切如來名海法。
388c18║ 或為說一世界海法。或為說一切世界海法。
388c19║ 或為說一佛授記海法。或為說一切佛授記
388c20║ 海法。

简体字

"又，善男子，我如是正念思惟，得如来十种大威德陀罗尼轮。何者为十？所谓：普入一切法陀罗尼轮、普持一切法陀罗尼轮、普说一切法陀罗尼轮、普念十方一切佛陀罗尼轮、普说一切佛名号陀罗尼轮、普入三世诸佛愿海陀罗尼轮、普入一切诸乘海陀罗尼轮、普入一切众生业海陀罗尼轮、疾转一切业陀罗尼轮、疾生一切智陀罗尼轮。善男子，此十陀罗尼轮，以十千陀罗尼轮而为眷属，恒为众生演说妙法。

"善男子，我或为众生说闻慧法，或为众生说思慧法，或为众生说修慧法，或为众生说一有法，或为众生说一切有法，或为说一如来名海法，或为说一切如来名海法，或为说一世界海法，或为说一切世界海法，或为说一佛授记海法，或为说一切佛授记海法，

Also, Son of Good Family, as I engaged with right mindfulness in reflections such as these, I acquired ten of the Tathāgata's immensely awesome *dhāraṇī maṇḍalas*. What are those ten? They are:

The *dhāraṇī maṇḍala* of the comprehensive entry into all dharmas;
The *dhāraṇī maṇḍala* of the comprehensive retention of all dharmas;
The *dhāraṇī maṇḍala* of the comprehensive teaching of all dharmas;
The *dhāraṇī maṇḍala* of the comprehensive mindfulness of all buddhas of the ten directions;
The *dhāraṇī maṇḍala* of the comprehensive recitation of the names of all buddhas;
The *dhāraṇī maṇḍala* of the comprehensive entry into the ocean of the vows of all buddhas throughout the three periods of time;
The *dhāraṇī maṇḍala* of the comprehensive entry into the ocean of all vehicles;
The *dhāraṇī maṇḍala* of the comprehensive entry into the ocean of all beings' karmic actions;
The *dhāraṇī maṇḍala* of the swift transformation of all karma; and
The *dhāraṇī maṇḍala* of the swift production of all-knowledge.

Son of Good Family, these ten *dhāraṇī maṇḍalas* have a retinue of a myriad *dhāraṇī maṇḍalas*. With their assistance, I constantly expound on the sublime Dharma for the benefit of beings.

Son of Good Family:

I sometimes teach beings the dharma of wisdom acquired by listening;
I sometimes teach beings the dharma of wisdom acquired by contemplative reflection;
I sometimes teach beings the dharma of wisdom acquired by meditative cultivation;[145]
I sometimes teach beings the dharma of a single existence;
I sometimes teach beings the dharma of all existences;
I sometimes teach beings the dharma of the ocean of a single *tathāgata*'s names;
I sometimes teach beings the dharma of the oceans of all *tathāgatas*' names;
I sometimes teach beings the dharma of a single ocean of worlds;
I sometimes teach beings the dharma of the oceans of all worlds;
I sometimes teach beings the dharma of the ocean of a single buddha's predictions;
I sometimes teach beings the dharma of the oceans of all buddhas' predictions;

正體字

或為說一如來眾會道場海法。或為說
388c21 一切如來眾會道場海法。或為說一如來法
388c22 輪海法。或為說一切如來法輪海法。或為說
388c23 一如來修多羅法。或為說一切如來修多羅
388c24 法。或為說一如來集會法。或為說一切如來
388c25 集會法。或為說一薩婆若心海法。或為說一
388c26 切薩婆若心海法。或為說一乘出離法。或為
388c27 說一切乘出離法。善男子。我以如是等不可
388c28 說法門。為眾生說。善男子。我入如來無差別
388c29 法界門海。說無上法。普攝眾生。盡未來劫。
389a01 住普賢行。善男子。我成就此甚深自在妙音
389a02 解脫。於念念中。增長一切諸解脫門。念念充
389a03 滿一切法界。時善財童子。白夜神言。奇哉天
389a04 神。此解脫門。如是希有。聖者證得。其已久
389a05 如。夜神言。善男子。乃往古世。過世界轉微塵
389a06 數劫。有劫名離垢光明。有世界名法界功
389a07 德雲。

简体字

或为说一如来众会道场海法，或为说一切如来众会道场海法，或为说一如来法轮海法，或为说一切如来法轮海法，或为说一如来修多罗法，或为说一切如来修多罗法，或为说一如来集会法，或为说一切如来集会法，或为说一萨婆若心海法，或为说一切萨婆若心海法，或为说一乘出离法，或为说一切乘出离法。善男子，我以如是等不可说法门，为众生说。

“善男子，我入如来无差别法界门海，说无上法，普摄众生，尽未来劫，住普贤行。善男子，我成就此甚深自在妙音解脱，于念念中增长一切诸解脱门，念念充满一切法界。”

时，善财童子白夜神言：“奇哉！天神，此解脱门如是希有！圣者证得，其已久如？”

夜神言：“善男子，乃往古世，过世界转微尘数劫，有劫名离垢光明，有世界名法界功德云，

I sometimes teach beings the dharma of the ocean of a single *tathāgata*'s congregations;
I sometimes teach beings the dharma of the oceans of all *tathāgatas*' congregations;
I sometimes teach beings the dharma of the Dharma wheel of a single *tathāgata*;
I sometimes teach beings the dharma of the Dharma wheel of all *tathāgatas*;
I sometimes teach beings the dharma of a single *tathāgata*'s sutras;
I sometimes teach beings the dharma of all *tathāgatas*' sutras;
I sometimes teach beings the dharma of the gathering of a single *tathāgata*'s assembly;
I sometimes teach beings the dharma of the gathering of all *tathāgatas*' assemblies;
I sometimes teach beings the dharma of the ocean of a single omniscient mind;
I sometimes teach beings the dharma of the oceans of all omniscient minds;
I sometimes teach beings the dharma of emancipation through a single vehicle; and
I sometimes teach beings the dharma of emancipation through all vehicles.

Son of Good Family, I teach beings with an ineffable number of Dharma gateways such as these.

Son of Good Family, I have entered the ocean of the Tathāgata's gateways to the undifferentiated Dharma realm by which I teach the unexcelled Dharma to everywhere attract beings and dwell in the practices of Samantabhadra to the very end of all future kalpas.

Son of Good Family, I have perfected this "extremely profound and miraculous sublime sound" liberation with which, in each successive mind-moment, I bring about the growth of all gateways of liberation which in every mind-moment completely fill the entire Dharma realm.

Sudhana the Youth then addressed the Night Spirit, saying, "O Celestial Spirit, this is extraordinary indeed! This liberation gateway is so rare. How long has it been since the Āryā realized it?"

The Night Spirit then replied:

Son of Good Family, it was long ago, in the ancient past, back beyond a number of kalpas equal to the atoms in a world transformation[146] that there was a kalpa named Pristine Radiance in which there was a world known as Cloud of the Dharma Realm's Meritorious Qualities. Its substance was composed of an ocean of

正體字

以現一切眾生業摩尼王海為體。形如
389a08║ 蓮華。住四天下微塵數香摩尼須彌山網中。
389a09║ 以出一切如來本願音蓮華。而為莊嚴。須
389a10║ 彌山微塵數蓮華。而為眷屬。須彌山微塵數
389a11║ 香摩尼。以為間錯。有須彌山微塵數四天下。
389a12║ 一一四天下。有百千億那由他不可說不可
389a13║ 說城。善男子。彼世界中有四天下。名為妙幢。
389a14║ 中有王都。名普寶華光。去此不遠。有菩提場。
389a15║ 名普顯現法王宮殿。須彌山微塵數如來。於
389a16║ 中出現。其最初佛。名法海雷音光明王。彼佛
389a17║ 出時。有轉輪王。名清淨日光明面。於其佛所。
389a18║ 受持一切法海旋修多羅。佛涅槃後。其王出
389a19║ 家。護持正法。法欲滅時。有千部[1]異千種說
389a20║ 法。近於末劫。業惑障重。諸惡比丘。多有鬪
389a21║ 諍。樂著境界。不求功德。樂說王論賊論女論。
389a22║ 國論海論。及以一切世間之論。時王比丘。而
389a23║ 語之言。奇哉苦哉。佛於無量諸大劫海。集此
389a24║ 法炬。云何汝等。而共毀滅。作是說已。上昇虛
389a25║ 空。高七多羅樹。身出無量諸色焰雲。

简体字

以现一切众生业摩尼王海为体，形如莲华，住四天下微尘数香摩尼须弥山网中，以出一切如来本愿音莲华而为庄严，须弥山微尘数莲华而为眷属，须弥山微尘数香摩尼以为间错，有须弥山微尘数四天下，一一四天下有百千亿那由他不可说不可说城。

“善男子，彼世界中，有四天下，名为妙幢；中有王都，名普宝华光；去此不远，有菩提场，名普显现法王宫殿。须弥山微尘数如来于中出现，其最初佛，名法海雷音光明王。彼佛出时，有转轮王，名清净日光明面，于其佛所，受持一切法海旋修多罗。佛涅槃后，其王出家，护持正法。法欲灭时，有千部异众千种说法。近于末劫，业惑障重；诸恶比丘多有斗诤，乐著境界，不求功德，乐说王论、贼论、女论、国论、海论，及以一切世间之论。

“时，王比丘而语之言：‘奇哉！苦哉！佛于无量诸大劫海集此法炬，云何汝等而共毁灭？’作是说已，上升虚空，高七多罗树，身出无量诸色焰云，

sovereign *maṇi* jewels that reveal the karmic actions of all beings. It was shaped like a lotus flower and dwelt within a net of fragrant *maṇī* jewel Sumeru Mountains as numerous as the atoms in four continents. It was adorned with lotus flowers that emanated the sounds of the original vows of all *tathāgatas* and it had a retinue of lotus flowers as numerous as the atoms in Mount Sumeru. It was also inlaid with fragrant *maṇi* jewels as numerous as the atoms in Mount Sumeru. It had sets of four-continent lands as numerous as the atoms in Mount Sumeru and every one of those four-continent lands had a number of cities equal to a hundred thousand *koṭīs* of *nayutas* of ineffable-ineffables.

Son of Good Family, that world had a four-continent land known as Marvelous Banner in which there was a royal capital known as Universal Jewels' Floral Light. Not far from there was a site of enlightenment known as Everywhere Manifesting the Dharma King's Palace in which *tathāgatas* appeared that were as numerous as the atoms in Mount Sumeru.

The very first of those buddhas was known as Radiant King of the Dharma Ocean's Thunderous Sound. When that buddha appeared in the world, there was a wheel-turning king named Pure Solar Radiance Countenance who received and learned a scripture from that buddha that was called Whirlpool in the Ocean of All Dharmas Sutra. After that Buddha had entered nirvāṇa, that king left the householder's life and devoted himself to protecting and preserving right Dharma.

When the Dharma was on the verge of disappearing, there were a thousand heterodox sects adhering to a thousand ways of explaining the Dharma. Toward the end of the kalpa, the obstacles arising from karma and afflictions became so heavy that evil bhikshus were extensively engaged in quarrelsome disputation. They delighted in attachment to sense objects, did not seek to develop the meritorious qualities, and delighted in discussions about kings, in discussions about insurgents, in discussions about women, in discussions about the state, in discussions about the ocean, and in all kinds of other worldly discussions.

That king who had become a bhikshu then spoke to them, saying, "This is strange indeed and painful indeed! For an ocean of countless great kalpas, the Buddha strived to create this Dharma torch. How then can it be that you are all now joining in extinguishing it?" Having said this, he then rose into the sky to the height of seven *tāla* trees and sent forth from his body a flaming-light cloud shining with countless colors after which he emanated an immense web of

正體字

放種種
389a26‖ 色大光明網。令無量眾生。除煩惱熱。令無量
389a27‖ 眾生。發菩提心。以是因緣。彼如來教。復於六
389a28‖ 萬五千歲中。而得興盛。時有比丘尼。名法
389a29‖ 輪化光。是此王女。百千比丘尼。而為眷屬。聞
389b01‖ 父王語。及見神力。發菩提心。永不退轉。得三
389b02‖ 昧。名一切佛教燈。又得此甚深自在妙音解
389b03‖ 脫。得已。身心柔軟。即得現見法海雷音光明
389b04‖ 王如來一切神力。善男子。於汝意云何。彼
389b05‖ 時轉輪聖王。隨於如來。轉正法輪。佛涅槃後。
389b06‖ 興隆末法者。豈異人乎。今普賢菩薩是。其法
389b07‖ 輪化光比丘尼。即我身是。我於彼時。守護佛
389b08‖ 法。令十萬比丘尼。於阿耨多羅三藐三菩提。
389b09‖ 得不退轉。又令得現見一切佛三昧。又令得
389b10‖ 一切佛法輪金剛光明陀羅尼。又令得普入
389b11‖ 一切法門海般若波羅蜜。次有佛興。名離垢
389b12‖ 法光明。次有佛興。名法輪光明髻。次有佛興。
389b13‖ 名法日功德雲。次有佛興。名法海妙音王。次
389b14‖ 有佛興。名法日智慧燈。次有佛興。名法華
389b15‖ 幢雲。

简体字

放种种色大光明网，令无量众生除烦恼热，令无量众生发菩提心。以是因缘，彼如来教，复于六万五千岁中而得兴盛。

“时，有比丘尼，名法轮化光，是此王女，百千比丘尼而为眷属，闻父王语及见神力，发菩提心永不退转，得三昧，名一切佛教灯，又得此甚深自在妙音解脱；得已，身心柔软，即得现见法海雷音光明王如来一切神力。

“善男子，于汝意云何？彼时转轮圣王随于如来转正法轮，佛涅槃后兴隆末法者，岂异人乎？今普贤菩萨是。其法轮化光比丘尼，即我身是。我于彼时，守护佛法，令十万比丘尼于阿耨多罗三藐三菩提得不退转，又令得现见一切佛三昧，又令得一切佛法轮金刚光明陀罗尼，又令得普入一切法门海般若波罗蜜。

“次有佛兴，名离垢法光明；次有佛兴，名法轮光明髻；次有佛兴，名法日功德云；次有佛兴，名法海妙音王；次有佛兴，名法日智慧灯；次有佛兴，名法华幢云；

light rays in all different colors. These enabled countless beings to rid themselves of the heat of the afflictions and enabled countless beings to resolve to attain bodhi. For this reason, the teachings of that *tathāgata* then flourished in all their fullness for an additional sixty-five thousand years.

At that time, there was a bhikshuni named Dharma Wheel Transformation Radiance. She was the daughter of the king and was attended by a retinue of a hundred thousand bhikshunis. Having heard those words spoken by her father, the king, and having also witnessed his spiritual powers, she then made the ever-irreversible resolve to attain bodhi and acquired a samādhi known as "the lamp of all buddhas' teachings." She also acquired "the extremely profound and miraculous sublime sound liberation." Having acquired it, she also attained a state of pliancy of body and mind and then directly witnessed all the spiritual powers of that *tathāgata,* Radiant King of the Dharma Ocean's Thunderous Sound.

Son of Good Family, what do you think? As for that wheel-turning sage king who came along after that *tathāgata* and continued to turn the wheel of right Dharma, thereby enabling its flourishing resurgence during the Dharma ending age after that buddha's *parinirvāṇa,* could it have been anyone else? It was none other than our present era's Samantabhadra Bodhisattva.

As for that Dharma Wheel Transformation Radiance Bhikshuni, she was none other than myself. At that time, I preserved and protected the Buddha's Dharma and enabled ten myriads of bhikshunis to achieve irreversibility in progressing toward *anuttara-samyak-saṃbodhi.* I also enabled them to acquire "the samādhi of the direct seeing of all buddhas," also enabled them to acquire "the *dhāraṇī* of the vajra light of all buddhas' turning of the Dharma wheel," and also enabled them to acquire the *prajñāpāramitā* that everywhere enters the ocean of all gateways into the Dharma.

Next there appeared a buddha known as Stainless Dharma Radiance.

Next there appeared a buddha known as Dharma Wheel's Radiant Crest.

Next there appeared a buddha known as Dharma Sun's Cloud of Qualities.

Next there appeared a buddha known as King of the Dharma Ocean's Wondrous Voices.

Next there appeared a buddha known as Dharma Sun's Lamp of Wisdom.

Next there appeared a buddha known as Cloud of Dharma Flower Banners.

正體字

次有佛興。名法焰山幢王。次有佛興。名
389b16║ 甚深法功德月。次有佛興。名法智普光藏。次
389b17║ 有佛興。名開示普智藏。次有佛興。名功德
389b18║ 藏山王。次有佛興。名普門須彌賢。次有佛興。
389b19║ 名一切法精進幢。次有佛興。名法寶華功德
389b20║ 雲。次有佛興。名寂靜光明髻。次有佛興。名法
389b21║ 光明慈悲月。次有佛興。名功德焰海。次有佛
389b22║ 興。名智日普光明。次有佛興。名普賢圓滿智。
389b23║ 次有佛興。名神通智光王。次有佛興。名福德
389b24║ 華光燈。次有佛興。名智師子幢王。次有佛興。
389b25║ 名日光普照王。次有佛興。名須彌寶莊嚴相。
389b26║ 次有佛興。名日光普照。次有佛興。名法王功
389b27║ 德月。次有佛興。名開敷蓮華妙音雲。次有佛
389b28║ 興。名日光明相。

简体字

次有佛兴，名法焰山幢王；次有佛兴，名甚深法功德月；次有佛兴，名法智普光藏；次有佛兴，名开示普智藏；次有佛兴，名功德藏山王；次有佛兴，名普门须弥贤；次有佛兴，名一切法精进幢；次有佛兴，名法宝华功德云；次有佛兴，名寂静光明髻；次有佛兴，名法光明慈悲月；次有佛兴，名功德焰海；次有佛兴，名智日普光明；次有佛兴，名普贤圆满智；次有佛兴，名神通智光王；次有佛兴，名福德华光灯；次有佛兴，名智师子幢王；次有佛兴，名日光普照王；次有佛兴，名须弥宝庄严相；次有佛兴，名日光普照；次有佛兴，名法王功德月；次有佛兴，名开敷莲华妙音云；次有佛兴，名日光明相；

Next there appeared a buddha known as Banner King of the Mountain of Flaming Dharma.

Next there appeared a buddha known as Moon of Extremely Profound Dharma Qualities.

Next there appeared a buddha known as Treasury of Dharma Wisdom's Universal Light.

Next there appeared a buddha known as Explainer of the Treasury of Universal Wisdom.

Next there appeared a buddha known as Treasury of Qualities Mountain King.

Next there appeared a buddha known as Paragon of the Universal Gateway's Sumeru.

Next there appeared a buddha known as Banner of Vigor in All Dharmas.

Next there appeared a buddha known as Cloud of the Qualities of the Dharma Jewel's Flower.

Next there appeared a buddha known as Crest of Quiescent Light.

Next there appeared a buddha known as Dharma Light of the Moon of Kindness and Compassion.

Next there appeared a buddha known as Meritorious Qualities' Ocean of Flaming Light.

Next there appeared a buddha known as Universal Light of the Sun of Wisdom.

Next there appeared a buddha known as Universal Worthy's Perfectly Full Wisdom.

Next there appeared a buddha known as King of the Light of Spiritual Superknowledges and Wisdom.

Next there appeared a buddha known as Lamp of the Light of the Flower of Merit.

Next there appeared a buddha known as Banner King of the Lion of Wisdom.

Next there appeared a buddha known as King of the Sunlight's Universal Illumination.

Next there appeared a buddha known as Signs of Sumeru's Jewel Adornment.

Next there appeared a buddha known as Sunlight's Universal Illumination.

Next there appeared a buddha known as Moon of the Dharma King's Qualities.

Next there appeared a buddha known as Cloud of the Marvelous Sounds of the Blooming Lotus.

Next there appeared a buddha known as Sunlight's Shining Signs.

正體字

次有佛興。名普光明妙法音。
389b29‖ 次有佛興。名師子金剛那羅延無畏。次有佛
389c01‖ 興。名普智勇猛幢。次有佛興。名普開法蓮
389c02‖ 華身。次有佛興。名功德妙華海。次有佛興。名
389c03‖ 道場功德月。次有佛興。名法炬熾然月。次有
389c04‖ 佛興。名普光明髻。次有佛興。名法幢燈。次有
389c05‖ 佛興。名金剛海幢雲。次有佛興。名名稱山功
389c06‖ 德雲。次有佛興。名栴檀妙月。次有佛興。名普
389c07‖ 妙光明華。次有佛興。名照一切眾生光明王。
389c08‖ 次有佛興。名功德蓮華藏。次有佛興。名香焰
389c09‖ 光明王。次有佛興。名波頭摩華因。次有佛
389c10‖ 興。名眾相山普光明。次有佛興。名普名稱幢。
389c11‖ 次有佛興。名須彌普門光。次有佛興。名功德
389c12‖ 法城光。次有佛興。名大樹山光明。

简体字

次有佛兴，名普光明妙法音；次有佛兴，名师子金刚那罗延无畏；次有佛兴，名普智勇猛幢；次有佛兴，名普开法莲华身；次有佛兴，名功德妙华海；次有佛兴，名道场功德月；次有佛兴，名法炬炽然月；次有佛兴，名普光明髻；次有佛兴，名法幢灯；次有佛兴，名金刚海幢云；次有佛兴，名名称山功德云；次有佛兴，名栴檀妙月；次有佛兴，名普妙光明华；次有佛兴，名照一切众生光明王；次有佛兴，名功德莲华藏；次有佛兴，名香焰光明王；次有佛兴，名波头摩华因；次有佛兴，名众相山普光明；次有佛兴，名普名称幢；次有佛兴，名须弥普门光；次有佛兴，名功德法城光；次有佛兴，名大树山光明；

Next there appeared a buddha known as Universal Radiance and Sublime Voice of Dharma.

Next there appeared a buddha known as Lion Vajra's Nārāyaṇa Fearlessness.

Next there appeared a buddha known as Banner of Universal Wisdom's Courage.

Next there appeared a buddha known as Body of the Universally Opening Dharma Lotus.

Next there appeared a buddha known as Ocean of Wondrous Flowers of Meritorious Qualities.

Next there appeared a buddha known as Moon of the Site of Enlightenment's Qualities.

Next there appeared a buddha known as Moon of the Dharma Torch's Blazing Flames.

Next there appeared a buddha known as Crest of Universal Radiance.

Next there appeared a buddha known as Dharma Banner Lamp.

Next there appeared a buddha known as Banner Cloud of the Vajra Ocean.

Next there appeared a buddha known as Cloud of the Qualities of the Famous Mountain.

Next there appeared a buddha known as Marvelous Sandalwood Moon.

Next there appeared a buddha known as Universally Marvelous Flower of Radiance.

Next there appeared a buddha known as King of the Light That Illuminates All Beings.

Next there appeared a buddha known as Treasury of the Lotuses of Meritorious Qualities.

Next there appeared a buddha known as King of Fragrant Flaming Light.

Next there appeared a buddha known as Cause of the Padma's Blossoming.

Next there appeared a buddha known as Universal Light of the Mountain of Many Signs.

Next there appeared a buddha known as Banner of Universal Fame.

Next there appeared a buddha known as Light of Sumeru's Universal Gateway.

Next there appeared a buddha known as Light of the Dharma City of Meritorious Qualities.

Next there appeared a buddha known as Light of Big Tree Mountain.

正體字

次有佛興。
389c13 名普德光明幢。次有佛興。名功德吉祥相。次
389c14 有佛興。名勇猛法力幢。次有佛興。名法輪光
389c15 明音。次有佛興。名功德山智慧光。次有佛興。
389c16 名無上妙法月。次有佛興。名法蓮華淨光幢。
389c17 次有佛興。名寶蓮華光明藏。次有佛興。名光
389c18 焰雲山燈。次有佛興。名普覺華。次有佛興。
389c19 名種種功德焰須彌藏。次有佛興。名圓滿光
389c20 山王。次有佛興。名福德雲莊嚴。次有佛興。名
389c21 法山雲幢。次有佛興。名功德山光明。次有佛
389c22 興。名法日雲燈王。次有佛興。名法雲名稱王。
389c23 次有佛興。名法輪雲。次有佛興。名開悟菩提
389c24 智光幢。次有佛興。名普照法輪月。次有佛興。
389c25 名寶山威德賢。次有佛興。名賢德廣大光。

简体字

次有佛兴，名普德光明幢；次有佛兴，名功德吉祥相；次有佛兴，名勇猛法力幢；次有佛兴，名法轮光明音；次有佛兴，名功德山智慧光；次有佛兴，名无上妙法月；次有佛兴，名法莲华净光幢；次有佛兴，名宝莲华光明藏；次有佛兴，名光焰云山灯；次有佛兴，名普觉华；次有佛兴，名种种功德焰须弥藏；次有佛兴，名圆满光山王；次有佛兴，名福德云庄严；次有佛兴，名法山云幢；次有佛兴，名功德山光明；次有佛兴，名法日云灯王；次有佛兴，名法云名称王；次有佛兴，名法轮云；次有佛兴，名开悟菩提智光幢；次有佛兴，名普照法轮月；次有佛兴，名宝山威德贤；次有佛兴，名贤德广大光；

Next there appeared a buddha known as Radiant Banner of Universal Virtue.

Next there appeared a buddha known as Auspicious Sign of Meritorious Qualities.

Next there appeared a buddha known as Banner of Courageous Dharma Power.

Next there appeared a buddha known as Light and Sound of the Wheel of Dharma.

Next there appeared a buddha known as Wisdom Light of the Mountain of Meritorious Qualities.

Next there appeared a buddha known as Moon of the Unsurpassably Wondrous Dharma.

Next there appeared a buddha known as Banner of the Pure Light of the Dharma Lotus.

Next there appeared a buddha known as Treasury of Jeweled Lotus Flower Light.

Next there appeared a buddha known as Lamp of the Mountain of Flaming Radiance Clouds.

Next there appeared a buddha known as Flower of Universal Enlightenment.

Next there appeared a buddha known as Treasury of a Sumeru of Various Qualities' Flaming Radiance.

Next there appeared a buddha known as King of the Mountain of Perfected Radiance.

Next there appeared a buddha known as Merit Cloud Adornment.

Next there appeared a buddha known as Cloud Banner of the Mountain of Dharma Mountain.

Next there appeared a buddha known as Light of the Mountain of Meritorious Qualities.

Next there appeared a buddha known as Dharma Sun Cloud Lamp King.

Next there appeared a buddha known as Famous King of the Dharma Cloud.

Next there appeared a buddha known as Dharma Wheel Cloud.

Next there appeared a buddha known as Banner of the Bodhi Awakening Wisdom Light.

Next there appeared a buddha known as Universally Illuminating Dharma Wheel Moon.

Next there appeared a buddha known as Awesomely Virtuous Worthy of the Mountain of Jewels.

Next there appeared a buddha known as Vast Radiance of Worthy Virtue.

正體字

次
389c26‖ 有佛興。名普智雲。次有佛興。名法力功德山。
389c27‖ 次有佛興。名功德香焰王。次有佛興。名金色
389c28‖ 摩尼山妙音聲。次有佛興。名頂髻出一切法
389c29‖ 光明雲。次有佛興。名法輪熾盛光。次有佛
390a01‖ 興。名無上功德山。次有佛興。名精進炬光明
390a02‖ 雲。次有佛興。名三昧印廣大光明冠。次有佛
390a03‖ 興。名寶光明功德王。次有佛興。名法炬寶蓋
390a04‖ 音。次有佛興。名普照虛空界無畏法光明。次
390a05‖ 有佛興。名月相莊嚴幢。次有佛興。名光明焰
390a06‖ 山雲。次有佛興。名照無障礙法虛空。次有佛
390a07‖ 興。名開顯智光身。次有佛興。名世主德光明
390a08‖ 音。次有佛興。名一切法三昧光明音。次有佛
390a09‖ 興。名法音功德藏。次有佛興。名熾然焰法海
390a10‖ 雲。次有佛興。名普照三世相大光明。

简体字

次有佛兴，名普智云；次有佛兴，名法力功德山；次有佛兴，名功德香焰王；次有佛兴，名金色摩尼山妙音声；次有佛兴，名顶髻出一切法光明云；次有佛兴，名法轮炽盛光；次有佛兴，名无上功德山；次有佛兴，名精进炬光明云；次有佛兴，名三昧印广大光明冠；次有佛兴，名宝光明功德王；次有佛兴，名法炬宝盖音；次有佛兴，名普照虚空界无畏法光明；次有佛兴，名月相庄严幢；次有佛兴，名光明焰山云；次有佛兴，名照无障碍法虚空；次有佛兴，名开显智光身；次有佛兴，名世主德光明音；次有佛兴，名一切法三昧光明音；次有佛兴，名法音功德藏；次有佛兴，名炽然焰法海云；次有佛兴，名普照三世相大光明；

Next there appeared a buddha known as Universal Wisdom Cloud.

Next there appeared a buddha known as Mountain of Qualities of the Power of Dharma.

Next there appeared a buddha known as King of the Qualities' Fragrance and Flaming Radiance.

Next there appeared a buddha known as Sublime Sound of the Golden Maṇi Jewel Mountain.

Next there appeared a buddha known as Uṣṇīṣa Emanating Clouds of the Light of All Dharmas.

Next there appeared a buddha known as Flourishing Radiance of the Wheel of Dharma.

Next there appeared a buddha known as Mountain of Peerless Qualities.

Next there appeared a buddha known as Cloud of Light from the Torch of Vigor.

Next there appeared a buddha known as Crown of Vast Radiance from the Seal of Samādhi.

Next there appeared a buddha known as Jewel Light Qualities King.

Next there appeared a buddha known as Sound of the Dharma Torch's Jeweled Canopy.

Next there appeared a buddha known as Fearless Dharma Radiance Everywhere Illuminating the Realm of Space.

Next there appeared a buddha known as Banner of the Lunar Signs' Adornment.

Next there appeared a buddha known as Cloud of the Mountain of Flaming Radiance.

Next there appeared a buddha known as Illumination of the Sky of Unimpeded Dharma.

Next there appeared a buddha known as Body Revealing the Light of Wisdom.

Next there appeared a buddha known as Light and Sound of the World Leader's Qualities.

Next there appeared a buddha known as Light and Sound of the Samādhi of All Dharmas.

Next there appeared a buddha known as Treasury of the Sound of Dharma's Meritorious Qualities.

Next there appeared a buddha known as The Dharma Ocean's Cloud of Blazing Light.

Next there appeared a buddha known as Great Radiance Everywhere Illuminating the Signs of the Three Periods of Time.

正體字

次有佛
390a11‖ 興。名普照法輪山。次有佛興。名法界師子光。
390a12‖ 次有佛興。名須彌華光明。次有佛興。名一
390a13‖ 切三昧海師子焰。次有佛興。名普智光明燈。
390a14‖ 善男子。如是等須彌山微塵數如來。其最後
390a15‖ 佛。名法界城智慧燈。並於離垢光明劫中。出
390a16‖ 興于世。我皆尊重。親近供養。聽聞受持所說
390a17‖ 妙法。亦於彼一切諸如來所。出家學道護持
390a18‖ 法教。入此菩薩甚深自在妙音解脫。種種方
390a19‖ 便。教化成熟無量眾生。從是已來。於佛刹
390a20‖ 微塵數劫。所有諸佛。出興於世。我皆供養。修
390a21‖ 行其法。善男子。我從是來。於生死夜無明昏
390a22‖ 寐諸眾生中。而獨覺悟。令諸眾生。守護心城。
390a23‖ 捨三界城。住一切智無上法城。善男子。我唯
390a24‖ 知此甚深自在妙音解脫。令諸世間。離戲論
390a25‖ 語。不作二語。常真實語。恒清淨語。如諸菩薩
390a26‖ 摩訶薩。能知一切語言自性。於念念中。自在
390a27‖ 開悟一切眾生。

简体字

次有佛兴，名普照法轮山；次有佛兴，名法界师子光；次有佛兴，名须弥华光明；次有佛兴，名一切三昧海师子焰；次有佛兴，名普智光明灯。

“善男子，如是等须弥山微尘数如来，其最后佛，名法界城智慧灯，并于离垢光明劫中，出兴于世。我皆尊重，亲近供养，听闻受持所说妙法；亦于彼一切诸如来所，出家学道，护持法教，入此菩萨甚深自在妙音解脱，种种方便教化成熟无量众生。从是已来，于佛刹微尘数劫，所有诸佛出兴于世；我皆供养，修行其法。

“善男子，我从是来，于生死夜无明昏寐诸众生中而独觉悟；令诸众生，守护心城，舍三界城，住一切智无上法城。

“善男子，我唯知此甚深自在妙音解脱，令诸世间，离戏论语，不作二语，常真实语，恒清净语。如诸菩萨摩诃萨，能知一切语言自性，于念念中自在开悟一切众生，

Next there appeared a buddha known as Universally Illuminating Dharma Wheel Mountain.

Next there appeared a buddha known as Light of the Lion of the Dharma Realm.

Next there appeared a buddha known as Sumeru Flower Light.

Next there appeared a buddha known as Flaming Radiance of the Lion of the Ocean of All Samādhis.

And next there appeared a buddha known as Lamp of the Light of Universal Wisdom.

Son of Good Family, *tathāgatas* such as these as numerous as the atoms in Mount Sumeru appeared in this way. The very last of those buddhas was named Wisdom Lamp of the City of the Dharma Realm. He too appeared in the world during that Pristine Radiance kalpa.

I revered, drew near to, and made offerings to them all, listened to, absorbed, and retained the sublime Dharma that they proclaimed, and also, in the presence of all those *tathāgatas*, left the home life, studied the path, and guarded and preserved their Dharma teachings.

Having entered this bodhisattva's "extremely profound and miraculous sublime sound liberation," I used many different skillful means to teach and ripen countless beings. From this point on forward to the present, as all buddhas in kalpas as numerous as the atoms in a buddha *kṣetra* have appeared in the world, I have made offerings to them all and cultivated their Dharma.

Son of Good Family, from this point on, throughout the nighttime of *saṃsāra*, in the midst of beings submerged in their confused slumber of ignorance, when I alone have awakened, I have enabled those beings to guard the city of the mind, abandon the city of the three realms of existence, and dwell in the city of the unexcelled Dharma of all-knowledge.

Son of Good Family, I know only this "extremely profound and miraculous sublime sound liberation" by which I enable those in the world to abandon lewd and frivolous speech, to refrain from duplicitous speech, to always engage in truthful speech, and to constantly abide in pure speech.

As for the bodhisattva-mahāsattvas, how could I know of or be able to speak about the meritorious qualities and practices of they:

Who are able to realize the essential nature of all speech;

Who in every mind-moment exercise mastery in awakening all beings;

正體字

入一切眾生言音海。於一切
390a28 言[1]辭。悉皆[2]辨了。明見一切諸法門海。於普
390a29 攝一切法陀羅尼。已得自在。隨諸眾生心之
390b01 所疑。而為說法。究竟調伏一切眾生。能普攝
390b02 受一切眾生。巧修菩薩諸無上業。深入菩薩
390b03 諸微細智。能善觀察諸菩薩藏。能自在說諸
390b04 菩薩法。何以故。已得成就一切法輪陀羅尼
390b05 故。而我云何能知能說彼功德行。善男子。此
390b06 佛會中。有主夜神。名開敷一切樹華。汝詣彼
390b07 問。菩薩云何學一切智。云何安立一切眾生。
390b08 住一切智。爾時守護一切城主夜神。欲重宣
390b09 此解脫義。為善財童子。而說頌言
390b10 菩薩解脫深難見　虛空如如平等相
390b11 普見無邊法界內　一切三世諸如來
390b12 出生無量勝功德　證入難思真法性
390b13 增長一切自在智　開通三世解脫道
390b14 過於剎轉微塵劫　爾時有劫名淨光
390b15 世界名為法焰雲　其城號曰寶華光
390b16 其中諸佛興於世　[3]量與須彌塵數等

简体字

入一切众生言音海，于一切言辞悉皆辩了，明见一切诸法门海，于普摄一切法陀罗尼已得自在，随诸众生心之所疑而为说法，究竟调伏一切众生，能普摄受一切众生，巧修菩萨诸无上业，深入菩萨诸微细智，能善观察诸菩萨藏，能自在说诸菩萨法。何以故？已得成就一切法轮陀罗尼故。而我云何能知能说彼功德行？

“善男子，此佛会中，有主夜神，名开敷一切树华。汝诣彼问：菩萨云何学一切智？云何安立一切众生住一切智？”

尔时，守护一切城主夜神，欲重宣此解脱义，为善财童子而说颂言：

“菩萨解脱深难见，虚空如如平等相，
普见无边法界内，一切三世诸如来。
出生无量胜功德，证入难思真法性，
增长一切自在智，开通三世解脱道。
过于刹转微尘劫，尔时有劫名净光，
世界名为法焰云，其城号曰宝华光。
其中诸佛兴于世，无量须弥尘数等；

Who enter the ocean of all beings' languages and completely distinguish the import of all their phrasings;

Who clearly perceive the ocean of all gateways into the Dharma;

Who have already achieved sovereign mastery in their use of the *dhāraṇī* that everywhere subsumes all dharmas;

Who adapt to the doubts in the minds of beings as they teach the Dharma for them;

Who bring about the ultimate training of all beings;

Who are able to everywhere attract and sustain all beings;

Who skillfully cultivate all of the bodhisattva's unsurpassed karmic deeds;

Who deeply enter the bodhisattva's subtle wisdom;

Who are able to skillfully contemplate the canon of all bodhisattvas; and

Who are able to speak with sovereign mastery on all bodhisattva dharmas?

And why [are they able to do all this]? This is because they have already perfected the *dhāraṇī* of the *maṇḍala* of all dharmas.

Son of Good Family, in this Buddha's congregation, there is a night spirit by the name of Sarvavṛkṣapraphullanasukhasaṃvāsā, or "Bringing Forth the Blossoms of All Trees." You should go there, pay your respects, and ask, "How should the bodhisattva train in his quest to attain all-knowledge and how should he go about establishing all beings in all-knowledge?"

At that time, wishing to once again proclaim the meaning of this liberation, the Night Spirit, Sarvanagararaksāsambhavatejahśrī, spoke these verses for Sudhana the Youth:

This liberation of the bodhisattvas is extremely difficult to perceive,
for it has the character of space, true suchness, and uniform equality.
With it they see everywhere within the boundless Dharma realm
all the *tathāgatas* of the three periods of time.

They produce countless supreme meritorious qualities
and realize and penetrate the inconceivable true nature of dharmas.
They grow in all forms of sovereign wisdom
and open up the path of liberation of the three periods of time.

Back beyond kalpas as many as the atoms in a *kṣetra* transformation,[147]
there was at that time a kalpa named Pristine Radiance
and a world named Cloud of Dharma's Flaming Radiance
that had a city named Jewel Flower Light.

In it, all the buddhas who appeared in the world
were as numerous as the atoms contained in Mount Sumeru.

正體字

390b17 有佛名為法海音　於此劫中[4]先出現
390b18 乃至其中最後佛　名為法界焰燈王
390b19 如是一切諸如來　我皆供養聽受法
390b20 我見法海雷音佛　其身普作真金色
390b21 諸相莊嚴如寶山　發心願得成如來
390b22 我暫見彼如來身　即發菩提廣大心
390b23 誓願勤求一切智　性與法界虛空等
390b24 由斯普見三世佛　及以一切菩薩眾
390b25 亦見國[5]王眾生海　而普攀緣起大悲
390b26 隨諸眾生心所樂　示現種種無量身
390b27 普遍十方諸國土　動地舒光悟含識
390b28 見第二佛而親近　亦見十方剎海佛
390b29 乃至最後佛出興　如是須彌塵數等
390c01 於諸剎轉微塵劫　所有如來照世燈
390c02 我皆親近而瞻奉　令此解脫得清淨
390c03 爾時善財童子。得入此菩薩甚深自在妙音
390c04 解脫故。入無邊三昧海。入廣大總持海。得菩
390c05 薩大神通。獲菩薩大辯才。心大歡喜。觀察守
390c06 護一切城主夜神。以偈讚曰
390c07 已行廣大妙慧海　已度無邊諸有海

简体字

有佛名为法海音，于此劫中先出现；
乃至其中最后佛，名为法界焰灯王；
如是一切诸如来，我皆供养听受法。
我见法海雷音佛，其身普作真金色，
诸相庄严如宝山，发心愿得成如来。
我暂见彼如来身，即发菩提广大心，
誓愿勤求一切智，性与法界虚空等。
由斯普见三世佛，及以一切菩萨众；
亦见国土众生海，而普攀缘起大悲。
随诸众生心所乐，示现种种无量身，
普遍十方诸国土，动地舒光悟含识。
见第二佛而亲近，亦见十方刹海佛，
乃至最后佛出兴，如是须弥尘数等。
于诸刹转微尘劫，所有如来照世灯；
我皆亲近而瞻奉，令此解脱得清净。”

尔时，善财童子得入此菩萨甚深自在妙音解脱故，入无边三昧海，入广大总持海，得菩萨大神通，获菩萨大辩才；心大欢喜，观察守护一切城主夜神，以偈赞曰：

“已行广大妙慧海，已度无边诸有海，

Among them was a Buddha named Dharma Ocean Sound
who was the very first of them to appear in that kalpa.

This continued until the last buddha appeared there
who was named Dharma Realm's Flaming Radiance Lamp King.
To all these *tathāgatas* who appeared in this way,
I presented offerings and listened to the Dharma they taught.

I saw Dharma Ocean Thunder Sound Buddha
whose body everywhere shone with the color of real gold.
Adorned with all the marks, he resembled a mountain of jewels.
It was then that I made the resolve and vowed to become a *tathāgata*.

When I had but briefly seen the body of that *tathāgata,*
I immediately summoned the vast resolve to attain bodhi,
vowed to diligently seek to realize all-knowledge
and the nature that is like the Dharma realm's empty space.

Because of this, I everywhere saw all buddhas of the three times
as well as all their bodhisattva congregations.
I also saw the oceans of lands and their beings
and took them all as the focus for developing the great compassion.

In accordance with whatever befits the inclinations of beings,
I manifest countless bodies of many different types
that everywhere pervade all lands of the ten directions,
shake the earth, emanate light, and awaken sentient beings.

When I saw the second buddha, I then drew near to him
and also saw the buddhas in the oceans of *kṣetras* of the ten directions.
And so I continued in this way until that very last buddha appeared.
In this way, they came to equal all the atoms in Mount Sumeru.

For kalpas as numerous as the atoms in a *kṣetra* transformation,
I drew near to all those *tathāgatas,* those world-illuminating lamps,
and, as I gazed up at them in admiration, I served them
and thus brought about the purification of this liberation.

At that time, because he was able to enter this bodhisattva's "extremely profound and miraculous sublime sound" liberation, Sudhana the Youth then entered an ocean of boundless samādhis, entered an ocean of vast complete-retention *dhāraṇīs,* acquired the bodhisattva's great spiritual superknowledges, acquired the bodhisattva's immense capacities for eloquence, and then, with a mind of great joyous delight, he contemplated the Night Spirit, Sarvanagararaksāsam bhavatejahśrī, and spoke these verses of praise:

You have already sailed on the vast ocean of sublime wisdom,
have already gone beyond the boundless ocean of existence,

正體字

390c08 ║ 長壽無患智藏身　威德光明住此眾
390c09 ║ 了達法性如虛空　普入三世皆無礙
390c10 ║ 念念攀緣一切境　心心永斷諸分別
390c11 ║ 了達眾生無有性　而於眾生起大悲
390c12 ║ 深入如來解脫門　廣度群迷無量眾
390c13 ║ 觀察思惟一切法　了知證入諸法性
390c14 ║ 如是修行佛智慧　普化眾生令解脫
390c15 ║ 天是眾生調御師　開示如來智慧道
390c16 ║ 普為法界諸含識　說離世間眾怖行
390c17 ║ 已住如來諸願道　已受菩提廣大教
390c18 ║ 已修一切遍行力　已見十方佛自在
390c19 ║ 天神心淨如虛空　普離一切諸煩惱
390c20 ║ 了知三世無量剎　諸佛菩薩及眾生
390c21 ║ 天神一念悉了知　晝夜日月年劫海
390c22 ║ 亦知一切眾生類　種種名相各差別
390c23 ║ 十方眾生生死處　有色無色想無想
390c24 ║ 隨順世俗悉了知　引導使入菩提路
390c25 ║ 已生如來誓願家　已入諸佛功德海
390c26 ║ 法身清淨心無礙　隨眾生樂現眾色
390c27 ║ 時善財童子。說此頌已。禮夜神足。

简体字

长寿无患智藏身，威德光明住此众。
了达法性如虚空，普入三世皆无碍；
念念攀缘一切境，心心永断诸分别。
了达众生无有性，而于众生起大悲；
深入如来解脱门，广度群迷无量众。
观察思惟一切法，了知证入诸法性；
如是修行佛智慧，普化众生令解脱。
天是众生调御师，开示如来智慧道，
普为法界诸含识，说离世间众怖行。
已住如来诸愿道，已受菩提广大教，
已修一切遍行力，已见十方佛自在。
天神心净如虚空，普离一切诸烦恼，
了知三世无量刹，诸佛菩萨及众生。
天神一念悉了知，昼夜日月年劫海；
亦知一切众生类，种种名相各差别。
十方众生生死处，有色无色想无想，
随顺世俗悉了知，引导使入菩提路。
已生如来誓愿家，已入诸佛功德海，
法身清净心无碍，随众生乐现众色。”
时，善财童子说此颂已，礼夜神足，

have a long-lived body free of disasters that is a treasury of wisdom,
and, with the radiance of awesome virtue, dwell in this assembly.

Fully comprehending dharmas' nature as like empty space,
you everywhere unimpededly enter the three periods of time.
In each successive mind-moment, you focus on all objective spheres
while, in every thought, you forever sever all discriminations.

Fully comprehending that beings have no inherent nature at all,
you nevertheless arouse the great compassion for beings.
You deeply enter the Tathāgata's gateways of liberation
and extensively liberate countless beings submerged in confusion.

Contemplating and reflecting upon all dharmas,
you fully know and realize entry into the nature of all dharmas.
It is in this way that you cultivate the wisdom of the Buddha
and everywhere teach beings, thereby enabling their liberation.

O Goddess, you are the teacher who guides and trains beings,
and who reveals to them the path to the Tathāgata's wisdom.
Everywhere, for all of the sentient beings of the Dharma realm,
you explain the practices for leaving behind the world's many terrors.

You already abide in the path of all vows of the Tathāgata
and you have already taken on the vast teachings leading to bodhi.
You have already cultivated the pervasively effective powers
and have seen the sovereign mastery of the ten directions' buddhas.

O Goddess, your mind has become as pure as space
and it has everywhere transcended all of the afflictions.
It fully knows the countless *kṣetras* of the three periods of time
as well as all buddhas, all bodhisattvas, and all beings.

O Goddess, in but a single mind-moment, you fully know
the ocean of all days and nights, all days, months, years, and kalpas
while also knowing with regard to all types of beings
each of their many different names and features.

The stations of rebirth of the beings of the ten directions,
whether with form, formless, with perception or without perception,
you fully comprehend in accordance with their worldly ways,
lead them all forth, and then enable them to enter the path to bodhi.

Having already been born into the house of the Tathāgata's vows,
having already entered the ocean of all buddhas' meritorious qualities,
and having acquired a purified Dharma body and unimpeded mind,
adapting to beings' inclinations, you then appear in many forms.

At that time, having spoken these verses, Sudhana the Youth then bowed down in reverence at the feet of the Night Spirit and

正體字

遶無量匝。
390c28 慇懃瞻仰。辭退而去
391a02 [1]大方廣佛華嚴經卷[2]第七十二
391a05 [6]入法界品第三十九之十三
391a06 爾時善財童子。入菩薩甚深自在妙音解脫
391a07 門修行增進。往詣開敷一切樹華夜神所。見
391a08 其身在眾寶香樹樓閣之內妙寶所成師子座
391a09 上。百萬夜神。所共圍遶。時善財童子。頂禮其
391a10 足。於前合掌。而作是言。聖者。我已先發阿耨
391a11 多羅三藐三菩提心。而未知菩薩云何學菩
391a12 薩行。云何得一切智。唯願垂慈。為我宣說。夜
391a13 神言。善男子。我於此娑婆世界。日光已沒。蓮
391a14 華覆合。諸人眾等。罷遊觀時。見其一切若山
391a15 若水。若城若野。如是等處。種種眾生。咸悉發
391a16 心。欲還所住。我皆密護。令得正道。達其處
391a17 所。宿夜安樂。善男子。若有眾生。盛年好色。
391a18 憍慢放逸。五欲自恣。我為示現老病死相。令
391a19 生恐怖。捨離諸惡。復為稱歎種種善根。使其
391a20 修習。為慳吝者讚歎布施。為破戒者稱揚淨
391a21 戒。有瞋恚者教住大慈。

简体字

绕无量匝，殷勤瞻仰，辞退而去。

大方广佛华严经卷第七十二

入法界品第三十九之十三

尔时，善财童子入菩萨甚深自在妙音解脱门，修行增进。

往诣开敷一切树华夜神所，见其身在众宝香树楼阁之内妙宝所成师子座上，百万夜神所共围绕。

时，善财童子顶礼其足，于前合掌而作是言：“圣者，我已先发阿耨多罗三藐三菩提心，而未知菩萨云何学菩萨行？云何得一切智？唯愿垂慈，为我宣说！”

夜神言：“善男子，我于此娑婆世界，日光已没，莲华覆合，诸人众等罢游观时，见其一切若山、若水、若城、若野，如是等处种种众生，咸悉发心欲还所住；我皆密护，令得正道，达其处所，宿夜安乐。

“善男子，若有众生，盛年好色，憍慢放逸，五欲自恣。我为示现老、病、死相，令生恐怖，舍离诸恶。复为称叹种种善根，使其修习；为悭吝者，赞叹布施；为破戒者，称扬净戒；有瞋恚者，教住大慈；

circumambulated her countless times as he gazed up at her in attentive admiration. He then respectfully withdrew and departed.

37 – Sarvavṛkṣapraphullanasukhasaṃvāsā

At that time, Sudhana the Youth entered the bodhisattva's "extremely profound and miraculous sublime sound" liberation gateway and cultivated and progressed into it. He then went to pay his respects to the night spirit, Sarvavṛkṣapraphullanasukhasaṁvāsā, or "Bringing Forth All Trees' Blossoms." He then saw her within a tower of many jewels and fragrant trees, seated on a lion throne made of marvelous jewels where she was surrounded by a hundred myriads of night spirits.

Sudhana the Youth then bowed down in reverence at her feet, stood before her with palms pressed together, and addressed her, saying:

> O Āryā, I have already resolved to attain *anuttara-samyak-saṃbodhi.* Even so, I do not yet know how the bodhisattva should train in the bodhisattva practices or how he is to attain all-knowledge. Please bestow your kindness on me and expound on these matters for my sake.

The Night Spirit then said:

> Son of Good Family, when, in this Sahā World, the light of the sun grows dim at sunset, the lotus flowers close their blossoms, and crowds of people stop wandering about and sightseeing, if I see anyone still out and about in such places as the mountains, rivers, cities, or wilderness and any of those various beings have decided they wish to return to their dwelling places, I secretly protect them and enable them to find the right path to reach their homes and then happily pass the night.
>
> Son of Good Family, if there are any beings who, in their prime, are fond of lustful indulgences, who have become arrogant and neglectful, or who have given themselves over to unrestrained pursuit of the five desires, I then reveal to them the signs of aging, sickness, and death, thereby arousing fear in them and motivating them to relinquish all such wrong behavior. For their benefit, I then also praise the many different kinds of roots of goodness to encourage them to cultivate them:
>
> For those who are miserly, I praise the practice of giving;
> For those who break the moral precepts, I praise and promote purity in the moral precepts;
> For those who are full of hatred, I teach them to abide in the great kindness;

正體字

懷惱害者令行忍辱。
391a22║ 若懈怠者令起精進。若散亂者令修禪定。住
391a23║ 惡慧者令學般若。樂小乘者令住大乘。樂著
391a24║ 三界諸趣中者。令住菩薩願波羅[7]蜜。若有
391a25║ 眾生。福智微劣。為諸結業之所逼迫多留礙
391a26║ 者。令住菩薩力波羅[*]蜜。若有眾生。其心[8]闇
391a27║ 昧。無有智慧。令住菩薩智波羅[*]蜜。善男子。
391a28║ 我已成就菩薩[9]出生廣大喜光明解脫門。善
391a29║ 財言。大聖。此解脫門境界云何。夜神言。善男
391b01║ 子。入此解脫。能知如來普攝眾生巧方便智。
391b02║ 云何普攝。善男子。一切眾生。所受諸樂。皆
391b03║ 是如來威德力故。順如來教故。行如來語故。
391b04║ [10]學如來行故。得如來所護力故。修如來所
391b05║ 印道故。種如來所行善故。依如來所說法
391b06║ 故。如來智慧日光之所照故。

简体字

怀恼害者，令行忍辱；若懈怠者，令起精进；若散乱者，令修禅定；住恶慧者，令学般若；乐小乘者，令住大乘；乐著三界诸趣中者，令住菩萨愿波罗蜜；若有众生，福智微劣，为诸结业之所逼迫多留碍者，令住菩萨力波罗蜜；若有众生，其心暗昧，无有智慧，令住菩萨智波罗蜜。

“善男子，我已成就菩萨出生广大喜光明解脱门。”

善财言：“大圣，此解脱门境界云何？”

夜神言：“善男子，入此解脱，能知如来普摄众生巧方便智。云何普摄？善男子，一切众生所受诸乐，皆是如来威德力故，顺如来教故，行如来语故，学如来行故，得如来所护力故，修如来所印道故，种如来所行善故，依如来所说法故，如来智慧日光之所照故，

For those who harbor the desire to torment or hurt others, I induce them to practice patience;

For those who are indolent, I induce them to summon vigor;

For those who have become scattered, I induce them to cultivate the *dhyāna* absorptions;

For those who abide in perverse uses of their intelligence, I induce them to train in *prajñā;*

For those who delight in the Small Vehicle, I induce them to abide in the Great Vehicle;

For those who are blissfully attached to the rebirth destinies of the three realms of existence, I induce them to abide in the bodhisattva's *pāramitā* of vows;

For those whose merit and wisdom are scant and inferior, who are influenced by the fetters and karma, and who encounter many obstacles, I induce them to abide in the bodhisattva's *pāramitā* of the powers; and

For beings whose minds are submerged in darkness and bereft of wisdom, I induce them to abide in the bodhisattva's *pāramitā* of knowledge.

Son of Good Family, I have already perfected the bodhisattva's liberation gateway of "the generation of the light of vast joy."

Sudhana then asked, "O great Āryā, what is this liberation gateway's sphere of experience like?"

The Night Spirit then replied:

Son of Good Family, when one enters this liberation, one is able to understand the Tathāgata's use of skillful means and wisdom in everywhere attracting beings. What is meant by "everywhere attracting them"?

Son of Good Family, as for the happiness enjoyed by all beings:

It is due to the power of the Tathāgata's awesome virtue;

It is due to according with the Tathāgata's teachings;

It is due to carrying out the Tathāgata's instructions;

It is due to training in the Tathāgata's practices;

It is due to acquiring the power of the Tathāgata's protection;

It is due to cultivating the path that has received the seal of the Tathāgata;

It is due to planting the same goodness as that practiced by the Tathāgata;

It is due to relying on the Dharma taught by the Tathāgata;

It is due to being illuminated by the light of the Tathāgata's wisdom sun; and

正體字

如來性淨業力
391b07║ 之所攝故。云何知然善男子。我入此[11]出生
391b08║ 廣大喜光明解脫。憶念毘盧遮那如來應正
391b09║ 等覺往昔所修菩薩行海。悉皆明見善男子。
391b10║ 世尊往昔。為菩薩時。見一切眾生。著我我
391b11║ 所。住無明闇室。入諸見稠林。為貪愛所[12]縛。
391b12║ 忿怒所壞。愚癡所亂。慳嫉所纏。生死輪迴。貧
391b13║ 窮困苦。不得值遇諸佛菩薩。見如是已。起大
391b14║ 悲心。利益眾生。所謂起願得一切妙寶資具。
391b15║ 攝眾生心。願一切眾生。皆悉具足資生之物
391b16║ 無所[13]乏心。[14]於一切眾事離執著心。於一切
391b17║ 境界無貪染心。於一切所有無慳吝心。於一
391b18║ 切果報無希望心。於一切榮好無羨慕心。於
391b19║ 一切因緣無迷惑心。起觀察真實法性心。起
391b20║ 救護一切眾生心。起深入一切法[15]漩澓心。起
391b21║ 於一切眾生住平等大慈心。起於一切眾生
391b22║ 行方便大[16]悲心。

简体字

如来性净业力之所摄故。云何知然？善男子，我入此出生广大喜光明解脱，忆念毗卢遮那如来、应、正等觉往昔所修菩萨行海，悉皆明见。

"善男子，世尊往昔为菩萨时，见一切众生，著我、我所，住无明暗室，入诸见稠林，为贪爱所缚、忿怒所坏、愚痴所乱、悭嫉所缠，生死轮回，贫穷困苦，不得值遇诸佛菩萨。见如是已，起大悲心利益众生，所谓：起愿得一切妙宝资具摄众生心；愿一切众生，皆悉具足资生之物无所乏心，于一切众事离执著心，于一切境界无贪染心，于一切所有无悭吝心，于一切果报无希望心，于一切荣好无羡慕心，于一切因缘无迷惑心；起观察真实法性心；起救护一切众生心；起深入一切法漩澓心；起于一切众生住平等大慈心；起于一切众生行方便大悲心；

It is due to being attracted by the power of the pure deeds of the lineage of the Tathāgatas.

How does one know this is so? Son of Good Family, having entered this liberation of "the generation of the light of vast joy," I recall and clearly see the entire ocean of bodhisattva practices cultivated throughout the past by Vairocana, the Tathāgata, the Arhat, the One of Right and Universal Enlightenment.

Son of Good Family, when, in the distant past, the Bhagavat was a bodhisattva, he observed with regard to all beings:

That they are attached to "I" and "mine";
That they dwell in the dark house of ignorance;
That they have entered the dense forest of the various views;
That they are tied up by desire;
That they are destroyed by anger;
That they are kept in confusion by delusion;
That they are entangled in jealousy;
That they are oppressed by the poverty and suffering of *saṃsāra;* and
That they are unable to encounter the buddhas or the bodhisattvas.

Having observed this, he aroused the mind of great compassion to benefit beings. In particular:

He resolved to acquire all the marvelous jewels and means of sustenance useful in attracting beings;
He resolved to ensure that all beings would be well equipped with the means of sustenance and never experience scarcity;
He resolved to abandon attachments for all things;
He resolved to remain free of the defilement of desires for objects of the senses;
He resolved to remain free of miserliness regarding any of his possessions;
He resolved to have no hopes for karmic rewards;
He resolved to not cherish honor or benefit;
He resolved to remain free of any delusion regarding any causes or conditions;
He resolved to contemplate the true nature of dharmas;
He resolved to rescue all beings;
He resolved to deeply enter the whirlpool of all dharmas;
He resolved to abide in impartiality and great kindness toward all beings;
He resolved to implement skillful means and great compassion for all beings;

正體字

起為大法蓋普覆眾生心。起
391b23 以大智金剛杵破一切眾生煩惱障山心。起
391b24 令一切眾生。增長喜樂心。起願一切眾生究
391b25 竟安樂心。起隨眾生所欲雨一切財寶心。起
391b26 以平等方便成熟一切眾生心。起令一切眾
391b27 生滿足聖財心。起願一切眾生究竟皆得十
391b28 力智果心。起如是心已。得菩薩力。現大神
391b29 變。遍法界虛空界。於一切眾生前。普雨一切
391c01 資生之物。隨其所欲。悉滿其意。皆令歡喜。不
391c02 悔不吝。無間無斷。以是方便。普攝眾生。教化
391c03 成熟。皆令得出生死苦難。不求其報。淨治一
391c04 切眾生心寶。令其生起一切諸佛同一善根。
391c05 增一切智福德大海。菩薩如是。念念成熟一
391c06 切眾生。念念嚴淨一切佛剎。念念普入一切
391c07 法界。念念[17]悉皆遍虛空界。念念普入一切
391c08 三世。念念成就調伏一切諸眾生智。念念恒
391c09 轉一切法輪。

简体字

起为大法盖普覆众生心；起以大智金刚杵破一切众生烦恼障山心；起令一切众生增长喜乐心；起愿一切众生究竟安乐心；起随众生所欲雨一切财宝心；起以平等方便成熟一切众生心；起令一切众生满足圣财心；起愿一切众生究竟皆得十力智果心。

“起如是心已，得菩萨力，现大神变；遍法界、虚空界，于一切众生前，普雨一切资生之物，随其所欲悉满其意皆令欢喜，不悔不吝，无间无断。以是方便，普摄众生，教化成熟，皆令得出生死苦难，不求其报；净治一切众生心宝，令其生起一切诸佛同一善根，增一切智福德大海。

“菩萨如是念念成熟一切众生，念念严净一切佛刹，念念普入一切法界，念念皆悉遍虚空界，念念普入一切三世，念念成就调伏一切诸众生智，念念恒转一切法轮，

He resolved to serve as a great canopy of Dharma that everywhere shelters all beings;

He resolved to use the vajra pestle of great wisdom to smash all beings' mountains of affliction-based obstacles;

He resolved to enable all beings to experience increasing joy and bliss;

He resolved that all beings shall experience ultimate happiness;

He resolved to rain down all kinds of wealth and jewels in accordance with whatever beings desire;

He resolved to use impartial skillful means to ripen all beings;

He resolved to enable all beings to fully acquire the wealth of the *āryas*;[148] and

He resolved to enable all beings to ultimately acquire the fruits of the wisdom of the ten powers.

Having made types of resolve such as these, he then acquired the powers of the bodhisattva and manifested great spiritual transformations that reached throughout the Dharma realm and the realm of empty space. Directly before all beings, he everywhere rained down all of the life-sustaining provisions and, in accordance with whatever they desired, he fulfilled all their wishes and made them all feel happy. With no regrets or inclinations to be sparing in his efforts, he continuously and ceaselessly used these skillful means to everywhere attract beings and then teach them, ripen them, and enable them all to escape from the sufferings and difficulties of *saṃsāra*. In so doing he never sought the gratitude of anyone. He purified the jewels of all beings' minds, enabled them to develop roots of goodness identical to those of all buddhas, and increased the great ocean of merit associated with all-knowledge. It was in these ways that, as a bodhisattva:

In every mind-moment, he ripened all beings;

In every mind-moment, he purified all buddha *kṣetras;*

In every mind-moment, he everywhere entered the entire Dharma realm;

In every mind-moment, he everywhere pervaded the realm of empty space;

In every mind-moment, he everywhere entered all three periods of time;

In every mind-moment, he perfected the knowledge of how to train all beings;

In every mind-moment, he constantly turned all the wheels of the Dharma;

正體字

念念恒以一切智道利益眾生。
391c10‖ 念念普於一切世界種種差別諸眾生前。盡
391c11‖ 未來劫。現一切佛成等正覺。念念普於一切
391c12‖ 世界一切諸劫。修菩薩行。不生二想。所謂普
391c13‖ 入一切廣大世界海一切世界種中。種種際
391c14‖ 畔諸世界。種種莊嚴諸世界。種種體性諸世
391c15‖ 界。種種形狀諸世界。種種分布諸世界。或有
391c16‖ 世界穢而兼淨。或有世界淨而兼穢。或有世
391c17‖ 界一向雜穢。或有世界一向清淨。或小或大。
391c18‖ 或麁或細。或正或側。或覆或仰。如是一切諸
391c19‖ 世界中念念修行諸菩薩行。入菩薩[18]位。現菩
391c20‖ 薩力。亦[19]現三世一切佛身。隨眾生心。普使
391c21‖ 知見。善男子。毘盧遮那如來。於過去世。如
391c22‖ 是修行菩薩行時。見諸眾生。不修功德。無有
391c23‖ 智慧。著我我所無明翳障。不正思惟。入諸邪
391c24‖ 見。不識因果。順煩惱業。墮於生死險難深
391c25‖ 坑。具受種種無量諸苦。起大悲心。具修一切
391c26‖ 波羅[*]蜜行。為諸眾生。

简体字

念念恒以一切智道利益众生，念念普于一切世界种种差别诸众生前尽未来劫现一切佛成等正觉，念念普于一切世界、一切诸劫修菩萨行不生二想。所谓：普入一切广大世界海一切世界种中，种种际畔诸世界，种种庄严诸世界，种种体性诸世界，种种形状诸世界，种种分布诸世界，或有世界秽而兼净，或有世界净而兼秽，或有世界一向杂秽，或有世界一向清净，或小或大，或粗或细，或正或侧，或覆或仰；如是一切诸世界中，念念修行诸菩萨行，入菩萨位，现菩萨力，亦现三世一切佛身，随众生心普使知见。

“善男子，毗卢遮那如来，于过去世，如是修行菩萨行时，见诸众生——不修功德，无有智慧，著我、我所，无明翳障，不正思惟，入诸邪见，不识因果，顺烦恼业，堕于生死险难深坑，具受种种无量诸苦。——起大悲心，具修一切波罗蜜行，为诸众生

In every mind-moment, he constantly used the path to all-knowledge to benefit beings;

In every mind-moment, in the presence of the many different kinds of beings in all worlds, he everywhere manifested all buddhas' realization of the universal and right enlightenment and continued to do so to the very end of all future kalpas; and

In every mind-moment, everywhere in all worlds and throughout all kalpas, he cultivated the bodhisattva practices without ever having a second thought.

In particular, in all the vast oceans of worlds, he everywhere entered all world systems, worlds containing many different kinds of boundaries, worlds with many different kinds of adornments, worlds with many different kinds of natures, worlds with many different kinds of shapes and appearances, and worlds having many different arrangements. Some were defiled worlds with pure aspects, some were pure worlds with defiled aspects, some were pervasively defiled worlds, some were pervasively pure worlds, some were small and some were large, some were coarse and some were fine, some were erect and some were tilted, and some were inverted and some were upward facing.

So it was that, in all these worlds, in every mind-moment, he cultivated the bodhisattva practices, entered the bodhisattva stages, manifested the bodhisattva powers, and also manifested the bodies of all buddhas of the three periods of time. Then, adapting to the minds of beings, he everywhere enabled them to know and see them.

Son of Good Family, so it was that, in the past, when Vairocana Tathāgata was cultivating the bodhisattva practices in these ways, he observed with regard to beings that:

They do not cultivate meritorious qualities;

They are bereft of wisdom;

They are attached to "I" and "mine";

Their vision is blocked by the cataracts of ignorance;

They do not pursue right thought;

They enter all the wrong views;

They do not recognize the existence of cause and effect;

They follow along with the karma of the afflictions;

They fall into the dangerous, difficult, and deep abyss of *saṃsāra*; and

They fully experience all kinds of measureless suffering.

He then aroused the mind of great compassion, completely cultivated all the *pāramitā* practices, and, for the sake of beings:

正體字

稱揚讚歎堅固善根。
391c27‖ 令其安住遠離生死貧窮之苦。勤修福智助
391c28‖ 道之法。為說種種諸因果門。為說業報不相
391c29‖ 違反。為說於法證入之處。為說一切眾生欲
392a01‖ 解。及說一切受生國土。令其不斷一切佛種。
392a02‖ 令其守護一切佛教。令其捨離一切諸惡。[1]又
392a03‖ 為稱讚趣一切智助道之法。令諸眾生。心生
392a04‖ 歡喜。令行法施。普攝一切。令其發起一切智
392a05‖ 行。令其修學諸大菩薩波羅[*]蜜道。令其增
392a06‖ 長成一切智諸善根海。令其滿足一切聖財。
392a07‖ 令其得入佛自在門。令其攝取無量方便。令
392a08‖ 其觀見如來威德。令其安住菩薩智慧。善財
392a09‖ 童子言。聖者。發阿耨多羅三藐三菩提心。其
392a10‖ 已久如。夜神言。善男子。此處難信。難知難
392a11‖ 解。難入

简体字

称扬赞叹坚固善根，令其安住远离生死、贫穷之苦，勤修福智助道之法；为说种种诸因果门，为说业报不相违反，为说于法证入之处，为说一切众生欲解，及说一切受生国土，令其不断一切佛种，令其守护一切佛教，令其舍离一切诸恶；又为称赞趣一切智助道之法，令诸众生心生欢喜，令行法施普摄一切，令其发起一切智行，令其修学诸大菩萨波罗蜜道，令其增长成一切智诸善根海，令其满足一切圣财，令其得入佛自在门，令其摄取无量方便，令其观见如来威德，令其安住菩萨智慧。”

善财童子言：“圣者发阿耨多罗三藐三菩提心，其已久如？”

夜神言：“善男子，此处难信、难知、难解、难入、

He widely praised solid roots of goodness and enabled them to securely abide in them;
He enabled them to safely escape the suffering of poverty-stricken lives in *saṃsāra* and diligently cultivate the provisions for enlightenment consisting of merit and wisdom;
He taught them about the many different methods of understanding cause and effect;
He taught them about the noncontradictory nature of karmic actions and their retributions;
He taught them about the stations in which one realizes and enters the Dharma;
He taught them about all beings' dispositions;
He taught them about all the lands in which one may be reborn;
He enabled them to prevent the severance of the lineage of all buddhas;
He enabled them to preserve and protect the teachings of all buddhas; and
He enabled them to abandon every kind of evil deed.

Moreover, for their sakes, he praised the provisions for the path to all-knowledge. So it was that:

He enabled beings to feel happy in mind;
He induced them to practice the giving of Dharma and thereby attract everyone;
He induced them to initiate the practices leading to all-knowledge;
He induced them to cultivate and train in the great bodhisattvas' path of the *pāramitās*;
He induced them to enlarge the ocean of roots of goodness leading to the realization of all-knowledge;
He induced them to fulfill all the qualities constituting the wealth of the *āryas*;
He enabled them to enter the gateway of the Buddha's transformative powers;[149]
He enabled them to assimilate countless skillful means;
He enabled them to witness the Tathāgata's awesome virtue; and
He enabled them to become established in the bodhisattva's wisdom.

Sudhana the Youth then asked, "O Āryā, how long has it been now since you first resolved to attain *anuttara-samyak-saṃbodhi*?"

The Night Spirit replied:

Son of Good Family, this matter is difficult to believe, difficult to know, difficult to understand, difficult to penetrate, and difficult to

正體字

難說。一切世間。及以二乘。皆不能
392a12║ 知。唯除諸佛神力所護。善友所攝。集勝功德。
392a13║ 欲樂清淨。無下劣心。[2]無雜染心。無諂曲心。
392a14║ 得普照耀智光明心。發普饒益諸眾生心。一
392a15║ 切煩惱。及以眾魔。無能壞心。起必成就一切
392a16║ 智心。不樂一切生死樂心。能求一切諸佛妙
392a17║ 樂。能滅一切眾生苦惱。能修一切佛功德海。
392a18║ 能觀一切諸法實性。能具一切清淨信解。能
392a19║ 超一切生死暴流。能入一切如來智海。能決
392a20║ 定到無上法城。能勇猛入如來境界。能速疾
392a21║ 趣諸佛地位。能即成就一切智力。能於十力。
392a22║ 已得究竟。如是之人。於此能持。能入能了。何
392a23║ 以故。此是如來智慧境界。一切菩薩。尚不
392a24║ 能知。況餘眾生。

简体字

难说，一切世间及以二乘皆不能知。唯除诸佛神力所护，善友所摄，集胜功德，欲乐清净，无下劣心，无杂染心，无谄曲心，得普照耀智光明心，发普饶益诸众生心、一切烦恼及以众魔无能坏心，起必成就一切智心，不乐一切生死乐心，能求一切诸佛妙乐，能灭一切众生苦恼，能修一切佛功德海，能观一切诸法实性，能具一切清净信解，能超一切生死暴流，能入一切如来智海，能决定到无上法城，能勇猛入如来境界，能速疾趣诸佛地位，能即成就一切智力，能于十力已得究竟；如是之人，于此能持、能入、能了。何以故？此是如来智慧境界，一切菩萨尚不能知，况余众生？

describe. It is something that no one in the world or any practitioner of the two vehicles could ever know with the exception of:

Those who are protected by the spiritual powers of the buddhas;
Those who have been attracted by good spiritual guides;
Those who have accumulated excellent meritorious qualities;
Those who have purified their mental inclinations;
Those whose minds are free of inferior motivations;
Those whose minds are free of defilements;
Those whose minds are free of flattery and deviousness;
Those who have developed minds that everywhere shine with the brilliant light of wisdom;
Those who have resolved to everywhere benefit all beings;
Those whose minds are invulnerable to destruction by any of the afflictions or by any of the many *māras*;
Those who have resolved to definitely succeed in realizing all-knowledge;
Those whose minds do not delight in any of the pleasures of *saṃsāra*;
Those who are able to seek the sublime bliss of all buddhas;
Those who are able to extinguish the suffering and anguish of all beings;
Those who are able to cultivate the ocean of all buddhas' meritorious qualities;
Those who are able to contemplate the true nature of all dharmas;
Those who are able to possess all forms of pure resolute faith;
Those who are able to traverse the flood of *saṃsāra*;
Those who are able to enter the ocean of all buddhas' wisdom;
Those who are able to definitely reach the city of the unexcelled Dharma;
Those who are able to courageously enter the realm of the Tathāgata;
Those who are able to swiftly progress toward the ground of all buddhas;
Those who are able to immediately perfect the power of all-knowledge; or
Those who have already been able to acquire the ultimate realization of the ten powers.

It is people such as these who are able to grasp, able to enter, and able to completely understand this. And why is this so? This is a sphere of the Tathāgata's wisdom that not even all bodhisattvas could know, how much the less could other beings do so.

正體字

然我今者。以佛威力。欲令調
392a25 ‖ 順可化眾生意速清淨。欲令修習善根眾生。
392a26 ‖ 心得自在。隨汝所問。為汝宣說。爾時開敷一
392a27 ‖ 切樹華夜神。欲重明其義。觀察三世如來境
392a28 ‖ 界。而說頌言
392a29 ‖ 佛子汝所問　甚深佛境界
392b01 ‖ 難思剎塵劫　說之不可盡
392b02 ‖ 非是貪恚癡　憍慢惑所覆
392b03 ‖ 如是眾生等　能知佛妙法
392b04 ‖ 非是住慳嫉　諂誑諸濁意
392b05 ‖ 煩惱業所覆　能知佛境界
392b06 ‖ 非著蘊界處　及計於有身
392b07 ‖ 見倒想倒人　能知佛所覺
392b08 ‖ 佛境界寂靜　性淨離分別
392b09 ‖ 非著諸有者　能知此法性
392b10 ‖ 生於諸佛家　為佛所守護
392b11 ‖ 持佛法藏者　智眼之境界
392b12 ‖ [3] 親近善知識　愛樂白淨法
392b13 ‖ 勤求諸佛力　聞此法歡喜
392b14 ‖ 心淨無分別　猶如[4]大虛空
392b15 ‖ 慧燈破諸闇　是彼之境界

简体字

然我今者，以佛威力，欲令调顺可化众生意速清净，欲令修习善根众生心得自在，随汝所问，为汝宣说。”

尔时，开敷一切树华夜神，欲重明其义，观察三世如来境界而说颂言：

“佛子汝所问，甚深佛境界，
难思刹尘劫，说之不可尽。
非是贪恚痴，憍慢惑所覆，
如是众生等，能知佛妙法。
非是住悭嫉，谄诳诸浊意，
烦恼业所覆，能知佛境界。
非著蕴界处，及计于有身，
见倒想倒人，能知佛所觉。
佛境界寂静，性净离分别，
非著诸有者，能知此法性。
生于诸佛家，为佛所守护，
持佛法藏者，智眼之境界。
亲近善知识，爱乐白净法，
勤求诸佛力，闻此法欢喜。
心净无分别，犹如太虚空，
慧灯破诸暗，是彼之境界。

Even so, now, with the aid of the Buddha's awesome powers, wishing to enable well-trained and teachable beings to swiftly purify their minds and wishing to enable beings who cultivate roots of goodness to gain sovereign mastery of their minds, in response to your question, I shall expound on this matter for you.

Then, wishing to once again clarify her meaning, the Night Spirit, Sarvavṛkṣapraphullanasukhasaṃvāsā, contemplated the realm of all buddhas of the three periods of time and spoke these verses:

Son of the Buddha, as for what you have asked about,
namely the extremely profound realm of the Buddha, even doing so
for inconceivably many kalpas as numerous as a *kṣetra*'s atoms,
one could still never completely describe it.

It is not the case that beings
who are covered over by the afflictions
of greed, hatred, delusion, and arrogance
could ever thus know the sublime Dharma of the Buddha.

It is not the case that those who dwell in envy and miserliness,
whose minds harbor flattery, deception, and the turbidities,
or who are covered over by afflictions and karma
could ever thus know the realm of the Buddha.

It is not the case that those attached to the aggregates, sense realms,
and sense bases, those imputing a truly existent person in them,
or those with inverted views and inverted perceptions
could ever thus know that to which the Buddha has awakened.

The realm of the Buddha is quiescent,
pure in its nature, and beyond discriminations.
It is not the case that those attached to any stations of existence
could ever thus know the nature of this Dharma.

This is the realm of the wisdom eye as possessed by
those who have been born into the clan of the Tathāgatas,
who receive the protection of the Buddha,
and who preserve the treasury of the Buddha's Dharma.

Those who have drawn near to good spiritual guides,
those who cherish and delight in the pure dharmas,
those who diligently seek to acquire the powers of all buddhas,
those who, hearing this Dharma, are filled with joyous delight,

those who in their purity of mind and freedom from discriminations
are like the immense realm of empty space,
and those who, as lamps of wisdom, dispel all darkness—
This is the sphere of those such as these.

正體字

392b16 以大慈悲意　普覆諸世間
392b17 一切皆平等　是彼之境界
392b18 歡喜心無著　一切皆能捨
392b19 平等施眾生　是彼之境界
392b20 心淨離諸惡　究竟無所悔
392b21 順行諸佛教　是彼之境界
392b22 了知法自性　及以諸業種
392b23 其心無動亂　是彼之境界
392b24 勇猛勤精進　安住心不退
392b25 勤修一切智　是彼之境界
392b26 其心寂靜住三昧　究竟清涼無熱惱
392b27 已修一切智海因　此證悟者之解脫
392b28 善知一切真實相　深入無邊法界門
392b29 普度群生靡有餘　此慧燈者之解脫
392c01 了達眾生真實性　不著一切諸有海
392c02 如影普現心水中　此正道者之解脫
392c03 從於一切三世佛　方便願種而出生
392c04 盡諸劫剎勤修行　此普賢者之解脫
392c05 普入一切法界門　悉見十方諸剎海
392c06 亦見其中劫成壞　而心畢竟無分別

简体字

以大慈悲意，普覆诸世间，
一切皆平等，是彼之境界。
欢喜心无著，一切皆能舍，
平等施众生，是彼之境界。
心净离诸恶，究竟无所悔，
顺行诸佛教，是彼之境界。
了知法自性，及以诸业种，
其心无动乱，是彼之境界。
勇猛勤精进，安住心不退，
勤修一切智，是彼之境界。
其心寂静住三昧，究竟清凉无热恼，
已修一切智海因，此证悟者之解脱。
善知一切真实相，深入无边法界门，
普度群生靡有余，此慧灯者之解脱。
了达众生真实性，不著一切诸有海，
如影普现心水中，此正道者之解脱。
从于一切三世佛，方便愿种而出生，
尽诸劫刹勤修行，此普贤者之解脱。
普入一切法界门，悉见十方诸刹海，
亦见其中劫成坏，而心毕竟无分别。

Those whose minds are motivated by great kindness and compassion
that everywhere extend to and shelter all worlds,
impartially including everyone equally—
This is the sphere of those such as these.

Those who abide in joyous delight and are free of attachment,
those who are able to give away everything,
and those who bestow gifts on beings impartially—
This is the sphere of those such as these.

Those with pure mind who have abandoned all evil,
those who are ultimately free of anything they might regret,
and those who compliantly practice the teachings of all buddhas—
This is the sphere of those such as these.

Those who completely know the inherent nature of dharmas
as well as all the types of karmic actions
and those whose minds are unshakable and unconfused—
This is the sphere of those such as these.

Those who are heroically brave in their diligent vigor,
those who are securely established in irreversible resolve,
and those who diligently cultivate the means to gain all-knowledge—
This is the sphere of those such as these.

Those whose minds quiescently abide in samādhi,
those living in ultimate clarity and coolness free of feverish torment,
and those who have cultivated causes for the ocean of omniscience—
This is the liberation gained by those attaining realized awakening.

Those who well know the true character of everything,
those deeply entering the gateways into the boundless Dharma realm,
and those liberating all types of beings without exception—
This is the liberation gained by these lamps of wisdom.

Those who fully comprehend the true nature of beings
and those who are not attached to anything in the ocean of existence,
seeing them all like reflections appearing in the waters of the mind—
This is the liberation of those on the right path.

Those born from the lineage of the skillful means and vows
of all buddhas of the three periods of time
who diligently cultivate throughout all kalpas and *kṣetras*—
This is the liberation of those who are universally worthy.[150]

Those who everywhere enter all gateways of the Dharma realm,
those who see the entire ocean of the *kṣetras* of the ten directions
and also see the arising and destruction of all the kalpas within it
even as their minds remain ultimately free of discriminations,

正體字

392c07 ‖ 法界所有微塵中　悉見如來坐道樹
392c08 ‖ 成就菩提化群品　此無礙眼之解脫
392c09 ‖ 汝於無量大劫海　親近供養善知識
392c10 ‖ 為利群生求正法　聞已憶念無遺忘
392c11 ‖ 毘盧遮那廣大境　無量無邊不可思
392c12 ‖ 我承佛力為汝說　令汝深心轉清淨
392c13 ‖ 善男子。乃往古世。過世界海微塵數劫。有世
392c14 ‖ 界海。名普光明真金摩尼山。其世界海中。有
392c15 ‖ 佛出現。名普照法界智慧山寂靜威德王。善
392c16 ‖ 男子。其佛往修菩薩行時。淨彼世界海。其世
392c17 ‖ 界海中。有世界微塵數世界種。[5]一一世界
392c18 ‖ 種。有世界微塵數世界。一一世界。皆有如
392c19 ‖ 來出興於世。一一如來。說世界海微塵數修
392c20 ‖ 多羅。一一修多羅。授佛剎微塵數諸菩薩記。
392c21 ‖ 現種種神力。說種種法門。度無量眾生。善男
392c22 ‖ 子。彼普光明真金摩尼山世界海中。有世界
392c23 ‖ 種。名普莊嚴幢。[6]此世界種中。有世界名一
392c24 ‖ 切寶色普光明。以現一切化佛影摩尼王為
392c25 ‖ 體。形如天城。以現一切如來道場影像摩尼
392c26 ‖ 王。為其下際。

简体字

法界所有微尘中，悉见如来坐道树，
成就菩提化群品，此无碍眼之解脱。
汝于无量大劫海，亲近供养善知识，
为利群生求正法，闻已忆念无遗忘。
毗卢遮那广大境，无量无边不可思，
我承佛力为汝说，令汝深心转清净。

“善男子，乃往古世，过世界海微尘数劫，有世界海，名普光明真金摩尼山；其世界海中，有佛出现，名普照法界智慧山寂静威德王。善男子，其佛往修菩萨行时，净彼世界海。其世界海中，有世界微尘数世界种；一一世界种，有世界微尘数世界；一一世界，皆有如来出兴于世；一一如来，说世界海微尘数修多罗；一一修多罗，授佛刹微尘数诸菩萨记，现种种神力，说种种法门，度无量众生。

“善男子，彼普光明真金摩尼山世界海中，有世界种，名普庄严幢。此世界种中，有世界，名一切宝色普光明，以现一切化佛影摩尼王为体，形如天城；以现一切如来道场影像摩尼王为其下际，

and those seeing all *tathāgatas* at the enlightenment tree
in all the motes of dust throughout the Dharma realm
where they realize bodhi and teach the many kinds of beings—
This is the liberation of those with the unimpeded eyes.

Throughout the ocean of countless kalpas,
you have drawn near to and made offerings to good spiritual guides
and, to benefit the many kinds of beings, have sought right Dharma
and, having heard it, remember it without ever forgetting anything.

The vast realm of Vairocana
is measureless, boundless, and inconceivable.
Aided by the Buddha's power, I speak about this for you
to enable your deep resolve to become ever more purified.

Son of Good Family, long ago in the ancient past, back beyond a number of kalpas as numerous as the atoms in an ocean of worlds, there was an ocean of worlds known as Universally Radiant Mountain of Gold and Maṇi Jewels. In that ocean of worlds, there was a buddha who appeared there named King of Serene and Awesome Virtue Whose Mountain of Wisdom Everywhere Illuminates the Dharma Realm.

Son of Good Family, when, in the past, that buddha was cultivating the bodhisattva path, he purified that ocean of worlds. Within that ocean of worlds, there were different world systems as numerous as a world's atoms. In every one of those world systems, there were worlds as numerous as a world's atoms. In every one of those worlds, there was a *tathāgata* who appeared in the world. Every one of those *tathāgatas* proclaimed sutras as numerous as the atoms in an ocean of worlds, and every one of those sutras contained within it transmissions of predictions of bodhisattvas' future buddhahood as numerous as the atoms in a buddha *kṣetra* and also contained manifestations of many different kinds of spiritual powers, explanations of many different kinds of Dharma gateways, and the liberation of countless beings.

Son of Good Family, within that ocean of worlds known as Universally Radiant Mountain of Gold and Maṇi Jewels, there was a world system known as Banner of Universal Adornment. Among the worlds in that world system, there was a world named Universally Illuminating Radiance of the Colors of All Jewels, the substance of which consisted of sovereign *maṇi* jewels displaying images of all the transformation buddhas. It had the shape of a celestial city. Its lower regions were made of sovereign *maṇi* jewels that displayed the images of all *tathāgatas'* sites of enlightenment. It

正體字

住一切寶華海上。淨穢相雜。此
392c27 世界中。有須彌山微塵數四天下。有一四天
392c28 下。最處其中。名一切寶山幢。其四天下。一一
392c29 縱廣十萬由旬。一一各有一萬大城。其閻浮
393a01 提中。有一王都。名堅固妙寶莊嚴雲燈。一萬
393a02 大城。周匝圍繞。閻浮提人壽萬歲時。其中有
393a03 王。名一切法音圓滿蓋。有五百大臣。六萬
393a04 [1]采女。七百王子。其諸王子。皆端正勇健。有
393a05 大威力。爾時彼王。威德普被閻浮提內。無有
393a06 怨敵。時彼世界。劫欲盡時。有五濁起。一切人
393a07 眾。壽命短促。資財乏少。形色鄙陋。多苦少
393a08 樂。不修十善。專作惡業。更相忿諍。互相毀
393a09 辱。離他眷屬。妬他榮好。任情起見。非法貪
393a10 求。以是因緣。風雨不時。苗稼不登。園林草
393a11 樹。一切枯槁。人民匱乏。多諸疫病。馳走四
393a12 方。靡所依怙。[2]咸來共遶王都大城。

简体字

住一切宝华海上，净秽相杂。此世界中，有须弥山微尘数四天下，有一四天下最处其中，名一切宝山幢。其四天下，一一纵广十万由旬，一一各有一万大城。其阎浮提中，有一王都，名坚固妙宝庄严云灯，一万大城周匝围绕。阎浮提人寿万岁时，其中有王，名一切法音圆满盖，有五百大臣、六万采女、七百王子；其诸王子皆端正勇健，有大威力。尔时，彼王威德普被阎浮提内，无有冤敌。

“时，彼世界劫欲尽时，有五浊起。一切人众，寿命短促，资财乏少，形色鄙陋，多苦少乐，不修十善，专作恶业，更相忿诤，互相毁辱，离他眷属，妒他荣好，任情起见，非法贪求。以是因缘，风雨不时，苗稼不登，园林、草树一切枯槁，人民匮乏，多诸疫病，驰走四方，靡所依怙，咸来共绕王都大城，

dwelt on an ocean of all kinds of jeweled flowers and was characterized by an admixture of both pure and defiled aspects.

Within that world, there were sets of four-continent lands as numerous as the atoms in Mount Sumeru, among which there was a four-continent land in the very middle named Banner of the Mountains of All Jewels. Each one of those four-continent lands was a hundred thousand *yojanas* in length and breadth and each one of these had ten thousand great cities. In the middle of that Jambudvīpa continent, there was a royal capital named Lamp of Clouds Adorned by Solid and Marvelous Jewels that was surrounded by ten thousand great cities. The people on that Jambudvīpa continent had a life span of ten thousand years. Among them was a king known as Perfect Canopy of all Dharma Sounds who had five hundred state ministers, sixty thousand female attendants, and seven hundred royal princes. Those princes were all handsome, courageous, and possessed of great awesome strength.

At that time, the awesome virtue of that king extended throughout the continent of Jambudvīpa so completely that he had no adversaries. At that time, that world was reaching the point where the kalpa was coming to an end, the five turbidities had arisen, and all of its people had developed the following characteristics:

Their lifetimes were short and passed by quickly;
They were deficient in the wealth necessary for subsistence;
Their physical appearances were ugly;
They experienced much suffering and little happiness;
They did not cultivate the ten courses of good karmic action;
They exclusively engaged in bad karmic actions;
They engaged in mutual anger and disputation;
They disparaged and vilified each other;
They caused others' families to separate;
They were envious of others' glory and good fortune;
They gave free rein to their emotions and developed [wrong] views; and
They indulged in desires contrary to the Dharma.

For these reasons, the winds and rains did not accord with their seasons, the crop seedlings failed to grow, the gardens, groves, shrubs, and trees all dried up and withered, the people ran short of basic necessities, and there was much epidemic illness. They ran off to the four directions and had no one they could rely on. Then they all came and surrounded the royal capital's great city. Gathering together on all four sides in a crowd consisting of

正體字

無量無
393a13‖ 邊百千萬億。四面周匝。高聲大呼。或舉其手。
393a14‖ 或合其掌。或以頭扣地。或以手搥胸。或屈膝
393a15‖ 長號。或[3]踊身大叫。頭髮蓬亂。衣裳弊惡。皮
393a16‖ 膚皺裂。面目無光。而向王言。大王大王。我等
393a17‖ 今者。貧窮孤露。飢渴寒凍。疾病衰羸。眾苦所
393a18‖ 逼。命將不久。無依無救。無所控告。我等今
393a19‖ 者。來歸大王。我觀大王。仁慈智慧。於大王
393a20‖ 所。生得安樂想。[4]得所愛想。得活命想。得攝
393a21‖ 受想。得寶藏想。遇津梁想。逢道路想。值船筏
393a22‖ 想。見寶洲想。獲財利想。昇天宮想。爾時大
393a23‖ 王。聞此語已。得百萬阿僧祇大悲門。一心
393a24‖ 思惟。發十種大悲語。其十者何。所謂哀哉
393a25‖ 眾生。墮於無底生死大坑。我當云何而速勉
393a26‖ 濟。令其得住一切智地。哀哉眾生。為諸煩
393a27‖ 惱之所逼迫。我當云何而作救護。令其安住
393a28‖ 一切善業。哀哉眾生。生老病死之所恐怖。我
393a29‖ 當云何為作歸依。令其永得身心安隱。哀哉
393b01‖ 眾生。常為世間眾怖所逼。我當云何而為祐
393b02‖ 助。令其得住一切智道。

简体字

无量无边百千万亿，四面周匝高声大呼；或举其手，或合其掌，或以头扣地，或以手捶胸，或屈膝长号，或踊身大叫；头发蓬乱，衣裳弊恶，皮肤皴裂，面目无光，而向王言：‘大王，大王，我等今者，贫穷孤露，饥渴寒冻，疾病衰羸，众苦所逼，命将不久，无依无救，无所控告。我等今者来归大王，我观大王仁慈智慧，于大王所生得安乐想、得所爱想、得活命想、得摄受想、得宝藏想、遇津梁想、逢道路想、值船筏想、见宝洲想、获财利想、升天宫想。’

“尔时，大王闻此语已，得百万阿僧祇大悲门，一心思惟，发十种大悲语。其十者何？所谓：‘哀哉众生！堕于无底生死大坑；我当云何而速勉济，令其得住一切智地？哀哉众生！为诸烦恼之所逼迫；我当云何而作救护，令其安住一切善业？哀哉众生！生老病死之所恐怖；我当云何为作归依，令其永得身心安隐？哀哉众生！常为世间众怖所逼；我当云何而为祐助，令其得住一切智道？

countless hundreds of thousands of myriads of *koṭīs* of people, they began to shout and yell, or raise up their hands, or press their palms together in supplication, or bow their heads down to earth, or beat their chests with their fists, or fall to their knees and howl forth long wails, or jump up and down and shout. Their hair was shaggy and disheveled, their robes were dirty and loathsome, their skin had become wrinkled and cracked, and their countenances had lost their radiance.

They said to the king:

> O Great King, Great King. We have all now become poor, destitute, solitary, exposed to the elements, hungry, thirsty, cold, freezing, sick, weak, wasted, and oppressed by the many kinds of sufferings. Our lives will not last much longer. We have no one to rely on, no one to rescue us from our plight, and no place where we can express our grievances. We have all now come to take refuge in our great king. We look to our great king for humanity, kindness, and wisdom.

As they looked upon the king, they thought of him as a source of happiness, thought of him as the source of what they cherished, thought of him as the means for their survival, thought of him as one who would take them in, thought of him as a treasury of precious jewels, thought of him as a bridge across the waters, thought of him as a road to their destination, thought of him as a boat or a raft, thought of him as an isle of jewels, thought of him as a source of the benefits of wealth, and thought of him as if he were a means to ascend to the celestial palaces.

Then, when that great king heard what they had told him, he acquired hundreds of myriads of *asaṃkhyeyas* of gateways to the great compassion and, single-mindedly reflecting on them, he made ten proclamations of great compassion. What were those ten proclamations? They were as follows:

> Alas! These beings have fallen down into the immense and bottomless chasm of *saṃsāra*. How can I swiftly rescue them and enable them to dwell on the ground of all-knowledge?
>
> Alas! These beings are driven along by the afflictions. How can I rescue them and enable them to dwell securely in all types of good karmic actions?
>
> Alas! These beings are terrorized by birth, aging, sickness, and death. How can I serve as a refuge for them and enable them to forever attain peace and security of body and mind?
>
> Alas! These beings are forever oppressed by the world's many fears. How can I be a protector for them and enable them to dwell in the path to all-knowledge?

正體字

哀哉眾生。無有智眼。
393b03‖ 常為身見疑惑所覆。我當云何為作方便。令
393b04‖ 其得決。疑見翳膜。哀哉眾生。常為癡闇之所
393b05‖ 迷惑。我當云何為作明炬。令其照見一切智
393b06‖ 城。哀哉眾生。常為慳嫉諂誑所濁。我當云何
393b07‖ 而為開曉。令其證得清淨法身。哀哉眾生。長
393b08‖ 時漂沒生死大海。我當云何而普運度。令其
393b09‖ 得上菩提彼岸。哀哉眾生。諸根剛[5]彊。難可
393b10‖ 調伏。我當云何而為調御。令其具足諸佛神
393b11‖ 力。哀哉眾生。猶如盲瞽不見道路。我當云何
393b12‖ 而為引導。令其得入一切智門。作是語已。擊
393b13‖ 鼓宣令。我今普施一切眾生。隨有所須悉令
393b14‖ 充足。即時[頌>頒]下閻浮提內大小諸城。及諸聚
393b15‖ 落。悉開庫藏。出種種物。置四衢道。所謂金銀
393b16‖ 瑠璃。摩尼等寶。衣服飲食。華香[6]瓔珞。宮殿
393b17‖ 屋宅。床榻敷具。建大光明。摩尼寶幢。其光觸
393b18‖ 身。悉使安隱。亦施一切病緣湯藥。種種寶器。
393b19‖ 盛眾雜寶。金剛器中。盛種種香。寶香器中。
393b20‖ 盛種種衣。輦輿車乘。幢幡繒蓋。如是一切資
393b21‖ 生之物。悉開庫藏。而以給施。亦施一切村營
393b22‖ 城邑。

简体字

哀哉众生！无有智眼，常为身见疑惑所覆；我当云何为作方便，令其得决疑见翳膜？哀哉众生！常为痴暗之所迷惑；我当云何为作明炬，令其照见一切智城？哀哉众生！常为悭嫉谄诳所浊；我当云何而为开晓，令其证得清净法身？哀哉众生！长时漂没生死大海；我当云何而普运度，令其得上菩提彼岸？哀哉众生！诸根刚强，难可调伏；我当云何而为调御，令其具足诸佛神力？哀哉众生！犹如盲瞽，不见道路；我当云何而为引导，令其得入一切智门？’

“作是语已，击鼓宣令：‘我今普施一切众生，随有所须悉令充足。’即时颁下阎浮提内大小诸城及诸聚落，悉开库藏，出种种物，置四衢道，所谓：金、银、琉璃、摩尼等宝；衣服、饮食、华香、璎珞、宫殿、屋宅、床榻、敷具；建大光明摩尼宝幢，其光触身，悉使安隐；亦施一切病缘汤药；种种宝器盛众杂宝，金刚器中盛种种香，宝香器中盛种种衣；辇舆、车乘、幢幡、缯盖。如是一切资生之物，悉开库藏而以给施。亦施一切村营、城邑、

Alas! These beings do not have the eye of wisdom and their vision is forever obscured by the view of real personhood and by doubts. How can I produce skillful means that will enable them to do away with the cataracts of doubts and views?

Alas! These beings are forever confused by the darkness of their delusion. How can I serve them as a brightly shining torch that enables them to illuminate and see the city of all-knowledge?

Alas! These beings are forever sullied by miserliness, jealously, flattery, and deception. How can I awaken their understanding and enable them to realize and acquire the pure Dharma body?

Alas! These beings have for so long now been drifting about and sinking in the great ocean of *saṃsāra*. How can I ferry them all across and enable them to ascend the far shore of bodhi?

Alas! These beings' faculties are so stubbornly resistant and they are so difficult to train. How can I serve them as a trainer and guide and enable them to perfect the spiritual powers of the buddhas?

Alas! These beings are as if blind and unable to see the road. How can I serve them as a guide and enable them to enter the gates of all-knowledge?

Having spoken in this way, he then beat the drums and issued a proclamation, saying, "I shall now engage in universal giving to all beings so that they will all be enabled to obtain a sufficient amount of whatever they need." He then immediately had this edict distributed to all the cities, towns, and villages throughout the continent of Jambudvīpa and ordered all the storehouses to be opened up and the many kinds of material supplies to brought forth and set out at the crossroads. These included gold, silver, lapis lazuli, *maṇi* jewels, other kinds of precious jewels, clothing, drink and food, flowers, incense, jewel necklaces, palaces, buildings, homes, beds, couches, and cushions.

He erected brilliantly radiant *maṇi* jewel banners that, whenever their light touched anyone, it caused them to feel safe and secure. He also provided medicines for all illnesses, provided many kinds of jeweled vessels full of many kinds of assorted jewels, including vajra vessels full of many kinds of incense, and jeweled and fragrant vessels full of many kinds of clothing. He also provided hand-drawn carriages, carts, and other such vehicles as well as banners, pennants, streamers, and canopies.

So it was that he opened up all the storehouses and treasuries and provided all such life-sustaining material possessions. He also provided all kinds of hamlets, encampments, cities, mountains,

正體字

山澤林藪。妻子眷屬。及以王位。頭目耳
393b23║ 鼻。脣舌牙齒。手足皮肉。心腎肝肺。內外所
393b24║ 有。悉皆能捨。其堅固妙寶。莊嚴雲燈城。東
393b25║ 面有門。名摩尼山光明。於其門外。有施會
393b26║ 處。其地廣博。清淨平坦。無諸坑坎。荊棘沙
393b27║ 礫。一切皆以妙寶所成。散眾寶華。熏諸妙
393b28║ 香。然諸寶燈。一切香雲。充滿虛空。無量寶
393b29║ 樹。次第行列。無量華網。無量香網。彌覆其
393c01║ 上。無量百千億那由他諸音樂器。恒出妙
393c02║ 音。如是一切。皆以妙寶而為莊嚴。悉是菩薩
393c03║ 淨業果報。於彼會中。置師子座。[7]十寶為地。
393c04║ 十寶欄楯。十種寶樹。周匝圍遶。金剛寶輪。以
393c05║ 承其下。以一切寶。為龍神像。而共捧持。種種
393c06║ 寶物。以為嚴飾。幢幡間列。眾網覆上。無量寶
393c07║ 香常出香雲。種種寶衣處處分布。百千種樂
393c08║ 恒奏美音。復於其上張施寶蓋。常放無量寶
393c09║ 焰光明。如閻浮金熾然清淨。覆以寶網。垂
393c10║ 諸[*]瓔珞摩尼寶帶。周迴間列。種種寶鈴。恒
393c11║ 出妙音。勸諸眾生。修行善業。時彼大王。處師
393c12║ 子座。形容端正。人相具足。

简体字

山泽、林薮、妻子、眷属及以王位，头、目、耳、鼻、唇、舌、牙、齿、手、足、皮、肉、心、肾、肝、肺，内外所有，悉皆能舍。

“其坚固妙宝庄严云灯城，东面有门，名摩尼山光明。于其门外，有施会处。其地广博，清净平坦，无诸坑坎、荆棘、沙砾，一切皆以妙宝所成，散众宝华，熏诸妙香，燃诸宝灯，一切香云充满虚空，无量宝树次第行列，无量华网、无量香网弥覆其上，无量百千亿那由他诸音乐器恒出妙音。如是一切，皆以妙宝而为庄严，悉是菩萨净业果报。

“于彼会中，置师子座，十宝为地，十宝栏楯，十种宝树周匝围绕，金刚宝轮以承其下，以一切宝为龙神像而共捧持，种种宝物以为严饰，幢幡间列，众网覆上，无量宝香常出香云，种种宝衣处处分布，百千种乐恒奏美音。复于其上张施宝盖，常放无量宝焰光明，如阎浮金炽然清净；覆以宝网，垂诸璎珞，摩尼宝带周回间列，种种宝铃恒出妙音，劝诸众生修行善业。时，彼大王处师子座，形容端正，人相具足，

marshes, forests, and wild lands while even being able to relinquish his wives, sons, retinue, the royal throne, and his own head, eyes, ears, nose, lips, tongue, teeth, feet, hands, feet, skin, flesh, heart, kidneys, liver, lungs, and all other parts of his inward and outward possessions.

That city, Lamp of Clouds Adorned by Solid and Marvelous Jewels, had an eastern gate known as Maṇi Jewel Mountain Radiance. Outside the gates, a distribution center was set up. Its grounds were vast, immaculate, level, free of holes or pits, thorn bushes, sand, or gravel. Everything there was made entirely of various jewels. There he distributed many kinds of jewel flowers, scented the air with marvelous incenses, and lit jeweled lanterns.

Clouds of all kinds of incense filled the air there. Countless jewel trees were arranged there in rows. Draped overhead, there were nets of countless floral adornments and nets of countless kinds of incense. There were countless hundreds of thousands of *koṭīs* of *nayutas* of musical instruments constantly emanating marvelous sounds. All of these things were adorned with wondrous jewels and all of them were karmic rewards produced by this bodhisattva's pure karma.

In the center of this assembly there was a lion throne that had been set up. The ground beneath it was made of the ten precious things and it was encircled by railings made of the ten precious things and by trees made of the ten kinds of precious things. It was supported by a sphere made of vajra and jewels that was held up by images of dragons and spirits made from all kinds of jewels. It was adorned with many different kinds of precious things. There were regularly spaced arrays of flags and banners, many kinds of nets that stretched across overhead, and countless types of precious incense always sending forth clouds of incense. There were many different kinds of jeweled robes arrayed all about as adornments and hundreds of thousands of types of music that constantly played, sending forth their exquisite sounds.

In addition, above, there was a jeweled canopy that had been set up which always emanated flaming radiance from countless jewels that shone with a pure blazing light like that reflected by *jambūnada* gold. It was also sheltered by a jeweled net draped with jewel necklaces and streamers made of *maṇi* jewels that hung down, evenly spaced all around its circumference. There were also bells made of many different kinds of jewels that constantly emanated marvelous voices encouraging beings to cultivate good karmic deeds.

Just then, that king was sitting on the lion throne presenting a handsome appearance complete with the marks of a great man. His

正體字

光明妙寶。以為其
393c13 冠。那羅延身。不可沮壞。一一[8]肢分。悉皆圓
393c14 滿。性普賢善。王種中生。於財及法。悉得自
393c15 在。辯才無礙。智慧明達。以政治國。無違命
393c16 者。爾時閻浮提無量無數百千萬億那由他
393c17 眾生。種種國土。種種族類。種種形貌。種種衣
393c18 服。種種言辭。種種欲樂。俱來此會。觀察彼
393c19 王。咸言此王是大智人。是福須彌。是功德月。
393c20 住菩薩願。行廣大施。時王見彼諸來乞者。生
393c21 悲愍心。生歡喜心。生尊重心。生善友心。生廣
393c22 大心。生相續心。生精進心。生不退心。生捨施
393c23 心。生周遍心。善男子爾時彼王。見諸乞者。心
393c24 大歡喜。經須臾頃。假使忉利天王。夜摩天王。
393c25 兜率陀天王。盡百千億那由他劫。所受快樂
393c26 亦不能及。善化天王。於無數劫。所受快樂。自
393c27 在天王。於無量劫。所受快樂。大梵天王。於無
393c28 邊劫。所受梵樂。光音天王。於難思劫。所受天
393c29 樂。遍淨天王。於無盡劫。所受天樂。淨居天
394a01 王。不可說劫。住寂靜樂。悉不能及。

简体字

光明妙宝以为其冠，那罗延身不可沮坏，一一肢分悉皆圆满，性普贤善，王种中生，于财及法悉得自在，辩才无碍，智慧明达，以政治国，无违命者。

“尔时，阎浮提无量无数百千万亿那由他众生——种种国土、种种族类、种种形貌、种种衣服、种种言辞、种种欲乐，俱来此会，观察彼王，咸言：‘此王是大智人、是福须弥、是功德月，住菩萨愿，行广大施。’时，王见彼诸来乞者，生悲愍心，生欢喜心，生尊重心，生善友心，生广大心，生相续心，生精进心，生不退心，生舍施心，生周遍心。

“善男子，尔时，彼王见诸乞者，心大欢喜经须臾顷；假使忉利天王、夜摩天王、兜率陀天王，尽百千亿那由他劫所受快乐，亦不能及。善化天王于无数劫所受快乐，自在天王于无量劫所受快乐，大梵天王于无边劫所受梵乐，光音天王于难思劫所受天乐，遍净天王于无尽劫所受天乐，净居天王不可说劫住寂静乐，悉不能及。

crown was made of marvelous radiant jewels. His *nārāyaṇa* body was invincible. All of his limbs were perfectly developed and he was by nature possessed of the goodness of Samantabhadra. He had been born into a lineage of kings and had achieved complete sovereign mastery in both wealth and Dharma. He was possessed of unimpeded eloquence and wisdom that was bright and penetrating. In his implementation of policies to rule the country, no one opposed his edicts.

At that time, Jambudvīpa's countless hundreds of thousands of myriads of *koṭīs* of *nayutas* of beings from their many different countries, of many different clans and classes, of many different forms and appearances, wearing their many different kinds of clothing, speaking their many different languages, and possessed of their many different sorts of dispositions all came and attended this assembly. Gazing up at that king, they said, "This king is a man of great wisdom, a Mount Sumeru of merit, and a moon of meritorious qualities, one who abides in the bodhisattva vows and carries out vast acts of generosity."

The king then looked out at all of those who had come as supplicants and aroused a mind of compassion, a joyous mind, a reverential mind, a mind regarding them as good friends, a vast mind, a persistent mind, a vigorous mind, an irreversible mind, a charitable mind, an all-encompassing mind.

Son of Good Family, when that king saw those supplicants, his mind was filled with such joyous delight that a mere instant of it could not be matched by all the bliss enjoyed in a hundred thousand *koṭīs* of *nayutas* of kalpas by the Trāyastriṃśa Heaven King, the Yāma Heaven King, or the Tuṣita Heaven King.

It was also such that it could not be approached by all the bliss enjoyed in countless kalpas by the king of the Skillful Transformations Heaven, could not be approached by the bliss enjoyed in measureless kalpas by the king of the Vaśavartin Heaven, could not be approached by the bliss enjoyed in boundlessly many kalpas by the king of the Great Brahma Heaven, could not be approached by the bliss enjoyed in an inconceivable number of kalpas by the king of the Light and Sound Heaven, could not be approached by the celestial bliss enjoyed in endless kalpas by the king of the Universal Purity Heaven, and could not be approached by the quiescent bliss enjoyed in an ineffable number of kalpas by the king of the Pure Dwelling Heaven, for the quiescent bliss in which he dwelt was such that no other bliss could even approach it.

正體字

善男子。
394a02‖ 譬如有人仁慈孝友。遭逢世難。父母妻息。兄
394a03‖ 弟姊妹。竝皆散失。忽於曠野道路之間。而相
394a04‖ 值遇。瞻奉撫對。情無厭足。時彼大王。見來
394a05‖ 求者。心生歡喜。亦復如是。善男子。其王爾
394a06‖ 時。因善知識。於佛菩提。解欲增長。諸根成
394a07‖ 就。信心清淨。歡喜圓滿。何以故。此菩薩勤
394a08‖ 修諸行。求一切智。願得利益一切眾生。願
394a09‖ 獲菩提無量妙樂。[1]捨離一切諸不善心。常
394a10‖ 樂積集一切善根。常願救護一切眾生。常樂
394a11‖ 觀察薩婆若道。常樂修行一切智法。滿足一
394a12‖ 切眾生所願。入一切佛功德大海。破一切魔
394a13‖ 業惑障山。隨順一切如來教行。行一切智無
394a14‖ 障礙道。已能深入一切智流。一切法流。常現
394a15‖ 在前。大願無盡。為大丈夫。住大人法。積集
394a16‖ 一切普門善藏。離一切著。不染一切世間境
394a17‖ 界。知諸法性。猶如虛空。

简体字

“善男子，譬如有人仁慈孝友，遭逢世难，父母、妻息、兄弟、姊妹并皆散失，忽于旷野道路之间而相值遇，瞻奉抚对，情无厌足。时，彼大王见来求者，心生欢喜，亦复如是。

“善男子，其王尔时，因善知识，于佛菩提，解欲增长，诸根成就，信心清净，欢喜圆满。何以故？此菩萨勤修诸行，求一切智，愿得利益一切众生，愿获菩提无量妙乐，舍离一切诸不善心，常乐积集一切善根，常愿救护一切众生，常乐观察萨婆若道，常乐修行一切智法，满足一切众生所愿，入一切佛功德大海，破一切魔业惑障山，随顺一切如来教行，行一切智无障碍道，已能深入一切智流，一切法流常现在前，大愿无尽，为大丈夫，住大人法，积集一切普门善藏，离一切著，不染一切世间境界，知诸法性犹如虚空。

Son of Good Family, it is as if a humane, kindly, filial, and friendly person were to meet with some generational disaster in which he became separated from his parents, wife, children, brothers, and sisters, all of whom had become scattered, but then, when out on the road in a desolate wilderness, he suddenly came upon them there and was overcome with irrepressible emotions of delight and mutual concern. The joyous delight that arose in the mind of that great king on seeing those coming as supplicants was of this very sort.

Son of Good Family, because of his good spiritual guides, that king's resolute faith in the bodhi of the Buddha increased, his faculties developed, his mind of faith was purified, and his happiness became perfectly complete. Why? As for this bodhisattva:

He diligently cultivated the practices with which to seek all-knowledge;
He wished to benefit all beings;
He wished to acquire the measureless sublime bliss of bodhi;
He abandoned all unwholesome thoughts;
He always delighted in accumulating all roots of goodness;
He always wished to rescue all beings;
He always delighted in contemplating the path to all-knowledge;
He always delighted in cultivating the dharmas leading to all-knowledge;
He fulfilled the wishes of all beings;
He entered the immense ocean of all buddhas' meritorious qualities;
He destroyed the mountain of all obstacles caused by Māra, karma, and afflictions;
He accorded in his practice with the teachings of all *tathāgatas*;
He traveled the unimpeded path to all-knowledge;
He was already able to deeply enter the stream of all-knowledge;
He always had the flow of all dharmas manifesting directly before him;
He had made great vows that were endless;
He had become a great man dwelling in the Dharma of the great men;
He had accumulated the treasuries of goodness of all universal gateways;
He had abandoned all attachments;
He remained undefiled by any of the world's sense realms; and
He realized that the nature of all dharmas was like empty space.

正體字

於來乞者。生一子
394a18‖ 想。生父母想。生福田想。生難得想。生恩益
394a19‖ 想。生堅固想。師想佛想。不[2]揀方處。不擇
394a20‖ 族類。不選形貌。隨有來至。如其所欲。以大
394a21‖ 慈心。平等無礙一切普施皆令滿足。求飲食
394a22‖ 者。施與飲食。求衣服者施與衣服。求香華者
394a23‖ 施與香華。求鬘蓋者施與鬘蓋。幢幡[3]瓔珞。
394a24‖ 宮殿園苑。象馬車乘。床座被褥。金銀摩尼。諸
394a25‖ 珍寶物。一切庫藏。及諸眷屬。城邑聚落。皆悉
394a26‖ 如是。普施眾生。時此會中。有長者女。名寶光
394a27‖ 明。與六十童女俱端正[4]姝妙。人所喜見。皮
394a28‖ 膚金色。目髮紺青。身出妙香口演梵音。上
394a29‖ 妙寶衣以為莊嚴。常懷慚愧正念不亂。具足
394b01‖ 威儀恭敬師長。

简体字

“于来乞者，生一子想，生父母想，生福田想，生难得想，生恩益想，生坚固想、师想、佛想。不简方处，不择族类，不选形貌，随有来至，如其所欲，以大慈心，平等无碍，一切普施，皆令满足：求饮食者，施与饮食；求衣服者，施与衣服；求香华者，施与香华；求鬘盖者，施与鬘盖；幢幡、璎珞、宫殿、园苑、象马、车乘、床座、被褥、金、银、摩尼、诸珍宝物、一切库藏，及诸眷属、城邑、聚落，皆悉如是普施众生。

“时，此会中有长者女，名宝光明，与六十童女俱，端正殊妙，人所喜见，皮肤金色，目发绀青，身出妙香；口演梵音，上妙宝衣以为庄严，常怀惭愧，正念不乱，具足威仪，恭敬师长，

With regard to all those supplicants who had come there:

He thought of them as he would his only son;
He thought of them as he would his own parents;
He thought of them as fields of merit;
He thought of them as rarely encountered opportunities;
He thought of them as benefactors;
He thought of them as solid supports [on the path to bodhi];[151]
He thought of them as teachers; and
He thought of them as if they were buddhas.

He made no distinction regarding their region of origin, did not discriminate on the basis of clan, and did not judge them on the basis of their physical appearance. Rather, whoever came, with a mind of great kindness, he was impartial and unrestrained in giving everything to everyone in accordance with their wishes to completely satisfy them all. Thus:

For those who had come seeking food and drink, he provided them with food and drink;
For those who had come seeking clothing, he provided them with clothing;
For those who had come seeking incense and flowers, he provided them with incense and flowers;
For those who had come seeking garlands or canopies, he provided them with garlands or canopies; and
So too, in this very same way, for those who had come seeking to acquire banners, pennants, necklaces, palaces, parks, gardens, elephants, horses, carts, carriages, beds, seats, blankets, cushions, gold, silver, *maṇi* jewels, other such precious things, the contents of all kinds of storehouses, or even retinues, cities, towns, or villages—in every case he practiced universal giving of all these things to all these beings.

At that time, within this assembly, there was an elder's daughter by the name of Ratnaprabhā or "Jewel Light" who was attended by sixty young maidens. She possessed especially marvelous beauty and was one whom people delighted in seeing. She had golden skin and indigo hair. Her body exuded a marvelous fragrance and she spoke with a voice like Brahmā.

She was adorned with supremely marvelous jeweled robes and was one who always retained a sense of shame, a dread of blame, and unconfused right mindfulness. With perfect deportment, she treated her teachers and elders with reverential respect and was always mindfully compliant in her practice of the most profound

正體字

常念順行甚深妙行。所聞之
394b02║ 法憶持不忘。宿世善根流潤其心。清淨廣大
394b03║ 猶如虛空等安眾生。常見諸佛求一切智。時
394b04║ 寶光明女。去王不遠。合掌頂禮。作如是念。我
394b05║ 獲善利我獲善利。我今得見大善知識。於彼
394b06║ 王所。生大師想。善知識想。具慈悲想。能攝受
394b07║ 想。其心正直。生大歡喜。脫身[*]瓔珞。持奉彼
394b08║ 王。作是願言。今此大王。為無量無邊無明眾
394b09║ 生。作所依處。願我未來亦復如是。[5]如彼大
394b10║ 王所知之法。所載之乘。所修之道。所具色相。
394b11║ 所有財產。所攝眾會。無邊無盡。難勝難壞。願
394b12║ 我未來悉得如是。隨所生處。皆隨往生。爾時
394b13║ 大王。知此童女。發如是心。而告之言。童女隨
394b14║ 汝所欲。我皆與汝。我今所有。一切皆捨。令諸
394b15║ 眾生。普得滿足。時寶光明女。信心清淨。生大
394b16║ 歡喜。即以偈頌。而讚王言
394b17║ 往昔此城邑　大王未出時
394b18║ 一切不可樂　猶如餓鬼處
394b19║ 眾生相殺害　竊盜縱婬佚
394b20║ 兩舌不實語　無義麁惡言

简体字

常念顺行、甚深妙行，所闻之法忆持不忘，宿世善根流润其心，清净广大犹如虚空，等安众生，常见诸佛，求一切智。

"时，宝光明女去王不远，合掌顶礼，作如是念：'我获善利！我获善利！我今得见大善知识。'于彼王所，生大师想、善知识想、具慈悲想、能摄受想。其心正直，生大欢喜，脱身璎珞，持奉彼王，作是愿言：'今此大王为无量无边无明众生作所依处，愿我未来亦复如是。如彼大王所知之法、所载之乘、所修之道、所具色相、所有财产、所摄众会，无边无尽，难胜难坏，愿我未来悉得如是。随所生处，皆随往生。'

"尔时，大王知此童女发如是心，而告之言：'童女！随汝所欲，我皆与汝。我今所有，一切皆舍；令诸众生，普得满足。'时，宝光明女，信心清净，生大欢喜，即以偈颂而赞王言：

"'往昔此城邑，大王未出时，
一切不可乐，犹如饿鬼处。
众生相杀害，窃盗纵淫佚，
两舌不实语，无义粗恶言，

and marvelous practices. Whatever Dharma teaching she heard, she retained it in memory and never forgot it.

Her roots of goodness developed in previous lives flowed into and moistened her mind so that it was as pure and vast as empty space. She treated beings equally, was always able to see the buddhas, and sought the attainment of all-knowledge.

At that time, that maiden, Ratnaprabhā, was not far away from the king. She pressed her palms together, bowed down to him in reverence, and then thought, "I have acquired such a splendid benefit! I have acquired such a splendid benefit! I have now been able to see a great good spiritual guide." She then thought of that king as a great teacher, thought of him as a good spiritual guide, thought of him as embodying kindness and compassion, and thought of him as one who is able to attract and sustain others.

With upright and virtuous intentions, she became filled with great joy, whereupon she took off the necklace she was wearing, offered it up to that king, and then made this vow:

> This great king has now become a refuge for measurelessly and boundlessly many beings who have fallen under the sway of ignorance. In the future, may I too be just like this. May I acquire the Dharma this great king knows, the vehicle in which he travels, the path that he cultivates, the physical signs he has, the wealth he possesses, and the congregation he has attracted, all in such boundlessness, endlessness, invincibility, and indestructibility. In the future, may I always be able in this way to follow him and be reborn wherever he is reborn.

The great king then knew that this maiden had made such a resolve and told her, "Whatever the young lady wishes for, I shall give it all to you. All that I now possess, I shall relinquish to allow all beings to be satisfied."

Then, with a mind of pure faith, the maiden, Ratnaprabhā, became filled with joyous delight and spoke these verses in praise of the king:

In the past, this city,
before the great king appeared,
was a place no one could delight in,
for it was like a land of the hungry ghosts.

The beings engaged in mutual murder and harm,
thievery, sexual profligacy,
divisive speech, lying,
and meaningless, coarse, and abusive speech.

正體字	394b21	貪愛他財物	瞋恚懷毒心
	394b22	邪見不善行	命終墮惡道
	394b23	以是等眾生	愚癡所覆蔽
	394b24	住於顛倒見	天旱不降澤
	394b25	以無時雨故	百穀悉不生
	394b26	草[6]本皆枯槁	泉流亦乾竭
	394b27	大王未興世	津池悉枯涸
	394b28	園苑多骸骨	望之如曠野
	394b29	大王昇寶位	廣濟諸群生
	394c01	油雲被八方	普雨皆充洽
	394c02	大王臨庶品	普斷諸暴虐
	394c03	刑獄皆止措	惸獨悉安隱
	394c04	往昔諸眾生	各各相殘害
	394c05	飲血而噉肉	今悉起慈心
	394c06	往昔諸眾生	貧窮少衣服
	394c07	以草自遮蔽	飢羸如餓鬼
	394c08	大王既興世	[7]秔米自然生
	394c09	樹中出妙衣	男女皆嚴飾
	394c10	昔日競微利	非法相[8]陵奪
	394c11	今時竝豐足	如遊帝釋園
简体字		贪爱他财物，	瞋恚怀毒心，
		邪见不善行，	命终堕恶道。
		以是等众生，	愚痴所覆蔽，
		住于颠倒见，	天旱不降泽。
		以无时雨故，	百谷悉不生，
		草木皆枯槁，	泉流亦干竭。
		大王未兴世，	津池悉枯涸，
		园苑多骸骨，	望之如旷野。
		大王升宝位，	广济诸群生，
		油云被八方，	普雨皆充洽。
		大王临庶品，	普断诸暴虐，
		刑狱皆止措，	茕独悉安隐。
		往昔诸众生，	各各相残害，
		饮血而啖肉，	今悉起慈心。
		往昔诸众生，	贫穷少衣服，
		以草自遮蔽，	饥羸如饿鬼。
		大王既兴世，	粳米自然生，
		树中出妙衣，	男女皆严饰。
		昔日竞微利，	非法相陵夺；
		今时并丰足，	如游帝释园。

They lusted after the wealth and possessions of others,
harbored hatred and anger, cherished cruel thoughts,
held wrong views, and engaged in unwholesome actions,
whereupon, at life's end, they fell into the wretched destinies.

Because of beings such as these
who were so covered over and blinded by delusion
and who dwelt in the inverted views,
drought came and the heavens failed to send down their rains.

Because there were no seasonal rains,
the hundred kinds of grains all failed to sprout,
the shrubs and trees all withered,[152]
and the flow of the springs all dried up as well.

Before the great king appeared in this world,
the streams and ponds had all dried up,
the parks and gardens were filled with many skeletons,
and, as one looked upon it, it appeared like a desolate wilderness.

Since the great king has ascended to the throne,
he has extensively rescued all the many kinds of beings.
The dense rain clouds[153] have blanketed the eight directions
and have rained everywhere so that everything is fully drenched.

Since the great king has drawn near to the masses,
he has everywhere put an end to violence and cruelty,
and has abandoned corporal punishments and harsh imprisonments
so that the orphaned and the solitary are all comforted and made safe.

In the past, all these beings
inflicted cruelties and injury on each other,
drinking blood and feasting on flesh,
but now they have all aroused minds of kindness.

In the past, all these beings
were poor, destitute, and wanting even for clothing.
They had to cloak themselves with the grasses
and became so wasted with hunger as to resemble the hungry ghosts.

Since the great king came into this world,
the rice has spontaneously grown,
the trees have produced marvelous robes,
and men and women have all worn splendid adornments.

In days past, they struggled with each other over paltry benefits,
and, contravening the Dharma, robbed each other of possessions.
In the present era, however, they all enjoy flourishing abundance
and it has become as if we roamed through the gardens of Indra.

正體字

394c12 | 昔時人作惡　非分生貪染
394c13 | 他妻及童女　種種相侵逼
394c14 | 今見他婦人　端正妙嚴飾
394c15 | 而心無染著　猶如知足天
394c16 | 昔日諸眾生　妄言不真實
394c17 | 非法無利益　諂曲取人意
394c18 | 今日群生類　悉離諸惡言
394c19 | 其心既柔軟　發語亦調順
394c20 | 昔日諸眾生　種種行邪法
394c21 | 合掌恭敬禮　牛羊犬豚類
394c22 | 今聞王正法　悟解除邪見
394c23 | 了知苦樂報　悉從因緣起
394c24 | 大王演妙音　聞者皆欣樂
394c25 | 梵釋音聲等　一切無能及
394c26 | 大王眾寶蓋　迥處虛空中
394c27 | 擎以瑠璃幹　覆以摩尼網
394c28 | 金鈴自然出　如來和雅音
394c29 | 宣揚微妙法　除滅眾生惑
395a01 | 次復廣演說　十方諸佛剎
395a02 | 一切諸劫中　如來并眷屬

简体字

昔时人作恶，非分生贪染，
他妻及童女，种种相侵逼。
今见他妇人，端正妙严饰，
而心无染著，犹如知足天。
昔日诸众生，妄言不真实，
非法无利益，谄曲取人意。
今日群生类，悉离诸恶言，
其心既柔软，发语亦调顺。
昔日诸众生，种种行邪法，
合掌恭敬礼，牛羊犬豚类。
今闻王正法，悟解除邪见，
了知苦乐报，悉从因缘起。
大王演妙音，闻者皆欣乐；
梵释音声等，一切无能及。
大王众宝盖，迥处虚空中，
擎以琉璃干，覆以摩尼网。
金铃自然出，如来和雅音，
宣扬微妙法，除灭众生惑。
次复广演说，十方诸佛刹，
一切诸劫中，如来并眷属。

In the past, these people committed evil deeds
and lusted after and were defiled by craving what was not their own.
The wives and maiden daughters of others
were subjected to all kinds of forced violations.

Now, when they see the wives of others,
beautiful and marvelously adorned,
their minds are as free of defiling lust
as those of the Tuṣita Heaven devas.

In days past, these beings
engaged in false speech, saying what is not true,
speaking what was contrary to Dharma and unbeneficial,
and using flattery and deviousness to manipulate others' minds.

These days, however, the many kinds of beings
have all abandoned all forms of evil speech.
Since their minds have become pliant and gentle,
their speech has also become restrained and harmonious.

In days past, these beings practiced
many different kinds of deviant dharmas:
With joined palms, they even reverently bowed
to the likes of cows, sheep, dogs, and pigs.

Now, having heard the king's teachings on right Dharma,
they have awakened, understood, and rid themselves of wrong views.
They completely understand the painful and blissful results of karma
all arise from its causes and conditions.

The great king expounds with a sublime voice
that delights all who hear it
and which cannot be matched
even by the voices of Brahmā, Indra, or other such devas.

The great king's canopy of the many kinds of jewels
that hangs above, up in the sky,
is supported by poles of lapis lazuli
and is covered by a net of *maṇi* jewels.

Its bells of gold spontaneously emanate
the harmonious and elegant sounds of the Tathāgata
and thus spread forth the sublime Dharma
that extinguishes beings' afflictions.

In addition, they extensively expound
on the *kṣetras* of all buddhas of the ten directions
and on their *tathāgatas* and their retinues
as they have arisen in all kalpas.

正體字	395a03 又復次第說　過去十方剎 395a04 及彼國土中　一切諸如來 395a05 又出微妙音　普遍閻浮界 395a06 廣說人天等　種種業差別 395a07 眾生聽聞已　自知諸業藏 395a08 離惡勤修行　迴向佛菩提 395a09 王父淨光明　王母蓮華光 395a10 五濁出現時　處位治天下 395a11 時有廣大園　園有五百池 395a12 一一千樹遶　各各華彌覆 395a13 於其池岸上　建立千柱堂 395a14 欄楯等莊嚴　一切無不備 395a15 末世惡法起　積年不降雨 395a16 池流悉乾竭　草樹皆枯槁 395a17 王生七日前　先現靈瑞相 395a18 見者咸心念　救世今當出 395a19 爾時於中夜　大地六種動 395a20 有一寶華池　光明猶日現 395a21 五百諸池內　功德水充滿 395a22 枯樹悉生枝　華葉皆榮茂
简体字	又复次第说，过去十方刹， 及彼国土中，一切诸如来。 又出微妙音，普遍阎浮界， 广说人天等，种种业差别。 众生听闻已，自知诸业藏， 离恶勤修行，回向佛菩提。 王父净光明，王母莲华光， 五浊出现时，处位治天下。 时有广大园，园有五百池， 一一千树绕，各各华弥覆。 于其池岸上，建立千柱堂， 栏楯等庄严，一切无不备。 末世恶法起，积年不降雨， 池流悉干竭，草树皆枯槁。 王生七日前，先现灵瑞相； 见者咸心念：救世今当出。 尔时于中夜，大地六种动； 有一宝华池，光明犹日现。 五百诸池内，功德水充满， 枯树悉生枝，华叶皆荣茂。

They speak in accordance with their sequence
about the past *kṣetras* throughout the ten directions,
about the lands within them,
and about all of their *tathāgatas*.

[Those bells] also emanate sublime sounds
that everywhere pervade the realms of Jambudvīpa,
speaking extensively about humans, the devas, and others,
and on their many different kinds of karmic deeds.

After beings have listened to this,
they know for themselves about the storehouse of all karma,
whereupon they abandon evil, diligently cultivate,
and dedicate it to the realization of the bodhi of the Buddha.

The king's father was Pure Light
and the king's mother was Lotus Light.
He occupied the throne and ruled the realm
when the five turbidities first emerged.

At that time, there was a vast park,
and in that park there were five hundred ponds,
each of which was surrounded by a thousand trees,
and each of which was covered with flowers.

On the shores of those ponds
were built halls supported by a thousand pillars
with railings and other such adornments,
none of which were not fully embellished.

With the onset of the Dharma-ending age, evil dharmas arose,
and then, for many years, no rain fell.
Then the ponds and streams all dried up
and the shrubs and trees all withered.

Seven days before this king was born,
there first appeared auspicious portents.
All those who saw them then thought,
"A savior of the world is now bound to emerge!"

At that time, in the middle of the night,
the great earth moved and shook in six ways,
whereupon one jeweled flower pond
emanated radiance rivaling the rising sun.

Then all of those five hundred ponds
filled with waters possessed of the excellent qualities.
Those withered trees all produced branches
whose flowers and leaves all flourished with radiant lushness.

正體字

395a23 池水既盈滿　流演一切處
395a24 普及閻浮地　靡不皆霑洽
395a25 藥草及諸樹　百穀苗稼等
395a26 枝葉華果實　一切皆繁盛
395a27 溝坑及堆阜　種種高下處
395a28 如是一切地　莫不皆平坦
395a29 荊棘沙礫等　所有諸雜穢
395b01 皆於一念中　變[1]成眾寶玉
395b02 眾生見是已　歡喜而讚歎
395b03 咸言得善利　如渴飲[2]美水
395b04 時彼光明王　眷屬無量眾
395b05 僉然備法駕　遊觀諸園苑
395b06 五百諸池內　有池名[3]慶喜
395b07 池上有法堂　父王於此住
395b08 先王語夫人　我念七夜前
395b09 中[4]宵地震動　此中有光現
395b10 時彼華池內　千葉蓮華出
395b11 光如千日照　上徹須彌頂
395b12 金剛以為莖　閻浮金為臺
395b13 眾寶為華葉　妙香作鬚蘂

简体字

池水既盈满，流演一切处，
普及阎浮地，靡不皆沾洽。
药草及诸树，百谷苗稼等，
枝叶华果实，一切皆繁盛。
沟坑及塠阜，种种高下处，
如是一切地，莫不皆平坦。
荆棘沙砾等，所有诸杂秽，
皆于一念中，变成众宝玉。
众生见是已，欢喜而赞叹，
咸言得善利，如渴饮美水。
时彼光明王，眷属无量众，
佥然备法驾，游观诸园苑。
五百诸池内，有池名庆喜，
池上有法堂，父王于此住。
先王语夫人：我念七夜前，
中宵地震动，此中有光现。
时彼华池内，千叶莲华出，
光如千日照，上彻须弥顶。
金刚以为茎，阎浮金为台，
众宝为华叶，妙香作须蕊。

The waters of the ponds having become completely filled,
their waters flowed forth to all places
so that, throughout the ground of Jambudvīpa,
no place was not then soaked with their moisture.

The herbs, shrubs, and trees
the hundred kinds of cereals, seedlings, grains, and such,
as well as the branches laden with leaves, flowers, and fruit
all became fully flourishing.

From the ravines to the hillocks,
all the many different high and low places—
of all such aspects of the land such as these,
there were none that did not then become level.

The brambles and thorns, the sand, rubble, and such,
as well as all of the various kinds of filth—
in but a brief moment, they all transformed
into the many kinds of jewels and jade.

Having seen this, the beings there
were filled with joyous delight and exclaimed in praise.
All of them said they had acquired such a fine benefit,
it was as if a thirsty person had drunk from sweet waters.

Then that King, Pure Light,
together with a retinue of countless followers
all prepared the Dharma excursion carriages
and roamed about, sightseeing in the parks and gardens.

Among those five hundred ponds,
there was a pond known as "Felicitous Joy."
On that pond, there was a Dharma Hall
in which the king's father dwelt.

That former king then said to his wife:
"I recall that, seven nights ago,
the earth quaked and shook in the middle of the night,
whereupon a light appeared in this place."

Then, in the middle of that flower pond,
a thousand-petaled lotus flower emerged
that emanated a radiance like that of a thousand suns
whose light penetrated all the way up to the top of Mount Sumeru.

Its stem was made of vajra
and its seed pod was made of *jambūnada* gold.
The many kinds of jewels formed its flower petals
and marvelous incense formed its stamens.

正體字

395b14 王生彼華上　端身結[5]跏坐
395b15 相好以莊嚴　天神所恭敬
395b16 先王大歡喜　入池自撫[6]掬
395b17 持以授夫人　汝子應欣慶
395b18 寶藏皆[7]涌出　寶樹生妙衣
395b19 天樂奏美聲　充滿虛空中
395b20 一切諸眾生　皆生大歡喜
395b21 合掌稱希有　善哉救護世
395b22 王時放身光　普照於一切
395b23 能令四天下　闇盡病除滅
395b24 夜叉毘舍闍　毒蟲諸惡獸
395b25 所欲害人者　一切自藏匿
395b26 惡名失善利　橫事病所持
395b27 如是眾苦滅　一切皆歡喜
395b28 凡是眾生類　相視如父母
395b29 離惡起慈心　專求一切智
395c01 關[8]閉諸惡趣　開示人天路
395c02 宣揚薩婆若　度脫諸群生
395c03 我等見大王　普獲於善利
395c04 無歸無導者　一切悉安樂

简体字

王生彼华上，端身结跏坐，
相好以庄严，天神所恭敬。
先王大欢喜，入池自抚鞠，
持以授夫人：汝子应欣庆。
宝藏皆涌出，宝树生妙衣，
天乐奏美声，充满虚空中。
一切诸众生，皆生大欢喜，
合掌称希有：善哉救护世！
王时放身光，普照于一切，
能令四天下，暗尽病除灭。
夜叉毗舍阇，毒虫诸恶兽，
所欲害人者，一切自藏匿。
恶名失善利，横事病所持，
如是众苦灭，一切皆欢喜。
凡是众生类，相视如父母，
离恶起慈心，专求一切智。
关闭诸恶趣，开示人天路，
宣扬萨婆若，度脱诸群生。
我等见大王，普获于善利，
无归无导者，一切悉安乐。’

The king was born atop that flower
with his body sitting straight up in the lotus posture,
adorned with the major marks and secondary signs.
He was revered there by the devas and spirits.

The former king was then filled with such great joy
that he then entered that pond and, gently lifting up the child,
carried him back and passed him to his wife, saying,
"This is your son. You should rejoice."

The jewel treasuries then gushed forth jewels,
jeweled trees produced exquisite robes,
and the devas played exquisite music
that then filled up all of space.

All those beings were then filled
with great joyous delight.
Pressing their palms together, they exclaimed about the marvel:
"This is excellent indeed, a rescuer and protector of the world!"

The king then emanated a light from his body
that everywhere illuminated everything.
Throughout the four continents, it was everywhere able
to dispel all darkness and extinguish all illness.

The *yakṣas*, the *piśācas*,
the poisonous insects, the fearsome beasts,
and any other beings intent on harming people
all then hid themselves away.

Those who had a bad reputation, who had lost their good fortune,
who had fallen victim to misfortune, or who were gripped by illness—
All such types of suffering disappeared
and everyone was then filled with joyous delight.

All of the various kinds of beings
then looked upon each other as they would their own parents
and, abandoning evil, then aroused the mind of loving-kindness
and whole-heartedly pursued the quest for all-knowledge.

The gates to the wretched destinies were closed
and the road to the human and deva realms was opened.
There was then the proclamation of the path to all-knowledge
and the liberation of all the many kinds of beings.

By our being able to see the great king,
we have all acquired good fortune.
Those without a refuge or a guide
have all been established in happiness.

正體字

395c05‖ 爾時寶光明童女。以偈讚歎一切法音圓滿
395c06‖ 蓋王已。遶無量匝。合掌頂禮。曲躬恭敬。却住
395c07‖ 一面。時彼大王。告童女言。善哉童女。汝能
395c08‖ 信知他人功德。是為希有。童女。一切眾生。不
395c09‖ 能信知他人功德。童女。一切眾生。不知報恩。
395c10‖ 無有智慧。其心濁亂。性不明了。本無志力。又
395c11‖ 退修行。如是之人。不信不知菩薩如來所有
395c12‖ 功德神通智慧。童女。汝今決定求趣菩提。能
395c13‖ 知菩薩如是功德。汝今生此閻浮提中。發勇
395c14‖ 猛心。普攝眾生。功不唐捐。亦當成就如是功
395c15‖ 德。王讚女已。以無價寶衣。手自授與寶光童
395c16‖ 女并其眷屬一一告言。汝著此衣。時諸童女。
395c17‖ 雙膝著地。兩手承捧。置於頂上。然後而著。既
395c18‖ 著衣已。右遶於王。諸寶衣中。普出一切星宿
395c19‖ 光明。眾人見之。咸作是言。此諸女等皆悉端
395c20‖ 正。如淨夜天星宿莊嚴。善男子。爾時一切
395c21‖ 法音圓滿蓋王者。豈異人乎。今毘盧遮那如
395c22‖ 來應正等覺是也。光明王者。淨飯王是。蓮華
395c23‖ 光夫人者。摩耶夫人是。寶光童女者。即我身
395c24‖ 是。

简体字

“尔时，宝光明童女，以偈赞叹一切法音圆满盖王已，绕无量匝，合掌顶礼，曲躬恭敬，却住一面。时，彼大王告童女言：‘善哉！童女！汝能信知他人功德，是为希有。童女！一切众生，不能信知他人功德。童女！一切众生，不知报恩，无有智慧，其心浊乱，性不明了，本无志力，又退修行；如是之人，不信不知菩萨如来所有功德神通智慧。童女！汝今决定求趣菩提，能知菩萨如是功德。汝今生此阎浮提中，发勇猛心，普摄众生，功不唐捐，亦当成就如是功德。’王赞女已，以无价宝衣，手自授与宝光童女并其眷属，一一告言：‘汝著此衣。’时，诸童女双膝著地，两手承捧，置于顶上，然后而著；既著衣已，右绕于王，诸宝衣中普出一切星宿光明。众人见之，咸作是言：‘此诸女等，皆悉端正，如净夜天星宿庄严。’

“善男子，尔时一切法音圆满盖王者，岂异人乎？今毗卢遮那如来、应、正等觉是也。光明王者，净饭王是。莲华光夫人者，摩耶夫人是。宝光童女者，即我身是。

At that time, after the maiden, Ratnaprabhā, had finished speaking these verses in praise of the king, Perfect Canopy of all Dharma Sounds, she circumambulated him countless times, pressed her palms together respectfully, and bowed down before him in reverence. Then, with her body held in a stooped posture as a gesture of reverence, she stood off to one side. That great king then spoke to the maiden, saying:

> It is good indeed, maiden, that you are able to believe in and recognize others' meritorious qualities. This is a rarity. Maiden, beings are unable to believe in and recognize others' meritorious qualities.
>
> Maiden, beings do not know to repay kindnesses extended to them. They are bereft of wisdom, their minds are turbid and confused, their nature is to fail to completely understand, they are fundamentally lacking in any power of resolve, and they also retreat from their cultivation. People such as these do not believe in or recognize the meritorious qualities, spiritual superknowledges, and wisdom of the bodhisattvas and the *tathāgatas*.
>
> Maiden, you, however, are now resolutely pursuing your quest to attain bodhi and are able to recognize such meritorious qualities of bodhisattvas. Now that you have taken birth in Jambudvīpa, you have aroused the courageous resolve to gather in all beings. Your efforts have not been expended in vain, for you too are now bound to perfect just such meritorious qualities.

Having praised the maiden, the king personally passed priceless jeweled robes to the maiden, Ratnaprabhā, and to all the attendants in her retinue, telling each of them, "You are to wear this robe."

All of those maidens then knelt with both knees touching the ground, received their robes with both hands. They then raised them up to touch the top of their heads, after which they donned the robes. Having put on the robes, they circumambulated the king in a rightward direction.

From each of those jeweled robes, there shone the light of all the stars and constellations. When the crowd saw this they all exclaimed, "All these maidens are so beautiful! It is as if they were adorned with the stars and constellations of the clear night sky."

Son of Good Family, as for the king at that time, Perfect Canopy of all Dharma Sounds, could it have been anyone else? Indeed, it was our present Vairocana Tathāgata, the Arhat, the One of Right and Universal Enlightenment. As for that former king, Pure Light, he was none other than this era's King Śuddhodana. As for his wife, Lotus Light, she was this era's Lady Māyā. And, as for that young maiden, Ratnaprabhā, that was myself.

正體字

其王爾時。以四攝法。所攝眾生。即此會中
395c25‖ 一切菩薩是。皆於阿耨多羅三藐三菩提。得
395c26‖ 不退轉。或住初地乃至十地。[9]具種種大願。
395c27‖ 集種種助道。修種種妙行。備種種莊嚴。得種
395c28‖ 種神通。住種種解脫。於此會中。處於種種妙
395c29‖ 法宮殿。爾時開敷一切樹華主夜神。為善財
396a01‖ 童子。欲重宣此解脫義。而說頌言
396a02‖ 我有廣大眼　普見於十方
396a03‖ 一切剎海中　五趣輪迴者
396a04‖ 亦見彼諸佛　菩提樹下坐
396a05‖ 神通遍十方　說法度眾生
396a06‖ 我有清淨耳　普聞一切聲
396a07‖ 亦[1]聞佛說法　歡喜而信受
396a08‖ 我有他心智　無二無所礙
396a09‖ 能於一念中　悉了諸心海
396a10‖ 我得宿命智　能知一切劫
396a11‖ 自身及他人　分別悉明了
396a12‖ 我於一念知　剎海微塵劫
396a13‖ 諸佛及菩薩　五道眾生類

简体字

其王尔时以四摄法所摄众生，即此会中一切菩萨是，皆于阿耨多罗三藐三菩提得不退转，或住初地乃至十地，具种种大愿，集种种助道，修种种妙行，备种种庄严，得种种神通，住种种解脱，于此会中处于种种妙法宫殿。”

尔时，开敷一切树华主夜神，为善财童子，欲重宣此解脱义而说颂言：

“我有广大眼，普见于十方，
一切刹海中，五趣轮回者。
亦见彼诸佛，菩提树下坐，
神通遍十方，说法度众生。
我有清净耳，普闻一切声，
亦闻佛说法，欢喜而信受。
我有他心智，无二无所碍，
能于一念中，悉了诸心海。
我得宿命智，能知一切劫，
自身及他人，分别悉明了。
我于一念知，刹海微尘劫，
诸佛及菩萨，五道众生类。

All those beings who were gathered in at that time by that king's use of the four means of attraction, those are just all the bodhisattvas who are now in attendance here in this very congregation, all of whom have achieved irreversibility in their progress toward *anuttara-samyak-saṃbodhi* and all of whom dwell on one of the grounds, from the first ground up to the tenth bodhisattva ground. They are equipped with many different kinds of great vows, have accumulated many different kinds of provisions for enlightenment, have cultivated many different kinds of marvelous practices, have completely developed many different kinds of adorning practices, have acquired many different kinds of spiritual superknowledges, and have come to abide in many different kinds of liberations so that, in this assembly, they reside in many different kinds of palaces of the sublime Dharma.

At that time, wishing to once again proclaim the meaning of this liberation, the Night Spirit Sarvavṛkṣapraphullanasukhasajvāsā spoke these verses for Sudhana the Youth:

I possess the eye of vast vision
with which I see throughout the ten directions,
within the ocean of all *kṣetras*,
those in the five rebirth destinies of cyclic existence.

I also see all those buddhas,
sitting beneath their respective bodhi trees,
pervading the ten directions with their spiritual superknowledges,
proclaiming the Dharma to liberate beings.

I possess the purified ear
with which I everywhere hear all sounds
and also hear the Buddha teaching the Dharma
that I joyfully accept out of faith.

I possess the knowledge of others' thoughts
that is non-dual and unimpeded.
I am able in but a single mind-moment
to completely know the ocean of all thoughts.

I have acquired the knowledge of previous existences
by which I can know them as they have transpired in all kalpas
for myself and also for other people,
clearly distinguishing them all.

In but a single mind-moment, I know these matters
transpiring in the ocean of *kṣetras* for kalpas as numerous as atoms
as they occur for the buddhas, for the bodhisattvas,
and for all types of beings in the five rebirth destinies.

正體字

396a14| [2] 憶知彼諸佛　始發菩提願
396a15| 乃至修諸行　一一悉圓滿
396a16| 亦知彼諸佛　成就菩提道
396a17| 以種種方便　為眾轉法輪
396a18| 亦知彼諸佛　所有諸乘海
396a19| 正法住久近　眾生度多少
396a20| 我於無量劫　修習此法門
396a21| 我今為汝說　佛子汝應學
396a22| 善男子。我唯知此菩薩出生廣大喜光明解
396a23| 脫門。如諸菩薩摩訶薩。親近供養一切諸佛。
396a24| 入一切智大願海。滿一切佛諸願海。得勇猛
396a25| 智。於一菩薩地。普入一切菩薩地海。得清淨
396a26| 願。於一菩薩行。普入一切菩薩行海。得自在
396a27| 力。於一菩薩解脫門。普入一切菩薩解脫門
396a28| 海。而我云何能知能說彼功德行。善男子。此
396a29| 道場中。有一夜神。名大願精進力救護一切
396b01| 眾生。汝詣彼問。菩薩云何教化眾生。令趣
396b02| 阿耨多羅三藐三菩提。云何嚴淨一切佛剎。
396b03| 云何承事一切如來。云何修行一切佛法。

简体字

忆知彼诸佛，始发菩提愿，
乃至修诸行，一一悉圆满。
亦知彼诸佛，成就菩提道，
以种种方便，为众转法轮。
亦知彼诸佛，所有诸乘海，
正法住久近，众生度多少。
我于无量劫，修习此法门；
我今为汝说，佛子汝应学。

“善男子，我唯知此菩萨出生广大喜光明解脱门。如诸菩萨摩诃萨，亲近供养一切诸佛，入一切智大愿海，满一切佛诸愿海；得勇猛智，于一菩萨地，普入一切菩萨地海；得清净愿，于一菩萨行，普入一切菩萨行海；得自在力，于一菩萨解脱门，普入一切菩萨解脱门海。而我云何能知能说彼功德行？

“善男子，此道场中，有一夜神，名大愿精进力救护一切众生。汝诣彼问：菩萨云何教化众生，令趣阿耨多罗三藐三菩提？云何严净一切佛刹？云何承事一切如来？云何修行一切佛法？”

So it is that I recall with regard to all those buddhas
everything from their initial resolve to reach bodhi
on through to their cultivation of the practices
and their perfect fulfillment of every one of them.

I also know with regard to all those buddhas
their complete fulfillment of the path to bodhi
and their use of many different kinds of skillful means
as they turned the Dharma wheel for the benefit of the multitudes.

I also know with regard to all those buddhas
all that is contained in their ocean of the vehicles,
the length or brevity of their right Dharma ages,
and the number of beings they have liberated.

Throughout the course of countless kalpas,
I have cultivated this gateway into the Dharma.
I have now described it for your sake.
Hence, O Son of the Buddha, you should train in it.

Son of the Buddha, I know only this bodhisattva's liberation gateway of "the generation of the light of vast joy." As for the bodhisattva-mahāsattvas:

Who have drawn near to and made offerings to all buddhas;
Who have entered the ocean of great vows to attain all-knowledge;
Who have fulfilled the ocean of vows of all buddhas;
Who have acquired courageous wisdom;
Who, in but one of the bodhisattva grounds, have everywhere entered the ocean of all bodhisattva grounds and purified their vows;
Who, in but one of the bodhisattva practices, have everywhere entered the ocean of all bodhisattva practices and attained the power of sovereign mastery in them; and
Who, in but one of the bodhisattva gateways to liberation, have everywhere entered the ocean of all bodhisattva gateways to liberation—

How could I know of or be able to speak about their meritorious qualities and practices?

Son of the Buddha, in this very site of enlightenment, there is a night spirit known as Sarvajagadrakṣāpraṇidhānavīryaprabhā or "Power of Vigor in the Great Vows to Rescue and Protect all Beings." You should go there, pay your respects, and ask, "How should the bodhisattva teach beings and enable them to progress toward *anuttara-samyak-saṃbodhi*? How should they purify all buddha *kṣetras*? How should they serve all *tathāgatas*? And how should they cultivate the Dharma of all buddhas?

正體字

時
396b04‖ 善財童子。頂禮其足。遶無數匝。慇懃瞻仰。辭
396b05‖ 退而去

简体字

时，善财童子顶礼其足，绕无数匝，殷勤瞻仰，辞退而去。

Sudhana the Youth then bowed down in reverence at the feet of the Night Spirit and circumambulated her countless times as he gazed up at her in attentive admiration. He then respectfully withdrew and departed.

Volume Five Endnotes

1. "Benefactor of Orphans and the Solitary" (給孤獨園) is a literal translation of the name given to the benefactor who arranged for Prince Jeta to donate the Jeta Grove to the Buddha and the Sangha. (Sanskrit: Anāthapiṇḍada. Pali: Anāthapiṇḍika.)
2. The bodhisattva names listed below are grouped according to common elements in their names ("banner," "eye," "sound," etc.)
3. Although the SA Chinese text would appear to be referring to "adornment and purification" (嚴淨), as pointed out by VB, the *Gaṇḍavyūha* Sanskrit text's antecedent term for this Chinese compound is *pariśodhayati* (and variant grammatical forms) which refer exclusively to "purification." Hence the idea of "adornment" as a separate concept is not at all intended.
4. Although at first glance the "inconceivable" (不思議) and "ineffable" (不可說) in the Chinese text might appear to describe the marvelousness of the clouds described in this list, as verified by the Sanskrit text, these are actually just huge cardinal numbers. All three denominations of enumeration in this list, "inconceivably many" (*acintya*), "countless" (*asaṃkhyeya*), and "ineffably many" (*anabhilāpya*), are immensely large Buddhist Sanskrit numbers the size of which is explained in Chapter 30, the Asaṃkhyeya Chapter.
5. This refers to a kind of tree such as that seen in the Trāyastriṃśa Heaven, the branches of which produce marvelously fine heavenly robes.
6. Although, looking solely at the Chinese text, one would think this list consisted of ten kinds of "perfectly full light clouds" (圓滿光明雲), looking at the Sanskrit, we see that this Chinese phrase was instead attempting to translate *prabhāmaṇḍalamegha*, "clouds of light spheres," or (depending on context), "halos," "nimbuses," "auras," etc.
7. Later in this section, when this bodhisattva speaks a series of verses, he is instead referred to as "King of the Banner of the Light of Vows and Wisdom Bodhisattva" (願智光明幢王菩薩).
8. As pointed out by VB, *zizai* (自在) is often used in SA's translation to translate not only the usual *vaśī*, "mastery," but also *adhipateya*, "dominance," or, as in this case, *vikurvita*, "magic" or "feats of spiritual power."
9. At the end of this section, when this bodhisattva speaks a series of verses, he is instead referred to as "King of the Different Vows, Wisdom, and Spiritual Superknowledges of the Dharma Realm" (法界差別願智神通王菩薩).

10. Although perhaps not so immediately obvious, as briefly noted in passing by QL, each member of the following tenfold list corresponds in standard order to one of the ten *pāramitās* and also, again in standard order, to one of the ten bodhisattva grounds.
11. "*Dāna pāramitā*" refers to the perfection of giving.
12. "*Śīla pāramitā*" refers to the perfection of moral virtue.
13. "*Kṣānti pāramitā*" refers to the perfection of patience.
14. "*Dhyāna pāramitā*" refers to the perfection of skill in meditation.
15. Lest "inapprehensibility" seem somewhat obscure, this is simply a reference to the absence of inherent existence in any and all phenomena.
16. The Sanskrit adds: "*yena tāni buddhavikurvitāni paśyeyuḥ,*" "by which they might have seen those miraculous transformations of the Buddha."
17. The Sanskrit adds: "*yena parīttālambane vipulavikurvitādhiṣṭhānānyavat areyuḥ,*" "by which they might have entered upon the resolutions of miraculously tranforming a small object to become vast."
18. "Apex of reality" here translates "*bhūtakoṭi.*"
19. The Sanskrit (*ātmakāryaparipråptāḥ*) is more like: "They had achieved the completion of their own task."
20. The DSBC Sanskrit clarifies that "wisdom" refers here to the wisdom of all-knowledge (*sarvajñatājñāna*) as possessed by the Buddha.
21. The Sanskrit specifies "those world rulers directed toward bodhi" (*te ca lokendrā bodhyabhimukhā*).
22. The Sanskrit specifies "man" (*puruṣa*).
23. Although the Chinese *fodao* (佛道) in this line appears to refer to "the Buddha path," the extant edition of the Sanskrit indicates that, as is commonly the case in these texts, *fodao* is instead translating *buddhabodhi,* "the Buddha's enlightenment."
24. "Unsurpassed Eminence" here translates *wushangshi* (無上士), one of the ten titles of the Buddha (*sattvasāra*).
25. "The fullness of his vast sphere of wisdom" (廣大智圓滿) is a sino-Buddhist approximation of the Sanskrit's "vast sphere of wisdom" (*vipulaṁ jñānamaṇḍalam*).
26. The Indian subcontinent's Amanta tradition of establishing the lunar calendar ended each month on the no moon day. Hence, under that system, the full moon was brightest on the fifteenth of the month. (This system was in effect between the end of the Vedic period (roughly 500 BCE) and 57 BCE, this per V. R. Ramachandra Dikshitar (1993). *The Gupta Polity.* Motilal Banarsidass. pp. 24–35. ISBN 978-81-208-1024-2. (Wikipedia. 2019. "Hindu Calendar." Last modified February 7, 2020, this at: https://en.wikipedia.org/wiki/Hindu_calendar.)

27. "White dharmas of pristine purity" translates the Chinese "white dharmas" (白法) which is a literal translation of the Sanskrit *śukladharma*. In traditional Buddhist writings, "white dharmas" represent pure dharmas and "black dharmas" (黑法 / *kṛṣṇadharma*) represent unwholesome or defiled dharmas.

28. As the antecedent phrases for the Chinese "sphere (or "wheel") of water" (水輪) and "sphere of wisdom" (智慧輪), the Sanskrit text has "aggregation (or "mass") of water" (*apskandha*) and "aggregation of wisdom" (*jñānaskandha*). This is a reflection of ancient Indian cosmology which conceived of the earth's continents as resting on water.

29. Here the Chinese *zizai* (自在) again translates the Sanskrit antecedent *vikurvita* which has the special sense of "a miraculous or supernormal power of transformation."

30. The DSBC Sanskrit makes it clear that *zuisheng* (最勝), "supremely victorious" is translating "*jina*," one of the names used to describe the Buddha, hence my choice to render it as such here.

31. For what I translate here as "miraculous powers" (and *not* as "powers of sovereign mastery" as one might otherwise expect), the DSBC text gives "*vikurvita*" as the Sanskrit antecedent.

32. As VB points out, "dragon king" (*mahānāga*) is used in Indian literature as an epithet of "great beings." Hence, even in this simile, it is perhaps not actually intended to refer to a king of dragons *per se*, but is instead meant to refer to a particularly heroic and extraordinary being. The BB translation reflects this idea and is somewhat closer to the extant Sanskrit (*bhūriprajñā mahānāgāḥ sarvalokapramocanāḥ*) with "The Great Dragon King possessed of genuine wisdom liberates all beings" (實智大龍王度脫一切眾 / T09n0278_p0682a04).

33. Although the Sanskrit makes it clear that the subject in this series of verses is plural and refers to bodhisattvas, one would not easily deduce this from the SA text.

34. The BB translation has "serves as an unsurpassably supreme field of merit."

35. Although ambiguous in the BB, SA, and Prajñā translations' Chinese, the Sanskrit specifies the plural "Tathāgatas" (*tathāgatāḥ*).

36. As is often the case, the Chinese *fangbian* (方便) as used in this subsection does *not* translate the Sanskrit *upāya* or *upāya-kauśalya* (skillful or expedient means). Rather it instead corresponds here to *naya* ("method," "means," "way," "prudent or fitting actions," etc.).

37. "Commensurate with" here and hereafter is an attempt to translate into English diction the Chinese text's rather opaque and terse "equal to" (等) which in turn translates the equally opaque Sanskrit *samatā* which also refers to equality or sameness.

38. Again, "on a scale commensurate with" translates the Chinese text's "equal to" (等).

39. I add the "however" and "solely" here to preserve the disjunctive sense that is clear in the Sanskrit (because of the initial *api tu*), but lost from the Chinese by which we are reminded that the circumstances described by these "Dharma instructions" are the exclusive domain of a buddha's knowledge (*api tu khalu punarbho jinaputrāḥ tathāgatajñānagocara eṣaḥ*). Thanks to VB for pointing out this subtlety in his critical comments on the first draft translation.

40. An "ineffable" (*anabhilapya*) is an ineffably great number defined in the "Asaṃkhyeya" chapter of this sutra.

41. Although the Chinese that I translate here as "methods" is more usually translated as "skillful means" (方便), here it corresponds to the Sanskrit *naya*.

42. Following the S,Y,M, and G editions, I emend the reading of the text here by preferring *xiang*1 (相) to *xiang*3 (想), this to correct a fairly obvious scribal error as disclosed by the Sanskrit text which shows this character was intended to translate the Sanskrit word *dhvaja*, or "banner."

43. Per the Sanskrit, *zizai* (自在), more commonly "sovereign mastery," is instead translating *vikurvita* which, in a Buddhist context, refers instead to feats of spiritual power.

44. "Apex of reality" (真實際) here = DSBC "*bhūtakoṭī*." VB notes: "[In contrast to the Chinese 'unveiled' {示}], interestingly, here the extant Sanskrit text has -*vipaśyakānāṁ*, 'contemplated with insight,' 'saw clearly into.'"

45. The DSBC text's antecedent for "dharma of baselessness" (無依處法) is *anālayadharma*. This is just another reference to the absence of inherent existence in any and all dharmas, i.e., "emptiness."

46. "Apex of reality" (真實際) corresponds to DSBC's *bhūtakoṭi* which is a synonym for ultimate or absolute truth or ultimate reality.

47. The term I choose to translate here as "resounding emanation" (發) corresponds to the DSBC Sanskrit's *nigarjamānāḥ*, a form of *nigarjati*, which, as pointed out by VB, per BHSD, may mean "to roar," "cry forth," or "proclaim loudly" (BHSD, p. 293-4).

48. I follow the BB translation's much less ambiguous idea here: "[portrayed] all dharmas as being like dreams." (一切諸法皆悉如夢。 / T09n0278_p0708c25–26)

49. This most likely refers to buddhas and/or bodhisattvas presenting the appearance of taking birth in the world for the purpose of teaching the Dharma to beings.

50. Beginning here, the gateways refer (in standard order) primarily to the practice of the six *pāramitās* (perfections): *dāna* (giving); *śīla* (moral virtue); *kṣānti* (patience); *vīrya* (vigor); *dhyāna* (meditative practices); and *prajñā* (wisdom).

51. "Master physician" (醫王), is literally "physician king," but, at least in this context, as revealed by the Sanskrit (*vaidya*), this is just an idiomatic way of referring to an excellent physician.

52. Noting that these are simply "road spirits," QL notes that these "foot-travel spirits"(足行神 / *pada-kāyikābhir devatābhiḥ, pada-kāyika devatā**) exist in relationship to those who travel by foot, serving them as their protectors. For example, there are foot-travel spirits who support each footstep of buddhas and other holy beings with "stepping stones" consisting of immense flower blossoms.

53. Here and immediately below, *zizai* (自在), (more usually *vaśitā*, "sovereign mastery"), is instead translating *vikurvita*, "miraculous powers of transformation," or, more simply, "spiritual powers." The Prajñā translation states this more explicitly by including both meanings of *zizai* (無量自在神通菩薩圍遶) "... surrounded by countless bodhisattvas possessed of freely manifested spiritual powers ...."

54. QL indicates that this refers to all buddhas' accumulation of the myriad practices.

55. HH says this refers to "all buddhas' continual and uninterrupted transmittal and receipt of the wisdom life of the buddhas" [from past buddhas to present buddhas to future buddhas].

56. Here Sudhana is metaphorically referring to Mañjuśrī as Indra, the ruler of the gods who dwells in the Trāyastriṃṣa Heaven on the summit of Mount Sumeru where he defends his celestial realm from the attacks of the *asuras* or demi-gods.

57. QL clarifies here that what might otherwise be read as "universal practices" (普行) is instead intended to refer to "the practices of Samantabhadra" (普賢之行). (L130n1557_0385b11).

58. HH states that it is the bodhi resolve that is as solid as vajra, whereas QL states that it is *prajñā*'s realization of the noumenal that is as solid as vajra's keen-edged sharpness in its solid severance of the delusions arising from confusion with regard to the noumenal. (般若證理如金剛堅斷迷理惑如金剛利). It may be helpful to recall that "noumenon" in the Huayan school's terminology most readily corresponds to the ultimate truth of emptiness of all conditioned things.

59. I emend the reading of the text here by preferring the *yuan* (願) of the Song, Yuan, and Ming editions to the Taisho text's *lei* (類), this to correct an obvious graphic-similarity scribal error.

60. QL notes that, of these eleven list items, this first item ("Seeking the bodhisattva practices") is the "general" topic whereas the following ten items are the particular bodhisattva practices that constitute the specific subtopics to which it refers.

61. QL notes: "Not dwelling in *nirvāṇa* is the gateway to *saṃsāra*; not dwelling in *saṃsāra* is the gateway to *nirvāṇa*."

62. It may be useful to the reader to realize that all of the above descriptors such as "numberlessly many," "measurelessly many," "boundlessly many," "incomparably many," "innumerably many," "indescribably many," "inconceivably many," "immeasurably many," "ineffably many," and "ineffably-ineffably many" are all translations of their corresponding precisely defined Buddhist Sanskrit numbers that refer to actual quantities (i.e., they are not merely hyperbolic adjectives). There are one hundred and twenty-four of these numbers, all of which are defined in Chapter Thirty, "Asaṃkhyeyas," where we find that each of these terms is the square of the immediately previous number. (The smallest number, a *lakṣa*, is one hundred thousand.) The result of one hundred and twenty-three squarings of the immediately previous number is that the largest number is inconceivably large.

63. HH suggests that this refers to "using right mindfulness to contemplate the number of bodhisattvas as being like a great ocean." (以正念來觀察菩薩的數量猶如大海似的. / HYQS) Then, by way of paraphrase, he approvingly echoed the assessment of QL who wrote: "Fourth, he brought to mind the many different constituents of the earlier congregation." (四念前種種眾會 / L130n1557_0405b13) The BB translation says: "He contemplated the ocean of all bodhisattvas' skillful means." (觀察一切菩薩諸方便海。 / T09n0278_p0690b27–28)

64. QL says: "Sixth, this is just the 'ten directions' as mentioned earlier." (六即前十方 / T09n0278_p0690b27–28)

65. According to MW (p. 168, Column 3), an *indranīla* is a sapphire.

66. As VB points out *zizai* (自在) is again translating *vikurvita* ("miraculous powers") and *chengdao* (成道) is again translating *abhisaṃbhodhi* ("attainment of enlightenment"). The Sanskrit for this line is *acintyamabhisaṁbodhivikurvitaṁ paśyāmi.*

67. VB points out here that, in the phrase "*ziranzhe fa* - 自然者法 (*svayaṃbhūdharmān*)," *ziran* (自然) is translating *svayaṃbhū* which "is a technical term for one who achieves the goal on his own, without depending on the guidance of an existing buddha."

68. *Kṣaṇas, lavas,* and *muhūrtas* are short increments of time measurement in ancient Sanskrit enumeration somewhat analogous to milliseconds, seconds, and hours respectively.

69. "Karmic inaction" (無作) here is translating *anabhisaṃskāra* which refers to refraining from the creation of any *saṃskāras* or karmic formative factors. Per BHSD's definition number one (p. 20, Column 2), among other closely related ideas, this can mean *"non-accumulation* (of *karman*)" or *"having or characterized by no accumulation* (of *karman*)."

70. "Vaṣitā" here is a reconstruction of the name used to translate this city's name in the two earliest editions of this scripture (the BB and SA translations). The name found in later editions (the Sanskrit and Prajñā editions) is "Vajrapura." There is no way that "Vajrapura" could have been the Sanskrit in the source texts used by BB and SA since there is no way that one could translate *vajrapura* into Chinese as *zizai* (自在), the translation chosen by both BB and SA. Hence my inclination to reconstruct the name here.

71. "Praised the lineage of dispassion" (歎離欲性) corresponds to the Sanskrit edition's *virāgavaṁśamudīrayan* in which SA is using *xing* (性) to translate *vaṃśa* ("lineage").

72. "The Adornments of the Syllabary Wheel" translates the Sanskrit *cakrākṣaraparivartavyūha.*

73. "The difficulties" refers to "the eight difficulties" which consist of: rebirths in the hells; rebirths among hungry ghosts, rebirths among animals; rebirths in the long-life heavens (where bliss is so overwhelming there is no motivation to cultivate the path); rebirths on the continent of Uttarakuru (where, again, life is so pleasant there is no path motivation); rebirths as deaf, dumb, or blind; rebirths as someone possessed of merely worldly knowledge and eloquence (who is thus inclined to be a spiritual philistine insensitive to the preciousness of the Dharma); and rebirths either before or after a buddha appears in the world (which prevent one from encountering the Dharma).

74. An "ineffable-ineffable" (*anabhilāpya-anabhilāpya*) is the next-to-highest number of one hundred and twenty-four numbers in this Sutra's numbering schema, each number of which is the result of the successive squaring of the immediately previous number. The first and smallest of these numbers known as a *lakṣa* is one hundred thousand. These numbers are all defined in Chapter Thirty, "Asaṃkhyeyas."

75. A *nārāyaṇa* (那羅延) is usually a kind of vajra-bearing Dharma protector spirit or deva.

76. HH indicates this refers to having the same Dharma body as all bodhisattvas.

77. *"Brahmacarya"* (梵行) refers to pure spiritual practice in which celibacy is strictly observed.

78. "Meditation on impurity" or, more literally, "meditation on the unlovely" (不淨觀, *asubha-bhāvanā*) is a reference to the various meditations on the inherently unattractive or impure nature of the bodies of those to whom one might otherwise find sexually attractive.

79. VB points out here that, instead of SA's "they taught the dharma of the nonexistence of anything whatsoever" (說無所有法), the BB translation has "they taught the dharma of nonattachment" (說無著法) and the Sanskrit also has "they taught nonattachment" (*anālayatāṁ kathayamānān*).

80. I am presuming here that "progressing toward the stages of right abiding" (向正住) and "already reached the stages of right abiding" (正住) are references to those who have not yet achieved irreversibility on the path and those who have already achieved irreversibility on the path. As I understand it, being a member of one or the other of these categories is a function of whether or not the practitioner in question has already obtained fruits of either the *śrāvaka*-vehicle path or the bodhisattva path by which he could never again fall back down into the status of a "foolish common person" (*pṛthagjana*) who wanders aimlessly in *saṃsāra*. The corresponding Sanskrit edition's text has *sarvasamyagn[iy]atasamyakpratipanna*. (VB recommends the [*iy*] emendation which I have included.)

81. VB points out that the Chinese *mianmen* (面門), literally "gateway of the face" is actually translating the Sanskrit *mukhadvāra* which just means "mouth." (BB translates as *cong qi kou* [從其口], "from his mouth."

82. I emend the Taisho text's reading here by replacing *bian* (辨) with S, Y, M, and G's *ban* (辦), this to correct an obvious graphic-similarity scribal error.

83. Again, I emend the Taisho text's reading here by replacing *bian* (辨) with S, Y, M, and G's *ban* (辦), this to correct an obvious graphic-similarity scribal error.

84. Again, I emend the Taisho text's reading here by replacing *bian* (辨) with S, Y, M, and G's *ban* (辦), this to correct an obvious graphic-similarity scribal error.

85. HH and QL both point out that "difficulties" here refers to the eight difficulties and related circumstances.

86. This is another reference to the eight difficulties.

87. Both the BB translation (智慧究竟一切法趣) and the Sanskrit (*sarvadhar magatyanusṛtijñāninānāṁ*) make it clear that SA's *yiqie qu* (一切趣) "all destinies" is meant to refer to *yiqie faqu* (一切法趣) which I take to mean "destinies of all dharmas," i.e., "where all dharmas eventually lead."

88. I emend the reading of the text by replacing Taisho's *bian* (辨), "distinguish," with SYMG's *bian* (辯), "discuss" or "explain," this to correct an apparent graphic-similarity scribal error. Both the BB translation and the Sanskrit seem to support this emendation.

89. The"understanding" character (解) of the SA text's "dwelling in pure *understanding*" (住清淨解) may originally have instead been meant to refer either to "liberations" (解脫) as rendered by the earlier BB translation's "pure liberations" (淨解脫) or else to "resolute faith" (信解), a standard Chinese translation of the *adhimukti* which we find in the later Sanskrit text's "the attainment of pure resolute faith" (*adhimuktiviśuddhayanugata*).

90. Because it is clear from the structure of the grammar here that this single mention of "the bodhisattva" is intended to apply to all statements down through 344c26, I have added it to all of those statements.

91. The Sanskrit: *"anabhilāpya-anabhilāpya-parivarta."* See Chapter Thirty entitled "Asaṃkhyeyas" for a sense of the size of this indescribably large number, the largest of them all. This number results from the successive squaring of each of the one hundred and twenty-three previous numbers in this numbering system, the smallest of which is a *lakṣa* (one hundred thousand).

92. For "the banner of sorrowless security," the Sanskrit text has *"aśokakṣemadhvajo."*

93. A "same-practice" good spiritual friend is one of the three main types of "good spiritual friends" or "good spiritual guides" (*kalyānamitra*): a) the good spiritual guide who serves as one's Dharma teacher; b) the "same-practice" good spiritual friend; and c) the "outwardly protective" good spiritual friend who assists with one's material needs (food, robes, medical care, etc.).

94. MW equates *utpala* with "the blue lotus (*Nymphaea Caerulea*)" and *padma* with "a lotus (esp. the flower of the lotus-plant [*Nelumbium Speciosum*] which closes towards evening."

95. VB notes that this refers "to lighting fires in the four cardinal points while remaining in the middle, at noon, with sun at its apex above."

96. Although the BB and SA translations refer here to "non-buddhist youths" (外道童子), the Sanskrit has *udāraṃ māṇavaka* or "noble [non-Buddhist] religious students."

97. DSBC has *"buddhasamādhivikurvaṇamukhaṁ."*

98. The Sanskrit here for the somewhat misleading SA text has: *"sudurlab hāścaryāśayaratnapratilabdho"*.

99. The Sanskrit for this passage as we have it now has *"dharmamaṇḍala-viśuddhimatiparamaḥ."*

100. DSBC has "*niryāṇa*." The BB translation has "same path of cultivation" (同修道).

101. DSBC has "*ekādhimukti*." The BB translation has "same nature of aspirations" (同欲性).

102. DSBC has "budhyapramāṇāni."

103. DSBC has "cittaspharaṇāni."

104. A note in the Ming edition says, "'Elder' in the generally circulating text is instead 'householder'" (明註曰長者流布本作居士).

105. I follow HH whose interpretation follows easily from the SA text without forcing the grammar: "Because the [influence of the] good spiritual guides permeated his mind, it caused his determination to draw near to the good spiritual guides to become even more solid" (他以善知識，來熏習他的心，使其親近善知識的志願更加堅固。 / HYQS).

106. VB points out that the SA translation's "merit dharma" may be a corruption, for both the Sanskrit (*tatpuṇyanidhim-avalokayan*) and the BB translation (觀彼功德藏) suggest instead: "...contemplated his treasure of merit" or "...contemplated his store of merit."

107. The "Great Unification Hells" (眾合大地獄, *saṃghāta-naraka*) are hells where beings are crushed between two collapsing mountains.

108. Both the Sanskrit and Prajñā editions refer to "devas" in the plural.

109. "Five turbidities" ("五濁," or, in KJ translations: "五濁惡世") generally refers to historical times characterized by deterioration in the quality of five phenomena: kalpas, views, afflictions, beings, and life spans.

110. In his Treatise on the Ten Bodhisattva Grounds otherwise known as the Daśabhūmika Vibhāṣā (T1521: 十住毘婆沙論), Nāgārjuna speaks repeatedly of "the four bases of meritorious qualities" (四功四處) consisting of truth, relinquishment, quiescence, and wisdom (諦捨及滅慧。 / T26n1521_p0022b28).

111. The eight classes of spiritual beings (八部衆, *aṣṭa-gatyaḥ*) consist of: devas, *nāgas*, *yakṣas*, *gandharvas*, *asuras*, *garuḍas*, *kiṃnaras*, and *mahoragas*.

112. Regarding what one would otherwise translate as "one's own body" (自身), I instead follow the implications of this comment offered by VB: "Skt: *ekacittotpādam-adhyātmadṛṣṭisahagatam-utpādayitum*. It seems that '自身' is intended to capture the prefix *adhi* -> *adhy*, *adhyātma* is an internal self. This has a wider significance than 'body.'"

113. Again, per VB's comments: "無記心 = avyākṛtacitta. This is a technical Abhidharma term. Cittas are classified as good, bad, and indeterminate (*kuśala, akuśala, avyākṛta*). So she is saying that she never gave rise to bad (defiled) thoughts or indeterminate thoughts, only to good (wholesome) thoughts."

114. The "ten eyes" are listed in Chapter 38, the "Transcending the World" chapter (T10n0279_302c17–25), as follows:

Sons of the Buddha, the bodhisattva-mahāsattva has ten kinds of eyes, namely:

The fleshly eye, so-called because it sees all forms;

The heavenly eye, so-called because it sees all beings' minds;

The wisdom eye, so-called because it sees all beings' faculties and spheres of cognition;

The Dharma eye, so-called because it sees all dharmas in a manner consistent with their true character;

The Buddha eye, so-called because it sees the Tathāgata's ten powers;

The eye of knowledge, so-called because it knows and sees all dharmas;

The radiance eye, so-called because it sees the Buddha's light;

The eye that transcends saṃsāra, so-called because it sees nirvāṇa;

The unimpeded eye, so-called because it has unimpeded vision of everything it sees;

The eye of all-knowledge, so-called because it sees the "universal gateway" Dharma realm.

These are the ten. If bodhisattvas securely abide in these dharmas, then they acquire the Tathāgata's eye of unexcelled great wisdom.

115. As pointed out by VB in review notes, for "受持," "took in and retained," the Sanskrit text verb here is *vibantī*, "drank in" which has also been captured in the BB translation's "悉飲," "I have completely imbibed."

116. VB points out that the Sanskrit for 一切眾生所樂, "whatever all beings find pleasing," is *sarvasattvayathāśaya*, or "inclinations of beings."

117. VB mentions in his review notes that, "Both Chinese translations (by which he means the BB and SA editions) miss the most important phrase in the Sanskrit text, *'apaśyat sudhanaḥ śreṣṭhidārako,'* 'the youth Sudhana saw.' It occurs several times in the paragraph and underscores that this was an inner experience of Sudhana."

Actually, since not only the BB and SA translations to which VB referred here seem to "miss" this phrase, I checked the Prajñā translation and found that it does not include it, either. This leads me to suspect that this very helpful phrase may have instead been *added* at a later time into the Sanskrit text which, in earlier editions, required the readers to conclude for themselves that Acalā's samādhi-precipitated scenarios were directly seen by Sudhana.

118. This simile is not found in the BB translation. The Prajñā translation reads: "They are like the king of the *asuras* who is everywhere able to agitate the ocean of afflictions of the great city of the three realms of existence, thereby everywhere causing beings to reach ultimate quiescence.

119. Although both the SA and BB translations refer to Sarvagāmin as a "non-buddhist renunciate" (出家外道), the Sanskrit is actually *parivrājika* which is more like MW's "wandering religious mendicant" or, as VB suggests, "wandering ascetic."

120. I emend the reading of the text here by replacing 德 with 得 in accordance with the reading in two other editions of the text (Song and Gong) to correct an apparent scribal error and to preserve a precise translation of the Sanskrit name for this mountain (*sulabha* = "Good Gain") otherwise lost in the current edition of the Taisho text.

121. In his review notes, VB points out that "King Yama's realms" is a reference to the *preta* or "hungry ghost" realm.

122. In his review notes, VB points out that "the Good Dharma Hall" (*sudharmadevasabhā*) is not a distinct heaven [as suggested by the syntax of the SA translation's Chinese which would read "Good Dharma Heaven"], but rather is the assembly hall of the Trayastriṃśa Heaven. (The BB and Prajñā translations as well as the DSBC Sanskrit all refer specifically to "the Good Dharma Hall" (善法堂 / *sudharmadevasabhā*).

123. "Evil mental tendencies" corresponds here to the DSBC Sanskrit's "*viṣama-mati*."

124. Although, unlike the BB translation's "wrong views" (邪見), Prajñā's "evil views" (惡見), and the DSBC Sanskrit's "unwholesome views" (*akuśaladṛṣṭi*), SA does not qualify "views" (諸見) at all, it may help to recall here that, in Buddhist texts in general, all by itself, "views" is *already* usually an implicit reference to "*wrong* views"(even without further adjectival qualification).

125. Although the SA translation does not include it, both the BB and Sanskrit editions specify "the sufferings of *saṃsāra*."

126. As phrased, it is clear that this is specifically referring to halting all of the ten courses of unwholesome karma (*daśa-akuśala-karma-patha*), the standard listing of which begins with "killing" and ends with "wrong views."

127. VB points out in his review notes that the presence of "buddhas" or "*tathāgatas*" at this point in the BB translation, the Prajñā translation, and the DSBC Sanskrit demonstrates that this character was accidentally dropped from the SA translation. That is why I have included it in brackets here.

128. DSBC = *virāga koṭīgato nāma bodhisattvavimokṣaḥ.*

129. I emend the reading of the Taisho text here by preferring the *shou* (受), "receiving," variant found in the S, Y, M, and G editions to Taisho's *shou* (授), "transmitting," doing so based on consulting the DSBC Sanskrit (*sarvatathāgatavyākaraṇasaṃpratīcchanatāṃ*) and the Prajñā translation while also noting the presence of the same variant in the S, Y, and M editions of the BB translation.

130. "Easeful mastery" as a translation of the Chinese *youxi* (遊戲), "roaming playfully," translates the Sanskrit *vikrīḍita*, which, per BHSD, literally means "sport," but which, per BHSD (p. 482, column 1) is more often meant to mean "something like *easy mastery*."

131. The *jie* (解) which I render here as "beliefs" is SA's contracted Chinese translation of the Sanskrit *adhimukti* which is much more commonly translated into Chinese as *xinjie* (信解), "resolute belief," "resolute faith," "conviction," etc.

132. "The mind that induces them to establish themselves in the path to all-knowledge" (for which SA has "住一切智心") corresponds to the Sanskrit's "*sarvajñatāmārgapratiṣṭhāpanacitta.*"

133. This is clearly a reference to the ten courses of bad karmic action. In fact, the Sanskrit lists all ten of them here.

134. The five nefarious karmic offenses (五逆罪, *pañcânantarya*) are matricide, patricide, killing an arhat, drawing the blood of a buddha, and creating a schism in the Sangha.

135. This is a reference to "the wide and long tongue," one of the thirty-two marks of a buddha's body.

136. For "Good Dharma Bridge" (善法度), DSBC has "*sudharmatīrtho.*"

137. For this incredibly long bodhi tree name, "the body emanating the light of all buddhas' spiritual powers that is adorned with omni-radiant sovereign *maṇi* jewels" (一切光摩尼王莊嚴身出生一切佛神力光明), DSBC has "*sarvavyūhaprabhāmaṇirājaśarīre sarvabuddhavikurvitaprabhave mahābodhivṛkṣe.*"

138. A *rākṣasī* is a female *rākṣasa*. The female form of this flesh-eating rapidly flying demon is renowned for her ability to transform into the shape of a beautiful woman to seduce and destroy cultivators of the path.

139. "Difficulties" here refers to the eight difficulties.

140. Here, the Chinese *zizai* (自在) is translating the Sanskrit *vikurvita* which, per MW [p. 954, column 3], means "the assuming of various shapes."

141. "Lesser Vastness Heaven devas" translates the Chinese *shaoguang* (少廣 [天]) for which I could not find a Sanskrit antecedent in the usual sources. There is no counterpart in the DSBC Sanskrit. VB suggests it seems to be a gratuitous interpolation.

142. Here "the One with Ten Powers" is a common name for the Buddha.

143. Lest the meaning of this seem unclear, in his HYQS, HH offers the example of a person having to always live in close proximity to a tiger.

144. The Chinese (調御) makes it clear that this is a reference to one of the ten epithets of the Buddha, namely "the Tamer of Men" (*purusadamya-sārathi* [調御丈夫]).

145. These first three list items together constitute "the three kinds of wisdom" (*trividhā prajñā* or 三慧) consisting of *śrutamayī prajñā, cintāmayī prajñā*, and *bhāvanāmayī*.

146. In his HYQS, commenting on this passage, HH explains that a "world transformation" (*lokadhātuparivarta* / 世界轉) is a number calculated from supposing that one ground a world to dust, then allowed each one of those motes of dust to represent a *kṣetra* that one then in turn also ground to dust. The resulting number of dust motes produced from grinding up all those *kṣetras* equals this very large number known as a "world transformation."

147. "*Kṣetra* transformation" (*buddhakṣetraparivarta* / 剎轉). See the previous note regarding "world transformation." This verse is simply restating that earlier textual passage.

148. "Wealth of the *āryas*" (聖財, *ārya-dhāna*) or "the seven kinds of wealth of the *āryas*" (七聖財, *saptāryadhāna*), or "seven kinds of Dharma wealth" (七法財), refers to personal qualities of awakened beings. Lists vary somewhat, but they usually include: faith; moral virtue; a sense of shame; a dread of blame; abundant Dharma learning; generosity; and wisdom.

149. According to the DSBC Sanskrit, SA's *zizai* (自在) which I render here as "transformative powers" is translating *vikurvita* for which MW gives "the assuming of various shapes" and BHSD gives "miracle."

150. Here, "universally worthy" is a play on the Chinese translation of the name of Samantabhadra Bodhisattva. Hence it could be construed to mean: "This is the liberation of those who are like Samantabhadra."

151. DSBC has "*bodhimārgopastambhasaṃjñā*" which, per VB in review notes translates as "He conceived of them as solid supports on the path to bodhi."

152. I emend the reading by replacing Taisho's 本 with 木 to correct a fairly obvious scribal error arising through graphic similarity, this in accordance with two alternative editions and the BB translation.

153. What I translate here as "dense rain clouds" is literally "oily clouds" (油雲).

www.ingramcontent.com/pod-product-compliance
Lightning Source LLC
Chambersburg PA
CBHW030236170426
43202CB00007B/22
9781935413523